1970	1971	1972	1973	1974	1975	1976	1977	1978	1979	1980	1981	1982
648.5	701.9	770.6	852.4	933.4	1,034.4	1,151.9	1,278.6	1,428.5	1,592.2	1,757.1	1,941.1	2,077.3
152.4	178.2	207.6	244.5	249.4	230.2	292.0	361.3	438.0	492.9	479.3	572.4	517.2
233.8	246.5	263.5	281.7	317.9	357.7	383.0	414.1	453.6	500.8	566.2	627.5	680.5
59.7	63.0	70.8	95.3	126.7	138.7	149.5	159.4	186.9	230.1	280.8	305.2	283.2
55.8	62.3	74.2	91.2	127.5	122.7	151.1	182.4	212.3	252.7	293.8	317.8	303.2
1,038.5	1,127.1	1,238.3	1,382.7	1,500.0	1,638.3	1,825.3	2,030.9	2,294.7	2,563.3	2,789.5	3,128.4	3,255.0
617.2	658.9	725.1	811.2	890.2	949.1	1,059.3	1,180.5	1,336.1	1,500.8	1,651.8	1,825.8	1,925.8
222.5	249.2	279.3	318.5	324.0	359.7	403.4	459.9	520.4	566.0	587.1	679.4	696.0
839.7	908.1	1,004.4	1,129.7	1,214.2	1,308.8	1,462.7	1,640.4	1,856.5	2,066.8	2,238.9	2,505.2	2,621.8
84.8	92.4	98.3	105.1	112.4	124.1	132.3	138.2	149.3	150.4	166.2	204.2	206.0
106.7	115	126.5	139.3	162.5	187.7	205.2	230.0	262.3	300.1	343.0	388.1	426.9
1,031.2	1,115.5	1,229.2	1,374.1	1,489.1	1,620.6	1,800.2	2,008.6	2,268.1	2,517.3	2,748.1	3,097.5	3,254.7
7.3	11.6	9.1	8.6	10.9	17.7	25.1	22.3	26.6	46.0	41.4	30.9	0.3
1,038.5	1,127.1	1,238.3	1,382.7	1,500.0	1,638.3	1,825.3	2,030.9	2,294.7	2,563.3	2,789.5	3,128.4	3,255.0
3,771.9	3,898.6	4,105.0	4,341.5	4,319.6	4,311.2	4,540.9	4,750.5	5,015.0	5,173.4	5,161.7	5,291.7	5,189.3
0.2	3.4	5.3	5.8	−0.5	−0.2	5.3	4.6	5.6	3.2	−0.2	2.5	−1.9
205.1	207.7	209.9	211.9	213.9	216.0	218.0	220.2	222.6	225.1	227.7	230.0	232.2
82.8	84.4	87.0	89.4	91.9	93.8	96.2	99.0	102.3	105.0	106.9	108.7	110.2
78.7	79.4	82.2	85.1	86.8	85.8	88.8	92.0	96.0	98.8	99.3	100.4	99.5
4.1	5.0	4.9	4.4	5.2	7.9	7.4	7.0	6.2	6.1	7.6	8.3	10.7
60.4	60.2	60.4	60.8	61.3	61.2	61.6	62.3	63.2	63.7	63.8	63.9	64.0
4.9	5.9	5.6	4.9	5.6	8.5	7.7	7.1	6.1	5.8	7.1	7.6	9.7
18,395	18,774	19,557	20,488	20,199	19,962	20,826	21,570	22,531	22,987	22,666	23,011	22,350
−1.0	2.1	4.2	4.8	−1.4	−1.2	4.3	3.6	4.5	2.0	−1.4	1.5	−2.9
626.5	710.3	802.3	855.5	902.1	1,016.2	1,152.0	1,270.3	1,366.0	1,473.7	1,599.8	1,755.4	1,910.3
27.5	28.9	30.2	31.8	34.7	38.0	40.2	42.8	45.8	49.5	54.0	59.1	62.7
5.3	5.0	4.3	5.6	9.0	9.4	5.8	6.4	7.0	8.3	9.1	9.4	6.1
38.8	40.5	41.8	44.4	49.3	53.8	56.9	60.6	65.2	72.6	82.4	90.9	96.5
5.7	4.4	3.2	6.2	11.0	9.1	5.8	6.5	7.6	11.3	13.5	10.3	6.7
2.3	−1.4	−5.8	7.1	2.0	18.1	4.3	−14.3	−15.1	−0.3	2.3	5.0	−5.3

EIGHTH EDITION

MACROECONOMICS

PARKIN

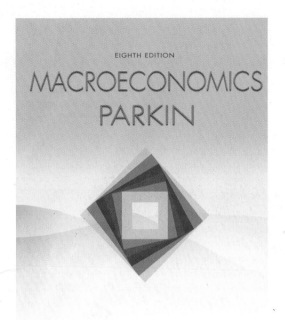

EIGHTH EDITION

MACROECONOMICS
PARKIN

To change the way students see the world—that has been my aim throughout the eight editions of this book.

The cover depicts a landscape viewed through a geometric icon.

The landscape is the economic world. And the icon represents the clarity that economic science brings to our view and understanding of the economic world.

When we view the landscape without the economic lens, we see questions but not answers. The lens provides answers by enabling us to focus on the unseen forces that shape our world. It is a tool that enables us to see the invisible.

This book equips students with the economic lens, shows them how to use it, and enables them to gain their own informed and structured view of the economic world.

to Robin

Michael Parkin received his training as an economist at the Universities of Leicester and Essex in England. Currently in the Department of Economics at the University of Western Ontario, Canada, Professor Parkin has held faculty appointments at Brown University, the University of Manchester, the University of Essex, and Bond University. He is a past president of the Canadian Economics Association and has served on the editorial boards of the *American Economic Review* and the *Journal of Monetary Economics* and as managing editor of the *Canadian Journal of Economics*. Professor Parkin's research on macroeconomics, monetary economics, and international economics has resulted in over 160 publications in journals and edited volumes, including the *American Economic Review,* the *Journal of Political Economy,* the *Review of Economic Studies,* the *Journal of Monetary Economics,* and the *Journal of Money, Credit and Banking.* He became most visible to the public with his work on inflation that discredited the use of wage and price controls. Michael Parkin also spearheaded the movement toward European monetary union. Professor Parkin is an experienced and dedicated teacher of introductory economics.

This book presents economics as a serious, lively, and evolving science. Its goal is to open students' eyes to the "economic way of thinking" and to help them gain insights into how the economy works and how it might be made to work better.

I provide a thorough and complete coverage of the subject, using a straightforward, precise, and clear writing style.

Because I am conscious that many students find economics hard, I place the student at center stage and write for the student. I use language that doesn't intimidate and that allows the student to concentrate on the substance.

I open each chapter with a clear statement of learning objectives, a real-world student-friendly vignette to grab attention, and a brief preview. I illustrate principles with examples that are selected to hold the student's interest and to make the subject lively. And I put principles to work by using them to illuminate current real-world problems and issues.

I explain modern topics, such as dynamic comparative advantage, game theory, the principal-agent problem, and the modern theory of the firm, public choice theory, information and uncertainty, rational expectations, new growth theory, and real business cycle theory, using the familiar core ideas and tools.

Today's course springs from today's issues—the information revolution and the new economy, the economic shockwaves after 9/11 that continue to affect our lives, and the expansion of global trade, investment, and offshore outsourcing. But the principles that we use to understand these issues remain the core principles of our science.

Governments and international agencies place continued emphasis on long-term fundamentals as they seek to promote economic growth. This book reflects this emphasis.

To help promote a rich, active learning experience, I have developed a comprehensive online learning environment featuring a dynamic e-book, interactive tests, study plans, and tutorials, daily news updates, and more.

The Eighth Edition Revision

Macroeconomics, eighth edition, retains all of the improvements achieved in its predecessor with its thorough and detailed presentation of modern economics, emphasis on real-world examples and critical thinking skills, diagrams renowned for pedagogy and precision, and path-breaking technology.

Highlights of the Macro Revision

In this edition, extensive and detailed changes have been made.

The organizing principle behind the revision of *Macroeconomics* is the distinction between the forces that determine the long-run trends and those that bring short-run fluctuations. Part Four now focuses on the economy in the long run, Part Five on the economy in the short run, and Part Six on macroeconomic policy issues in both the long run and the short run.

In addition to thorough and extensive updating, the macroeconomics chapters feature the following seven major revisions:

1. **At Full Employment: The Classical Model** (Chapter 7): The explanation of the demand for labor has been made clearer; the distinction between potential GDP as an equilibrium quantity and the *PPF* as a physical limit is explained; the capital market is explained using the demand for and supply of loanable funds; applications of the classical model contrast the U.S. economy at full employment in 1981 and 2001 and the U.S. economy and European economy.

2. **Economic Growth** (Chapter 8): The chapter now opens with an explanation of the rule of 70 and the significance of maintaining a higher growth rate. The material on growth accounting and growth theories is simplified to focus on the core ideas and de-emphasize the technical aspects of these topics.

3. **Money, the Price Level, and Inflation** (Chapter 9): The coverage of money is now divided between Chapter 9, which has an institutional and long-run focus, and Chapter 15 (described below). Chapter 9 describes the money and banking system including the Federal Reserve. It also explains how, in the long run, the quantity of money determines the price level and the growth rate of the quantity of money determines the inflation rate.

4. **The Exchange Rate and Balance of Payments** (Chapter 10): This chapter on international finance is now integrated into the main macro sequence. Placing the chapter at this point of the course serves to emphasize that in the long run, the exchange rate, like the price level, is a monetary phenomenon. It also serves to emphasize that the balance of payments is determined by saving and investment (private plus public).

   This chapter addresses the current policy concerns of the falling dollar and the persistent current account deficit. The chapter also explains China's foreign exchange market policies and their consequences both for China and the United States.

   The material in this chapter has been kept as self-contained as possible to enable the chapter to be either skipped or covered at the end of the course.

5. **Aggregate Supply and Aggregate Demand** (Chapter 11): This chapter opens the part on the economy in the short run and is only slightly different from the seventh edition in that the short section on cycles and growth in the U.S. economy has been moved to open the new Chapter 13 (described below). Chapter 11 may be studied right at the outset for those who prefer this way of organizing the course.

6. **U.S. Inflation, Unemployment, and Business Cycle** (Chapter 13): This chapter combines and shortens the material in the seventh edition chapters on inflation and the business cycle. The chapter begins by using the *AS-AD* model to interpret inflation, growth, and cycles in the U.S. economy. It then explains demand-pull and cost-push inflation using the *AS-AD* model; the short-run tradeoff using the Phillips curve; and the business cycle using both the traditional (or mainstream) *AS-AD* approach and the new approach of real business cycle theory.

7. **Monetary Policy** (Chapter 15): This chapter explains the goal, intermediate targets, and instruments of monetary policy. The chapter also explains exactly how the Fed goes about the business of determining its monetary policy strategy and daily operations. Finally, the chapter places the Fed's choices in the broader context of the debate about the appropriate way in which to conduct monetary policy.

   My aim with this chapter has been to explain the Fed's actions and their effects as accurately and objectively as possible and then, in the final part of the chapter, to widen the scope of the discussion but avoid taking a strong position.

Features to Enhance Teaching and Learning

Here I describe the chapter features that are designed to enhance the learning process. Each chapter contains the following learning aids.

Chapter Opener

Each chapter opens with a one-page student-friendly, attention-grabbing vignette. The vignette raises questions that both motivate the student and focus the chapter. I carry this story into the main body of the chapter and relate it to the chapter-ending *Reading Between the Lines* feature for a cohesive learning experience.

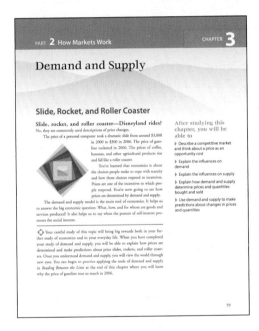

Chapter Objectives

A list of learning objectives enables students to see exactly where the chapter is going and to set their goals before they begin the chapter. I link these goals directly to the chapter's major headings.

In-Text Review Quizzes

A review quiz at the end of most major sections enables students to determine whether a topic needs further study before moving on. This feature includes a reference to the appropriate MyEconLab study plan to help students further test their understanding.

> ### REVIEW QUIZ
> 1 What is the distinction between a money price and a relative price?
> 2 Explain why a relative price is an opportunity cost.
> 3 Think of examples of goods whose relative price has risen or fallen by a large amount.
>
> myeconlab **Study Plan 3.1**

Key Terms

Highlighted terms within the text simplify the student's task of learning the vocabulary of economics. Each highlighted term appears in an end-of-chapter list with page numbers, in an end-of-book glossary with page numbers, boldfaced in the index, in the Web glossary, and in the Web Flash Cards.

leads to an increase in the demand for *most* goods, it does not lead to an increase in the demand for *all* goods. A **normal good** is one for which demand increases as income increases. An **inferior good** is one for which demand decreases as income increases. Transportation has examples of both normal and inferior goods. As incomes increase, rail travel (a normal good) increases and long-distance bus trips (an infe-

Key Terms

Change in demand, 62
Change in supply, 67
Change in the quantity demanded, 65
Change in the quantity supplied, 68
Competitive market, 60
Complement, 63
Demand, 61
Demand curve, 62
Equilibrium price, 70
Equilibrium quantity, 70
Inferior good, 64
Law of demand, 61
Law of supply, 66
Money price, 60
Normal good, 64
Quantity demanded, 61
Quantity supplied, 66

Normal good A good for which demand increases as income increases. (p. 64)

North American Free Trade Agreement An agreement, which became effective on January 1, 1994, to eliminate all barriers to international trade between the United States, Canada, and Mexico after a 15-year phasing-in period. (p. 408)

Diagrams That Show the Action

Through eight editions, this book has set new standards of clarity in its diagrams. My goal has always been to show "where the economic action is." The diagrams in this book continue to generate an enormously positive response, which confirms my view that graphical analysis is the most powerful tool available for teaching and learning economics. But many students find graphs hard to work with. For this reason, I have developed the entire art program with the study and review needs of the student in mind.

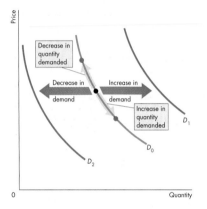

The diagrams feature

- Original curves consistently shown in blue
- Shifted curves, equilibrium points, and other important features highlighted in red
- Color-blended arrows to suggest movement
- Graphs paired with data tables
- Diagrams labeled with boxed notes
- Extended captions that make each diagram and its caption a self-contained object for study and review.

End-of-Chapter Study Material

Each chapter closes with a concise summary organized by major topics, lists of key terms (all with page references), problems, critical thinking questions, and Web Activities.

The end-of-chapter problem section includes news-based and real-world problems that are new to this edition. Solutions to the odd-numbered problems are provided on MyEconLab; the even-numbered problems are left for students to solve on their own. This arrangement offers help to students and flexibility to instructors who want to assign problems for credit.

Reading Between the Lines

In *Reading Between the Lines*, which appears at the end of each chapter, I show the student how to apply the tools they have just learned by analyzing an article from a newspaper or news Web site. The eighth edition features 16 new articles. I have chosen each article so that it sheds additional light on the questions first raised in the Chapter Opener.

Special "You're the Voter" sections in selected chapters invite students to analyze typical campaign topics and to probe their own stances on key public policy issues. Critical Thinking questions about the article appear with the end-of-chapter questions and problems.

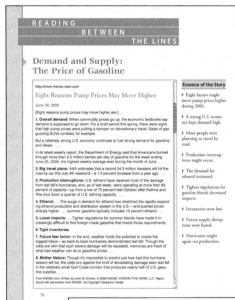

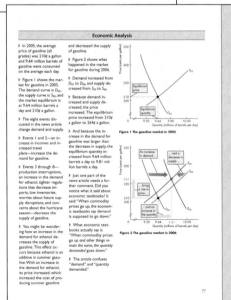

For the Instructor

This book enables you to achieve three objectives in your principles course:

- Focus on the economic way of thinking
- Explain the issues and problems of our time
- Choose your own course structure

Focus on the Economic Way of Thinking

You know how hard it is to encourage a student to think like an economist. But that is your goal. Consistent with this goal, the text focuses on and repeatedly uses the central ideas: choice; tradeoff; opportunity cost; the margin; incentives; the gains from voluntary exchange; the forces of demand, supply, and equilibrium; the pursuit of economic rent; the tension between self-interest and the social interest; and the scope and limitations of government actions.

Explain the Issues and Problems of Our Time

Students must *use* the central ideas and tools if they are to begin to *understand* them. There is no better way to motivate students than by using the tools of economics to explain the issues that confront today's world. Issues such as globalization and the emergence of China as a major economic force; the new economy with new near-monopolies such as eBay and the widening income gap between rich and poor; the post-9/11 economy and the reallocation of resources toward counterterrorism and the defense that it entails; corporate scandals and the principal-agent problems and incentives faced by corporate managers; HIV/AIDS and the enormous cost of drugs for treating it; the disappearing tropical rainforests and the challenge that this problem of the commons creates; the challenge of managing the world's water resources; the persistent unemployment during the nation's jobless recovery of 2002 and 2003; the looming debt that arises from our newly emerged federal budget deficit and the even greater fiscal problems that arise from the Social Security obligations to an aging population; our vast and rising international deficit; and the tumbling value of the dollar on the foreign exchange market.

Choose Your Own Course Structure

You want to teach your own course. I have organized this book to enable you to do so. I demonstrate the book's flexibility in the flexibility chart and alternative sequences table that appear on pp. xxv–xxvi. You can use this book to teach a traditional course that blends theory and policy or a current policy issues course. You can structure your macro course to emphasize long-term growth and supply-side fundamentals. Or you can follow a traditional macro sequence and emphasize short-term fluctuations. The choice is yours.

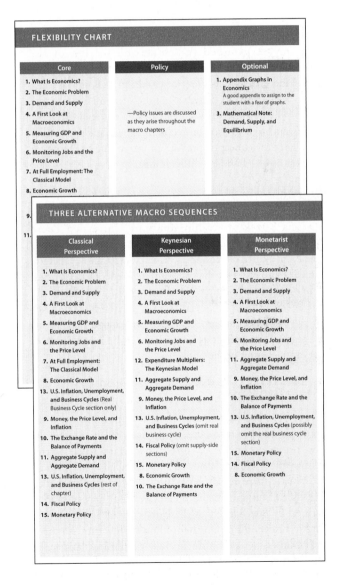

FLEXIBILITY CHART

Core	Policy	Optional
1. What Is Economics?		1. Appendix Graphs in Economics A good appendix to assign to the student with a fear of graphs.
2. The Economic Problem		
3. Demand and Supply	—Policy issues are discussed as they arise throughout the macro chapters	3. Mathematical Note: Demand, Supply, and Equilibrium
4. A First Look at Macroeconomics		
5. Measuring GDP and Economic Growth		
6. Monitoring Jobs and the Price Level		
7. At Full Employment: The Classical Model		
8. Economic Growth		
9.		
11.		

THREE ALTERNATIVE MACRO SEQUENCES

Classical Perspective	Keynesian Perspective	Monetarist Perspective
1. What Is Economics?	1. What Is Economics?	1. What Is Economics?
2. The Economic Problem	2. The Economic Problem	2. The Economic Problem
3. Demand and Supply	3. Demand and Supply	3. Demand and Supply
4. A First Look at Macroeconomics	4. A First Look at Macroeconomics	4. A First Look at Macroeconomics
5. Measuring GDP and Economic Growth	5. Measuring GDP and Economic Growth	5. Measuring GDP and Economic Growth
6. Monitoring Jobs and the Price Level	6. Monitoring Jobs and the Price Level	6. Monitoring Jobs and the Price Level
7. At Full Employment: The Classical Model	12. Expenditure Multipliers: The Keynesian Model	11. Aggregate Supply and Aggregate Demand
8. Economic Growth	11. Aggregate Supply and Aggregate Demand	9. Money, the Price Level, and Inflation
13. U.S. Inflation, Unemployment, and Business Cycles (Real Business Cycle section only)	9. Money, the Price Level, and Inflation	10. The Exchange Rate and the Balance of Payments
9. Money, the Price Level, and Inflation	13. U.S. Inflation, Unemployment, and Business Cycles (omit real business cycle)	13. U.S. Inflation, Unemployment, and Business Cycles (possibly omit the real business cycle section)
10. The Exchange Rate and the Balance of Payments	14. Fiscal Policy (omit supply-side sections)	15. Monetary Policy
11. Aggregate Supply and Aggregate Demand	15. Monetary Policy	14. Fiscal Policy
13. U.S. Inflation, Unemployment, and Business Cycles (rest of chapter)	8. Economic Growth	8. Economic Growth
14. Fiscal Policy	10. The Exchange Rate and the Balance of Payments	
15. Monetary Policy		

Instructor's Manual

The Instructor's Manual integrates the teaching and learning package and serves as a guide to all the supplements. Each chapter contains a chapter outline, what's new in the eighth edition, teaching suggestions, a look at where we have been and where we are going, a list of available overhead transparencies, a description of the electronic supplements, additional discussion questions, answers to the Review Quizzes, solutions to end-of-chapter problems, additional problems, and solutions to the additional problems. The chapter outline and teaching suggestions sections are keyed to the PowerPoint lecture notes.

Lecture Notes   Ready to use lecture notes from each chapter are grouped in the second section of the Instructor's Manual. These notes run approximately 3 to 5 pages and enable a new user of Parkin to walk into a classroom well armed to deliver a polished lecture. The lecture notes provide concise statements of key material, alternate tables and figures, key terms, definitions, and boxes that highlight key concepts, provide an interesting anecdote, or suggest how to handle a difficult idea.

Worksheets   Another innovative feature of the Instructor's Manual is a set of Worksheets prepared by Patricia Kuzyk of Washington State University. These Worksheets ask students to contemplate real-world problems that illustrate economic principles. Examples include showing the effect of the catastrophic events of 9/11 using a marginal cost/marginal benefit diagram, and calculating the effects of funding Social Security for the huge number of baby-boomer retirees. Instructors can assign these as in-class group projects or as homework. There is a Worksheet for every chapter of the book.

Three Test Banks

Three Test Banks with nearly 6,500 questions, provide multiple-choice, true-false, numerical, fill-in-the-blank, short-answer, and essay questions. Mark Rush of the University of Florida reviewed and edited all existing questions to ensure their clarity and consistency with the eighth edition and incorporated over 500 new questions written by Sue Bartlett of the University of South Florida and Jeff Reynolds of Northern Illinois University. All three test banks are available in Test Generator Software (TestGen with QuizMaster). Fully networkable, it is available for Windows and Macintosh. TestGen's graphical interface enables instructors to view, edit, and add questions; transfer questions to tests; and print different forms of tests. Tests can be formatted with varying fonts and styles, margins, and headers and footers, as in any word-processing document. Search and sort features let the instructor quickly locate questions and arrange them in a preferred order. QuizMaster, working with your school's computer network, automatically grades the exams, stores the results on disk, and allows the instructor to view or print a variety of reports. These Test Banks are available in hard copy and electronically on the Instructor's Resource Disk and in the instructors' resources section of MyEconLab and the Instructors' Resource Center.

PowerPoint Resources

Robin Bade and I have developed a full-color Microsoft PowerPoint Lecture Presentation for each chapter that includes all the figures from the text, animated graphs, and speaking notes. The slide outlines are based on the chapter outlines in the Instructor's Manual, and the speaking notes are based on the Instructor's Manual teaching suggestions. The presentations can be used electronically in the classroom or can be printed to create hard-copy transparency masters. This item is available for Macintosh and Windows.

Clicker-Ready PowerPoint Resources

This edition features the addition of clicker-ready PowerPoint slides for the Personal Response System you use. Each chapter of the text includes ten multiple-choice questions that test important concepts. Instructors can assign these as in-class assignments or review quizzes.

Overhead Transparencies

Full-color overhead transparencies of over 100 figures from the text will improve the clarity of your lectures. They are available to qualified adopters of the text (contact your Addison-Wesley sales representative).

Instructor's Resource Disk

Fully compatible with Windows and Macintosh computers, this CD-ROM contains electronic files of every instructor supplement for the eighth edition. Files included are: Microsoft® Word and Adobe® PDF files of the Instructor's Manual and Test Bank; complete PowerPoint® slides; and the Computerized TestGen® Test Bank. Add this useful resource to your exam copy book-bag, or locate your local Addison-Wesley sales representative at www.aw-bc.com/replocator to request a copy.

MyEconLab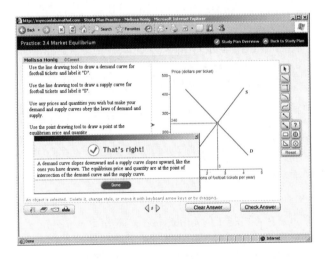

MyEconLab is an online course management, testing, and tutorial resource. Instructors choose how much, or how little, time they want to spend setting up and using MyEconLab.

For each chapter, and requiring no instructor set-up, students get two preloaded Sample Tests, a Study Plan, and tutorial help. The online Gradebook records each student's time spent and performance on the Tests and Study Plan. Instructors can access the Gradebook at any time during the course and obtain reports by student or by chapter.

Instructors can assign Tests, Quizzes, and Homework in MyEconLab using five resources:

- Pre-loaded Sample Test questions
- Study Plan questions
- Test Bank questions
- Self-authored questions using Econ Exercise Builder
- Problems similar to the end-of-chapter problems

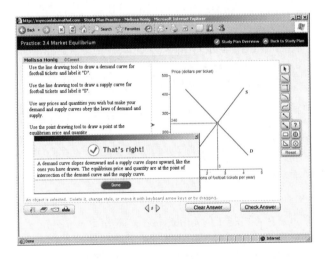

These test resources provide ample material from which the instructor can create assignments. Tests use multiple-choice, graph drawing, and free response questions and some questions are generated algorithmically so that they present differently each time they are worked.

MyEconLab grades every problem, even those with graphs, and students get immediate feedback with links to additional learning tools.

Customization and Communication MyEconLab in CourseCompass provides additional optional customization and communication tools. Instructors who teach distance-learning courses or very large lecture sections find the CourseCompass format useful because they can upload course documents and assignments, customize the order of chapters, and use communication features such as Digital Dropbox and Discussion Board.

For the Student

Four outstanding support tools for the student are

- Study Guide
- MyEconLab
- Student PowerPoint Lecture Notes
- Econ Tutor Center

Study Guide

The eighth edition Study Guide by Mark Rush of the University of Florida is carefully coordinated with the text, MyEconLab, and the Test Banks. Each chapter of the Study Guide contains

- Key concepts
- Helpful hints
- True/false/uncertain questions
- Multiple-choice questions
- Short-answer questions
- Common questions or misconceptions that the student explains as if he or she were the teacher

Each part allows students to test their cumulative understanding with questions that go across chapters and work a sample midterm examination.

MyEconLab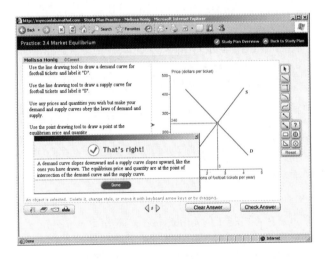

MyEconLab puts students in control of their own learning through a suite of testing, practice, and study tools tied to the online, interactive version of the textbook and other media resources.

Within MyEconLab's structured environment, students practice what they learn, test their understanding, and pursue a personal Study Plan generated from their performance on sample tests.

At the core of MyEconLab are the following features:

- Sample Tests, two per chapter
- Personal Study Plan
- Tutorial Instruction
- Graphing Tool

Sample Tests Two Sample Tests for each chapter are preloaded in MyEconLab, enabling students to practice what they have learned, test their understanding, and identify areas in which they need to do further work. Students can study on their own or they can complete assignments created by their instructor.

Personal Study Plan Based on a student's performance on a Test, a personal Study Plan is generated that shows where further study is needed. The Study Plan consists of a series of additional practice exercises with detailed feedback and guided solutions and keyed to other tutorial resources.

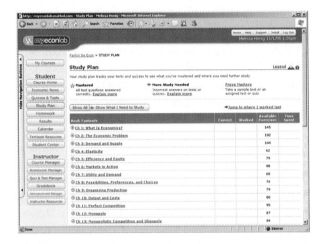

Tutorial Instruction Launched from the exercises in the Study Plan, tutorial instruction is provided in the form of step-by-step solutions and other media-based explanations.

Graphing Tool A graphing tool integrated into the Tests and Study Plan exercises enables students to make and manipulate graphs so that they better understand how concepts, numbers, and graphs connect. Questions that

use the graphing tool (like all the other questions) are automatically graded.

Additional MyEconLab Tools

1. eText

2. Animated figures—every figure from the textbook in step-by-step animations with audio explanations of the action

3. Glossary—a searchable version of the textbook glossary with additional examples and links to related terms

4. Glossary Flashcards—every key term as a flashcard, allowing students to quiz themselves on vocabulary from one or more chapters at a time

5. Office Hours—email economic-related questions to the authors

6. *Economics in the News*—daily updates during the school year of news items with links to sources for further reading and discussion questions

7. Links for Web Activities—all the links needed for the Web Activities in the textbook

8. eThemes of the Times—archived articles from *The New York Times*, correlated to each textbook chapter and paired with Critical Thinking questions

9. Research Navigator (CourseCompass version only)—extensive help on the research process and four exclusive databases of credible and reliable source material including *The New York Times*, the *Financial Times*, and peer-reviewed journals

PowerPoint Lecture Notes

Robin Bade and I have prepared a set of PowerPoint lecture notes especially for students. These notes contain an outline of each chapter with the textbook figures animated. Students can download these lecture notes from MyEconLab, print them, and bring them to class or use them in creating their own set of notes for use when preparing for tests and exams.

Econ Tutor Center

Staffed by qualified, experienced college economics instructors, the Econ Tutor Center is open five days a week, seven hours a day. Tutors can be reached by phone, fax, e-mail or White Board technology. The Econ Tutor Center hours are designed to meet your students' study schedules, with evening hours Sunday through Thursday. Students receive one-on-one tutoring on examples, related exercises, and problems.

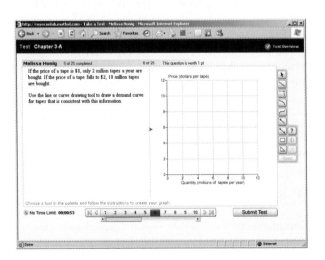

Special Editions

Three special editions of the eighth edition text are available:

- Economist.com Edition
- The Wall Street Journal Edition
- Financial Times Edition

Economist.com Edition

The premier online source of economic news analysis, Economist.com provides your students with insight and opinion on current economic events. Through an agreement between Addison Wesley and *The Economist,* your students can receive a low-cost subscription to this premium Web site for 12 weeks, including the complete text of the current issue of *The Economist* and access to *The Economist's* searchable archives. Other features include Web-only weekly articles, news feeds with current world and business news, and stock market and currency data. Professors who adopt this special edition will receive a complimentary one-year subscription to Economist.com.

The Wall Street Journal Edition

Addison Wesley is also pleased to provide your students with access to *The Wall Street Journal,* the most respected and trusted daily source for information on business and economics. For a small additional charge, Addison Wesley offers your students a subscription to *The Wall Street Journal* and WSJ.com. Ten-week and 15-week subscriptions are available. Adopting professors will receive a complimentary one-year subscription to *The Wall Street Journal* as well as access to WSJ.com.

Financial Times Edition

Featuring international news and analysis from FT journalists in more than 50 countries, the *Financial Times* will provide your students with insights and perspectives on economic developments around the world. The Financial Times Edition provides your students with a 15-week subscription to one of the world's leading business publications. Adopting professors will receive a complimentary one-year subscription to the *Financial Times* as well as access to FT.com.

PearsonChoices Alternative Editions . . . Your Text Your Way!

With ever-increasing demands on time and resources, today's college faculty and students want greater value, innovation, and flexibility in products designed to meet teaching and learning goals. We've responded to that need by creating PearsonChoices, a unique program that allows faculty and students to choose from a range of text and media formats that match their teaching and learning styles and students' budgets.

Books à la Carte Edition For today's student on the go, we've created a portable version of *Macroeconomics* that is three-hole punched. Students can take only what they need to class, incorporate their own notes, and save money! Each Books à la Carte text arrives with a laminated study card, perfect for students to use when preparing for exams, plus access to MyEconLab.

SafariX Textbooks Online SafariX Textbooks Online is an exciting new service for college students looking to save money on required or recommended textbooks for academic courses. By subscribing to Web books through SafariX Textbooks Online, students can save up to 50 percent off the suggested list price of print textbooks. Log on to www.safarix.com for details about purchasing *Macroeconomics.*

Acknowledgments

I thank my current and former colleagues and friends at the University of Western Ontario who have taught me so much. They are Jim Davies, Jeremy Greenwood, Ig Horstmann, Peter Howitt, Greg Huffman, David Laidler, Phil Reny, Chris Robinson, John Whalley, and Ron Wonnacott. I also thank Doug McTaggart and Christopher Findlay, co-authors of the Australian edition, and Melanie Powell and Kent Matthews, co-authors of the European edition. Suggestions arising from their adaptations of earlier editions have been helpful to me in preparing this edition.

I thank the several thousand students whom I have been privileged to teach. The instant response that comes from the look of puzzlement or enlightenment has taught me how to teach economics.

It is a special joy to thank the many outstanding editors, media specialists, and others at Addison Wesley who contributed to the concerted publishing effort that brought this edition to completion. Denise Clinton, Editor-in-Chief for Economics and Finance, was a constant source of inspiration and encouragement and provided overall direction to the project. Adrienne D'Ambrosio, Acquisitions Editor for Economics and my sponsoring editor, played a major role in shaping this revision and the many outstanding supplements that accompany it. Adrienne brings intelligence and insight to her work and is the unchallengeably pre-eminent economics editor. Kay Ueno, Director of Development, brought her huge professional experience to managing the development effort. Cynthia Sheridan, Development Editor, worked tirelessly to bring reviews in on time and consolidate and summarize them. Michelle Neil, Director of Media, continued her remarkable work to improve MyEconLab and Melissa Honig, Senior Media Producer and Doug Ruby, Content Lead for MyEconLab, ensured that all our media assets were correctly assembled. Roxanne Hoch, Senior Marketing Manager, provided inspired marketing strategy and direction. Barbara Willette provided a superbly careful and consistent copy edit. Charles Spaulding, Senior Designer, designed the cover and package and yet again surpassed the challenge of ensuring that we meet the highest design standards. Joe Vetere provided endless technical help with the text and art files. And Ingrid Benson with the other members of an outstanding editorial and production team at Elm Street kept the project on track on an impossibly tight schedule. I thank all of these wonderful people. It has been inspiring to work with them and to share in creating what I believe is a truly outstanding educational tool.

I thank our talented eighth edition supplements authors—Sue Bartlett, University of South Florida; Pat Kuzyk, Washington State University; and Jeff Reynolds, Northern Illinois University.

I especially thank Mark Rush, who yet again played a crucial role in creating another edition of this text and package. Mark has been a constant source of good advice and good humor. I thank the many exceptional reviewers who have shared their insights through the various editions of this book. Their contribution has been invaluable. I particularly thank Barry Falk and Kenneth Christianson for their extraordinarily careful accuracy reviews.

I thank the people who work directly with me. Jeannie Gillmore provided outstanding research assistance on many topics, including the *Reading Between the Lines* news articles. Richard Parkin created the electronic art files and offered many ideas that improved the figures in this book. And Laurel Davies managed an ever-growing and ever more complex MyEconLab database.

As with the previous editions, this one owes an enormous debt to Robin Bade. I dedicate this book to her and again thank her for her work. I could not have written this book without the unselfish help she has given me. My thanks to her are unbounded.

Classroom experience will test the value of this book. I would appreciate hearing from instructors and students about how I can continue to improve it in future editions.

Michael Parkin
London, Ontario, Canada
michael.parkin@uwo.ca

Reviewers

Eric Abrams, Hawaii Pacific University

Christopher Adams, Federal Trade Commission

Tajudeen Adenekan, Bronx Community College

Syed Ahmed, Cameron University

Frank Albritton, Seminole Community College

Milton Alderfer, Miami-Dade Community College

William Aldridge, Shelton State Community College

Donald L. Alexander, Western Michigan University

Terence Alexander, Iowa State University

Stuart Allen, University of North Carolina, Greensboro

Sam Allgood, University of Nebraska, Lincoln

Neil Alper, Northeastern University

Alan Anderson, Fordham University

Lisa R. Anderson, College of William and Mary

Jeff Ankrom, Wittenberg University

Fatma Antar, Manchester Community Technical College

Kofi Apraku, University of North Carolina, Asheville

Moshen Bahmani-Oskooee, University of Wisconsin, Milwaukee

Donald Balch, University of South Carolina

Mehmet Balcilar, Wayne State University

Paul Ballantyne, University of Colorado

Sue Bartlett, University of South Florida

Jose Juan Bautista, Xavier University of Louisiana

Valerie R. Bencivenga, University of Texas, Austin

Ben Bernanke, Chairman of Federal Reserve

Margot Biery, Tarrant County Community College South

John Bittorowitz, Ball State University

David Black, University of Toledo

Kelly Blanchard, Purdue University

S. Brock Blomberg, Claremont McKenna College

William T. Bogart, Case Western Reserve University

Giacomo Bonanno, University of California, Davis

Tan Khay Boon, Nanyard Technological University

Sunne Brandmeyer, University of South Florida

Audie Brewton, Northeastern Illinois University

Baird Brock, Central Missouri State University

Byron Brown, Michigan State University

Jeffrey Buser, Columbus State Community College

Alison Butler, Florida International University

Tania Carbiener, Southern Methodist University

Kevin Carey, American University

Kathleen A. Carroll, University of Maryland, Baltimore County

Michael Carter, University of Massachusetts, Lowell

Edward Castronova, California State University, Fullerton

Subir Chakrabarti, Indiana University-Purdue University

Joni Charles, Texas State University

Adhip Chaudhuri, Georgetown University

Gopal Chengalath, Texas Tech University

Daniel Christiansen, Albion College

Kenny Christianson, Binghampton University

John J. Clark, Community College of Allegheny County, Allegheny Campus

Meredith Clement, Dartmouth College

Michael B. Cohn, U. S. Merchant Marine Academy

Robert Collinge, University of Texas, San Antonio

Carol Condon, Kean University

Doug Conway, Mesa Community College

Larry Cook, University of Toledo

Bobby Corcoran, Middle Tennessee State University, retired

Kevin Cotter, Wayne State University

James Peery Cover, University of Alabama, Tuscaloosa

Erik Craft, University of Richmond

Eleanor D. Craig, University of Delaware

Jim Craven, Clark College

Elizabeth Crowell, University of Michigan, Dearborn

Stephen Cullenberg, University of California, Riverside

David Culp, Slippery Rock University

Norman V. Cure, Macomb Community College

Dan Dabney, University of Texas, Austin

Andrew Dane, Angelo State University

Joseph Daniels, Marquette University

Gregory DeFreitas, Hofstra University

David Denslow, University of Florida

Mark Dickie, University of Central Florida

James Dietz, California State University, Fullerton

Carol Dole, State University of West Georgia

Ronald Dorf, Inver Hills Community College

John Dorsey, University of Maryland, College Park

Eric Drabkin, Hawaii Pacific University

Amrik Singh Dua, Mt. San Antonio College

Thomas Duchesneau, University of Maine, Orono

Lucia Dunn, Ohio State University

Donald Dutkowsky, Syracuse University

John Edgren, Eastern Michigan University

David J. Eger, Alpena Community College

Harry Ellis, Jr., University of North Texas

Ibrahim Elsaify, Goldey-Beacom College

Kenneth G. Elzinga, University of Virginia

Antonina Espiritu, Hawaii Pacific University

Gwen Eudey, University of Pennsylvania

Barry Falk, Iowa State University

M. Fazeli, Hofstra University

Philip Fincher, Louisiana Tech University

F. Firoozi, University of Texas, San Antonio

Nancy Folbre, University of Massachusetts at Amherst

Kenneth Fong, Temasek Polytechnic (Singapore)

Steven Francis, Holy Cross College

David Franck, University of North Carolina, Charlotte

Roger Frantz, San Diego State University

Mark Frascatore, Clarkson University

Alwyn Fraser, Atlantic Union College

Marc Fusaro, East Carolina University

James Gale, Michigan Technological University

Susan Gale, New York University

Roy Gardner, Indiana University

Eugene Gentzel, Pensacola Junior College

Scott Gilbert, Southern Illinois University at Carbondale

Andrew Gill, California State University, Fullerton

Robert Giller, Virginia Polytechnic Institute and State University

Robert Gillette, University of Kentucky

James N. Giordano, Villanova University

Maria Giuili, Diablo College

Susan Glanz, St. John's University

Robert Gordon, San Diego State University

Richard Gosselin, Houston Community College

John Graham, Rutgers University

John Griffen, Worcester Polytechnic Institute

Wayne Grove, Syracuse University

Robert Guell, Indiana State University

Jamie Haag, Pacific University, Oregon

Gail Heyne Hafer, Lindenwood University

Rik W. Hafer, Southern Illinois University, Edwardsville

Daniel Hagen, Western Washington University

David R. Hakes, University of Northern Iowa

Craig Hakkio, Federal Reserve Bank, Kansas City

Bridget Gleeson Hanna, Rochester Institute of Technology

Ann Hansen, Westminster College

Seid Hassan, Murray State University

Jonathan Haughton, Suffolk University

Randall Haydon, Wichita State University

Denise Hazlett, Whitman College

Julia Heath, University of Memphis

Jac Heckelman, Wake Forest University

Jolien A. Helsel, Kent State University

James Henderson, Baylor University

Jill Boylston Herndon, University of Florida

Gus Herring, Brookhaven College

John Herrmann, Rutgers University

John M. Hill, Delgado Community College

Jonathan Hill, Florida International University

Lewis Hill, Texas Tech University

Steve Hoagland, University of Akron

Tom Hoerger, Fellow, Research Triangle Institute

Calvin Hoerneman, Delta College

George Hoffer, Virginia Commonwealth University

Dennis L. Hoffman, Arizona State University

Paul Hohenberg, Rensselaer Polytechnic Institute

Jim H. Holcomb, University of Texas, El Paso

Harry Holzer, Georgetown University

Linda Hooks, Washington and Lee University

Jim Horner, Cameron University

Djehane Hosni, University of Central Florida

Harold Hotelling, Jr., Lawrence Technical University

Calvin Hoy, County College of Morris

Ing-Wei Huang, Assumption University, Thailand

Julie Hunsaker, Wayne State University

Beth Ingram, University of Iowa

Jayvanth Ishwaran, Stephen F. Austin State University

Michael Jacobs, Lehman College

S. Hussain Ali Jafri, Tarleton State University

Dennis Jansen, Texas A&M University

Garrett Jones, Southern Florida University

Frederick Jungman, Northwestern Oklahoma State University

Paul Junk, University of Minnesota, Duluth

Leo Kahane, California State University, Hayward

Veronica Kalich, Baldwin-Wallace College

John Kane, State University of New York, Oswego

Eungmin Kang, St. Cloud State University

Arthur Kartman, San Diego State University

Gurmit Kaur, Universiti Teknologi (Malaysia)

Louise Keely, University of Wisconsin at Madison

Manfred W. Keil, Claremont McKenna College

Elizabeth Sawyer Kelly, University of Wisconsin at Madison

Rose Kilburn, Modesto Junior College

Robert Kirk, Indiana University—Purdue University, Indianapolis

Norman Kleinberg, City University of New York, Baruch College

Robert Kleinhenz, California State University, Fullerton

John Krantz, University of Utah

Joseph Kreitzer, University of St. Thomas

Patricia Kuzyk, Washington State University

David Lages, Southwest Missouri State University

W. J. Lane, University of New Orleans

Leonard Lardaro, University of Rhode Island

Kathryn Larson, Elon College

Luther D. Lawson, University of North Carolina, Wilmington

Elroy M. Leach, Chicago State University

Jim Lee, Texas A & M, Corpus Christi

Sang Lee, Southeastern Louisiana University

Robert Lemke, Florida International University

Mary Lesser, Iona College

Jay Levin, Wayne State University

Arik Levinson, University of Wisconsin, Madison

Tony Lima, California State University, Hayward

William Lord, University of Maryland, Baltimore County

Nancy Lutz, Virginia Polytechnic Institute and State University

Murugappa Madhavan, San Diego State University

K. T. Magnusson, Salt Lake Community College

Mark Maier, Glendale Community College

Jean Mangan, Staffordshire University Business School

Michael Marlow, California Polytechnic State University

Akbar Marvasti, University of Houston

Wolfgang Mayer, University of Cincinnati

John McArthur, Wofford College

Amy McCormick, Mary Baldwin College

Russel McCullough, Iowa State University

Gerald McDougall, Wichita State University

Stephen McGary, Brigham Young University-Idaho

Richard D. McGrath, Armstrong Atlantic State University

Richard McIntyre, University of Rhode Island

John McLeod, Georgia Institute of Technology

Mark McLeod, Virginia Tech

B. Starr McMullen, Oregon State University

Mary Ruth McRae, Appalachian State University

Kimberly Merritt, Cameron University

Charles Meyer, Iowa State University

Peter Mieszkowski, Rice University

John Mijares, University of North Carolina, Asheville

Richard A. Miller, Wesleyan University

Judith W. Mills, Southern Connecticut State University

Glen Mitchell, Nassau Community College

Jeannette C. Mitchell, Rochester Institute of Technology

Khan Mohabbat, Northern Illinois University

Bagher Modjtahedi, University of California, Davis

W. Douglas Morgan, University of California, Santa Barbara

William Morgan, University of Wyoming

James Morley, Washington University in St. Louis

William Mosher, Clark University

Joanne Moss, San Francisco State University

Nivedita Mukherji, Oakland University

Francis Mummery, Fullerton College

Edward Murphy, Southwest Texas State University

Kevin J. Murphy, Oakland University

Kathryn Nantz, Fairfield University

William S. Neilson, Texas A&M University

Bart C. Nemmers, University of Nebraska, Lincoln

Melinda Nish, Orange Coast College

Anthony O'Brien, Lehigh University

Norman Obst, Michigan State University

Constantin Ogloblin, Georgia Southern University

Mary Olson, Tulane University

Terry Olson, Truman State University

James B. O'Neill, University of Delaware

Farley Ordovensky, University of the Pacific

Z. Edward O'Relley, North Dakota State University

Donald Oswald, California State University, Bakersfield

Jan Palmer, Ohio University

Michael Palumbo, Chief, Federal Reserve Board

Chris Papageorgiou, Louisiana State University

G. Hossein Parandvash, Western Oregon State College

Randall Parker, East Carolina University

Robert Parks, Washington University

David Pate, St. John Fisher College

James E. Payne, Illinois State University

Donald Pearson, Eastern Michigan University

Steven Peterson, University of Idaho

Mary Anne Pettit, Southern Illinois University, Edwardsville

William A. Phillips, University of Southern Maine

Dennis Placone, Clemson University

Charles Plot, California Institute of Technology, Pasadena

Mannie Poen, Houston Community College

Kathleen Possai, Wayne State University

Ulrika Praski-Stahlgren, University College in Gavle-Sandviken, Sweden

Edward Price, Oklahoma State University

Rula Qalyoubi, University of Wisconsin, Eau Claire

K. A. Quartey, Talladega College

Herman Quirmbach, Iowa State University

Jeffrey R. Racine, University of South Florida

Peter Rangazas, Indiana University-Purdue University, Indianapolis

Vaman Rao, Western Illinois University

Laura Razzolini, University of Mississippi

Rob Rebelein, University of Cincinnati

J. David Reed, Bowling Green State University

Robert H. Renshaw, Northern Illinois University

Javier Reyes, University of Arkansas

Jeff Reynolds, Northern Illinois University

Rupert Rhodd, Florida Atlantic University

W. Gregory Rhodus, Bentley College

Jennifer Rice, Indiana University, Bloomington

John Robertson, Paducah Community College

Malcolm Robinson, University of North Carolina, Greensboro

Richard Roehl, University of Michigan, Dearborn

Carol Rogers, Georgetown University

William Rogers, University of Northern Colorado

Thomas Romans, State University of New York, Buffalo

David R. Ross, Bryn Mawr College

Thomas Ross, Baldwin Wallace College

Robert J. Rossana, Wayne State University

Jeffrey Rous, University of North Texas

Rochelle Ruffer, Youngstown State University

Mark Rush, University of Florida

Allen R. Sanderson, University of Chicago

Gary Santoni, Ball State University

John Saussy, Harrisburg Area Community College

Don Schlagenhauf, Florida State University

David Schlow, Pennsylvania State University

Paul Schmitt, St. Clair County Community College

Jeremy Schwartz, Hampden-Sydney College

Martin Sefton, University of Nottingham

Esther-Mirjam Sent, University of Notre Dame

Rod Shadbegian, University of Massachusetts, Dartmouth

Gerald Shilling, Eastfield College

Dorothy R. Siden, Salem State College

Mark Siegler, California State University at Sacramento

Scott Simkins, North Carolina Agricultural and Technical State University

Chuck Skoro, Boise State University

Phil Smith, DeKalb College

William Doyle Smith, University of Texas, El Paso

Sarah Stafford, College of William and Mary

Frank Steindl, Oklahoma State University

Jeffrey Stewart, New York University

Allan Stone, Southwest Missouri State University

Courtenay Stone, Ball State University

Paul Storer, Western Washington University

Richard W. Stratton, University of Akron

Mark Strazicich, Ohio State University, Newark

Michael Stroup, Stephen F. Austin State University

Robert Stuart, Rutgers University

Della Lee Sue, Marist College

Abdulhamid Sukar, Cameron University

Terry Sutton, Southeast Missouri State University

Gilbert Suzawa, University of Rhode Island

David Swaine, Andrews University

Jason Taylor, Central Michigan University

Mark Thoma, University of Oregon

Janet Thomas, Bentley College

Kiril Tochkov, SUNY at Binghamton

Kay Unger, University of Montana

Anthony Uremovic, Joliet Junior College

David Vaughn, City University, Washington

Don Waldman, Colgate University

Francis Wambalaba, Portland State University

Rob Wassmer, California State University, Sacramento

Paul A. Weinstein, University of Maryland, College Park

Lee Weissert, St. Vincent College

Robert Whaples, Wake Forest University

David Wharton, Washington College

Mark Wheeler, Western Michigan University

Charles H. Whiteman, University of Iowa

Sandra Williamson, University of Pittsburgh

Brenda Wilson, Brookhaven Community College

Larry Wimmer, Brigham Young University

Mark Witte, Northwestern University

Willard E. Witte, Indiana University

Mark Wohar, University of Nebraska, Omaha

Laura Wolff, Southern Illinois University, Edwardsville

Cheonsik Woo, Vice President, Korea Development Institute

Douglas Wooley, Radford University

Arthur G. Woolf, University of Vermont

John T. Young, Riverside Community College

Michael Youngblood, Rock Valley College

Peter Zaleski, Villanova University

Jason Zimmerman, South Dakota State University

David Zucker, Martha Stewart Living Omnimedia

Supplements Authors

Sue Bartlett, University of South Florida

James Cobbe, Florida State University

Carol Dole, State University of West Georgia

John Graham, Rutgers University

Jill Herndon, University of Florida

Sang Lee, Southeastern Louisiana University

Patricia Kuzyk, Washington State University

James Morley, Washington University, St. Louis

William Mosher, Clark University

Constantin Ogloblin, Georgia Southern University

Edward Price, Oklahoma State University

Jeff Reynolds, Northern Illinois University

Mark Rush, University of Florida

Della Lee Sue, Marist College

Michael Stroup, Stephen F. Austin State University

FLEXIBILITY CHART

Core

1. What Is Economics?

2. The Economic Problem

3. Demand and Supply

4. A First Look at Macroeconomics

5. Measuring GDP and Economic Growth

6. Monitoring Jobs and the Price Level

7. At Full Employment: The Classical Model

8. Economic Growth
   This chapter may be delayed and studied at any desired point.

9. Money, the Price Level, and Inflation

11. Aggregate Supply and Aggregate Demand
    This chapter may be covered at any point after Chapter 5.

Policy

—Policy issues are discussed as they arise throughout the macro chapters

14. Fiscal Policy
15. Monetary Policy

Optional

1. Appendix Graphs in Economics
   A good appendix to assign to the student with a fear of graphs.

3. Mathematical Note: Demand, Supply, and Equilibrium

10. The Exchange Rate and the Balance of Payments
    This chapter may be delayed and studied at end of the course.

12. Expenditure Multipliers: The Keynesian Model
    This chapter may be brought forward and studied at any point after Chapter 5.

13. U.S. Inflation, Unemployment, and Business Cycles

16. Trading with the World

THREE ALTERNATIVE MACRO SEQUENCES

Classical Perspective

1. What Is Economics?
2. The Economic Problem
3. Demand and Supply
4. A First Look at Macroeconomics
5. Measuring GDP and Economic Growth
6. Monitoring Jobs and the Price Level
7. At Full Employment: The Classical Model
8. Economic Growth
13. U.S. Inflation, Unemployment, and Business Cycles (Real Business Cycle section only)
9. Money, the Price Level, and Inflation
10. The Exchange Rate and the Balance of Payments
11. Aggregate Supply and Aggregate Demand
13. U.S. Inflation, Unemployment, and Business Cycles (rest of chapter)
14. Fiscal Policy
15. Monetary Policy

Keynesian Perspective

1. What Is Economics?
2. The Economic Problem
3. Demand and Supply
4. A First Look at Macroeconomics
5. Measuring GDP and Economic Growth
6. Monitoring Jobs and the Price Level
12. Expenditure Multipliers: The Keynesian Model
11. Aggregate Supply and Aggregate Demand
9. Money, the Price Level, and Inflation
13. U.S. Inflation, Unemployment, and Business Cycles (omit real business cycle)
14. Fiscal Policy (omit supply-side sections)
15. Monetary Policy
8. Economic Growth
10. The Exchange Rate and the Balance of Payments

Monetarist Perspective

1. What Is Economics?
2. The Economic Problem
3. Demand and Supply
4. A First Look at Macroeconomics
5. Measuring GDP and Economic Growth
6. Monitoring Jobs and the Price Level
11. Aggregate Supply and Aggregate Demand
9. Money, the Price Level, and Inflation
10. The Exchange Rate and the Balance of Payments
13. U.S. Inflation, Unemployment, and Business Cycles (possibly omit the real business cycle section)
15. Monetary Policy
14. Fiscal Policy
8. Economic Growth

BRIEF CONTENTS

CONTENTS

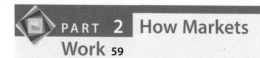

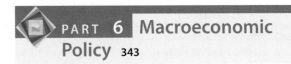

EIGHTH EDITION

MACROECONOMICS

PARKIN

CHAPTER 1

What Is Economics?

Understanding Our Changing World

You are studying economics at a time of enormous change. Much of the change is for the better. The information age with its lap-

top computers, wireless Internet connections, iPods, DVD movies, cell phones, video games, and a host of other gadgets and toys has transformed the way we work and play. And as we crank up the rate of production of these high-tech goods and services, our incomes and the incomes of people in China, India, and other countries are expanding rapidly.

But some change is for the worse. As the new millennium began, the U.S. economy slipped into recession. Businesses fired hundreds of thousands of workers and cut production. Then, on September 11, 2001, terrorist attacks generated shockwaves that are still reverberating around the global economy and have no visible end. Natural disasters such as Hurricane Katrina and the Indian Ocean tsunami wiped out the homes and devastated the lives of millions. And the onslaught of AIDS has lowered the life expectancy in some African nations to just 33 years.

◆ The events and forces that we've just described are changing today's world. Your course in economics will help you to understand how these powerful forces shape our world. This chapter takes the first step. It describes the questions that economists try to answer, the way they think about those questions, and the methods they use in the search for answers. And an appendix explains the types of graphs that economists use in their search for answers.

After studying this chapter, you will be able to

▶ Define economics and distinguish between microeconomics and macroeconomics

▶ Explain the two big questions of economics

▶ Explain the key ideas that define the economic way of thinking

▶ Explain how economists go about their work as social scientists

Definition of Economics

All economic questions arise because we want more than we can get. We want a peaceful and secure world. We want clean air, lakes, and rivers. We want long and healthy lives. We want good schools, colleges, and universities. We want spacious and comfortable homes. We want an enormous range of sports and recreational gear from running shoes to jet skis. We want the time to enjoy sports, games, novels, movies, music, travel, and hanging out with our friends.

What each one of us can get is limited by time, by the incomes we earn, and by the prices we must pay. Everyone ends up with some unsatisfied wants. What we can get as a society is limited by our productive resources. These resources include the gifts of nature, human labor and ingenuity, and tools and equipment that we have produced.

Our inability to satisfy all our wants is called **scarcity**. The poor and the rich alike face scarcity. A child wants a $1.00 can of soda and two 50¢ packs of gum but has only $1.00 in his pocket. He faces scarcity. A millionaire wants to spend the weekend playing golf *and* spend the same weekend at the office attending a business strategy meeting. She faces scarcity. A society wants to provide improved health care, install a computer in every classroom, explore space, clean polluted lakes and rivers, and so on. Society faces scarcity. Even parrots face scarcity!

Faced with scarcity, we must *choose* among the available alternatives. The child must *choose* the soda *or* the gum. The millionaire must *choose* the golf game *or* the meeting. As a society, we must *choose* among health care, national defense, and education.

The choices that we make depend on the incentives that we face. An **incentive** is a reward that encourages an action or a penalty that discourages one. If the price of soda falls, the child has an *incentive* to choose more soda. If a profit of $10 million is at stake, the millionaire has an *incentive* to skip the golf game. As computer prices tumble, school boards have an *incentive* to connect more classrooms to the Internet.

Economics is the social science that studies the *choices* that individuals, businesses, governments, and entire societies make as they cope with *scarcity* and the *incentives* that influence and reconcile those choices. The subject divides into two main parts

- Microeconomics
- Macroeconomics

Microeconomics

Microeconomics is the study of the choices that individuals and businesses make, the way these choices interact in markets, and the influence of governments. Some examples of microeconomic questions are: Why are people buying more DVDs and fewer movie tickets? How would a tax on e-commerce affect eBay?

Macroeconomics

Macroeconomics is the study of the performance of the national economy and the global economy. Some examples of macroeconomic questions are: Why did incomes in the United States grow rapidly in 2006? Can the Federal Reserve keep incomes growing by cutting interest rates?

Not only do I want a cracker—we all want a cracker!

© The New Yorker Collection 1985
Frank Modell from cartoonbank.com. All Rights Reserved.

REVIEW QUIZ

1 List some examples of scarcity in the United States today.
2 Use the headlines in today's news to provide some examples of scarcity around the world.
3 Use today's news to illustrate the distinction between microeconomics and macroeconomics.

myeconlab Study Plan 1.1

Two Big Economic Questions

Two big questions summarize the scope of economics:

■ How do choices end up determining *what, how,* and *for whom* goods and services get produced?

■ When do choices made in the pursuit of *self-interest* also promote the *social interest*?

What, How, and For Whom?

Goods and services are the objects that people value and produce to satisfy human wants. Goods are physical objects such as golf balls. Services are tasks performed for people such as haircuts. By far the largest part of what the United States produces today is services such as retail and wholesale trade, health care, and education. Goods are a small part of total production.

What? What we produce changes over time. Seventy years ago, 25 percent of Americans worked on farms. That number has shrunk to 3 percent today. Over the same period, the number of people who produce goods—in mining, construction, and manufacturing—has shrunk from 31 percent to 17 percent. The decrease in farming and manufacturing is reflected in an increase in services. Seventy years ago, 45 percent of the population produced services. Today, more than 80 percent of working Americans have service jobs. Figure 1.1 shows these trends.

What determines the quantities of corn, DVDs, and haircuts and all the other millions of items that we produce?

How? Goods and services are produced by using productive resources that economists call **factors of production**. Factors of production are grouped into four categories:

■ Land

■ Labor

■ Capital

■ Entrepreneurship

Land The "gifts of nature" that we use to produce goods and services are called **land**. In economics, land is what in everyday language we call *natural resources*.

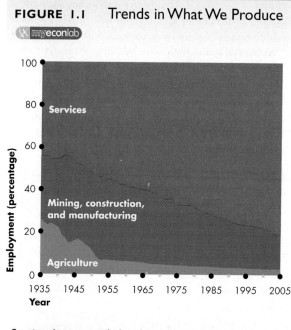

FIGURE 1.1   Trends in What We Produce

Services have expanded, and agriculture, mining, construction, and manufacturing have shrunk.

Source of data: U.S. Census Bureau, *Statistical Abstract of the United States.*

It includes land in the everyday sense together with metal ores, oil, gas and coal, water, and air.

Our land surface and water resources are renewable and some of our mineral resources can be recycled. But the resources that we use to create energy are nonrenewable—they can be used only once.

Labor The work time and work effort that people devote to producing goods and services is called **labor**. Labor includes the physical and mental efforts of all the people who work on farms and construction sites and in factories, shops, and offices.

The *quality* of labor depends on **human capital**, which is the knowledge and skill that people obtain from education, on-the-job training, and work experience. You are building your own human capital right now as you work on your economics course, and your human capital will continue to grow as you gain work experience.

Human capital expands over time. Today, 86 percent of the population of the United States has completed high school and 28 percent have a college or university degree. Figure 1.2 shows these measures of the growth of human capital in the United States over the past century.

Capital The tools, instruments, machines, build-ings, and other constructions that businesses use to produce goods and services are called **capital.**

In everyday language, we talk about money, stocks, and bonds as being capital. These items are *financial* capital. Financial capital plays an important role in enabling businesses to borrow the funds that they use to buy capital. But financial capital is not used to produce goods and services. Because it is not a productive resource, it is not capital.

Entrepreneurship The human resource that organizes labor, land, and capital is called **entrepreneurship.** Entrepreneurs come up with new ideas about what and how to produce, make business decisions, and bear the risks that arise from these decisions.

How do the quantities of factors of production that get used to produce the many different goods and services get determined?

For Whom? Who gets the goods and services that are produced depends on the incomes that people earn. A large income enables a person to buy large quantities of goods and services. A small income leaves a person with few options and small quantities of goods and services.

People earn their incomes by selling the services of the factors of production they own:

- Land earns **rent.**
- Labor earns **wages.**
- Capital earns **interest.**
- Entrepreneurship earns **profit.**

Which factor of production earns the most income? The answer is labor. Wages and fringe benefits are around 70 percent of total income. Land, capital, and entrepreneurship share the rest. These percentages have been remarkably constant over time.

Knowing how income is shared among the factors of production doesn't tell us how it is shared among individuals. You know of lots of people who earn very large incomes. Movie director Steven Spielberg made $332 million in 2005. And Bill Gates' wealth increased by $5 billion in 2005 from the operations of Microsoft.

You know of even more people who earn very small incomes. Servers at McDonald's average around $6.35 an hour; checkout clerks, bartenders, cleaners, and textile and leather workers all earn less than $10 an hour.

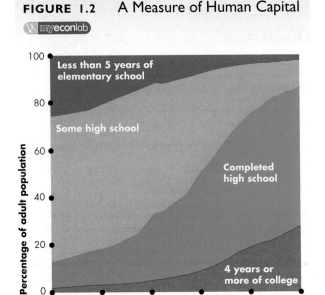

FIGURE 1.2   A Measure of Human Capital

Today, 28 percent of the population has 4 years or more of college, up from 2 percent in 1905. A further 58 percent have completed high school, up from 10 percent in 1905.

Source of data: U.S. Census Bureau, *Statistical Abstract of the United States.*

You probably know about other persistent differences in incomes. Men, on the average, earn more than women; whites earn more than minorities; college graduates earn more than high-school graduates.

We can get a good sense of who consumes the goods and services produced by looking at the percentages of total income earned by different groups of people. The 20 percent of people with the lowest incomes earn about 5 percent of total income, while the richest 20 percent earn close to 50 percent of total income. So on the average, people in the top 20 percent earn more than 10 times the incomes of those in the bottom 20 percent.

Why is the distribution of income so unequal? Why do women and minorities earn less than white males?

Economics provides some answers to these questions about what, how, and for whom goods and services get produced.

The second big question of economics that we'll now examine is a harder question both to appreciate and to answer.

When Is the Pursuit of Self-Interest in the Social Interest?

Every day, you and 300 million other Americans, along with 6.6 billion people in the rest of the world, make economic choices that result in *what*, *how*, and *for whom* goods and services get produced.

Are the goods and services produced, and the quantities in which they are produced, the right ones? Do the factors of production employed get used in the best possible way? And do the goods and services that we produce go to the people who benefit most from them?

You know that your own choices are the best ones for you—or at least you think they're the best at the time that you make them. You use your time and other resources in the way that makes most sense to you. But you don't think much about how your choices affect other people. You order a home delivery pizza because you're hungry and want to eat. You don't order it thinking that the delivery person or the cook needs an income. You make choices that are in your **self-interest**—choices that you think are best for you.

When you act on your economic decisions, you come into contact with thousands of other people who produce and deliver the goods and services that you decide to buy or who buy the things that you sell. These people have made their own decisions—what to produce and how to produce it, who to hire or whom to work for, and so on. Like you, everyone else makes choices that they think are best for them. When the pizza delivery person shows up at your door, he's not doing you a favor. He's earning his income and hoping for a good tip.

Could it be possible that when each one of us makes choices that are in our own best interest, it turns out that these choices are also the best for society as a whole? Choices that are the best for society as a whole are said to be in the **social interest**.

Economists have been trying to find the answer to this question since 1776, the year of American independence and the year in which Adam Smith's monumental book, *The Nature and the Causes of the Wealth of Nations*, was published. The question is a hard one to answer, but a lot of progress has been made. Much of the rest of this book helps you to learn what we know about this question and its answer. To help you start thinking about the question, we're going to illustrate it with ten topics that generate heated discussion in today's world. You're already at least a little bit familiar with each one of them. They are

- Privatization
- Globalization
- The new economy
- Economic response to 9/11
- Corporate scandals
- HIV/AIDS
- Disappearing tropical rainforests
- Water shortages
- Unemployment
- Deficits and debts

Privatization November 9, 1989, is a date that will long be recalled in the world's economic history books. On that day, the Berlin Wall tumbled, and with its destruction, two Germanys embarked on a path toward unity.

West Germany was a nation designed on the model of the United States and Western Europe. In these nations, people own property and operate businesses. Privately owned businesses produce goods and services and trade them freely with customers in shops and markets. All this economic activity is conducted by people who pursue their own self-interest.

East Germany was a nation designed on the model of the Soviet Union—a centrally-planned economy. In such an economy, people are not free to operate businesses and trade freely with each other. The government owns the factories, shops, and offices, and it decides what to produce, how to produce it, and for whom to produce. Economic life is managed in detail by a government economic planning agency, and each individual follows instructions. The entire economy is operated like one giant firm.

The Soviet Union collapsed soon after the fall of the Berlin Wall and splintered into a number of independent states, each of which embarked on a process of privatization. China, another centrally-planned economy, began to encourage private enterprise and move away from sole reliance on public ownership and central economic planning during the 1980s.

Today, only Cuba, North Korea, and Vietnam remain centrally-planned economies.

Do publicly owned businesses coordinated by central economic planning serve the social interest better than private businesses that trade freely in markets as they do in the United States? Or is it possible that our economic system serves the social interest more effectively?

Globalization When world leaders meet, anti-globalization protests accompany them. *Globalization*—the expansion of international trade and investment—has been going on for centuries, but during the 1990s, advances in microchip, satellite, and fiber-optic technologies brought a dramatic fall in the cost of communication and accelerated the process. A phone call or even a video-conference with people who live 10,000 miles apart has become an everyday and easily affordable event. Every day, 20,000 people travel by air between the United States and Asia, and a similar number travel between the United States and Europe.

The explosion of communication has globalized production decisions. When Nike produces more sports shoes, people in China, Indonesia, or Malaysia get more work. When more people use credit cards, people in Barbados key in the data from sales slips. When Sony creates a new game for PlayStation 3, or Steven Spielberg creates an animation sequence in a movie, programmers in India write the code. And when China Airlines buys new airplanes, Americans who work for Boeing build them.

As part of the process of globalization, the United States produces more services and fewer manufactured goods. And China and the small economies in East Asia produce an expanding volume of manufactures.

Some economies of Asia are also growing more rapidly than are those of the United States and Europe. And on current trends, China will be the world's largest economy by 2013. The rapid economic expansion in Asia will bring further changes to the global economy as the wealthier Chinese and other Asians travel and buy more of the goods and services that the United States and other parts of the world produce. Globalization will proceed at an accelerated pace.

But globalization is leaving some behind. The nations of Africa and parts of South America are not sharing in the prosperity that globalization is bringing to other parts of the world.

Is globalization a good thing? Whom does it benefit? Globalization is clearly in the interest of the owners of multinational firms that profit by producing in low-cost regions and selling in high-price regions. But is globalization in *your* interest and the interest of the young worker in Malaysia who sews your new running shoes? Is it in the social interest?

The New Economy The 1980s and 1990s were years of extraordinary economic change that have been called the *Information Revolution*. Economic revolutions don't happen very often. The previous one, the *Industrial Revolution*, occurred between 1760 and 1830 and saw the transformation from rural farm life to urban industrial life for most people. The revolution before that, the *Agrarian Revolution*, occurred around 12,000 years ago and saw the transformation from a life of hunting and gathering to a life of settled farming.

According the events of the last 25 years the status of those two previous revolutions might be a stretch. But the changes that occurred during those 25 years were incredible. And they were based on one major technology: the microprocessor or computer chip. Gordon Moore of Intel predicted in 1965 that the number of transistors that could be placed on one integrated chip would double every 18 months (Moore's law). This prediction turned out to be remarkably accurate. In 1980, a PC chip had 60,000 transistors. By 2000, chips with more than 40 million transistors were in machines like the one you use.

The spinoffs from faster and cheaper computing were widespread. Telecommunications became much faster and cheaper, music and movie recording became more realistic and cheaper, millions of routine tasks that previously required human decision and action were automated. You encounter these automated tasks every day when you check out at the supermarket, call directory assistance, or call a government department or large business.

All the new products and processes and the low-cost computing power that made them possible were produced by people who made choices in the pursuit of self-interest. They did not result from any grand design or government economic plan.

When Gordon Moore set up Intel and started making chips, no one had told him to do so, and he wasn't thinking how much easier it would be for you to turn in your essay on time if you had a faster PC. When Bill Gates quit Harvard to set up Microsoft, he wasn't trying to create an operating system to improve people's computing experience. Moore and Gates and thousands of other entrepreneurs were in hot pursuit of the big payoffs that many of them achieved. Yet their actions did make millions of people better off. They did advance the social interest.

But were resources used in the best possible way during the information revolution? Did Intel make the right quality of chips and sell them in the right quantities for the right prices? Or was the quality too low and the price too high? And what about Microsoft? Did Bill Gates have to be paid $30 billion to produce the successive generations of Windows? Was this program developed in the social interest?

The Economic Response to 9/11

The awful events of September 11, 2001, created economic shockwaves that will last for some years and changed *what*, *how*, and *for whom*.

The biggest changes in production occurred in travel, accommodation, and security. Much business travel was replaced by teleconferencing. Many vacationers left the air and went onto the highway. Foreign trips were cut back. Airlines lost business and ordered fewer new airplanes. Banks wrote off millions of dollars in losses on loans to airlines.

But sales of SUVs and RVs increased. And airports, although operating at lower capacity, beefed up their security services. Tens of thousands of new security agents were hired, and state-of-the-art scanners were installed.

Thousands of people made choices in pursuit of their self-interest that led to these changes in production. But were these changes also in the social interest?

Corporate Scandals

In 2000, the names Enron and WorldCom meant corporate integrity and spectacular success. Today, they are tainted with scandal.

Founded in 1985, Enron expanded to become America's seventh largest business by 2001. But its expansion was built on an elaborate web of lies, deceit, and fraud. In October 2001, after revelations by one of its former executives, Enron's directors acknowledged that by inflating reported income and hiding debts, they had made the firm appear to be worth much more than it actually was. Enron executives Jeffrey Skilling and Kenneth Lay were convicted of fraud that made them millions of dollars but wiped out the stockholders' wealth.

Scott Sullivan, a highly respected financial officer, joined WorldCom in 1992 and helped to turn it into one of the world's telecommunications giants. In his last year with the company, Sullivan's salary was $700,000 and his bonus (in stock options) was $10 million. But just ten years after joining the company, Sullivan was fired and arrested for allegedly falsifying the company's accounts, inflating its book profits by almost $4 billion, and inflating his own bonus in the process. Shortly after these events, WorldCom filed for bankruptcy protection in the largest bankruptcy filing in U.S. history, laid off 17,000 workers, and wiped out its stockholders' wealth.

These cases illustrate the fact that sometimes, in the pursuit of self-interest, people break the law. Such behavior is not in the social interest. Indeed, the law was established precisely to limit such behavior.

But some corporate behavior that is legal is regarded by some as inappropriate. For example, many people think that the salaries of top executives are out of control. In some cases, executives who receive huge incomes bring ruin to the companies that they manage.

The people who hired the executives acted in their own self-interest and appointed the best people they could find. The executives acted in their own self-interest. But what became of the self-interest of the stockholders and the customers of these firms? Didn't they suffer? Aren't these glaring examples of conflict between self-interest and the social interest?

HIV/AIDS

The World Health Organization and the United Nations estimate that about 40 million people were suffering from HIV/AIDS in 2005. During that year, 3 million died from the disease and there were 4 million new cases. Most of the HIV/AIDS cases—25 million of them in 2005—were in Africa, where incomes average around $7 a day. The most effective treatment for this disease is an antiretroviral drug made by large multinational drug companies. The cost of this treatment is around $2,700 a year—more than $7 a day. For sales to poor countries, the cost has been lowered to around $1,200 a year—$3.30 a day.

Developing new drugs is a high-cost and high-risk activity, and if it were not in the self-interest of the drug companies, they would stop the effort. But once a drug is developed, the cost of producing it is just a few cents a dose. Would it be in the social interest for drugs to be made available at the low cost of producing them?

Disappearing Tropical Rainforests

Tropical rainforests in South America, Africa, and Asia support the lives of 30 million species of plants, animals, and insects—approaching 50 percent of all species on the planet. These rainforests provide us with the ingredients for many goods, including soaps, mouthwashes, shampoos, food preservatives, rubber, nuts, and fruits. The Amazon rainforest alone converts about 1 trillion pounds of carbon dioxide into oxygen each year.

Yet tropical rainforests cover less than 2 percent of the earth's surface and are heading for extinction. Logging, cattle ranching, mining, oil extraction, hydroelectric dams, and subsistence farming are destroying an area the size of two football fields every second, or larger than New York City every day. At the current rate of destruction, almost all the tropical rainforest ecosystems will be gone by 2030.

Each one of us makes economic choices that are in our self-interest to consume products, some of which are destroying this natural resource. Are our choices damaging the social interest? If they are, what can be done to change the incentives we face and change our behavior?

Water Shortages The world is awash with water—it is our most abundant resource. But 97 percent of it is seawater. Another 2 percent is frozen in glaciers and ice. The 1 percent of the earth's water that is available for human consumption would be sufficient if only it were in the right places. Finland, Canada, and a few other places have more water than they can use, but Australia, Africa, and California (and many other places) could use much more water than they can get.

Some people pay less for water than others. California farmers, for example, pay less than California households. Some of the highest prices for water are faced by people in the poorest countries who must either buy from a water dealer's truck or carry water in buckets over many miles.

In the United Kingdom, water is provided by private water companies. In the United States, public enterprises deliver the water.

In India and Bangladesh, plenty of rain falls, but it falls during a short wet season and the rest of the year is dry. Dams could help, but not enough have been built in those countries.

Are the nation's and the world's water resources being managed properly? Are the decisions that we each make in our self-interest to use, conserve, and transport water also in the social interest?

Unemployment During the 1930s, in a period called the *Great Depression*, more than 20 percent of the U.S. labor force was unemployed. Even today, about 30 percent of the African American teenage labor force is unemployed. Why can't everyone who wants a job find one? If economic choices arise from scarcity, how can resources be left unused?

People get jobs because other people expect to make a profit by hiring them. And people accept jobs when they think the pay and other conditions are good enough. So the number of people with jobs is determined by the self-interest of employers and workers. But is the number of jobs also in the social interest?

Deficits and Debts On a typical day since September 30, 2002, the U.S. government has run a budget deficit of $1.71 billion, which means that the government's debt has increased each day by that amount. On July 11, 2006, the day these words were written, your personal share of the outstanding government debt was $28,140.

Also, during 2006, Americans bought goods and services from the rest of the world in excess of what foreigners bought from the United States to the tune of almost $800 billion. To pay for these goods and services, we borrowed from the rest of the world.

These enormous deficits and the debts they create cannot persist indefinitely, and the debt will somehow have to be repaid. And it will most likely be repaid by you, not by your parents.

Are the choices that we vote for and make through our federal government and the choices we make when we buy from and sell to the rest of the world in the social interest?

We've just looked at ten topics that illustrate the big question: Do choices made in the pursuit of self-interest also serve the social interest?

You'll discover, as you work through this book, that much of what we do in the pursuit of our self-interest does indeed further the social interest. But there are areas in which the social interest and self-interest come into conflict. You'll discover the principles that help economists to figure out when the social interest is being served, when it is not, and what might be done when it is not.

REVIEW QUIZ

1 Describe the broad facts about *what*, *how*, and *for whom* goods and services get produced.
2 Use headlines from the recent news to illustrate the potential for conflict between self-interest and the social interest.

 myeconlab Study Plan 1.2

The Economic Way of Thinking

The questions that economics tries to answer tell us about the *scope of economics.* But they don't tell us how economists *think* about these questions and go about seeking answers to them.

You're now going to begin to see how economists approach economic questions. First, in this section, we'll look at the ideas that define the *economic way of thinking.* This way of thinking needs practice, but it is powerful, and as you become more familiar with it, you'll begin to see the world around you with a new and sharp focus.

Choices and Tradeoffs

Because we face scarcity, we must make choices. And when we make a choice, we select from the available alternatives. For example, you can spend the weekend studying for your next economics test and having fun with your friends, but you can't do both of these activities at the same time. You must choose how much time to devote to each. Whatever choice you make, you could have chosen something else instead.

You can think about your choice as a tradeoff. A **tradeoff** is an exchange—giving up one thing to get something else. When you choose how to spend your weekend, you face a tradeoff between studying and hanging out with your friends.

Guns Versus Butter The classic tradeoff is between guns and butter. "Guns" and "butter" stand for any pair of goods. They might actually be guns and butter. Or they might be broader categories such as national defense and food. Or they might be any pair of specific goods or services such as cola and bottled water, baseball bats and tennis rackets, colleges and hospitals, realtor services and career counseling.

Regardless of the specific objects that guns and butter represent, the guns-versus-butter tradeoff captures a hard fact of life: If we want more of one thing, we must trade something else in exchange for it.

The idea of a tradeoff is central to the whole of economics. We'll look at some examples, beginning with the big questions: What, How, and For Whom? We can view each of these questions about goods and services in terms of tradeoffs.

What, How, and *For Whom* Tradeoffs

The questions what, how, and for whom goods and services are produced all involve tradeoffs that are similar to that between guns and butter.

***What* Tradeoffs** What goods and services get produced depends on choices made by each one of us, by our government, and by the businesses that produce the things we buy.

Each of these choices involves a tradeoff. Each one of us faces a tradeoff when we choose how to spend our income. You go to the movies this week, but you forgo a few cups of coffee to buy the ticket. You trade off coffee for a movie.

The federal government faces a tradeoff when it chooses how to spend our tax dollars. Congress votes for more national defense but cuts back on educational programs. Congress trades off education for national defense.

Businesses face a tradeoff when they decide what to produce. Nike hires Tiger Woods and allocates resources to designing and marketing a new golf ball but cuts back on its development of a new running shoe. Nike trades off running shoes for golf balls.

***How* Tradeoffs** How goods and services get produced depends on choices made by the businesses that produce the things we buy. These choices involve a tradeoff. For example, Krispy Kreme opens a new doughnut store that has an automated production line and closes an older store with a traditional kitchen. Krispy Kreme trades off labor for capital.

***For Whom* Tradeoffs** For whom goods and services are produced depends on the distribution of buying power. Buying power can be redistributed—transferred from one person to another—in three ways: by voluntary payments, by theft, or through taxes and benefits organized by government. Redistribution brings tradeoffs.

Each of us faces a *for whom* tradeoff when we choose how much to contribute to the United Nations' famine relief fund. You donate $50 and cut your spending. You trade off your own spending for a small increase in economic equality.

We face a *for whom* tradeoff when we vote to increase the resources for catching thieves and enforcing the law. We trade off goods and services for an increase in the security of our property.

We also face a *for whom* tradeoff when we vote for taxes and social programs that redistribute buying power from the rich to the poor. These redistribution programs confront society with what has been called the **big tradeoff**—the tradeoff between equality and efficiency. Taxing the rich and making transfers to the poor bring greater economic equality. But taxing productive activities such as running a business, working hard, and saving and investing in capital discourages these activities. So taxing productive activities means producing less. A more equal distribution means there is less to share.

Think of the problem of how to share a pie that everyone contributes to baking. If each person receives a share of the pie that is proportional to her or his effort, everyone will work hard and the pie will be as large as possible. But if the pie is shared equally, regardless of contribution, some talented bakers will slack off and the pie will shrink. The big tradeoff is one between the size of the pie and how equally it is shared. We trade off some pie for increased equality.

Choices Bring Change

What, how, and for whom goods and services are produced changes over time. And choices bring change. The quantity and range of goods and services available today in the United States are much greater than those in Africa. And the economic condition of the United States today is much better than it was a generation ago. But the quality of economic life (and its rate of improvement) doesn't depend purely on nature and on luck. It depends on many of the choices made by each one of us, by governments, and by businesses. And these choices involve tradeoffs.

One choice is that of how much of our income to consume and how much to save. Our saving can be channeled through the financial system to finance businesses and to pay for new capital that increases production. The more we save and invest, the more goods and services we'll be able to produce in the future. When you decide to save an extra $1,000 and forgo a vacation, you trade off the vacation for a higher future income. If everyone saves an extra $1,000 and businesses invest in more equipment that increases production, future consumption per person rises. As a society, we trade off current consumption for economic growth and higher future consumption.

A second choice is how much effort to devote to education and training. By becoming better educated

and more highly skilled, we become more productive and are able to produce more goods and services. When you decide to remain in school for another two years to complete a professional degree and forgo a huge chunk of leisure time, you trade off leisure today for a higher future income. If everyone becomes better educated, production increases and income per person rises. As a society, we trade off current consumption and leisure time for economic growth and higher future consumption.

A third choice is how much effort to devote to research and the development of new products and production methods. Ford Motor Company can hire people either to design a new robotic assembly line or to operate the existing plant and produce cars. The robotic plant brings greater productivity in the future but means smaller current production—a tradeoff of current production for greater future production.

Seeing choices as tradeoffs emphasizes the idea that to get something, we must give up something. What we give up is the cost of what we get. Economists call this cost the *opportunity cost*.

Opportunity Cost

"There's no such thing as a free lunch" expresses the central idea of economics: Every choice has a cost. The **opportunity cost** of something is the highest-valued alternative that we give up to get it.

You can quit school, or you can remain in school. If you quit school and take a job at McDonald's, you earn enough to buy some CDs, go to the movies, and spend lots of free time with your friends. If you remain in school, you can't afford these things. You will be able to buy these things when you graduate and get a job, and that is one of the payoffs from being in school. But for now, when you've bought your books, you have nothing left for CDs and movies. And doing assignments leaves no time for hanging around with your friends. The opportunity cost of being in school is the highest-valued alternative that you would have done if you had quit school.

All the *what, how,* and *for whom* tradeoffs that we've just considered involve opportunity cost. The opportunity cost of some guns is the butter forgone; the opportunity cost of a movie ticket is the number of cups of coffee forgone.

And the choices that bring change also involve opportunity cost. The opportunity cost of more goods and services in the future is less consumption today.

Choosing at the Margin

You can allocate the next hour between studying and e-mailing your friends. But the choice is not all or nothing. You must decide how many minutes to allocate to each activity. To make this decision, you compare the benefit of a little bit more study time with its cost—you make your choice at the **margin**.

The benefit that arises from an increase in an activity is called **marginal benefit**. For example, suppose that you're spending four nights a week studying and your grade point average (GPA) is 3.0. You decide that you want a higher GPA and decide to study an extra night each week. Your GPA rises to 3.5. The marginal benefit from studying for one extra night a week is the 0.5 increase in your GPA. It is *not* the 3.5. You already have a 3.0 from studying for four nights a week, so we don't count this benefit as resulting from the decision you are now making.

The cost of an increase in an activity is called **marginal cost**. For you, the marginal cost of increasing your study time by one night a week is the cost of the additional night not spent with your friends (if that is your best alternative use of the time). It does not include the cost of the four nights you are already studying.

To make your decision, you compare the marginal benefit from an extra night of studying with its marginal cost. If the marginal benefit exceeds the marginal cost, you study the extra night. If the marginal cost exceeds the marginal benefit, you do not study the extra night.

By evaluating marginal benefits and marginal costs and choosing only those actions that bring greater benefit than cost, we use our scarce resources in the way that makes us as well off as possible.

Responding to Incentives

Our choices respond to incentives. A change in marginal cost or a change in marginal benefit changes the incentives that we face and leads us to change our choice.

For example, suppose your economics instructor gives you a problem set and tells you that all the problems will be on the next test. The marginal benefit from working these problems is large, so you diligently work them all. In contrast, if your math instructor gives you a problem set and tells you that none of the problems will be on the next test, the marginal benefit from working these problems is lower, so you skip most of them.

The central idea of economics is that we can predict how choices will change by looking at changes in incentives. More of an activity is undertaken when its marginal cost falls or its marginal benefit rises; less of an activity is undertaken when its marginal cost rises or its marginal benefit falls.

Incentives are also the key to reconciling self-interest and social interest. When our choices are *not* in the social interest, it is because of the incentives we face. One of the challenges for economists is to figure out the incentive systems that result in self-interested choices being in the social interest.

Human Nature, Incentives, and Institutions

Economists take human nature as given and view people as acting in their self-interest. All people—consumers, producers, politicians, and public servants—pursue their self-interest.

Self-interested actions are not necessarily *selfish* actions. You might decide to use your resources in ways that bring pleasure to others as well as to yourself. But a self-interested act gets the most value for *you* based on *your* view about value.

If human nature is given and if people act in their self-interest, how can we take care of the social interest? Economists answer this question by emphasizing the crucial role that institutions play in influencing the incentives that people face as they pursue their self-interest.

Private property protected by a system of laws and markets that enable voluntary exchange are the fundamental institutions. You will learn as you progress with your study of economics that where these institutions exist, self-interest can indeed promote the social interest.

REVIEW QUIZ

1 Provide three everyday examples of tradeoffs and describe the opportunity cost involved in each.
2 Provide three everyday examples to illustrate what we mean by choosing at the margin.
3 How do economists predict changes in choices?
4 What do economists say about the role of institutions in promoting the social interest?

myeconlab Study Plan 1.3

Economics: A Social Science

Economics is a social science (along with political science, psychology, and sociology). Economists try to discover how the economic world works, and in pursuit of this goal (like all scientists), they distinguish between two types of statements:

- What *is*
- What *ought to be*

Statements about what *is* are called *positive* statements, and they might be right or wrong. We can test a positive statement by checking it against the facts. When a chemist does an experiment in her laboratory, she is attempting to check a positive statement against the facts.

Statements about what *ought to be* are called *normative* statements. These statements depend on values and cannot be tested. When Congress debates a motion, it is ultimately trying to decide what ought to be. It is making a normative statement.

To see the distinction between positive and normative statements, consider the controversy over global warming. Some scientists believe that centuries of the burning of coal and oil are increasing the carbon dioxide content of the earth's atmosphere and leading to higher temperatures that eventually will have devastating consequences for life on this planet. "Our planet is warming because of an increased carbon dioxide buildup in the atmosphere" is a positive statement. It can (in principle and with sufficient data) be tested. "We ought to cut back on our use of carbon-based fuels such as coal and oil" is a normative statement. You can agree or disagree with this statement, but you can't test it. It is based on values.

Health-care reform provides another economic example of the distinction. "Universal health care will cut the amount of work time lost to illness" is a positive statement. "Every American should have equal access to health care" is a normative statement.

The task of economic science is to discover positive statements that are consistent with what we observe and that help us to understand the economic world. This task can be broken into three steps:

- Observation and measurement
- Model building
- Testing models

Observation and Measurement

The first step toward understanding how the economic world works is to observe it. All science needs data. Economists observe and measure data on all aspects of economic behavior, some examples of which are the quantities of resources available, wage rates and work hours, the quantities of goods and services produced and consumed and their prices.

Model Building

The second step toward understanding how the economic world works is to build a model. An **economic model** is a description of some aspect of the economic world that includes only those features of the world that are needed for the purpose at hand. A model is simpler than the reality it describes. What a model includes and ignores result from assumptions about what is essential and what are inessential details.

You can see how ignoring details is useful—even essential—to our understanding by thinking about a model that you probably see every day: the TV weather map. The weather map is a model that helps to predict the temperature, wind speed and direction, and precipitation over a future period. The weather map shows lines called isobars—lines of equal barometric pressure. It doesn't show the interstate highways. The reason is that our theory of the weather tells us that the pattern of air pressure, not the location of the highways, determines the weather.

An economic model is similar to a weather map. For example, an economic model of a cell phone network might tell us the effects of the development of a new low-cost technology on the number of cell phone subscribers and the volume of cell phone use. But the model would ignore such details as the colors of the covers on people's cell phones and the tunes they use for ringtones.

Testing Models

The third step is testing models. A model's predictions might correspond to the facts or be in conflict with them. By comparing the model's predictions with the facts, we can test a model and develop an economic theory. An **economic theory** is a generalization that summarizes what we think we understand about the economic choices that people make and the performance of industries and entire economies. It is a bridge between an economic model and the real economy.

The process of building and testing models creates theories. For example, meteorologists have a theory that if the isobars form a particular pattern at a particular time of the year (a model), then it will snow (reality). They have developed this theory by repeated observation and by carefully recording the weather that follows specific pressure patterns.

Economics is a young science. It was born in 1776 with the publication of Adam Smith's *Wealth of Nations* (see p. 54). Over the years since then, economists have discovered many useful theories. But in many areas, economists are still looking for answers. The gradual accumulation of economic knowledge gives most economists some faith that their methods will, eventually, provide usable answers to the big economic questions.

But progress in economics comes slowly. Let's look at some of the obstacles to progress in economics.

Obstacles and Pitfalls in Economics

We cannot easily do economic experiments. And most economic behavior has many simultaneous causes. For these two reasons, it is difficult in economics to unscramble cause and effect.

Unscrambling Cause and Effect By changing one factor at a time and holding all the other relevant factors constant, we isolate the factor of interest and are able to investigate its effects in the clearest possible way. This logical device, which all scientists use to identify cause and effect, is called *ceteris paribus*. **Ceteris paribus** is a Latin term that means "other things being equal" or "if all other relevant things remain the same." Ensuring that other things are equal is crucial in many activities, and all successful attempts to make scientific progress use this device.

Economic models (like the models in all other sciences) enable the influence of one factor at a time to be isolated in the imaginary world of the model. When we use a model, we are able to imagine what would happen if only one factor changed. But *ceteris paribus* can be a problem in economics when we try to test a model.

Laboratory scientists, such as chemists and physicists, perform experiments by actually holding all the relevant factors constant except for the one under investigation. In non-experimental sciences such as economics (and meteorology), we usually observe the outcomes of the simultaneous operation of many factors. Consequently, it is hard to sort out the effects of each individual factor and to compare them with what a model predicts. To cope with this problem, economists take three complementary approaches.

First, they look for pairs of events in which other things were equal (or similar). An example might be to study the effects of unemployment insurance on the unemployment rate by comparing the United States with Canada on the presumption that the people in the two economies are sufficiently similar. Second, economists use statistical tools—called econometrics. Third, when economists can, they perform experiments. This relatively new approach puts real subjects (usually students) in a decision-making situation and varies their incentives in some way to discover how they respond to a change in one factor at a time.

Economists try to avoid fallacies—errors of reasoning that lead to a wrong conclusion. But two fallacies are common, and you need to be on your guard to avoid them. They are the

- Fallacy of composition
- *Post hoc* fallacy

Fallacy of Composition The fallacy of composition is the (false) statement that what is true of the parts is true of the whole or that what is true of the whole is true of the parts. There are many everyday examples of this fallacy. Standing at a ball game to get a better view works for one person but not for all—what is true for a part of a crowd is not true for the whole crowd.

The fallacy of composition arises in many economic situations that stem from the fact that the parts interact with each other to produce an outcome for the whole that might differ from the intent of the parts.

For example, a firm fires some workers to cut costs and improve its profits. If all firms take similar actions, income falls and so does spending. The firm sells less, and its profits don't improve.

Or suppose that a firm thinks it can gain market share by cutting its price and mounting a large advertising campaign. Again, if the one firm takes these actions, they work. But if all firms in an industry take the same actions, the firms end up with the same market share as before and lower profits.

Post Hoc **Fallacy** Another Latin phrase—*post hoc, ergo propter hoc*—means "after this, therefore because of this." The *post hoc* fallacy is the error of reasoning that a first event *causes* a second event because the first occurred before the second. Suppose you are a visitor from a far-off world. You observe lots of people shopping in early December, and then you see them opening gifts and partying in the holiday season. "Does the shopping cause the holiday season?," you wonder. After a deeper study, you discover that the holiday season causes the shopping. A later event causes an earlier event.

Unraveling cause and effect is difficult in economics. And just looking at the timing of events often doesn't help. For example, the stock market booms, and some months later the economy expands—jobs and incomes grow. Did the stock market boom cause the economy to expand? Possibly, but perhaps businesses started to plan the expansion of production because a new technology that lowered costs had become available. As knowledge of the plans spread, the stock market reacted to *anticipate* the economic expansion. To disentangle cause and effect, economists use economic models and data and, to the extent that they can, perform experiments.

Economics is a challenging science. Does the difficulty of getting answers in economics mean that anything goes and that economists disagree on most questions? Perhaps you've heard the joke "If you laid all the economists in the world end to end, they still wouldn't reach agreement." Surprisingly, perhaps, the joke does not describe reality.

Agreement and Disagreement

Economists agree on a remarkably wide range of questions. And often the agreed-upon view of economists disagrees with the popular and sometimes politically correct view. When Federal Reserve Chairman Ben Bernanke testifies before the Senate Banking Committee, his words are rarely controversial among economists, even if they generate endless debate in the media and Congress.

Here are 12 propositions with which at least 7 out of every 10 economists broadly agree:

- Tariffs and import restrictions make most people worse off.
- A large budget deficit has an adverse effect on the economy.
- A minimum wage increases unemployment among young workers and low-skilled workers.

- Cash payments to welfare recipients make them better off than do transfers-in-kind of equal cash value.
- A tax cut can help to lower unemployment when the unemployment rate is high.
- The distribution of income in the United States should be more equal.
- Inflation is primarily caused by a rapid rate of money creation.
- The government should restructure welfare along the lines of a "negative income tax."
- Rent controls cut the availability of housing.
- Pollution taxes are more effective than pollution limits.
- The redistribution of income is a legitimate role for the U.S. government.
- The federal budget should be balanced on the average over the business cycle but not every year.

Which of these propositions are positive and which are normative? Notice that economists are willing to offer their opinions on normative issues as well as their professional views on positive issues. Be on the lookout for normative propositions dressed up as positive propositions.

REVIEW QUIZ

1 What is the distinction between a positive statement and a normative statement? Provide an example (different from those in the chapter) of each type of statement.
2 What is a model? Can you think of a model that you might use (probably without thinking of it as a model) in your everyday life?
3 What is a theory? Why is the statement "It might work in theory, but it doesn't work in practice" a silly statement?
4 What is the *ceteris paribus* assumption and how is it used?
5 Try to think of some everyday examples of the fallacy of composition and the *post hoc* fallacy.

myeconlab Study Plan 1.4

SUMMARY

Key Points

Definition of Economics (p. 2)

- All economic questions arise from scarcity—from the fact that wants exceed the resources available to satisfy them.
- Economics is the social science that studies the choices that people make as they cope with scarcity.
- The subject divides into microeconomics and macroeconomics.

Two Big Economic Questions (pp. 3–8)

- Two big questions summarize the scope of economics:
  1. How do choices end up determining *what*, *how*, and *for whom* goods and services get produced?
  2. When do choices made in the pursuit of *self-interest* also promote the *social interest*?

The Economic Way of Thinking (pp. 9–11)

- Every choice is a tradeoff—exchanging more of something for less of something else.
- The classic guns-versus-butter tradeoff represents all tradeoffs.
- All economic questions involve tradeoffs.
- The big social tradeoff is that between equality and efficiency.
- The highest-valued alternative forgone is the opportunity cost of what is chosen.
- Choices are made at the margin and respond to incentives.

Economics: A Social Science (pp. 12–14)

- Economists distinguish between positive statements—what is—and normative statements—what ought to be.
- To explain the economic world, economists develop theories by building and testing economic models.
- Economists use the *ceteris paribus* assumption to try to disentangle cause and effect and are careful to avoid the fallacy of composition and the *post hoc* fallacy.
- Economists agree on a wide range of questions about how the economy works.

Key Terms

Big tradeoff, 10
Capital, 4
Ceteris paribus, 13
Economic model, 12
Economics, 2
Economic theory, 12
Entrepreneurship, 4
Factors of production, 3
Goods and services, 3
Human capital, 3
Incentive, 2
Interest, 4
Labor, 3
Land, 3
Macroeconomics, 2
Margin, 11
Marginal benefit, 11
Marginal cost, 11
Microeconomics, 2
Opportunity cost, 10
Profit, 4
Rent, 4
Scarcity, 2
Self-interest, 5
Social interest, 5
Tradeoff, 9
Wages, 4

PROBLEMS

myeconlab Tests, Study Plan, Solutions*

1. Apple Computer Inc. decides to make iTunes freely available in unlimited quantities.
   a. Does Apple's decision mean that tunes are no longer scarce?
   b. Does Apple's decision change the incentives that people face?
   c. Is Apple's decision an example of a microeconomic or a macroeconomic issue?
   d. How does Apple's decision change the opportunity cost of a tune?

2. Which of the following pairs does not match:
   a. Labor and wages?
   b. Land and rent?
   c. Entreprenuership and profit?
   d. Capital and profit?

3. Explain how the following news headlines concern self-interest and the social interest:
   a. Wal-Mart Expands in Europe
   b. Taco Bell Opens in Canada
   c. McDonald's Moves into Salads
   d. Food Must Be Labeled with Nutrition Information

4. The night before an economics exam, you decide to go to the movies instead of staying home and working your MyEconLab study plan. You get 50 percent on your exam compared with the 70 percent that you normally score.
   a. Did you face a tradeoff?
   b. What was the opportunity cost of your evening at the movies?

5. Which of the following statements is positive, which is normative, and which can be tested?
   a. The U.S. government should cut its imports.
   b. China is the United States' largest trading partner.
   c. If the price of antiretroviral drugs increases, HIV/AIDS sufferers will decrease their consumption of the drug.

6. Which statement illustrates the fallacy of composition and which the *post hoc* fallacy?
   a. You'll see more if you stand on your toes.
   b. Everyone should leave home an hour earlier to avoid the rush hour traffic.
   c. People who smoke cigarettes face an increased risk of lung and heart diseases.

*Solutions to odd-numbered problems are provided.

CRITICAL THINKING

1. As London prepares to host the 2012 Olympic Games, concern about the cost of the event increases. An example:

   Costs Soar for London Olympics—The regeneration of East London is set to add extra £1.5 billion to taxpayers' bill.
   The Times, London, July 6, 2006

   Is the cost of regenerating East London an opportunity cost of hosting the 2012 Olympic Games? Explain why or why not.

WEB ACTIVITIES

myeconlab Links to Web sites

1. Visit CNNMoney.com
   a. What is the top economic news story today?
   b. With which of the big questions does it deal? (It must deal with at least one of them and might deal with more than one.)
   c. What tradeoffs does the news item discuss?
   d. Write a brief summary of the news item in a few bulleted points using as much as possible of the economic vocabulary that you have learned in this chapter and that is in the key terms list on p. 15.

2. Visit *Resources for Economists on the Internet.* This Web site is a good place from which to search for economic information on the Internet. Click on "Blogs, Commentaries, and Podcasts."
   a. Click on the Becker-Posner Blog and read the latest blog by these two outstanding economists.
   b. As you read this blog, think about what it is saying about "what," "how," and "for whom" questions.
   c. As you read this blog, think about what it is saying about self-interest and the social interest.

3. Visit the Bureau of Labor Statistics and find information about employment, unemployment, and earnings in your state. Also find information about employment, unemployment, and earnings for the United States and compare your state with the nation as a whole.

APPENDIX

Graphs in Economics

After studying this appendix, you will be able to

▶ Make and interpret a time-series graph, a cross-section graph, and a scatter diagram

▶ Distinguish between linear and nonlinear relationships and between relationships that have a maximum and a minimum

▶ Define and calculate the slope of a line

▶ Graph relationships among more than two variables

Graphing Data

A graph represents a quantity as a distance on a line. In Fig. A1.1, a distance on the horizontal line represents temperature, measured in degrees Fahrenheit. A movement from left to right shows an increase in temperature. The point 0 represents zero degrees Fahrenheit. To the right of 0, the temperature is positive. To the left of 0 (as indicated by the minus sign), the temperature is negative. A distance on the vertical line represents altitude or height, measured in thousands of feet. The point 0 represents sea level. Points above 0 represent feet above sea level. Points below 0 (indicated by a minus sign) represent feet below sea level.

By setting two scales perpendicular to each other, as in Fig. A1.1, we can visualize the relationship between two variables. The scale lines are called *axes*. The vertical line is the *y*-axis, and the horizontal line is the *x*-axis. Each axis has a zero point, which is shared by the two axes and called the *origin*.

We need two bits of information to make a two-variable graph: the value of the *x* variable and the value of the *y* variable. For example, off the coast of Alaska, the temperature is 32 degrees—the value of *x*. A fishing boat is located at 0 feet above sea level—the value of *y*. These two bits of information appear as point *A* in Fig. A1.1. A climber at the top of Mount McKinley on a cold day is 20,320 feet above sea level in a zero-degree gale. These two pieces of information appear as

FIGURE A1.1   Making a Graph

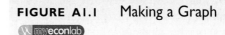

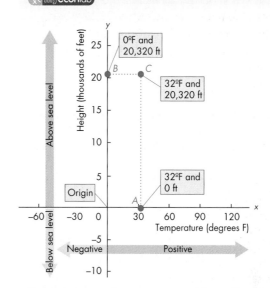

Graphs have axes that measure quantities as distances. Here, the horizontal axis (*x*-axis) measures temperature, and the vertical axis (*y*-axis) measures height. Point *A* represents a fishing boat at sea level (0 on the *y*-axis) on a day when the temperature is 32°F. Point *B* represents a climber at the top of Mt. McKinley, 20,320 feet above sea level at a temperature of 0°F. Point *C* represents a climber at the top of Mt. McKinley, 20,320 feet above sea level at a temperature of 32°F.

point *B*. On a warmer day, a climber might be at the peak of Mt. McKinley when the temperature is 32 degrees, at point *C*.

We can draw two lines, called *coordinates*, from point *C*. One, called the *y*-coordinate, runs from *C* to the horizontal axis. Its length is the same as the value marked off on the *y*-axis. The other, called the *x*-coordinate, runs from *C* to the vertical axis. Its length is the same as the value marked off on the *x*-axis. We describe a point in a graph by the values of its *x*-coordinate and its *y*-coordinate.

Graphs like that in Fig. A1.1 can show any type of quantitative data on two variables. Economists use three types of graphs based on the principles in Fig. A1.1 to reveal and describe the relationships among variables. They are

■ Time-series graphs

■ Cross-section graphs

■ Scatter diagrams

Time-Series Graphs

A **time-series graph** measures time (for example, months or years) on the *x*-axis and the variable or variables in which we are interested on the *y*-axis. Figure A1.2 is an example of a time-series graph. It provides some information about the price of gasoline. In this figure, we measure time in years starting in 1973. We measure the price of gasoline (the variable that we are interested in) on the *y*-axis.

The point of a time-series graph is to enable us to visualize how a variable has changed over time and how its value in one period relates to its value in another period.

A time-series graph conveys an enormous amount of information quickly and easily, as this example illustrates. It shows

- The *level* of the price of gasoline—when it is *high* and *low*. When the line is a long way from the *x*-axis, the price is high, as it was, for example, in 1981. When the line is close to the *x*-axis, the price is low, as it was, for example, in 1998.

- How the price *changes*—whether it *rises* or *falls*. When the line slopes upward, as in 1979, the price is rising. When the line slopes downward, as in 1986, the price is falling.

- The *speed* with which the price changes—whether it rises or falls *quickly* or *slowly*. If the line is very steep, then the price rises or falls quickly. If the line is not steep, the price rises or falls slowly. For example, the price rose quickly between 1978 and 1980 and slowly between 1994 and 1996. The price fell quickly between 1985 and 1986 and slowly between 1990 and 1994.

A time-series graph also reveals whether there is a **trend**—a general tendency for a variable to move in one direction. A trend might be upward or downward. In Fig. A1.2, the price of gasoline had a general tendency to fall during the 1980s and 1990s. That is, although the price rose and fell, the general tendency was for it to fall—the price had a downward trend. During the 2000s, the trend has been upward.

A time-series graph also helps us to detect fluctuations in a variable around its trend. You can see some peaks and troughs in the price of gasoline in Fig. A1.2.

Finally, a time-series graph also lets us compare the variable in different periods quickly. Figure A1.2 shows that the 1970s and 1980s were different from

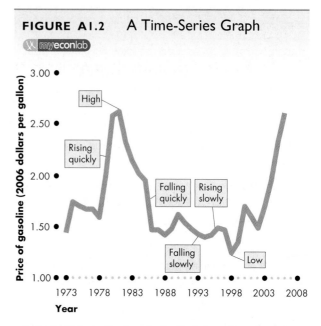

FIGURE A1.2   A Time-Series Graph

A time-series graph plots the level of a variable on the *y*-axis against time (day, week, month, or year) on the *x*-axis. This graph shows the price of gasoline (in 2006 dollars per gallon) each year from 1973 to 2006. It shows us when the price of gasoline was *high* and when it was *low*, when the price *increased* and when it *decreased*, and when the price changed *quickly* and when it changed *slowly*.

the 1990s. The price of gasoline fluctuated more during the 1970s and 1980s than it did in the 1990s.

You can see that a time-series graph conveys a wealth of information. And it does so in much less space than we have used to describe only some of its features. But you do have to "read" the graph to obtain all this information.

Cross-Section Graphs

A **cross-section graph** shows the values of an economic variable for different groups or categories at a point in time. Figure A1.3, called a *bar chart*, is an example of a cross-section graph.

The bar chart in Fig. A1.3 shows 10 leisure pursuits and the percentage of the U. S. population that participated in them during 2005. The length of each bar indicates the percentage of the population. This figure enables you to compare the popularity of these 10 activities. And you can do so much more quickly and clearly than by looking at a list of numbers.

FIGURE A1.3   A Cross-Section Graph

Ⓧ myeconlab

Dining out
Surfing the Internet
Playing cards
Baking
Doing crossword puzzles
Playing video games
Going to the zoo
Dancing
Attending rock concerts
Playing a musical instrument

0   10   20   30   40   50
Percentage of population

A cross-section graph shows the level of a variable across categories or groups. This bar chart shows 10 popular leisure activities and the percentage of the U.S. population that engages in each of them.

Scatter Diagrams

A **scatter diagram** plots the value of one variable against the value of another variable. Such a graph reveals whether a relationship exists between two variables and describes their relationship. Figure A1.4(a) shows the relationship between expenditure and income. Each point shows expenditure per person and income per person in a given year from 1990 to 2000. The points are "scattered" within the graph. The point labeled *A* tells us that in 1996, income per person was $20,613 and expenditure per person was $18,888. The dots in this graph form a pattern, which reveals that as income increases, expenditure increases.

Figure A1.4(b) shows the relationship between the number of international phone calls and the price of a call. This graph shows that as the price per minute falls, the number of calls increases.

Figure A1.4(c) shows a scatter diagram of inflation and unemployment in the United States. Here, the dots show no clear relationship between these two variables. The dots in this graph reveal that there is no simple relationship between these variables.

FIGURE A1.4   Scatter Diagrams

Ⓧ myeconlab

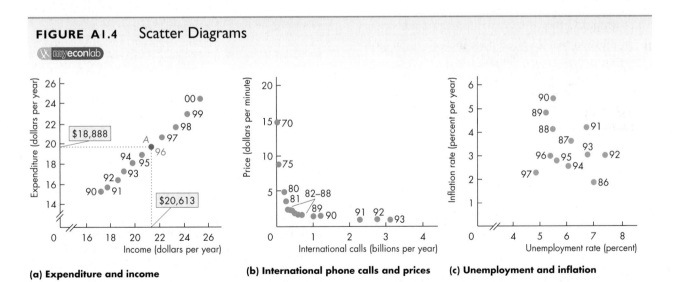

(a) Expenditure and income

(b) International phone calls and prices

(c) Unemployment and inflation

A scatter diagram reveals the relationship between two variables. Part (a) shows the relationship between expenditure and income. Each point shows the values of the two variables in a specific year. For example, point A shows that in 1996, average income was $20,613 and average expenditure was $18,888. The pattern formed by the points shows that as income increases, expenditure increases.

Part (b) shows the relationship between the price of an international phone call and the number of calls made. This graph shows that as the price of a phone call falls, the number of calls made increases. Part (c) shows a scatter diagram of the inflation rate and unemployment rate in the United States. This graph shows that inflation and unemployment are not closely related.

Breaks in the Axes Two of the graphs you've just looked at, Fig. A1.4(a) and Fig. A1.4(c), have breaks in their axes, as shown by the small gaps. The breaks indicate that there are jumps from the origin, 0, to the first values recorded.

In Fig. A1.4(a), the breaks are used because the lowest value of expenditure exceeds $14,000 and the lowest value of income exceeds $16,000. With no breaks in the axes, there would be a lot of empty space, all the points would be crowded into the top right corner, and we would not be able to see whether a relationship exists between these two variables. By breaking the axes, we are able to bring the relationship into view.

Putting a break in the axes is like using a zoom lens to bring the relationship into the center of the graph and magnify it so that the relationship fills the graph.

Misleading Graphs Breaks can be used to highlight a relationship. But they can also be used to mislead—to make a graph that lies. The most common way of making a graph lie is to use axis breaks and to either stretch or compress a scale. For example, suppose that in Fig. A1.4(a), the y-axis that measures expenditure ran from zero to $45,000 while the x-axis was the same as the one shown. The graph would now create the impression that despite a huge increase in income, expenditure had barely changed.

To avoid being misled, it is a good idea to get into the habit of always looking closely at the values and the labels on the axes of a graph before you start to interpret it.

Correlation and Causation A scatter diagram that shows a clear relationship between two variables, such as Fig. A1.4(a) or Fig. A1.4(b), tells us that the two variables have a high correlation. When a high correlation is present, we can predict the value of one variable from the value of the other variable. But correlation does not imply causation.

Sometimes a high correlation is a coincidence, but sometimes it does arise from a causal relationship. It is likely, for example, that rising income causes rising expenditure (Fig. A1.4a) and that the falling price of a phone call causes more calls to be made (Fig. A1.4b).

You've now seen how we can use graphs in economics to show economic data and to reveal relationships. Next, we'll learn how economists use graphs to construct and display economic models.

Graphs Used in Economic Models

The graphs used in economics are not always designed to show real-world data. Often they are used to show general relationships among the variables in an economic model.

An *economic model* is a stripped-down, simplified description of an economy or of a component of an economy such as a business or a household. It consists of statements about economic behavior that can be expressed as equations or as curves in a graph. Economists use models to explore the effects of different policies or other influences on the economy in ways that are similar to the use of model airplanes in wind tunnels and models of the climate.

You will encounter many different kinds of graphs in economic models, but there are some repeating patterns. Once you've learned to recognize these patterns, you will instantly understand the meaning of a graph. Here, we'll look at the different types of curves that are used in economic models, and we'll see some everyday examples of each type of curve. The patterns to look for in graphs are the four cases in which

■ Variables move in the same direction.

■ Variables move in opposite directions.

■ Variables have a maximum or a minimum.

■ Variables are unrelated.

Let's look at these four cases.

Variables That Move in the Same Direction

Figure A1.5 shows graphs of the relationships between two variables that move up and down together. A relationship between two variables that move in the same direction is called a **positive relationship** or a **direct relationship**. A line that slopes upward shows such a relationship.

Figure A1.5 shows three types of relationships, one that has a straight line and two that have curved lines. But all the lines in these three graphs are called curves. Any line on a graph—no matter whether it is straight or curved—is called a *curve*.

A relationship shown by a straight line is called a **linear relationship**. Figure A1.5(a) shows a linear

FIGURE A1.5   Positive (Direct) Relationships

myeconlab

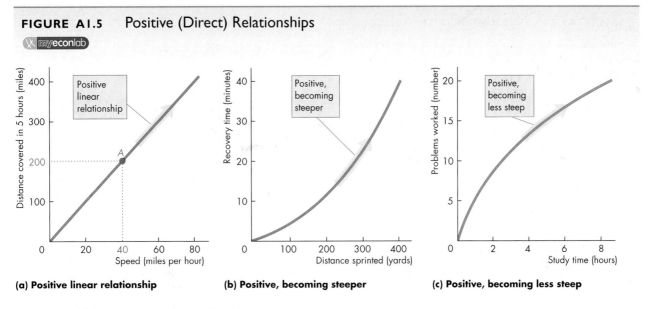

(a) Positive linear relationship   **(b) Positive, becoming steeper**   **(c) Positive, becoming less steep**

Each part of this figure shows a positive (direct) relationship between two variables. That is, as the value of the variable measured on the x-axis increases, so does the value of the variable measured on the y-axis. Part (a) shows a linear relationship—as the two variables increase together, we move along a straight line. Part (b) shows a positive relationship such that as the two variables increase together, we move along a curve that becomes steeper. Part (c) shows a positive relationship such that as the two variables increase together, we move along a curve that becomes flatter.

relationship between the number of miles traveled in 5 hours and speed. For example, point A shows that we will travel 200 miles in 5 hours if our speed is 40 miles an hour. If we double our speed to 80 miles an hour, we will travel 400 miles in 5 hours.

Figure A1.5(b) shows the relationship between distance sprinted and recovery time (the time it takes the heart rate to return to its normal resting rate). This relationship is an upward-sloping one that starts out quite flat but then becomes steeper as we move along the curve away from the origin. The reason this curve slopes upward and becomes steeper is because the additional recovery time needed from sprinting an additional 100 yards increases. It takes less than 5 minutes to recover from sprinting 100 yards but more than 10 minutes to recover from sprinting 200 yards.

Figure A1.5(c) shows the relationship between the number of problems worked by a student and the amount of study time. This relationship is an upward-sloping one that starts out quite steep and becomes flatter as we move away from the origin. Study time becomes less productive as the student spends more hours studying and becomes more tired.

Variables That Move in Opposite Directions

Figure A1.6 shows relationships between things that move in opposite directions. A relationship between variables that move in opposite directions is called a **negative relationship** or an **inverse relationship**.

Figure A1.6(a) shows the relationship between the number of hours available for playing squash and the number of hours for playing tennis when the total is 5 hours. One extra hour spent playing tennis means one hour less playing squash and vice versa. This relationship is negative and linear.

Figure A1.6(b) shows the relationship between the cost per mile traveled and the length of a journey. The longer the journey, the lower is the cost per mile. But as the journey length increases, even though the cost per mile decreases, the fall in the cost is smaller the longer the journey. This feature of the relationship is shown by the fact that the curve slopes downward, starting out steep at a short journey length and then becoming flatter as the journey length increases. This relationship arises because some of the costs are fixed, such as auto insurance, and the fixed costs are spread over a longer journey.

FIGURE A1.6   Negative (Inverse) Relationships

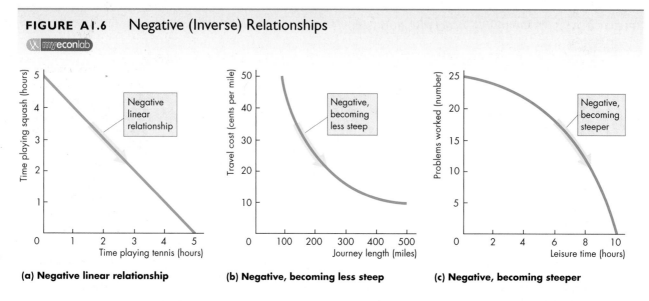

(a) Negative linear relationship   **(b) Negative, becoming less steep**   **(c) Negative, becoming steeper**

Each part of this figure shows a negative (inverse) relationship between two variables. That is, as the value of the variable measured on the *x*-axis increases, the value of the variable measured on the *y*-axis decreases. Part (a) shows a linear relationship. The total time spent playing tennis and squash is 5 hours. As the time spent playing tennis increases, the time spent playing squash decreases, and we move along a straight line. Part (b) shows a negative relationship such that as the journey length increases, the travel cost decreases as we move along a curve that becomes less steep. Part (c) shows a negative relationship such that as leisure time increases, the number of problems worked decreases as we move along a curve that becomes steeper.

Figure A1.6(c) shows the relationship between the amount of leisure time and the number of problems worked by a student. Increasing leisure time produces an increasingly large reduction in the number of problems worked. This relationship is a negative one that starts out with a gentle slope at a small number of leisure hours and becomes steeper as the number of leisure hours increases. This relationship is a different view of the idea shown in Fig. A1.5(c).

Variables That Have a Maximum or a Minimum

Many relationships in economic models have a maximum or a minimum. For example, firms try to make the maximum possible profit and to produce at the lowest possible cost. Figure A1.7 shows relationships that have a maximum or a minimum.

Figure A1.7(a) shows the relationship between rainfall and wheat yield. When there is no rainfall, wheat will not grow, so the yield is zero. As the rainfall increases up to 10 days a month, the wheat yield

increases. With 10 rainy days each month, the wheat yield reaches its maximum at 40 bushels an acre (point *A*). Rain in excess of 10 days a month starts to lower the yield of wheat. If every day is rainy, the wheat suffers from a lack of sunshine and the yield decreases to zero. This relationship is one that starts out sloping upward, reaches a maximum, and then slopes downward.

Figure A1.7(b) shows the reverse case—a relationship that begins sloping downward, falls to a minimum, and then slopes upward. Most economic costs are like this relationship. An example is the relationship between the cost per mile and speed for a car trip. At low speeds, the car is creeping in a traffic snarl-up. The number of miles per gallon is low, so the cost per mile is high. At high speeds, the car is traveling faster than its efficient speed, using a large quantity of gasoline, and again the number of miles per gallon is low and the cost per mile is high. At a speed of 55 miles an hour, the cost per mile is at its minimum (point *B*). This relationship is one that starts out sloping downward, reaches a minimum, and then slopes upward.

FIGURE A1.7   Maximum and Minimum Points

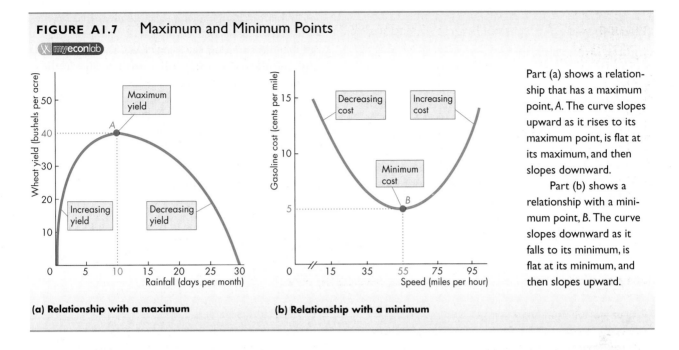

(a) Relationship with a maximum

(b) Relationship with a minimum

Part (a) shows a relationship that has a maximum point, A. The curve slopes upward as it rises to its maximum point, is flat at its maximum, and then slopes downward.

Part (b) shows a relationship with a minimum point, B. The curve slopes downward as it falls to its minimum, is flat at its minimum, and then slopes upward.

Variables That Are Unrelated

There are many situations in which no matter what happens to the value of one variable, the other variable remains constant. Sometimes we want to show the independence between two variables in a graph, and Fig. A1.8 shows two ways of achieving this.

In describing the graphs in Fig. A1.5 through A1.7, we have talked about curves that slope upward or slope downward, and curves that become less steep or steeper. Let's spend a little time discussing exactly what we mean by slope and how we measure the slope of a curve.

FIGURE A1.8   Variables That Are Unrelated

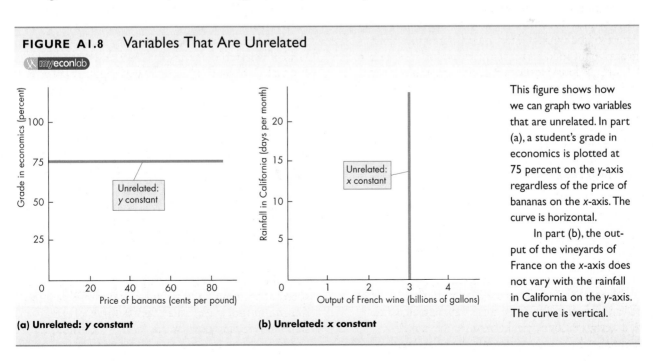

(a) Unrelated: y constant

(b) Unrelated: x constant

This figure shows how we can graph two variables that are unrelated. In part (a), a student's grade in economics is plotted at 75 percent on the y-axis regardless of the price of bananas on the x-axis. The curve is horizontal.

In part (b), the output of the vineyards of France on the x-axis does not vary with the rainfall in California on the y-axis. The curve is vertical.

The Slope of a Relationship

We can measure the influence of one variable on another by the slope of the relationship. The **slope** of a relationship is the change in the value of the variable measured on the y-axis divided by the change in the value of the variable measured on the x-axis. We use the Greek letter Δ (*delta*) to represent "change in." Thus Δy means the change in the value of the variable measured on the y-axis, and Δx means the change in the value of the variable measured on the x-axis. Therefore the slope of the relationship is

$$\Delta y / \Delta x.$$

If a large change in the variable measured on the y-axis (Δy) is associated with a small change in the variable measured on the x-axis (Δx), the slope is large and the curve is steep. If a small change in the variable measured on the y-axis (Δy) is associated with a large change in the variable measured on the x-axis (Δx), the slope is small and the curve is flat.

We can make the idea of slope clearer by doing some calculations.

The Slope of a Straight Line

The slope of a straight line is the same regardless of where on the line you calculate it. The slope of a straight line is constant. Let's calculate the slopes of the lines in Fig. A1.9. In part (a), when x increases from 2 to 6, y increases from 3 to 6. The change in

FIGURE A1.9   The Slope of a Straight Line

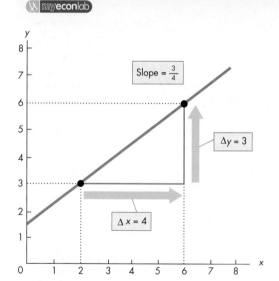

(a) Positive slope

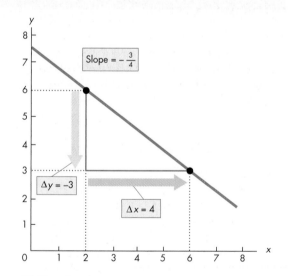

(b) Negative slope

To calculate the slope of a straight line, we divide the change in the value of the variable measured on the y-axis (Δy) by the change in the value of the variable measured on the x-axis (Δx), as we move along the curve. Part (a) shows the calculation of a positive slope. When x increases from 2 to 6, Δx equals 4. That change in x brings about an increase in y from 3 to 6, so Δy equals 3. The slope ($\Delta y/\Delta x$) equals 3/4. Part (b) shows the calculation of a negative slope. When x increases from 2 to 6, Δx equals 4. That increase in x brings about a decrease in y from 6 to 3, so Δy equals –3. The slope ($\Delta y/\Delta x$) equals –3/4.

x is +4—that is, Δx is 4. The change in y is +3—that is, Δy is 3. The slope of that line is

$$\frac{\Delta y}{\Delta x} = \frac{3}{4}.$$

In part (b), when x increases from 2 to 6, y decreases from 6 to 3. The change in y is *minus* 3—that is, Δy is –3. The change in x is *plus* 4—that is, Δx is 4. The slope of the curve is

$$\frac{\Delta y}{\Delta x} = \frac{-3}{4}.$$

Notice that the two slopes have the same magnitude (3/4) but the slope of the line in part (a) is positive (+3/+4 = 3/4), while that in part (b) is negative (–3/+4 = 3/4). The slope of a positive relationship is positive; the slope of a negative relationship is negative.

The Slope of a Curved Line

The slope of a curved line is trickier. The slope of a curved line is not constant, so the slope depends on where on the curved line we calculate it. There are two ways to calculate the slope of a curved line: You can calculate the slope at a point, or you can calculate the slope across an arc of the curve. Let's look at the two alternatives.

Slope at a Point To calculate the slope at a point on a curve, you need to construct a straight line that has the same slope as the curve at the point in question. Figure A1.10 shows how this is done. Suppose you want to calculate the slope of the curve at point A. Place a ruler on the graph so that it touches point A and no other point on the curve, then draw a straight line along the edge of the ruler. The straight red line is this line, and it is the tangent to the curve at point A. If the ruler touches the curve only at point A, then the slope of the curve at point A must be the same as the slope of the edge of the ruler. If the curve and the ruler do not have the same slope, the line along the edge of the ruler will cut the curve instead of just touching it.

Now that you have found a straight line with the same slope as the curve at point A, you can calculate the slope of the curve at point A by calculating the slope of the straight line. Along the straight line, as x

FIGURE A1.10   Slope at a Point

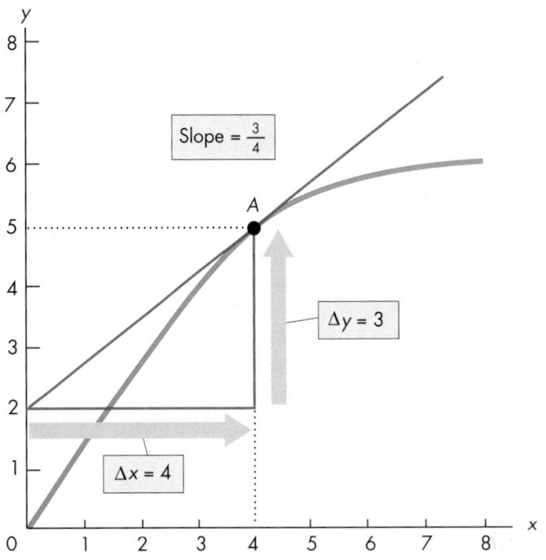

To calculate the slope of the curve at point A, draw the red line that just touches the curve at A—the tangent. The slope of this straight line is calculated by dividing the change in y by the change in x along the line. When x increases from 0 to 4, Δx equals 4. That change in x is associated with an increase in y from 2 to 5, so Δy equals 3. The slope of the red line is 3/4. So the slope of the curve at point A is 3/4.

increases from 0 to 4 ($\Delta x = 4$) y increases from 2 to 5 ($\Delta y = 3$). Therefore the slope of the straight line is

$$\frac{\Delta y}{\Delta x} = \frac{3}{4}.$$

So the slope of the curve at point A is 3/4.

Slope Across an Arc An arc of a curve is a piece of a curve. In Fig. A1.11, you are looking at the same curve as in Fig. A1.10. But instead of calculating the slope at point A, we are going to calculate the slope across the arc from B to C. You can see that the slope at B is greater than at C. When we calculate the slope across an arc, we are calculating the average slope between two points. As we move along the arc from B to C, x increases from 3 to 5 and y increases from 4 to 5.5. The change in x is 2 ($\Delta x = 2$), and the change

FIGURE A1.11   Slope Across an Arc

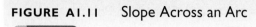

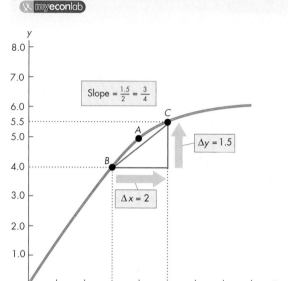

To calculate the average slope of the curve along the arc *BC*, draw a straight line from *B* to *C*. The slope of the line *BC* is calculated by dividing the change in *y* by the change in *x*. In moving from *B* to *C*, Δx equals 2 and Δy equals 1.5. The slope of the line *BC* is 1.5 divided by 2, or 3/4. So the slope of the curve across the arc *BC* is 3/4.

in *y* is 1.5 ($\Delta y = 1.5$). Therefore the slope is

$$\frac{\Delta y}{\Delta x} = \frac{1.5}{2} = \frac{3}{4}.$$

So the slope of the curve across the arc *BC* is 3/4.

This calculation gives us the slope of the curve between points *B* and *C*. The actual slope calculated is the slope of the straight line from *B* to *C*. This slope approximates the average slope of the curve along the arc *BC*. In this particular example, the slope across the arc *BC* is identical to the slope of the curve at point *A*. But the calculation of the slope of a curve does not always work out so neatly. You might have some fun constructing some more examples and some counterexamples.

You now know how to make and interpret a graph. But so far, we've limited our attention to graphs of two variables. We're now going to learn how to graph more than two variables.

Graphing Relationships Among More Than Two Variables

We have seen that we can graph the relationship between two variables as a point formed by the *x*- and *y*-coordinates in a two-dimensional graph. You might be thinking that although a two-dimensional graph is informative, most of the things in which you are likely to be interested involve relationships among many variables, not just two. For example, the amount of ice cream consumed depends on the price of ice cream and the temperature. If ice cream is expensive and the temperature is low, people eat much less ice cream than when ice cream is inexpensive and the temperature is high. For any given price of ice cream, the quantity consumed varies with the temperature; and for any given temperature, the quantity of ice cream consumed varies with its price.

Figure A1.12 shows a relationship among three variables. The table shows the number of gallons of ice cream consumed each day at various temperatures and ice cream prices. How can we graph these numbers?

To graph a relationship that involves more than two variables, we use the *ceteris paribus* assumption.

Ceteris Paribus   We noted in the chapter (see p. 13) that every laboratory experiment is an attempt to create *ceteris paribus* and isolate the relationship of interest. We use the same method to make a graph when more than two variables are involved.

Figure A1.12(a) shows an example. There, you can see what happens to the quantity of ice cream consumed when the price of ice cream varies when the temperature is held constant. The line labeled 70°F shows the relationship between ice cream consumption and the price of ice cream if the temperature remains at 70°F. The numbers used to plot that line are those in the third column of the table in Fig. A1.12. For example, if the temperature is 70°F, 10 gallons are consumed when the price is 60¢ a scoop, and 18 gallons are consumed when the price is 30¢ a scoop. The curve labeled 90°F shows consumption as the price varies if the temperature remains at 90°F.

We can also show the relationship between ice cream consumption and temperature when the price of ice cream remains constant, as shown in

FIGURE A1.12   Graphing a Relationship Among Three Variables

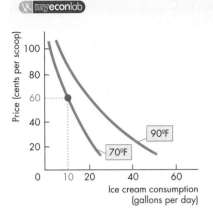

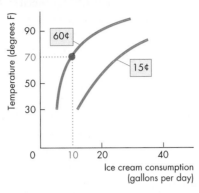

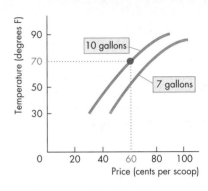

(a) Price and consumption at a given temperature

(b) Temperature and consumption at a given price

(c) Temperature and price at a given consumption

Price (cents per scoop)	Ice cream consumption (gallons per day)			
	30°F	**50°F**	**70°F**	**90°F**
15	12	18	25	50
30	10	12	18	37
45	7	10	13	27
60	5	7	10	20
75	3	5	7	14
90	2	3	5	10
105	1	2	3	6

Ice cream consumption depends on its price and the temperature. The table tell us how many gallons of ice cream are consumed each day at different prices and different temperatures. For example, if the price is 60¢ a scoop and the temperature is 70°F, 10 gallons of ice cream are consumed. This set of values is highlighted in the table and each part of the figure.

To graph a relationship among three variables, the value of one variable is held constant. Part (a) shows the relationship between price and consumption when temperature is held constant. One curve holds temperature at 90°F and the other holds it at 70°F. Part (b) shows the relationship between temperature and consumption when price is held constant. One curve holds the price at 60¢ a scoop and the other holds it at 15¢ a scoop. Part (c) shows the relationship between temperature and price when consumption is held constant. One curve holds consumption at 10 gallons and the other holds it at 7 gallons.

Fig. A1.12(b). The curve labeled 60¢ shows how the consumption of ice cream varies with the temperature when the price of ice cream is 60¢ a scoop, and a second curve shows the relationship when the price is 15¢ a scoop. For example, at 60¢ a scoop, 10 gallons are consumed when the temperature is 70°F and 20 gallons when the temperature is 90°F.

Figure A1.12(c) shows the combinations of temperature and price that result in a constant consumption of ice cream. One curve shows the combinations that result in 10 gallons a day being consumed, and the other shows the combinations that result in 7

gallons a day being consumed. A high price and a high temperature lead to the same consumption as a lower price and a lower temperature. For example, 10 gallons of ice cream are consumed at 70°F and 60¢ a scoop, at 90°F and 90¢ a scoop, and at 50°F and 45¢ a scoop.

◆ With what you have learned about graphs, you can move forward with your study of economics. There are no graphs in this book that are more complicated than those that have been explained in this appendix.

Mathematical Note:
Equations of Straight Lines

If a straight line in a graph describes the relationship between two variables, we call it a linear relationship. Figure 1 shows the *linear relationship* between a person's expenditure and income. This person spends $100 a week (by borrowing or spending previous savings) when income is zero. And out of each dollar earned, this person spends 50 cents (and saves 50 cents).

All linear relationships are described by the same general equation. We call the quantity that is measured on the horizontal axis (or x-axis) *x,* and we call the quantity that is measured on the vertical axis (or y-axis) *y.* In the case of Fig. 1, *x* is income and *y* is expenditure.

A Linear Equation

The equation that describes a straight-line relationship between *x* and *y* is

$$y = a + bx.$$

In this equation, *a* and *b* are fixed numbers and they are called constants. The values of *x* and *y* vary so these numbers are called variables. Because the equation describes a straight line, the equation is called a *linear equation.*

The equation tells us that when the value of *x* is zero, the value of *y* is *a.* We call the constant *a* the y-axis intercept. The reason is that on the graph the straight line hits the y-axis at a value equal to *a.* Figure 1 illustrates the y-axis intercept.

For positive values of *x,* the value of *y* exceeds *a.* The constant *b* tells us by how much *y* increases above *a* as *x* increases. The constant *b* is the slope of the line.

Slope of Line

As we explain in the chapter, the *slope* of a relationship is the change in the value of *y* divided by the change in the value of *x.* We use the Greek letter Δ (delta) to represent "change in." So Δy means the change in the value of the variable measured on the y-axis, and Δx means the change in the value of the variable measured on the x-axis. Therefore the slope of the relationship is

$$\Delta y / \Delta x.$$

To see why the slope is *b,* suppose that initially the value of *x* is x_1, or $200 in Fig. 2. The corresponding value of *y* is y_1, also $200 in Fig. 2. The equation of the line tells us that

$$y_1 = a + bx_1. \tag{1}$$

Now the value of *x* increases by Δx to $x_1 + \Delta x$ (or $400 in Fig. 2). And the value of *y* increases by Δy to $y_1 + \Delta y$ (or $300 in Fig. 2).

The equation of the line now tells us that

$$y_1 + \Delta y = a + b(x_1 + \Delta x) \tag{2}$$

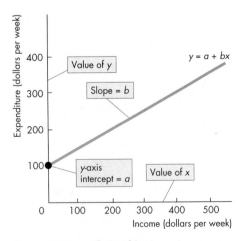

Figure 1 Linear relationship

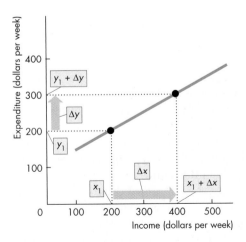

Figure 2 Calculating slope

To calculate the slope of the line, subtract equation (1) from equation (2) to obtain

$$\Delta y = b\Delta x \qquad (3)$$

and now divide equation (3) by Δx to obtain

$$\Delta y/\Delta x = b.$$

So the slope of the line is b.

Position of Line

The y-axis intercept determines the position of the line on the graph. Figure 3 illustrates the relationship between the y-axis intercept and the position of the line on the graph. In this graph, the y-axis measures saving and the x-axis measures income.

When the y-axis intercept, a, is positive, the line hits the y-axis at a positive value of y—as the blue line does. Its y-axis intercept is 100. When the y-axis intercept, a, is zero, the line hits the y-axis at the origin—as the purple line does. Its y-axis intercept is 0. When the y-axis intercept, a, is negative, the line hits the y-axis at a negative value of y—as the red line does. Its y-axis intercept is -100.

As the equations of the three lines show, the value of the y-axis intercept does not influence the slope of the line. All three lines have a slope equal to 0.5.

Positive Relationships

Figure 1 shows a positive relationship—the two variables x and y move in the same direction. All positive relationships have a slope that is positive. In the equation of the line, the constant b is positive. In this example, the y-axis intercept, a, is 100. The slope b equals $\Delta y/\Delta x$, which is 100/200 or 0.5. The equation of the line is

$$y = 100 + 0.5x.$$

Negative Relationships

Figure 4 shows a negative relationship—the two variables x and y move in the opposite direction. All negative relationships have a slope that is negative. In the equation of the line, the constant b is negative. In the example in Fig. 4, the y-axis intercept, a, is 30. The slope, b, equals $\Delta y/\Delta x$, which is $-20/2$ or -10. The equation of the line is

$$y = 30 + (-10)x$$

or

$$y = 30 - 10x.$$

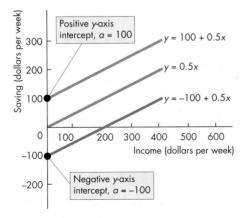

Figure 3 The y-axis intercept

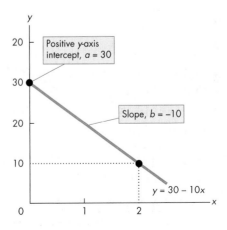

Figure 4 Negative relationship

Key Points

Graphing Data (pp. 17–20)

- A time-series graph shows the trend and fluctuations in a variable over time.
- A cross-section graph shows how variables change across the members of a population.
- A scatter diagram shows the relationship between two variables. It shows whether two variables are positively related, negatively related, or unrelated.

Graphs Used in Economic Models (pp. 20–23)

- Graphs are used to show relationships among variables in economic models.
- Relationships can be positive (an upward-sloping curve), negative (a downward-sloping curve), positive and then negative (have a maximum point), negative and then positive (have a minimum point), or unrelated (a horizontal or vertical curve).

The Slope of a Relationship (pp. 24–26)

- The slope of a relationship is calculated as the change in the value of the variable measured on the y-axis divided by the change in the value of the variable measured on the x-axis—that is, $\Delta y/\Delta x$.
- A straight line has a constant slope.
- A curved line has a varying slope. To calculate the slope of a curved line, we calculate the slope at a point or across an arc.

Graphing Relationships Among More Than Two Variables (pp. 26–27)

- To graph a relationship among more than two variables, we hold constant the values of all the variables except two.
- We then plot the value of one of the variables against the value of another.

Key Figures

Key Terms

1. What are the three types of graphs used to show economic data?
2. Give an example of a time-series graph.
3. List three things that a time-series graph shows quickly and easily.
4. Give three examples, different from those in the chapter, of scatter diagrams that show a positive relationship, a negative relationship, and no relationship.
5. Draw some graphs to show the relationships between two variables
   a. That move in the same direction.
   b. That move in opposite directions.
   c. That have a maximum.
   d. That have a minimum.
6. Which of the relationships in question 5 is a positive relationship and which a negative relationship?
7. What are the two ways of calculating the slope of a curved line?
8. How do we graph a relationship among more than two variables?

myeconlab Study Plan 1.A

PROBLEMS

myeconlab Tests, Study Plan, Solutions*

The spreadsheet provides data on the U.S. economy: Column A is the year, column B is the inflation rate, column C is the interest rate, column D is the growth rate, and column E is the unemployment rate. Use this spreadsheet to answer problems 1, 2, 3, and 4.

	A	B	C	D	E
1	1995	2.8	7.6	2.5	5.6
2	1996	2.9	7.4	3.7	5.4
3	1997	2.3	7.3	4.5	4.9
4	1998	1.6	6.5	4.2	4.5
5	1999	2.2	7.0	4.4	4.2
6	2000	3.4	7.6	3.7	4.0
7	2001	2.8	7.1	0.8	4.7
8	2002	1.6	6.5	1.6	5.8
9	2003	2.3	5.7	2.7	6.0
10	2004	2.7	5.6	4.2	5.5
11	2005	3.4	5.2	3.5	5.1

1. a. Draw a time-series graph of the inflation rate.
   b. In which year(s) (i) was inflation highest, (ii) was inflation lowest, (iii) did it increase, (iv) did it decrease, (v) did it increase most, and (vi) did it decrease most?
   c. What was the main trend in inflation?

2. a. Draw a time-series graph of the interest rate.
   b. In which year(s) (i) was the interest rate highest, (ii) was the interest rate lowest, (iii) did it increase, (iv) did it decrease, (v) did it increase most, and (vi) did it decrease most.
   c. What was the main trend in the interest rate?

3. Draw a scatter diagram to show the relationship between the inflation rate and the interest rate. Describe the relationship.

4. Draw a scatter diagram to show the relationship between the growth rate and the unemployment rate. Describe the relationship.

5. Draw a graph to show the relationship between the two variables x and y:

x	0	1	2	3	4	5	6	7	8
y	0	1	4	9	16	25	36	49	64

   a. Is the relationship positive or negative?
   b. Does the slope of the relationship increase or decrease as the value of x increases?

*Solutions to odd-numbered problems are provided.

c. Think of some economic relationships that might be similar to this one.

6. Draw a graph that shows the relationship between the two variables x and y:

x	0	1	2	3	4	5
y	25	24	22	16	8	0

   a. Is the relationship positive or negative?
   b. Does the slope of the relationship increase or decrease as the value of x increases?
   c. Think of some economic relationships that might be similar to this one.

7. In problem 5, calculate the slope of the relationship between x and y when x equals 4.

8. In problem 6, calculate the slope of the relationship between x and y when x equals 3.

9. In problem 5, calculate the slope of the relationship across the arc when x increases from 3 to 4.

10. In problem 6, calculate the slope of the relationship across the arc when x increases from 4 to 5.

11. Calculate the slope of the relationship shown at point A in the following figure.

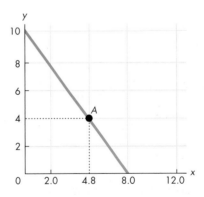

12. Calculate the slope of the relationship shown at point A in the following figure.

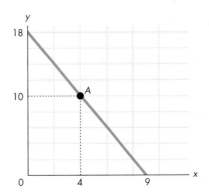

13. Use the following figure to calculate the slope of the relationship.

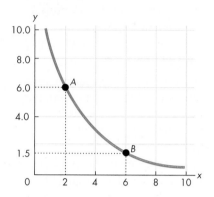

a. At points *A* and *B*.
b. Across the arc *AB*.

14. Use the following figure to calculate the slope of the relationship.

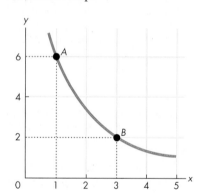

a. At points *A* and *B*.
b. Across the arc *AB*.

15. The table gives the price of a balloon ride, the temperature, and the number of rides a day.

Price	Balloon rides (number per day)		
(dollars per ride)	50°F	70°F	90°F
5.00	32	40	50
10.00	27	32	40
15.00	18	27	32
20.00	10	18	27

Draw graphs to show the relationship between
a. The price and the number of rides, holding the temperature constant.
b. The number of rides and temperature, holding the price constant.

c. The temperature and price, holding the number of rides constant.

16. The table gives the price of an umbrella, the amount of rainfall, and the number of umbrellas purchased.

Price	Umbrellas (number per day)		
(dollars per umbrella)	0	1	2
	(inches of rainfall)		
10	7	8	12
20	4	7	8
30	2	4	7
40	1	2	4

Draw graphs to show the relationship between
a. The price and the number of umbrellas purchased, holding the amount of rainfall constant.
b. The number of umbrellas purchased and the amount of rainfall, holding the price constant.
c. The amount of rainfall and the price, holding the number of umbrellas purchased constant.

WEB ACTIVITIES

myeconlab Links to Web sites

1. Find Consumer Price Index (CPI) for the latest 12 months. Make a graph of the CPI. During the most recent month, was the CPI rising or falling? Was the rate of rise or fall increasing or decreasing?
2. Find the unemployment rate for the latest 12 months. Graph the unemployment rate. During the most recent month, was it rising or falling? Was the rate of rise or fall increasing or decreasing?
3. Use the data that you obtained in questions 1 and 2. Make a graph to show whether the CPI and the unemployment rate are related to each other.
4. Use the data that you obtained in questions 1 and 2. Calculate the percentage change in the CPI each month. Make a graph to show whether the percentage change in the CPI and the unemployment rate are related to each other.

CHAPTER 2

The Economic Problem

Good, Better, Best!

We live in a style that surprises our grandparents and would have astonished our great-grandparents. MP3s, video games, cell

phones, gene splicing, and personal computers, which didn't exist even 25 years ago, have transformed our daily lives. For most of us, life is good and getting better. But we still make choices and face costs.

Perhaps the biggest choice that you will make is when to quit school and begin full-time work. When you've completed your current program, will you remain in school and work toward a postgraduate degree or a professional degree? What are the costs and consequences of this choice? We'll return to this question in *Reading Between the Lines* at the end of this chapter.

When we make our choices, we pursue our self-interest. Do our choices also serve the social interest? And what do we mean by the social interest?

We see an incredible amount of specialization and trade in the world. Each one of us specializes in a particular job—as a lawyer, a journalist, a homemaker. Why? How do we benefit from specialization and trade?

Over many centuries, social institutions have evolved that we take for granted. They include firms, markets, and a political and legal system that protects private property. Why have these institutions evolved?

◆ These are the questions that we study in this chapter. We begin with the core economic problem—scarcity and choice—and the concept of the production possibilities frontier. We then learn about the central idea of economics: that the pursuit of the social interest means using resources efficiently. We also discover how we can expand production by accumulating capital, expanding our knowledge, and specializing and trading with each other. What you will learn in this chapter is the foundation on which all economics is built.

After studying this chapter, you will be able to

▶ Define the production possibilities frontier and calculate opportunity cost

▶ Distinguish between production possibilities and preferences and describe an efficient allocation of resources

▶ Explain how current production choices expand future production possibilities

▶ Explain how specialization and trade expand our production possibilities

▶ Describe the economic institutions that coordinate decisions

Production Possibilities and Opportunity Cost

Every working day, in mines, factories, shops, and offices and on farms and construction sites across the United States, 138 million people produce a vast variety of goods and services valued at $50 billion. But the quantities of goods and services that we can produce are limited both by our available resources and by technology. And if we want to increase our production of one good, we must decrease our production of something else—we face tradeoffs. You are going to learn about the production possibilities frontier, which describes the limit to what we can produce and provides a neat way of thinking about and illustrating the idea of a tradeoff.

The **production possibilities frontier** (*PPF*) is the boundary between those combinations of goods and services that can be produced and those that cannot. To illustrate the *PPF*, we focus on two goods at a time and hold the quantities produced of all the other goods and services constant. That is, we look at a *model* economy in which everything remains the same (*ceteris paribus*) except for the production of the two goods we are considering.

Let's look at the production possibilities frontier for CDs and pizza, which stand for *any* pair of goods or services.

Production Possibilities Frontier

The *production possibilities frontier* for CDs and pizza shows the limits to the production of these two goods, given the total resources available to produce them. Figure 2.1 shows this production possibilities frontier. The table lists some combinations of the quantities of pizzas and CDs that can be produced in a month given the resources available. The figure graphs these combinations. The *x*-axis shows the quantity of pizzas produced, and the *y*-axis shows the quantity of CDs produced.

The *PPF* illustrates *scarcity* because we cannot attain the points outside the frontier. They are points that describe wants that can't be satisfied. We can produce at any point *inside* the *PPF* and *on* the *PPF*. These points are attainable. Suppose that in a typical month, we produce 4 million pizzas and 5 million CDs. Figure 2.1 shows this combination as point *E* and as possibility *E* in the table. The figure also

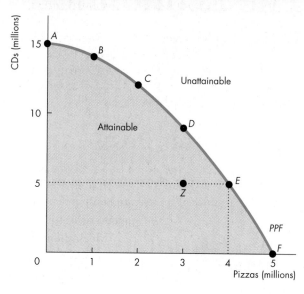

FIGURE 2.1   Production Possibilities Frontier

Possibility	Pizzas (millions)		CDs (millions)
A	0	and	15
B	1	and	14
C	2	and	12
D	3	and	9
E	4	and	5
F	5	and	0

The table lists six points on the production possibilities frontier for CDs and pizzas. Row *A* tells us that if we produce no pizza, the maximum quantity of CDs we can produce is 15 million. Points *A, B, C, D, E,* and *F* in the figure represent the rows of the table. The line passing through these points is the production possibilities frontier (*PPF*).

The *PPF* separates the attainable from the unattainable. Production is possible at any point *inside* the orange area or *on* the frontier. Points outside the frontier are unattainable. Points inside the frontier such as point *Z* are inefficient because resources are wasted or misallocated. At such points, it is possible to use the available resources to produce more of either or both goods.

shows other production possibilities. For example, we might stop producing pizza and move all the people who produce it into producing CDs. Point *A* in the figure and possibility *A* in the table show this case. The quantity of CDs produced increases to 15 million, and pizza production dries up. Alternatively, we might close the CD factories and switch all the resources into producing pizza. In this situation, we produce 5 million pizzas. Point *F* in the figure and possibility *F* in the table show this case.

Production Efficiency

We achieve **production efficiency** if we cannot produce more of one good without producing less of some other good. When production is efficient, we are at a point *on* the *PPF*. If we are at a point *inside* the *PPF*, such as point *Z* in Fig. 2.1, production is *inefficient* because we have some *unused* resources or we have some *misallocated* resources or both.

Resources are unused when they are idle but could be working. For example, we might leave some of the factories idle or some workers unemployed.

Resources are *misallocated* when they are assigned to tasks for which they are not the best match. For example, we might assign skilled pizza makers to work in a CD factory and skilled CD makers to work in a pizza shop. We could get more pizzas *and* more CDs from these same workers if we reassigned them to the tasks that more closely match their skills.

If we produce at a point inside the *PPF* such as *Z* in Fig. 2.1, we can use our resources more efficiently to produce more pizzas, more CDs, or more of *both* pizzas and CDs. But if we produce at a point *on* the *PPF*, we are using our resources efficiently. We can produce more of one good only if we produce less of the other. That is, along the *PPF*, we face a *tradeoff*.

Tradeoff Along the *PPF*

Every choice *along* the *PPF* involves a *tradeoff*—we must give up something to get something else. On the *PPF* in Fig. 2.1, we must give up some CDs to get more pizzas or give up some pizzas to get more CDs.

Tradeoffs arise in every imaginable real-world situation, and you reviewed several of them in Chapter 1. At any given point in time, we have a fixed amount of labor, land, capital, and entrepreneurship. By using our available technologies, we can employ these resources to produce goods and services. But we are limited in what we can produce. This limit defines a boundary between what we can attain and what we cannot attain. This boundary is the real-world's production possibilities frontier, and it defines the tradeoffs that we must make. On our real-world *PPF*, we can produce more of any one good or service only if we produce less of some other goods or services.

When doctors say that we must spend more on AIDS and cancer research, they are suggesting a tradeoff: more medical research for less of some other things. When the President says that he wants to spend more on education and health care, he is suggesting a tradeoff: more education and health care for less national defense or less private spending (because of higher taxes). When an environmental group argues for less logging, it is suggesting a tradeoff: greater conservation of endangered wildlife for less paper. When your parents say that you should study more, they are suggesting a tradeoff: more study time for less leisure or sleep.

All tradeoffs involve a cost—an opportunity cost.

Opportunity Cost

The *opportunity cost* of an action is the highest-valued alternative forgone. The *PPF* helps us to make the concept of opportunity cost precise and enables us to calculate it. Along the *PPF*, there are only two goods, so there is only one alternative forgone: some quantity of the other good. Given our current resources and technology, we can produce more pizzas only if we produce fewer CDs. The opportunity cost of producing an additional pizza is the number of CDs we *must* forgo. Similarly, the opportunity cost of producing an additional CD is the quantity of pizzas we *must* forgo.

For example, at point *C* in Fig. 2.1, we produce fewer pizzas and more CDs than at point *D*. If we choose point *D* over point *C*, the additional 1 million pizzas *cost* 3 million CDs. One pizza costs 3 CDs.

We can also work out the opportunity cost of choosing point *C* over point *D* in Fig. 2.1. If we move from point *D* to point *C*, the quantity of CDs produced increases by 3 million and the quantity of pizzas produced decreases by 1 million. So if we choose point *C* over point *D*, the additional 3 million CDs *cost* 1 million pizzas. One CD costs 1/3 of a pizza.

Opportunity Cost Is a Ratio Opportunity cost is a ratio. It is the decrease in the quantity produced of one good divided by the increase in the quantity produced of another good as we move along the production possibilities frontier.

Because opportunity cost is a ratio, the opportunity cost of producing an additional CD is equal to the *inverse* of the opportunity cost of producing an additional pizza. Check this proposition by returning to the calculations we've just worked through. When we move along the *PPF* from *C* to *D*, the opportunity cost of a pizza is 3 CDs. The inverse of 3 is 1/3, so if we decrease the production of pizza and increase the production of CDs by moving from *D* to *C*, the opportunity cost of a CD must be 1/3 of a pizza. You can check that this number is correct. If we move from *D* to *C*, we produce 3 million more CDs and 1 million fewer pizzas. Because 3 million CDs cost 1 million pizzas, the opportunity cost of 1 CD is 1/3 of a pizza.

Increasing Opportunity Cost The opportunity cost of a pizza increases as the quantity of pizzas produced increases. Also, the opportunity cost of a CD increases as the quantity of CDs produced increases. This phenomenon of increasing opportunity cost is reflected in the shape of the *PPF*—it is bowed outward.

When a large quantity of CDs and a small quantity of pizzas are produced—between points *A* and *B* in Fig. 2.1—the frontier has a gentle slope. A given increase in the quantity of pizzas *costs* a small decrease in the quantity of CDs, so the opportunity cost of a pizza is a small quantity of CDs.

When a large quantity of pizzas and a small quantity of CDs are produced—between points *E* and *F* in Fig. 2.1—the frontier is steep. A given increase in the quantity of pizzas *costs* a large decrease in the quantity of CDs, so the opportunity cost of a pizza is a large quantity of CDs.

The *PPF* is bowed outward because resources are not all equally productive in all activities. People with several years of experience working for Sony are good at producing CDs but not very good at making pizzas. So if we move some of these people from Sony to Domino's, we get a small increase in the quantity of pizzas but a large decrease in the quantity of CDs.

Similarly, people who have spent years working at Domino's are good at producing pizzas, but they have no idea how to produce CDs. So if we move some of these people from Domino's to Sony, we get a small increase in the quantity of CDs but a large decrease in the quantity of pizzas. The more of either good we try to produce, the less productive are the additional resources we use to produce that

good and the larger is the opportunity cost of a unit of that good.

Increasing Opportunity Costs Are Everywhere Just about every activity that you can think of is one with an increasing opportunity cost. We allocate the most skillful farmers and the most fertile land to the production of food. And we allocate the best doctors and the least fertile land to the production of health-care services. If we shift fertile land and tractors away from farming to hospitals and ambulances and ask farmers to become hospital porters, the production of food drops drastically and the increase in the production of health-care services is small. The opportunity cost of a unit of health-care services rises. Similarly, if we shift our resources away from health care toward farming, we must use more doctors and nurses as farmers and more hospitals as hydroponic tomato factories. The decrease in the production of health-care services is large, but the increase in food production is small. The opportunity cost of a unit of food rises.

This example is extreme and unlikely, but these same considerations apply to any pair of goods that you can imagine.

REVIEW QUIZ

1 How does the production possibilities frontier illustrate scarcity?
2 How does the production possibilities frontier illustrate production efficiency?
3 How does the production possibilities frontier show that every choice involves a tradeoff?
4 How does the production possibilities frontier illustrate opportunity cost?
5 Why is opportunity cost a ratio?
6 Why does the *PPF* for most goods bow outward so that opportunity cost increases as the quantity produced of a good increases?

myeconlab Study Plan 2.1

We've seen that what we can produce is limited by the production possibilities frontier. We've also seen that production on the *PPF* is efficient. But we can produce many different quantities on the *PPF*. How do we choose among them? How do we know which point on the *PPF* is the best one?

Using Resources Efficiently

You've seen that we achieve production efficiency at every point on the *PPF*. But which point is best? What quantities of CDs and pizzas best serve the social interest?

This question is an example of real-world questions of enormous consequence such as: How much should we spend on treating AIDS and how much on cancer research? Should we expand education and health-care programs or cut taxes? Should we spend more on the preservation of rainforests and the conservation of endangered wildlife?

To answer these questions, we must find a way of measuring and comparing costs and benefits.

The *PPF* and Marginal Cost

The **marginal cost** of a good is the opportunity cost of producing one more unit of it. We calculate marginal cost from the slope of the *PPF*. As the quantity of pizzas produced increases, the *PPF* gets steeper and marginal cost of a pizza increases. Figure 2.2 illustrates the calculation of the marginal cost of a pizza.

Begin by finding the opportunity cost of pizza in blocks of 1 million pizzas. The first million pizzas cost 1 million CDs, the second million pizzas cost 2 million CDs, the third million pizzas cost 3 million CDs, and so on. The bars in part (a) illustrate these calculations.

The bars in part (b) show the cost of an average pizza in each of the 1 million pizza blocks. Focus on the third million pizzas—the move from *C* to *D* in part (a). Over this range, because the 1 million pizzas cost 3 million CDs, one of these pizzas, on the average, costs 3 CDs—the height of the bar in part (b).

Next, find the opportunity cost of each additional pizza—the marginal cost of a pizza. The marginal cost of a pizza increases as the quantity of pizza produced increases. The marginal cost at point *C* is less than it is at point *D*. On the average over the range from *C* to *D*, the marginal cost of a pizza is 3 CDs. But it exactly equals 3 CDs only in the middle of the range between *C* and *D*.

The red dot in part (b) indicates that the marginal cost of a pizza is 3 CDs when 2.5 million pizzas are produced. Each black dot in part (b) is interpreted in the same way. The red curve that passes through these dots, labeled *MC*, is the marginal cost curve. It shows the marginal cost of a pizza at each quantity of pizza as we move along the *PPF*.

FIGURE 2.2   The *PPF* and Marginal Cost

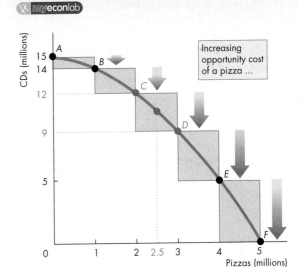

(a) PPF and opportunity cost

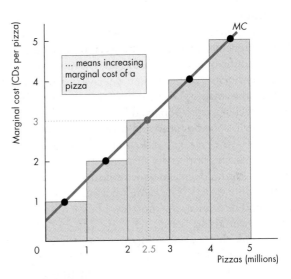

(b) Marginal cost

Marginal cost is calculated from the slope of the *PPF*. As the quantity of pizzas produced increases, the *PPF* gets steeper and the marginal cost of a pizza increases. The bars in part (a) show the opportunity cost of pizza in blocks of 1 million pizzas. The bars in part (b) show the cost of an average pizza in each of these 1 million blocks. The red curve, *MC*, shows the marginal cost of a pizza at each point along the *PPF*. This curve passes through the center of each of the bars in part (b).

Preferences and Marginal Benefit

Look around your classroom and notice the wide variety of shirts, caps, pants, and shoes that you and your fellow students are wearing today. Why is there such a huge variety? Why don't you all wear the same styles and colors? The answer lies in what economists call preferences. **Preferences** are a description of a person's likes and dislikes.

You've seen that we have a concrete way of describing the limits to production: the *PPF*. We need a similarly concrete way of describing preferences. To describe preferences, economists use the concept of marginal benefit. The **marginal benefit** from a good or service is the benefit received from consuming one more unit of it.

We measure the marginal benefit from a good or service by the most that people are *willing to pay* for an additional unit of it. The idea is that you are not willing to pay more for a good than it is worth to you. But you are willing to pay an amount up to what it is worth. So the willingness to pay for something measures its marginal benefit.

Economists use the marginal benefit curve to illustrate preferences. The **marginal benefit curve** shows the relationship between the marginal benefit from a good and the quantity of that good consumed. It is a general principle that the more we have of any good or service, the smaller is its marginal benefit and the less we are willing to pay for an additional unit of it. This tendency is so widespread and strong that we call it a principle—the *principle of decreasing marginal benefit.*

The basic reason why marginal benefit from a good or service decreases as we consume more of it is that we like variety. The more we consume of any one good or service, the more we can see other things that we would like better.

Think about your willingness to pay for pizza (or any other item). If pizza is hard to come by and you can buy only a few slices a year, you might be willing to pay a high price to get an additional slice. But if pizza is all you've eaten for the past few days, you are willing to pay almost nothing for another slice.

In everyday life, we think of what we pay for goods and services as the money that we give up—dollars. But you've learned to think about cost as other goods or services forgone, not a dollar cost. You can think about willingness to pay in the same terms. The price you are willing to pay for something is the quantity of other goods and services that you are willing to forgo. Let's continue with the example of CDs and pizzas and illustrate preferences this way.

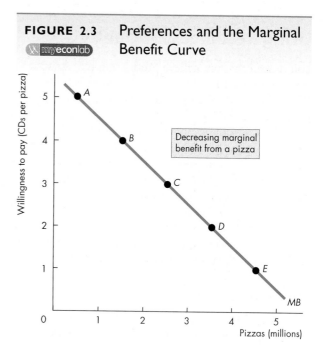

FIGURE 2.3   Preferences and the Marginal Benefit Curve

Possibility	Pizzas (millions)	Willingness to pay (CDs per pizza)
A	0.5	5
B	1.5	4
C	2.5	3
D	3.5	2
E	4.5	1

The smaller the quantity of pizzas produced, the more CDs people are willing to give up for an additional pizza. If pizza production is 0.5 million, people are willing to pay 5 CDs per pizza. But if pizza production is 4.5 million, people are willing to pay only 1 CD per pizza. Willingness to pay measures marginal benefit. And decreasing marginal benefit is a universal feature of people's preferences.

Figure 2.3 illustrates preferences as the willingness to pay for pizza in terms of CDs. In row *A*, pizza production is 0.5 million, and at that quantity, people are willing to pay 5 CDs per pizza. As the quantity of pizza produced increases, the amount that people are willing to pay for it falls. When pizza production is 4.5 million, people are willing to pay only 1 CD per pizza.

Let's now use the concepts of marginal cost and marginal benefit to describe the efficient quantity of pizzas to produce.

FIGURE 2.4   Efficient Use of Resources

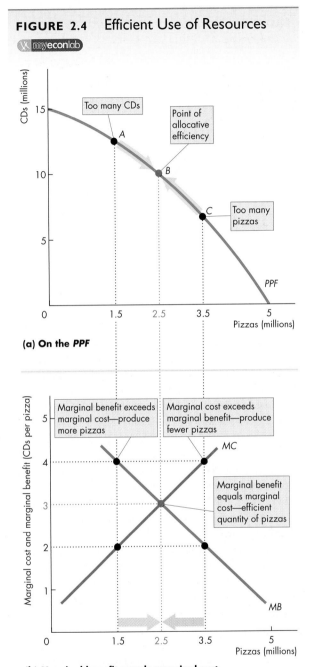

(a) On the PPF

(b) Marginal benefit equals marginal cost

The greater the quantity of pizzas produced, the smaller is the marginal benefit (MB) from pizza—the fewer CDs people are willing to give up to get an additional pizza. But the greater the quantity of pizzas produced, the greater is the marginal cost (MC) of pizza—the more CDs people must give up to get an additional pizza. When marginal benefit equals marginal cost, resources are being used efficiently.

Efficient Use of Resources

When we cannot produce more of any one good without giving up some other good, we have achieved *production efficiency*, and we're producing at a point on the *PPF*. When we cannot produce more of any good without giving up some other good that we *value more highly*, we have achieved **allocative efficiency** and we are producing at the point on the *PPF* that we prefer above all other points.

Suppose in Fig. 2.4, we produce 1.5 million pizzas. The marginal cost of a pizza is 2 CDs, and the marginal benefit from a pizza is 4 CDs. Because someone values an additional pizza more highly than it costs to produce, we can get more value from our resources by moving some of them out of producing CDs and into producing pizzas.

Now suppose we produce 3.5 million pizzas. The marginal cost of a pizza is now 4 CDs, but the marginal benefit from a pizza is only 2 CDs. Because the additional pizza costs more to produce than anyone thinks it is worth, we can get more value from our resources by moving some of them away from producing pizzas and into producing CDs.

But suppose we produce 2.5 million pizzas. Marginal cost and marginal benefit are now equal at 3 CDs. This allocation of resources between pizzas and CDs is efficient. If more pizzas are produced, the forgone CDs are worth more than the additional pizzas. If fewer pizzas are produced, the forgone pizzas are worth more than the additional CDs.

REVIEW QUIZ

1 What is marginal cost? How is it measured?
2 What is marginal benefit? How is it measured?
3 How does the marginal benefit from a good change as the quantity produced of that good increases?
4 What is allocative efficiency and how does it relate to the production possibilities frontier?
5 What conditions must be satisfied if resources are used efficiently?

(X) myeconlab **Study Plan 2.2**

You now understand the limits to production and the conditions under which resources are used efficiently. Your next task is to study the expansion of production possibilities.

Economic Growth

During the past 30 years, production per person in the United States has doubled. Such an expansion of production is called **economic growth**. Economic growth increases our *standard of living*, but it doesn't overcome scarcity and avoid opportunity cost. To make our economy grow, we face a tradeoff—the faster we make production grow, the greater is the opportunity cost of economic growth.

The Cost of Economic Growth

Economic growth comes from technological change and capital accumulation. **Technological change** is the development of new goods and of better ways of producing goods and services. **Capital accumulation** is the growth of capital resources, including *human capital*.

Because of technological change and capital accumulation, we have an enormous quantity of cars that enable us to produce more transportation than was available when we had only horses and carriages; we have satellites that make global communications possible on a scale that is much larger than that produced by the earlier cable technology. But if we use our resources to develop new technologies and produce capital, we must decrease our production of consumption goods and services. New technologies and new capital have an opportunity cost. Let's look at this opportunity cost.

Instead of studying the *PPF* of pizzas and CDs, we'll hold the quantity of CDs produced constant and examine the *PPF* for pizzas and pizza ovens. Figure 2.5 shows this *PPF* as the blue curve *ABC*. If we devote no resources to producing pizza ovens, we produce at point *A*. If we produce 3 million pizzas, we can produce 6 pizza ovens at point *B*. If we produce no pizza, we can produce 10 ovens at point *C*.

The amount by which our production possibilities expand depends on the resources we devote to technological change and capital accumulation. If we devote no resources to this activity (point *A*), our *PPF* remains at *ABC*—the blue curve in Fig. 2.5. If we cut the current production of pizza and produce 6 ovens (point *B*), then in the future, we'll have more capital and our *PPF* will rotate outward to the position shown by the red curve. The fewer resources we devote to producing pizza and the more resources we devote to producing ovens, the

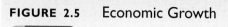

FIGURE 2.5   Economic Growth

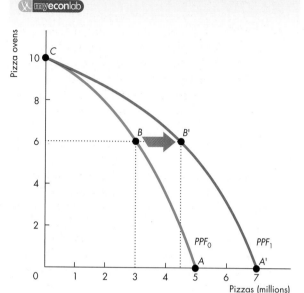

PPF_0 shows the limits to the production of pizza and pizza ovens, with the production of all other goods and services remaining the same. If we devote no resources to producing pizza ovens and produce 5 million pizzas, our production possibilities will remain the same PPF_0. But if we decrease pizza production to 3 million and produce 6 ovens, at point *B*, our production possibilities expand. After one period, the *PPF* rotates outward to PPF_1 and we can produce at point *B'*, a point outside the original PPF_0. We can rotate the *PPF* outward, but we cannot avoid opportunity cost. The opportunity cost of producing more pizzas in the future is fewer pizzas today.

greater is the future expansion of our production possibilities.

Economic growth is not free. To make it happen, we devote resources to producing new ovens and less to producing pizza. In Fig. 2.5, we move from *A* to *B*. There is no free lunch. The opportunity cost of more pizzas in the future is fewer pizzas today. Also, economic growth is no magic formula for abolishing scarcity. On the new production possibilities frontier, we continue to face a tradeoff and opportunity cost.

The ideas about economic growth that we have explored in the setting of the pizza industry also apply to nations. Let's look at two examples.

Economic Growth in the United States and Hong Kong

If a nation devotes all its resources to producing consumption goods and none to advancing technology and accumulating capital, its production possibilities in the future will be the same as they are today. To expand production possibilities in the future, we must devote fewer resources to producing consumption goods and some resources to accumulating capital and developing technologies. The decrease in today's consumption is the opportunity cost of tomorrow's increase in consumption.

The experiences of the United States and Hong Kong make a striking example of the effects of our choices on the rate of economic growth. In 1966, the production possibilities per person in the United States were more than four times those in Hong Kong (see Fig. 2.6). The United States devoted one fifth of its resources to accumulating capital and the other four fifths to consumption. In 1966, the United States was at point *A* on its *PPF*. Hong Kong devoted one third of its resources to accumulating capital and two thirds to consumption. In 1966, Hong Kong was at point *A* on its *PPF*.

Since 1966, both countries have experienced economic growth, but growth in Hong Kong has been more rapid than that in the United States. Because Hong Kong devoted a bigger fraction of its resources to accumulating capital, its production possibilities have expanded more quickly.

By 2006, the production possibilities per person in Hong Kong had reached 80 percent of those in the United States. If Hong Kong continues to devote more resources to accumulating capital than we do (at point *B* on its 2006 *PPF*), it will continue to grow more rapidly than the United States. But if Hong Kong increases consumption and decreases capital accumulation (moving to point *D* on its 2006 *PPF*), then its rate of economic growth will slow.

The United States is typical of the rich industrial countries, which include Western Europe and Japan. Hong Kong is typical of the fast-growing Asian economies, which include Taiwan, Thailand, South Korea, and China. Growth in these countries slowed during the Asia crisis of 1998 but quickly rebounded. Production possibilities expand in these countries by between 5 and almost 10 percent a year. If such high growth rates are maintained, these other Asian countries will eventually close the gap between them and the United States, as Hong Kong has done.

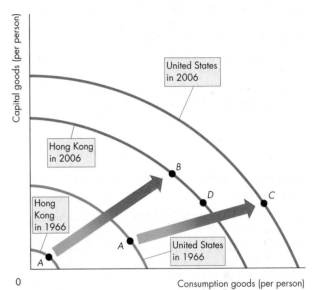

FIGURE 2.6   Economic Growth in the United States and Hong Kong

In 1966, the production possibilities per person in the United States were much larger than those in Hong Kong. But Hong Kong devoted more of its resources to accumulating capital than did the United States, so its production possibilities frontier has shifted outward more quickly than has that of the United States. In 2006, Hong Kong's production possibilities per person were 80 percent of those in the United States.

REVIEW QUIZ

1 What generates economic growth?
2 How does economic growth influence the production possibilities frontier?
3 What is the opportunity cost of economic growth?
4 Why has Hong Kong experienced faster economic growth than the United States?

myeconlab Study Plan 2.3

Next, we're going to study another way in which we expand our production possibilities—the amazing fact that *both* buyers and sellers gain from specialization and trade.

Gains from Trade

People can produce for themselves all the goods that they consume, or they can concentrate on producing one good (or perhaps a few goods) and then trade with others—exchange some of their own goods for those of others. Concentrating on the production of only one good or a few goods is called *specialization*. We are going to discover how people gain by specializing in the production of the good in which they have a *comparative advantage* and trading with each other.

Comparative Advantage and Absolute Advantage

A person has a **comparative advantage** in an activity if that person can perform the activity at a lower opportunity cost than anyone else. Differences in opportunity costs arise from differences in individual abilities and from differences in the characteristics of other resources.

No one excels at everything. One person is an outstanding pitcher but a poor catcher; another person is a brilliant lawyer but a poor teacher. In almost all human endeavors, what one person does easily, someone else finds difficult. The same applies to land and capital. One plot of land is fertile but has no mineral deposits; another plot of land has outstanding views but is infertile. One machine has great precision but is difficult to operate; another is fast but often breaks down.

Although no one excels at everything, some people excel and can outperform others in a large number of activities—perhaps even in all activities. A person who is more productive than others has an **absolute advantage**.

Absolute advantage involves comparing productivities—production per hour—while comparative advantage involves comparing opportunity cost.

Notice that a person who has an absolute advantage does not have a *comparative* advantage in every activity. John Grisham is a better lawyer and a better author of fast-paced thrillers than most people. He has an absolute advantage in these two activities. But compared to others, he is a better writer than lawyer, so his *comparative* advantage is in writing.

Because people's abilities and the quality of their resources differ, they have different opportunity costs of producing various goods. These differences in opportunity cost are the source of comparative advantage.

Let's explore the idea of comparative advantage by looking at two smoothie bars: one operated by Liz and the other operated by Joe.

Liz's Smoothie Bar Liz produces smoothies and salads. In Liz's high-tech bar, she can turn out either a smoothie or a salad every 90 seconds—see Table 2.1. If Liz spends all her time making smoothies, she can produce 40 an hour. And if she spends all her time making salads, she can also produce 40 an hour. If she splits her time equally between the two, she can produce 20 smoothies and 20 salads an hour. For each additional smoothie Liz produces, she must decrease her production of salads by one, and for each additional salad she produces, she must decrease her production of smoothies by one. So

Liz's opportunity cost of producing 1 smoothie is 1 salad,

and

Liz's opportunity cost of producing 1 salad is 1 smoothie.

Liz's customers buy smoothies and salads in equal quantities, so she splits her time equally between the two items and produces 20 smoothies and 20 salads an hour.

Joe's Smoothie Bar Joe also produces both smoothies and salads. But Joe's bar is smaller than Liz's. Also, Joe has only one blender, and it's a slow old machine. Even if Joe uses all his resources to produce smoothies, he can produce only 6 an hour—see Table 2.2. But Joe is good in the salad department, so if he uses all his resources to make salads, he can produce 30 an hour.

TABLE 2.1   Liz's Production Possibilities

Item	Minutes to produce 1	Quantity per hour
Smoothies	1.5	40
Salads	1.5	40

TABLE 2.2   Joe's Production Possibilities

Item	Minutes to produce 1	Quantity per hour
Smoothies	10	6
Salads	2	30

Joe's ability to make smoothies and salads is the same regardless of how he splits an hour between the two tasks. He can make a salad in 2 minutes or a smoothie in 10 minutes. For each additional smoothie Joe produces, he must decrease his production of salads by 5. And for each additional salad he produces, he must decrease his production of smoothies by 1/5 of a smoothie. So

Joe's opportunity cost of producing 1 smoothie is 5 salads,

and

Joe's opportunity cost of producing 1 salad is 1/5 of a smoothie.

Joe's customers, like Liz's, buy smoothies and salads in equal quantities. So Joe spends 50 minutes of each hour making smoothies and 10 minutes of each hour making salads. With this division of his time, Joe produces 5 smoothies and 5 salads an hour.

Liz's Absolute Advantage You can see from the numbers that describe the two smoothie bars that Liz is four times as productive as Joe—her 20 smoothies and salads an hour are four times Joe's 5. Liz has an absolute advantage—she is more productive than Joe in producing both smoothies and salads. But Liz has a comparative advantage in only one of the activities.

Liz's Comparative Advantage In which of the two activities does Liz have a comparative advantage? Recall that comparative advantage is a situation in which one person's opportunity cost of producing a good is lower than another person's opportunity cost of producing that same good. Liz has a comparative advantage in producing smoothies. Her opportunity cost of a smoothie is 1 salad, whereas Joe's opportunity cost of a smoothie is 5 salads.

Joe's Comparative Advantage If Liz has a comparative advantage in producing smoothies, Joe must have a comparative advantage in producing salads. His opportunity cost of a salad is 1/5 of a smoothie, while Liz's opportunity cost of a salad is 1 smoothie.

Achieving the Gains from Trade

Liz and Joe run into each other one evening in a singles bar. After a few minutes of getting acquainted, Liz tells Joe about her amazingly profitable smoothie business that is selling 20 smoothies and 20 salads an hour. Her only problem, she tells Joe, is that she wishes she could produce more because potential customers leave when her lines get too long.

Joe isn't sure whether to risk spoiling his chances by telling Liz about his own struggling business. But he takes the risk. When he explains to Liz that he spends 50 minutes of every hour making 5 smoothies and 10 minutes making 5 salads, Liz's eyes pop. "Have I got a deal for you!" she exclaims.

Here's the deal that Liz sketches on a table napkin. Joe stops making smoothies and allocates all his time to producing salads. And Liz increases her production of smoothies to 35 an hour and cuts her production of salads to 5 an hour—see Table 2.3(a).

TABLE 2.3   Liz and Joe Gain from Trade

(a) Production	Liz	Joe
Smoothies	35	0
Salads	5	30

(b) Trade	Liz	Joe
Smoothies	sell 10	buy 10
Salads	buy 20	sell 20

(c) After trade	Liz	Joe
Smoothies	25	10
Salads	25	10

(d) Gains from trade	Liz	Joe
Smoothies	+5	+5
Salads	+5	+5

They then trade. Liz sells Joe 10 smoothies and Joe sells Liz 20 salads—the price of a smoothie is 2 salads—see Table 2.3(b).

After the trade, Joe has 10 salads—the 30 he produces minus the 20 he sells to Liz. And he has the 10 smoothies that he buys from Liz. So Joe doubles the quantities of smoothies and salads he can sell—see Table 2.3(c).

Liz has 25 smoothies—the 35 she produces minus the 10 she sells to Joe. And she has 25 salads—the 5 she produces plus the 20 she buys from Joe—see Table 2.3(c). Both Liz and Joe gain 5 smoothies and 5 salads—see Table 2.3(d).

Liz draws a graph (Fig. 2.7) to illustrate her suggestion. The blue *PPF* in part (a) shows Joe's production possibilities. He is producing 5 smoothies and 5 salads an hour at point *A*. The blue *PPF* in part (b)

shows Liz's production possibilities. She is producing 20 smoothies and 20 salads an hour at point *A*.

Liz's proposal is that they each produce more of the good in which they have a comparative advantage. Joe produces 30 salads and no smoothies at point *B* on his *PPF*. Liz produces 35 smoothies and 5 salads at point *B* on her *PPF*.

Liz and Joe then trade—exchange—smoothies and salads at a price of 2 salads per smoothie or 1/2 of a smoothie per salad. Joe gets smoothies for 2 salads each, which is less than the 5 salads it costs him to produce them. And Liz gets salads for 1/2 a smoothie each, which is less than the 1 smoothie that it costs her to produce them.

With trade, Joe has 10 smoothies and 10 salads at point *C*—a gain of 5 smoothies and 5 salads. Joe moves to a point *outside* his *PPF*.

FIGURE 2.7   The Gains from Trade

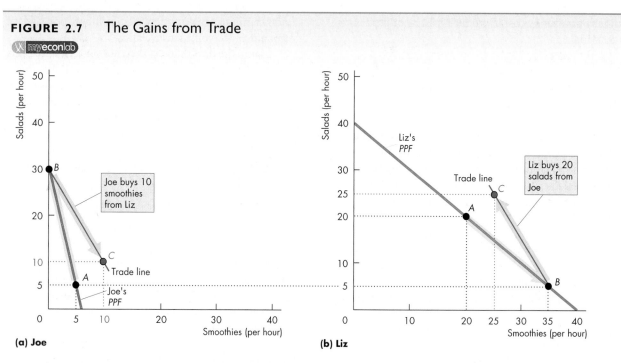

(a) Joe

(b) Liz

Joe initially produces at point *A* on his *PPF* in part (a), and Liz initially produces at point *A* on her *PPF* in part (b). Joe's opportunity cost of producing a salad is less than Liz's, so Joe has a comparative advantage in producing salads. Liz's opportunity cost of producing a smoothie is less than Joe's, so Liz has a comparative advantage in producing smoothies. If Joe specializes in salad, he produces 30 salads and no smoothies at point *B* on his *PPF*. If Liz produces 25 smoothies

and 5 salads, she produces at point *B* on her *PPF*. They exchange salads for smoothies along the red "Trade line." Liz buys salads from Joe for less than her opportunity cost of producing them. And Joe buys smoothies from Liz for less than his opportunity cost of producing them. Each goes to point *C*—a point outside his or her *PPF*. Both Joe and Liz increase production by 5 smoothies and 5 salads with no change in resources.

With trade, Liz has 25 smoothies and 25 salads at point *C*—a gain of 5 smoothies and 5 salads. Liz moves to a point *outside* her *PPF*.

Despite Liz's absolute advantage in producing smoothies and salads, both Liz and Joe gain from producing more of the good in which they have a comparative advantage and trading.

The gains that we achieve from international trade are similar to those achieved by Joe and Liz in this example. When Americans buy T-shirts from China and when China buys Boeing aircraft from the United States, both countries gain. We get our shirts at a lower cost than that at which we can produce them, and China gets its aircraft at a lower cost than that at which it can produce them.

Dynamic Comparative Advantage

At any given point in time, the resources and technologies available determine the comparative advantages that individuals and nations have. But just by repeatedly producing a particular good or service, people become more productive in that activity, a phenomenon called **learning-by-doing**. Learning-by-doing is the basis of *dynamic* comparative advantage. **Dynamic comparative advantage** is a comparative advantage that a person (or country) possesses as a result of having specialized in a particular activity and, as a result of learning-by-doing, having become the producer with the lowest opportunity cost.

Singapore, for example, pursued dynamic comparative advantage when it decided to begin a biotechnology industry in which it initially didn't have a comparative advantage.

REVIEW QUIZ

1 What gives a person a comparative advantage?
2 Distinguish between comparative advantage and absolute advantage.
3 Why do people specialize and trade?
4 What are the gains from specialization and trade?
5 What is the source of the gains from trade?
6 How does dynamic comparative advantage arise?

 myeconlab Study Plan 2.4

Economic Coordination

People gain by specializing in the production of those goods and services in which they have a comparative advantage and then trading with each other. Liz and Joe, whose production of salads and smoothies we studied earlier in this chapter, can get together and make a deal that enables them to enjoy the gains from specialization and trade. But for billions of individuals to specialize and produce millions of different goods and services, their choices must somehow be coordinated.

Two competing economic coordination systems have been used: central economic planning and decentralized markets.

Central economic planning might appear to be the best system because it can express national priorities. But when this system was tried, as it was for 60 years in Russia and for 30 years in China, it was a miserable failure. Today, these and most other previously planned economies are adopting a decentralized market system.

To make decentralized coordination work, four complementary social institutions that have evolved over many centuries are needed. They are

- Firms
- Markets
- Property rights
- Money

Firms

A **firm** is an economic unit that hires factors of production and organizes those factors to produce and sell goods and services. Examples of firms are your local gas station, Wal-Mart, and General Electric.

Firms coordinate a huge amount of economic activity. A Starbucks coffee shop, for example, might buy the machines and labor services of Liz and Joe and start to produce salads and smoothies at all its outlets.

But if a firm gets too big, it can't keep track of all the information that is needed to coordinate its activities. For this reason, firms themselves specialize and trade with each other. For example, Wal-Mart could produce all the things that it sells in its stores. And it could produce all the raw materials that are used to produce the things that it sells. But Sam Walton would not have become one of the wealthiest people in the world if he had followed that path. Instead, Wal-Mart buys from other firms that specialize in the production of a narrow range of items. And this trade takes place in markets.

Markets

In ordinary speech, the word *market* means a place where people buy and sell goods such as fish, meat, fruits, and vegetables. In economics, a *market* has a more general meaning. A **market** is any arrangement that enables buyers and sellers to get information and to do business with each other. An example is the market in which oil is bought and sold—the world oil market. The world oil market is not a place. It is the network of oil producers, oil users, wholesalers, and brokers who buy and sell oil. In the world oil market, decision makers do not meet physically. They make deals throughout the world by telephone, fax, and direct computer link.

Markets have evolved because they facilitate trade. Without organized markets, we would miss out on a substantial part of the potential gains from trade. Enterprising individuals and firms, each pursuing their own self-interest, have profited from making markets—standing ready to buy or sell the items in which they specialize. But markets can work only when property rights exist.

Property Rights

The social arrangements that govern the ownership, use, and disposal of anything that people value are called **property rights**. *Real property* includes land and buildings—the things we call property in ordinary speech—and durable goods such as plant and equipment. *Financial property* includes stocks and bonds and money in the bank. *Intellectual property* is the intangible product of creative effort. This type of property includes books, music, computer programs, and inventions of all kinds and is protected by copyrights and patents.

Where property rights are enforced, people have the incentive to specialize and produce the goods in which they have a comparative advantage. Where people can steal the production of others, resources are devoted not to production but to protecting possessions. Without property rights, we would still be hunting and gathering like our Stone Age ancestors.

Money

Money is any commodity or token that is generally acceptable as a means of payment. Liz and Joe didn't use money in the example above. They exchanged salads and smoothies. In principle, trade in markets can exchange any item for any other item. But you can perhaps imagine how complicated life would be if we exchanged goods for other goods. The "invention" of money makes trading in markets much more efficient.

Circular Flows Through Markets

Figure 2.8 shows the flows that result from the choices that households and firms make. Households specialize and choose the quantities of labor, land, capital, and entrepreneurship to sell or rent to firms. Firms choose the quantities of factors of production to hire. These (red) flows go through the *factor markets*. Households choose the quantities of goods and services to buy, and firms choose the quantities to produce. These (red) flows go through the *goods markets*. Households receive incomes and make expenditures on goods and services (the green flows).

How do markets coordinate all these decisions?

Coordinating Decisions

Markets coordinate decisions through price adjustments. To see how, think about your local market for hamburgers. Suppose that some people who want to buy hamburgers are not able to do so. To make the choices of buyers and sellers compatible, buyers must scale down their appetites or more hamburgers must be offered for sale (or both must happen). A rise in the price of a hamburger produces this outcome. A higher price encourages producers to offer more hamburgers for sale. It also encourages some people to change their lunch plans. Fewer people buy hamburgers, and more buy hot dogs. More hamburgers (and more hot dogs) are offered for sale.

Alternatively, suppose that more hamburgers are available than people want to buy. In this case, to make the choices of buyers and sellers compatible, more hamburgers must be bought or fewer hamburgers must be offered for sale (or both). A fall in the price of a hamburger achieves this outcome. A lower price encourages firms to produce a smaller quantity of hamburgers. It also encourages people to buy more hamburgers.

FIGURE 2.8   Circular Flows in the Market Economy

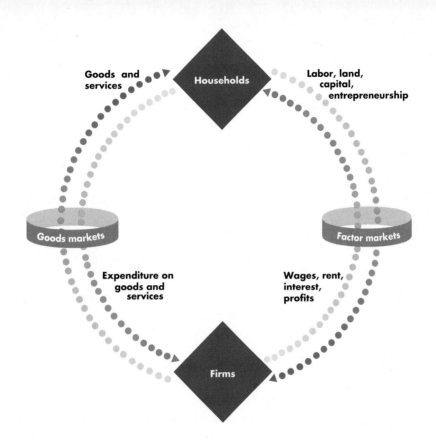

Households and firms make economic choices and markets coordinate these choices.

Households choose the quantities of labor, land, capital, and entrepreneurship to sell or rent to firms in exchange for wages, rent, interest, and profit. Households also choose how to spend their incomes on the various types of goods and services available.

Firms choose the quantities of factors of production to hire and the quantities of goods and services to produce.

Goods markets and factor markets coordinate these choices of households and firms.

The clockwise red flows are real flows—the flow of factors of production from households to firms and the flow of goods and services from firms to households.

The counterclockwise green flows are the payments for the red flows. They are the flow of incomes from firms to households and the flow of expenditure on goods and services from households to firms.

REVIEW QUIZ

1 Why are social institutions such as firms, markets, property rights, and money necessary?
2 What are the main functions of markets?
3 What are the flows in the market economy that go from firms to households and from households to firms?

 myeconlab Study Plan 2.5

◆ You have now begun to see how economists approach economic questions. Scarcity, choice, and divergent opportunity costs explain why we specialize and trade and why firms, markets, property rights, and money have developed. You can see all around you the lessons you've learned in this chapter. *Reading Between the Lines* on pp. 48–49 gives an example. It explores the *PPF* of a student like you and the choices that students must make that influence their own economic growth—the growth of their incomes.

The Cost and Benefit of Education

http://bostonworks.boston.com

MBA Grads May See Higher Compensation

May 29, 2005

Good news, business school graduates: That MBA will likely land you a fat salary.

Those are the findings of Consultants News, a publication of New Hampshire-based Kennedy Information Inc. that serves the consulting industry. It found that graduates of the nation's top business schools are expecting higher pay for their degree and some just might get it.

The newsletter said MBA students from top business schools expect to receive up to 20 percent more in total compensation this year based on their interviews with consulting firms.

"On average, base salary for this year's MBAs is almost $110,000, up about 10 percent over last year," said the newsletter. It noted that some firms, hoping to temper the salary rise, increased signing bonuses by nearly 30 percent.

The newsletter based its findings on information collected from 85 MBA students from a dozen high-ranked business schools, including Yale University, the University of Pennsylvania, the University of Chicago and the University of California at Los Angeles. It found that the average salary this year will be $109,000, up from $98,751 in 2004. The increase is the first since 2002, when salaries rose to $99,082, up from $92,253 in 2000.

Essence of the Story

▶ Consultants News reports the results of a survey of 85 MBA graduates from 12 top business schools.

▶ The average compensation of MBA graduates was expected to be 20 percent higher than in the previous year.

▶ The average base salary for a 2005 MBA was $109,000, up about 10 percent over the previous year.

▶ Recent average salaries were $92,253 in 2000, $99,082 in 2002, and $98,751 in 2004.

▶ Education increases human capital and expands production possibilities.

▶ The opportunity cost of a degree is forgone consumption. The payoff is an increase in lifetime production possibilities.

▶ Figure 1 shows the tradeoff facing a high school graduate between education goods and services and consumption goods and services on the blue *PPF*.

▶ Working full time, this person is at point *A* on the blue *PPF* in Fig. 1.

▶ By attending a university, the student moves from point *A* to point *B* along her *PPF*, forgoes current consumption (the opportunity cost of education), and increases the use of educational goods and services.

▶ On graduating from the university, earnings jump, so production possibilities expand to the red *PPF* in Fig. 1.

▶ Figure 2 shows a university graduate's tradeoff. The blue curve is the same *PPF* as the red *PPF* in Fig. 1.

▶ Working full time, this person earns enough to consume at point C on the blue *PPF* in Fig. 2.

▶ By pursuing an MBA, the student moves from point *C* to point *D* along her *PPF*, forgoes current consumption (the opportunity cost of an MBA), and increases the use of educational goods and services.

▶ With an MBA, a person's earnings jump again, so production possibilities expand to the red *PPF* in Fig. 2.

▶ For people who have the required ability, the benefits of postsecondary and postgraduate education are large.

You're the Voter

▶ With the huge return from postsecondary and postgraduate education, why don't more people remain in school longer?

▶ Would you vote for higher taxes to provide public scholarships to encourage more people to pursue postgraduate education? Explain why or why not.

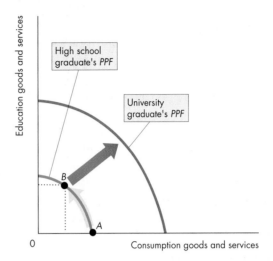

Figure 1 High school graduate's choices

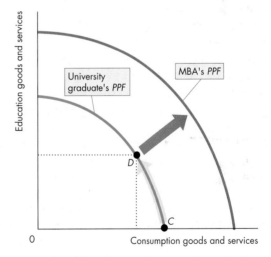

Figure 2 University graduate's choices

SUMMARY

Key Points

Production Possibilities and Opportunity Cost (pp. 34–36)

- The production possibilities frontier, *PPF*, is the boundary between production levels that are attainable and those that are not attainable when all the available resources are used to their limit.

- Production efficiency occurs at points on the *PPF*.

- Along the *PPF*, the opportunity cost of producing more of one good is the amount of the other good that must be given up.

- The opportunity cost of all goods increases as the production of the good increases.

Using Resources Efficiently (pp. 37–39)

- The marginal cost of a good is the opportunity cost of producing one more unit.

- The marginal benefit from a good is the maximum amount of another good that a person is willing to forgo to obtain more of the first good.

- The marginal benefit of a good decreases as the amount of the good available increases.

- Resources are used efficiently when the marginal cost of each good is equal to its marginal benefit.

Economic Growth (pp. 40–41)

- Economic growth, which is the expansion of production possibilities, results from capital accumulation and technological change.

- The opportunity cost of economic growth is forgone current consumption.

Gains from Trade (pp. 42–45)

- A person has a comparative advantage in producing a good if that person can produce the good at a lower opportunity cost than everyone else.

- People gain by specializing in the activity in which they have a comparative advantage and trading with others.

- Dynamic comparative advantage arises from learning-by-doing.

Economic Coordination (pp. 45–47)

- Firms coordinate a large amount of economic activity, but there is a limit to the efficient size of a firm.

- Markets coordinate the economic choices of people and firms.

- Markets can work efficiently only when property rights exist.

- Money makes trading in markets more efficient.

Key Figures

Key Terms

PROBLEMS

myeconlab Tests, Study Plan, Solutions*

1. Use the figure to calculate Wendell's opportunity cost of one hour of tennis when he increases the time he plays tennis from
   a. 4 to 6 hours a week.
   b. 6 to 8 hours a week.

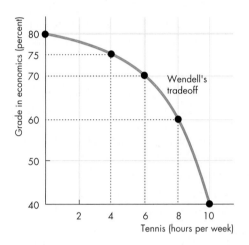

2. Wendell, whose *PPF* is shown in problem 1, has the following marginal benefit curve.

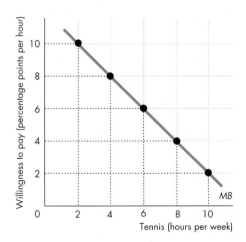

   a. If Wendell uses his time efficiently, what is his grade and how many hours of tennis does he play?
   b. Explain why Wendell would be worse off getting a higher grade.

*Solutions to odd-numbered problems are provided.

3. Sunland's production possibilities are

Food (pounds per month)		Sunscreen (gallons per month)
300	and	0
200	and	50
100	and	-100
0	and	150

   a. Draw a graph of Sunland's *PPF*.
   b. What is Sunland's opportunity cost of producing 1 pound of food?
   c. What is Sunland's opportunity cost of producing 1 gallon of sunscreen?

4. In Sunland, which has the production possibilities shown in the table in problem 3, preferences are described by the following table.

Sunscreen (gallons per month)	Willingness to pay (pounds per gallons)
25	3
75	2
125	1

   a. Draw a graph of Sunland's marginal benefit from sunscreen.
   b. What is the quantity of sunscreen produced in Sunland if it achieves allocative efficiency?

5. A farm grows wheat and produces pork. The marginal cost of producing each of these products increases as more of it is produced.
   a. Make a graph that illustrates the farm's *PPF*.
   b. The farm adopts a new technology that allows it to use fewer resources to fatten pigs. Use your graph to illustrate the impact of the new technology on the farm's *PPF*.
   c. With the farm using the new technology described in part b, has the opportunity cost of producing a ton of wheat increased, decreased, or remained the same? Explain and illustrate your answer.
   d. Is the farm more efficient with the new technology than it was with the old one?

6. Tom can produce 40 balls per hour or 4 bats per hour. Tessa can produce 80 balls per hour or 4 bats per hour.
   a. Calculate Tom's opportunity cost of producing a ball.
   b. Calculate Tessa's opportunity cost of producing a ball.
   c. Who has a comparative advantage in producing balls?

d. If Tom and Tessa specialize in producing the good in which each of them has a comparative advantage, and they trade 1 bat for 15 balls, who gains from the specialization and trade?

Suppose Tessa buys a new machine for making bats that enables her to make 20 bats per hour. (She can still make only 80 balls per hour.)

e. Now who has a comparative advantage in producing bats?

f. Can Tom and Tessa still gain from trade?

g. Would Tom and Tessa still be willing to trade 1 bat for 15 balls?

CRITICAL THINKING

1. After you have studied *Reading Between the Lines* on pp. 48–49, answer the following questions:
   a. At what point on the blue *PPF* in Fig. 1 on p. 49 are resources allocated efficiently? Explain and illustrate your answer.
   b. Suppose that tuition rises. How does higher tuition change the opportunity cost of education and how does it change the student's *PPF*s in Fig. 1 and Fig. 2?
   c. Do you think that people obtain an efficient quantity of education? Explain why.
2. Before the Civil War, the South traded with the North and with England. It sold cotton and bought manufactured goods and food. During the war, one of Lincoln's first actions was to blockade the ports, which prevented this trade. The South had to increase its production of munitions and food.
   a. In what did the South have a comparative advantage?
   b. Draw a graph to illustrate production, consumption, and trade in the South before the Civil War. Was the South consuming inside, on, or outside its *PPF*?
   c. Draw a graph to show the effects of the Civil War on consumption and production in the South.
   d. Did the Civil War change any opportunity costs in the South? Did the opportunity cost of everything rise? Or did items cost less? Use graphs to illustrate your answer.

3. Ethanol can be produced from either sugar or corn. A gallon of ethanol costs 90¢ to produce from Brazilian sugarcane and $1 to produce from U.S. corn. The U. S. Department of Agriculture expects 20 percent of the corn harvest to be used to produce ethanol in 2007, an increase of 34 percent from 2006.
   a. Does the United States have a comparative advantage in producing ethanol?
   b. Will the opportunity cost of producing ethanol in the United States increase in 2007?
   c. Could the United States gain by importing ethanol (or sugarcane) from Brazil?
4. "America's baby-boomers are embracing tea for its health benefits," said *The Economist* (July 8, 2005, p. 65). The article went on to say: "Even though the climate is suitable, tea-growing [in the United States] is simply too costly, since the process is labor-intensive and resists automation." Using the information provided:
   a. Sketch two *PPF*s for the production of tea and other goods and services: one in the United States and the other in India.
   b. Sketch the marginal benefit curve for tea in the United States before and after the baby-boomers appreciated the health benefits of tea.
   c. Does the United States produce tea or import it?
   d. Does the change in preferences toward tea have any effect on the opportunity cost of producing tea?

WEB ACTIVITIES

myeconlab **Links to Web sites**

1. Obtain data on the tuition and other costs of enrolling in the MBA program at a school that interests you.
   a. Draw a *PPF* that shows the tradeoff that you would face if you decided to enroll in the MBA program.
   b. Do you think the marginal benefit of an MBA exceeds the marginal cost?

Your Economic Revolution

You are making progress in your study of economics. You've already encountered the big questions and big ideas of economics. And you've learned about the key insight of Adam Smith, the founder of economics: Specialization and exchange create economic wealth.

You are studying economics at a time that future historians will call the *information revolution*. We reserve the word "revolution" for big events that influence all future generations.

During the *Agricultural Revolution*, which occurred 10,000 years ago, people learned to domesticate animals and plant crops. They stopped roaming in search of food and settled in villages and eventually towns and cities, where they developed markets in which to exchange their products.

During the *Industrial Revolution*, which began 240 years ago, people used science to create new technologies. This revolution brought extraordinary wealth for some but created conditions in which others were left behind. It brought social and political tensions that we still face today.

During today's *Information Revolution*, people who embraced the new technologies prospered on an unimagined scale. But the incomes and living standards of the less educated are falling behind, and social and political tensions are increasing. Today's revolution has a global dimension. Some of the winners live in previously poor countries in Asia, and some of the losers live here in the United States.

So you are studying economics at an interesting time. Whatever *your* motivation is for studying economics, *my* objective is to help you do well in your course, enjoy it, and develop a deeper understanding of the economic world around you.

There are three reasons why I hope that we both succeed: First, a decent understanding of economics will help you to become a full participant in the information revolution. Second, an understanding of economics will help you to play a more effective role as a citizen and voter and enable you to add your voice to those who are looking for solutions to our social and political problems. Third, you will enjoy the sheer fun of *understanding* the forces at play and how they are shaping our world.

If you are finding economics interesting, think seriously about majoring in the subject. A degree in economics gives the best training available in problem solving, offers lots of opportunities to develop conceptual skills, and opens doors to a wide range of graduate courses, including the MBA, and to a wide range of jobs.

Economics was born during the Industrial Revolution. We'll look at its birth and meet its founder, Adam Smith. Then we'll talk about the progress that economists have made and some of the outstanding policy problems of today with one of today's most distinguished economists, Robert Barro of Harvard University.

The Sources of Economic Wealth

"It is not from the benevolence of the butcher, the brewer, or the baker that we expect our dinner, but from their regard to their own interest."

ADAM SMITH
The Wealth of Nations

The Father of Economics

Adam Smith *was a giant of a scholar who contributed to ethics and jurisprudence as well as economics. Born in 1723 in Kirkcaldy, a small fishing town near Edinburgh, Scotland, Smith was the only child of the town's customs officer (who died before Adam was born).*

His first academic appointment, at age 28, was as Professor of Logic at the University of Glasgow. He subsequently became tutor to a wealthy Scottish duke, whom he accompanied on a two-year grand European tour, following which he received a pension of £300 a year—ten times the average income at that time.

With the financial security of his pension, Smith devoted ten years to writing An Inquiry into the Nature and Causes of the **Wealth of Nations**, *which was published in 1776. Many people had written on economic issues before Adam Smith, but he made economics a science. Smith's account was so broad and authoritative that no subsequent writer on economics could advance ideas without tracing their connections to those of Adam Smith.*

The Issues

Why are some nations wealthy while others are poor? This question lies at the heart of economics. And it leads directly to a second question: What can poor nations do to become wealthy?

Adam Smith, who is regarded by many scholars as the founder of economics, attempted to answer these questions in his book *The Wealth of Nations*, published in 1776. Smith was pondering these questions at the height of the Industrial Revolution. During these years, new technologies were invented and applied to the manufacture of cotton and wool cloth, iron, transportation, and agriculture.

Smith wanted to understand the sources of economic wealth, and he brought his acute powers of observation and abstraction to bear on the question. His answer:

- The division of labor
- Free markets

The division of labor—breaking tasks down into simple tasks and becoming skilled in those tasks—is the source of "the greatest improvement in the productive powers of labor," said Smith. The division of labor became even more productive when it was applied to creating new technologies. Scientists and engineers, trained in extremely narrow fields, became specialists at inventing. Their powerful skills accelerated the advance of technology, so by the 1820s, machines could make consumer goods faster and more accurately than any craftsman could. And by the 1850s, machines could make other machines that labor alone could never have made.

But, said Smith, the fruits of the division of labor are limited by the extent of the market. To make the market as large as possible, there must be no impediments to free trade both within a country and among countries. Smith argued that when each person makes the best possible economic choice, that choice leads as if by "an invisible hand" to the best outcome for society as a whole. The butcher, the brewer, and the baker each pursue their own interests but, in doing so, also serve the interests of everyone else.

Then

Adam Smith speculated that one person, working hard, using the hand tools available in the 1770s, might possibly make 20 pins a day. Yet, he observed, by using those same hand tools but breaking the process into a number of individually small operations in which people specialize —by the *division of labor*—ten people could make a staggering 48,000 pins a day. One draws out the wire, another straightens it, a third cuts it, a fourth points it, a fifth grinds it. Three specialists make the head, and a fourth attaches it. Finally, the pin is polished and packaged. But a large market is needed to support the division of labor: One factory employing ten workers would need to sell more than 15 million pins a year to stay in business.

Now

If Adam Smith were here today, the computer chip would fascinate him. He would see it as an extraordinary example of the productivity of the division of labor and of the use of machines to make machines that make other machines. From a design of a chip's intricate circuits, cameras transfer an image to glass plates that work like stencils. Workers prepare silicon wafers on which the circuits are printed. Some slice the wafers, others polish them, others bake them, and yet others coat them with a light-sensitive chemical. Machines transfer a copy of the circuit onto the wafer. Chemicals then etch the design onto the wafer. Further processes deposit atom-sized transistors and aluminum connectors. Finally, a laser separates the hundreds of chips on the wafer. Every stage in the process of creating a computer chip uses other computer chips. And like the pin of the 1770s, the computer chip of today benefits from a large market—a global market—to buy chips in the huge quantities in which they are produced efficiently.

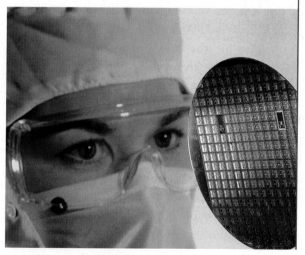

Many economists have worked on the big themes that Adam Smith began. One of these is Robert J. Barro of Harvard University, whom you can meet on the following pages.

Robert J. Barro

Robert J. Barro is Paul M. Warburg Professor of Economics at Harvard University and a senior fellow at the Hoover Institution of Stanford University. Born in 1944 in New York City, he was a physics undergraduate at the California Institute of Technology and an economics graduate student at Harvard.

Professor Barro is one of the world's leading economists and has done research on every aspect of macroeconomics, with a focus in recent years on economic growth and the interaction of economics and religion. Currently, he is studying the impact on stock markets and other asset markets of rare disasters—world wars, great depressions, epidemics, natural disasters. In addition to his many scholarly books and articles, his books, Getting it Right: Markets and Choices in a Free Society *(MIT Press, 1996) and* Nothing Is Sacred: Economic Ideas for the New Millennium *(MIT Press, 2002), explain, in nontechnical language, the importance of property rights and free markets for achieving economic growth and a high standard of living. He has just completed a new intermediate macroeconomics book,* Macroeconomics: A Modern Approach, *to be published by Thomson Learning. His articles in* Business Week *and the* Wall Street Journal *provide an accessible analysis of an incredible range of current economic issues.*

Michael Parkin talked with Robert Barro about his work and the progress that economists have made since the pioneering work of Adam Smith.

Professor Barro, your first degree was in physics. Why did you switch to economics when you went to graduate school?

For me, economics provided an ideal combination of technical analysis with applications to social problems and policies. Physics—or really mathematics—provided a strong background for economic theory and econometrics, but it was not until later in graduate school that I thought I acquired good economic insights. Overall, the transition from physics to economics was a relatively easy one for me, and I have never regretted the choice to switch fields. (Perhaps it also helped that, after taking courses from the great Richard Feynman at Caltech, I recognized that I would never be an outstanding theoretical physicist.)

Let's talk first about markets and choices in a free society. What is the central theme and message of your books on these vital issues?

In the long run, the central distinction between successful and unsuccessful economies is the extent to which they foster free markets and provide functioning institutions that support property rights and the rule of law. These points were highlighted by the failure of Communist economies, notably the former Soviet Union and China under Mao, in comparison with the successes of western societies, which relied more on markets and choices. These days China has arguably become the most capitalistic country on earth. For example, on a recent trip there, I saw a statue of Adam Smith on the campus of the South-Western University of Finance and Economics in Chengdu. As far as I know, there is no such statue at any U.S. or Canadian university.

Much of your research has focused on the same question that Adam Smith addressed in his. How do Adam Smith's speculations look today in light of what econo-

mists have discovered over the past two centuries? What are some of the key things we know today that Adam Smith didn't know?

Smith's topic about the source of the wealth of nations is often rephrased in modern research in terms of which factors determine the long-term rate of economic growth. Of course, for an economy to become wealthy, it has to sustain strong economic growth over a long period. A lot of progress has been made since the early 1990s in attaining an empirical understanding of the determinants of economic growth. There are no "silver bullets" for growth, but there are a number of favorable policies, institutions, and national characteristics that have been identified.

For example, growth is stimulated by strong rule of law, high levels of human capital in the forms of education and health, low levels of nonproductive government spending (and associated taxes), international openness, low fertility rates, and macroeconomic stability (including low and stable inflation). Given these and other factors, growth tends to be higher if a country starts off poorer. That is, convergence—in the sense of the poor tending to grow faster than the rich—holds in a conditional sense, when one holds constant an array of policies and national characteristics. However, convergence does not apply in an absolute sense because the poorest countries tend to have the worst policies and characteristics (which explains why they are poor).

Is there anything that rich countries can do to help poor countries grow faster? Or does successful economic growth come only from self-help?

Mostly, economic growth has to come from internal improvements in institutions and policies and from domestic accumulations of human and physical capital. There is no evidence that the rich countries can help through welfare programs, such as foreign aid and debt relief. On the contrary, there is some evidence that, because of the low quality of governance in most developing countries, foreign aid goes mainly to increased government spending and corruption. In the bad old days, the rich countries also provided governance (though not aimed especially at the interests of the governed). However, no one wants to return to the era of colonialism.

How does international trade influence economic growth? Could the rich countries do more by opening themselves to free trade with poor countries? Or is it enough for poor countries to just get on with opening their doors to free trade as Hong Kong did?

The rich countries could help to spur economic development by opening themselves more to trade in goods and services, technology, and financial transactions. Protectionist policies, notably in agriculture and textiles, are harmful to developing countries as well as to consumers in rich countries. President Bush's policies have been a mixed bag in this area; negative aspects were protectionism for steel, agriculture, and timber, as well as threats of protectionism against Chinese goods, especially textiles. Of course, on agricultural protectionism, Western Europe is even worse than the United States.

Inflation was subdued in the United States for most of the 1990s and early 2000s. Is inflation still a problem of the past or should we start worrying about again?

I am optimistic that the monetary authorities of the United States and many other countries have become committed to price stability and have learned that high inflation does not stimulate growth. Central banks seem also to have learned a lot about the mechanics of achieving price stability. The appointment of

> There are no 'silver bullets' for growth, but there are a number of favorable policies, institutions, and national characteristics that have been identified.

> I am optimistic that the monetary authorities of the United States and many other countries have become committed to price stability and have learned that high inflation does not stimulate growth.

Ben Bernanke as U.S. Federal Reserve chair was an excellent move. I think he will move the United States over time toward a more formal regime of inflation targeting, and this will be a good idea.

Some of your recent work has been on the interaction of religion and economic performance. Does religion influence the economy? Or does economic performance influence religion?

My coauthor (and wife), Rachel McCleary, and I have found that both directions of causation are important. Economic development tends to reduce religious participation and beliefs, though the effect is not strong, and the United States is an exception to the usual pattern. Subsidy to organized religion through establishment of state religion tends to increase participation, but some forms of regulation of the religion market tend to reduce participation. Religious beliefs related to an after-life—notably, beliefs in hell and heaven—tend to foster growth (a result reminiscent of the theorizing by the sociologist Max Weber). However, for given beliefs, greater participation in formal religion seems to reduce growth. We think the last effect involves the time and other resources used up in religious participation.

What remains in today's macroeconomics of the contribution of Keynes?

Probably, Keynesian economics is most influential today in analyses that stress the real effects of monetary policy—either as sources of business fluctuations or as ways to smooth out the cycle. This situation is ironic because Keynes himself deemphasized monetary shocks as a source of fluctuations. He stressed the excesses of the private economy—including the amplifying effects of multipliers and the sensitivity of investment to shifting expectations—and the potentially beneficial role of offsetting fiscal policies. Empirically, the multiplier seems to have existed only in the mind of Keynes.

What advice do you have for a student who is just starting to study economics? Is it a good subject in which to major? If so, what other subjects would you urge students to study alongside economics? Or is the path that you followed, starting with physics (or perhaps math) and then moving to economics for graduate school, more effective?

Economics is an excellent field for an undergraduate to study whether one chooses to become an economist or—more likely—if one goes into other fields, such as business or law. Economists have found the framework or methodology that makes economics the core social science, and its impact has been felt greatly by other fields, such as political science, law, and history.

These days, economic reasoning is being applied to the study of an array of social topics, including marriage and fertility, crime, democracy, and legal structure. As another example, I am currently participating in a project that involves the interactions between economics and religion (see www.wcfia.harvard.edu/religion for a description). This work is partly about how economic development and government policies affect religiosity and partly about how religious beliefs and participation influence economic and political outcomes. So perhaps in the future, economics will also be important for studies in theology. No doubt, many economists (including me) have imperialistic tendencies, but this is because they have a great product to sell. As for other complementary subjects to study, the most valuable one is probably mathematics, which provides many of the useful tools to carry out theoretical and empirical inquiries.

> Economists have found the framework or methodology that makes economics the core social science, and its impact has been felt greatly by other fields, such as political science, law, and history.

Demand and Supply

Slide, Rocket, and Roller Coaster

Slide, rocket, and roller coaster—Disneyland rides?

No, they are commonly used descriptions of price changes.

The price of a personal computer took a dramatic slide from around $3,000 in 2000 to $300 in 2006. The price of gasoline rocketed in 2006. The prices of coffee, bananas, and other agricultural products rise and fall like a roller coaster.

You've learned that economics is about the choices people make to cope with scarcity and how those choices respond to incentives. Prices are one of the incentives to which people respond. You're now going to see how prices are determined by demand and supply.

The demand and supply model is the main tool of economics. It helps us to answer the big economic question: What, how, and for whom are goods and services produced? It also helps us to say when the pursuit of self-interest promotes the social interest.

◆ Your careful study of this topic will bring big rewards both in your further study of economics and in your everyday life. When you have completed your study of demand and supply, you will be able to explain how prices are determined and make predictions about price slides, rockets, and roller coasters. Once you understand demand and supply, you will view the world through new eyes. You can begin to practice applying the tools of demand and supply in *Reading Between the Lines* at the end of this chapter where you will learn why the price of gasoline rose so much in 2006.

After studying this chapter, you will be able to

▶ Describe a competitive market and think about a price as an opportunity cost

▶ Explain the influences on demand

▶ Explain the influences on supply

▶ Explain how demand and supply determine prices and quantities bought and sold

▶ Use demand and supply to make predictions about changes in prices and quantities

Markets and Prices

When you need a new pair of running shoes, want a bagel and a latte, plan to upgrade your cell phone, or need to fly home for Thanksgiving, you must find a place where people sell those items or offer those services. The place in which you find them is a *market.* You learned in Chapter 2 (p. 46) that a market is any arrangement that enables buyers and sellers to get information and to do business with each other.

A market has two sides: buyers and sellers. There are markets for *goods* such as apples and hiking boots, for *services* such as haircuts and tennis lessons, for *resources* such as computer programmers and earth-movers, and for other manufactured *inputs* such as memory chips and auto parts. There are also markets for money such as Japanese yen and for financial securities such as Yahoo! stock. Only our imagination limits what can be traded in markets.

Some markets are physical places where buyers and sellers meet and where an auctioneer or a broker helps to determine the prices. Examples of this type of market are the New York Stock Exchange and the wholesale fish, meat, and produce markets.

Some markets are groups of people spread around the world who never meet and know little about each other but are connected through the Internet or by telephone and fax. Examples are the e-commerce markets and currency markets.

But most markets are unorganized collections of buyers and sellers. You do most of your trading in this type of market. An example is the market for basketball shoes. The buyers in this $3 billion-a-year market are the 45 million Americans who play basketball (or who want to make a fashion statement). The sellers are the tens of thousands of retail sports equipment and footwear stores. Each buyer can visit several different stores, and each seller knows that the buyer has a choice of stores.

Markets vary in the intensity of competition that buyers and sellers face. In this chapter, we're going to study a **competitive market**—a market that has many buyers and many sellers, so no single buyer or seller can influence the price.

Producers offer items for sale only if the price is high enough to cover their opportunity cost. And consumers respond to changing opportunity cost by seeking cheaper alternatives to expensive items.

We are going to study how people respond to *prices* and the forces that determine prices. But to pursue these tasks, we need to understand the relationship between a price and an opportunity cost.

In everyday life, the *price* of an object is the number of dollars that must be given up in exchange for it. Economists refer to this price as the **money price**.

The *opportunity cost* of an action is the highest-valued alternative forgone. If, when you buy a cup of coffee, the highest-valued thing you forgo is some gum, then the opportunity cost of the coffee is the *quantity* of gum forgone. We can calculate the quantity of gum forgone from the money prices of the coffee and the gum.

If the money price of coffee is $1 a cup and the money price of gum is 50¢ a pack, then the opportunity cost of one cup of coffee is two packs of gum. To calculate this opportunity cost, we divide the price of a cup of coffee by the price of a pack of gum and find the *ratio* of one price to the other. The ratio of one price to another is called a **relative price**, and a *relative price is an opportunity cost.*

We can express the relative price of coffee in terms of gum or any other good. The normal way of expressing a relative price is in terms of a "basket" of all goods and services. To calculate this relative price, we divide the money price of a good by the money price of a "basket" of all goods (called a *price index*). The resulting relative price tells us the opportunity cost of the good in terms of how much of the "basket" we must give up to buy it.

The theory of demand and supply that we are about to study determines *relative prices,* and the word "price" means *relative* price. When we predict that a price will fall, we do not mean that its *money* price will fall—although it might. We mean that its *relative* price will fall. That is, its price will fall *relative* to the average price of other goods and services.

REVIEW QUIZ

1 What is the distinction between a money price and a relative price?
2 Explain why a relative price is an opportunity cost.
3 Think of examples of goods whose relative price has risen or fallen by a large amount.

myeconlab Study Plan 3.1

Let's begin our study of demand and supply, starting with demand.

Demand

If you demand something, then you

1. Want it,
2. Can afford it, and
3. Plan to buy it.

Wants are the unlimited desires or wishes that people have for goods and services. How many times have you thought that you would like something "if only you could afford it" or "if it weren't so expensive"? Scarcity guarantees that many—perhaps most—of our wants will never be satisfied. Demand reflects a decision about which wants to satisfy.

The **quantity demanded** of a good or service is the amount that consumers plan to buy during a given time period at a particular price. The quantity demanded is not necessarily the same as the quantity actually bought. Sometimes the quantity demanded exceeds the amount of goods available, so the quantity bought is less than the quantity demanded.

The quantity demanded is measured as an amount per unit of time. For example, suppose that you buy one cup of coffee a day. The quantity of coffee that you demand can be expressed as 1 cup per day, as 7 cups per week, or as 365 cups per year.

Many factors influence buying plans, and one of them is the price. We look first at the relationship between the quantity demanded of a good and its price. To study this relationship, we keep all other influences on buying plans the same and we ask: How, other things remaining the same, does the quantity demanded of a good change as its price changes?

The law of demand provides the answer.

The Law of Demand

The **law of demand** states

Other things remaining the same, the higher the price of a good, the smaller is the quantity demanded; and the lower the price of a good, the greater is the quantity demanded.

Why does a higher price reduce the quantity demanded? For two reasons:

■ Substitution effect
■ Income effect

Substitution Effect When the price of a good rises, other things remaining the same, its *relative* price—its opportunity cost—rises. Although each good is unique, it has *substitutes*—other goods that can be used in its place. As the opportunity cost of a good rises, people buy less of that good and more of its substitutes.

Income Effect When a price rises and all other influences on buying plans remain unchanged, the price rises *relative* to people's incomes. So faced with a higher price and an unchanged income, people cannot afford to buy all the things they previously bought. They must decrease the quantities demanded of at least some goods and services, and normally, the good whose price has increased will be one of the goods that people buy less of.

To see the substitution effect and the income effect at work, think about the effects of a change in the price of an energy bar. Several different goods are substitutes for an energy bar. For example, an energy drink could be consumed instead of an energy bar.

Suppose that an energy bar initially sells for $3 and then its price falls to $1.50. People now substitute energy bars for energy drinks—the substitution effect. And with a budget that now has some slack from the lower price of an energy bar, people buy even more energy bars—the income effect. The quantity of energy bars demanded increases for these two reasons.

Now suppose that an energy bar initially sells for $3 each and then the price doubles to $6. People now buy fewer energy bars and more energy drinks—the substitution effect. And faced with a tighter budget, people buy even fewer energy bars—the income effect. The quantity of energy bars demanded decreases for these two reasons.

Demand Curve and Demand Schedule

You are now about to study one of the two most used curves in economics: the demand curve. And you are going to encounter one of the most critical distinctions: the distinction between *demand* and *quantity demanded*.

The term **demand** refers to the entire relationship between the price of the good and the quantity demanded of the good. Demand is illustrated by the demand curve and the demand schedule. The term *quantity demanded* refers to a point on a demand curve—the quantity demanded at a particular price.

Figure 3.1 shows the demand curve for energy bars. A **demand curve** shows the relationship between the quantity demanded of a good and its price when all other influences on consumers' planned purchases remain the same.

The table in Fig. 3.1 is the demand schedule for energy bars. A *demand schedule* lists the quantities demanded at each price when all the other influences on consumers' planned purchases remain the same. For example, if the price of a bar is 50¢, the quantity demanded is 22 million a week. If the price is $2.50, the quantity demanded is 5 million a week. The other rows of the table show the quantities demanded at prices of $1.00, $1.50, and $2.00.

We graph the demand schedule as a demand curve with the quantity demanded on the *x*-axis and the price on the *y*-axis. The points on the demand curve labeled *A* through *E* correspond to the rows of the demand schedule. For example, point *A* on the graph shows a quantity demanded of 22 million energy bars a week at a price of 50¢ a bar.

Willingness and Ability to Pay   Another way of looking at the demand curve is as a willingness-and-ability-to-pay curve. And the willingness and ability to pay is a measure of *marginal benefit.*

If a small quantity is available, the highest price that someone is willing and able to pay for one more unit is high. But as the quantity available increases, the marginal benefit of each additional unit falls and the highest price that someone is willing and able to pay also falls along the demand curve.

In Fig. 3.1, if only 5 million energy bars are available each week, the highest price that someone is willing to pay for the 5 millionth bar is $2.50. But if 22 million energy bars are available each week, someone is willing to pay 50¢ for the last bar bought.

A Change in Demand

When any factor that influences buying plans other than the price of the good changes, there is a **change in demand**. Figure 3.2 illustrates an increase in demand. When demand increases, the demand curve shifts rightward and the quantity demanded at each price is greater. For example, at a price of $2.50, on the original (blue) demand curve, the quantity demanded is 5 million energy bars a week and on the new (red) demand curve, the quantity demanded is 15 million energy bars a week. Look closely at the numbers in the table and check that the quantity demanded at each price is greater.

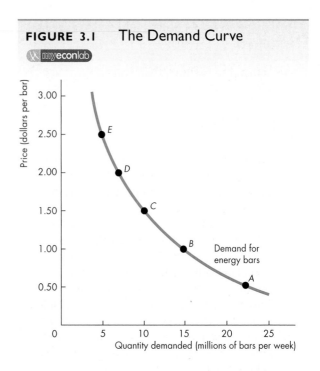

FIGURE 3.1   The Demand Curve

	Price (dollars per bar)	**Quantity demanded** (millions of bars per week)
A	0.50	22
B	1.00	15
C	1.50	10
D	2.00	7
E	2.50	5

The table shows a demand schedule for energy bars. At a price of 50¢ a bar, 22 million bars a week are demanded; at a price of $1.50 a bar, 10 million bars a week are demanded. The demand curve shows the relationship between quantity demanded and price, other things remaining the same. The demand curve slopes downward: As price decreases, the quantity demanded increases.

The demand curve can be read in two ways. For a given price, the demand curve tells us the quantity that people plan to buy. For example, at a price of $1.50 a bar, people plan to buy 10 million bars a week. For a given quantity, the demand curve tells us the maximum price that consumers are willing and able to pay for the last bar available. For example, the maximum price that consumers will pay for the 15 millionth bar is $1.00.

Six main factors bring changes in demand. They are changes in

- The prices of related goods
- Expected future prices
- Income
- Expected future income
- Population
- Preferences

Prices of Related Goods The quantity of energy bars that consumers plan to buy depends in part on the prices of substitutes for energy bars. A **substitute** is a good that can be used in place of another good. For example, a bus ride is a substitute for a train ride; a hamburger is a substitute for a hot dog; and an energy drink is a substitute for an energy bar. If the price of a substitute for an energy bar rises, people buy less of the substitute and more energy bars. For example, if the price of an energy drink rises, people buy fewer energy drinks and more energy bars. The demand for energy bars increases.

The quantity of energy bars that people plan to buy also depends on the prices of complements with energy bars. A **complement** is a good that is used in conjunction with another good. Hamburgers and fries are complements, and so are energy bars and exercise. If the price of an hour at the gym falls, people buy more gym time *and more* energy bars.

Expected Future Prices If the price of a good is expected to rise in the future and if the good can be stored, the opportunity cost of obtaining the good for future use is lower today than it will be when the price has increased. So people retime their purchases—they substitute over time. They buy more of the good now before its price is expected to rise (and less afterward), so the demand for the good today increases.

For example, suppose that a Florida frost damages the season's orange crop. You expect the price of orange juice to rise, so you fill your freezer with enough frozen juice to get you through the next six months. Your current demand for frozen orange juice has increased, and your future demand has decreased.

Similarly, if the price of a good is expected to fall in the future, the opportunity cost of buying the good today is high relative to what it is expected to be in the future. So again, people retime their purchases. They buy less of the good now before its price

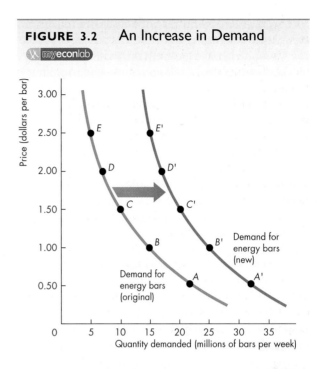

FIGURE 3.2   An Increase in Demand

Original demand schedule			New demand schedule		
Original income			New higher income		
	Price (dollars per bar)	Quantity demanded (millions of bars per week)		Price (dollars per bar)	Quantity demanded (millions of bars per week)
A	0.50	22	A'	0.50	32
B	1.00	15	B'	1.00	25
C	1.50	10	C'	1.50	20
D	2.00	7	D'	2.00	17
E	2.50	5	E'	2.50	15

A change in any influence on buyers' plans other than the price of the good itself results in a new demand schedule and a shift of the demand curve. A change in income changes the demand for energy bars. At a price of $1.50 a bar, 10 million bars a week are demanded at the original income (row C of the table) and 20 million bars a week are demanded at the new higher income. A rise in income increases the demand for energy bars. The demand curve shifts *rightward*, as shown by the shift arrow and the resulting red curve.

falls, so the demand for the good decreases today and increases in the future.

Computer prices are constantly falling, and this fact poses a dilemma. Will you buy a new computer now, in time for the start of the school year, or will you wait until the price has fallen some more? Because people expect computer prices to keep falling, the current demand for computers is less (the future demand is greater) than it otherwise would be.

Income Consumers' income influences demand. When income increases, consumers buy more of most goods; and when income decreases, consumers buy less of most goods. Although an increase in income leads to an increase in the demand for *most* goods, it does not lead to an increase in the demand for *all* goods. A **normal good** is one for which demand increases as income increases. An **inferior good** is one for which demand decreases as income increases. Long-distance transportation has examples of both normal goods and inferior goods. As incomes increase, the demand for air travel (a normal good) increases and the demand for long-distance bus trips (an inferior good) decreases.

Expected Future Income When income is expected to increase in the future, demand might increase now. For example, a salesperson gets the news that she will receive a big bonus at the end of the year, so she decides to buy a new car right now.

Population Demand also depends on the size and the age structure of the population. The larger the population, the greater is the demand for all goods and services; the smaller the population, the smaller is the demand for all goods and services.

For example, the demand for parking spaces or movies or energy bars or just about anything that you can imagine is much greater in New York City (population 7.5 million) than it is in Boise, Idaho (population 150,000).

Also, the larger the proportion of the population in a given age group, the greater is the demand for the goods and services used by that age group.

For example, during the 1990s, a decrease in the college-age population decreased the demand for college places. During those same years, the number of Americans aged 85 years and over increased by more than 1 million. As a result, the demand for nursing home services increased.

TABLE 3.1   The Demand for Energy Bars

The Law of Demand

The quantity of energy bars demanded

Decreases if:	Increases if:
■ The price of an energy bar rises	■ The price of an energy bar falls

Changes in Demand

The demand for energy bars

Decreases if:	Increases if:
■ The price of a substitute falls	■ The price of a substitute rises
■ The price of a complement rises	■ The price of a complement falls
■ The price of an energy bar is expected to fall in the future	■ The price of an energy bar is expected to rise in the future
■ Income falls*	■ Income rises*
■ Expected future income falls	■ Expected future income rises
■ The population decreases	■ The population increases

*An energy bar is a normal good.

Preferences Demand depends on preferences. *Preferences* determine the value that people place on each good and service. Preferences depend on such things as the weather, information, and fashion. For example, greater health and fitness awareness has shifted preferences in favor of energy bars, so the demand for energy bars has increased.

Table 3.1 summarizes the influences on demand and the direction of those influences.

A Change in the Quantity Demanded Versus a Change in Demand

Changes in the factors that influence buyers' plans cause either a change in the quantity demanded or a change in demand. Equivalently, they cause either a movement along the demand curve or a shift of the demand curve. The distinction between a change in the quantity demanded and a change in demand is the same as that between a movement along the demand curve and a shift of the demand curve.

A point on the demand curve shows the quantity demanded at a given price. So a movement along the demand curve shows a **change in the quantity demanded**. The entire demand curve shows demand. So a shift of the demand curve shows a *change in demand*. Figure 3.3 illustrates these distinctions.

Movement Along the Demand Curve

If the price of a good changes but everything else remains the same, there is a movement along the demand curve. Because the demand curve slopes downward, a fall in the price of a good increases the quantity demanded of it and a rise in the price of the good decreases the quantity demanded of it—the law of demand.

In Fig. 3.3, if the price of a good falls when everything else remains the same, the quantity demanded of that good increases and there is a movement down the demand curve D_0. If the price rises when everything else remains the same, the quantity demanded of that good decreases and there is a movement up the demand curve D_0.

A Shift of the Demand Curve

If the price of a good remains constant but some other influence on buyers' plans changes, there is a change in demand for that good. We illustrate a change in demand as a shift of the demand curve. For example, if more people work out at the gym, consumers buy more energy bars regardless of the price of a bar. That is what a rightward shift of the demand curve shows—more energy bars are demanded at each price.

In Fig. 3.3, when any influence on buyers' planned purchases changes, other than the price of the good, there is a *change in demand* and the demand curve shifts. Demand *increases* and the demand curve *shifts rightward* (to the red demand curve D_1) if the price of a substitute rises, the price of a complement falls, the expected future price of the good rises, income increases (for a normal good), expected future income increases, or the population increases. Demand *decreases* and the demand curve *shifts leftward* (to the red demand curve D_2) if the price of a substitute falls, the price of a complement rises, the expected future price of the good falls, income decreases (for a normal good), expected future income decreases, or the population decreases. (For an inferior good, the effects of changes in income are in the direction opposite to those described above.)

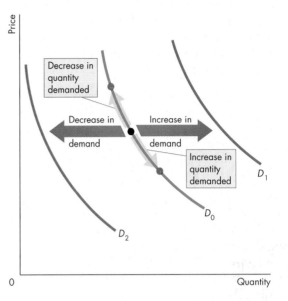

FIGURE 3.3   A Change in the Quantity Demanded Versus a Change in Demand

When the price of the good changes, there is a movement along the demand curve and *a change in the quantity demanded,* shown by the blue arrows on demand curve D_0. When any other influence on buyers' plans changes, there is a shift of the demand curve and a *change in demand.* An increase in demand shifts the demand curve rightward (from D_0 to D_1). A decrease in demand shifts the demand curve leftward (from D_0 to D_2).

REVIEW QUIZ

1 Define the quantity demanded of a good or service.
2 What is the law of demand and how do we illustrate it?
3 What does the demand curve tell us about the price that consumers are willing to pay?
4 List all the influences on buying plans that change demand, and for each influence, say whether it increases or decreases demand.
5 Why does demand not change when the price of a good changes with no change in the other influences on buying plans?

myeconlab Study Plan 3.2

Supply

If a firm supplies a good or service, the firm

1. Has the resources and technology to produce it,
2. Can profit from producing it, and
3. Plans to produce it and sell it.

A supply is more than just having the *resources* and the *technology* to produce something. *Resources and technology* are the constraints that limit what is possible.

Many useful things can be produced, but they are not produced unless it is profitable to do so. Supply reflects a decision about which technologically feasible items to produce.

The **quantity supplied** of a good or service is the amount that producers plan to sell during a given time period at a particular price. The quantity supplied is not necessarily the same amount as the quantity actually sold. Sometimes the quantity supplied is greater than the quantity demanded, so the quantity bought is less than the quantity supplied.

Like the quantity demanded, the quantity supplied is measured as an amount per unit of time. For example, suppose that GM produces 1,000 cars a day. The quantity of cars supplied by GM can be expressed as 1,000 a day, 7,000 a week, or 365,000 a year. Without the time dimension, we cannot tell whether a particular number is large or small.

Many factors influence selling plans, and again one of them is the price. We look first at the relationship between the quantity supplied of a good and its price. And again, as we did when we studied demand, to isolate this relationship, we keep all other influences on selling plans the same and we ask: How, other things remaining the same, does the quantity supplied of a good change as its price changes?

The law of supply provides the answer.

The Law of Supply

The **law of supply** states:

Other things remaining the same, the higher the price of a good, the greater is the quantity supplied; and the lower the price of a good, the smaller is the quantity supplied.

Why does a higher price increase the quantity supplied? It is because *marginal cost increases*. As the quantity produced of any good increases, the marginal cost of producing the good increases. (You can refresh your memory of increasing marginal cost in Chapter 2, p. 37.)

It is never worth producing a good if the price received for the good does not at least cover the marginal cost of producing it. So when the price of a good rises, other things remaining the same, producers are willing to incur a higher marginal cost and increase production. The higher price brings forth an increase in the quantity supplied.

Let's now illustrate the law of supply with a supply curve and a supply schedule.

Supply Curve and Supply Schedule

You are now going to study the second of the two most used curves in economics: the supply curve. And you're going to learn about the critical distinction between *supply* and *quantity supplied*.

The term **supply** refers to the entire relationship between the price of a good and the quantity supplied of it. Supply is illustrated by the supply curve and the supply schedule. The term *quantity supplied* refers to a point on a supply curve—the quantity supplied at a particular price.

Figure 3.4 shows the supply curve of energy bars. A **supply curve** shows the relationship between the quantity supplied of a good and its price when all other influences on producers' planned sales remain the same. The supply curve is a graph of a supply schedule.

The table in Fig. 3.4 sets out the supply schedule for energy bars. A *supply schedule* lists the quantities supplied at each price when all the other influences on producers' planned sales remain the same. For example, if the price of a bar is 50¢, the quantity supplied is zero—in row A of the table. If the price of a bar is $1.00, the quantity supplied is 6 million energy bars a week—in row B. The other rows of the table show the quantities supplied at prices of $1.50, $2.00, and $2.50.

To make a supply curve, we graph the quantity supplied on the *x*-axis and the price on the *y*-axis, just as in the case of the demand curve. The points on the supply curve labeled A through E correspond to the rows of the supply schedule. For example, point A on the graph shows a quantity supplied of zero at a price of 50¢ an energy bar.

FIGURE 3.4   The Supply Curve

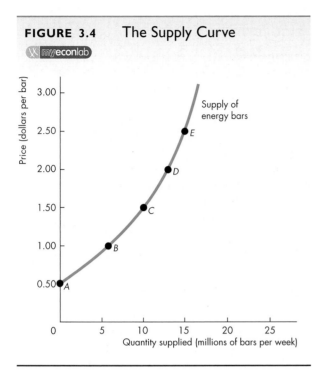

The table shows the supply schedule of energy bars. For example, at a price of $1.00, 6 million bars a week are supplied; at a price of $2.50, 15 million bars a week are supplied. The supply curve shows the relationship between the quantity supplied and price, other things remaining the same. The supply curve slopes upward: As the price of a good increases, the quantity supplied increases.

A supply curve can be read in two ways. For a given price, the supply curve tells us the quantity that producers plan to sell at that price. For example, at a price of $1.50 a bar, producers are willing to supply 10 million bars a week. For a given quantity, the supply curve tells us the minimum price that producers are willing to sell one more bar. For example, if 15 million bars are produced each week, the lowest price at which someone is willing to sell the 15 millionth bar is $2.50.

Minimum Supply Price   Just as the demand curve has two interpretations, so too does the supply curve. The demand curve can be interpreted as a willingness-and-ability-to-pay curve. The supply curve can be interpreted as a minimum-supply-price curve—a curve that shows the lowest price at which someone is willing to sell. And this lowest price is *marginal cost*.

If a small quantity is produced, the lowest price at which someone is willing to sell one more unit is low. But as the quantity produced increases, the marginal cost of each additional unit rises and the lowest price at which someone is willing to sell also rises along the supply curve.

In Fig. 3.4, if 15 million bars are produced each week, the lowest price at which someone is willing to sell the 15 millionth bar is $2.50. But if 10 million bars are produced each week, someone is willing to accept $1.50 for the last bar sold.

A Change in Supply

When any factor that influences selling plans other than the price of the good changes, there is a **change in supply**.

Five main factors bring changes in supply. They are changes in

- The prices of productive resources
- The prices of related goods produced
- Expected future prices
- The number of suppliers
- Technology

Prices of Productive Resources   The prices of the productive resources used to produce a good influence its supply. The easiest way to see this influence is to think about the supply curve as a minimum-supply-price curve. If the price of a productive resource rises, the lowest price a producer is willing to accept rises, so supply decreases. For example, during 2006, as the price of jet fuel increased, the supply of air transportation decreased. Similarly, a rise in the minimum wage decreases the supply of hamburgers.

Prices of Related Goods Produced   The prices of related goods and services that firms produce influence supply. For example, if the price of energy gel rises, the supply of energy bars decreases. Energy bars and energy gel are *substitutes in production*—goods that can be produced by using the same resources. If the price of beef rises, the supply of cowhide increases. Beef and cowhide are *complements in production—* goods that must be produced together.

Expected Future Prices If the price of a good is expected to rise, the return from selling the good in the future is higher than it is today. So supply decreases today and increases in the future.

The Number of Suppliers The larger the number of firms that produce a good, the greater is the supply of the good. And as firms enter an industry, the supply in that industry increases. As firms leave an industry, the supply in that industry decreases.

Technology The term "technology" is used broadly to mean the way that factors of production are used to produce a good. Technology changes both positively and negatively. A positive technology change occurs when a new method is discovered that lowers the cost of producing a good. An example is new methods used in the factories that make computer chips. A negative technology change occurs when an event such as extreme weather or natural disaster increases the cost of producing a good. A positive technology change increases supply, and a negative technology change decreases supply.

Figure 3.5 illustrates an increase in supply. When supply increases, the supply curve shifts rightward and the quantity supplied at each price is larger. For example, at $1.00 per bar, on the original (blue) supply curve, the quantity supplied is 6 million bars a week. On the new (red) supply curve, the quantity supplied is 15 million bars a week. Look closely at the numbers in the table in Fig. 3.5 and check that the quantity supplied is larger at each price.

Table 3.2 summarizes the influences on supply and the directions of those influences.

A Change in the Quantity Supplied Versus a Change in Supply

Changes in the factors that influence producers' planned sales cause either a change in the quantity supplied or a change in supply. Equivalently, they cause either a movement along the supply curve or a shift of the supply curve.

A point on the supply curve shows the quantity supplied at a given price. A movement along the supply curve shows a **change in the quantity supplied**. The entire supply curve shows supply. A shift of the supply curve shows a *change in supply*.

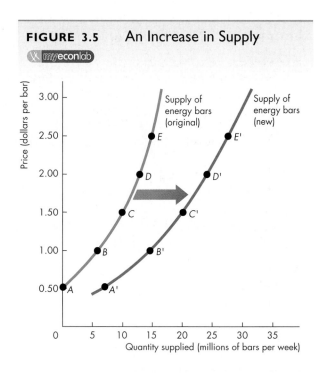

FIGURE 3.5   An Increase in Supply

| Original supply schedule | | New supply schedule | |
| Old technology | | New technology | |
Price (dollars per bar)	Quantity supplied (millions of bars per week)	Price (dollars per bar)	Quantity supplied (millions of bars per week)
A 0.50	0	A' 0.50	7
B 1.00	6	B' 1.00	15
C 1.50	10	C' 1.50	20
D 2.00	13	D' 2.00	25
E 2.50	15	E' 2.50	30

A change in any influence on sellers' plans other than the price of the good itself results in a new supply schedule and a shift of the supply curve. For example, with a new, cost-saving technology for producing energy bars, the supply of energy bars changes. At a price of $1.50 a bar, 10 million bars a week are supplied when producers use the old technology (row *C* of the table) and 20 million energy bars a week are supplied when producers use the new technology. An advance in technology *increases* the supply of energy bars. The supply curve shifts *rightward*, as shown by the shift arrow and the resulting red curve.

Figure 3.6 illustrates and summarizes these distinctions. If the price of a good falls and everything else remains the same, the quantity supplied of that good decreases and there is a movement down the supply curve S_0. If the price of a good rises and everything else remains the same, the quantity supplied increases and there is a movement up the supply curve S_0. When any other influence on selling plans changes, the supply curve shifts and there is a *change in supply*. If the supply curve is S_0 and if production costs fall, supply increases and the supply curve shifts to the red supply curve S_1. If production costs rise, supply decreases and the supply curve shifts to the red supply curve S_2.

TABLE 3.2   The Supply of Energy Bars

The Law of Supply

The quantity of energy bars supplied

Decreases if:	*Increases if:*
■ The price of an energy bar falls	■ The price of an energy bar rises

Changes in Supply

The supply of energy bars

Decreases if:	*Increases if:*
■ The price of a resource used to produce energy bars rises	■ The price of a resource used to produce energy bars falls
■ The price of a substitute in production rises	■ The price of a substitute in production falls
■ The price of a complement in production falls	■ The price of a complement in production rises
■ The price of an energy bar is expected to rise in the future	■ The price of an energy bar is expected to fall in the future
■ The number of bar producers decreases	■ The number of bar producers increases
■ A negative technology change in energy bar production occurs	■ A positive technology change in energy bar production occurs

FIGURE 3.6   A Change in the Quantity Supplied Versus a Change in Supply

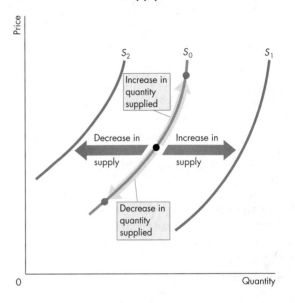

When the price of the good changes, there is a movement along the supply curve and *a change in the quantity supplied,* shown by the blue arrows on supply curve S_0. When any other influence on selling plans changes, there is a shift of the supply curve and a *change in supply.* An increase in supply shifts the supply curve rightward (from S_0 to S_1), and a decrease in supply shifts the supply curve leftward (from S_0 to S_2).

REVIEW QUIZ

1 Define the quantity supplied of a good or service.
2 What is the law of supply and how do we illustrate it?
3 What does the supply curve tell us about the producer's minimum supply price?
4 List all the influences on selling plans, and for each influence, say whether it changes supply.
5 What happens to the quantity of Palm Pilots supplied and the supply of Palm Pilots if the price of a Palm Pilot falls?

Ⓧ myeconlab Study Plan 3.3

Now we're going to combine demand and supply and see how prices and quantities are determined.

Market Equilibrium

We have seen that when the price of a good rises, the quantity demanded *decreases* and the quantity supplied *increases*. We are now going to see how prices coordinate the plans of buyers and sellers and achieve an equilibrium.

An *equilibrium* is a situation in which opposing forces balance each other. Equilibrium in a market occurs when the price balances the plans of buyers and sellers. The **equilibrium price** is the price at which the quantity demanded equals the quantity supplied. The **equilibrium quantity** is the quantity bought and sold at the equilibrium price. A market moves toward its equilibrium because

- Price regulates buying and selling plans.
- Price adjusts when plans don't match.

Price as a Regulator

The price of a good regulates the quantities demanded and supplied. If the price is too high, the quantity supplied exceeds the quantity demanded. If the price is too low, the quantity demanded exceeds the quantity supplied. There is one price at which the quantity demanded equals the quantity supplied. Let's work out what that price is.

Figure 3.7 shows the market for energy bars. The table shows the demand schedule (from Fig. 3.1) and the supply schedule (from Fig. 3.4). If the price of a bar is 50¢, the quantity demanded is 22 million bars a week but no bars are supplied. There is a shortage of 22 million bars a week. This shortage is shown in the final column of the table. At a price of $1.00 a bar, there is still a shortage but only of 9 million bars a week. If the price of a bar is $2.50, the quantity supplied is 15 million bars a week but the quantity demanded is only 5 million. There is a surplus of 10 million bars a week. The one price at which there is neither a shortage nor a surplus is $1.50 a bar. At that price, the quantity demanded is equal to the quantity supplied: 10 million bars a week. The equilibrium price is $1.50 a bar, and the equilibrium quantity is 10 million bars a week.

Figure 3.7 shows that the demand curve and the supply curve intersect at the equilibrium price of $1.50 a bar. At each price *above* $1.50 a bar, there is a surplus of bars. For example, at $2.00 a bar, the surplus is 6

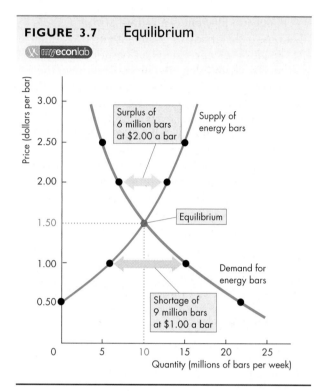

FIGURE 3.7   Equilibrium

Price (dollars per bar)	Quantity demanded	Quantity supplied	Shortage (–) or surplus (+)
	(millions of bars per week)		
0.50	22	0	–22
1.00	15	6	–9
1.50	10	10	0
2.00	7	13	+6
2.50	5	15	+10

The table lists the quantity demanded and the quantity supplied as well as the shortage or surplus of bars at each price. If the price is $1.00 a bar, 15 million bars a week are demanded and 6 million are supplied. There is a shortage of 9 million bars a week, and the price rises.

If the price is $2.00 a bar, 7 million bars a week are demanded and 13 million are supplied. There is a surplus of 6 million bars a week, and the price falls.

If the price is $1.50 a bar, 10 million bars a week are demanded and 10 million are supplied. There is neither a shortage nor a surplus. Neither buyers nor sellers have any incentive to change the price. The price at which the quantity demanded equals the quantity supplied is the equilibrium price. And 10 million bars a week is the equilibrium quantity.

million bars a week, as shown by the blue arrow. At each price *below* $1.50 a bar, there is a shortage of bars. For example, at $1.00 a bar, the shortage is 9 million bars a week, as shown by the red arrow.

Price Adjustments

You've seen that if the price is below equilibrium, there is a shortage and that if the price is above equilibrium, there is a surplus. But can we count on the price to change and eliminate a shortage or surplus? We can, because such price changes are beneficial to both buyers and sellers. Let's see why the price changes when there is a shortage or a surplus.

A Shortage Forces the Price Up Suppose the price of an energy bar is $1. Consumers plan to buy 15 million bars a week, and producers plan to sell 6 million bars a week. Consumers can't force producers to sell more than they plan, so the quantity that is actually offered for sale is 6 million bars a week. In this situation, powerful forces operate to increase the price and move it toward the equilibrium price. Some producers, noticing lines of unsatisfied consumers, raise the price. Some producers increase their output. As producers push the price up, the price rises toward its equilibrium. The rising price reduces the shortage because it decreases the quantity demanded and increases the quantity supplied. When the price has increased to the point at which there is no longer a shortage, the forces moving the price stop operating and the price comes to rest at its equilibrium.

A Surplus Forces the Price Down Suppose the price of a bar is $2. Producers plan to sell 13 million bars a week, and consumers plan to buy 7 million bars a week. Producers cannot force consumers to buy more than they plan, so the quantity that is actually bought is 7 million bars a week. In this situation, powerful forces operate to lower the price and move it toward the equilibrium price. Some producers, unable to sell the quantities of energy bars they planned to sell, cut their prices. In addition, some producers scale back production. As producers cut the price, the price falls toward its equilibrium. The falling price decreases the surplus because it increases the quantity demanded and decreases the quantity supplied. When the price has fallen to the point at which there is no longer a surplus, the forces moving the price stop operating and the price comes to rest at its equilibrium.

The Best Deal Available for Buyers and Sellers When the price is below equilibrium, it is forced upward. Why don't buyers resist the increase and refuse to buy at the higher price? Because they value the good more highly than the current price and they can't satisfy their demand at the current price. In some markets—for example, the markets that operate on eBay—the buyers might even be the ones who force the price up by offering to pay a higher price.

When the price is above equilibrium, it is bid downward. Why don't sellers resist this decrease and refuse to sell at the lower price? Because their minimum supply price is below the current price and they cannot sell all they would like to at the current price. Normally, it is the sellers who force the price down by offering lower prices to gain market share.

At the price at which the quantity demanded and the quantity supplied are equal, neither buyers nor sellers can do business at a better price. Buyers pay the highest price they are willing to pay for the last unit bought, and sellers receive the lowest price at which they are willing to supply the last unit sold.

When people freely make offers to buy and sell and when demanders try to buy at the lowest possible price and suppliers try to sell at the highest possible price, the price at which trade takes place is the equilibrium price—the price at which the quantity demanded equals the quantity supplied. The price coordinates the plans of buyers and sellers, and no one has an incentive to change it.

REVIEW QUIZ

1 What is the equilibrium price of a good or service?
2 Over what range of prices does a shortage arise?
3 Over what range of prices does a surplus arise?
4 What happens to the price when there is a shortage?
5 What happens to the price when there is a surplus?
6 Why is the price at which the quantity demanded equals the quantity supplied the equilibrium price?
7 Why is the equilibrium price the best deal available for both buyers and sellers?

 myeconlab **Study Plan 3.4**

Predicting Changes in Price and Quantity

The demand and supply theory that we have just studied provides us with a powerful way of analyzing influences on prices and the quantities bought and sold. According to the theory, a change in price stems from a change in demand, a change in supply, or a change in both demand and supply. Let's look first at the effects of a change in demand.

An Increase in Demand

When more and more people join health clubs, the demand for energy bars increases. The table in Fig. 3.8 shows the original and new demand schedules for energy bars (the same as those in Fig. 3.2) as well as the supply schedule of energy bars.

When demand increases, there is a shortage at the original equilibrium price of $1.50 a bar. To eliminate the shortage, the price must rise. The price that makes the quantity demanded and quantity supplied equal again is $2.50 a bar. At this price, 15 million bars are bought and sold each week. When demand increases, both the price and the quantity increase.

Figure 3.8 shows these changes. The figure shows the original demand for and supply of energy bars. The original equilibrium price is $1.50 an energy bar, and the quantity is 10 million energy bars a week. When demand increases, the demand curve shifts rightward. The equilibrium price rises to $2.50 an energy bar, and the quantity supplied increases to 15 million energy bars a week, as highlighted in the figure. There is an *increase in the quantity supplied* but *no change in supply*—a movement along, but no shift of, the supply curve.

A Decrease in Demand

We can reverse this change in demand. Start at a price of $2.50 a bar with 15 million energy bars a week being bought and sold, and then work out what happens if demand decreases to its original level. Such a decrease in demand might arise if people switch to energy gel (a substitute for energy bars). The decrease in demand shifts the demand curve leftward. The equilibrium price falls to $1.50 a bar, and the equilibrium quantity decreases to 10 million bars a week.

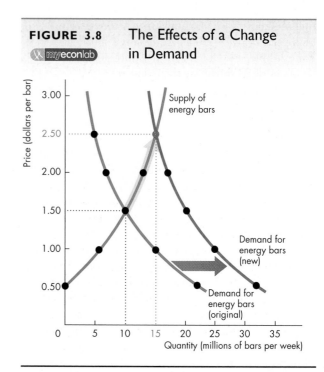

FIGURE 3.8   The Effects of a Change in Demand

Price (dollars per bar)	Quantity demanded (millions of bars per week)		Quantity supplied (millions of bars per week)
	Original	New	
0.50	22	32	0
1.00	15	25	6
1.50	**10**	20	**10**
2.00	7	17	13
2.50	5	15	15

Initially, the demand for energy bars is the blue demand curve. The equilibrium price is $1.50 a bar, and the equilibrium quantity is 10 million bars a week. When more health-conscious people do more exercise, the demand for energy bars increases and the demand curve shifts rightward to become the red curve.

At $1.50 a bar, there is now a shortage of 10 million bars a week. The price of a bar rises to a new equilibrium of $2.50. As the price rises to $2.50, the quantity supplied increases—shown by the blue arrow on the supply curve—to the new equilibrium quantity of 15 million bars a week. Following an increase in demand, the quantity supplied increases but supply does not change—the supply curve does not shift.

We can now make our first two predictions:

1. When demand increases, both the price and the quantity increase.

2. When demand decreases, both the price and the quantity decrease.

An Increase in Supply

When Nestlé (the producer of PowerBar) and other energy bar producers switch to a new cost-saving technology, the supply of energy bars increases. Figure 3.9 shows the new supply schedule (the same one that was shown in Fig. 3.5). What are the new equilibrium price and quantity? The price falls to $1.00 a bar, and the quantity increases to 15 million a week. You can see why by looking at the quantities demanded and supplied at the old price of $1.50 a bar. The quantity supplied at that price is 20 million bars a week, and there is a surplus of bars. The price falls. Only when the price is $1.00 a bar does the quantity supplied equal the quantity demanded.

Figure 3.9 illustrates the effect of an increase in supply. It shows the demand curve for energy bars and the original and new supply curves. The initial equilibrium price is $1.50 a bar, and the quantity is 10 million bars a week. When the supply increases, the supply curve shifts rightward. The equilibrium price falls to $1.00 a bar, and the quantity demanded increases to 15 million bars a week, highlighted in the figure. There is an *increase in the quantity demanded* but *no change in demand*—a movement along, but no shift of, the demand curve.

A Decrease in Supply

Start out at a price of $1.00 a bar with 15 million bars a week being bought and sold. Then suppose that the cost of labor or raw materials rises and the supply of energy bars decreases. The decrease in supply shifts the supply curve leftward. The equilibrium price rises to $1.50 a bar, and the equilibrium quantity decreases to 10 million bars a week.

We can now make two more predictions:

1. When supply increases, the quantity increases and the price falls.

2. When supply decreases, the quantity decreases and the price rises.

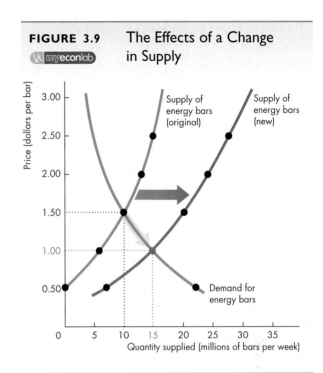

FIGURE 3.9   The Effects of a Change in Supply

Price (dollars per bar)	Quantity demanded (millions of bars per week)	Quantity supplied (millions of bars per week)	
		Original	New
0.50	22	0	7
1.00	15	6	15
1.50	10	10	20
2.00	7	13	25
2.50	5	15	30

Initially, the supply of energy bars is shown by the blue supply curve. The equilibrium price is $1.50 a bar, and the equilibrium quantity is 10 million bars a week. When the new cost-saving technology is adopted, the supply of energy bars increases and the supply curve shifts rightward to become the red curve.

At $1.50 a bar, there is now a surplus of 10 million bars a week. The price of an energy bar falls to a new equilibrium of $1.00 a bar. As the price falls to $1.00, the quantity demanded increases—shown by the blue arrow on the demand curve—to the new equilibrium quantity of 15 million bars a week. Following an increase in supply, the quantity demanded increases but demand does not change—the demand curve does not shift.

All the Possible Changes in Demand and Supply

You can now predict the effects of a change in either demand or supply on the price and the quantity. And with what you've learned, you can also predict what happens if *both* demand and supply change together. To see what happens when both demand and supply change, let's summarize what you already know.

Change in Demand with No Change in Supply The first row of Fig. 3.10, parts (a), (b), and (c), summarizes the effects of a change in demand with no change in supply. In part (a), with no change in either demand or supply, neither the price nor the quantity changes. With an *increase* in demand and no change in supply in part (b), both the price and quantity increase. And with a *decrease* in demand and no change in supply in part (c), both the price and the quantity decrease.

Change in Supply with No Change in Demand The first column of Fig. 3.10, parts (a), (d), and (g), summarizes the effects of a change in supply with no change in demand. With an increase in supply and no change in demand in part (d), the price falls and quantity increases. And with a decrease in supply and no change in demand in part (g), the price rises and the quantity decreases.

Increase in Both Demand and Supply You've seen that an increase in demand raises the price and increases the quantity. And you've seen that an increase in supply lowers the price and increases the quantity. Fig. 3.10(e) combines these two changes. Because either an increase in demand or an increase in supply increases the quantity, the quantity also increases when both demand and supply increase. But the effect on the price is uncertain. An increase in demand raises the price and an increase in supply lowers the price, so we can't say whether the price will rise or fall when both demand and supply increase. We need to know the magnitudes of the changes in demand and supply to predict the effects on price. In the example in Fig. 3.10(e), the price does not change. But notice that if demand increases by slightly more than the amount shown in the figure, the price will rise. And if supply increases by slightly more than the amount shown in the figure, the price will fall.

Decrease in Both Demand and Supply Figure 3.10(i) shows the case in which demand and supply *both decrease*. For the same reasons as those we've just reviewed, when both demand and supply decrease, the quantity decreases, and again the direction of the price change is uncertain.

Decrease in Demand and Increase in Supply You've seen that a decrease in demand lowers the price and decreases the quantity. And you've seen that an increase in supply lowers the price and increases the quantity. Fig. 3.10(f) combines these two changes. Both the decrease in demand and the increase in supply lower the price. So the price falls. But a decrease in demand decreases the quantity and an increase in supply increases the quantity, so we can't predict the direction in which the quantity will change unless we know the magnitudes of the changes in demand and supply. In the example in Fig. 3.10(f), the quantity does not change. But notice that if demand decreases by slightly more than the amount shown in the figure, the quantity will decrease. And if supply increases by slightly more than the amount shown in the figure, the quantity will increase.

Increase in Demand and Decrease in Supply Figure 3.10(h) shows the case in which demand increases and supply decreases. Now, the price rises, and again the direction of the quantity change is uncertain.

REVIEW QUIZ

1 What is the effect on the price of an MP3 player (such as the iPod) and the quantity of MP3 players if (a) the price of a PC falls or (b) the price of an MP3 download rises or (c) more firms produce MP3 players or (d) electronics workers' wages rise or (e) any two of these events occur together? (Draw the diagrams!)

myeconlab Study Plan 3.5

Now that you understand the demand and supply model and the predictions that it makes, try to get into the habit of using the model in your everyday life. To see how you might use the model, take a look at *Reading Between the Lines* on pp. 76–77, which uses the tools of demand and supply to explain the rising price of gasoline in 2006.

FIGURE 3.10   The Effects of All the Possible Changes in Demand and Supply

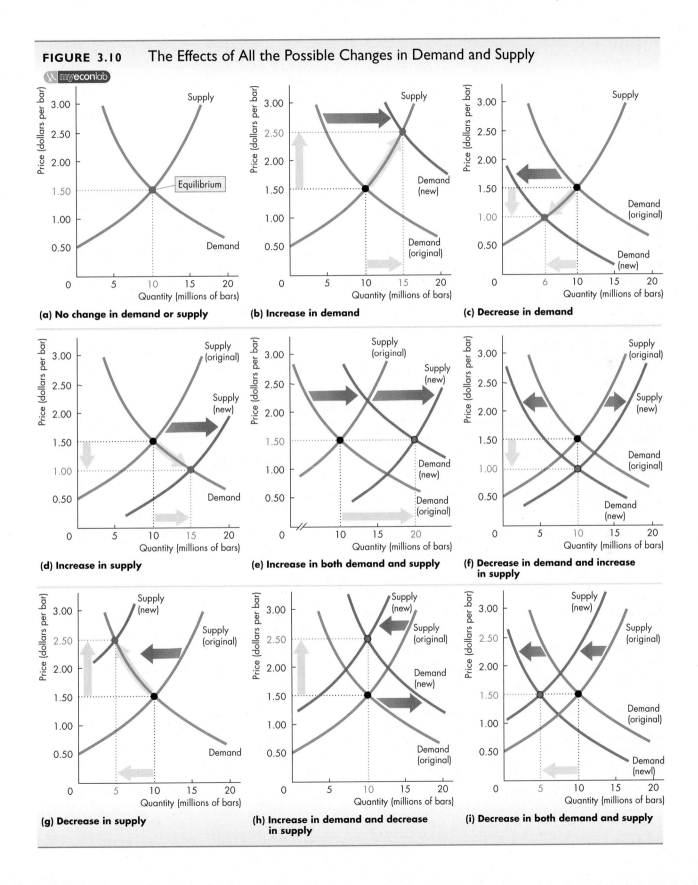

(a) No change in demand or supply

(b) Increase in demand

(c) Decrease in demand

(d) Increase in supply

(e) Increase in both demand and supply

(f) Decrease in demand and increase in supply

(g) Decrease in supply

(h) Increase in demand and decrease in supply

(i) Decrease in both demand and supply

Demand and Supply:
The Price of Gasoline

Eight Reasons Pump Prices May Move Higher

June 30, 2006

[Eight reasons pump prices may move higher are:] . . .

1. Overall demand: When commodity prices go up, the economic textbooks say demand is supposed to go down. For a brief period this spring, there were signs that high pump prices were putting a damper on discretionary travel. Sales of gas guzzling SUVs tumbled, for example.

But a relatively strong U.S. economy continues to fuel strong demand for gasoline and diesel. . . .

In its latest weekly report, the Department of Energy said that Americans burned through more than 9.5 million barrels per day of gasoline for the week ending June 23, 2006, the highest weekly average ever during the month of June. . . .

2. Big travel plans: AAA estimates that a record 34.3 million travelers will hit the road by car this July 4th weekend—a 1.3 percent increase from a year ago. . . .

3. Production interruptions: U.S. refiners have repaired most of the damage from last fall's hurricanes, and, as of last week, were operating at more than 93 percent of capacity—up from a low of 75 percent last October after Katrina and Rita shut down a quarter of U.S. refining capacity. . . .

4. Ethanol: . . .The surge in demand for ethanol has stretched the rapidly expanding ethanol production and distribution system in the U.S.—and pushed prices sharply higher. . . . summer gasoline typically includes 10 percent ethanol . . .

5. Lower imports: . . .Tighter regulations for summer blends have made it increasingly difficult to find foreign-made gasoline that meets those requirements.

6. Tight inventories

7. Future fear factor: In the end, weather holds the potential to create the biggest havoc—as back-to-back hurricanes demonstrated last fall. Though the odds are slim that such severe damage will be repeated, memories are fresh of what bad weather can do to gasoline prices. . . .

8. Mother Nature: Though it's impossible to predict just how bad this hurricane season will be, the odds are against the kind of devastating damage seen last fall in the relatively small Gulf Coast corridor that produces nearly half of U.S. gasoline supplies. . . .

Essence of the Story

▶ Eight factors might move pump prices higher during 2006.

▶ A strong U.S. economy kept demand high.

▶ More people were planning to travel by road.

▶ Production interruptions might occur.

▶ The demand for ethanol increased.

▶ Tighter regulations for gasoline blends decreased imports.

▶ Inventories were low.

▶ Future supply disruptions were feared.

▶ Hurricanes might again cut production.

▶ In 2005, the average price of gasoline (all grades) was 210¢ a gallon and 9.64 million barrels of gasoline were consumed on the average each day.

▶ Figure 1 shows the market for gasoline in 2005. The demand curve is D_{05}, the supply curve is S_{05}, and the market equilibrium is at 9.64 million barrels a day and 210¢ a gallon.

▶ The eight events discussed in the news article change demand and supply.

▶ Events 1 and 2—an increase in incomes and increased travel plans—increase the demand for gasoline.

▶ Events 3 through 8—production interruptions, an increase in the demand for ethanol, tighter regulations that decrease imports, low inventories, worries about future supply disruptions, and concerns about the hurricane season—decrease the supply of gasoline.

▶ You might be wondering how an increase in the demand for ethanol decreases the supply of gasoline. This effect occurs because ethanol is an additive in summer gasoline. With an increase in the demand for ethanol, its price increased, which increased the cost of producing summer gasoline

and decreased the supply of gasoline.

▶ Figure 2 shows what happened in the market for gasoline during 2006.

▶ Demand increased from D_{05} to D_{06}, and supply decreased from S_{05} to S_{06}.

▶ Because demand increased and supply decreased, the price increased. The equilibrium price increased from 210¢ a gallon to 264¢ a gallon.

▶ And because the increase in the demand for gasoline was larger than the decrease in supply, the equilibrium quantity increased from 9.64 million barrels a day to 9.81 million barrels a day.

▶ Just one part of the news article needs a further comment. Did you notice what it said about economic textbooks? It said: "When commodity prices go up, the economic textbooks say demand is supposed to go down."

▶ What economic textbooks actually say is "When commodity prices go up *and other things remain the same, the quantity demanded* goes down."

▶ The article confuses "demand" and "quantity demanded."

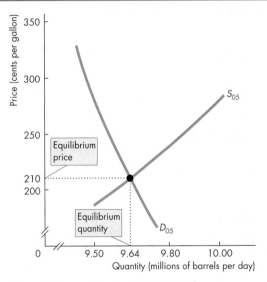

Figure 1 The gasoline market in 2005

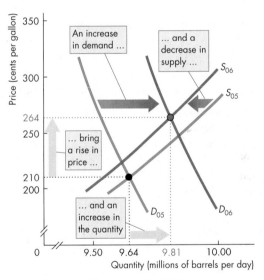

Figure 2 The gasoline market in 2006

Mathematical Note
Demand, Supply, and Equilibrium

Demand Curve

The law of demand says that as the price of a good or service falls, the quantity demanded of that good or service increases. We can illustrate the law of demand by drawing a graph of the demand curve or writing down an equation. When the demand curve is a straight line, the following equation describes it:

$$P = a - bQ_D,$$

where P is the price and Q_D is the quantity demanded. The a and b are positive constants.

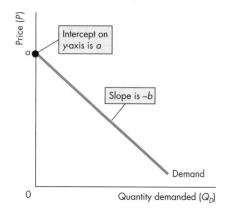

The demand equation tells us three things:

1. The price at which no one is willing to buy the good (Q_D is zero). That is, if the price is a, then the quantity demanded is zero. You can see the price a on the graph. It is the price at which the demand curve hits the y-axis—what we call the demand curve's "intercept on the y-axis."

2. As the price falls, the quantity demanded increases. If Q_D is a positive number, then the price P must be less than a. And as Q_D gets larger, the price P becomes smaller. That is, as the quantity increases, the maximum price that buyers are willing to pay for the last unit of the good falls.

3. The constant b tells us how fast the maximum price that someone is willing to pay for the good falls as the quantity increases. That is, the constant b tells us about the steepness of the demand curve. The equation tells us that the slope of the demand curve is $-b$.

Supply Curve

The law of supply says that as the price of a good or service rises, the quantity supplied of that good or service increases. We can illustrate the law of supply by drawing a graph of the supply curve or writing down an equation. When the supply curve is a straight line, the following equation describes it:

$$P = c + dQ_S,$$

where P is the price and Q_S is the quantity supplied. The c and d are positive constants.

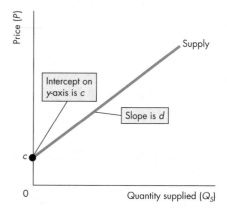

The supply equation tells us three things:

1. The price at which sellers are not willing to supply the good (Q_S is zero). That is, if the price is c, then no one is willing to sell the good. You can see the price c on the graph. It is the price at which the supply curve hits the y-axis—what we call the supply curve's "intercept on the y-axis."

2. As the price rises, the quantity supplied increases. If Q_S is a positive number, then the price P must be greater than c. And as Q_S increases, the price P get larger. That is, as the quantity increases, the minimum price that sellers are willing to accept for the last unit rises.

3. The constant d tells us how fast the minimum price at which someone is willing to sell the good rises as the quantity increases. That is, the constant d tells us about the steepness of the supply curve. The equation tells us that the slope of the supply curve is d.

Market Equilibrium

Demand and supply determine market equilibrium. The figure shows the equilibrium price (P^*) and equilibrium quantity (Q^*) at the intersection of the demand curve and the supply curve.

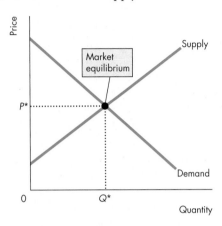

We can use the equations to find the equilibrium price and equilibrium quantity. The price of a good adjusts until the quantity demanded equals the quantity supplied. That is,

$$Q_D = Q_S.$$

So at the equilibrium price (P^*) and equilibrium quantity (Q^*),

$$Q_D = Q_S = Q^*.$$

To find the equilibrium price and equilibrium quantity, substitute Q^* for Q_D in the demand equation and Q^* for Q_S in the supply equation. Then the price is the equilibrium price (P^*), which gives

$$P^* = a - bQ^*$$
$$P^* = c + dQ^*.$$

Notice that

$$a - bQ^* = c + dQ^*.$$

Now solve for Q^*:

$$a - c = bQ^* + dQ^*$$
$$a - c = (b + d)Q^*$$
$$Q^* = \frac{a - c}{b + d}.$$

To find the equilibrium price, (P^*), substitute for Q^* in either the demand equation or the supply equation.

Using the demand equation, we have

$$P^* = a - b\left(\frac{a - c}{b + d}\right)$$
$$P^* = \frac{a(b + d) - b(a - c)}{b + d}$$
$$P^* = \frac{ad + bc}{b + d}.$$

Alternatively, using the supply equation, we have

$$P^* = c + d\left(\frac{a - c}{b + d}\right)$$
$$P^* = \frac{c(b + d) + d(a - c)}{b + d}$$
$$P^* = \frac{ad + bc}{b + d}.$$

An Example

The demand for ice-cream cones is

$$P = 800 - 2Q_D.$$

The supply of ice-cream cones is

$$P = 200 + 1Q_S.$$

The price of a cone is expressed in cents, and the quantities are expressed in cones per day.

To find the equilibrium price (P^*) and equilibrium quantity (Q^*), substitute Q^* for Q_D and Q_S and P^* for P. That is,

$$P^* = 800 - 2Q^*$$
$$P^* = 200 + 1Q^*.$$

Now solve for Q^*:

$$800 - 2Q^* = 200 + 1Q^*$$
$$600 = 3Q^*$$
$$Q^* = 200.$$

And

$$P^* = 800 - 2(200)$$
$$= 400.$$

The equilibrium price is $4 a cone, and the equilibrium quantity is 200 cones per day.

SUMMARY

Key Points

Markets and Prices (p. 60)

- A competitive market is one that has so many buyers and sellers that no one can influence the price.
- Opportunity cost is a relative price.
- Demand and supply determine relative prices.

Demand (pp. 61–65)

- Demand is the relationship between the quantity demanded of a good and its price when all other influences on buying plans remain the same.
- The higher the price of a good, other things remaining the same, the smaller is the quantity demanded—the law of demand.
- Demand depends on the prices of related goods (substitutes and complements), expected future prices, income, expected future income, population, and preferences.

Supply (pp. 66–69)

- Supply is the relationship between the quantity supplied of a good and its price when all other influences on selling plans remain the same.
- The higher the price of a good, other things remaining the same, the greater is the quantity supplied—the law of supply.
- Supply depends on the prices of resources used to produce a good, the prices of related goods produced, expected future prices, the number of suppliers, and technology.

Market Equilibrium (pp. 70–71)

- At the equilibrium price, the quantity demanded equals the quantity supplied.
- At prices above equilibrium, there is a surplus and the price falls.
- At prices below equilibrium, there is a shortage and the price rises.

Predicting Changes in Price and Quantity (pp. 72–75)

- An increase in demand brings a rise in the price and an increase in the quantity supplied. A decrease in demand brings a fall in the price and a decrease in the quantity supplied.

- An increase in supply brings a fall in the price and an increase in the quantity demanded. A decrease in supply brings a rise in the price and a decrease in the quantity demanded.
- An increase in demand and an increase in supply bring an increased quantity but an uncertain price change. An increase in demand and a decrease in supply bring a higher price but an uncertain change in quantity.

Key Figures

Key Terms

PROBLEMS

myeconlab Tests, Study Plan, Solutions*

1. William Gregg owned a mill in South Carolina. In December 1862, he placed a notice in the *Edgehill Advertiser* announcing his willingness to exchange cloth for food and other items. Here is an extract:

   1 yard of cloth for 1 pound of bacon
   2 yards of cloth for 1 pound of butter
   4 yards of cloth for 1 pound of wool
   8 yards of cloth for 1 bushel of salt

   a. What is the price of butter in terms of wool?
   b. If the price of bacon was 20¢ a pound, what do you predict was the price of butter?
   c. If the price of bacon was 20¢ a pound and the price of salt was $2.00 a bushel, do you think anyone would accept Mr. Gregg's offer of cloth for salt?

2. Classify the following pairs of goods and services as substitutes, complements, substitutes in production, or complements in production.
   a. Bottled water and health club memberships
   b. French fries and baked potatoes
   c. Leather purses and leather shoes
   d. SUVs and pickup trucks
   e. Diet coke and regular coke
   f. Low-fat milk and cream

3. "As more people buy computers, the demand for Internet service increases and the price of Internet service decreases. The fall in the price of Internet service decreases the supply of Internet service." Is this statement true or false? Explain your answer.

4. What is the effect on the price of a recordable CD and the quantity of recordable CDs sold if
   a. The price of an MP3 download rises?
   b. The price of an iPod falls?
   c. The supply of CD players increases?
   d. Consumers' incomes increase?
   e. Workers who make CDs get a pay raise?
   f. The events in (a) and (e) occur together?

5. The following events occur one at a time:
   (i)   The price of crude oil rises.
   (ii) The price of a car rises.
   (iii) All speed limits on highways are abolished.
   (iv) Robots cut car production costs.

Which of these events will increase or decrease (state which occurs)
   a. The demand for gasoline?
   b. The supply of gasoline?
   c. The quantity of gasoline demanded?
   d. The quantity of gasoline supplied?

6. The figure illustrates the market for pizza.

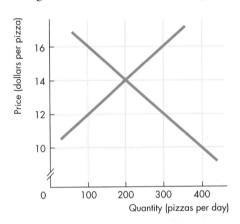

Label the curves and explain what happens if
   a. The price of a pizza is $16.
   b. The price of a pizza is $12.

7. The table sets out the demand and supply schedules for gum.

Price (cents per pack)	Quantity demanded (millions of packs a week)	Quantity supplied (millions of packs a week)
20	180	60
40	140	100
60	100	140
80	60	180

   a. Draw a graph of the gum market, label the axes and the curves, and mark in the equilibrium price and quantity.
   b. Suppose that the price of gum is 70¢ a pack. Describe the situation in the gum market and explain how the price adjusts.
   c. Suppose that the price of gum is 30¢ a pack. Describe the situation in the gum market and explain how the price adjusts.
   d. If a fire destroys some factories producing gum and the the quantity of gum supplied decreases by 40 million packs a week at each price, explain what happens in the market for gum and illustrate the changes in your graph of the gum market.

*Solutions to odd-numbered problems are provided.

e. If an increase in the teenage population increases the quantity of gum demand by 40 million packs a week at each price at the same time as the fire occurs, what are the new equilibrium price and quantity of gum? Illustrate these changes in your graph.

8. The table sets out the demand and supply schedules for potato chips.

Price (cents per bag)	Quantity demanded (millions of bags per week)	Quantity supplied (millions of bags per week)
50	160	130
60	150	140
70	140	150
80	130	160
90	120	170
100	110	180

a. Draw a graph of the potato chip market and mark in the equilibrium price and quantity.
b. Describe the situation in the market for chips and explain how the price adjusts if chips are 60¢ a bag.
c. If a new dip increases the quantity of potato chips demanded by 30 million bags per week at each price, how does the price and quantity of chips change?
d. If a virus destroys potato crops and the quantity of potato chips supplied decreases by 40 million bags a week at each price at the same time as the dip comes onto the market, how does the price and quantity of chips change?

CRITICAL THINKING

1. After you have studied *Reading Between the Lines* on pp. 76–77, answer the following questions:
   a. How does the news article confuse the concepts of "a change in demand" and "a change in the quantity demanded"?
   b. Which of the eight reasons for a rise in the price of gasoline would increase the demand for gasoline and why?
   c. Which of the eight reasons for a rise in the price of gasoline would decrease the supply of gasoline and why?
   d. How do we know that the demand for gasoline increased by more than the supply of gasoline decreased in the summer of 2006?

2. **Eurostar boosted by Da Vinci Code**
   Eurostar, the train service linking London to Paris. . . , said on Wednesday first-half sales rose 6 per cent, boosted by devotees of the blockbuster Da Vinci movie.
   CNN, July 26, 2006
   a. Explain how Da Vinci Code fans helped to raise Eurostar's sales.
   b. CNN commented on the "fierce competition from budget airlines." Explain the effect of this competition on Eurostar's sales.
   c. What markets in Paris do you think these fans influenced? Explain the influence on three markets.

3. **Of gambling, grannies and good sense**
   Nevada has the fastest growing elderly population of any state. . . . Las Vegas has . . . plenty of jobs for the over 50s.
   The Economist, July 26, 2006
   Explain how grannies have influenced the
   a. Demand side of some Las Vegas markets.
   b. Supply side of other Las Vegas markets.

WEB ACTIVITIES

[myeconlab] Links to Web sites

1. Obtain data on the prices and quantities of bananas in 1985 and 2002.
   a. Make a graph to illustrate the market for bananas in 1985 and 2002.
   b. On the graph, show the changes in demand and supply and the changes in the quantity demanded and the quantity supplied that are consistent with the price and quantity data.
   c. Why do you think demand and supply changed?

2. Obtain data on the price of oil since 2000.
   a. Describe how the price of oil changed.
   b. Use a demand-supply graph to explain what happens to the price when supply increases or decreases and demand is unchanged.
   c. What do you predict would happen to the price of oil if a new drilling technology permitted deeper ocean sources to be used?
   d. What do you predict would happen to the price of oil if a clean and safe nuclear technology were developed?

The Amazing Market

The four chapters that you've just studied explain how markets work. The market is an amazing instrument. It enables people who have never met and who know nothing about each other to interact and do business. It also enables us to allocate our scarce resources to the uses that we value most highly. Markets can be very simple or highly organized.

A simple market is one that the American historian Daniel J. Boorstin describes in *The Discoverers* (p. 161). In the late fourteenth century,

> *The Muslim caravans that went southward from Morocco across the Atlas Mountains arrived after twenty days at the shores of the Senegal River. There the Moroccan traders laid out separate piles of salt, of beads from Ceutan coral, and cheap manufactured goods. Then they retreated out of sight. The local tribesmen, who lived in the strip mines where they dug their gold, came to the shore and put a heap of gold beside each pile of Moroccan goods. Then they, in turn, went out of view, leaving the Moroccan traders either to take the gold offered for a particular pile or to reduce the pile of their merchandise to suit the offered price in gold. Once again the Moroccan traders withdrew, and the process went on. By this system of commercial etiquette, the Moroccans collected their gold.*

An organized market is the New York Stock Exchange, which trades many millions of stocks each day. Another is an auction at which the U.S. government sells rights to broadcasters and cellular telephone companies for the use of the airwaves.

All of these markets determine the prices at which exchanges take place and enable both buyers and sellers to benefit.

Everything and anything that can be exchanged is traded in markets. There are markets for goods and services; for resources such as labor, capital, and raw materials; for dollars, pounds, and yen; for goods to be delivered now and for goods to be delivered in the future. Only the imagination places limits on what can be traded in markets.

You began your study of markets in Chapter 3 by learning about the laws of demand and supply. There, you discovered the forces that make prices adjust to coordinate buying plans and selling plans.

The laws of demand and supply that you've learned and used in this chapter were discovered during the nineteenth century by some remarkable economists. We conclude our study of demand and supply and markets by looking at the lives and times of some of these economists and by talking to one of today's most influential economists who studies markets using experimental methods.

Discovering the Laws of Demand and Supply

The Economist

Alfred Marshall *(1842–1924) grew up in an England that was being transformed by the railroad and by the expansion of manufacturing. Mary Paley was one of Marshall's students at Cambridge, and when Alfred and Mary married, in 1877, celibacy rules barred Alfred from continuing to teach at Cambridge. By 1884, with more liberal rules, the Marshalls returned to Cambridge, where Alfred became Professor of Political Economy.*

Many others had a hand in refining the theory of demand and supply, but the first thorough and complete statement of the theory as we know it today was set out by Alfred Marshall, with the acknowledged help of Mary Paley Marshall. Published in 1890, this monumental treatise, The Principles of Economics, *became the textbook on economics on both sides of the Atlantic for almost half a century. Marshall was an outstanding mathematician, but he kept mathematics and even diagrams in the background. His supply and demand diagram appears only in a footnote.*

The Issues

The laws of demand and supply that you studied in Chapter 3 were discovered during the 1830s by Antoine-Augustin Cournot (1801–1877), a professor of mathematics at the University of Lyon, France. Although Cournot was the first to use demand and supply, it was the development and expansion of the railroads during the 1850s that gave the newly emerging theory its first practical applications. Railroads then were at the cutting edge of technology just as airlines are today. And as in the airline industry today, competition among the railroads was fierce.

Dionysius Lardner (1793–1859), an Irish professor of philosophy at the University of London, used demand and supply to show railroad companies how they could increase their profits by cutting rates on long-distance business on which competition was fiercest and by raising rates on short-haul business on which they had less to fear from other transportation suppliers. Today, economists use the principles that Lardner worked out during the 1850s to calculate the freight rates and passenger fares that will give airlines the largest possible profit. And the rates calculated have a lot in common with the railroad rates of the nineteenth century. On local routes on which there is little competition, fares per mile are highest, and on long-distance routes on which the airlines compete fiercely, fares per mile are lowest.

Known satirically among scientists of the day as "Dionysius Diddler," Lardner worked on an amazing range of problems from astronomy to railway engineering to economics. A colorful character, he would have been a regular guest of David Letterman if late-night talk shows had been around in the 1850s. Lardner visited the École des Ponts et Chaussées (School of Bridges and Roads) in Paris and must have learned a great deal from Jules Dupuit.

In France, Jules Dupuit (1804–1866), a French engineer/economist, used demand to calculate the benefits from building a bridge and, once the bridge was built, for calculating the toll to charge for its use. His work was the forerunner of what is today called *cost-benefit analysis.* Working with the principles invented by Dupuit, economists today calculate the costs and benefits of highways, airports, dams, and power stations.

Then

Dupuit used the law of demand to determine whether a bridge or canal would be valued enough by its users to justify the cost of building it. Lardner first worked out the relationship between the cost of production and supply and used demand and supply theory to explain the costs, prices, and profits of railroad operations. He also used the theory to discover ways of increasing revenue by raising rates on short-haul business and lowering them on long-distance freight.

Now

Today, using the same principles that Dupuit devised, economists calculate whether the benefits of expanding airports and air-traffic control facilities are sufficient to cover their costs. Airline companies use the principles developed by Lardner to set their prices and to decide when to offer "seat sales." Like the railroads before them, the airlines charge a high price per mile on short flights, for which they face little competition, and a low price per mile on long flights, for which competition is fierce.

Markets do an amazing job. And the laws of demand and supply help us to understand how markets work. But in some situations, a market must be designed and institutions must be created to enable the market to operate. In recent years, economists have begun to use experiments to design and create markets. One of the chief architects of experimental methods in economics is Charles Holt, whom you can meet on the following pages.

Charles A. Holt

Charles A. Holt is the A. Willis Robertson Professor of Political Economy and Director of the Thomas Jefferson Center for Political Economy at the University of Virginia.

Born in 1948 in Richmond, he was an undergraduate at Washington and Lee University and a graduate student at Carnegie-Mellon University. Professor Holt became interested in laboratory experiments as part of his work on auctions and discovered that the data generated by experiments often rejected standard theories. These discoveries sent him on the path of developing new theories that are consistent with experimental data in areas that include rent seeking, auctions, bargaining, and public goods. His research has produced more than a hundred articles and several books.

Professor Holt is also a committed teacher. He has written a series of interactive games and experimental markets for teaching on his Veconlab Web site.

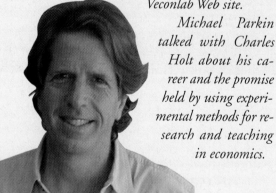

Michael Parkin talked with Charles Holt about his career and the promise held by using experimental methods for research and teaching in economics.

What sparked your interest in economics and led to your decision to become an economist?

When I was taking a summer school history class, the high school coach who was teaching the class remarked, "I don't understand why one baseball team would trade a player with another, don't they see that one person always gets the short end of a deal?" This comment caused me think about how voluntary trade can benefit both parties. For example, a team with two good first basemen could trade one for a pitcher from a team with a full bullpen but nobody at first, and both teams might end up winning more games that season. In the same manner, each trade between willing partners in an economy can make both better off, and lots of trades can create lots of wealth. I later enjoyed reading the ideas of economists like Adam Smith, Milton Friedman, and John Maynard Keynes, who were able to transform a jumble of everyday economic events into a large picture with a coherent organization and purpose.

Based on the wide experience you have with experimental markets, how does the demand and supply model of Alfred Marshall stand up today?

When I first took economics in college, we had to memorize a list of assumptions underlying the model of perfect competition that is represented by the supply and demand graph. These assumptions included "large numbers of buyers and sellers" and "perfect information." The professor would invariably end up by admitting that few actual markets fit this model exactly, but that some markets, for example wheat, might come close.

Vernon Smith's early market experiments, run in his class, showed that prices track the supply-and-demand predictions surprisingly well, even with as few as 3 or 4 traders on each side of the market, and with nobody having any direct information about others' values and costs for the commodity being traded. I ran some experiments of my own to try to stress the model, by giving "power" to one side of the market, but the outcomes were surprisingly competitive. This experience in the laboratory added confidence and enthusiasm to my teaching.

What can we learn about how competitive markets work in classroom experiments?

My coauthor Doug Davis and I ran some experiments in which we let sellers discuss prices while buyers were out of the room, and they invariably tried to fix prices at high levels. When prices were publicly posted for all to see, these conspiracies would raise sellers' earnings and harm buyers, but attempts at collusion generally failed when sellers were able to offer secret discounts to buyers that could not be seen by other sellers. In this case, rampant discounting would drive discounted prices down to near-competitive levels. I remember one group that ended up "fixing" a price, but unknown to them, the price that they fixed was at about the level of the supply and demand intersection. In the experiments, as in actual markets, consumers benefit from lower prices, and the combined benefit of buyers and earnings of sellers rise as prices approach competitive levels.

Can we learn even more by doing web-based experiments? What in particular are the gains from running web-based experiments like those that you've created?

You only have to look at the computer screens of traders in many markets to see that they have large amounts of information available, and yet that they have to rely on arms-length negotiations. Web-based experiments can add this kind of realistic complexity to classroom markets.

For example, the programs can keep track of your cash, interest earnings, dividends, and stock shares while you buy and sell quickly. Often "insiders" have sources of private information, and the web-based experiments can generate and preserve the privacy of this information, as students use it to guide their trading decisions. In particular, I could only dream of doing realistic macroeconomics experiments before I began writing web-based programs, and now these programs allow "workers" and "firms" to interact in markets that are connected by the "circular flow" of money, goods, and labor. In this setting, one can see how a contraction in the money supply may stifle transactions and lead to a "general glut" in which unsold labor and goods results in low levels of consumption and production. It is an exhilarating experience to see how an increase in the money supply in such cases may have "real effects" that pull it out of a slump.

Another example involves the work that I've been doing for the Federal Communications Commission (the FCC) on auction design. Their auctions involve hundreds or thousands of broadcast licenses, and these auctions are run in a series of "rounds" as prices continue to rise. These auctions involve bidders around the country, and naturally, they are controlled by computer software, just as our auction experiments are run in the lab, with bidding screens that have the same "look and feel" as that used in the actual auctions.

You might be wondering why would anyone be concerned about a laboratory setting with students like yourself (earning fairly large amounts of cash) when a real auction occurs every 6 months or so? Think of it this way, an auction may involve billions of dollars of trade, and some auctions have failed badly, with prices that barely get "off the ground." You wouldn't want to try a new auction design without extensive laboratory testing, any more than you would want to launch a multi-billion dollar space shuttle without lots of tests here on earth.

I remember wearing a "NASA Mission Acquisition" nametag at a meeting at Caltech, where results of laboratory experiments were discussed. I later got a chance to talk candidly with some of the NASA officials on the "red-eye" flight back to the East Coast. In particular, I got to ask them what they really hoped to learn from small-scale simulations of the procurement process. Their response was that the amounts of money involved were so large, and the budgeting/procurement process was so complex, that they had a fear of "losing control," and any

> **You wouldn't want to try a new auction design without extensive laboratory testing, any more than you would want to launch a multi-billion dollar space shuttle without lots of tests here on earth.**

insights gleaned from controlled laboratory experiments could be extremely valuable.

Many students have been introduced to game theory watching Russell Crowe as mathematics professor John Nash in A Beautiful Mind. What have we learned about games from experiments?

Game theory is an elegant apparatus that can yield strikingly accurate predictions of human behavior, especially where the "players" are driven by the profit motive to make careful decisions and to acquire extensive information about what their competitors are doing. One criticism of game theory, however, is that it is all too often based on an assumption that the players are "perfectly rational" and perfectly selfish, not caring much about others' economic well-being.

We all think of ourselves as being rational, but most of us have doubts about the rationality of others. In "Ten Little Treasures of Game Theory, and Ten Intuitive Contradictions," (*American Economic Review*, 2001) Professor Jacob Goeree (Caltech) and I use experiments to show that game theoretic "Nash equilibrium" predictions tend to work well in some games (the "treasures") and badly in others. The intuition here is that games are interactions of thinking humans, so reactions to uncertainty about others may cause "feedback effects" that take behavior away from theoretical predictions based on perfect knowledge and rationality.

Some people are skeptical about experiments. What are some of the easily disposed of criticisms? Are there any compelling criticisms of the experimental approach? How do you respond to them?

Experiments with real people can be used to inject realistic elements into the study of economic behavior. Many economic movements (depressions) are like the movements of planets that cannot be undone or repeated exactly, but controlled experiments allow us the opportunity to obtain repeated observations under controlled conditions. For example, the work for the FCC on auction design involved over 900 student "subjects" who participated in hundreds of auctions, which permitted us to see the major patterns that emerge from random variations due to individual differences and interactions. Some of what we learned seems obvious after the fact, but the experiments gave us the confidence to argue strongly for and against particular changes in auction procedures. Much of the alternative analysis considered by the FCC officials involved computer simulations, which are necessarily based on somewhat mechanical assumptions. Computer simulations can also be quite useful, especially when laboratory experiments are used to refine the assumed behavior rules.

One critique of laboratory experiments is that the subject population is narrowly selected. Hence some economists and political scientists have used "field experiments" in which the participants are in their native environment. This involves some loss of control, but the added realism can be justified when "social context" is important. For example, the effects of appeals to vote on voter turnout are probably best studied in field experiments, where random samples of households are exposed to different "appeal" treatments—a phone call or a knock on the door.

What is your advice to a student who is just setting out to become an economist? Is economics a good subject in which to major? What other subjects work well with economics?

I enjoyed both politics and economics courses in college, but I chose to study economics because I felt that the theories I was learning would still be largely intact in 20 years, which has turned out to be true. Economics offers a nice combination of a firm scientific basis that can be applied to important social problems. These problems are fascinating because of the forward-looking, strategic nature of humans, which are inherently less mechanical than what you might be studying in physical sciences. And the tools that you learn in economics, a mix of theory, intuition, data analysis, and experiments, can be profitably transported to the study of a wide range of social issues. The experimental side of economics has a close tie to psychology, and many of the most interesting policy applications occur in setting where a deep understanding of political processes is helpful.

A First Look at Macroeconomics

What Will Your World Be Like?

During the past 100 years, the quantity of goods and services produced in the nation's farms, factories, shops, and offices has expanded more than twentyfold. As a result, we have a much higher standard of living than our grandparents had. Will production always expand?

For most of us, a high standard of living means finding a good job. What

kind of job will you find when you graduate? Will you have lots of choices, or will you face a labor market with a high unemployment rate in which jobs are hard to find?

A high standard of living means being able to afford to buy life's necessities and have some fun. If prices rise too quickly, some people get left behind and must cut back on what they buy. What will the dollar buy next year, in 10 years when you are paying off your student loan, and in 50 years when you are spending your life's savings in retirement?

Almost every year since 1970, the U.S. government has spent more than it has raised in taxes. And most years, the United States has spent more on imports from other countries than it has earned from exports. We have large and persistent government and international deficits and growing debts. Are debts and deficits a problem?

To keep production expanding and prevent an economic slowdown, the federal government and the Federal Reserve Board—the nation's financial managers—take policy actions. How do their actions influence production, jobs, prices, the value of the dollar, and our ability to compete in the global marketplace?

◆ These are the questions of macroeconomics that you are about to study. With what you learn in these chapters, you will be able to understand the economic world that you will enter when you graduate and in which you will earn your living. *Reading Between the Lines* at the end of the chapter gives you some practice by looking at our expanding economy in 2006.

After studying this chapter, you will be able to

▶ Describe the origins and issues of macroeconomics

▶ Describe the trends and fluctuations in economic growth and explain the benefits and costs of economic growth

▶ Describe the trends and fluctuations in unemployment and explain why unemployment is a problem

▶ Describe the trends and fluctuations in inflation and the value of the dollar and explain why inflation is a problem

▶ Describe the trends and fluctuations in surpluses, deficits, and debts and explain why they matter

▶ Identify the macroeconomic policy challenges and list the tools available for meeting them

89

Origins and Issues of Macroeconomics

Economists began to study economic growth, inflation, and international finance as long ago as the 1750s, and this work was the origin of macroeconomics. But modern macroeconomics did not emerge until the **Great Depression,** a decade (1929–1939) of high unemployment and stagnant production throughout the world economy. In the Depression's worst year, 1933, the production of U.S. farms, factories, shops, and offices was only 70 percent of its 1929 level and 25 percent of the labor force was unemployed. These were years of human misery on a scale that is hard to imagine today. They were also years of extreme pessimism about the ability of markets to work properly. Many people believed that private ownership, free markets, and democratic political institutions could not survive.

The science of economics had no solutions to the Great Depression. The major alternative system of socialism and central planning seemed attractive to many people. It was in this climate of economic depression and political and intellectual turmoil that modern macroeconomics emerged with the publication in 1936 of John Maynard Keynes' *The General Theory of Employment, Interest, and Money.*

Short-Term Problems Versus Long-Term Goals

Keynes' theory was that depression and high unemployment result from insufficient private spending and that to cure these problems, the government must increase its spending. Keynes focused on the *short term.* He wanted to cure an immediate problem regardless of the *long-term* consequences of the cure. "In the long run," said Keynes, "we're all dead."

But Keynes believed that after his cure for depression had restored full employment, the long-term problems of inflation and slow economic growth would return. And he suspected that his cure for depression—increased government spending—might trigger inflation and slow long-term growth. With a lower long-term growth rate, the economy would create fewer jobs. If this outcome did occur, a policy aimed at lowering unemployment in the short run might end up increasing it in the long run.

By the late 1960s and through the 1970s, Keynes' predictions became a reality. Inflation increased, economic growth slowed, and in some countries, unemployment became persistently high. The causes of these developments are complex. But they point to an inescapable conclusion: The long-term problems of inflation, slow growth, and persistent unemployment and the short-term problems of depression and economic fluctuations intertwine and are most usefully studied together. So although macroeconomics was reborn during the Great Depression, it has now returned to its older tradition. Today, macroeconomics is a subject that studies long-term economic growth and inflation as well as short-term business fluctuations and unemployment.

The Road Ahead

There is no unique way to study macroeconomics. Because its rebirth was a product of depression, the common practice for many years was to pay most attention to short-term output fluctuations and unemployment but never to completely lose sight of the long-term issues. When a rapid inflation emerged during the 1970s, this topic returned to prominence. During the 1980s, when long-term growth slowed in the United States and other rich industrial countries but exploded in East Asia, economists redirected their energy toward economic growth. During the 1990s, as information technologies further shrank the globe, the international dimension of macroeconomics became more prominent. The result of these developments is that modern macroeconomics is a broad subject that studies all the issues we've just identified: economic growth, unemployment, and inflation. Macroeconomics also studies fluctuating currencies and government budget and international deficits and debts.

Over the past 40 years, economists have developed a clearer understanding of the forces that determine macroeconomic performance and have devised policies that they hope will improve this performance. Your main goal is to become familiar with the theories of macroeconomics and the policies that they make possible. To set you on your path toward this goal, we're going to take a first look at economic growth, unemployment, inflation and the dollar, and surpluses, deficits, and debts and learn why these macroeconomic phenomena merit our attention.

 myeconlab **Study Plan 4.1**

Economic Growth and Fluctuations

Your parents are richer than your grandparents were when they were young. But are you going to be richer than your parents are? And are your children going to be richer than you? The answers depend on the rate of economic growth.

Economic growth is the expansion of the economy's production possibilities. It can be pictured as an outward shift of the production possibilities frontier (*PPF*).

We measure economic growth by the increase in real gross domestic product. We define *real gross domestic product* (also called *real GDP*) and how it is measured in Chapter 5 (see pp. 112–116) but for now, you can think of it as the value of the economy's total production measured in the prices of a single year. Real GDP in the United States is currently measured in the prices of 2000 (called 2000 dollars). We use the dollar prices of a single year to eliminate the influence of *inflation*—the increase in the average level of prices—and determine how much production has grown from one year to another.

Real GDP is not a perfect measure of total production because it does not include everything that is produced. It excludes the things we produce for ourselves at home (preparing meals, doing laundry, house painting, gardening, and so on). It also excludes production that people hide to avoid taxes or because the activity is illegal—the underground economy. But despite its shortcomings, real GDP is the best measure of total production available. Let's see what it tells us about economic growth.

Economic Growth in the United States

Figure 4.1 shows real GDP in the United States from 1960 to 2005 and highlights two features of economic growth:

- The growth of potential GDP
- Fluctuations of real GDP around potential GDP

The Growth of Potential GDP When all the economy's labor, capital, land, and entrepreneurial ability are fully employed, the value of production is called **potential GDP**. Real GDP fluctuates around potential GDP, and the long-term economic growth rate is measured by the growth rate of potential GDP. It is shown by the steepness of the potential GDP line (the black line) in Fig. 4.1.

During the 1960s, potential GDP grew at an unusually rapid rate. But the growth rate of output per person slowed during the 1970s, a phenomenon called the **productivity growth slowdown**. Potential GDP began to grow more rapidly during the late 1980s and through the 1990s and 2000s. But the high growth rate of the 1960s did not return.

Why did the productivity growth slowdown occur? The answer to this question is controversial. One possible cause is a sharp rise in the relative price of energy. We explore the causes of the productivity growth slowdown in Chapter 8. Whatever its cause, a productivity growth slowdown means that we all have smaller incomes today than we would have had if the economy had continued to grow at its rate of the 1960s.

Let's now look at GDP fluctuations.

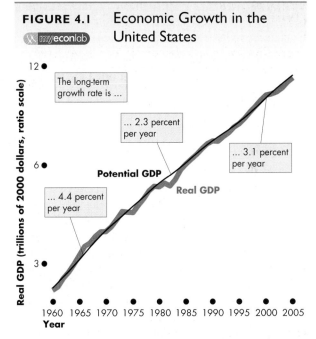

FIGURE 4.1   Economic Growth in the United States

The economic growth rate, measured by the growth of potential GDP, was 4.4 percent a year during the 1960s. Growth slowed to 2.3 percent during the 1970s. Growth speeded up during the late 1980s through the 1990s and 2000s, but it did not return to its 1960s rate. Real GDP fluctuates around potential GDP.

Source of data: U.S. Department of Commerce, *National Income and Product Accounts of the United States.*

Fluctuations of Real GDP Around Potential GDP Real GDP fluctuates around potential GDP in a business cycle. A **business cycle** is the periodic but irregular up-and-down movement in production. The business cycle is measured by fluctuations in real GDP around potential GDP. When real GDP is less than potential GDP, some resources are underused. For example, some labor is unemployed and capital is underutilized. When real GDP is greater than potential GDP, resources are overused. Many people work longer hours than they are willing to put up with in the long run, capital is worked so intensively that it is not maintained in prime working order, delivery times lengthen, bottlenecks occur, and backorders increase.

Business cycles are not regular, predictable, or repeating cycles like the phases of the moon. Their timing changes unpredictably, but they do have some things in common. Every business cycle has two phases:

1. A recession
2. An expansion

and two turning points:

1. A peak
2. A trough

Figure 4.2 shows these features of the most recent business cycle in the United States. A common definition of **recession** is a period during which real GDP decreases—its growth rate is negative—for at least two successive quarters. The most recent recession, which is highlighted in the figure, began in the first quarter of 2001 and ended in the third quarter of 2001. This recession lasted for three quarters. An **expansion** is a period during which real GDP increases. The most recent expansion began in the fourth quarter of 2001. The earlier expansion that began in the second quarter of 1991 was the longest expansion on record.

When an expansion ends and a recession begins, the turning point is called a *peak*. The most recent peak occurred in the fourth quarter of 2000. When a recession ends and an expansion begins, the turning point is called a *trough*. The most recent trough occurred in the fourth quarter of 2001.

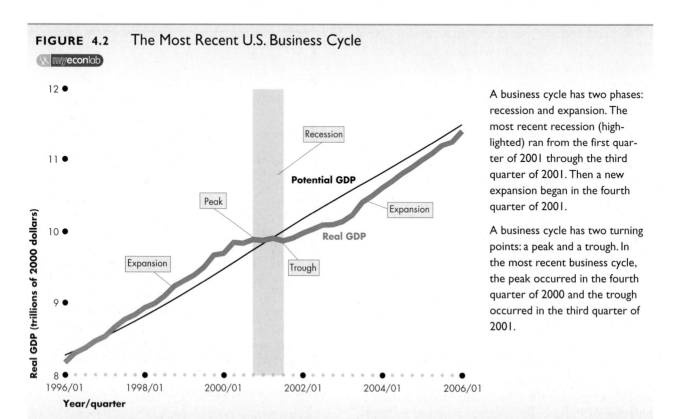

FIGURE 4.2   The Most Recent U.S. Business Cycle

A business cycle has two phases: recession and expansion. The most recent recession (highlighted) ran from the first quarter of 2001 through the third quarter of 2001. Then a new expansion began in the fourth quarter of 2001.

A business cycle has two turning points: a peak and a trough. In the most recent business cycle, the peak occurred in the fourth quarter of 2000 and the trough occurred in the third quarter of 2001.

Source of data: U.S. Department of Commerce, *National Income and Product Accounts of the United States* and Congressional Budget Office.

The Most Recent Recession in Historical Perspective
The recession of 2001 was milder than the recessions of 1990–1991 and 1982, but compared to earlier recessions these recessions were mild. You can see how mild they were by looking at Fig. 4.3, which shows a longer history of U.S. economic growth. The biggest decrease in real GDP occurred during the Great Depression of the 1930s. A large decrease also occurred in 1946 and 1947, after a huge World War II expansion. In more recent times, serious recessions occurred during the mid-1970s and during the early 1980s.

Each of these economic downturns was more severe than those in 1990–1991 and 2001. But you can see that the Great Depression was much more severe than anything that followed it. This episode was so extreme that we don't call it a recession. We call it a *depression*.

This last truly great depression occurred before the government started taking policy actions to stabilize the economy. It also occurred before the birth of modern macroeconomics. Is the absence of another great depression a sign that macroeconomics has contributed to economic stability? Some people believe it

is. Others doubt it. We'll evaluate these opinions on a number of occasions in this book.

We've looked at real GDP growth and fluctuations in the United States. But is the U.S. experience typical? Do other countries share our experience? Let's see whether they do.

Economic Growth Around the World

All countries experience economic growth, but the growth rate varies both over time and across countries. The fluctuations in economic growth rates over time tend to be correlated across countries, but some countries experience greater volatility in growth rates than others. And some growth rate differences across countries persist over a number of years.

We'll compare U.S. economic growth over time with that in other countries. And we'll look at longer-term differences in growth rates among countries and groups of countries.

Growth Rates over Time First, we'll compare the growth rate of real GDP in the United States with that for the rest of the world as a whole. Figure 4.4(a)

FIGURE 4.3   Long-Term Economic Growth in the United States

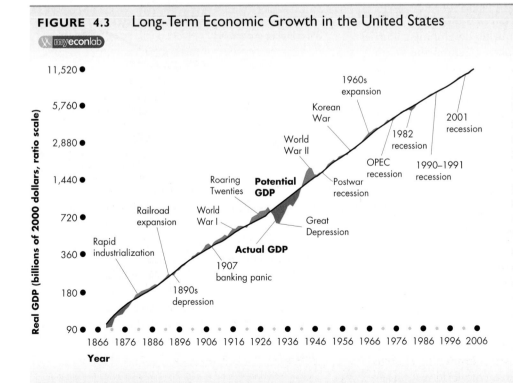

The thin black line shows potential GDP. Along this line, real GDP grew at an average rate of 3.7 percent a year between 1870 and 2005. The blue areas show when real GDP was above potential GDP, and the red areas show when it was below potential GDP. During some periods, such as World War II, real GDP expanded quickly. During other periods, such as the Great Depression and more recently in 1975, 1982, 1990–1991, and 2001, real GDP declined.

Sources of data: 1869–1928, Christina Romer, "The Prewar Business Cycle Reconsidered: New Estimates of Gross National Product, 1869–1908," *Journal of Political Economy* 97, (1989) 1–37. 1929–2005, U.S. Department of Commerce, *National Income and Product Accounts of the United States.*

shows these two growth rates from 1976 to 2005. (Note that this figure graphs *growth rates* of real GDP and not *levels* of real GDP that the three previous figures showed. So the number on the *y*-axis of this graph is a growth rate expressed as percent per year.)

You can see a striking fact in Fig. 4.4(a). The U.S. real GDP growth rate fluctuates much more than the real GDP growth rate in the rest of the world as a whole. In several years, U.S. real GDP actually falls—a negative growth rate—but economic growth in the rest of the world was never negative during the 30 years shown in the figure.

Persistent Differences in Growth Rates Second, we'll look at persistent longer-term differences across countries. Figure 4.4(b) compares the growth rate of the U.S. economy with that of several other countries and regions from 1996 through 2006. Among the advanced economies (the red bars), Japan has grown the slowest and the newly industrialized Asian economies have grown the fastest. The United States is in the middle of these two growth rates. The European Union has grown at the average rate of the advanced economies.

Among the developing economies (the green bars), the most rapid growth has occurred in Asia, where the average growth rate was more than 7 percent a year. The slowest growing developing countries are in the Western Hemisphere (Central and South America). The average growth rates of the developing countries of Central and Eastern Europe and Africa were close to the world average growth rate.

World average growth (the blue bar) has been 4 percent a year and slightly greater than the average U.S. growth rate.

Consequences of Persistent Differences The persistent differences in growth rates are bringing dramatic change to some nations' shares of world real GDP. Because the U.S. real GDP growth rate is slightly less than that of the rest of the world, the U.S. share of world real GDP has decreased from 21 percent in 1980 to 20 percent in 2005. But some fast-growing nations such as China are becoming a significantly bigger part of the global economy. China's share of world real GDP increased from 3 percent in 1980 to 15 percent in 2005 and its share continues to grow. Africa is growing close to the world average, so its share of world real GDP remains constant at about 3 percent.

FIGURE 4.4   Economic Growth Around the World

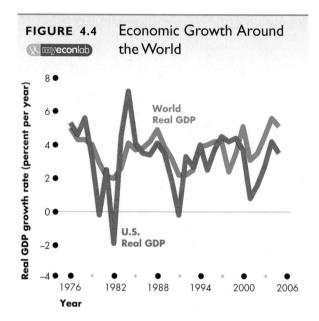

(a) The United States and the rest of the world: 1976–2005

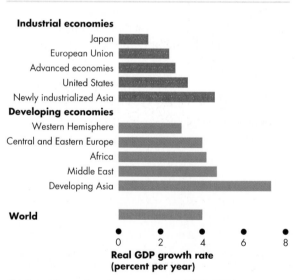

(b) Countries and regions compared: 1996–2006 average

In part (a), U.S. economic growth fluctuates much more than that in the rest of the world as a whole, but U.S. fluctuations and those in the rest of the world are correlated.

In part (b), growth rate differences persist. On the average between 1996 and 2006, developing Asian economies grew fastest and Japan grew slowest. The U.S. growth rate is in the middle of the pack but is slightly lower than the world average growth rate.

Source of data: International Monetary Fund, *World Economic Outlook*, April 2006, Washington, D.C.

The Lucas Wedge and the Okun Gap

You've seen that productivity growth slowed during the 1970s. And you've seen that real GDP growth fluctuates, so real GDP falls below potential GDP from time to time. How costly are the growth slowdown and lost output over the business cycle?

The answers are provided by two measures:

- The Lucas wedge
- The Okun gap

The Lucas Wedge The *Lucas wedge* is the accumulated loss of output that results from a slowdown in the growth rate of real GDP per person. It is given this name because Robert E. Lucas, Jr., a leading macroeconomist, drew attention to it and remarked that once you begin to think about the benefits of faster economic growth, it is hard to think about anything else!

Figure 4.5(a) shows the Lucas wedge that arises from the productivity growth slowdown of the 1970s. The black line in the figure tracks the path that potential GDP would have followed if its 1960s growth rate had been maintained through the next 35 years to 2005.

The Lucas wedge is a staggering $72 trillion— almost 6.5 years of real GDP at the 2005 level. This number is a measure of the cost of slower productivity growth.

The Okun Gap Real GDP minus potential GDP is the **output gap**. When the output gap is negative, it is called the *Okun gap*. It is given this name because Arthur M. Okun, a policy economist who was chairman of President Lyndon Johnson's Council of Economic Advisors during the 1960s, drew attention to it as a source of loss from economic fluctuations.

Figure 4.5(b) shows the Okun gap from the recessions that occurred over the same years as those for which we've just calculated the Lucas wedge.

The Okun gap is $3.3 trillion—about 30 percent of real GDP in 2005. This number is a measure of the cost of business cycle fluctuations.

You can see that the Lucas wedge is a much bigger deal than the Okun gap—more than *twenty* times as big a deal! Smoothing the business cycle saves spells of high unemployment and lost output. But maintaining a high rate of productivity growth makes a dramatic difference to the standard of living over a number of years.

FIGURE 4.5   The Lucas Wedge and the Okun Gap

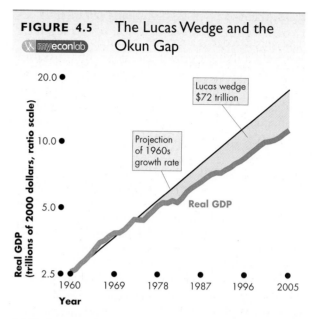

(a) The Lucas wedge

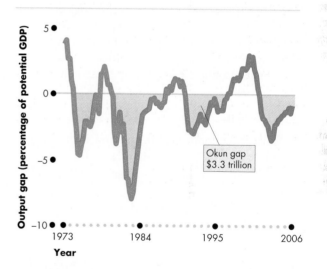

(b) The Okun gap

In part (a), the Lucas wedge that arises from the productivity growth slowdown of the 1970s is a staggering $72 trillion, or 6.5 times the real GDP of 2005.

In part (b), the Okun gap that arises from the lost production in recessions since the early 1970s amounts to $3.3 trillion, or about 30 percent of real GDP in 2005.

Over this 35-year period, the Lucas wedge is more than 20 times as large as the Okun gap.

Source of data: Bureau of Economic Analysis and author's assumptions.

Benefits and Costs of Economic Growth

The Lucas wedge is a measure of the dollar value of lost real GDP if the growth rate slows. But this cost translates into real goods and services. It is a cost in terms of less health care for the poor and elderly, less cancer and AIDS research, less space research and exploration, worse roads, and less housing. We even have less to spend on cleaner lakes, more trees, and cleaner air.

But fast growth is also costly. Its main cost is for-gone *current* consumption. To sustain a high growth rate, resources must be devoted to advancing technology and accumulating capital rather than to *current* consumption. This cost cannot be avoided. But it brings the benefit of greater consumption in the future. (See Chapter 2, p. 40.)

Two other possible costs of faster growth are a more rapid depletion of nonrenewable natural resources such as oil and natural gas and increased pollution of the air, rivers, and oceans. But neither of these two costs is inevitable. The technological advances that bring economic growth help us to economize on natural resources and to clean up the environment. For example, more efficient auto engines cut gasoline use and tailpipe emissions.

REVIEW QUIZ

1 What is economic growth and how is the long-term economic growth rate measured?
2 What is the distinction between real GDP and potential GDP?
3 What is a business cycle and what are its phases?
4 What is a recession?
5 In what phase of the business cycle was the U.S. economy during 2005?
6 What happened to economic growth in the United States during the 1970s?
7 What are the benefits and the costs of long-term economic growth?

   myeconlab Study Plan 4.2

We've seen that real GDP grows and that it fluctuates over the business cycle. The business cycle brings fluctuations in jobs and unemployment. Let's now examine these core macroeconomic problems.

Jobs and Unemployment

What kind of labor market will you enter when you graduate? Will there be plenty of good jobs to choose from, or will there be so much unemployment that you will be forced to take a low-paying job that does not use your education? The answer depends, to a large degree, on the total number of jobs available and on the unemployment rate.

Jobs

The U.S. economy is an incredible job-creating machine. In 2006, 143 million people had jobs—16 million more than in 1996 and 33 million more than in 1986. But the pace of job creation fluctuates, and during a recession, the number of jobs shrinks. For example, during the recession of 1990–1991, more than 1 million jobs were lost, and during the 2001 recession, 2 million jobs disappeared.

Through the expansion that follows a recession, more jobs are created than the number previously lost. For example, during the expansion of the 1990s, 2 million jobs were created each year. During the current expansion, job creation was slow and the number of jobs returned to its 2001 peak only toward the end of 2003.

The jobs created are not the same as those lost. Most new jobs are in the service industries. Jobs in manufacturing shrink each year because we buy more of our consumer goods from cheaper foreign sources. Some people worry that we are exporting our best jobs, but the truth is that, on the average, the new jobs are better than the ones lost and pay higher wages.

Unemployment

Not everyone who wants a job can find one. On any day in a normal or average year, 7 million people are unemployed, and during a recession or depression, unemployment rises above this level. For example, in the 1990–1991 recession and again in 2003, 9 million people were looking for jobs. In the booming economic conditions of 1999, the number of job seekers fell to 6 million.

These unemployment numbers are large. The number of people unemployed during a recession is equivalent to the population of Los Angeles. And even in a boom, the number is equivalent to the population of Chicago!

To place the number of unemployed people in perspective, we use a measure called the unemployment rate. The **unemployment rate** is the number of unemployed people expressed as a percentage of all the people who have jobs or are looking for one. (The concept of the unemployment rate, along with some other measures of the labor market, is explained more fully in Chapter 6.)

The unemployment rate is not a perfect measure of the underutilization of labor for two main reasons. First, it excludes people who are so discouraged that they've given up the effort to find work. Second, the unemployment rate measures unemployed people rather than unemployed labor hours. So the unemployment rate doesn't tell us about the numbers of part-time workers who want full-time jobs.

Despite these two limitations, the unemployment rate is the best available measure of underused labor resources. Let's look at some facts about unemployment.

Unemployment in the United States

Figure 4.6 shows the unemployment rate in the United States from 1929 through 2006. Three features stand out. First, during the Great Depression of the 1930s, the unemployment rate climbed to an all-time high of 25 percent in 1933 and remained high throughout the 1930s. After 1934, the official rate probably overstates unemployment because it counts as unemployed the people who had make-work jobs created by the government.

Second, although in recent years we have not experienced anything as devastating as the Great Depression, we have seen some high unemployment rates during four recessions: the OPEC recession of the mid-1970s, the 1982 recession, the 1990–1991 recession, and the 2001 recession.

Third, unemployment never falls to zero. In the period since World War II, the average unemployment rate has been close to 5.5 percent.

How does U.S. unemployment compare with unemployment in other countries?

FIGURE 4.6   Unemployment in the United States

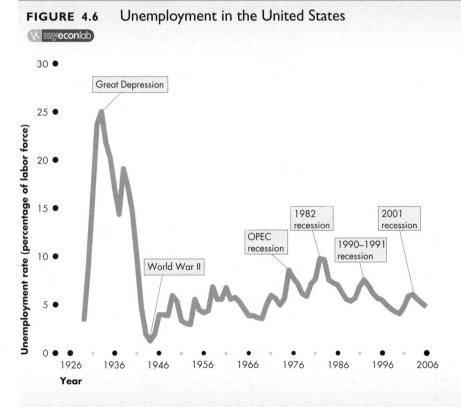

Unemployment is a persistent feature of economic life, but its rate varies. At its worst—during the Great Depression—25 percent of the labor force was unemployed. In the OPEC recession, the unemployment rate climbed to almost 8 percent, and in the 1982 recession, it climbed toward 10 percent. In the 1990–1991 and 2001 recessions, the unemployment rate climbed above 5 percent. Between the late 1960s and 1982, there was a general tendency for the unemployment rate to increase. Since then, the unemployment rate has remained below its 1982 peak. The unemployment rate fell during the expansions of the 1990s and 2000s.

Source of data: Bureau of Labor Statistics.

Unemployment Around the World

Figure 4.7 shows the unemployment rates in Western Europe, Canada, and Japan and compares them with the unemployment rate in the United States. Over the period shown in the figure, U.S. unemployment averaged 6.2 percent, much higher than Japanese unemployment, which averaged 3.3 percent, but lower than Canadian unemployment, which averaged 8.9 percent and European unemployment, which averaged 8.6 percent.

U.S. unemployment fluctuates over the business cycle. It increases during a recession and decreases during an expansion. Like U.S. unemployment, both Canadian and European unemployment increase during recessions and decrease during expansions. The cycle in Canadian unemployment is similar to that in U.S. unemployment, but the European cycle is out of phase with the U.S. cycle. Also, European unemployment was on a rising trend through the 1980s. In contrast with other countries, Japanese unemployment remained low and relatively stable until the mid-1990s but since then has drifted upward.

We've looked at some facts about unemployment. Let's now look at some of the consequences of unemployment that make it a serious problem.

Why Unemployment Is a Problem

Unemployment is a serious economic, social, and personal problem for two main reasons:

- Lost production and incomes
- Lost human capital

Lost Production and Incomes The loss of a job brings a loss of income and production. These losses are devastating for the people who bear them and make unemployment a frightening prospect for everyone. Employment benefits creates a safety net, but it doesn't fully replace lost earnings.

Lost Human Capital Prolonged unemployment permanently damages a person's job prospects. For example, a manager loses his job when his employer downsizes. Short of income, he becomes a taxi driver. After a year in this work, he discovers that he can't compete with new MBA graduates. He eventually gets hired as a manager but in a small firm and at a low wage. He has lost some of his human capital.

The costs of unemployment are spread unequally,

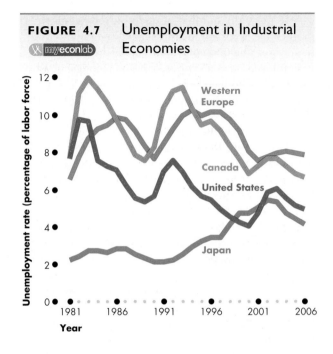

FIGURE 4.7 Unemployment in Industrial Economies

The unemployment rate in the United States has been lower than that in Western Europe and Canada but higher than that in Japan. The cycle in Canadian unemployment is similar to that in the United States. Western European unemployment has a cycle that is out of phase with the U.S. unemployment cycle. Unemployment in Japan has drifted upward since the mid-1990s.

Source of data: International Monetary Fund, *World Economic Outlook*, April 2006, Washington, D.C.

which makes it a highly charged political problem as well as a serious economic problem.

REVIEW QUIZ

1. What is unemployment?
2. What have been the main trends and cycles in the U.S. unemployment rate since 1929?
3. How does unemployment in the United States compare with unemployment in Canada, Western Europe, and Japan?
4. What are the main costs of unemployment that make it a serious problem?

myeconlab Study Plan 4.3

Let's now turn to the third major topic of macroeconomics: inflation and the dollar.

Inflation and the Dollar

What will it really cost you to pay off your student loan? What will your parent's life savings buy when they retire? The answers depend on what happens to prices and the value of the dollar.

We measure the *level* of prices—the **price level**—as the average of the prices that people pay for all the goods and services that they buy. A common measure of the price level is the *Consumer Price Index* (CPI), which is explained in Chapter 6.

We measure the **inflation rate** as the annual percentage change in price level. For example, if the CPI (the price *level*) rises from 200 to 208 in a year, the inflation rate is 4 percent a year.

Inflation occurs when the price level is rising persistently. A one-time jump in the price of gasoline isn't inflation. Inflation is a *persistent* rise in the *average* of all prices.

If the inflation rate is negative, the price *level* is falling and we have **deflation**.

Inflation in the United States

Figure 4.8 shows the U.S. inflation rate from 1960 through 2006. Notice that the inflation rate is always positive—we have not experienced *deflation*. (The last time deflation occurred was during the 1930s.)

During the early 1960s, the inflation rate was between 1 and 2 percent a year. It began to increase during the late 1960s at the time of the Vietnam War. But the largest increases occurred in 1974 and 1980 when the Organization of Petroleum Exporting Countries (OPEC) forced the price of oil up and triggered a period of more broadly rising prices that the Federal Reserve (the Fed) failed to contain. Inflation fell in the early 1980s when Fed Chairman Paul Volcker raised the interest rate and choked off spending.

Inflation was mild through the 1990s until 2002. But after 2002, the inflation rate gradually increased. By 2006, it was above 4 percent a year, a rate that most economists regard as too high and that might force the current Fed Chairman Ben Bernanke to follow Paul Volcker's path and keep raising the interest rate.

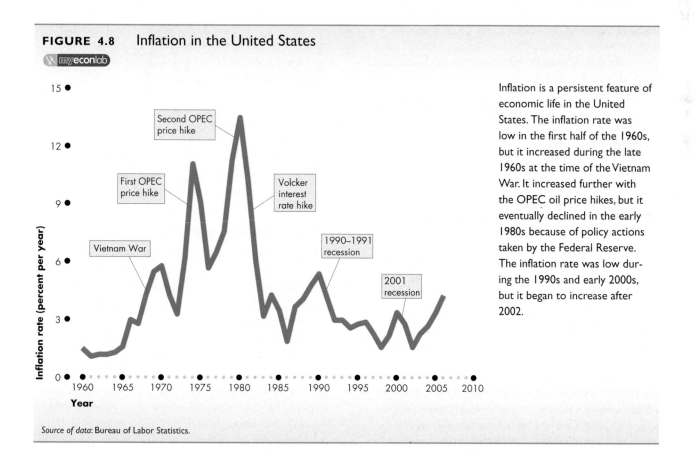

FIGURE 4.8   Inflation in the United States

Inflation is a persistent feature of economic life in the United States. The inflation rate was low in the first half of the 1960s, but it increased during the late 1960s at the time of the Vietnam War. It increased further with the OPEC oil price hikes, but it eventually declined in the early 1980s because of policy actions taken by the Federal Reserve. The inflation rate was low during the 1990s and early 2000s, but it began to increase after 2002.

Source of data: Bureau of Labor Statistics.

Inflation Around the World

Figure 4.9 shows inflation around the world from 1980 to 2005. It also shows the U.S. inflation rate in a broader perspective. Part (a) shows that U.S. inflation has been similar to that of other industrial countries. All industrial countries, including the United States, had falling inflation during the early 1980s, rising inflation during the late 1980s, falling inflation during the 1990s, and low but rising inflation in the 2000s.

Part (b) shows that the average inflation rate of industrial countries has been very low compared with that of the developing countries. Among the developing countries, the most extreme inflation in recent times occurred in Zimbabwe, where its rate in 2006 was 17 percent per *month,* or 1,200 percent per year.

Hyperinflation

Inflation in Zimbabwe today is serious. But even that inflation rate doesn't match the worst that has occurred. The most serious type of inflation is called **hyperinflation**—an inflation rate that exceeds 50 percent a month. At the height of a hyperinflation, workers are often paid twice a day because money loses its value so quickly. As soon as workers are paid, they rush out to spend their wages before the money loses too much value.

Hyperinflation is rare, but several European countries experienced it during the 1920s after World War I and again during the 1940s after World War II. In 1994, the African nation of Zaire had a hyperinflation that peaked at a *monthly* inflation rate of 76 percent, which is 88,000 percent a year! And in Brazil, a cup of coffee that cost 15 cruzeiros in 1980 cost 22 *billion* cruzeiros in 1994.

Why Inflation Is a Problem

Inflation is a problem for several reasons, but the main one is that once it takes hold, its rate is unpredictable. Unpredictable inflation brings serious social and personal problems because it

- Redistributes income and wealth
- Diverts resources from production

Redistributes Income and Wealth Inflation makes the economy behave like a casino in which some people gain and some lose and no one can predict where the gains and losses will fall. Gains and losses occur

FIGURE 4.9   Inflation Around the World

(a) The United States and other industrial countries

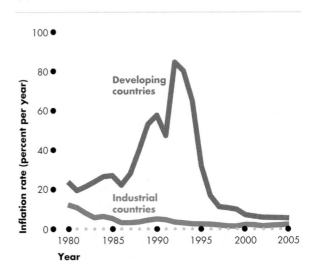

(b) Industrial countries and developing countries

Inflation in the United States is similar to that in the other industrial countries. Compared with the developing countries, the inflation rate in the industrial countries is low.

Source of data: International Monetary Fund, *World Economic Outlook,* 2006.

because of unpredictable changes in the value of money. Money is used as a measuring rod of value in the transactions that we undertake. Borrowers and lenders, workers and employers, all make contracts in terms of money. If the value of money varies unpredictably over time, then the amounts *really* paid and received—the quantities of goods that the money will buy—also fluctuate unpredictably. Measuring value with a measuring rod whose units vary is a bit like trying to measure a piece of cloth with an elastic ruler. The size of the cloth depends on how tightly the ruler is stretched.

Diverts Resources from Production In a period of rapid, unpredictable inflation, resources get diverted from productive activities to forecasting inflation. It becomes more profitable to forecast the inflation rate correctly than to invent a new product. Doctors, lawyers, accountants, farmers—just about everyone—can make themselves better off, not by specializing in the profession for which they have been trained but by spending more of their time dabbling as amateur economists and inflation forecasters and managing their investment portfolios.

From a social perspective, this diversion of talent resulting from inflation is like throwing scarce resources onto the garbage heap. This waste of resources is a cost of inflation.

The Value of the Dollar Abroad

When you spend money in the United States, you pay more when the prices in the stores rise. Inflation lowers the value of the money in your wallet and bank account. But suppose you take a vacation in Canada, Mexico, Europe, Asia, or Australia. How much will your dollar buy in these parts of the world?

The answer depends partly on inflation in these places. But it also depends on the **exchange rate**—the value of the U.S. dollar in terms of other currencies. An example of an exchange rate is the number of Canadian dollars that 1 U.S dollar will buy. The exchange rate bounces around from day to day and from year to year.

The Fluctuating Dollar In July 2006, 1 U.S. dollar would buy 1.14 Canadian dollars. But five years earlier, in July 2001, the same 1 U.S. dollar would have bought 1.51 Canadian dollars. So the U.S. dollar *depreciated* against the Canadian dollar. The U.S. dollar was worth less in Canada in 2006 than in 2001. And a ski vacation in Canada that cost $300 (U.S.) in 2001 would cost $400 in 2006 even if Canada had no inflation.

Since 2001, the U.S. dollar has depreciated against the currencies of all the major countries. It fell from 1.18 to 0.80 euros; from 71 to 54 British pence; from 1.94 to 1.34 Australian dollars, and from 124 to

TABLE 4.1	The Value of the U.S. Dollar in Other Currencies	
Currency	Exchange rate in July 2001	Exchange rate in July 2006
	(Units of foreign currency per U.S. dollar)	Percentage change
European euro	1.18	0.80	−32
Australian dollar	1.94	1.34	−31
Canadian dollar	1.51	1.14	−25
U.K. pound	0.71	0.54	−24
Japanese yen	124	117	−6
Mexican peso	9.00	10.90	21

Source of data: Economic Report of the President, 2006.

117 yen. Table 4.1 summarizes these numbers and shows the percentage fall in the value of the dollar.

But the U.S. dollar didn't fall in value against all currencies. You can see in Table 4.1 that against the Mexican peso, the dollar rose in value—it *appreciated*. If you took a vacation in Cancun in 2001 that cost $300, with no change in Mexican prices, that vacation would cost only $250 in 2006.

Because there are many different currencies and exchange rates, we track the value of the dollar against an average of currencies. Figure 4.10 shows this value as an average of the major currencies, which include the euro, British pound, Japanese yen, Canadian dollar, and Australian dollar. In the figure, this index equals 100 in 1985.

You can see that the dollar depreciated sharply over the 10 years from 1985 to 1995. It then *appreciated*—rose in value—until 2001 before depreciating again during the 2000s.

Why the Exchange Rate Matters

When the U.S. dollar depreciates, other things remaining the same, we must pay more for the things that we import. And when the dollar appreciates, we pay less for the things that we import. So a lower dollar hurts consumers; a higher dollar benefits them.

But what is good for the consumer can make life tough for the producer. A higher dollar makes it

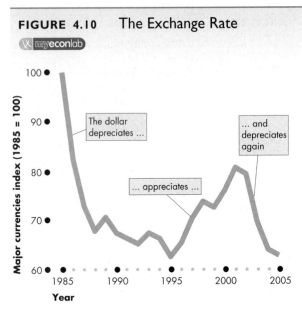

FIGURE 4.10   The Exchange Rate

The value of the U.S. dollar fluctuates against other major currencies on the foreign exchange market. The U.S. dollar depreciated between 1985 and 1995 and after 2001. It appreciated between 1995 and 2001.

Source of data: Economic Report of the President, 2006.

harder for a U.S. producer to compete in foreign markets and a lower dollar makes it easier to compete.

Chapter 10 explores these effects of the exchange rate more fully and explains what determines the exchange rate.

REVIEW QUIZ

1 What is inflation and how does it influence the value of money?

2 How is inflation measured?

3 What has been the U.S. inflation record since 1960?

4 How does inflation in the United States compare with inflation in other industrial countries and in developing countries?

5 Why is inflation a problem?

6 What has happened to the U.S. dollar exchange rate over the past 20 years?

Study Plan 4.4

Let's now examine the federal government's and the nation's surpluses, deficits, and debts.

Surpluses, Deficits, and Debts

In 1998, for the first time in almost 30 years, the U.S. federal government had a budget surplus. But the surplus was short-lived. By 2002, the budget was again in deficit. The United States also has a large and growing international deficit.

What happens when a government or a nation spends more than it receives and has a deficit? Do governments and nations face the problem that you and I would face if we spent more than we earned? Do governments and nations run out of funds? Let's look at these questions.

Government Budget Balance

If a government collects more in taxes than it spends, it has a surplus—a **government budget surplus**. If a government spends more than it collects in taxes, it has a deficit—a **government budget deficit**.

Figure 4.11(a) shows the federal government budget surplus and deficit measured as a percentage of GDP from 1960 to 2005.

We measure the budget surplus or deficit as a percentage of GDP so that we can compare the surplus or deficit in one year with that in another year. You can think of this measure as the number of cents of surplus or deficit per dollar of income earned by an average person.

The government had a budget surplus in the 1960s and from 1998 to 2001. In every year from 1970 through 1997, the government had a deficit that fluctuated and swelled during recessions. From 1980 through 1995, the deficit was never less than 2 percent of GDP.

After 1992 the government budget deficit shrank, and in 1998, a budget surplus emerged. In 2000, the government budget surplus was a bit more than 2 percent of GDP. In 2001, the government budget surplus turned into a budget deficit again.

International Deficit

When we import goods and services from the rest of the world, we make payments to foreigners. When we export goods and services to the rest of the world, we receive payments from foreigners. If our imports exceed our exports, we have an international deficit.

Figure 4.11(b) shows the history of the U.S. international balance from 1960 to 2005. The figure

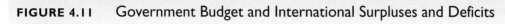

FIGURE 4.11   Government Budget and International Surpluses and Deficits

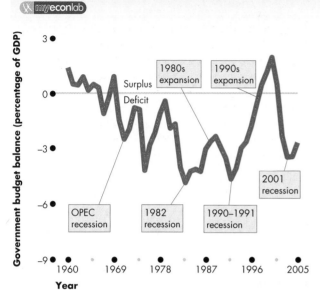

(a) U.S. government budget deficit

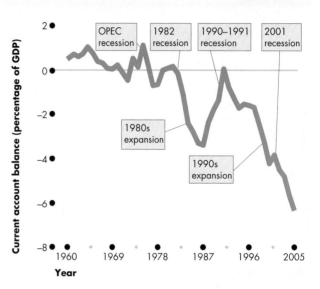

(b) U.S. international deficit

In part (a), the federal government budget deficit as a percentage of GDP increased during recessions and shrank during the expansions. A budget surplus emerged in 1998, but in 2001, the budget deficit reappeared.

In part (b), the U.S. current account shows the balance

of U.S exports minus U.S imports. Until the early 1980s, the U.S. current account was generally in surplus. During the 1980s expansion, a large current account deficit emerged. It almost disappeared during the 1990–1991 recession, but it reappeared during the 1990s expansion.

Source of data: The U.S. federal government's budget and *Economic Report of the President*, 2006.

---

shows the balance on the **current account**, which includes U.S. exports minus U.S. imports but also takes into account interest payments paid to and received from the rest of the world. (Again, to compare one year with another, the figure shows the current account as a percentage of GDP.)

The U.S. current account has fluctuated between a surplus of 1 percent of GDP and a deficit of more than 6 percent of GDP. But since 1980, the current account has been in deficit. And since 1991, the deficit has grown. By 2005, the current account deficit had reached 6.3 percent of GDP.

Deficits Bring Debts

A deficit is the amount by which spending exceeds income during a given period. Suppose that you charge everything that you buy to your credit card and when you receive your monthly credit card statement, you pay only the minimum balance. You have a personal budget deficit.

A *debt* is an amount that is owed. It is the total of all the past deficits minus the total of all past surpluses. The total amount outstanding on your credit card account is a debt. It is the amount that you owe to the issuer of the card.

What happens to your credit card balance—your debt—if you charge more than you pay off? Your debt grows.

The government and the nation face the same problem that you face. When a government or a nation has a deficit, its debt grows.

The government's debt is called the **national debt**. It is the amount that the government owes to all the people who have made loans to cover the government deficits. Today, your share of the U.S. national debt is approaching $30,000!

Figure 4.12(a) shows the history of U.S. national debt since 1945, the year in which World War II ended. In that year, the national debt exceeded 100 percent of GDP. Budget surpluses and economic growth lowered the ratio of the national debt to GDP

FIGURE 4.12   Government and International Debts

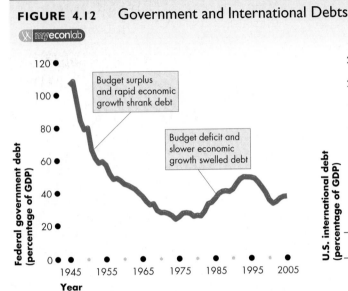

(a) U.S. government debt

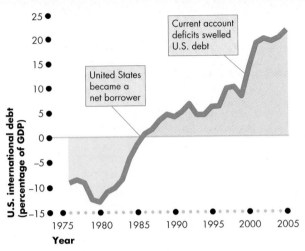

(b) U.S. international debt

In part (a), budget surpluses and economic growth decreased the government debt from more than 100 percent of GDP in 1945 to 24 percent in 1974. Then budget deficits increased government debt until 1995. For a few years, government

debt fell, but it started to rise again in 2003. Part (b) shows that the United States was a net lender until 1986 when it became a net borrower. Since 1986, current account deficits have increased U.S. international debt.

Source of data: Economic Report of the President, 2006.

---

to 24 percent in 1974. But through the 1970s and 1980s, budget deficits brought a rising level of debt. The debt to GDP ratio fell for a few years in the late 1990s and early 2000s but then started to rise again.

Figure 4.12(b) shows the U.S. international debt. This debt is the amount that U.S. residents owe to foreigners. When U.S international debt is negative, foreigners owe U.S. residents. The United States became a net borrower from the rest of the world in 1986. Since then, the U.S. current account deficit has swelled the international debt.

Why Deficits and Debts Matter

What happens when a government cannot cover its spending with taxes, or when a country buys more from other countries than it sells to them?

Whether borrowing and paying out huge amounts of interest is a good idea depends on what the borrowed funds are used for. If you borrow to finance a vacation, you must eventually tighten your belt, cut spending, and repay your debt as well as pay interest on the debt.

But if you borrow to invest in a business that earns a large profit, you might be able to repay your debt and pay the interest on it while continuing to increase your spending. It is the same with a government and a nation. A government or a nation that borrows to increase its consumption might be heading for trouble later. But a government or a nation that borrows to buy assets that earn a profit might be making a sound investment.

You will learn more about the government budget in Chapter 14 and about the international current account deficit in Chapter 10.

Macroeconomic Policy Challenges and Tools

Now that you have reviewed the performance of the economy, you've seen that economic growth has slowed, we always have some unemployment and in a recession its rate is high, inflation persistently erodes the value of our money, and government and international deficits persistently swell our debts. You are perhaps wondering whether something can be done to improve our macroeconomic performance.

Economists think that much can be done, but they don't agree on the most effective approach. Their views fall into two broad schools: classical and Keynesian.

The Classical and Keynesian Views

The *classical* view, first stated in Adam Smith's *Wealth of Nations* published in 1776, is that the only economic role for government is to enforce property rights. The economy behaves best, in the classical view, if the government leaves people free to pursue their own self-interest. Attempts by government to improve macroeconomic performance will not succeed.

The *Keynesian* view, which originated in Keynes' *General Theory of Employment, Interest, and Money* published in 1936 and was inspired by the Great Depression, is that the economy behaves badly if left alone and that government action is needed to achieve and maintain full employment.

We'll explore these views in greater detail at a number of points in the chapters that follow.

Policy Challenges and Tools

Today, the five widely agreed challenges for macroeconomic policy are to

1. Boost economic growth
2. Keep inflation low
3. Stabilize the business cycle
4. Reduce unemployment
5. Reduce government and international deficits

But how can we do all these things? What are the tools available to pursue the macroeconomic policy challenges? Macroeconomic policy tools are divided into two broad categories:

- Fiscal policy
- Monetary policy

Fiscal Policy Making changes in tax rates and in government spending programs is called **fiscal policy**. This range of actions is under the control of the federal government. Fiscal policy can be used to try to boost long-term growth by creating incentives that encourage saving, investment, and technological change. Fiscal policy can also be used to try to smooth out the business cycle. When the economy is in a recession, the government might cut taxes or increase its spending. Conversely, when the economy is in a rapid expansion, the government might increase taxes or cut its spending in an attempt to slow real GDP growth and prevent inflation from increasing. Fiscal policy is discussed in Chapter 14.

Monetary Policy Changing interest rates and changing the amount of money in the economy is called **monetary policy**. These actions are under the control of the Fed. The principal aim of monetary policy is to keep inflation in check. To achieve this objective, the Fed prevents the quantity of money from expanding too rapidly. Monetary policy can also be used to smooth the business cycle. When the economy is in recession, the Fed might lower interest rates and inject money into the economy. And when the economy is in a rapid expansion, the Fed might increase interest rates in an attempt to slow real GDP growth and prevent inflation from increasing. We study the Fed in Chapter 9 and monetary policy in Chapter 15.

REVIEW QUIZ

1 What are the main challenges of macroeconomic policy?
2 List the main macroeconomic policy tools.
3 Distinguish between fiscal policy and monetary policy.

myeconlab Study Plan 4.6

◆ In the following chapters, you will learn about the causes of economic growth, business cycles, unemployment, inflation, and deficits as well as the policy choices and challenges that the government and the Fed face. But first, *Reading Between the Lines* on pp. 106–107 gives you a close-up view of the 2006 expansion in the U.S. economy.

The 2006 Expansion

http://www.latimes.com

U.S. Economic Growth Surges in 1st Quarter

April 29, 2006

The U.S. economy grew briskly in the first three months of this year, the government reported Friday, but new evidence suggested that ordinary workers were still not keeping pace with inflation.

Shaking off the effects of Hurricane Katrina, the economy grew at an annual inflation-adjusted rate of 4.8% in the first quarter, the Commerce Department said. The burst offset a meager 1.7% growth rate in the last three months of last year after the hurricane struck the Gulf Coast.

Only once in George W. Bush's presidency—when the economy grew at a 7.2% rate in the third quarter of 2003—has economic growth been more robust than in the first quarter.

"The economy was firing on all cylinders," said Mark Zandi, chief economist for Moody's Economy.com. Consumer spending and business investment were strong, and U.S. exports rose smartly, Zandi said. . . .

Analysts generally agree that the economy can't sustain for long the first quarter's torrid pace.

Brian Bethune, U.S. economist for Global Insight, said the average growth rate of the last six months—3.25%—represented the economy's current potential of "solid growth but not over the top." . . .

Essence of the Story

▶ Hurricane Katrina slowed the real GDP growth rate to a 1.7 percent annual rate during the fourth quarter of 2005.

▶ The real GDP growth rate surged during the first quarter of 2006 to a 4.8 percent annual rate.

▶ Real GDP has grown faster only once during George W. Bush's presidency: a 7.2 percent annual rate during the third quarter of 2003.

▶ Consumer spending, business investment, and exports all contributed to the faster growth.

▶ A U.S. economist says that the real GDP growth rate will slow to a sustainable rate of 3.25 percent per year.

▶ The final estimate of the real GDP growth rate during the first quarter of 2006 was 5.6 percent, not 4.8 percent as reported in the news article.

▶ This growth rate is expressed as a percentage *annual* growth rate.

▶ Real GDP actually grew by $153 billion, which is 1.4 percent of its level during the fourth quarter of 2005.

▶ How does the first-quarter growth rate compare with those for earlier quarters?

▶ The figure provides the answer.

▶ During 2001, the U.S. economy was in recession and real GDP shrank—the real GDP growth rate was negative.

▶ From the fourth quarter of 2001 when the expansion began through the fourth quarter of 2005, real GDP grew at an average annual rate of 2.8 percent.

▶ During one quarter in 2003, real GDP grew by an exceptional 7.2 percent annual rate.

▶ So the growth rate in the fourth quarter of 2006 was not the fastest on record, but it was faster than the average of the previous five years.

▶ The black line in the figure is potential GDP.

▶ Potential GDP grows at an annual average rate of a bit more than 3 percent.

▶ Until the third quarter of 2003, real GDP was growing below its potential growth rate and the Okun gap—the gap between actual and potential GDP—widened.

▶ An expansion that widens the Okun gap, or even leaves it constant, doesn't create enough new jobs to lower the unemployment rate. Such an episode is called a *jobless recovery*.

▶ The accumulated value of lost output—the accumulated Okun gap—during 2002 and 2003 was about $1 trillion, or 10 percent of annual real GDP.

▶ Can a growth rate of around 5.6 percent a year be maintained over a number of years? Or will growth become more subdued, as predicted by economist Brian Bethune in the news article?

▶ The figure shows a reason why Brian Bethune is almost certainly correct.

▶ In the long run, real GDP growth cannot exceed the growth rate of potential GDP.

▶ A growth rate of 4.8 percent for just two more quarters would take real GDP above potential GDP.

▶ Eventually, real GDP growth must slow to average the growth rate of potential GDP.

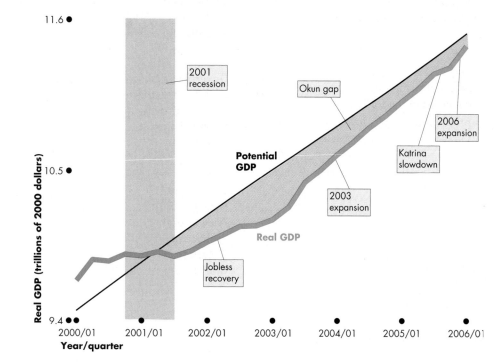

Figure 1 The 2001 recession and jobless recovery

SUMMARY

Key Points

Origins and Issues of Macroeconomics (p. 90)

- Macroeconomics studies economic growth and fluctuations, unemployment, inflation, the exchange rate, and surpluses, deficits, and debts.

Economic Growth and Fluctuations (pp. 91–96)

- Economic growth is the expansion of potential GDP. Real GDP fluctuates around potential GDP in a business cycle.
- A slowdown in productivity growth is more costly than business cycle recessions.
- Economic growth increases future consumption but lowers current consumption.

Jobs and Unemployment (pp. 96–98)

- The U.S. economy creates millions of jobs every year, but unemployment persists.
- Unemployment increases during a recession and decreases during an expansion.
- The U.S. unemployment rate is lower than that in Canada and Europe but higher than that in Japan.
- Unemployment can permanently damage a person's job prospects.

Inflation and the Dollar (pp. 99–102)

- Inflation, a process of rising prices, is measured by the percentage change in the CPI.
- Inflation is a problem because it lowers the value of money and makes money less useful as a measuring rod of value.
- The dollar fluctuates on the foreign exchange market and has depreciated in recent years.

Surpluses, Deficits, and Debts (pp. 102–104)

- When the government collects more in taxes than it spends, it has a budget surplus. When the government spends more than it collects in taxes, it has a budget deficit.
- When imports exceed exports, a nation has an international deficit.
- Deficits are financed by borrowing, which creates debts.

Macroeconomic Policy Challenges and Tools (p. 105)

- The macroeconomic policy challenge is to use fiscal policy and monetary policy to boost long-term growth, keep inflation low, stabilize the business cycle, reduce unemployment, and reduce government and international large deficits.

Key Figures

Key Terms

PROBLEMS

1. Use the Data Grapher to answer the following questions. In which country in 2005 was
   a. The growth rate of real GDP highest: Canada, Japan, or the United States?
   b. The unemployment rate highest: Canada, Japan, the United Kingdom, or the United States?

2. Use the Data Grapher to answer the following questions. In which country in 2005 was
   a. The inflation rate lowest: Canada, the United Kingdom, Japan, or the United States?
   b. The government budget surplus (as a percentage of GDP) smallest: Canada, the United Kingdom, or the United States?

3. The figure shows the real GDP growth rates in India and Pakistan from 1989 to 1996.

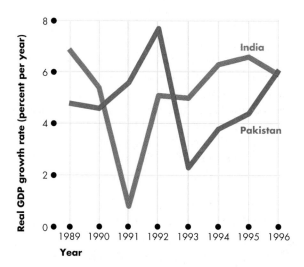

In which years did economic growth in
   a. India increase? And in which year was growth the fastest?
   b. Pakistan decrease? And in which year was growth the slowest?
   c. Compare the paths of economic growth in India and Pakistan during this period.

4. The figure shows the growth rate of real GDP per person in Australia and Japan from 1989 to 1996.

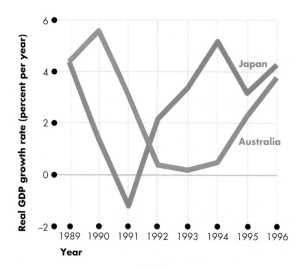

In which years did economic growth in
   a. Australia increase? And in which year was growth the fastest?
   b. Japan decrease? And in which year was growth the slowest?
   c. Compare the paths of economic growth in Australia and Japan during this period.

5. The figure shows real GDP in Germany from the first quarter of 1991 to the fourth quarter of 1994.

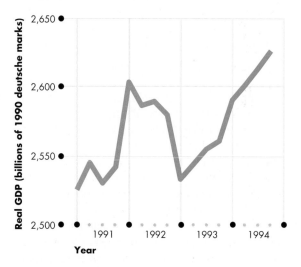

   a. How many recessions did Germany experience during this period?
   b. In which quarters, if any, did Germany experience a business cycle peak?
   c. In which quarters, if any, did Germany experience a business cycle trough?
   d. In which quarters, if any, did Germany experience an expansion?

6. Use the Data Grapher to answer the following questions. Which country, in 2002, had
   a. The largest budget deficit: Canada, Japan, the United Kingdom, or the United States?
   b. A current account deficit: Canada, Japan, Germany, or the United States?
7. Use the Data Grapher to make a scatter diagram of the inflation rate and the unemployment rate in the United States.
   a. Describe the relationship.
   b. Do you think that low unemployment brings an increase in the inflation rate?
8. Use the Data Grapher to make a scatter diagram of the government budget deficit as a percentage of GDP and the unemployment rate in the United States.
   a. Describe the relationship.
   b. Do you think that low unemployment brings a decrease in the budget deficit?

CRITICAL THINKING

1. Study *Reading Between the Lines* on pp. 106–107 and then answer the following questions:
   a. When did the most recent recession end and expansion begin?
   b. Why was the expansion in 2002 and 2003 called a jobless recovery?
   c. Why do you expect the growth rate of the first quarter of 2006 to be temporary?
   d. Can you think of reasons why the growth rate of potential GDP might have increased?
   e. Can you think of reasons why the growth rate during the first quarter of 2006 was faster than normal?

2. **Suddenly Rich, Poor Old Ireland Seems Bewildered**
   It was not so long ago, . . . that Ireland was a threadbare nation, barely relevant in European affairs. . . . In a little more than a decade, the so-called Celtic Tiger was transformed from one of the poorest countries in Western Europe to one of the richest in the world. Its gross domestic product per person, not quite 70 percent of the European Union average in 1987, sprang to 136 percent of the union's average by 2003, while the unemployment rate sank to 4 percent from 17 percent.
   The New York Times, February 2, 2005
   a. In what phase of the business cycle was Ireland in 2005?

   b. Is there a relationship between the phase of the business cycle and unemployment?
   c. Compare the change in unemployment in Ireland with that in the United States over the last decade. Give some reasons for the differences in unemployment rates between the two countries.

WEB ACTIVITIES

myeconlab **Links to Web sites**

1. Visit the Bureau of Economic Analysis and Bureau of Labor Statistics and obtain the latest data on real GDP, unemployment, and inflation.
   a. Update Figs. 4.2, 4.6, and 4.8.
   b. What dangers do you think the U.S. economy faces today?
2. Visit the Bureau of Labor Statistics and obtain data on unemployment in your state.
   a. Compare unemployment in your home state with that in the United States as a whole.
   b. Why do you think your state might have a higher or a lower unemployment rate than the U.S. average?
3. Visit the Bureau of Labor Statistics and obtain data on the Consumer Price Index for the capital city in your home state.
   a. Compare the inflation rate in your home state with that in the United States as a whole.
   b. Compare the inflation rate in your home state with that of the capital cities in neighboring states.
4. Visit the Board of Governors of the Federal Reserve and look at the most recent *Beige Book*. Read the summary and the section on the part of the country in which you live.
   a. Write a brief summary of the Fed's report.
   b. Compare your own region with the United States as a whole.
   c. Does the *Beige Book* confirm or contradict what you discovered in your answers to questions 1, 2, and 3 above?
5. Visit the Board of Governors of the Federal Reserve and look at the most recent *Monetary Policy Report to the Congress*.
   a. Write a brief summary of the report.
   b. Does the *Report to Congress* confirm or contradict what you discovered in your answers to questions 1, 2, and 3 above? Explain any contradictions that you find.

CHAPTER 5

Measuring GDP and Economic Growth

An Economic Barometer

Will our economy keep expanding through 2007 and

2008? If so, will the expansion be rapid or slow? Or are we going to slip into

recession again? Many U.S. corporations wanted to know the answers to these questions at the beginning of 2006. Google wanted to know whether to expand its server network and introduce new services or delay for a while. Amazon.com wanted to know whether to increase its warehousing facilities. To assess the state of the economy and to make big decisions about business expansion, firms such as Google and Amazon use forecasts of GDP. What exactly is GDP and what does it tell us about the state of the economy?

To reveal the rate of growth or shrinkage of GDP, we must remove the effects of inflation and assess how *real* GDP is changing. How do we remove the inflation component of GDP to reveal real GDP?

Some countries are rich while others are poor. How do we compare economic well-being in one country with that in another? How can we make international comparisons of GDP?

◈ In this chapter, you will find out how economic statisticians at the Bureau of Economic Analysis measure GDP, real GDP, and the economic growth rate. You will also learn about the uses and the limitations of these measures. In *Reading Between the Lines* at the end of the chapter, we'll look at real GDP growth during the business cycle expansion that began in 2002 and was still going in 2006.

After studying this chapter, you will be able to

▶ Define GDP and use the circular flow model to explain why GDP equals aggregate expenditure and aggregate income

▶ Explain the two methods used by the Bureau of Economic Analysis to measure U.S. GDP

▶ Explain how the Bureau of Economic Analysis measures *real* GDP and the GDP deflator to separate economic growth and inflation

▶ Explain the uses and the limitations of real GDP

Gross Domestic Product

What exactly is GDP, how is it calculated, what does it mean, and why do we care about it? You are going to discover the answers to these questions in this chapter. First, what *is* GDP?

GDP Defined

GDP, or **gross domestic product**, is the market value of all the final goods and services produced within a country in a given time period. This definition has four parts:

- Market value
- Final goods and services
- Produced within a country
- In a given time period

We'll examine each in turn.

Market Value To measure total production, we must add together the production of apples and oranges, computers and popcorn. Just counting the items doesn't get us very far. For example, which is the greater total production: 100 apples and 50 oranges or 50 apples and 100 oranges?

GDP answers this question by valuing items at their *market values*—the prices at which each item is traded in markets. If the price of an apple is 10 cents, the market value of 50 apples is $5. If the price of an orange is 20 cents, the market value of 100 oranges is $20. By using market prices to value production, we can add the apples and oranges together. The market value of 50 apples and 100 oranges is $5 plus $20, or $25.

Final Goods and Services To calculate GDP, we value the *final goods and services* produced. A **final good** (or service) is an item that is bought by its final user during a specified time period. It contrasts with an **intermediate good** (or service), which is an item that is produced by one firm, bought by another firm, and used as a component of a final good or service.

For example, a Ford SUV is a final good, but a Firestone tire on the SUV is an intermediate good. A Dell computer is a final good, but an Intel Pentium chip inside it is an intermediate good.

If we were to add the value of intermediate goods and services produced to the value of final goods and services, we would count the same thing many times—a problem called *double counting*. The value of an SUV already includes the value of the tires, and the value of a Dell PC already includes the value of the Pentium chip inside it.

Some goods can be an intermediate good in some situations and a final good in other situations. For example, the ice cream that you buy on a hot summer day is a final good, but the ice cream that a restaurant buys and uses to make sundaes is an intermediate good. The sundae is the final good. So whether a good is an intermediate good or a final good depends on what it is used for, not what it is.

Some items that people buy are neither final goods nor intermediate goods. Examples of such items include financial assets—stocks and bonds—and secondhand goods—used cars or existing homes.

These items are not part of GDP. But a used car and an existing home were part of GDP in the year in which they were produced.

Produced Within a Country Only goods and services that are produced *within a country* count as part of that country's GDP. Nike Corporation, a U.S. firm, produces sneakers in Vietnam, and the market value of those shoes is part of Vietnam's GDP, not part of U.S. GDP. Toyota, a Japanese firm, produces automobiles in Georgetown, Kentucky, and the value of this production is part of U.S. GDP, not part of Japan's GDP.

In a Given Time Period GDP measures the value of production *in a given time period*—normally either a quarter of a year—called the quarterly GDP data—or a year—called the annual GDP data.

GDP measures not only the value of total production but also total income and total expenditure. The equality between the value of total production and total income is important because it shows the direct link between productivity and living standards. Our standard of living rises when our incomes rise and we can afford to buy more goods and services. But we must produce more goods and services if we are to be able to buy more goods and services.

Rising incomes and a rising value of production go together. They are two aspects of the same phenomenon: increasing productivity. To see why, we study the circular flow of expenditure and income.

GDP and the Circular Flow of Expenditure and Income

Figure 5.1 illustrates the circular flow of expenditure and income. The economy consists of households, firms, governments, and the rest of the world (the dark blue diamonds), which trade in factor markets, goods (and services) markets, and financial markets. We focus first on households and firms.

Households and Firms Households sell and firms buy the services of labor, capital, and land in factor markets. For these factor services, firms pay income to households: wages for labor services, interest for the use of capital, and rent for the use of land. A fourth factor of production, entrepreneurship, receives profit.

Firms' retained earnings—profits that are not distributed to households—are part of the household sector's income. You can think of retained earnings as

being income that households save and lend back to firms. Figure 5.1 shows the total income—*aggregate income*—received by households, including retained earnings, by the blue dots labeled *Y*.

Firms sell and households buy consumer goods and services—such as inline skates and haircuts—in the goods market. The total payment for these goods and services is **consumption expenditure**, shown by the red dots labeled *C*.

Firms buy and sell new capital equipment—such as computer systems, airplanes, trucks, and assembly line equipment—in the goods market. Some of what firms produce is not sold but is added to inventory. For example, if GM produces 1,000 cars and sells 950 of them, the other 50 cars remain in GM's inventory of unsold cars, which increases by 50 cars. When a firm adds unsold output to inventory, we can think of the firm as buying goods from itself. The

FIGURE 5.1 The Circular Flow of Expenditure and Income

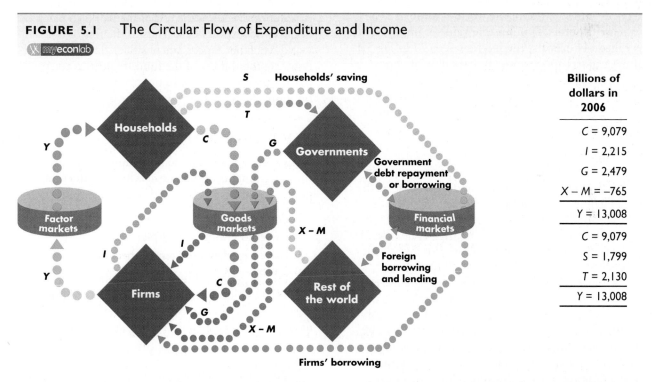

Billions of dollars in 2006
C = 9,079
I = 2,215
G = 2,479
X – M = –765
Y = 13,008
C = 9,079
S = 1,799
T = 2,130
Y = 13,008

In the circular flow of expenditure and income, households make consumption expenditures (*C*); firms make investment expenditures (*I*); governments buy goods and services (*G*); and the rest of the world buys net exports (*X* – *M*)—(the red flows). Households receive income (*Y*) from firms —(the blue flow).

Aggregate income (the blue flow) equals aggregate expenditure (the red flows). Households use their income to consume, (*C*), save (*S*), and pay net taxes (*T*). Firms borrow to finance their investment, and governments and the rest of the world borrow to finance their deficits or lend their surpluses (the green flows).

Source of data: U.S. Department of Commerce, Bureau of Economic Analysis. (The data are for the first quarter of 2006 annual rate.)

purchase of new plant, equipment, and buildings and the additions to inventories are **investment**, shown by the red dots labeled *I*.

Governments Governments buy goods and services from firms. The government expenditure on goods and services is called **government expenditure**. In Fig. 5.1, government expenditure is shown as the red flow *G*. Governments use taxes to pay for their expenditure. The green dots labeled *T* show taxes as net taxes. **Net taxes** are equal to taxes paid to governments minus transfer payments received from governments and minus interest payments on the governments' debt. *Transfer payments* are cash transfers from governments to households and firms such as social security benefits, unemployment compensation, and subsidies.

Rest of the World Firms sell goods and services to the rest of the world—**exports**—and buy goods and services from the rest of the world—**imports**. The value of exports (*X*) minus the value of imports (*M*) is called net exports, the red flow *X* − *M* in Fig 5.1. If net exports are positive, the net flow of goods and services is from U.S. firms to the rest of the world. If net exports are negative, the net flow of goods and services is from the rest of the world to U.S. firms.

GDP Equals Expenditure Equals Income Gross domestic product can be measured in two ways: By the total expenditure on goods and services or by the total income earned producing goods and services.

The total expenditure—*aggregate expenditure*—is the sum of the red flows in Fig. 5.1. Aggregate expenditure equals consumption expenditure plus investment plus government expenditure plus net exports.

Aggregate income earned producing goods and services is equal to the total amount paid for the factors of production used—wages, interest, rent, and profit. This amount is shown by the blue flow in Fig. 5.1. Because firms pay out as incomes (including retained profits) everything they receive from the sale of their output, income (the blue flow) equals expenditure (the sum of the red flows). That is,

$$Y = C + I + G + X - M.$$

The table in Fig. 5.1 shows the numbers for 2006. You can see that the sum of the expenditures is $13,008 billion, which also equals aggregate income.

Because aggregate expenditure equals aggregate

income, these two methods of measuring GDP give the same answer. So

GDP equals aggregate expenditure and equals aggregate income.

The circular flow model is the foundation on which the national economic accounts are built.

Financial Flows

The circular flow model also enables us to see the connection between the expenditure and income flows and flows through the financial markets that finance deficits and pay for investment. These flows are shown in green in Fig. 5.1. Household **saving** (*S*) is the amount that households have left after they have paid their taxes and bought their consumer goods and services. Government borrowing finances a government budget deficit. (Government lending arises when the government has a budget surplus.) A nation borrows from the rest of the world to pay for negative net exports (and lends to the rest of the world when net exports are positive). These financial flows are the sources of the funds that firms use to pay for their investment in new capital. Let's look a bit more closely at how investment is financed.

How Investment Is Financed

Investment adds to the stock of capital and is one of the determinants of the rate at which production grows. Investment is financed from three sources:

1. Private saving
2. Government budget surplus
3. Borrowing from the rest of the world

Private saving is the green flow labeled *S* in Fig. 5.1. Households' income is spent on consumption, saved, or paid in taxes. So income is equal to the sum of consumption expenditure, saving, and taxes:

$$Y = C + S + T.$$

But you've seen that *Y* also equals the sum of the components of aggregate expenditure:

$$Y = C + I + G + X - M.$$

By using these two equations, you can see that

$$I + G + X - M = S + T.$$

Now subtract *G* and *X* from both sides of the last

equation and add M to both sides to obtain

$$I = S + (T - G) + (M - X).$$

In this equation, $(T - G)$ is the government budget surplus and $(M - X)$ is borrowing from the rest of the world. If net taxes (T) exceed government expenditure (G), the government budget surplus contributes toward paying for investment. But if net taxes are less than government expenditure, the government budget deficit must be financed with funds that could otherwise have financed investment.

If U.S. imports (M) exceed U.S. exports (X), we borrow an amount equal to $(M - X)$ from the rest of the world. So part of the rest of the world's saving finances investment in the United States. If we export more than we import, we lend an amount equal to $(X - M)$ to the rest of the world. So part of U.S. saving finances investment in other countries.

The sum of private saving, S, and government saving, $(T - G)$, is called **national saving**. So national saving and foreign borrowing finance investment.

In 2006, investment of $2,270 billion and a government deficit (federal, state, and local combined) of $313 billion were financed by private saving of $1,799 billion and borrowing from the rest of the world of $784 billion.

Gross and Net Domestic Product

What does the "gross" in GDP mean? *Gross* means before the depreciation of capital. The opposite of gross is net, which means after the depreciation of capital. To understand the depreciation of capital and how it affects aggregate expenditure and income, we need to distinguish between flows and stocks.

Flows and Stocks in Macroeconomics A *flow* is a quantity per unit of time. The water that is running from an open faucet into a bathtub is a flow. So are the number of CDs that you buy during a month and the amount of income that you earn during a month. GDP is a flow—the value of the goods and services produced in a country *during a given time period*. Saving and investment are also flows.

A *stock* is a quantity that exists at a point in time. The water in a bathtub is a stock. So are the number of CDs that you own and the amount of money in your savings account today. The two key stocks in macroeconomics are wealth and capital. And the flows of saving and investment change these stocks.

Wealth and Saving **Wealth** is the value of all the things that people own. What people own, a stock, is related to what they earn, a flow. People earn an income, which is the amount they receive during a given time period from supplying the services of factors of production. Income that is left after paying taxes is either spent on consumption goods and services or saved. *Consumption expenditure* is the amount spent on consumption goods and services. *Saving* is the amount of income remaining after paying net taxes and making consumption expenditures. So saving adds to wealth.

For example, suppose that at the end of the school year, you have $250 in a savings account and some textbooks that are worth $300. That's all you own. Your wealth is $550. Suppose that you take a summer job and earn an income after taxes of $5,000. You are extremely careful and spend only $1,000 through the summer on consumption goods and services. At the end of the summer, when school starts again, you have $4,250 in your savings account. Your wealth is now $4,550. Your wealth has increased by $4,000, which equals your saving of $4,000. Your saving of $4,000 equals your income of $5,000 minus your consumption expenditure of $1,000.

National wealth and national saving work just like this personal example. The wealth of a nation at the start of a year equals its wealth at the start of the previous year plus its saving during the year. So a nation's saving equals its income minus its consumption expenditure.

Capital and Investment *Capital* is the plant, equipment, buildings, and inventories of raw materials and semifinished goods that are used to produce other goods and services. The amount of capital in the economy exerts a big influence on GDP.

Two flows change the stock of capital: investment and depreciation. *Investment*, the purchase of new capital, increases the stock of capital. (Investment includes additions to inventories.) **Depreciation** is the decrease in the stock of capital that results from wear and tear and obsolescence. Another name for depreciation is *capital consumption*. The total amount spent on purchases of new capital and on replacing depreciated capital is called **gross investment**. The amount by which the stock of capital increases is called **net investment**. Net investment equals gross investment minus depreciation.

Figure 5.2 illustrates these concepts. On January 1, 2006, Tom's CDs, Inc. had 3 machines. This quantity was its initial capital. During 2006, Tom's scrapped an older machine. This quantity is its depreciation. After depreciation, Tom's stock of capital was down to 2 machines. But also during 2006, Tom's bought 2 new machines. This amount is its gross investment. By December 31, 2006, Tom's CDs had 4 machines, so its capital had increased by 1 machine. This amount is Tom's net investment. Tom's net investment equals its gross investment (the purchase of 2 new machines) minus its depreciation (1 machine scrapped).

The example of Tom's CDs can be applied to the economy as a whole. The nation's capital stock decreases because capital depreciates and increases because of gross investment. The change in the nation's capital stock from one year to the next equals its net investment.

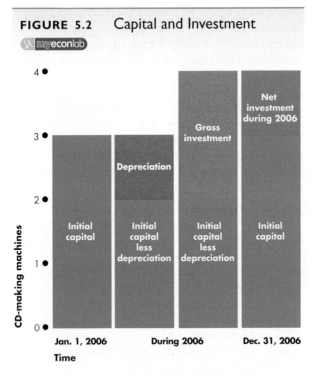

FIGURE 5.2   Capital and Investment

Tom's CDs has a capital stock at the end of 2006 that equals its capital stock at the beginning of the year plus its net investment. Net investment is equal to gross investment less depreciation. Tom's gross investment is the 2 new machines bought during the year, and its depreciation is the 1 machine that Tom's scrapped during the year. Tom's net investment is 1 machine.

Back to the Gross in GDP   We can now see the distinction between gross domestic product and net domestic product. On the income side of the flows that measure GDP, a firm's *gross* profit is its profit *before* subtracting *depreciation*. A firm's gross profit is part of aggregate income, so depreciation is counted as part of gross income and GDP. Similarly, on the expenditure side of the flows that measure GDP, a firm's *gross investment* includes depreciation, so depreciation is counted as part of aggregate expenditure and total expenditure is a gross measure.

Net domestic product excludes depreciation. Like GDP, it can be viewed as the sum of incomes or expenditures. Net income includes firms' *net* profits—profits *after* subtracting depreciation. And net expenditure includes *net* investment, which also excludes depreciation.

The Short Term Meets the Long Term   The flows and stocks that you've just studied influence GDP growth and fluctuations. One of the reasons why GDP grows is that the capital stock grows. Investment adds to capital, so GDP grows because of investment. But investment fluctuates, which brings fluctuations to GDP. So capital and investment are part of the key to understanding both the growth and the fluctuations of GDP.

Investment and saving interact with income and consumption expenditure in a circular flow of expenditure and income. In this circular flow, income equals expenditure, which also equals the value of production. This equality is the foundation on which a nation's economic accounts are built and from which its GDP is measured.

Let's now see how the ideas that you've just studied are used in practice. We'll see how GDP and its components are measured in the United States today.

Measuring U.S. GDP

The Bureau of Economic Analysis (BEA) uses the concepts in the circular flow model to measure GDP and its components in the *National Income and Product Accounts*. Because the value of aggregate output equals aggregate expenditure and aggregate income, there are two approaches available for measuring GDP, and both are used. They are

- The expenditure approach
- The income approach

The Expenditure Approach

The *expenditure approach* measures GDP as the sum of consumption expenditure (C), investment (I), government expenditure on goods and services (G), and net exports of goods and services ($X - M$), corresponding to the red flows in the circular flow model in Fig. 5.1. Table 5.1 shows the result of this approach for 2006. The table uses the terms in the *National Income and Product Accounts*.

Personal consumption expenditures are the expenditures by households on goods and services produced in the United States and in the rest of the world. They include goods such as CDs and books and services such as banking and legal advice. They do *not* include the purchase of new homes, which is counted as part of investment. But they do include the purchase of consumer durable goods, which technically are capital such as homes.

Gross private domestic investment is expenditure on capital equipment and buildings by firms and expenditure on new homes by households. It also includes the change in business inventories.

Government expenditure on goods and services is the expenditure on goods and services by all levels of government. This item includes expenditures on national defense and garbage collection. But it does *not* include *transfer payments* because they are not expenditures on goods and services.

Net exports of goods and services are the value of exports minus the value of imports. This item includes computers that IBM sells to Volkswagen, the German auto producer (a U.S. export), and Japanese DVD players that Circuit City buys from Sony (a U.S. import).

Table 5.1 shows the relative magnitudes of the four items of aggregate expenditure.

TABLE 5.1   GDP: The Expenditure Approach

Item	Symbol	Amount in 2006 (billions of dollars)	Percentage of GDP
Personal consumption expenditures	C	9,079	69.8
Gross private domestic investment	I	2,215	17.0
Government expenditure on goods and services	G	2,479	19.1
Net exports of goods and services	$X - M$	−765	−5.9
Gross domestic product	**Y**	**13,008**	**100.0**

The expenditure approach measures GDP as the sum of personal consumption expenditures (C), gross private domestic investment (I), government expenditure on goods and services (G), and net exports ($X - M$). In 2006, GDP measured by the expenditure approach was $13,008 billion. More than two thirds of aggregate expenditure is on personal consumption goods and services.

Source of data: U.S. Department of Commerce, Bureau of Economic Analysis.

The Income Approach

The *income approach* measures GDP by summing the incomes that firms pay households for the factors of production they hire—wages for labor, interest for capital, rent for land, and profit for entrepreneurship. The *National Income and Product Accounts* divide incomes into five categories:

1. Compensation of employees
2. Net interest
3. Rental income
4. Corporate profits
5. Proprietors' income

Compensation of employees is the payment for labor services. It includes net wages and salaries (called "take-home pay") that workers receive plus taxes withheld on earnings plus fringe benefits such as social security and pension fund contributions.

Net interest is the interest households receive on loans they make minus the interest households pay on their own borrowing.

Rental income is the payment for the use of land and other rented resources.

Corporate profits are the profits of corporations, some of which are paid to households in the form of dividends and some of which are retained by corporations as undistributed profits. They are all income.

Proprietors' income is the income earned by the owner-operator of a business, which includes compensation for the owner's labor, the use of the owner's capital, and profit.

Table 5.2 shows these five incomes and their relative magnitudes.

The sum of the incomes is called *net domestic income at factor cost*. The term "factor cost" is used because it is the cost of the factors of production used to produce final goods. When we sum the expenditures on final goods, we arrive at a total called *domestic product at market prices*. Market prices and factor cost diverge because of indirect taxes and subsidies.

An *indirect tax* is a tax paid by consumers when they buy goods and services. (In contrast, a *direct tax* is a tax on income.) State sales taxes and taxes on alcohol, gasoline, and tobacco products are indirect taxes. Because of indirect taxes, consumers pay more for some goods and services than producers receive. Market price exceeds factor cost. For example, if the sales tax is 7 percent, you pay $1.07 when you buy a $1 chocolate bar. The factor cost of the chocolate bar including profit is $1. The market price is $1.07.

A *subsidy* is a payment by the government to a producer. Payments made to grain growers and dairy farmers are subsidies. Because of subsidies, consumers pay less for some goods and services than producers receive. Factor cost exceeds market price.

To get from factor cost to market price, we add indirect taxes and subtract subsidies. Making this adjustment brings us one step closer to GDP, but it does not quite get us there.

The final step is to add depreciation. You can see the reason for this adjustment by recalling the distinction between gross and net profit and that between gross and net investment. Total income is a net number because it includes firms' net profits, which exclude depreciation. Total expenditure is a gross number because it includes gross investment. So to get from total income to GDP, we must add depreciation to total income.

TABLE 5.2   GDP: The Income Approach

Item	Amount in 2006 (billions of dollars)	Percentage of GDP
Compensation of employees	7,322	56.3
Net interest	706	5.4
Rental income	77	0.6
Corporate profits	1,343	10.3
Proprietors' income	1,008	7.8
Indirect taxes *less* subsidies	1,004	7.7
Depreciation	1,548	11.9
Gross domestic product	**13,008**	**100.0**

The sum of all incomes equals net domestic income at factor cost. GDP equals net domestic income at factor cost plus indirect taxes less subsidies plus depreciation. In 2006, GDP measured by the income approach was $13,008 billion. The compensation of employees—labor income—was by far the largest part of aggregate income.

Source of data: U.S. Department of Commerce, Bureau of Economic Analysis.

REVIEW QUIZ

1 What is the expenditure approach to measuring GDP?
2 What is the income approach to measuring GDP?
3 What adjustments must be made to total income to make it equal GDP?

 myeconlab Study Plan 5.2

You now know how GDP is defined and measured. Your next task is to learn how we unscramble two sources of change in GDP—inflation and economic growth—to reveal changes in the quantity of goods and services produced, changes in what we call *real* GDP.

Real GDP and the Price Level

You've seen that GDP measures total expenditure on final goods and services in a given period. In 2006, GDP was $13,008 billion. A year before, in 2005, GDP was $12,199 billion. Because GDP in 2006 was greater than that in 2005, we know that one or two things must have happened during 2006:

- We produced more goods and services in 2006 than we produced in 2005.
- We paid higher prices for our goods and services in 2006 than we paid in 2005.

Producing more goods and services contributes to an improvement in our standard of living. Paying higher prices means that our cost of living has increased but our standard of living has not. So it matters a great deal why GDP has increased.

You're now going to learn how economists at the Bureau of Economic Analysis split GDP into two parts. One part tells us the change in production, and the other part tells us the change in prices. The method that is used has changed in recent years, and you will learn both the old and the new methods.

We measure the change in production by using a number that we call real gross domestic product. **Real gross domestic product (real GDP)** is the value of final goods and services produced in a given year when valued at constant prices. By comparing the value of the goods and services produced at constant prices, we can measure the change in the quantity of production.

Calculating Real GDP

Table 5.3 shows the quantities produced and the prices in 2005 for an economy that produces only two goods: balls and bats. The first step toward calculating real GDP is to calculate **nominal GDP**, which is the value of the final goods and services produced in

a given year valued at the prices that prevailed in that same year. Nominal GDP is just a more precise name for GDP that we use when we want to be emphatic that we are not talking about real GDP.

Nominal GDP Calculation To calculate nominal GDP in 2005, sum the expenditures on balls and bats in 2005 as follows:

Expenditure on balls = 100 balls × $1   = $100.
Expenditure on bats = 20 bats × $5   = $100.
Nominal GDP in 2005 = $100 + $100 = $200.

Table 5.4 shows the quantities produced and the prices in 2006. The quantity of balls produced increased to 160, and the quantity of bats produced increased to 22. The price of a ball fell to 50¢, and the price of a bat increased to $22.50. To calculate nominal GDP in 2006, we sum the expenditures on balls and bats in 2006 as follows:

Expenditure on balls = 160 balls × $0.50 = $80.
Expenditure on bats = 22 bats × $22.50 = $495.
Nominal GDP in 2006 = $80 + $495   = $575.

To calculate real GDP, we choose one year, called the *base year*, against which to compare the other years. In the United States today, the base year is 2000. The choice of the base year is not important. It is just a common reference point. We'll use 2005 as the base year. By definition, in the base year, real GDP equals nominal GDP. So real GDP in 2005 is $200.

Base-Year Prices Value of Real GDP The base-year prices method of calculating real GDP, which is the old method, values the quantities produced in a year at the prices of the base year. Table 5.5 shows the prices for 2005 and the quantities in 2006 (based on the information in Tables 5.3 and 5.4). The value of

TABLE 5.3	GDP Data for 2005	
Item	Quantity	Price
Balls	100	$1.00
Bats	20	$5.00

TABLE 5.4	GDP Data for 2006	
Item	Quantity	Price
Balls	160	$0.50
Bats	22	$22.50

TABLE 5.5	2006 Quantities and 2005 Prices	
Item	**Quantity**	**Price**
Balls	160	$1.00
Bats	22	$5.00

the 2006 quantities at the 2005 prices is calculated as follows:

Expenditure on balls = 160 balls × $1.00 = $160.
Expenditure on bats = 22 bats × $5.00   = $110.
Value of the 2006 quantities at 2005 prices = $270.

If we use the old base-year prices method, $270 would be recorded as real GDP in 2006.

Chain-Weighted Output Index Calculation The **chain-weighted output index** method, which is the new method of calculating real GDP, uses the prices of two adjacent years to calculate the real GDP growth rate. So to find the real GDP growth rate in 2006, we compare the quantities produced in 2005 and 2006 by using both the 2005 prices and the 2006 prices. We then average the two sets of numbers in a way that we'll now describe.

To compare the quantities produced in 2005 and 2006 at 2006 prices, we need to calculate the value of 2005 quantities at 2006 prices. Table 5.6 summarizes these quantities and prices. The value of the 2005 quantities at the 2006 prices is calculated as follows:

Expenditure on balls = 100 balls × $0.50   = $50.
Expenditure on bats = 20 bats × $22.50   = $450.
Value of the 2005 quantities at 2006 prices = $500.

We now have two comparisons between 2005 and 2006. At the 2005 prices, the value of production

TABLE 5.6	2005 Quantities and 2006 Prices	
Item	**Quantity**	**Price**
Balls	100	$0.50
Bats	20	$22.50

increased from $200 in 2005 to $270 in 2006. The increase in value is $70, and the percentage increase is ($70 ÷ $200) × 100, which is 35 percent.

At the 2006 prices, the value of production increased from $500 in 2005 to $575 in 2006. The increase in value is $75, and the percentage increase is ($75 ÷ $500) × 100, which is 15 percent.

The new method of calculating real GDP uses the average of these two percentage increases. The average of 35 percent and 15 percent is (35 + 15) ÷ 2, which equals 25 percent. Real GDP in 2006 is 25 percent greater than it was in 2005. Real GDP in 2005 is $200, so real GDP in 2006 is $250.

Chain Linking The calculation that we've just described is repeated each year. Each year is compared with its preceding year. So in 2007, the calculations are repeated but using the prices and quantities of 2006 and 2007. Real GDP in 2007 equals real GDP in 2006 increased by the calculated percentage change in real GDP for 2007. For example, suppose that real GDP for 2007 is calculated to be 20 percent greater than that in 2006. You know that real GDP in 2006 is $250. So real GDP in 2007 is 20 percent greater than this value and is $300. In every year, real GDP is valued in base-year (2005) dollars.

By applying the calculated percentage change in real GDP in each year to the real GDP of the preceding year, real GDP in each year is linked back to the dollars of the base year like the links in a chain.

Calculating the Price Level

You've seen how real GDP reveals the change in the quantity of goods and services produced. We're now going to see how we can find the change in prices that increases our cost of living.

The average level of prices is called the **price level**. One measure of the price level is the **GDP deflator**, which is an average of current-year prices expressed as a percentage of base-year prices. To calculate the GDP deflator, we use the formula:

GDP deflator = (Nominal GDP ÷ Real GDP) × 100.

You can see why the GDP deflator measures the price level. If nominal GDP rises but real GDP remains unchanged, the price level must have risen. The larger the nominal GDP for a given real GDP, the higher is the price level and the larger is the GDP deflator.

TABLE 5.7   Calculating the GDP Deflator

Year	Nominal GDP	Real GDP	GDP Deflator
2005	$200	$200	100
2006	$575	$250	230

Table 5.7 shows how the GDP deflator is calculated. In 2005, the base year, real GDP equals nominal GDP, so the GDP deflator is 100. In 2006, it is 230, which equals nominal GDP of $575 divided by real GDP of $250 and then multiplied by 100.

Deflating the GDP Balloon

You can think of GDP as a balloon that is blown up by growing production and rising prices. In Fig. 5.3, the GDP deflator lets the inflation air—the contribution of rising prices—out of the nominal GDP balloon so that we can see what has happened to *real*

GDP. In this figure, the base year is 1986 and the red balloon for 1986 shows real GDP in that year. The green balloon shows *nominal* GDP in 2006. The red balloon for 2006 shows real GDP for that year. To see real GDP in 2006, we *deflate* nominal GDP by using the GDP deflator.

REVIEW QUIZ

1 What is the distinction between nominal GDP and real GDP?
2 What is the old method of calculating real GDP?
3 What is the new method of calculating real GDP?
4 How is the GDP deflator calculated?

myeconlab **Study Plan 5.3**

You now know how to calculate real GDP and the GDP deflator. Your next task is to learn how we use real GDP and to see some of its limitations.

FIGURE 5.3   The U.S. GDP Balloon

myeconlab

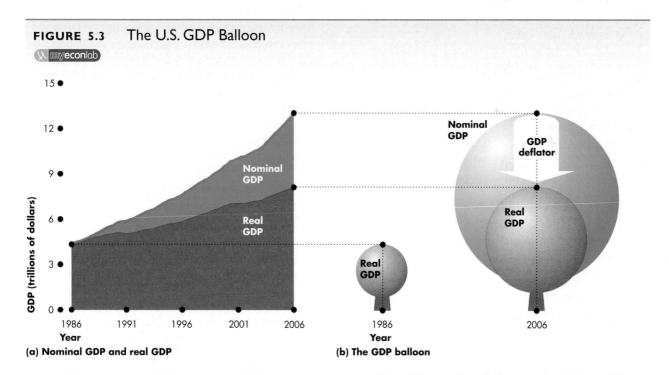

(a) Nominal GDP and real GDP

(b) The GDP balloon

Part of the rise in GDP comes from inflation, and part comes from increased production—an increase in real GDP.

The GDP deflator lets inflation air out of the GDP balloon so that we can see the extent to which production has increased.

Source of data: U.S. Department of Commerce, Bureau of Economic Analysis.

The Uses and Limitations of Real GDP

We use estimates of real GDP for three main purposes. They are to make

- Economic welfare comparisons over time
- Economic welfare comparisons across countries
- Business cycle forecasts

Although real GDP is used for these three purposes, it is not a perfect measure for any of them. But neither is it a seriously misleading measure. We'll describe the uses and evaluate the limitations of real GDP in each of the three cases.

Economic Welfare Comparisons Over Time

Economic welfare is a comprehensive measure of the general state of economic well-being. Economic welfare improves when the production of *all* goods and services grows. The goods and services that make up real GDP growth are only a part of all the items that influence economic welfare.

Today, because of real GDP growth, real GDP per person in the United States is twice what it was in 1971. But are we twice as well off? Does this growth of real GDP provide a full and accurate measure of the change in economic welfare?

It does not. The reason is that economic welfare depends on many other factors that are either not measured accurately by real GDP or not measured at all by real GDP. Some of these factors are

- Overadjustment for inflation
- Household production
- Underground economic activity
- Health and life expectancy
- Leisure time
- Environment quality
- Political freedom and social justice

Overadjustment for Inflation The price indexes that are used to measure inflation give an upward-biased estimate of true inflation. (You will learn about the sources of this bias on p. 145.) If we overestimate the rise in prices, we underestimate the growth of real

GDP. When car prices rise because cars have improved (safer, more fuel efficient, more comfortable), the GDP deflator counts the price increase as inflation. So what is really an increase in production is counted as an increase in price rather than an increase in real GDP. It is deflated away by the wrongly measured higher price level. The magnitude of this bias is probably less than 1 percentage point a year, but its exact magnitude is not known.

Household Production An enormous amount of production takes place every day in our homes. Preparing meals, cleaning the kitchen, changing a light bulb, cutting the grass, washing the car, and helping a high school student with homework are all examples of productive activities that do not involve market transactions and are not counted as part of GDP.

If these activities grew at the same rate as real GDP, not measuring them would not be a problem. But it is likely that market production, which is part of GDP, is increasingly replacing household production, which is not part of GDP. Two trends point in this direction. One is the number of people who have jobs, which has increased from 54 percent in 1970 to 62 percent in 2006. The other is the trend in the purchase of traditionally home-produced goods and services in the market. For example, more and more families now eat in fast-food restaurants—one of the fastest-growing industries in the United States—and use day-care services. This trend means that an increasing proportion of food preparation and child care that were part of household production are now measured as part of GDP. So real GDP grows more rapidly than does real GDP plus home production.

Underground Economic Activity The *underground economy* is the part of the economy that is purposely hidden from the view of the government to avoid taxes and regulations or because the goods and services being produced are illegal. Because underground economic activity is unreported, it is omitted from GDP.

The underground economy is easy to describe, even if it is hard to measure. It includes the production and distribution of illegal drugs, production that uses illegal labor that is paid less than the minimum wage, and jobs done for cash to avoid paying income taxes. This last category might be quite large and includes tips earned by cab drivers, hairdressers, and hotel and restaurant workers.

Estimates of the scale of the underground economy in the United States range between 9 and 30 percent of GDP ($1,200 billion to almost $4,000 billion). The underground economy is much larger in some countries, particularly in some Eastern European countries that are making a transition from centrally planned economies to market economies.

Provided that the underground economy is a reasonably stable proportion of the total economy, the growth rate of real GDP still gives a useful estimate of changes in economic welfare. But sometimes production shifts from the underground economy to the rest of the economy, and sometimes it shifts the other way. The underground economy expands relative to the rest of the economy if taxes become especially high or if regulations become especially restrictive. And the underground economy shrinks relative to the rest of the economy if the burdens of taxes and regulations are eased. During the 1980s, when tax rates were cut, there was an increase in the reporting of previously hidden income and tax revenues increased. So some part (but probably a very small part) of the expansion of real GDP during the 1980s represented a shift from the underground economy rather than an increase in production.

Health and Life Expectancy

Good health and a long life—the hopes of everyone—do not show up in real GDP, at least not directly. A higher real GDP does enable us to spend more on medical research, health care, a good diet, and exercise equipment. And as real GDP has increased, our life expectancy has lengthened—from 70 years at the end of World War II to approaching 80 years today. Infant deaths and death in childbirth, two fearful scourges of the nineteenth century, have been greatly reduced.

But we face new health and life expectancy problems every year. AIDS and drug abuse are taking young lives at a rate that causes serious concern. When we take these negative influences into account, we see that real GDP growth overstates the improvements in economic welfare.

Leisure Time

Leisure time is an economic good that adds to our economic welfare. Other things being equal, the more leisure we have, the better off we are. Our working time is valued as part of GDP, but our leisure time is not. Yet from the point of view of economic welfare, that leisure time must be at least as valuable to us as the wage that we earn on the last hour worked. If it were not, we would work instead of taking the leisure. Over the years, leisure time has steadily increased. The workweek has become shorter, more people take early retirement, and the number of vacation days has increased. These improvements in economic well-being are not reflected in real GDP.

Environment Quality

Economic activity directly influences the quality of the environment. The burning of hydrocarbon fuels is the most visible activity that damages our environment. But it is not the only example. The depletion of nonrenewable natural resources, the mass clearing of forests, and the pollution of lakes and rivers are other major environmental consequences of industrial production.

Resources that are used to protect the environment are valued as part of GDP. For example, the value of catalytic converters that help to protect the atmosphere from automobile emissions is part of GDP. But if we did not use such pieces of equipment and instead polluted the atmosphere, we would not count the deteriorating air that we were breathing as a negative part of GDP.

An industrial society possibly produces more atmospheric pollution than an agricultural society does. But pollution does not always increase as we become wealthier. Wealthy people value a clean environment and are willing to pay for one. Compare the pollution that was discovered in East Germany in the late 1980s with pollution in the United States. East Germany, a poor country, polluted its rivers, lakes, and atmosphere in a way that is unimaginable in the United States or in wealthy West Germany.

Political Freedom and Social Justice

Most people in the Western world value political freedoms such as those provided by the U.S. Constitution. And they value social justice or equity—equality of opportunity and of access to social security safety nets that protect people from the extremes of misfortune.

A country might have a very large real GDP per person but have limited political freedom and equity. For example, a small elite might enjoy political liberty and extreme wealth while the vast majority are effectively enslaved and live in abject poverty. Such an economy would generally be regarded as having less economic welfare than one that had the same amount of real GDP but in which political freedoms were enjoyed by everyone. Today, China has rapid real GDP growth but limited political freedoms, while Russia has slow real GDP growth and an emerging democratic political system. Economists have no easy way to determine which of these countries is better off.

The Bottom Line Do we get the wrong message about the growth in economic welfare by looking at the growth of real GDP? The influences that are omitted from real GDP are probably important and could be large. Developing countries have a larger underground economy and a larger amount of household production than do developed countries. So as an economy develops and grows, part of the apparent growth of real GDP might reflect a switch from underground to regular production and from home production to market production. This measurement error overstates the economic growth rate and the improvement in economic welfare.

Other influences on living standards include the amount of leisure time available, the quality of the environment, the security of jobs and homes, and the safety of city streets. It is possible to construct broader measures that combine the many influences that contribute to human happiness. Real GDP will be one element in those broader measures, but it will by no means be the whole of them.

Economic Welfare Comparisons Across Countries

All the problems we've just reviewed affect the economic welfare of every country. So to make international comparisons of economic welfare, factors in addition to real GDP must be used. But real GDP comparisons are major components of international welfare comparisons, and two special problems arise in making these comparisons. First, the real GDP of one country must be converted into the same currency units as the real GDP of the other country. Second, the same prices must be used to value the goods and services in the countries being compared. Let's look at these two problems by using a striking example: a comparison of the United States and China.

China and the United States Compared In 2006, GDP per person in the United States was almost $44,000. The official Chinese statistics published in the International Monetary Fund's (IMF) *World Economic Outlook* (WEO) says that GDP per person

in China in 2006 was 15,500 yuan. (The yuan is the currency of China.) On the average, during 2006, $1 U.S. was worth 9.9 yuan. If we use this exchange rate to convert 15,500 yuan into U.S. dollars, we get a value of $1,566. This comparison of China and the United States makes China look extremely poor. In 2006, GDP per person in the United States was 28 times that in China.

Figure 5.4 shows the story of real GDP in China from 1980 to 2006 based on converting the yuan to the U.S. dollar at the market exchange rate.

Purchasing Power Parity Comparison Figure 5.4 also shows another story based on an estimate of China's real GDP per person that is much larger than the measure we've just calculated. Let's see how this alternative measurement is made.

GDP in the United States is measured by using prices that prevail in the United States. China's GDP is measured by using prices that prevail in China. But the *relative* prices in the two countries are very different. Some goods that are expensive in the United States cost very little in China, so these items get a smaller weight in China's real GDP than they get in U.S. real GDP. If, instead of using China's prices, all the goods and services produced in China are valued at the prices prevailing in the United States, then a more valid comparison can be made of GDP in the two countries. Such a comparison uses prices called *purchasing power parity* prices, or PPP prices.

Alan Heston, Robert Summers, and Bettina Aten, economists in the Center for International Comparisons at the University of Pennsylvania, have used PPP prices to construct real GDP data for more than 100 countries. And the IMF now uses a method similar to that of Heston, Summers, and Aten to calculate PPP estimates of GDP in all countries. The PPP comparisons tell a remarkable story about China.

According to the PPP comparisons, GDP per person in the United States in 2006 was 5 times that of China, not the 28 times shown at the market exchange rate. Figure 5.4 shows the PPP view of China's real GDP and compares it with the market exchange rate view.

Uncertainty and Measurement Errors A prominent China scholar, Thomas Rawski of the University of Pittsburgh, doubts both sets of data shown in Fig. 5.4. He believes that the growth rate of China's real

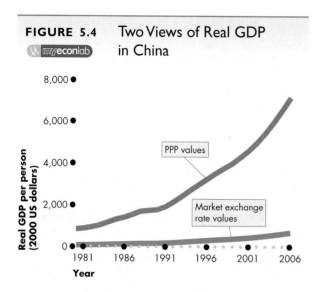

FIGURE 5.4   Two Views of Real GDP in China

When GDP is valued at the market exchange rate, China is a poor developing country in which income per person in 2006 is less than 4 percent of the U.S. level. But when GDP is valued at purchasing power parity prices, China's real GDP in 2006 is 20 percent of the U.S. level. Some China scholars think that even the market exchange rate numbers are too big. So there is much uncertainty about China's real GDP.

Sources of data: International Monetary Fund, *World Economic Outlook database*, April 2006 and Alan Heston, Robert Summers, and Bettina Aten, Penn World Table Version 6.1 Center for International Comparisons at the University of Pennsylvania (CICUP), October 2002.

GDP has been exaggerated for some years and that even the market exchange rate data overstate real GDP in China.

U.S. real GDP is measured reliably. But China's is not. The alternative measures of China's real GDP are unreliable, and the truth about GDP in China is not known. But China's real GDP is growing, and many businesses are paying close attention to the prospects of expanding their activities in China and other fast-growing Asian economies.

Business Cycle Forecasts

If policymakers plan to raise interest rates to slow an expansion that they believe is too strong, they look at the latest estimates of real GDP. But suppose that, for the reasons that we've just discussed, real GDP is mismeasured. Does this mismeasurement hamper our ability to identify the phases of the business cycle? It does not. The reason is that although the omissions

from real GDP do change over time, they probably do not change in a systematic way with the business cycle. So inaccurate measurement of real GDP does not necessarily cause a wrong assessment of the phase of the business cycle.

The fluctuations in economic activity measured by real GDP tell a reasonably accurate story about the phase of the business cycle that the economy is in. When real GDP grows, the economy is in a business cycle expansion; when real GDP shrinks (for two quarters), the economy is in a recession. Also, as real GDP fluctuates, so do production and jobs.

But real GDP fluctuations probably exaggerate or overstate the fluctuations in total production and economic welfare. The reason is that when business activity slows in a recession, household production increases and so does leisure time. When business activity speeds up in an expansion, household production and leisure time decrease. Because household production and leisure time increase in a recession and decrease in an expansion, real GDP fluctuations tend to overstate the fluctuations in both total production and economic welfare. But the directions of change of real GDP, total production, and economic welfare are probably the same.

REVIEW QUIZ

1   Does real GDP measure economic welfare? If not, why not?
2   Does real GDP measure total production of goods and services? If not, what are the main omissions?
3   How can we make valid international comparisons of real GDP?
4   Does the growth of real GDP measure the economic growth rate accurately?
5   Do the fluctuations in real GDP measure the business cycle accurately?

 myeconlab **Study Plan 5.4**

◆ You've now studied the methods used to measure GDP, economic growth, and the price level. And you've learned about some of the limitations of these measures. *Reading Between the Lines* on pp. 126–127 looks at real GDP in the 2006 U.S. expansion.

Your next task is to learn how we measure employment and unemployment and the CPI.

Real GDP in the Current Expansion

Economy Sets Fastest Pace Since the Summer of 2003

April 29, 2006

Propelled by a burst of consumer spending and vigorous business investment, the gross domestic product surged at a 4.8 percent rate in the first quarter of the year, the Commerce Department reported yesterday, the fastest pace of growth since the summer of 2003.

But the roaring American economy may be turning quieter. Even as the government report portrayed an economic engine firing on all cylinders, most economists argue that growth is poised to settle into a more moderate pace, slowed by high energy prices, rising interest rates and a softer housing market.

"This is the last big GDP number we are going to get in this economic cycle," said Ian Shepherdson, chief United States economist at High Frequency Economics in Valhalla, N.Y. "We are headed toward a slowing path."

Businesses and consumers started 2006 with remarkable vigor. Consumer spending expanded at an annualized rate of 5.5 percent compared with the last quarter of 2005. Business investment jumped 14.3 percent, the biggest increase since the second quarter of 2000. Even the government contributed to growth, powered by a 10 percent increase in military spending.

While residential construction slowed slightly, investment in commercial structures like factories, hospitals and office buildings jumped to 8.6 percent from 3.1 percent. "Everywhere people seem to be upbeat and extremely busy," said Kenneth D. Simonson, chief economist at the Associated General Contractors of America. . . .

Essence of the Story

▶ Real GDP grew at an annual rate of 4.8 percent from January through March 2006.

▶ It was the fastest quarterly growth since the summer of 2003.

▶ Business investment grew at an annual rate of 14.3 percent, the fastest since 2000.

▶ Investment in commercial buildings grew at an annual rate of 8.6 percent.

▶ Consumer spending grew at an annual rate of 5.5 percent.

▶ Government expenditure on defense increased at an annual rate of 10 percent.

▶ This news article reports real GDP numbers for the first quarter of 2006.*

▶ The data for this quarter show the second-largest percentage increase following the recession of 2001.

▶ Figure 1 shows the real GDP growth rate (annualized) quarter by quarter from the first quarter of 2000 to the first quarter of 2006.

▶ You can see very slow growth through 2002 and the beginning of 2003.

▶ You can also see the sharp increase in the growth rate in the third quarter of 2003 followed by continued strong growth.

▶ The growth rate dips in the fourth quarter of 2005—the Katrina effect—and then bounces back in the first quarter of 2006.

▶ Figure 2 shows the components of real GDP. You can see that most of the growth of real GDP comes from consumption expenditure and investment growth.

▶ The 2002–2006 expansion was a weak one.

▶ Figure 3 emphasizes the weakness of the 2002–2006 expansion.

▶ In the first quarter of 2006, after 18 quarters of expansion from the trough of 2001, real GDP was 16 percent above its trough level.

▶ At a similar point in the average of the previous five expansions, real GDP was 23 percent above its trough level.

▶ The current expansion is close to the weakest of the past five expansions.

▶ Since the trough of 2001, real GDP has grown at an average rate of 3.3 percent per year.

▶ Only the expansion of the 1990s was slower, and the expansion of the 1960s was almost twice as fast with an annual average growth rate of 5.8 percent.

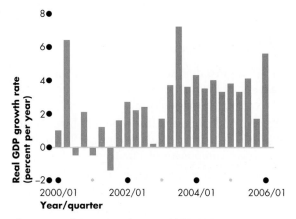

Figure 1 Real GDP growth rates: 2000–2006

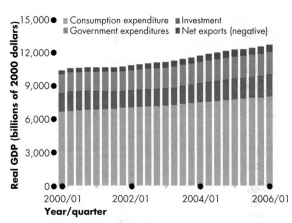

Figure 2 Real GDP and components: 2000–2006

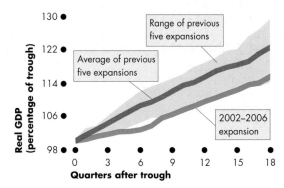

Figure 3 The slow recovery

---

* The growth rate was subsequently revised upward to 5.6 percent from the 4.8 percent in the news article and we use the revised data here.

SUMMARY

Key Points

Gross Domestic Product (pp. 112–116)

- GDP, or gross domestic product, is the market value of all the final goods and services produced in a country during a given period.
- A final good is an item that is bought by its final user, and it contrasts with an intermediate good, which is a component of a final good.
- GDP is calculated by using either the expenditure or income totals in the circular flow model.
- Aggregate expenditure on goods and services equals aggregate income and GDP.

Measuring U.S. GDP (pp. 117–118)

- Because aggregate expenditure, aggregate income, and the value of aggregate production are equal, we can measure GDP by using the expenditure approach or the income approach.
- The expenditure approach sums consumption expenditure, investment, government expenditure on goods and services, and net exports.
- The income approach sums wages, interest, rent, and profit (and indirect taxes less subsidies and depreciation).

Real GDP and the Price Level (pp. 119–121)

- Real GDP is measured by a chain-weighted output index that shows the percentage change in the value of production each year based on an average of the prices in the current year and previous year.
- The GDP deflator measures the price level based on the prices of the items that make up GDP.

The Uses and Limitations of Real GDP (pp. 122–125)

- Real GDP is used to compare economic welfare over time and across countries and to assess the phase of the business cycle.

- Real GDP growth is not a perfect measure of economic welfare because it excludes quality improvements, household production, the underground economy, health and life expectancy, leisure time, environmental damage, and political freedom and social justice.
- International comparisons use PPP prices.
- The growth rate of real GDP gives a good indication of the phases of the business cycle.

Key Figure and Tables

Key Terms

PROBLEMS

1. The figure below shows the flows of expenditure and income in the United States. During 2001, A was $2,200 billion, B was $7,064 billion, C was $1,840 billion, D was $1,624 billion, and E was −$330 billion. Calculate

   a. Aggregate expenditure.
   b. Aggregate income.
   c. GDP.
   d. Government budget deficit.
   e. Household saving.
   f. Government saving.
   g. National saving.
   h. Borrowing from the rest of the world.

2. In problem 1, during 2003, A was $1,507 billion, B was $7,274 billion, C was $2,054 billion, D was $1,624 billion, and E was −$505 billion.

   Calculate the quantities in problem 1 during 2003.

3. Martha owns a copy shop that has 10 copiers. One copier wears out each year and is replaced. In addition, this year Martha will expand her business to 14 copiers. Calculate Martha's initial capital stock, depreciation, gross investment, net investment, and final capital stock.

4. Martha in problem 3 buys paper from XYZ Paper Mills. Is Martha's expenditure on paper part of GDP? If not, how does the value of the paper get counted in GDP?

5. In the United Kingdom in 2005,

Item	Billions of pounds
Wages paid to labor	685
Consumption expenditure	791
Taxes	394
Transfer payments	267
Profits	273
Investment	209
Government expenditure	267
Exports	322
Saving	38
Imports	366

   a. Calculate GDP in the United Kingdom.
   b. Explain the approach (expenditure or income) that you used to calculate GDP.
   c. How is investment financed in the United Kingdom?

6. Tropical Republic produces only bananas and coconuts. The base year is 2005, and the tables give the quantities produced and prices.

Quantities	2005	2006
Bananas	1,000 bunches	1,100 bunches
Coconuts	500 bunches	525 bunches
Prices		
Bananas	$2 a bunch	$3 a bunch
Coconuts	$10 a bunch	$8 a bunch

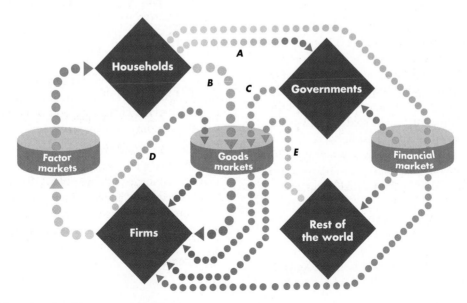

*Solutions to odd-numbered problems are provided.

a. Calculate Tropical Republic's nominal GDP in 2005 and 2006.

b. Calculate real GDP in 2006 using the base-year prices method.

c. Calculate the GDP deflator in 2006.

7. Tropical Republic (described in problem 6) decides to use the chain-weighted output index method to calculate real GDP. Using this method:

a. Calculate the growth rate of real GDP in 2006.

b. Calculate the GDP deflator in 2006.

c. Compare and comment on the differences in real GDP using the base-year prices and chain-weighted output index methods.

CRITICAL THINKING

1. Study *Reading Between the Lines* on pp. 126–127 and then answer the following questions:

a. Which components of aggregate expenditure increased at the fastest rate in the first quarter of 2006?

b. Which components of aggregate expenditure increased at the slowest rate in the first quarter of 2006?

c. For how long has the U.S. economy been expanding since the last business cycle trough?

d. How does the current expansion compare with previous expansions? Did it start out weak and then strengthen or did it start out strong and then weaken? Or has it been weak from the outset?

e. Can you think of any reasons why the current expansion might be weak?

2. **Boeing Bets the House**
Boeing plans to produce some components of its new 787 Dreamliner in Japan. The aircraft will be assembled in the United States, and much of the first year's production will be sold to ANA (All Nippon Airways), a Japanese airline.
The New York Times, May 7, 2006

a. Explain how Boeing's activities and its transactions affect GDP in the United States and Japan.

b. Explain how ANA's activities and its transactions affect GDP in the United States and Japan.

c. Use a circular flow diagram to illustrate your answers to parts (a) and (b).

3. The United Nations has created a Human Development Index (HDI) that is based on real GDP per person, life expectancy at birth, and indicators of the quality and quantity of education.

a. Explain why the HDI might be better than real GDP as a measure of economic welfare.

b. Which items in the HDI are part of real GDP and which items are not in real GDP?

c. Do you think the HDI should be expanded to include items such as pollution, resource depletion, and political freedom? Explain why.

d. Are there any other factors that influence economic welfare that you think should be included in a comprehensive measure?

WEB ACTIVITIES

myeconlab Links to Web sites

1. Visit the Bureau of Economic Analysis. There, you can obtain all the available data on GDP and the components of aggregate expenditure and aggregate income. The data are in current prices (nominal GDP) and constant prices (real GDP).

a. What is the value of nominal GDP in the current quarter?

b. What is the value of real GDP in the current quarter using the chain-weighted output index method?

c. What is the GDP deflator in the current quarter?

d. What was the value of real GDP in the same quarter of the previous year?

e. By how much has real GDP changed over the past year? (Express your answer as a percentage.)

f. Did real GDP increase or decrease and what does the change tell you about the state of the economy over the past year?

2. Visit the *World Economic Outlook*. There, you can obtain data on real GDP and other variables for 180 countries. Obtain real GDP data for the United States and any three other countries that you wish. Make a time-series graph of the real GDP growth rates and write a brief report that compares the growth and fluctuations in real GDP in these economies.

CHAPTER 6

Monitoring Jobs and the Price Level

Vital Signs

Each month, we chart the course of unemployment as a measure of U.S. economic health. How do we measure unemployment?

What does the unemployment rate tell us? Is it a reliable vital sign for the economy?

Every month, we also chart the number of people working, the number of hours they work, and the wages they receive. Are most new jobs full time or part time? And are they high-wage jobs or low-wage jobs?

As the U.S. economy expanded after 2002, job growth was weak and questions about the health of the labor market became of vital importance to millions of American families. We put the spotlight on the labor market during the past few years in *Reading Between the Lines* at the end of this chapter.

Having a good job that pays a decent wage is only half of the equation that translates into a good standard of living. The other half is the cost of living. We track the cost of the items that we buy with another number that is published every month, the Consumer Price Index, or CPI. What is the CPI? How is it calculated? And does it provide a reliable guide to the changes in our cost of living?

◆ These are the questions we study in this chapter. We begin by looking at the way we measure employment and unemployment.

After studying this chapter, you will be able to

▶ Define the unemployment rate, the labor force participation rate, the employment-to-population ratio, and aggregate hours

▶ Describe the sources of unemployment, its duration, the groups most affected by it, and how it fluctuates over a business cycle

▶ Explain how we measure the price level and the inflation rate using the CPI

Jobs and Wages

The state of the labor market has a large impact on our incomes and our lives. We become concerned when jobs are hard to find and more relaxed when they are plentiful. But we want a good job, which means that we want a well-paid and interesting job. You are now going to learn how economists track the health of the labor market.

Population Survey

Every month, the U.S. Census Bureau surveys 60,000 households and asks a series of questions about the age and job market status of the members of each household. This survey is called the Current Population Survey. The Census Bureau uses the answers to describe the anatomy of the labor force.

Figure 6.1 shows the population categories used by the Census Bureau and the relationships among the categories.

The population divides into two broad groups: the working-age population and others who are too young to work or who live in institutions and are unable to work. The **working-age population** is the total number of people aged 16 years and over who are not in jail, hospital, or some other form of institutional care.

The Census Bureau divides the working-age population into two groups: those in the labor force and those not in the labor force. It also divides the labor force into two groups: the employed and the unemployed. So the **labor force** is the sum of the employed and the unemployed.

To be counted as employed in the Current Population Survey, a person must have either a full-time job or a part-time job. To be counted as *un*employed, a person must be available for work and must be in one of three categories:

1. Without work but has made specific efforts to find a job within the previous four weeks
2. Waiting to be called back to a job from which he or she has been laid off
3. Waiting to start a new job within 30 days

Anyone surveyed who satisfies one of these three criteria is counted as unemployed. People in the working-age population who are neither employed nor unemployed are classified as not in the labor force.

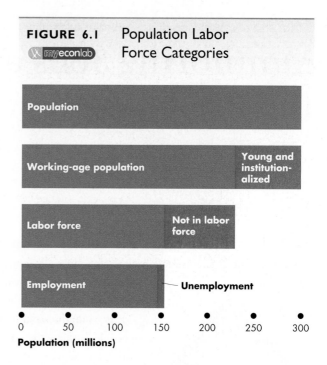

FIGURE 6.1 myeconlab   Population Labor Force Categories

The total population is divided into the working-age population and the young and institutionalized. The working-age population is divided into those in the labor force and those not in the labor force. The labor force is divided into the employed and the unemployed.

Source of data: Bureau of Labor Statistics.

In 2006, the population of the United States was 299.3 million. There were 70.6 million people under 16 years of age or living in institutions. The working-age population was 228.7 million. Of this number, 76.1 million were not in the labor force. Most of these people were in school full time or had retired from work. The remaining 152.6 million people made up the U.S. labor force. Of these, 145.3 million were employed and 7.3 million were unemployed.

Three Labor Market Indicators

The Census Bureau calculates three indicators of the state of the labor market, which are shown in Fig. 6.2. They are

- The unemployment rate
- The labor force participation rate
- The employment-to-population ratio

The Unemployment Rate The amount of unemployment is an indicator of the extent to which people who want jobs can't find them. The **unemployment rate** is the percentage of the people in the labor force who are unemployed. That is,

$$\text{Unemployment rate} = \frac{\text{Number of people unemployed}}{\text{Labor force}} \times 100$$

and

$$\text{Labor force} = \frac{\text{Number of people employed} + }{\text{Number of people unemployed}}.$$

In 2006, the number of people employed was 145.3 million and the number unemployed was 7.3 million. By using the above equations, you can verify that the labor force was 152.6 million (145.3 million plus 7.3 million) and the unemployment rate was 4.8 percent (7.3 million divided by 152.6 million, multiplied by 100).

Figure 6.2 shows the unemployment rate (graphed in orange and plotted against the right-hand scale) and two other labor market indicators from 1961 to 2006. The unemployment rate averaged 5.9 percent and it reached peak values at the end of the recessions of 1974, 1982, 1990–1991, and 2001.

The Labor Force Participation Rate The number of people who join the labor force is an indicator of the willingness of people of working age to take jobs. The **labor force participation rate** is the percentage of the working-age population who are members of the labor force. That is,

$$\text{Labor force participation rate} = \frac{\text{Labor force}}{\text{Working-age population}} \times 100.$$

In 2006, the labor force was 152.6 million and the working-age population was 228.7 million. By using the above equation, you can calculate the labor force participation rate. It was 66.7 percent (152.6 million divided by 228.7 million, multiplied by 100).

Figure 6.2 shows the labor force participation rate (graphed in red and plotted against the left-hand scale). It had an upward trend before 2000. But it fell slightly after 2000. It has also had some mild fluctuations, which result from unsuccessful job seekers becoming discouraged workers.

Discouraged workers are people who are available and willing to work but have not made specific efforts to find a job within the previous four weeks. These workers often temporarily leave the labor force during a recession and reenter during an expansion and become active job seekers.

FIGURE 6.2   Employment, Unemployment, and the Labor Force: 1961–2006

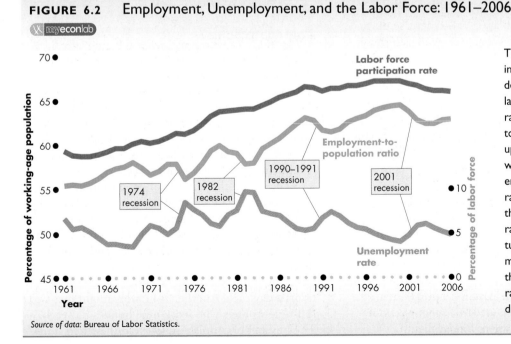

The unemployment rate increases in recessions and decreases in expansions. The labor force participation rate and the employment-to-population ratio have upward trends and fluctuate with the business cycle. The employment-to-population ratio fluctuates more than the labor force participation rate and reflects cyclical fluctuations in the unemployment rate. Fluctuations in the labor force participation rate arise mainly because of discouraged workers.

Source of data: Bureau of Labor Statistics.

The Employment-to-Population Ratio The number of people of working age who have jobs is an indicator of both the availability of jobs and the degree of match between people's skills and jobs. The **employment-to-population ratio** is the percentage of people of working age who have jobs. That is,

$$\text{Employment-to-population ratio} = \frac{\text{Number of people employed}}{\text{Working-age population}} \times 100.$$

In 2006, the number of people employed was 145.3 million and the working-age population was 228.7 million. By using the above equation, you can calculate the employment-to-population ratio. It was 63.5 percent (145.3 million divided by 228.7 million, multiplied by 100).

Figure 6.2 shows the employment-to-population ratio (graphed in blue and plotted against the left-hand scale). This indicator follows the same trends as the participation rate: upward before 2000 and downward after 2000. The increase before 2000 means that the U.S. economy created jobs at a faster rate than the working-age population grew. This indicator also fluctuates, and its fluctuations coincide with but are opposite to those in the unemployment rate. The employment-to-population ratio falls during a recession and increases during an expansion.

Why did the labor force participation rate and the employment-to-population ratio increase up to 2000 and then decrease? Women have driven these upward trends. Figure 6.3 shows that between 1961 and 2000, the female labor force participation rate increased from 38 percent to 60 percent. Shorter work hours, higher productivity, and an increased emphasis on white-collar jobs expanded the job opportunities and wages available to women. At the same time, technological advances increased productivity in the home, which freed up women's time and enabled them to take jobs outside the home. After 2000, the upward path ended.

Men have slowed the upward trend and turned the trend downward after 2000. Between 1961 and 2000, the male labor force participation rate decreased from 83 percent to 75 percent, and by 2006, it was 73 percent.

Male labor force participation decreased because increasing numbers of men are remaining in school longer and because some are retiring earlier.

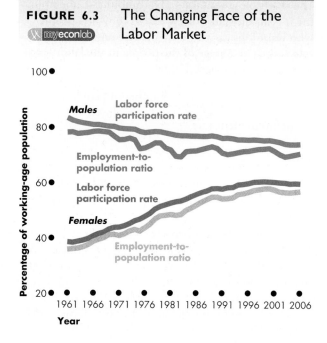

FIGURE 6.3 The Changing Face of the Labor Market

The upward trends in the labor force participation rate and the employment-to-population ratio are accounted for mainly by the increasing participation of women in the labor market. The male labor force participation rate and employment-to-population ratio have decreased.

Source of data: Bureau of Labor Statistics.

Aggregate Hours

The three labor market indicators that we've just examined are useful signs of the health of the economy and directly measure what matters to most people: jobs. But these three indicators don't tell us the quantity of labor used to produce real GDP, and we cannot use them to calculate the productivity of labor. The productivity of labor is significant because it influences the wages people earn.

The reason the number of people employed does not measure the quantity of labor employed is that all jobs are not the same. People in part-time jobs might work just a few hours a week. People in full-time jobs work around 35 to 40 hours a week. And some people regularly work overtime. For example, a 7-11 store might hire six students who work for three hours a day each. Another 7-11 store might hire two full-time workers who work nine hours a day each. The number of people employed in these two stores is eight, but the total hours worked by six of the eight is the same as the total hours worked by the other two. To determine the total amount of labor used to produce real GDP, we measure labor in hours rather than in jobs. **Aggregate hours** are the total number of hours worked by all the people employed, both full time and part time, during a year.

Figure 6.4(a) shows aggregate hours in the U.S. economy from 1961 to 2006. Like the employment-to-population ratio, aggregate hours have an upward trend. But aggregate hours have not grown as quickly as has the number of people employed. Between 1961 and 2006, the number of people employed in the U.S. economy increased by 120 percent. During that same period, aggregate hours increased by 90 percent. Why the difference? Because average hours per worker decreased.

Figure 6.4(b) shows average hours per worker. After hovering at almost 39 hours a week during the early 1960s, average hours per worker decreased to a bit less than 34 hours a week during the 2000s. The average workweek shortened partly because of a decrease in the average hours worked by full-time workers but also because the number of part-time jobs increased faster than the number of full-time jobs.

Fluctuations in aggregate hours and average hours per worker line up with the business cycle. Figure 6.4 highlights the past four recessions, during which aggregate hours decreased and average hours per worker decreased more quickly than trend.

Real Wage Rate

The **real wage rate** is the quantity of goods and services that an hour's work can buy. It is equal to the money wage rate (dollars per hour) divided by the price level. If we use the GDP deflator to measure the price level, the real wage rate is expressed in 2000 dollars because the GDP deflator is 100 in 2000. The real wage rate is a significant economic variable because it measures the reward for labor.

What has happened to the real wage rate in the United States? Figure 6.5 answers this question. It shows three measures of the average hourly real wage rate in the U.S. economy between 1961 and 2006.

The first measure of the real wage rate is the Department of Labor's calculation of the average hourly earnings of private manufacturing nonsupervisory workers. This measure increased to $12.44 in 1978 (in 2000 dollars) and then remained almost

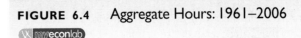

FIGURE 6.4   Aggregate Hours: 1961–2006

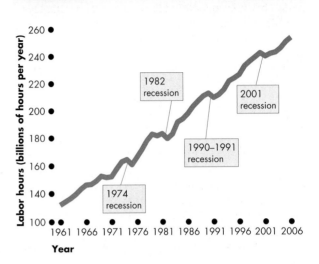

(a) Aggregate hours

(b) Average weekly hours per person

Aggregate hours in part (a) measure the total labor used to produce real GDP more accurately than does the number of people employed because an increasing proportion of jobs are part time. Between 1961 and 2006, aggregate hours increased by 90 percent. Fluctuations in aggregate hours coincide with the business cycle. Aggregate hours have increased at a slower rate than the number of jobs because the average workweek in part (b) has shortened.

Source of data: Bureau of Labor Statistics, and the author's calculations.

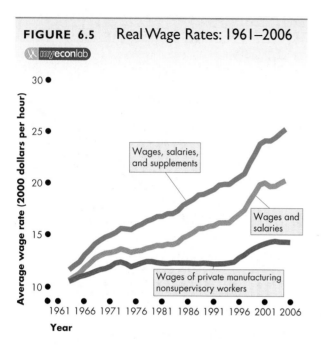

FIGURE 6.5   Real Wage Rates: 1961–2006

The average hourly real wage rate of private manufacturing nonsupervisory workers peaked in 1978, was constant through 1993, increased through 2001, and then remained constant. Broader measures of real wage rates increased, but all show a growth slowdown during the 1970s.

Sources of data: Bureau of Economic Analysis, Bureau of Labor Statistics, and the author's calculations.

constant at around $12.30 for 15 years. From the mid-1990s, the real wage rate increased and reached $14.44 by 2003, after which it again stopped rising.

The second measure of the real wage rate is calculated by dividing total wages and salaries in the *National Income and Product Accounts* by aggregate hours. This measure is broader than the first and includes the incomes of all types of labor, whether their rate of pay is calculated by the hour or not. This broader measure did not stop growing after 1978, but its growth rate slowed during the mid-1970s and remained low through the early 1980s. It then speeded up during the late 1980s, sagged during the early 1990s, and then grew very rapidly from 1996 through 2000. This measure of labor income per hour fell temporarily during the 2001 recession.

Fringe benefits such as pension contributions and the payment by employers of health insurance premiums have become an increasing part of labor

compensation. Figure 6.5 shows a third measure of the hourly real wage rate that reflects this trend. It is *total labor compensation*—wages, salaries, *and supplements*—divided by aggregate hours. This measure is the most comprehensive one available, and it shows that the real wage rate increased almost every year until 2000, then flatten before increasing again.

The data in Fig. 6.5 show us that no matter how we measure the real wage rate, its growth rate slowed during the 1970s. This slowdown in wage growth coincided with a slowdown in productivity growth—in the growth rate of real GDP per hour of work. The average real wage rate of workers in manufacturing was the most severely affected by the productivity growth slowdown, but the broader measures also slowed.

The fall in hourly compensation on the broader measures during the 2001 recession is unusual but not unknown. A small decrease occurred during the 1974 recession and real wage growth slowed temporarily in the other recessions.

REVIEW QUIZ

1 What are the trends in the unemployment rate, the labor force participation rate, and the employment-to-population ratio?
2 How do the unemployment rate, the labor force participation rate, and the employment-to-population ratio fluctuate over the business cycle?
3 Has the female labor force participation rate been similar to or different from the male labor force participation rate? If they differ, describe how.
4 How have aggregate hours changed since 1961?
5 How did average hourly real wage rates change during the 1990s and 2000s?

myeconlab Study Plan 6.1

You've now seen how we measure employment, unemployment, and real wage rate. Your next task is to study the anatomy of unemployment and see why it never disappears, even at full employment.

Unemployment and Full Employment

How do people become unemployed and how does a period of unemployment end? How long do people remain unemployed on the average? Who is at greatest risk of becoming unemployed? Let's answer these questions by looking at the anatomy of unemployment.

The Anatomy of Unemployment

People become unemployed if they

1. Lose their jobs and search for another job.
2. Leave their jobs and search for another job.
3. Enter or reenter the labor force to search for a job.

People end a spell of unemployment if they

1. Are hired or recalled.
2. Withdraw from the labor force.

People who are laid off, either permanently or temporarily, from their jobs are called *job losers*. Some job losers become unemployed, but some immediately withdraw from the labor force. People who voluntarily quit their jobs are called *job leavers*. Like job losers, some job leavers become unemployed and search for a better job while others either withdraw from the labor force temporarily or permanently retire from work. People who enter or reenter the labor force are called *entrants* and *reentrants*. Entrants are mainly people who have just left school. Some entrants get a job right away and are never unemployed, but many spend time searching for their first job, and during this period, they are unemployed. Reentrants are people who have previously withdrawn from the labor force. Most of these people are formerly discouraged workers. Figure 6.6 shows these labor market flows.

Let's see how much unemployment arises from the three different ways in which people can become unemployed.

The Sources of Unemployment Figure 6.7 shows unemployment by reason for becoming unemployed. Job losers are the biggest source of unemployment. On the average, they account for around half of total

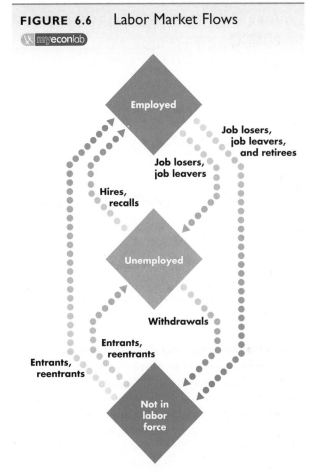

FIGURE 6.6 Labor Market Flows

Unemployment results from employed people losing or leaving their jobs (job losers and job leavers) and from people entering the labor force (entrants and reentrants). Unemployment ends because people get hired or recalled or because they withdraw from the labor force.

unemployment. Also, their number fluctuates a great deal. At the trough of the recession of 1990–1991, on any given day, more than 5 million of the 9.4 million unemployed were job losers. In contrast, at the business cycle peak in March 2001, only 3.3 million of the 6 million unemployed were job losers.

Entrants and reentrants also make up a large component of the unemployed. Their number fluctuates but more mildly than the fluctuations in the number of job losers.

Job leavers are the smallest and most stable source of unemployment. On any given day, fewer than 1 million people are unemployed because they

FIGURE 6.7   Unemployment by Reason

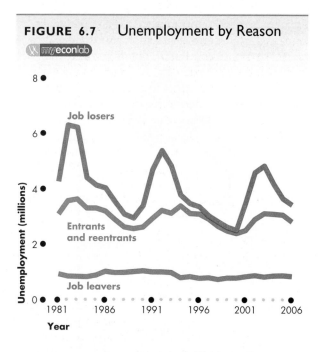

Everyone who is unemployed is a job loser, a job leaver, or an entrant or reentrant into the labor force. Most unemployment results from job loss. The number of job losers fluctuates more closely with the business cycle than do the numbers of job leavers and entrants and reentrants. Entrants and reentrants are the second most common type of unemployed people. Their number fluctuates with the business cycle because of discouraged workers. Job leavers are the least common type of unemployed people.

Source of data: Bureau of Labor Statistics.

FIGURE 6.8   Unemployment by Duration

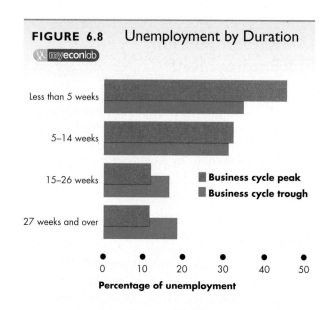

Close to a business cycle peak in 2000, when the unemployment rate was 4 percent, 45 percent of unemployment lasted for less than 5 weeks and 30 percent lasted for 5 to 14 weeks. So 75 percent of unemployment lasted for less than 15 weeks and 25 percent lasted for 15 weeks or more.

Close to a business cycle trough in 2002, when the unemployment rate was 5.8 percent, 35 percent of unemployment lasted for less than 5 weeks and 31 percent lasted for 5 to 14 weeks. So 66 percent of unemployment lasted for less than 15 weeks, and 34 percent lasted for 15 weeks or more.

Source of data: Bureau of Labor Statistics.

are job leavers. The number of job leavers is remarkably constant. To the extent that this number fluctuates, it does so in line with the business cycle: A slightly larger number of people leave their jobs in good times than in bad times.

The Duration of Unemployment Some people are unemployed for a week or two, and others are unemployed for periods of a year or more. The longer the spell of unemployment, the greater is the personal cost to the unemployed. The average duration of unemployment varies over the business cycle. Figure 6.8 compares the duration of unemployment close to a business cycle peak in 2000, when the unemployment rate was low, with that close to a business cycle trough in 2002, when the unemployment rate was high. In 2000, when the unemployment rate hit a

low of 4 percent, 45 percent of the unemployed were in that situation for less than 5 weeks and only 11 percent of the unemployed were jobless for more than 27 weeks. In 2002, when unemployment approached 5.8 percent, only 35 percent of the unemployed found a new job in less than 5 weeks and 18 percent were unemployed for more than 27 weeks. At both low and high unemployment rates, about 30 percent of the unemployed take between 5 weeks and 14 weeks to find a job.

The Demographics of Unemployment Figure 6.9 shows unemployment rates for different demographic groups. The figure shows that high unemployment rates occur among young workers and also among blacks. In the business cycle trough in 2002, the unemployment rate of black teenage males was 42 percent.

FIGURE 6.9 Unemployment by Demographic Group

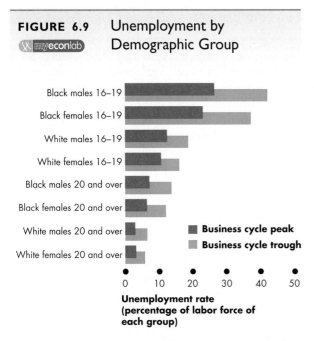

Black teenagers experience unemployment rates that average twice those of white teenagers, and teenage unemployment rates are much higher than those for people aged 20 years and over. Even in a business cycle trough, when unemployment is at its highest rate, only 6 percent of whites aged 20 years and over are unemployed.

Source of data: Bureau of Labor Statistics.

Even in 2000, when the unemployment rate was 4 percent, the black teenage unemployment rates were more than 20 percent. The unemployment rates for white teenagers are less than half those of black teenagers. The racial differences also exist for workers aged 20 years and over. The highest unemployment rates that whites 20 years and over experience are lower than the lowest rates experienced by the other groups.

Why are teenage unemployment rates so high? There are three reasons. First, young people are still in the process of discovering what they are good at and trying different lines of work. So they leave their jobs more frequently than do older workers. Second, firms sometimes hire teenagers on a short-term trial basis. So the rate of job loss is higher for teenagers than for other people. Third, most teenagers are in school and not in the labor force. This fact means that the percentage of the teenage population that is unemployed is much lower than the percentage of the teenage labor force that is unemployed. In 2003, for example, 1 mil-lion teenagers were unemployed and 6 million were employed. So the teenage unemployment rate (all races) was 14 percent. But 9 million teenagers were in school. If we considered being in school to be the equivalent of having a job and measured teenage unemployment as a percentage of the teenage labor force plus the school population, we would record that 6 percent of teenagers are unemployed.

Types of Unemployment

Unemployment is classified into three types that are based on its origins. They are

- Frictional
- Structural
- Cyclical

Frictional Unemployment The unemployment that arises from normal labor turnover—from people entering and leaving the labor force and from the ongoing creation and destruction of jobs—is **frictional unemployment**. Frictional unemployment is a permanent and healthy phenomenon in a dynamic, growing economy.

The unending flow of people into and out of the labor force and the processes of job creation and job destruction create the need for people to search for jobs and for businesses to search for workers. There are always businesses with unfilled jobs and people seeking jobs. Look in your local newspaper, and you will see that there are always some jobs being advertised. Businesses don't usually hire the first person who applies for a job, and unemployed people don't usually take the first job that comes their way. Instead, both firms and workers spend time searching out what they believe will be the best match available. By this process of search, people can match their own skills and interests with the available jobs and find a satisfying job and a good income. While these unemployed people are searching, they are frictionally unemployed.

The amount of frictional unemployment depends on the rate at which people enter and reenter the labor force and on the rate at which jobs are created and destroyed. During the 1970s, the amount of frictional unemployment increased as a consequence of the postwar baby boom that began during the 1940s. By the late 1970s, the baby boom had created a bulge in the number of people leaving school. As these people entered the labor force, the amount of frictional unemployment increased.

The amount of frictional unemployment is influenced by unemployment compensation. The greater the number of unemployed people covered by unemployment insurance and the more generous the unemployment benefit they receive, the longer is the average time taken in job search and the greater is the amount of frictional unemployment. In the United States in 2005, 35 percent of the unemployed received unemployment benefit. And the average benefit check was $266 a week. Canada and Western Europe have more generous benefits than those in the United States and have higher unemployment rates.

Structural Unemployment The unemployment that arises when changes in technology or international competition change the skills needed to perform jobs or change the locations of jobs is **structural unemployment**. Structural unemployment usually lasts longer than frictional unemployment because workers must usually retrain and possibly relocate to find a job. For example, when a steel plant in Gary, Indiana, is automated, some jobs in that city are eliminated. Meanwhile, new jobs for security guards, retail clerks, and life-insurance salespeople are created in Chicago, Indianapolis, and other cities. The unemployed former steelworkers remain unemployed for several months until they move, retrain, and get one of these jobs. Structural unemployment is painful, especially for older workers for whom the best available option might be to retire early or take a lower-skilled, lower-paying job.

At some times, the amount of structural unemployment is modest. At other times, it is large, and at such times, structural unemployment can become a serious long-term problem. It was especially large during the late 1970s and early 1980s. During those years, oil price hikes and an increasingly competitive international environment destroyed jobs in traditional U.S. industries, such as auto and steel, and created jobs in new industries, such as electronics and bioengineering, as well as in banking and insurance. Structural unemployment was also present during the early 1990s as many businesses and governments "downsized."

Cyclical Unemployment The fluctuating unemployment over the business cycle is **cyclical unemployment**. Cyclical unemployment increases during a recession and decreases during an expansion. An autoworker who is laid off because the economy is in a recession and who gets rehired some months later when the expansion begins has experienced cyclical unemployment.

Full Employment

There is always *some* unemployment—someone looking for a job or laid off and waiting to be recalled. So what do we mean by *full employment*? **Full employment** occurs when there is no cyclical unemployment or, equivalently, when all the unemployment is frictional and structural. The divergence of the unemployment rate from full employment is cyclical unemployment. The unemployment rate at full employment is called the **natural unemployment rate**.

There can be a lot of unemployment at full employment, and the term "full employment" is an example of a technical economic term that does not correspond with everyday language. The term "natural unemployment rate" is another technical economic term whose meaning does not correspond with everyday language. For most people—especially for unemployed workers—there is nothing *natural* about unemployment.

So why do economists call a situation with a lot of unemployment one of "full employment"? And why is the unemployment at full employment called "natural"?

The reason is that the economy is a complex mechanism that is always changing. In 2006, the U.S. economy employed 145 million people. More than 2.5 million workers retired during that year, and more than 3 million new workers entered the labor force. All these people worked in some 20 million businesses that produced goods and services valued at more than $13 trillion. Some of these businesses downsized and failed, and others expanded. This process of change creates frictions and dislocations that are unavoidable. And they create unemployment.

There is not much controversy about the existence of a natural unemployment rate. Nor is there much disagreement that it changes. The natural unemployment rate arises from the existence of frictional and structural unemployment, and it fluctuates because the frictions and the amount of structural change fluctuate.

But economists don't agree about the size of the natural unemployment rate and the extent to which it fluctuates. Some economists believe that the natural unemployment rate fluctuates frequently and that at times of rapid demographic and technological change, the natural unemployment rate can be high. Others think that the natural unemployment rate changes slowly.

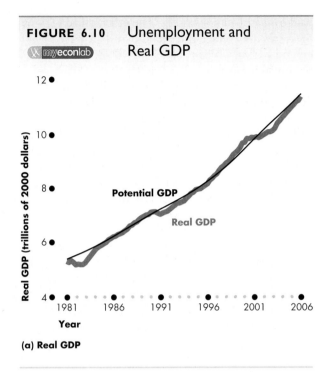

FIGURE 6.10 Unemployment and Real GDP

(a) Real GDP

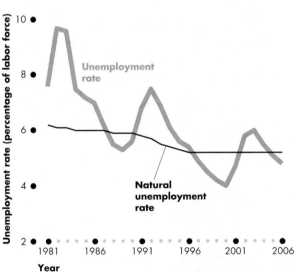

(b) Unemployment rate

As real GDP fluctuates around potential GDP (part a), the unemployment rate fluctuates around the natural unemployment rate (part b). At the end of the deep 1982 recession, the unemployment rate reached almost 10 percent. At the end of the milder 1990–1991 and 2001 recessions, unemployment peaked at lower rates. The natural unemployment rate decreased somewhat during the 1980s and 1990s.

Sources of data: Bureau of Economic Analysis, Bureau of Labor Statistics, and Congressional Budget Office.

Real GDP and Unemployment Over the Cycle

The quantity of real GDP at full employment is called **potential GDP.** You will study the forces that determine potential GDP in Chapter 7 (pp. 165–166). Over the business cycle, real GDP fluctuates around potential GDP and the unemployment rate fluctuates around the natural unemployment rate. Figure 6.10 illustrates these fluctuations in the United States between 1981 and 2006—real GDP in part (a) and the unemployment rate in part (b).

When the economy is at full employment, the unemployment rate equals the natural unemployment rate and real GDP equals potential GDP. When the unemployment rate is less than the natural unemployment rate, real GDP is greater than potential GDP. And when the unemployment rate is greater than the natural unemployment rate, real GDP is less than potential GDP.

Figure 6.10(b) shows one view of the natural unemployment rate. Keep in mind that economists do not know the magnitude of the natural unemployment rate and the natural rate shown in the figure is only one estimate. It shows that the natural unemployment rate was 6.2 percent in 1981 and that it fell steadily through the 1980s and 1990s to 5.2 percent by 1996. This estimate of the natural unemployment rate in the United States is one that many, but not all, economists would accept.

REVIEW QUIZ

1 What are the categories of people who become unemployed?
2 Define frictional unemployment, structural unemployment, and cyclical unemployment. Give examples of each type of unemployment.
3 What is the natural unemployment rate?
4 How does the natural unemployment rate change and what factors might make it change?
5 How does the unemployment rate fluctuate over the business cycle?

myeconlab Study Plan 6.2

Your final task in this chapter is to learn about another vital sign that gets monitored every month: the Consumer Price Index (CPI). What is the CPI, how do we measure it, and what does it mean?

The Consumer Price Index

The Bureau of Labor Statistics (BLS) calculates the Consumer Price Index every month. The **Consumer Price Index (CPI)** is a measure of the average of the prices paid by urban consumers for a fixed "basket" of consumer goods and services. What you learn in this section will help you to make sense of the CPI and relate it to your own economic life. The CPI tells you what has happened to the value of the money in your pocket.

Reading the CPI Numbers

The CPI is defined to equal 100 for a period called the **reference base period**. Currently, the reference base period is 1982–1984. That is, for the average of the 36 months from January 1982 through December 1984, the CPI equals 100.

In June 2006, the CPI was 202.9. This number tells us that the average of the prices paid by urban consumers for a fixed market basket of consumer goods and services was 102.9 percent higher in 2006 than it was on the average during 1982–1984.

In June 2006, the CPI was 202.9. A year earlier, it was 194.5. These numbers tell us that the index of the prices paid by urban consumers for a fixed basket of consumer goods and services increased between 2005 and 2006 by 8.4 points, or by 4.3 percent.

Constructing the CPI

Constructing the CPI is a huge operation that involves three stages:

■ Selecting the CPI basket
■ Conducting the monthly price survey
■ Calculating the CPI

The CPI Basket The first stage in constructing the CPI is to select what is called the *CPI basket*. This "basket" contains the goods and services represented in the index and the relative importance attached to each of them. The idea is to make the relative importance of the items in the CPI basket the same as that in the budget of an average urban household. For example, because people spend more on housing than on bus rides, the CPI places more weight on the price of housing than on the price of bus rides.

The BLS uses two baskets and calculates two CPIs. One, called CPI-U, measures the average price

paid by *all* urban households. The other, called CPI-W, measures the average price paid by urban wage earners and clerical workers. Here, we will focus on CPI-U, the broader measure.

To determine the spending patterns of households and to select the CPI basket, the BLS conducts a Consumer Expenditure Survey. This survey is costly and so is undertaken infrequently. Today's CPI basket is based on data gathered in a Consumer Expenditure Survey of 2001–2002. Until 1998, the CPI basket was based on a 1982–1984 Consumer Expenditure Survey but the BLS now updates the CPI basket more frequently.

Until 1998, the time period covered by the Consumer Expenditure Survey was also the reference base period. But now, when the BLS updates the CPI basket, it retains 1982–1984 as the reference base period.

Figure 6.11 shows the CPI basket at the end of 2005. The basket contains around 80,000 goods and

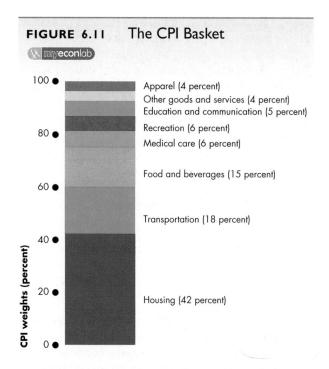

FIGURE 6.11   The CPI Basket

Apparel (4 percent)
Other goods and services (4 percent)
Education and communication (5 percent)
Recreation (6 percent)
Medical care (6 percent)
Food and beverages (15 percent)
Transportation (18 percent)
Housing (42 percent)

The CPI basket consists of the items that an average urban household buys. It consists mainly of housing (42 percent), transportation (18 percent), and food and beverages (15 percent). All other items add up to 25 percent of the total.

Sources of data: United States Census Bureau and Bureau of Labor Statistics.

services arranged in the eight large groups shown in the figure. The most important item in a household's budget is housing, which accounts for 42 percent of total expenditure. Transportation comes next at 18 percent. Third in relative importance are food and beverages at 15 percent. These three groups account for three quarters of the average household budget. Medical care and recreation each take 6 percent, and education and communication take 5 percent. Another 4 percent is spent on other goods and services, and apparel (clothing and footwear) takes 4 percent.

The BLS breaks down each of these categories into smaller ones. For example, the education and communication category breaks down into textbooks and supplies, tuition, telephone services, and personal computer services.

As you look at the relative importance of the items in the CPI basket, remember that they apply to the *average* household. *Individual* households are spread around the average. Think about your own expenditure and compare the basket of goods and services you buy with the CPI basket.

The Monthly Price Survey Each month, BLS employees check the prices of the 80,000 goods and services in the CPI basket in 30 metropolitan areas. Because the CPI aims to measure price *changes*, it is important that the prices recorded each month refer to exactly the same item. For example, suppose the price of a box of jelly beans has increased but a box now contains more beans. Has the price of jelly beans increased? The BLS employee must record the details of changes in quality or packaging so that price changes can be isolated from other changes.

Once the raw price data are in hand, the next task is to calculate the CPI.

Calculating the CPI The CPI calculation has three steps:

1. Find the cost of the CPI basket at base-period prices.
2. Find the cost of the CPI basket at current-period prices.
3. Calculate the CPI for the base period and the current period.

We'll work through these three steps for a simple example. Suppose the CPI basket contains only two goods and services: oranges and haircuts. We'll construct an annual CPI rather than a monthly CPI with the reference base period 2006 and the current period 2007.

Table 6.1 shows the quantities in the CPI basket and the prices in the base period and current period.

Part (a) contains the data for the base period. In that period, consumers bought 10 oranges at $1 each and 5 haircuts at $8 each. To find the cost of the CPI basket in the base-period prices, multiply the quantities in the CPI basket by the base-period prices. The cost of oranges is $10 (10 at $1 each), and the cost of haircuts is $40 (5 at $8 each). So total cost in the base period of the CPI basket is $50 ($10 + $40).

Part (b) contains the price data for the current period. The price of an orange increased from $1 to $2, which is a 100 percent increase—($1 ÷ $1) × 100 = 100. The price of a haircut increased from $8 to $10, which is a 25 percent increase—($2 ÷ $8) × 100 = 25.

The CPI provides a way of averaging these price increases by comparing the cost of the basket rather than the price of each item. To find the cost of the CPI basket in the current period, 2007, multiply the quantities in the basket by their 2007 prices. The cost of oranges is $20 (10 at $2 each), and the cost of haircuts is $50 (5 at $10 each). So total cost of the fixed CPI basket at current-period prices is $70 ($20 + $50).

TABLE 6.1   The CPI: A Simplified Calculation

(a) The cost of the CPI basket at base-period prices: 2006

Item	CPI basket Quantity	Price	Cost of CPI Basket
Oranges	10	$1.00	$10
Haircuts	5	$8.00	$40
Cost of CPI basket at base-period prices			$50

(b) The cost of the CPI basket at current-period prices: 2007

Item	CPI basket Quantity	Price	Cost of CPI Basket
Oranges	10	$2.00	$20
Haircuts	5	$10.00	$50
Cost of CPI basket at current-period prices			$70

You've now taken the first two steps toward calculating the CPI: calculating the cost of the CPI basket in the base period and the current period. The third step uses the numbers you've just calculated to find the CPI for 2006 and 2007.

The formula for the CPI is

$$\text{CPI} = \frac{\begin{array}{c}\text{Cost of CPI basket at}\\\text{current-period prices}\end{array}}{\begin{array}{c}\text{Cost of CPI basket at}\\\text{base-period prices}\end{array}} \times 100.$$

In Table 6.1, you established that in 2006, the cost of the CPI basket was $50 and in 2007, it was $70. You also know that the base period is 2006. So the cost of the CPI basket at base-year prices is $50. If we use these numbers in the CPI formula, we can find the CPI for 2006 and 2007. For 2006, the CPI is

$$\text{CPI in 2006} = \frac{\$50}{\$50} \times 100 = 100.$$

For 2007, the CPI is

$$\text{CPI in 2007} = \frac{\$70}{\$50} \times 100 = 140.$$

The principles that you've applied in this simplified CPI calculation apply to the more complex calculations performed every month by the BLS.

Measuring Inflation

A major purpose of the CPI is to measure *changes* in the cost of living and in the value of money. To measure these changes, we calculate the **inflation rate**, which is the annual percentage change in the price level. To calculate the inflation rate, we use the formula:

$$\begin{array}{c}\text{Inflation}\\\text{rate}\end{array} = \frac{(\text{CPI this year} - \text{CPI last year})}{\text{CPI last year}} \times 100.$$

We can use this formula to calculate the inflation rate in 2006. The CPI in June 2006 was 202.9, and the CPI in June 2005 was 194.5. So the inflation rate during the twelve months to June 2006 was

$$\begin{array}{c}\text{Inflation}\\\text{rate}\end{array} = \frac{(202.9 - 194.5)}{194.5} \times 100 = 4.3\%.$$

Figure 6.12 shows the CPI and the inflation rate in the United States during the 35 years between 1971 and 2006. The two parts of the figure are related.

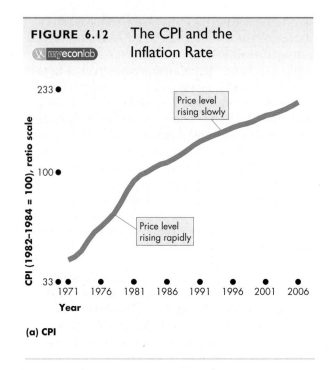

FIGURE 6.12   The CPI and the Inflation Rate

Price level rising slowly

Price level rising rapidly

(a) CPI

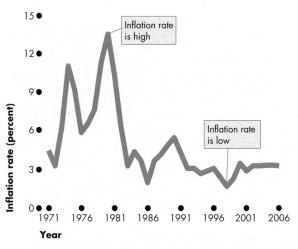

Inflation rate is high

Inflation rate is low

(b) Inflation rate

In part (a), the CPI (the price level) has increased every year. In part (b), the inflation rate has averaged 4.8 percent a year. During the 1970s and early 1980s, the inflation rate was high and sometimes exceeded 10 percent a year. But after 1983, the inflation rate fell to an average of 3 percent a year.

Source of data: Bureau of Labor Statistics.

Figure 6.12 shows that when the price *level* in part (a) rises rapidly, the inflation rate in part (b) is high, and when the price level in part (a) rises slowly, the inflation rate in part (b) is low. Notice in part (a) that the CPI increased every year during this period. During the late 1970s and 1980, the CPI was increasing rapidly, but its rate of increase slowed during the 1980s, 1990s, and 2000s.

The CPI is not a perfect measure of the price level, and changes in the CPI probably overstate the inflation rate. Let's look at the sources of bias.

The Biased CPI

The main sources of bias in the CPI are

- New goods bias
- Quality change bias
- Commodity substitution bias
- Outlet substitution bias

New Goods Bias If you want to compare the price level in 2007 with that in 1977, you must somehow compare the price of a computer today with that of a typewriter in 1977. Because a PC is more expensive than a typewriter was, the arrival of the PC puts an upward bias into the CPI and its inflation rate.

Quality Change Bias Cars, CD players, and many other items get better every year. Part of the rise in the prices of these items is a payment for improved quality and is not inflation. But the CPI counts the entire price rise as inflation and so overstates inflation.

Commodity Substitution Bias Changes in relative prices lead consumers to change the items they buy. For example, if the price of beef rises and the price of chicken remains unchanged, people buy more chicken and less beef. Suppose they switch from beef to chicken on a scale that provides the same amount of protein and the same enjoyment as before and their expenditure is the same as before. The price of protein has not changed. But because it ignores the substitution of chicken for beef, the CPI says the price of protein has increased.

Outlet Substitution Bias When confronted with higher prices, people use discount stores more frequently and convenience stores less frequently. This phenomenon is called *outlet substitution*. The CPI surveys do not monitor outlet substitutions.

The Magnitude of the Bias

You've reviewed the sources of bias in the CPI. But how big is the bias? This question was tackled in 1996 by a Congressional Advisory Commission on the Consumer Price Index chaired by Michael Boskin, an economics professor at Stanford University. This commission said that the CPI overstates inflation by 1.1 percentage points a year. That is, if the CPI reports that inflation is 3.1 percent a year, most likely inflation is actually 2 percent a year.

Some Consequences of the Bias

The bias in the CPI distorts private contracts and increases government outlays. Many private agreements, such as wage contracts, are linked to the CPI. For example, a firm and its workers might agree to a three-year wage deal that increases the wage rate by 2 percent a year *plus* the percentage increase in the CPI. Such a deal ends up giving the workers more real income than the firm intended.

Close to a third of federal government outlays, including Social Security checks, are linked directly to the CPI. And while a bias of 1 percent a year seems small, accumulated over a decade it adds up to almost a trillion dollars of additional expenditures.

Reducing the Bias To reduce the bias in the CPI, the BLS now undertakes consumer spending surveys at more frequent intervals and is experimenting with a chained CPI (see Chapter 5, p. 120).

REVIEW QUIZ

1 What is the CPI and how is it calculated?
2 How do we calculate the inflation rate and what is the relationship between the CPI and the inflation rate?
3 What are the four main ways in which the CPI is an upward-biased measure of the price level?
4 What problems arise from the CPI bias?

myeconlab Study Plan 6.3

You've now completed your study of the measurement of macroeconomic performance. Your task in the following chapters is to learn what determines that performance and how policy actions might improve it. But first, take a close-up look at the jobless recovery of 2002 and 2003 in *Reading Between the Lines* on pp. 146–147.

Jobs in the 2002–2006 Expansion

http://www.latimes.com

Solid Growth for U.S. Payrolls

April 8, 2006

The U.S. economy turned in a solid performance last month, adding a net 211,000 new jobs and driving the unemployment rate back to its lowest point in the current expansion, the government reported Friday.

March's unemployment rate fell to 4.7%—down from 4.8%—matching the level of two months earlier. That was the lowest rate since July 2001, when the economy was in recession.

The job gain exceeded economists' consensus forecast by 21,000. But the Labor Department revised downward its estimates of job growth in the prior two months by 34,000.

All major economic sectors added jobs in March except manufacturing, which lost 5,000. . . .

Friday's job report provided the latest evidence that the economy had rebounded strongly from a slump at the end of last year. . . .

The Bush administration, however, trumpeted the employment report as a rare and welcome piece of political good news. Within an hour of its release, President Bush said "These millions of new jobs are evidence of an economic resurgence that is strong, broad and benefiting all Americans." . . .

The administration made much of the fact that the March job report sent the economy's total job gain above 5 million since the low point in August 2003. The economy has added jobs at a rate of 167,000 a month since then.

By contrast, however, the economy generated 240,000 jobs a month during the second half of the 1990s. Job creation during the entire decade of the 1990s proceeded at an average of 180,000 a month—faster than in the current expansion even though the decade began with the 1990-91 recession. . . .

Essence of the Story

▶ The U.S. economy added a net 211,000 new jobs in March 2006.

▶ The unemployment rate fell to 4.7 percent, the lowest since July 2001.

▶ President Bush said that the job numbers were evidence of a strong economic resurgence.

▶ The administration emphasized that the economy had added jobs at a rate of 167,000 a month since August 2003.

▶ The economy generated 240,000 jobs a month during the second half of the 1990s.

▶ Job creation during the entire decade of the 1990s averaged 180,000 a month.

▶ This news article reports the number of jobs created in March 2006 and the average number of jobs created each month between 2003 and 2006, and during the 1990s expansion.

▶ The figures show the job creation performance of the U.S. economy during the expansion of 2002–2006 and place it in a longer-term historical perspective.

▶ In Fig. 1, the y-axis shows the level of employment as a percentage of its level at the business cycle trough and the x-axis shows the number of months since the business cycle trough.

▶ By March 2006, the expansion had been running for 54 months (4 1/2 years).

▶ The blue line in the figure shows the growth of employment during the 2002–2006 expansion.

▶ In March 2006, employment was only 6.5 percent higher than it had been at the cycle trough in November 2001.

▶ The red line in the figure shows the growth of employment on the average during the previous five expansions.

▶ On the average, after 54 months of expansion, employment has expanded by 12 percent—almost double that of the current expansion.

▶ The shaded area shows the range of experience over the previous five expansions.

▶ You can see that the current expansion follows the weakest of the previous ones.

▶ Figure 2 shows the same comparison for the unemployment rate.

▶ In an average expansion, the unemployment rate falls after 54 months to 70 percent of its trough level.

▶ But in the current expansions, the unemployment rate actually increased and after 18 months stood at 10 percent *above* its trough level.

▶ Again, the current expansion is the weakest of the past six expansions.

▶ The slow job recovery arises partly from a weaker-than-average recovery of production (see p. 127) and partly from an increase in output per worker.

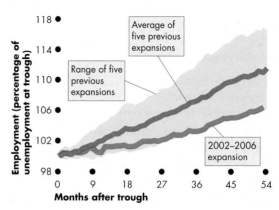

Figure 1 Employment during the 2002–2006 expansion

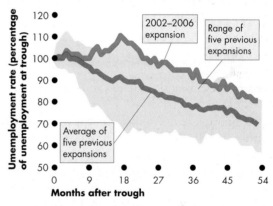

Figure 2 The unemployment rate during the 2002–2006 expansion

SUMMARY

Key Points

Jobs and Wages (pp. 132–136)

- The unemployment rate averaged 5.9 percent between 1961 and 2006. It increases in recessions and decreases in expansions.
- The labor force participation rate and the employment-to-population ratio have an upward trend and fluctuate with the business cycle.
- The labor force participation rate has increased for females and decreased for males.
- Aggregate hours have an upward trend, and they fluctuate with the business cycle.
- Real hourly wage rates grow, but their growth rates slowed during the 1970s.

Unemployment and Full Employment (pp. 137–141)

- People are constantly entering and leaving the state of unemployment.
- The duration of unemployment fluctuates over the business cycle. But the demographic patterns of unemployment are constant.
- Unemployment can be frictional, structural, or cyclical.
- When all unemployment is frictional and structural, the unemployment rate equals the natural unemployment rate, the economy is at full employment, and real GDP equals potential GDP.
- Over the business cycle, real GDP fluctuates around potential GDP and the unemployment rate fluctuates around the natural unemployment rate.

The Consumer Price Index (pp. 142–145)

- The Consumer Price Index (CPI) is a measure of the average of the prices paid by urban consumers for a fixed basket of consumer goods and services.
- The CPI is defined to equal 100 for a reference base period—currently 1982–1984.
- The inflation rate is the percentage change in the CPI from one period to the next.
- Changes in the CPI probably overstate the inflation rate because of the bias that arises from new goods, quality changes, commodity substitution, and outlet substitution.
- The bias in the CPI distorts private contracts and increases government outlays.

Key Figures

Key Terms

PROBLEMS

1. The Bureau of Labor Statistics reported the following data for May 2006:
   Labor force: 150,696,000
   Employment: 144,041,000
   Working-age population: 228,428,000
   Calculate for that month the
   a. Unemployment rate.
   b. Labor force participation rate.
   c. Employment-to-population ratio.

2. In the New Orleans metropolitan area in August 2005, the labor force was 634,512 and 35,222 people were unemployed. In September 2005 following Hurricane Katrina, the labor force fell by 156,518 and the number employed fell by 206,024. Calculate the unemployment rate in August 2005 and in September 2005.

3. In June 2003, the U.S. unemployment rate was 6.5 percent. In June 2006, the unemployment rate was 4.8 percent. Use this information to predict what happened between June 2003 and June 2006 to the numbers of
   a. Job losers and job leavers.
   b. Labor force entrants and reentrants.

4. In July 2007, in the economy of Sandy Island, 10,000 people were employed, 1,000 were unemployed, and 5,000 were not in the labor force. During August 2007, 80 people lost their jobs, 20 people quit their jobs, 150 people were hired or recalled, 50 people withdrew from the labor force, and 40 people entered or reentered the labor force. Calculate for July 2007
   a. The unemployment rate.
   b. The employment-to-population ratio.
   And calculate for the end of August 2007
   c. The number of people unemployed.
   d. The number of people employed.
   e. The unemployment rate.

5. The IMF *World Economic Outlook* reports the following unemployment rates:

Region	May 2005	May 2006
United States	5.1	4.6
Euro area	8.7	7.9
Japan	4.4	4.0

*Solutions to odd-numbered problems are provided.

a. What do these numbers tell you about the phase of the business cycle in the United States, Europe, and Japan in May 2006?
b. What do you think these numbers tell us about the relative size of the natural unemployment rates in the United States, the Euro area, and Japan?
c. Do these numbers tell us anything about the relative size of the labor force participation rates and employment-to-population ratios in the three regions?
d. Why might these unemployment numbers understate or overstate the true amount of unemployment?

6. The Bureau of Labor Statistics reported the following CPI data:
   June 2004   189.7
   June 2005   194.5
   June 2006   202.9
   a. What do these numbers tell you about the price level in these three years?
   b. Calculate the inflation rates for the years ended June 2005 and June 2006.
   c. How did the inflation rate change in 2006?
   d. Why might these CPI numbers be biased?
   e. What is the Bureau of Labor Statistics doing to minimize the bias in the CPI numbers?

7. A typical family on Sandy Island consumes only juice and cloth. Last year, which was the base year, the family spent $40 on juice and $25 on cloth. In the base year, juice was $4 a bottle and cloth was $5 a length. This year, juice is $4 a bottle and cloth is $6 a length. Calculate
   a. The CPI basket.
   b. The CPI in the current year.
   c. The inflation rate in the current year.

8. The IMF *World Economic Outlook* reports the following price level data (2000 = 100):

Region	2003	2004	2005
United States	106.8	109.7	113.4
Euro area	106.7	109.0	111.4
Japan	98.1	98.1	97.8

a. Which region had the highest inflation rate before 2004 and which has the highest inflation rate after 2004?
b. Describe the path of the price level in Japan.

CRITICAL THINKING

1. Study *Reading Between the Lines* on pp. 146–147 and then answer the following questions:
   a. Did the expansion of 2002–2006 create jobs at an unusually fast rate, an unusually slow rate, or an average rate?
   b. What did the Bush administration say about the March 2006 numbers and was its assessment correct?
   c. Can you think of reasons why the first two years of the expansion didn't create many jobs?
   d. Do you think the U.S. government should help to create more jobs? If so, why? How?

2. In 1929, U.S. real GDP was $865.2 billion, the CPI was 17.2, and the unemployment rate was 3.2 percent. In 1933 at the height of the Great Depression, real GDP was $635.5 billion, the CPI was 12.9, and the unemployment rate was 24.9 percent.
   a. Describe the change in the standard of living between 1929 and 1933.
   b. Calculate the inflation rate between 1929 and 1933.
   c. Explain what happened to the cost of living of the typical urban family.

3. You've seen in this chapter that the average work-week has shortened over the years. Do you think that shorter work hours are a problem or a benefit? Do you expect the average workweek to keep getting shorter? Why or why not?

4. An increasing number of jobs are part-time jobs. Can you think of some reasons for this trend? Who benefits from part-time jobs: the employer, the worker, or both? Explain with examples.

5. You've seen that the CPI is biased and overstates the true inflation rate. It would be a simple matter to adjust the CPI for the known average bias. Yet we continue to keep a flawed measure of inflation in place. Why do you think we don't adjust the CPI for the known average bias so that its measure of the inflation rate is more accurate? Explain who gains from the biased measure and who loses from it. Try to think of reasons why those who lose have not persuaded those who win to adopt a more accurate measure.

WEB ACTIVITIES

myeconlab Links to Web sites

1. Review the Federal Reserve's *Beige Book*. In which phase of the business cycle is the economy in your region? How does your region compare to the nation as a whole?

2. Visit the Bureau of Labor Statistics and find labor market data for your own state.
   a. What have been the trends in employment, unemployment, and labor force participation in your own state during the past two years?
   b. On the basis of what you know about your own region, how would you set about explaining these trends?
   c. Try to identify those industries that have expanded most and those that have shrunk.
   d. What are the problems with your own regional labor market that you think need state government action to resolve?
   e. What actions do you think your state government must take to resolve these problems? Answer this question by using the demand and supply model of the labor market and predict the effects of the actions you prescribe.
   f. Compare the labor market performance of your own state with that of the nation as a whole.
   g. If your state is performing better than the national average, to what do you attribute the success? If your region is performing worse than the national average, to what do you attribute its problems? What federal actions are needed in your state labor market?

3. Visit the Bureau of Labor Statistics and find CPI data for your own region.
   a. What have been the trends in the CPI in your region during the past two years?
   b. Compare the CPI performance of your own region with that of the nation as a whole.
   c. On the basis of what you know about your own region, how would you set about explaining its deviation from the national average?

The Big Picture

Macroeconomics is a large and controversial subject that is interlaced with political ideological disputes. And it is a field in which charlatans as well as serious thinkers have much to say. This page is a map that looks back at the road you've just traveled and forward at the path you will take from here.

You began your study of macroeconomics in Chapter 4 with a look at the origins and issues of macroeconomics. You also reviewed the core questions of the subject: What are the causes of

- Economic growth?
- Business cycles?
- Unemployment?
- Inflation?
- Exchange rate fluctuations?
- Surpluses, deficits, and debts?

Also, in Chapter 4, you previewed the macroeconomic policy challenges.

In Chapter 5, you learned how we measure the economy's output and one way of measuring the price level. We use these measures to calculate the rate of economic growth, business cycle fluctuations, and inflation. You discovered that making these measurements is not straightforward and that small measurement errors can have a big effect on our perceptions about how we are doing. In Chapter 6, you learned how we measure the state of the labor market—the levels of employment and unemployment and wages and another way of measuring the price level: the CPI.

The chapters that lie ahead of you explain the theories that economists have developed to explain macroeconomic performance.

In Chapters 7 through 10, you will study the economy in the long run when there is full employment. This material is central to the oldest question in macroeconomics that Adam Smith tried to answer: What are the causes of the wealth of nations? You'll begin in Chapter 7 by studying the forces that determine potential GDP, employment, and the real wage rate. You will also learn in this chapter how saving and lending finance borrowing and investment and determine the real interest rate. Then, in Chapter 8, you will study the growth process and the roles of capital accumulation and technological change in bringing about economic growth.

In Chapters 9 and 10, you will study three other old questions that Adam Smith's contemporary and friend David Hume first addressed: What causes inflation? What causes international deficits and surpluses? And why do exchange rates fluctuate?

Later chapters explain the business cycle as well as macroeconomic policy, both topics on which David Hume had some of the early insights.

Before continuing your study of macroeconomics, spend a few minutes with David Hume and with one of today's macroeconomists, Valerie Ramey of the University of California, San Diego.

Economists Versus Mercantilists

"... in every kingdom into which money begins to flow in greater abundance than formerly, everything takes a new face: labor and industry gain life; the merchant becomes more enterprising, the manufacturer more diligent and skillful, and even the farmer follows his plow with greater alacrity and attention."

DAVID HUME
Essays, Moral and Political

The Economist

David Hume, *who was born in Scotland in 1711 and died there in 1776, did not think of himself as an economist. "Philosophy and general learning" is how he described the subject of his life's work. Hume was an extraordinary thinker and writer. Published in 1742, his* Essays, Moral and Political, *range across economics, political science, moral philosophy, the arts, history, literature, ethics, and religion and explore such topics as love, marriage, divorce, suicide, death, and the immortality of the soul! But they also include some economic gems. His economic essays provide astonishing insights into the forces that cause inflation, business cycle fluctuations, balance of payments deficits, and interest rate fluctuations; and they explain the effects of taxes and government deficits and debts.*

Data were scarce in Hume's day, so he was not able to draw on detailed evidence to support his analysis. But he was empirical. He repeatedly appealed to experience and evidence as the ultimate judge of the validity of an argument.

Hume's fundamentally empirical approach dominates macroeconomics today.

The Issue

Mercantilism is the (incorrect) belief that a nation's wealth depends on the amount of gold (or more generally money) it possesses. Mercantilists say that by imposing tariffs to discourage imports and by encouraging exports, a nation can earn more than it spends in its trade with other nations and become richer by piling up the funds that its trade surplus earns.

The first steps toward the scientific study of macroeconomics were a reaction against mercantilism, and three of David Hume's essays on money, interest, and the balance of trade were directed toward debunking it.

In his essay "Of Money," Hume argued that the quantity of money (gold in his day) is unimportant. To make his point, he compared the amounts of money in ancient and contemporary societies and provided one of the first accounts of the quantity theory of money.

In his essay "Of Interest," he was struggling to understand the difference between the real interest rate and the nominal interest rate and argued that a low (real) interest rate enabled a nation to flourish.

But Hume's most important essay is "Of the Balance of Trade." In this essay, he explains why, if a nation lost most of its money or saw its money multiply to many times its initial level, forces would come into play that would restored the initial amount of money and leave everything else unchanged.

Hume laid out the reasons why an increase in the quantity of money couldn't make a nation rich and the forces that keep the distribution of money across the global economy in equilibrium, by drawing a parallel between money and water: Just as water remains at a level, so does money, he argued. He reached his conclusions by a powerful mixture of empirical evidence and thought experiments.

His classic thought experiment was to imagine that, by some miracle, "four fifths of all the money in

Great Britain ... [was] ... annihilated in one night." Imagining the consequences, he went on, "Must not the price of all labour and commodities sink in proportion? ... What nation could then ... sell manufactures at the same price, which to us would afford sufficient profit? In how little time, therefore, must this bring back the money which we had lost, and raise us to the level of all the neighbouring nations?"

Then

In 1776, the year in which David Hume died, William Playfair began to use economic data and display it in graphical form. He invented the time-series line graph, the bar chart, and the pie chart. Of the graphs we use today, only the scatter diagram came later. And the way we make graphs today is virtually unchanged since Playfair's day.

Some of Playfair's earliest graphs (like the one below) showed exports, imports, and the balance of trade—the item that was at the center of the disagreement between the economists and the mercantilists.

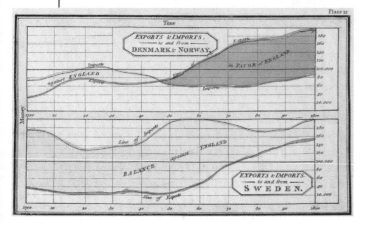

Now

Today, the Bureau of Economic Analysis compiles detailed data on the national accounts and international trade statistics. Advances in computer and communication technology have placed a huge economic database on everyone's desktop (or lap or even palm). At the click of a mouse, we can create graphs and explore data in ways that William Playfair could not have imagined.

At the Bureau of Economic Analysis Web site (shown below) and a similar Web site operated by the Bureau of Labor Statistics, you can view data and make graphs of thousands of variables that describe the health of the U.S. economy and its regions, states, and counties.

Valerie Ramey, whom you can meet on the following pages, is a macroeconomist. She has contributed to our understanding of economic growth, inflation, and the business cycle and played a significant role in using data to improve our understanding of how the economy works.

Valerie A. Ramey

Valerie A. Ramey is Professor of Economics and Chair of the UCSD Institute for Applied Economics Research at the University of California, San Diego, and an Associate of the National Bureau of Economic Research.

Born in 1959, Professor Ramey grew up in Panama. She obtained her B.A. in Economics and Spanish at the University of Arizona in 1981 and her Ph.D. in Economics at Stanford University in 1987.

Professor Ramey is an empirical macroeconomist. She has tested a number of important hypotheses about the channels of transmission of monetary policy, the role of technology shocks in driving the business cycle, and the relationship between the volatility and growth of real GDP.

All Professor Ramey's work uses data and employs statistical (econometric) tools to draw reliable conclusions. Her work has resulted in numerous important papers in the American Economic Review *and other leading journals.*

Michael Parkin talked with Valerie Ramey about her work and the progress that economists have made in understanding macroeconomic performance.

Professor Ramey, what attracted you to economics and in particular to macroeconomics?
I started college as a political science major, thinking it was a good preparation for law school. I was also on the debate team, and the topic my freshman year was: "Resolved: that the Federal Government should guarantee full employment." In the process of collecting evidence and writing cases, I had to learn a lot of macroeconomics quickly. I became so interested, that I switched majors. I was attracted to macroeconomics in particular because I thought that the questions, such as why some countries grow and others don't and why the Great Depression happened, were among the most important in economics.

You are an econometrician as well as a macroeconomist. What does an econometrician do?
Theoretical econometricians create new statistical methods for dealing with complications in estimating economic parameters and testing hypotheses.

Applied econometricians keep abreast of the latest methods and use them to answer questions. I am an applied econometrician. I use methods developed by theoretical econometricians to address data issues.

So data are crucial in your work. What kind of data do you use? Where does it come from?
Yes, data are crucial to my work. Looking for good data and analyzing a new data set are my favorite research activities. I use data from many sources. Some of my papers use publicly available government data, some use microeconomic data sets, and sometimes I collect my own data. For example, in one of my projects, I wanted to know what happens to the machinery after a plant closes down. At the time, we had a number of data sets that traced workers after factories closed down but none that traced capital. So in the mid-1990s, I went to several aerospace factories that were closing down and was able to gather data on every piece of equipment they

sold, what industry bought it, and how much they sold it for relative to the price at which they had bought it. I found that capital loses much more of its value when it switches industry than a worker does.

Currently, I am using time use studies going back to 1912 to determine whether leisure has increased over the last century. Keynes predicted that it would, but my research suggests that it hasn't changed much since 1900.

How have the data available to economists changed over the years?

Data availability has changed dramatically over the years. When classic economists such as Adam Smith and David Ricardo were writing, there were no measurements of the national economy. Governments began collecting macroeconomic data and forming national accounts in the 1940s. Over the last few decades, the amount of macroeconomic and microeconomic data has increased tremendously. The Internet has been a great help in disseminating data. When I wrote my dissertation, I had to input all my data by hand from hard copies!

Can you explain, perhaps with an example, how we use data to gain insights into macroeconomic performance?

We can obtain many insights into macroeconomic performance using data. Consider, for example, my work on the link between growth and volatility. In the late 1980s, Robert Lucas argued that the cost of business cycle volatility was very small and that macroeconomists should refocus their attention toward growth. My husband (who is also an economist) and I were talking about this at dinner one night, and he noted that perhaps business cycles were costly because they impeded growth.

To test this hypothesis, we used a cross-country data set to study the link between the volatility of the business cycle and the long-term growth rate. We found that countries with higher business cycle volatility had sig-

> We found that countries with higher business cycle volatility had significantly lower growth rates. Thus, you can't study growth separately from business cycles.

nificantly lower growth rates. Thus, you can't study growth separately from business cycles.

Keynes believed that the business cycle was driven by fluctuations in aggregate demand. Nobel Laureates Finn Kydland and Edward Prescott say that it is driven by technology shocks and aggregate supply fluctuations. What does your research say about the source of the business cycle?

Several of my recent papers have looked at this very issue: Are technology shocks an important source of aggregate fluctuations? All of my work on this subject answers this question with a resounding "no." On the other hand, I have found that government spending is one of the sources of fluctuations, but its role is relatively small.

> Are technology shocks an important source of aggregate fluctuations? All of my work on this subject answers this question with a resounding "no."

Whatever the source of the business cycle, there is little doubt that fluctuations have become milder. You tried to account for this phenomenon with a study of the auto industry. What did you discover?

Some researchers have hypothesized that fluctuations have become milder because firms now use information technology to manage their production and inventories better. I thought it would be interesting to analyze this hypothesis by doing a case study of the U.S. automobile industry, an industry that has incorporated a lot of information technology. Surprisingly, I found that the decrease in volatility in the automobile industry after 1984 came not from better production and inventory management, but rather from a more stable demand environment. In contrast to the period before 1984, the last couple of decades have had very stable monetary policy and, until recently, no significant oil price increases. This stability in the factors affecting sales is what accounts for the decline in the volatility of the business cycle. The recent events show that when the demand environment becomes more unstable again, output volatility also rises.

You've done a lot of work on money, its effects and transmission mechanisms? How would you summarize our current knowledge of the effects of money on the economy?

I think the bulk of research supports the following description: When the Federal Reserve raises the federal funds rate, it leads to a chain of events that lowers output and employment for a few years, and eventually lowers the inflation rate. Within four years, output and employment return to normal. However, movements in the federal funds rate that aren't just reactions to the economy are only a small part of economic fluctuations.

How do the Fed's monetary policy actions get transmitted?

We are less sure about the answer to this question. Some say that sticky prices and/or wages are important; others say that limited participation in the financial system is important. The impact may be solely through interest rates, or it may also be through a "credit channel." It is very difficult to get a clear answer from the data.

What is your assessment of the conduct of monetary policy under Chairman Greenspan? Do you expect Ben Bernanke to be an innovative Chairman of the Fed?

Alan Greenspan is already being hailed as one of the greatest chairmen in Federal Reserve history. I don't think this assessment will change as time goes by. His accomplishments are truly remarkable.

> ... stability in the factors affecting sales is what accounts for the decline in the volatility of the business cycle.

I was delighted when Ben Bernanke became the new chair. I do think he will be an innovative chair. He has a rare combination of a great research intellect and common sense about the economy. That bodes well for the conduct of monetary policy during his tenure.

What advice do you have for someone who is just beginning to study economics? What other subjects do you think work well alongside economics? Do you have some reading suggestions?

My advice for someone just beginning to study economics is to remember the importance of the questions when you are immersed in learning the tools. Many students are drawn into economics because of the topics discussed in the introductory classes. Once they begin taking the technically challenging intermediate classes, they sometimes forget why they liked economics.

As side reading, I recommend the book *The Economics of Public Issues* by Roger LeRoy Miller, Daniel K. Benjamin, and Douglass C. North, which I have used in my public policy class for some 15 years now. Students praise it, saying that it is truly eye-opening with respect to the relevance of economics to public issues.

Other subjects that work well alongside economics are math and political science. The math is particular important if one wants to do graduate work in economics. The political science is useful because it explains why actual government policy is so often different from the optimal policy.

At Full Employment: The Classical Model

Our Economy's Compass

The path followed by the economy is a bit like that of an explorer searching for a new route through unknown terrain. The explorer's

progress is like the economy's growth that brings an ever-rising standard of living. Sometimes the explorer strays off course to either the left or the right. These departures from the main course are like the alternation between recession and expansion as the economy fluctuates over the business cycle.

But the explorer has a compass that helps to keep finding the main path and avoid departing from it too far. The explorer's compass is like the forces that prevent the economy from fluctuating too wildly and keep returning it to its forward path. These are the forces that determine full-employment equilibrium.

The economy is a complex system that is hard to understand. Economists have made progress in their attempts to understand the economy and improve its performance by building macroeconomic models. There isn't a unique, all-embracing macroeconomic model that explains everything. Instead, there is a number of models, each of which works well for the special purpose for which it was developed.

You will study a model in this chapter—the *classical model*—that explains the forces that determine real GDP at full employment. The model also explains what determines the level of employment, the real wage rate, and the real interest rate and the allocation of real GDP between consumption and investment. In *Reading Between the Lines* at the end of the chapter, you will see how the classical model helps us to understand why real GDP per person is much higher in the United States than it is in Europe but why, at the same time, the real wage rate in the United States is almost the same as that in Europe.

After studying this chapter, you will be able to

▶ Explain the purpose of the classical model

▶ Describe the relationship between the quantity of labor employed and real GDP

▶ Explain what determines the full-employment level of employment and real wage rate and potential GDP

▶ Explain what determines unemployment when the economy is at full employment

▶ Explain how borrowing and lending decisions interact to determine the real interest rate, saving, and investment

▶ Apply the classical model to explain changes and international differences in potential GDP and the standard of living

The Classical Model: A Preview

Economists have made progress in understanding macroeconomic performance by distinguishing between *real* variables and *nominal* variables.

Real variables, which include real GDP, employment and unemployment, the real wage rate, consumption, saving, investment, and the real interest rate, measure quantities that tell us what is *really* happening to economic well-being.

Nominal variables, which include the price level (CPI or GDP deflator), the inflation rate, nominal GDP, the nominal wage rate, and the nominal interest rate, measure objects that tell us how *dollar values* and the cost of living are changing.

The separation of macroeconomic performance into a real part and a nominal part is the basis of a huge discovery called the **classical dichotomy**, which states:

> At full employment, the forces that determine real variables are independent of those that determine nominal variables.

In practical terms, the classical dichotomy means that we can explain why real GDP per person in the United States is 20 times that in Nigeria by looking only at the real parts of the two economies and ignoring differences in their price levels and inflation rates. Similarly, we can explain why real GDP per person in 2006 was around twice that in 1971 without considering what has happened to the value of the dollar between those two years.

The **classical model** is a model of an economy that determines the *real* variables—real GDP, employment and unemployment, the real wage rate, consumption, saving, investment, and the real interest rate—at full employment.

Most economists believe that the economy is rarely at full employment. They see the business cycle as the fluctuation of real GDP around its full-employment level. Classical economists see the economy as always being at full employment. They see the business cycle as the fluctuation of the full-employment level of real GDP. Regardless of which view of the business cycle an economist takes, all agree that the classical model that you're now going to study provides powerful insights into macroeconomic performance.

Ⓧ **myeconlab** Study Plan 7.1

Real GDP and Employment

To produce more real GDP, we must use more labor or more capital or develop technologies that are more productive. It takes time to change the quantity of capital and the state of technology. But the quantity of labor employed can change quickly. So we can change real GDP quickly by changing the quantity of labor employed. Let's look at the relationship between the quantity of labor and real GDP.

Production Possibilities

When you studied the limits to production in Chapter 2 (see p. 34), you learned that the *production possibilities frontier* is the boundary between the combinations of goods and services that can be produced and those that cannot. Let's think about the production possibilities frontier for two special items: real GDP and the quantity of leisure time.

Real GDP is a measure of the final goods and services produced in the economy in a given time period (see Chapter 5, p. 112). We measure real GDP as a number of 2000 dollars, but the measure is *real*. Real GDP is not a pile of dollars. It is a pile of goods and services. Think of it as a number of big shopping carts filled with goods and services. Each cart contains some of each kind of different goods and services produced, and one cartload of items costs $1 trillion. To say that real GDP is $12 trillion means that real GDP is 12 very big shopping carts of goods and services.

The quantity of leisure time is the number of hours we spend not working. It is the time we spend playing or watching sports, seeing movies, and hanging out with friends. It also includes the time we spend looking for a job if we don't have one.

Each leisure hour could have been spent working. When the quantity of leisure time increases by one hour, the quantity of labor employed decreases by one hour. If we spent all our time taking leisure, we would produce nothing. Real GDP would be zero. The more leisure we forgo, the greater is the quantity of labor employed and the greater is real GDP.

The relationship between leisure time and real GDP is a *production possibilities frontier* (*PPF*). Figure 7.1(a) shows an example of this frontier. The economy has 450 billion hours of time available. If people use all these hours to pursue leisure, no labor is

FIGURE 7.1   Production Possibilities and the Production Function

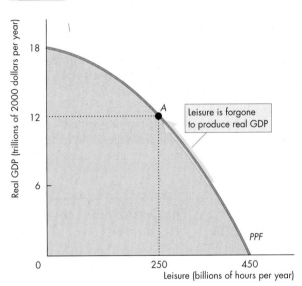

(a) Production possibilities frontier

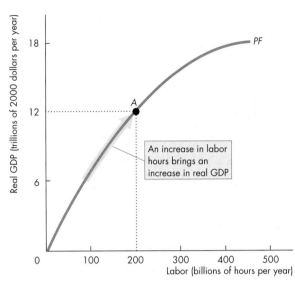

(b) Production function

On the *PPF* in part (a), if we enjoy 450 billion hours of leisure, we produce no real GDP. If we take 250 billion hours of leisure time and work for 200 billion hours, we

produce a real GDP of $12 trillion, at point *A*.

At point *A* on the production function in part (b), we work for 200 billion hours and produce $12 trillion of real GDP.

employed and real GDP is zero. As people forgo leisure and work more, real GDP increases. If people took 250 billion hours in leisure and spent 200 billion hours working, real GDP would be $12 trillion at point *A*. If people spent all the available hours working, real GDP would be $18 trillion.

The bowed-out *PPF* displays increasing opportunity cost. In this case, the opportunity cost of a given amount of real GDP is the amount of leisure time forgone to produce it. As real GDP increases, each additional unit of real GDP costs an increasing amount of forgone leisure. The reason is that we use the most productive labor first, and as we use more labor, we use increasingly less productive labor.

The Production Function

The **production function** is the relationship between real GDP and the quantity of labor employed when all other influences on production remain the same. The production function is like a mirror image of the *PPF* of leisure and real GDP. Figure 7.1(b) shows the production function for the economy whose *PPF* is shown in Fig. 7.1(a). When the quantity of labor

employed is zero, real GDP is also zero, and as the quantity of labor employed increases, so does real GDP. When 200 billion labor hours are employed, real GDP is $12 trillion (at point *A*).

A decrease in leisure hours and the corresponding increase in the quantity of labor employed bring movements along the *PPF* and the production function and an increase in real GDP. The arrows along the *PPF* and the production function in Fig. 7.1 show these movements. An example of such a movement occurred during World War II when employment and real GDP surged.

REVIEW QUIZ

1. What is the relationship between the leisure time–real GDP *PPF* and the production function?
2. What does the outward-bowed shape of the leisure time–real GDP *PPF* imply about the opportunity cost of real GDP and why is the *PPF* bowed outward?

myeconlab Study Plan 7.2

The Labor Market and Potential GDP

With a given amount of capital (physical and human) and a given state of technology, real GDP depends on the quantity of labor hours employed. The *PPF* shows us how much labor we must employ to produce a given level of real GDP. But what determines the levels of employment and real GDP at which the economy operates? Why don't we always produce the maximum possible output?

The quantity of real GDP produced depends on choices about how to allocate time between work and leisure. This choice is expressed in the **labor market**, which is the market in which households supply and firms demand labor services.

In the U.S. economy, there are many labor markets—markets for plumbers, dentists, economists, surgeons, and so on. In macroeconomics, we lump all the different types of labor together into one type, the quantity of which is measured by *aggregate hours*. The labor market determines the quantity of labor hours employed and the quantity of real GDP supplied. You will learn how by studying

- The demand for labor
- The supply of labor
- Labor market equilibrium
- Potential GDP

The Demand for Labor

The *quantity of labor demanded* is the number of labor hours hired by all the firms in the economy during a given period. This quantity depends on

1. The real wage rate
2. The marginal product of labor

We focus on the relationship between the quantity of labor demanded and the real wage rate and hold all the influences on labor hiring plans constant. We ask: How does the quantity of labor hired vary as the real wage rate varies?

Demand for Labor Schedule and Demand for Labor Curve The **demand for labor** is the relationship between the quantity of labor demanded and the real wage rate when all other influences on hiring plans remain the same.

We can represent the demand for labor as either a demand schedule or a demand curve. The table in Fig. 7.2 shows part of a demand for labor schedule. It tells us the quantity of labor demanded at three different real wage rates. For example, if the real wage rate is $40 an hour, the quantity of labor demanded is 150 billion hours a year in row *A*. The demand for labor curve is *LD*. Points *A*, *B*, and *C* on the curve correspond to rows *A*, *B*, and *C* of the demand schedule.

What is the real wage rate and why does the quantity of labor demanded depend on it rather than on the dollar wage rate? Let's answer these questions.

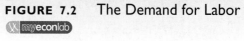

FIGURE 7.2   The Demand for Labor

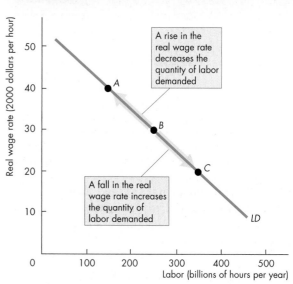

	Real wage rate (2000 dollars per hour)	**Quantity of labor demanded** (billions of hours per year)
A	40	150
B	30	250
C	20	350

The table shows part of a demand for labor schedule. Points *A*, *B*, and *C* on the demand for labor curve correspond to the rows of the table. The lower the real wage rate, the greater is the quantity of labor demanded.

The Real Wage Rate The **real wage rate** is the quantity of goods and services that an hour of labor earns. In contrast, the **money wage rate** is the number of dollars that an hour of labor earns. The real wage rate is equal to the money wage rate divided by the price level (and multiplied by 100). So the real wage rate is the wage rate expressed in constant dollars. (Today, we express the real wage rate in 2000 dollars.)

Like real GDP, the real wage rate is a pile of goods and services, not a pile of dollars. Think of it as a number of shopping baskets of goods and services. Each basket contains some of each kind of different goods and services produced, and one basket costs $10. If the real wage rate is $40 an hour, then it is really 4 baskets of goods and services.

The *real* wage rate influences the quantity of labor demanded because what matters to firms is not the number of dollars they pay (money wage rate) but how much output they must sell to earn those dollars.

The quantity of labor demanded *increases* as the real wage rate *decreases*. The demand for labor curve slopes downward. Why? To answer this question, we must learn about the productivity of labor and the marginal product of labor.

The Marginal Product of Labor The **marginal product of labor** is the change in real GDP that results from employing an additional hour of labor when all other influences on production remain the same. The marginal product of labor is governed by the **law of diminishing returns**, which states that as the quantity of labor increases, other things remaining the same, the marginal product of labor decreases.

The Law of Diminishing Returns Diminishing returns arise because the amount of capital is fixed. Two people operating one machine are not twice as productive as one person operating one machine. Eventually, as more labor hours are hired, workers get in each other's way and output increases barely at all.

Marginal Product Calculation We calculate the marginal product of labor as the change in real GDP divided by the change in the quantity of labor employed. Figure 7.3(a) shows some calculations, and Fig. 7.3(b) shows the marginal product curve.

In Fig. 7.3(a), when the quantity of labor employed increases from 100 billion hours to 200 billion hours, an increase of 100 billion hours, real GDP increases from $8 trillion to $12 trillion, an

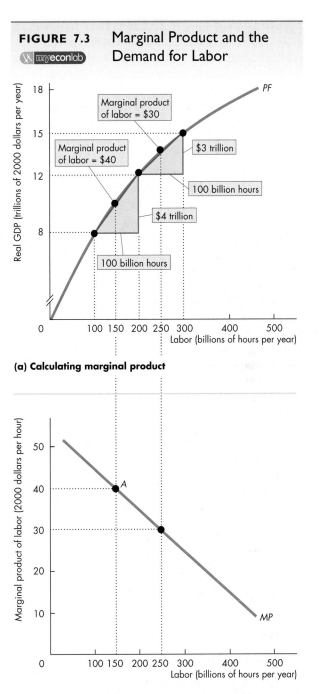

FIGURE 7.3 Marginal Product and the Demand for Labor

(a) Calculating marginal product

(b) The marginal product curve

Between 100 billion and 200 billion hours, the marginal product of labor is $40 an hour. Between 200 billion and 300 billion hours, the marginal product of labor is $30 an hour. At point A on the MP curve, the marginal product of labor is $40 an hour at 150 billion hours (between 100 billion and 200 billion). The MP curve is the demand for labor curve.

increase of $4 trillion, or $4,000 billion. The marginal product of labor equals the increase in real GDP ($4,000 billion) divided by the increase in the quantity of labor employed (100 billion hours), which is $40 an hour.

When the quantity of labor employed increases from 200 billion hours to 300 billion hours, an increase of 100 billion hours, real GDP increases from $12 trillion to $15 trillion, an increase of $3 trillion, or $3,000 billion. The marginal product of labor equals $3,000 billion divided by 100 billion hours, which is $30 an hour.

In Fig. 7.3(b), as the quantity of labor employed increases, the marginal product of labor diminishes. Between 100 billion and 200 billion hours (at 150 billion hours), marginal product of labor is $40 an hour. Between 200 billion and 300 billion hours (at 250 billion hours), marginal product is $30 an hour.

Diminishing Marginal Product and the Demand for Labor

The diminishing marginal product of labor limits the demand for labor. Firms aim to maximize profit. Each hour of labor hired increases output and adds to costs. Initially, an extra hour of labor produces more output than the real wage that it costs. Marginal product exceeds the real wage rate. But each additional hour of labor produces less additional output than the previous hour—marginal product diminishes.

As a firm hires more labor, eventually the extra output from an extra hour of labor is exactly what that hour of labor costs. At this point, marginal product equals the real wage rate. Hire one less hour, and marginal product exceeds the real wage rate. Hire one more hour, and the real wage rate exceeds the marginal product. In either case, profit is less.

Because marginal product diminishes as the quantity of labor employed increases, the lower the real wage rate, the greater is the quantity of labor that a firm can profitably hire. The demand for labor curve is the same as the marginal product curve.

You might better understand the demand for labor by thinking about an example. How does a soda factory decide how much labor to hire?

The Demand for Labor in a Soda Factory

Suppose that if a soda factory increases its labor from 98 hours to 99 hours, its output increases by 11 bottles and if it employs 100 hours, its output increases by 10 bottles. The marginal product of the 99th hour of labor is 11 bottles, and the marginal product of the 100th hour of labor is 10 bottles.

For the soda factory, the real wage rate is the money wage rate divided by the price of soda. If the money wage rate is $5.50 an hour and the price of soda is 50¢ a bottle, the real wage rate is 11 bottles an hour ($5.50 divided by 50¢ equals 11 bottles). At this real wage rate, the firm hires 99 hours of labor. But it doesn't hire 100 hours. The cost of the 100th hour is 11 bottles, and it produces only 10 bottles.

If the price of soda remains at 50¢ a bottle and the money wage rate falls to $5 an hour, the real wage rate falls to 10 bottles an hour. Similarly, if the money wage rate remains at $5.50 an hour and the price of soda rises to 55¢ a bottle, the real wage rate falls to 10 bottles an hour. In either case, when the real wage rate falls to 10 bottles an hour, the soda factory hires the 100th hour of labor.

Changes in the Demand for Labor

A change in the real wage rate brings a change in the quantity of labor demanded, which is shown by a movement along the demand curve. A change in any other influence on a firm's decision to hire labor brings a change in the demand for labor, which is shown by a shift of the demand curve.

All the other influences that change the demand for labor operate by changing the marginal product of labor. Labor becomes more productive when a new technology or new capital equipment or a combination of the two increases the labor's output per hour. Labor also becomes more productive as people acquire greater skills through education, on-the-job training, or job experience.

An advance in technology or an increase in capital (either physical capital or human capital) shifts the production function upward. These same forces increase the marginal product of labor, which increases the demand for labor and shifts the demand for labor curve rightward.

Some advances in technology bring labor-saving capital that decreases the demand for some types of labor. For example, voice recognition software and computers have replaced telephone operators. But such changes in technology increase the demand for the labor that makes the new machines and tools. Overall, advances in technology increase the demand for labor. You can see this fact by thinking about the extraordinary increase in labor during the information revolution of the 1990s.

The Supply of Labor

The *quantity of labor supplied* is the number of labor hours that all the households in the economy plan to work during a given period. This quantity depends on

1. The real wage rate
2. The working-age population
3. The value of other activities

We focus on the relationship between the quantity of labor supplied and the real wage rate when we hold all the influences on work decisions constant and ask: How does the quantity of labor supplied vary as the real wage rate varies?

Supply of Labor Schedule and Supply of Labor Curve

The **supply of labor** is the relationship between the quantity of labor supplied and the real wage rate when all other influences on work plans remain the same. We can represent the supply of labor as a supply schedule or a supply curve. The table in Fig. 7.4 shows a supply of labor schedule. It tells us the quantity of labor supplied at different real wage rates. For example, if the real wage rate is $15 an hour, the quantity of labor supplied is 150 billion hours a year in row *A*. The curve *LS* is a supply of labor curve. Points *A*, *B*, and *C* on the curve correspond to rows *A*, *B*, and *C* of the supply schedule.

The *real* wage rate influences the quantity of labor supplied because people care not how many dollars they earn but about what the dollars will buy.

Why does the quantity of labor supplied increase as the real wage rate increases? There are two reasons:

1. Hours per person increase
2. Labor force participation increases

Hours per Person

In choosing how many hours to work, a household considers the opportunity cost of not working. This opportunity cost is the real wage rate. The higher the real wage rate, the greater is the opportunity cost of taking leisure and not working. And as the opportunity cost of taking leisure rises and other things remain the same, the household chooses to work more hours.

But other things don't remain the same. The higher the real wage rate, the greater is the household's income. And the higher the household's income, the more it wants to consume. One item that it wants more of is leisure.

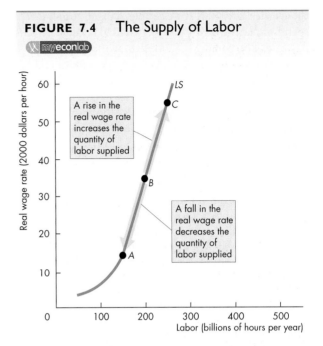

FIGURE 7.4   The Supply of Labor

A rise in the real wage rate increases the quantity of labor supplied

A fall in the real wage rate decreases the quantity of labor supplied

	Real wage rate (2000 dollars per hour)	Quantity of labor supplied (billions of hours per year)
A	15	150
B	35	200
C	55	250

The table shows part of a supply of labor schedule. Points A, B, and C on the supply of labor curve correspond to the rows of the table. The higher the real wage rate, the greater is the quantity of labor supplied.

So a rise in the real wage rate has two opposing effects. By increasing the opportunity cost of leisure, it makes the household want to take less leisure and to work more hours. And by increasing the household's income, it makes the household want to take more leisure and to work fewer hours. For most households, the opportunity cost effect is stronger than the income effect. So the higher the real wage rate, the greater is the number of hours that the household chooses to work.

Labor Force Participation

Some people have productive opportunities outside the labor force and choose to work only if the real wage rate exceeds the value of these other activities. For example, a parent might spend time caring for his or her child. The alternative is day care. The parent will choose to work only if he or she can earn enough per hour to pay the cost of child care and have enough left to make the work effort worthwhile.

The higher the real wage rate, the more likely it is that a parent will choose to work and so the greater is the labor force participation rate.

Labor Supply Response A rise in the real wage rate brings an increase in the quantity of labor supplied, which is shown by a movement along the supply curve. But as the real wage rate rises, a given percentage change in the real wage rate brings a smaller percentage change in the quantity of labor supplied.

Changes in the Supply of Labor A change in the real wage rate brings a change in the quantity of labor supplied, which is shown by a movement along the supply curve. A change in any other influence on a household's decision to work brings a change in the supply of labor, which is shown by a shift of the supply curve.

We've identified two factors that change the supply of labor: the working-age population and the value of other activities.

Over time, the working-age population increases because the number of births exceeds the number of deaths. In some countries—and the United States is a major example—immigration brings an even larger increase in the working-age population.

An increase in the working-age population means that more people are available to work, so the supply of labor increases and the supply of labor curve shifts rightward.

The value of other activities has a huge influence on the supply of labor and operates by changing the labor force participation rate. A major activity that competes with taking a job is producing goods and services in the home. Preparing meals, caring for children, and mowing a lawn are all examples of home production. Technological change in the home such as the arrival of washing machines, dishwashers, and microwave ovens has freed up time and increased the supply of labor, especially the supply of female labor. Changes in social attitudes have reinforced the effects of these advances in technology and further increased the supply of labor.

Labor Market Equilibrium

The forces of supply and demand operate in labor markets just as they do in the markets for goods and services. The price of labor is the real wage rate. A rise in the real wage rate eliminates a shortage of labor by decreasing the quantity demanded and increasing the quantity supplied. A fall in the real wage rate eliminates a surplus of labor by increasing the quantity demanded and decreasing the quantity supplied. If there is neither a shortage nor a surplus, the labor market is in equilibrium.

Figure 7.5 illustrates labor market equilibrium. The demand curve LD and the supply curve LS are the same as those in Fig. 7.2 and Fig. 7.4. This labor market is in equilibrium at a real wage rate of $35 an hour and employment of 200 billion hours a year.

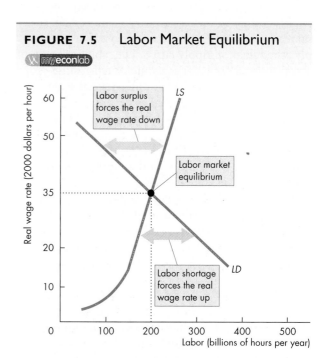

FIGURE 7.5   Labor Market Equilibrium

Labor market equilibrium occurs when the quantity of labor demanded equals the quantity of labor supplied. The equilibrium real wage rate is $35 an hour, and equilibrium employment is 200 billion hours per year.

At a wage rate above $35 an hour, there is a surplus of labor and the real wage rate falls to eliminate the surplus. At a wage rate below $35 an hour, there is a shortage of labor and the real wage rate rises to eliminate the shortage.

If the real wage rate exceeds $35 an hour, the quantity of labor supplied exceeds the quantity demanded and there is a surplus of labor. When there is a surplus of labor, the real wage rate falls toward the equilibrium real wage rate where the surplus is eliminated.

If the real wage rate is less than $35 an hour, the quantity of labor demanded exceeds the quantity supplied and there is a shortage of labor. When there is a shortage of labor, the real wage rate rises toward the equilibrium real wage rate where the shortage is eliminated.

If the real wage rate is $35 an hour, the quantity of labor demanded equals the quantity supplied and there is neither a shortage nor a surplus of labor. In this situation, there is no pressure in either direction on the real wage rate. So the real wage rate remains constant and the market is in equilibrium. At this equilibrium real wage rate and level of employment, the economy is at *full employment*.

Potential GDP

You've seen that the production function tells us how much real GDP a given amount of employment can produce—see Fig. 7.1(b), p. 159. The quantity of real GDP produced increases as the quantity of labor employed increases. At the equilibrium level of employment, the economy is at full employment. And the level of real GDP at full employment is potential GDP. So the full-employment quantity of labor produces potential GDP.

Figure 7.6 illustrates the determination of potential GDP. Part (a) shows labor market equilibrium. At the equilibrium real wage rate, the equilibrium level of employment is 200 billion hours.

Figure 7.6(b) shows the production function. The production function shows that 200 billion hours of labor can produce a real GDP of $12 trillion. This amount is potential GDP.

Potential GDP Not a Physical Limit Notice that potential GDP is not the highest level of real GDP that the economy can produce. Potential GDP is the *equilibrium quantity* produced at full employment. The *PPF* shows the limits to production, and the economy cannot produce more real GDP *and take more leisure* than the *PPF* permits. But potential GDP is one point on the *PPF*. If people are willing to work longer hours, as they did during World War II, real GDP can increase in a movement along the *PPF*.

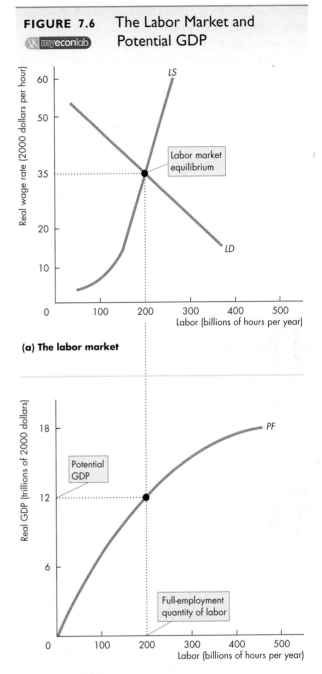

FIGURE 7.6   The Labor Market and Potential GDP

(a) The labor market

(b) Potential GDP

The economy is at full employment (part a) when the quantity of labor demanded equals the quantity of labor supplied. The real wage rate is $35 an hour, and employment is 200 billion hours a year. Part (b) shows potential GDP. It is the quantity of real GDP determined by the production function at the full-employment quantity of labor.

Potential GDP Is Production Efficient Recall that *production efficiency* occurs at all points *on* the *PPF* and that points *inside* the *PPF* are *inefficient* because some resources are *unused* or have been *misallocated* or both (see Chapter 2, p. 35). Because potential GDP occurs at a point on the *PPF*, production is efficient at potential GDP. As you will see in the next section, there is some unemployment at potential GDP. But that unemployment decreases employment in a movement along the *PPF.*

Allocative Efficiency at Potential GDP Recall that *allocative efficiency* occurs at *the one point on* the *PPF* where we cannot produce more of any good without giving up some other good that we *value more highly.* It is the point on the *PPF* that society prefers above all other points (see Chapter 2, p. 39). Potential GDP is such a point.

To see why, think about the allocation of time between labor and leisure. The lower the real wage rate, the smaller is the quantity of labor supplied and the greater is the quantity of leisure demanded. At any given quantity of leisure demanded, the real wage rate measures the marginal benefit of leisure.

The higher the real wage rate, the smaller is the quantity of labor demanded and the greater is the quantity of leisure supplied. At any given quantity of leisure supplied, the real wage rate measures the marginal cost of leisure.

At full employment, the quantity of labor demanded equals the quantity supplied and the quantity of leisure demanded equals the quantity of leisure supplied, so resources are allocated efficiently.

REVIEW QUIZ

1 Why does a rise in the real wage rate bring a decrease in the quantity of labor demanded?
2 Why does a rise in the real wage rate bring an increase in the quantity of labor supplied?
3 What happens in the labor market if the real wage rate is above or below its full-employment level?
4 How is potential GDP determined?
5 Why isn't potential GDP a physical limit?
6 Why might potential GDP be efficient?

Ⓧ myeconlab **Study Plan 7.3**

Unemployment at Full Employment

So far, we've focused on the forces that determine the real wage rate, the quantity of labor employed, and potential GDP. We're now going to bring unemployment into the picture and study the real factors that influence the natural unemployment rate.

In Chapter 6, you learned how unemployment is measured and how people become unemployed (they lose jobs, leave jobs, and enter or reenter the labor force); and we classified unemployment (it can be frictional, structural, or cyclical). You also learned that we call the unemployment rate at full employment the *natural unemployment rate.*

But measuring, describing, and classifying unemployment do not *explain* it. *Why* is there always some unemployment? Why does its rate vary across countries? Why is the unemployment rate in the United States lower than that in Europe and Canada? And why does the unemployment rate vary over time? Why was the unemployment rate higher during the 1970s and 1980s than in the 1960s and 2000s?

Here we look at the forces that determine the natural unemployment rate. (You will learn about the sources of cyclical unemployment in Chapter 11.)

Unemployment is always present for two broad reasons:

■ Job search
■ Job rationing

Job Search

Job search is the activity of looking for a suitable vacant job. There are always some people who have not yet found a suitable job and who are actively searching for one. The reason is that the labor market is in a constant state of change. The failure of existing businesses destroys jobs. The expansion of existing businesses and the startup of new businesses that use new technologies and develop new markets create jobs. As people pass through different stages of life, some enter or reenter the labor market. Others leave their jobs to look for better ones, and still others retire. This constant churning in the labor market means that there are always some people looking for jobs, and these people are the unemployed.

The amount of job search depends on a number of factors, one of which is the real wage rate. In Fig. 7.7, when the real wage rate is $35 an hour, the economy is at full-employment equilibrium. The amount of job search that takes place at this wage rate generates unemployment at the natural rate. If the real wage rate is above the full-employment equilibrium—for example, at $45 an hour—there is a surplus of labor. At this higher real wage rate, more job search takes place and unemployment exceeds the natural rate. If the real wage rate is below the full-employment equilibrium—for example, at $25 an hour—there is a shortage of labor. At this real wage rate, less job search takes place and unemployment falls below the natural rate.

The market forces of demand and supply move the real wage rate toward the full-employment equilibrium. And these same forces move the amount of job search toward the level that creates unemployment at the natural rate.

FIGURE 7.7   Job Search Unemployment

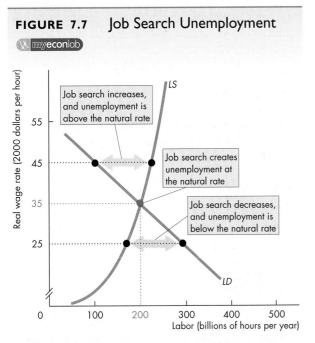

When the real wage rate is at its full-employment level—$35 an hour in this example—job search puts unemployment at the natural rate. If the real wage rate is above its full-employment level, there is a surplus of labor. Job search increases, and unemployment rises above the natural rate. If the real wage rate is below its full-employment level, there is a shortage of labor. Job search decreases, and unemployment falls below the natural rate.

But other influences on the amount of job search bring changes in the natural unemployment rate. The main sources of these changes are

- Demographic change
- Structural change
- Unemployment compensation

Demographic Change An increase in the proportion of the population that is of working age brings an increase in the entry rate into the labor force and an increase in the unemployment rate. The "baby boom"—the bulge in the birth rate that occurred from the late 1940s through the late 1950s—increased entry into the labor force during the 1970s and increased the natural unemployment rate.

As the birth rate declined, the bulge moved into higher age groups, and entry declined during the 1980s. During this period, the natural unemployment rate decreased.

Structural Change Sometimes, technological change brings a *structural slump*, a condition in which some industries and even regions die while other industries and regions are born and flourish. When these events occur, labor turnover is high—the flows between employment and unemployment increase and the number of unemployed people increases. The decline of industries in the "Rust Belt" and the rapid expansion of industries in the "Sun Belt" illustrate the effects of technological change and were a source of the increase in the natural unemployment rate during the 1970s and 1980s.

Unemployment Compensation The length of time that an unemployed person spends searching for a job depends, in part, on the opportunity cost of job search. An unemployed person who receives no unemployment compensation faces an opportunity cost of job search equal to the wage rate available without further search. Unemployment compensation lowers this opportunity cost.

An extension of unemployment compensation to larger groups of workers during the late 1960s and 1970s lowered the opportunity cost of job search and increased the natural unemployment rate.

Generous unemployment compensation in Europe and Canada is one of the factors that contributes to these economies having higher natural unemployment rates than the United States.

Job Rationing

Markets allocate scarce resources by adjusting the market price to make buying plans and selling plans agree. Another word that has a meaning similar to "allocate" is "ration." Markets *ration* scarce resources by adjusting prices. In the labor market, the real wage rate rations employment and therefore rations jobs. Changes in the real wage rate keep the number of people seeking work and the number of jobs available in balance.

But the real wage rate is not the only possible instrument for rationing jobs. And in some industries, the real wage rate is set above the market equilibrium level. **Job rationing** is the practice of paying a real wage rate above the equilibrium level and then rationing jobs by some method.

Two reasons why the real wage rate might be set above the equilibrium level are

- Efficiency wage
- Minimum wage

Efficiency Wage

An **efficiency wage** is a real wage rate set above the equilibrium real wage rate that balances the costs and benefits of this higher wage rate to maximize the firm's profit.

The cost of paying a higher wage is direct. It is the addition to the firm's wage bill. The benefits of paying a higher wage rate are indirect.

First, a firm that pays a high wage rate can attract the most productive workers. Second, the firm can get greater productivity from its work force if it threatens to fire those who do not perform at the desired standard. The threat of losing a well-paid job stimulates greater work effort. Third, workers are less likely to quit their jobs, so the firm faces a lower rate of labor turnover and lower training costs. Fourth, the firm's recruiting costs are lower. The firm always faces a steady stream of available new workers.

Faced with benefits and costs, a firm offers a wage rate that balances productivity gains from the higher wage rate against its additional cost. This wage rate maximizes the firm's profit and is the efficiency wage.

Minimum Wage

A **minimum wage** is the lowest wage rate at which a firm may legally hire labor. If the minimum wage is set *below* the equilibrium wage, the minimum wage has no effect. The minimum wage and market forces are not in conflict. But if a minimum wage is set *above* the equilibrium wage, the minimum wage is in conflict with the market forces and does have some effects on the labor market.

The U.S. federal minimum wage is set by the Fair Labor Standards Act and was last changed in 1997 when it was set at $5.15 an hour. The real minimum wage rate fell by 20 percent between 1997 and 2006. Some state governments have passed state minimum wage laws that exceed the federal minimum.

Job Rationing and Unemployment

Regardless of the reason, if the real wage rate is set above the equilibrium level, the natural unemployment rate increases. The above-equilibrium real wage rate decreases the quantity of labor demanded and increases the quantity of labor supplied. So even at full employment, the quantity of labor supplied exceeds the quantity of labor demanded.

The surplus of labor is an addition to the amount of unemployment. The unemployment that results from a nonmarket wage rate and job rationing increases the natural unemployment rate because it is added to the job search that takes place at full-employment equilibrium.

REVIEW QUIZ

1 Why does the economy experience unemployment at full employment?
2 Why does the natural unemployment rate fluctuate?
3 What is job rationing and why does it occur?
4 How does an efficiency wage influence the real wage rate, employment, and unemployment?
5 How does the minimum wage create unemployment?

ⓧ myeconlab Study Plan 7.4

You've now seen how the classical model explains the forces that determine the real wage rate, the quantity of labor employed, potential GDP, and the natural unemployment rate.

The classical model also explains the forces that determine the real interest rate and the allocation of real GDP between consumption and investment in new capital. The next section examines these forces by studying the market for loanable funds.

Loanable Funds and the Real Interest Rate

Potential GDP depends on the quantities of factors of production, one of which is capital. The **capital stock** is the total quantity of plant, equipment, buildings, and business inventories. The capital stock includes business capital such as communication satellites and computers as well as the inventories that businesses carry. It also includes houses and apartments. And it includes government-owned *social infrastructure capital* such as highways, dams and canals, and buildings and equipment in schools, state universities, the national defense system, and the legal system.

The capital stock is determined by investment decisions (see Chapter 5, pp. 115–116). And the funds that finance investment are obtained in the market for loanable funds.

The Market for Loanable Funds

The **market for loanable funds** is the market in which households, firms, governments, banks, and other financial institutions borrow and lend.

In the U.S. economy, there are many interrelated loans markets. There are markets in which the stocks of corporations are traded. Stocks are securities issued by corporations, and stock markets determine the prices and rates of return earned on stocks. The New York Stock Exchange is an example of this type of market. There are markets in which bonds are traded. Bonds are securities issued by corporations and governments. There are markets in all types of loans, such as credit card loans and student loans.

In macroeconomics, we lump all these individual markets for loans into the one big loanable funds market. Think of this market as the aggregate (or sum) of all the different markets in which people, businesses, and governments borrow and lend.

Flows in the Market for Loanable Funds The *circular flow model* (see Chapter 5, pp. 113–114) provides the accounting framework that explains the flows in the loanable funds market. Loanable funds are used for three purposes:

1. Business investment
2. Government budget deficit
3. International investment or lending

And loanable funds come from three sources:

1. Private saving
2. Government budget surplus
3. International borrowing

Firms often use retained earnings to finance business investment. These earnings belong to the firm's stockholders and are borrowed from the stockholders, rather than being paid to them as dividends. To keep the accounts in the clearest possible way, we think of these retained earning as being both demanded and supplied in the loanable funds market. They are included as business investment on the demand side and as private saving on the supply side.

We measure all the flows of loanable funds in *real* terms—in constant 2000 dollars.

You're now going to see how these real flows and their opportunity cost or price are determined by studying

- The demand for loanable funds
- The supply of loanable funds
- Equilibrium in the market for loanable funds

The Demand for Loanable Funds

The *quantity of loanable funds demanded* is the total quantity of funds demanded to finance investment, the government budget deficit, and international investment or lending during a given period. This quantity depends on

1. The real interest rate
2. The expected profit rate
3. Government and international factors

To focus on the demand for loanable funds, we ask: How does the quantity of loanable funds demanded vary as the real interest rate varies, with all other influences on borrowing plans remaining the same?

The Demand for Loanable Funds Curve The **demand for loanable funds** is the relationship between the quantity of loanable funds demanded and the real interest rate when all other influences on borrowing plans remain the same.

Business investment is the main item that makes up the demand for loanable funds, and the other two items—the government budget deficit and international investment and lending—can be thought of as amounts to be added to investment. Other things remaining the same, investment decreases if the real interest rate rises and increases if the real interest rate falls. Equivalently, the quantity of loanable funds demanded decreases if the real interest rate rises and increases if the real interest rate falls.

Figure 7.8 illustrates the demand for loanable funds when investment is the only source of demand (there is no government deficit or international investment or lending). The table shows investment at three real interest rates. Each point (A through C) on the demand for loanable funds curve corresponds to a row in the table. If the real interest rate is 6 percent a year, investment is

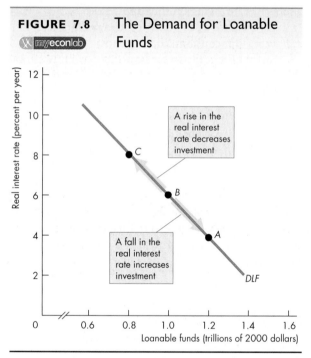

FIGURE 7.8   The Demand for Loanable Funds

myeconlab

	Real interest rate (percent per year)	Investment (trillions of 2000 dollars)
A	4	1.2
B	6	1.0
C	8	0.8

The demand for loanable funds curve shows the effects of a change in the real interest rate on investment and the quantity of loanable funds demanded, other things remaining the same. A change in the real interest rate brings a change in investment and a movement along the demand for loanable funds curve.

$1 trillion and the quantity of funds demanded is $1 trillion. A change in the real interest rate brings a movement along the demand for loanable funds curve. A rise in the real interest rate decreases investment and brings a movement up the demand curve. A fall in the real interest rate increases investment and brings a movement down the demand curve.

Why does the quantity of loanable funds demanded depend on the real interest rate? And what exactly is the *real* interest rate?

The Real Interest Rate and the Opportunity Cost of Loanable Funds The **real interest rate** is the quantity of goods and services that a unit of capital earns. In contrast, the **nominal interest rate** is the number of dollars that a unit of capital earns.

To measure the real interest rate, we begin with the nominal interest rate expressed as a percentage per year of the number of dollars loaned or borrowed. If your bank pays you $3 interest a year on a $100 savings deposit, you've earned a nominal interest rate of 3 percent per year.

The next step is to adjust the nominal interest rate for inflation. The real interest rate is approximately equal to the nominal interest rate minus the inflation rate.

You can see why if you think about what you can buy with the interest on a $100 savings deposit in one year. If the nominal interest rate is 3 percent a year, you will have $103 in your savings account after one year. Suppose that during the year, all prices increased by 2 percent—a 2 percent inflation rate. You need $102 to buy what a year earlier cost $100. So you can buy $1 worth more of goods and services than you could have bought a year earlier. You've earned goods and services worth $1, which is a real interest rate of 1 percent a year. And the bank has paid a real interest rate of 1 percent a year. So the real interest rate is the 3 percent nominal interest rate minus the 2 percent inflation rate.[1]

The real interest rate is the opportunity cost of loanable funds, and it is the opportunity cost of funds regardless of their source. The real interest *paid* on borrowed funds is an obvious cost. But the real

---

[1]The *exact* real interest rate formula, which allows for the change in the purchasing power of both the interest and the loan is: Real interest rate = (Nominal interest rate − Inflation rate) ÷ (1 + Inflation rate/100). If the nominal interest rate is 4 percent a year and the inflation rate is 3 percent a year, the real interest rate is (4 − 3) ÷ (1 + 0.03) = 0.97 percent a year.

interest rate is also the opportunity cost of using retained earnings. These funds could be loaned to another firm, so the real interest rate forgone is the opportunity cost of using retained earnings.

Now that you know what the real interest rate is, we can study its influence on the quantity of loanable funds demanded. To do so, we look at a firm's investment decision.

The Investment Decision How does Google decide how much to invest in servers and software to create a new Internet search system? Google's decision is influenced by the interplay of two factors:

1. The real interest rate
2. The expected profit rate

To decide whether to invest in a new Internet search system, Google compares the expected profit rate with the real interest rate. The expected profit rate is the benefit of the investment, and the real interest rate is the opportunity cost of the investment. Only if the benefit exceeds the cost, is it profitable to invest.

Imagine that Google is deciding how much to invest in a new Internet search system that will operate for one year and then be scrapped and replaced by an even better system. The firm believes that if it invests $100 million in a system to serve the U.S. market, it will earn a profit of $20 million, or 20 percent a year. Google also believes that if it invests another $100 million in a system to serve the European market, it will earn a profit of $10 million or 10 percent a year. And Google believes that if it invests yet another $100 million in a system to serve the Asian market, it will earn a profit of $5 million or 5 percent a year.

Suppose that Google can borrow in the loanable funds market at an interest rate of 9 percent a year. How much will it borrow and invest in the new search systems? The answer is that Google will borrow $200 million and build the U.S. and European systems but not the Asian system. If the interest rate increased to 15 percent a year, Google would drop the European plans and invest only $100 million in the U.S. system. And if the interest rate decreased to 4 percent a year, Google would go for all three projects and invest $300 million.

The higher the real interest rate, the smaller is the number of projects that are worth undertaking and the smaller is the amount of investment.

Changes in the Demand for Loanable Funds A change in the real interest rate brings a change in investment and a change in the quantity of loanable funds demanded, which is shown by a movement along the demand curve. A change in any other influence on a firm's decision to invest and borrow funds is shown by a shift of the demand curve. These other influences are all the factors that affect a firm's expected profit. Other things remaining the same, the greater the expected profit rate from new capital, the greater is the amount of investment and the greater is the demand for loanable funds.

Technology is a major influence of expected profit. Some firms strive to be first to market with a new technology. And some firms wait to see how a new technology performs before adopting it. But the profits of all firms are influenced by advances in technology, and investment plans must be constantly reassessed.

In a period of rapid and far-reaching technological change, such as that of the information revolution of the 1990s, firms become extremely optimistic about profits and investment booms.

The Supply of Loanable Funds

The *quantity of loanable funds supplied* is the total funds available from private saving, the government budget surplus, and international borrowing during a given period. This quantity depends on

- The real interest rate
- Disposable income
- Wealth
- Expected future income
- Government and international factors

To focus on the relationship between the quantity of loanable funds supplied and the real interest rate, we hold all other influences on lending plans constant and ask: How does the quantity of loanable funds supplied vary as the real interest rate varies?

The Supply of Loanable Funds Curve The **supply of loanable funds** is the relationship between the quantity of loanable funds supplied and the real interest rate when all other influences on lending plans remain the same.

Saving is the main item that makes up the supply of loanable funds, and the government budget surplus and international borrowing (when they are not zero) can be thought of as amounts to be added to saving.

Other things remaining the same, saving increases if the real interest rate rises and decreases if the real interest rate falls. Equivalently, the quantity of loanable funds supplied increases if the real interest rate rises and decreases if the real interest rate falls.

Figure 7.9 illustrates this relationship when saving is the only source of supply of funds (when there is no government budget surplus or international borrowing). The table shows saving at three real interest rates. Saving provides loanable funds, and the relationship between the quantity of loanable funds supplied and the real interest rate, other things remaining the same, is the supply of loanable funds.

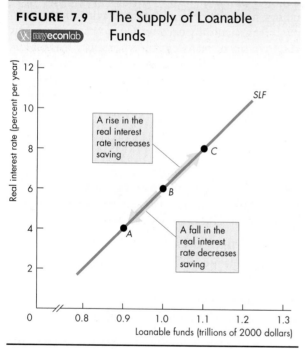

FIGURE 7.9   The Supply of Loanable Funds

A rise in the real interest rate increases saving

A fall in the real interest rate decreases saving

	Real interest rate (percent per year)	Saving (trillions of 2000 dollars)
A	4	0.9
B	6	1.0
C	8	1.1

The supply of loanable funds curve shows the effects of a change in the real interest rate on the quantity of loanable funds supplied, other things remaining the same. A change in the real interest rate brings a change in saving and a movement along the supply of loanable funds curve.

Each point (A through C) on the supply of loanable funds curve corresponds to a row in the table. If the real interest rate is 6 percent a year, saving is $1 trillion and the quantity of funds supplied is $1 trillion. A change in the real interest rate brings a movement along the supply of loanable funds curve. If the real interest rate rises, saving increases and there is a movement up the supply of loanable funds curve. If the real interest rate falls, saving decreases and there is a movement down the supply of loanable funds curve.

Saving increases when the real interest rate increases because the real interest rate is the opportunity cost of consumption. A dollar consumed is a dollar not saved, so the interest that could have been earned on that saving is forgone. This opportunity cost arises regardless of whether a person is a lender or a borrower. For a lender, saving less this year means receiving less interest next year. For a borrower, saving less this year means paying less off a loan this year and paying more interest next year.

You can see why the real interest rate influences saving by thinking about student loans. If the real interest rate on student loans jumps to 20 percent a year, students will save more (will buy cheaper food and find lower-rent accommodations) to pay off their loans as quickly as possible. If the real interest rate on student loans falls to 1 percent a year, students will save less and take out larger loans.

Changes in the Supply of Loanable Funds A change in the real interest rate brings a change in saving and a change in the quantity of loanable funds supplied, which is shown by a movement along the supply curve. A change in any other influence on saving and lending plans is shown by a shift of the supply curve. These other influences are disposable income, wealth, and expected future income.

Disposable Income The greater a household's disposable income, other things remaining the same, the greater is its saving. For example, suppose a student works during the summer and earns a disposable income of $10,000. She spends the entire $10,000 on consumption during the year and saves nothing. When she graduates as an economics major, her disposable income jumps to $20,000 a year. She now saves $4,000 and spends $16,000 on consumption. The increase in disposable income of $10,000 has increased saving by $4,000.

Wealth A household's *wealth* equals its assets (what it *owns*) minus its debts (what it *owes*). The purchasing power of a household's wealth is the *real* value of its wealth. It is the quantity of goods and services that the household's wealth can buy. The greater a household's real wealth, other things remaining the same, the less is its saving.

Patty is a department store executive who earns a disposable income of $30,000 a year. She has been saving and now has $15,000 in the bank and no debts. That is, Patty's wealth is $15,000. Patty's colleague, Tony, also earns a disposable income of $30,000, but he has no money in the bank and no debts. Tony's wealth is zero. Patty decides that this year, she will take a vacation and save only $1,000. But Tony decides to skip a vacation and save $5,000. With greater wealth and other things the same, Patty saves less than Tony.

Expected Future Income The higher a household's expected future income, other things remaining the same, the lower is its saving. That is, if two households have the same disposable income in the current year, the household with the larger expected future income will spend a larger portion of current disposable income on consumption goods and services and will save less.

Look at Patty and Tony again. Patty has just been promoted and will receive a $10,000 pay raise next year. Tony has just been told that he will be laid off at the end of the year. On receiving this news, Patty buys a new car—increases her consumption and decreases her saving. Tony sells his car and takes the bus—decreases his consumption and increases his saving.

A young household expects to have a higher future income for some years and then to have a lower income during retirement. Because of this life-cycle income pattern, young people and retired people save least and middle-aged people save most.

An increase in disposable income, a decrease in wealth, or a decrease in expected future income increases saving, which increases the supply of loanable funds and shifts the supply of loanable funds curve rightward. A decrease in disposable income, an increase in wealth, or an increase in expected future income decreases saving, which decreases the supply of loanable funds and shifts the supply of loanable funds curve leftward.

We're now going to see how borrowing decisions and lending decisions interact in the loanable funds market to determine the real interest rate.

Equilibrium in the Loanable Funds Market

You've seen that other things remaining the same, the quantities of loanable funds demanded and supplied depend on the real interest rate. The higher the real interest rate, the greater is the amount of saving and the larger is the quantity of loanable funds supplied and the smaller is the amount of investment and the smaller is the quantity of loanable funds demanded. There is one interest rate at which the quantities of loanable funds demanded and supplied are equal, and that is the equilibrium real interest rate.

Figure 7.10 shows how the demand for and supply of loanable funds determine the real interest rate. The *DLF* curve is the demand curve and the *SLF* curve is the supply curve. When the real interest rate

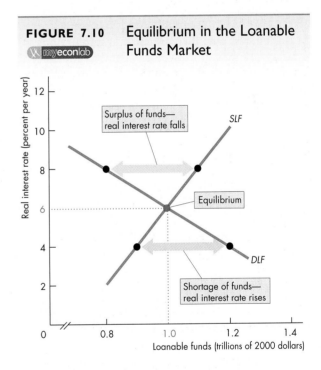

FIGURE 7.10   Equilibrium in the Loanable Funds Market

The figure shows the demand for loanable funds curve, *DLF*, and supply of loanable funds curve, *SLF*. If the real interest rate were 4 percent a year, the quantity of loanable funds demanded would exceed the quantity supplied and the real interest rate would rise. If the real interest rate were 8 percent a year, the quantity of loanable funds supplied would exceed the quantity demanded and the real interest rate would fall. When the real interest rate is 6 percent a year, the quantity of loanable funds demanded equals the quantity supplied, and the real interest rate is at its equilibrium. Saving equals investment.

exceeds 6 percent a year, saving exceeds investment. Borrowers have an easy time finding the funds they want, but lenders are unable to lend all the funds they have available. The real interest rate falls and continues to fall until the quantity of funds supplied equals the quantity of funds demanded. At this real interest rate, saving equals investment.

Alternatively, when the interest rate is less than 6 percent a year, saving is less than investment. Borrowers can't find the loans they want, but lenders are able to lend all the funds they have available. So the real interest rate rises and continues to rise until the supply of funds equals the demand for funds and saving equals investment.

Regardless of whether there is a surplus or a shortage of loanable funds, the real interest rate changes and is pulled toward an equilibrium level.

In Fig. 7.10, this equilibrium is 6 percent a year. At this interest rate, there is neither a surplus nor a shortage of funds. Borrowers can get the funds they demand, and lenders can lend all the funds they have available. The plans of borrowers (investors) and lenders (savers) are consistent with each other.

REVIEW QUIZ

1 What is the market for loanable funds?
2 What determines the demand for loanable funds?
3 How do firms make investment decisions?
4 What is the real interest rate?
5 Why is the real interest rate the opportunity cost of loanable funds?
6 What determines the supply of loanable funds?
7 How do households make saving decisions?
8 How is the real interest rate determined?
9 What happens if the real interest rate exceeds the equilibrium rate?
10 What happens if the real interest rate is below the equilibrium rate?

myeconlab Study Plan 7.5

You now know the components of the classical model and what the model determines. To complete your study of the classical model, let's see what it tells us about the U.S. economy today.

Using the Classical Model

The classical model is a powerful tool for understanding the forces that determine potential GDP, employment, the real wage rate, the real interest rate, and the amount of saving and investment, all of which play a crucial role in influencing our current and future standard of living. Because the model tells us about the economy at full employment, it omits the forces that make the economy fluctuate around full employment. So it doesn't completely describe the economy in any one year unless that year happens to be one in which the economy is at full employment. But because the economy fluctuates around full employment, you can think of the classical model as telling you about the average state of the economy over a business cycle.

We can apply the classical model to address two main questions: How does the present state of our economy compare with that at some earlier state, and how does our economy compare with that of some other country.

Here, we'll use the model to compare the U.S. economy in 2005 with its state almost 20 years earlier, in 1986. In *Reading Between the Lines*, on pp. 176–177, we'll use the classical model to explore the factors that make the U.S. economy different from the European economy.

The U. S. Economy Through the Eye of the Classical Model

The U.S. economy was close to full employment in 2005. It was also close to full employment 19 years earlier, in 1986. We're going to compare these two years and look at the forces that moved the economy from one full-employment equilibrium to another.

In 1986, employment was 198 billion hours, the real wage rate was $18 an hour, and real GDP in the United States was $6 trillion. (We are using 2000 dollars.)

By 2005, labor hours had increased to 254 billion, the real wage rate had risen to $26 an hour, and real GDP had increased to $11.8 trillion. (Again, we are using 2000 dollars.)

The classical model points us to the things that changed to increase employment, the real wage rate, and potential GDP.

First, advances in technology and the investment in capital that brought us the Internet, the cell phone,

FIGURE 7.11   Full Employment in the United States: 1986 and 2005

X myeconlab

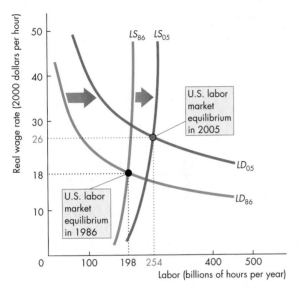

(a) The U.S. labor market in 1986 and 2005

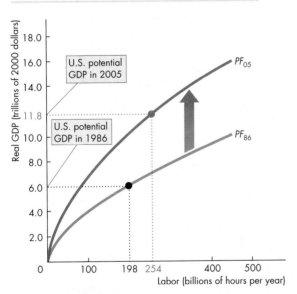

(b) The U.S. production functions in 1986 and 2005

In 1986, the real wage rate was $18 an hour and the quantity of labor employed was 198 billion hours in part (a). Potential GDP was $6 trillion on PF_{86} in part (b). By 2005, the real wage rate was $26 an hour and 254 billion hours of labor were employed. Potential GDP had increased to $11.8 trillion on PF_{05}.

MP3 audio, and MP4 video, as well as robots in factories and warehouses, increased productivity.

These same advances in technology and growth of capital increased the marginal product of labor and increased the demand for labor.

Second, the population expanded. In 1986, the working-age population was 170 million. By 2005, that number was 230 million. This increase in the working-age population increased the supply of labor.

The combined effects of technological advance, capital accumulation, and population growth increased employment, the real wage rate, and potential GDP.

Figure 7.11 illustrates these effects. In 1986, (shown in part a) the demand for labor was LD_{86}, the supply of labor was LS_{86}, the real wage rate was $18 an hour, and 198 billion hours of labor were employed. In part (b), the production function was PF_{86} and potential GDP was $6 trillion.

By 2005, the increase in the working-age population had increased the supply of labor and shifted the supply of labor curve to LS_{05}. And advances in technology and capital accumulation had increased the marginal product of labor, which shifted the demand for labor curve to LD_{05} and the production function upward to PF_{05}.

At the new 2005 full-employment equilibrium, the real wage rate had increased to $26 an hour, employment had increased to 254 billion hours, and potential GDP had increased to $11.8 trillion.

REVIEW QUIZ

1 How has the U.S. production function changed since 1986 and what brought about the change?
2 How has the U.S. demand for labor and supply of labor changed since 1986 and what brought about the changes?
3 Use the classical model to explain the change in U.S. employment, real wage rate, and potential GDP since 1986.

X myeconlab **Study Plan 7.6**

◆ You now know how the classical model can be used to explain changes in the economy over time. Before you leave this chapter, take a look at *Reading Between the Lines* on pp. 176–177 and see how the model also explains a curious international difference.

The United States Versus Europe

Euro-Zone Economy Holding Its Own Compared to Achievements of U.S.

June 26, 2004

There is a widespread belief . . . that continental Europe is a persistent underperformer relative to the United States—a "basket case", as some have put it. The U.S., it is pointed out, is richer than the euro zone and the gap is increasing.

In 2003, income per head in the euro zone—adjusted for price differences—was around 30 per cent less than in the U.S. . . .

Those who view continental Europe as an economic failure are also in no doubt as to why the United States is richer: . . .The advent of the "new economy" has resulted in technology-driven productivity gains in the U.S.

Europe, with its bureaucratic, over-regulated economies, has been slow to develop or take advantage of new technologies.

However, there's one problem with this conventional wisdom—it is contradicted by the evidence.

Through the use of a simple accounting framework, one can shine a light on the real sources of income [differences]: a higher level of GDP per head can be due either to higher productivity (GDP per hour worked) or to higher labour utilisation (total hours worked per head of population). . . .

The level of euro-zone productivity, when defined as output per hour, was only 4 per cent less than the U.S. in 2003, . . .

Labour utilisation (total hours worked per head of population), on the other hand, was 28 per cent lower in the euro zone in 2003 than in the U.S. Euro-zone employees worked 15 per cent less hours than their U.S. counterparts in 2003, accounting for one-half of the gap in labour utilisation.

The remaining gap was accounted for by a smaller proportion of people in employment. This is partly a function of higher structural unemployment (accounting for around one-quarter of the lower employment rate) but it is primarily a function of low labour participation, particularly among women. . . .

Extract from an article by Kevin Daly, an economist at Goldman Sachs investment bank, based on *Euroland's Secret Success Story*, Goldman Sachs Global Economics Paper, No 102, January 2004.

Essence of the Story

▶ In 2003, income per head in the euro zone was 30 percent less than that in the United States.

▶ Europe is thought to be bureaucratic, over-regulated, and slow to develop or take advantage of new technologies.

▶ The United States, in contrast, embraced the new technologies that increased productivity.

▶ The evidence contradicts the conventional wisdom.

▶ A higher level of GDP per person can be due to either higher productivity or longer work hours.

▶ Europe is almost as productive as the United States, but Europeans work shorter hours.

▶ The population of the United States is a bit smaller than that of the euro zone—300 million versus 313 million.

▶ But the United States produces a greater real GDP than the euro zone produces—$11.8 trillion versus $8 trillion.

▶ Despite this difference in production, the real wage rate in the United States is only $1 an hour higher than that in the euro zone.

▶ How can the United States produce much more than the euro zone when Americans earn almost the same hourly wage rate as Europeans?

▶ The news article has the answer: Americans work for many more hours than do Europeans.

▶ The workweek is longer, vacations are shorter, more people have jobs, and the natural unemployment rate is lower in the United States than it is in the euro zone.

▶ The figures use the classical model of the labor market to compare the U.S. and euro zone economies in 2005.

▶ Figure 1 shows the labor markets and Fig. 2 shows the production functions. The United States (US) is in red and the euro zone (EU) is in blue.

▶ The demand for labor in the United States is greater than that in the euro zone. The LD_{US} curve lies to the right of the LD_{EU} curve because the marginal product of labor is greater in the United States.

▶ The greater productivity in the United States is also reflected in the production functions in Fig. 2. With more capital and more advanced technologies (on the average), the U.S. production function PF_{US} lies above that of the euro zone PF_{EU}.

▶ The supply of labor in the euro zone is less than that in the United States. The LS_{EU} curve lies to the left of the LS_{US} curve.

▶ Equilibrium in the U.S. labor market occurs at a real wage rate of $26 an hour with 254 billion hours of labor. This labor produces a real GDP of $11.8 trillion.

▶ Equilibrium in the euro zone labor market occurs at a real wage rate of $25 an hour with 180 billion hours of labor. This labor produces a real GDP of $8 trillion.

▶ If Europeans worked the same number of hours as Americans work, the real wage rate and marginal product of labor in Europe would be much lower.

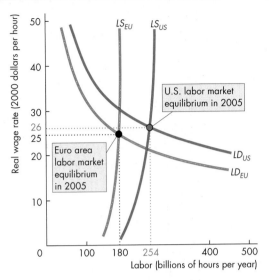

Figure 1 Labor markets in 2005

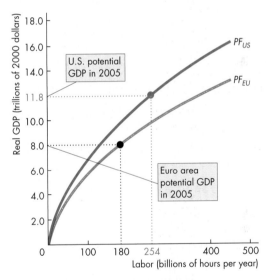

Figure 2 Production functions in 2005

▶ It is not known why the euro zone has a smaller supply of labor.

▶ Some economists say that higher taxes in Europe are the reason. Some say that stronger labor unions in Europe are the reason. And some say that

Europeans simply value leisure more highly than Americans do.

▶ Whatever the reason, Europeans enjoy more leisure than Americans, which Europeans regard as adequate compensation for lower real income.

SUMMARY

Key Points

The Classical Model: A Preview (p. 158)

- The classical model explains how real GDP, employment and unemployment, the real wage rate, investment, saving, and the real interest rate are determined at full employment.

Real GDP and Employment (pp. 158–159)

- To produce real GDP, we must forgo leisure time.
- As the quantity of labor increases, real GDP increases.

The Labor Market and Potential GDP (pp. 160–166)

- Other things remaining the same, as the real wage rate falls, the quantity of labor demanded increases and the quantity of labor supplied decreases.
- At full-employment equilibrium, the quantity of labor demanded equals the quantity of labor supplied and real GDP equals potential GDP.

Unemployment at Full Employment (pp. 166–168)

- The unemployment rate at full employment is the natural unemployment rate.
- Persistent unemployment arises from search and job rationing.

Loanable Funds and the Real Interest Rate (pp. 169–174)

- Other things remaining the same, as the real interest rate falls, investment and borrowing increase and saving and lending decrease.
- The equilibrium real interest rate makes the quantity of loanable funds demanded equal to the quantity of loanable funds supplied.

Using the Classical Model (pp. 174–175)

- The classical model can explain changes in an economy over time and differences among economies at a given time.
- In the U.S. economy, advances in technology and capital accumulation increase productivity and increase the demand for labor.

- Also, in the U.S. economy, population growth increases the supply of labor.
- The combined effect of technological advance, capital accumulation, and population growth is an increase in employment and potential GDP and a rise in the real wage rate.

Key Figures

Key Terms

PROBLEMS

myeconlab Tests, Study Plan, Solutions*

1. Robinson Crusoe lives on a desert island on the equator. He has 12 hours of daylight every day to allocate between leisure and work. The table shows seven alternative combinations of leisure and real GDP in Crusoe's economy:

Possibility	Leisure (hours per day)	Real GDP (dollars per day)
A	12	0
B	10	10
C	8	18
D	6	24
E	4	28
F	2	30
G	0	30

a. Make a table and a graph of Crusoe's production function.
b. Find the marginal product of labor for Crusoe at different quantities of labor.

2. Use the information about Robinson Crusoe's economy in problem 1 and the fact that at a real wage rate of $4.50 an hour, Crusoe is willing to work any number of hours between 0 and 12.

a. Make a table that shows Crusoe's demand for labor schedule and draw Crusoe's demand for labor curve.
b. Make a table that shows Crusoe's supply of labor schedule and draw Crusoe's supply of labor curve.
c. What are the equilibrium real wage rate and quantity of labor in Crusoe's economy?
d. Find Crusoe's potential GDP.

3. The figure (in the next column) describes the labor market on Cocoa Island. In addition (not shown in the figure), a survey tells us that when Cocoa Island is at full employment, people spend 1,000 hours a day in job search.
a. Find the full-employment equilibrium real wage rate and quantity of labor employed.
b. Calculate the natural unemployment rate.
c. If the government introduces a minimum wage of $4 an hour, how much unemployment is created?

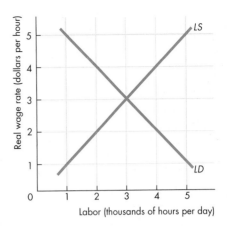

4. A cellular phone assembly plant costs $10 million and has a life of one year. The firm will have to hire labor at a cost of $3 million and buy parts and fuel at a cost of a further $3 million. If the firm builds the plant, it will be able to produce cellular telephones that will sell for a total revenue of $17 million. Does it pay the firm to invest in this new production line at the following real interest rates:
a. 5 percent a year?
b. 10 percent a year?
c. 15 percent a year?

5. In 1999, the Batman family (Batman and Robin) had a disposable income of $50,000, wealth of $100,000, and an expected future income of $50,000 a year. At an interest rate of 4 percent a year, the Batmans would save $10,000; at 6 percent a year, they would save $12,500; and at 8 percent a year, they would save $15,000.
a. Draw a graph of the Batman family's supply of loanable funds curve for 1999.
b. In 2000, everything remained the same as the year before except that the Batmans expected their future income to rise to $60,000 a year. Show the influence of this change on the Batman's supply of loanable funds curve.

6. If the United States cracked down on illegal immigrants and returned millions of workers to their countries of origin, what would happen in the United States to
a. Potential GDP.
b. Employment.
c. The real wage rate.

*Solutions to odd-numbered problems are provided.

7. If a large increase in investment increased the marginal product of labor, what would happen to
   a. Potential GDP.
   b. Employment.
   c. The real wage rate.

8. In 1973 the United Kingdom was at full employment. 47 billion hours of labor produced real GDP of £550 billion, and the real wage rate was £7.12 an hour. Between 1973 and 2003, capital per worker increased and technology advanced. At the same time, the population increased, but higher income taxes and more generous unemployment benefits decreased the supply of labor. In 2003, the full employment quantity of labor was the same as in 1973, but the real wage rate was £12.30 an hour and real GDP was £1,034 billion.

   a. Draw a graph of the U.K. labor market that shows the demand for labor, the supply of labor, and the real wage rate in 1973 and 2003.
   b. Draw a graph of the U.K. production function in 1973 and 2003. Make sure your graph shows potential GDP in both years.

CRITICAL THINKING

1. Study the news article about the differences between the U.S. and euro zone economies in *Reading Between the Lines* on pp. 176–177 and then
   a. Describe the key differences between the U.S. and euro zone economies.
   b. Why do you think the United States is more productive than Europe?
   c. Why do you think Europeans work fewer hours than Americans do?
   d. Explain the effects of the differences in productivity and work habits on U.S. and euro zone employment, potential GDP, and real wage rates.

2. You are working for the President's Council of Economic Advisors and must write a memo for the President that provides a checklist of policy initiatives that will increase potential GDP. Be as imaginative as possible, but justify each of your suggestions with reference to the concepts that you have learned about in this chapter.

3. **Tsunami social cost yet to come**
   Relief experts estimate it could take up to a decade for some places to fully recover, and reconstruction will cost about $9 billion. . . . An assessment by the Indonesian government estimated total damage from the tsunami at $4.5 billion to $5 billion. . . . Housing, commerce, agriculture, fisheries, and transport vehicles and services suffered losses of $2.8 billion, or 63 percent of the total. . . .

   CNN, 19 December 2005

   a. What happened to Indonesia's full-employment quantity of labor as a result of the December 2004 tsunami?
   b. Did Indonesia move along its production function or did its production function shift?
   c. What was the effect of the tsunami on Indonesia's potential GDP?
   d. According to the CNN news article, "people hardest-hit by the tsunami were those who fell outside the 'formal' economy—mainly fishermen, farmers, women and people running small businesses." Does this information change your answers to parts (a), (b), and (c)? Explain why.

WEB ACTIVITIES

(X) myeconlab **Links to Web sites**

1. Obtain information about the economy of Russia during the 1990s. Try to figure out what happened to the production possibilities frontier and production function and to the demand for labor and supply of labor in Russia during the 1990s. Tell a story about the Russian economy during those years using only the concepts and tools that you have learned about in this chapter.

2. Obtain information about the economy of China during the 1990s. Try to figure out what happened to the production possibilities frontier and production function and to the demand for labor and supply of labor in China during the 1990s. Tell a story about the Chinese economy during those years using only the concepts and tools that you have learned about in this chapter.

CHAPTER 8

Economic Growth

Transforming People's Lives

Real GDP *per person* in the United States almost tripled between 1960 and 2005. If you live in a dorm that was built during the

1960s, it is likely to have just two power sockets: one for a desk lamp and one for a bedside lamp. Today, with the help of a power bar (or two), your room bulges with a personal computer, television and DVD player, stereo system, microwave, refrigerator, coffeemaker, and toaster—and the list goes on. What has brought about this growth in production, incomes, and living standards?

We see even greater economic growth if we look at modern Asia. On the banks of the Li River in Southern China, Songman Yang breeds cormorants, amazing birds that he trains to fish and to deliver their catch to a basket on his simple bamboo raft. Songman's work, the capital equipment and technology he uses, and the income he earns are similar to those of his ancestors going back some 2,000 years. Yet all around Songman, in China's bustling cities, people are participating in an economic miracle. They are creating businesses, investing in new technologies, developing local and global markets, and transforming their lives. Why are incomes in China growing so rapidly?

◆ In this chapter, we study the forces that make real GDP grow, that make some countries grow faster than others, and that make our own growth rate sometimes slow down and sometimes speed up.

In *Reading Between the Lines* at the end of the chapter, we return to the economic growth of China and see how it compares with that of the United States.

After studying this chapter, you will be able to

▸ Define and calculate the economic growth rate and explain the implications of sustained growth

▸ Describe the economic growth trends in the United States and other countries and regions

▸ Identify the sources of economic growth

▸ Explain how we measure the effects of the sources of economic growth and identify why growth rates fluctuate

▸ Explain the main theories of economic growth

The Basics of Economic Growth

Economic growth is a sustained expansion of production possibilities measured as the increase in real GDP over a given period. Rapid economic growth maintained over a number of years can transform a poor nation into a rich one. Such has been the stories of Hong Kong, South Korea, Taiwan, and some other Asian economies. Slow economic growth or the absence of growth can condemn a nation to devastating poverty. Such has been the fate of Sierra Leone, Somalia, Zambia, and much of the rest of Africa.

The goal of this chapter is to help you to understand why some economies expand rapidly and others stagnate. We'll begin by learning how to calculate the economic growth rate and by discovering the magic of sustained growth.

Calculating Growth Rates

We express the **economic growth rate** as the annual percentage change of real GDP. To calculate this growth rate, we use the formula:

$$\text{Real GDP growth rate} = \frac{\text{Real GDP in current year} - \text{Real GDP in previous year}}{\text{Real GDP in previous year}} \times 100.$$

For example, if real GDP in the current year is $11 trillion and if real GDP in the previous year was $10 trillion, then the economic growth rate is 10 percent.

The growth rate of real GDP tells us how rapidly the *total* economy is expanding. This measure is useful for telling us about potential changes in the balance of economic power among nations. But it does not tell us about changes in the standard of living.

The standard of living depends on **real GDP per person** (also called *per capita* real GDP), which is real GDP divided by the population. So the contribution of real GDP growth to the change in the standard of living depends on the growth rate of real GDP per person. We use the above formula to calculate this growth rate, replacing real GDP with real GDP per person.

Suppose, for example, that in the current year, when real GDP is $11 trillion, the population is 202 million. Then real GDP per person is $11 trillion divided by 202 million, which equals $54,455. And suppose that in the previous year, when real GDP was $10 trillion, the population was 200 million. Then real GDP per person in that year was $10 trillion divided by 200 million, which equals $50,000.

Use these two real GDP per person values with the growth formula above to calculate the growth rate of real GDP per person. That is,

$$\text{Real GDP per person growth rate} = \frac{\$54,455 - \$50,000}{\$50,000} \times 100 = 8.9 \text{ percent.}$$

The growth rate of real GDP per person can also be calculated (approximately) by subtracting the population growth rate from the real GDP growth rate. In the example you've just worked through, the growth rate of real GDP is 10 percent. The population changes from 200 million to 202 million, so the population growth rate is 1 percent. The growth rate of real GDP per person is approximately equal to 10 percent minus 1 percent, which equals 9 percent.

Real GDP per person grows only if real GDP grows faster than the population grows. If the growth rate of the population exceeds the growth of real GDP, real GDP per person falls.

The Magic of Sustained Growth

Sustained growth of real GDP per person can transform a poor society into a wealthy one. The reason is that economic growth is like compound interest.

Compound Interest Suppose that you put $100 in the bank and earn 5 percent a year interest on it. After one year, you have $105. If you leave that $105 in the bank for another year, you earn 5 percent interest on the original $100 *and on the $5 interest that you earned last year*. You are now earning interest on interest! The next year, things get even better. Then you earn 5 percent on the original $100 and on the interest earned in the first year and the second year. You are even earning interest on the interest that you earned on the interest of the first year.

Your money in the bank is growing at a rate of 5 percent a year. Before too many years have passed, your initial deposit of $100 will have grown to $200. But after how many years?

The answer is provided by a formula called the **Rule of 70**, which states that the number of years it

FIGURE 8.1   The Rule of 70

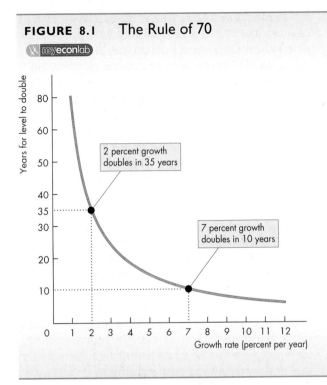

Growth rate (percent per year)	Years for level to double
1	70.0
2	35.0
3	23.3
4	17.5
5	14.0
6	11.7
7	10.0
8	8.8
9	7.8
10	7.0
11	6.4
12	5.8

The number of years it takes for the level of a variable to double is approximately 70 divided by the annual percentage growth rate.

takes for the level of any variable to double is approximately 70 divided by the annual percentage growth rate of the variable. Using the Rule of 70, you can now calculate how many years it takes your $100 to become $200. It is 70 divided by 5, which is 14 years.

Applying the Rule of 70

The Rule of 70 applies to any variable, so it applies to real GDP per person. Figure 8.1 shows the doubling time for growth rates of 1 percent per year to 12 percent per year.

You can see that real GDP per person doubles in 70 years (70 divided by 1)—an average human life span—if the growth rate is 1 percent a year. It doubles in 35 years if the growth rate is 2 percent a year and in just 10 years if the growth rate is 7 percent a year.

We can use the Rule of 70 to answer other questions about economic growth. For example, in 2000, U.S. real GDP per person was approximately 8 times that of China. China's recent growth rate of real GDP per person was 7 percent a year. If this growth rate were maintained, how long would it take China's real GDP per person to reach that of the United

States in 2000? The answer, provided by the Rule of 70, is 30 years. China's real GDP per person doubles in 10 (70 divided by 7) years. It doubles again to 4 times its current level in another 10 years. And it doubles yet again to 8 times its current level in another 10 years. So after 30 years of growth at 7 percent a year, China's real GDP per person is 8 times its current level and equals that of the United States in 2000. Of course, after 30 years, U.S. real GDP per person would have increased, so China would still not have caught up to the United States.

REVIEW QUIZ

1. What is economic growth and how do we calculate its rate?
2. What is the relationship between the growth rate of real GDP and the growth rate of real GDP per person?
3. Use the Rule of 70 to calculate the growth rate that leads to a doubling of real GDP per person in 20 years.

 myeconlab **Study Plan 8.1**

Economic Growth Trends

You have just seen the power of economic growth to increase incomes. At a 1 percent growth rate, it takes a human life span to double the standard of living. But at a 7 percent growth rate, the standard of living doubles every decade. How fast is our economy growing? How fast are other economies growing? Are poor countries catching up to rich ones, or do the gaps between the rich and poor persist or even widen? Let's answer these questions.

Growth in the U.S. Economy

Figure 8.2 shows real GDP per person in the United States for the hundred years from 1905 to 2005. In the middle of the graph are two extraordinary events: the Great Depression of the 1930s and World War II of the 1940s. The fall in real GDP per person during the depression and the bulge during the war obscure any changes in the long-term growth trend that might have occurred within these years.

For the century as a whole, the average growth rate was 2 percent a year. But from 1905 to the onset of the Great Depression in 1929, the average growth rate was only 1.4 percent a year. Between 1930 and 1950, averaging out the depression and the war, the long-term growth rate was 2.2 percent a year. Then, after World War II, the average growth rate was 2 percent a year. Growth was especially rapid during the 1960s and late 1990s and slower during the period from 1973 to 1983.

Figure 8.2 shows the productivity growth slow-down of 1973–1983 in a longer perspective. It also shows that productivity growth slowdowns have occurred before. The early years of the 1900s and the mid-1950s had even slower growth than we had during the 1970s and 1980s. The rapid growth of the 1960s and 1990s is not unusual either. The 1920s were years of similarly rapid growth.

A major goal of this chapter is to explain why our economy grows and why the long-term growth rate varies. Another goal is to explain variations in the economic growth rate across countries. Let's now look at growth rates in other countries.

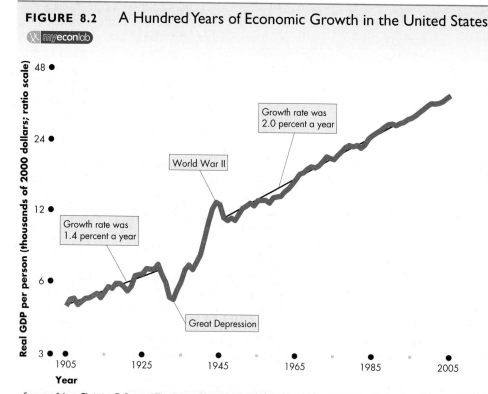

FIGURE 8.2   A Hundred Years of Economic Growth in the United States

During the 100 years from 1905 to 2005, real GDP per person in the United States grew by 2 percent a year, on the average. The growth rate was greater after World War II than before the Great Depression.

Sources of data: Christina D. Romer, "The Prewar Business Cycle Reconsidered: New Estimates of Gross National Product, 1869–1908," *Journal of Political Economy,* Vol. 97, 1989; Bureau of Economic Analysis; and author's calculations to link these two sources.

Real GDP Growth in the World Economy

Figure 8.3 shows real GDP per person in the United States and in other countries between 1960 and 2005. Part (a) looks at the seven richest countries—known as the G7 nations. Among these nations, the United States has the highest real GDP per person. In 2005, Canada had the second-highest real GDP per person, ahead of Japan and France, Germany, Italy, and the United Kingdom (collectively the Europe Big 4).

During the forty-five years shown here, the gaps between the United States, Canada, and the Europe Big 4 have been almost constant. But starting from a long way back, Japan grew fastest. It caught up to Europe in 1973 and to Canada in 1990. But during the 1990s, Japan's economy stagnated.

Many other countries are growing more slowly than, and falling farther behind, the United States. Figure 8.3(b) looks at some of these countries.

Real GDP per person in Central and South America was 28 percent of the U.S. level in 1960. It grew to 31 percent of the U.S. level by 1975 but then began to fall, and by 2005, real GDP per person in these countries had slipped to 22 percent of the U.S. level.

After a brief period of catch-up during the 1980s, the former Communist countries of Central Europe stagnated and fell increasingly behind the United States. More rapid growth resumed in these countries during the 1990s.

Real GDP per person in Africa, the world's poorest continent, slipped from 12 percent of the U.S. level in 1960 to 6 percent in 2005.

FIGURE 8.3   Economic Growth Around the World: Catch-Up or Not?

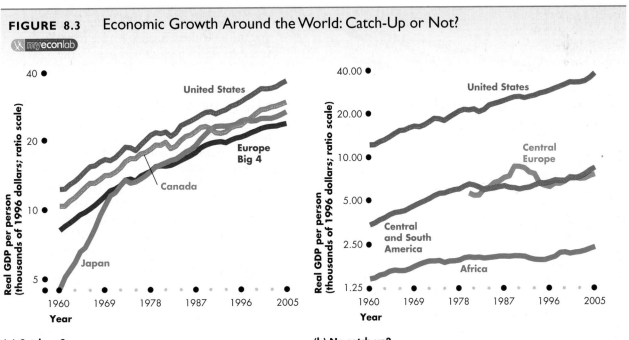

(a) Catch-up?

Real GDP per person has grown throughout the world economy. Among the rich industrial countries (part a), real GDP per person has grown slightly faster in the United States than in Canada and the four big countries of Europe (France, Germany, Italy, and the United Kingdom). Japan had the fastest growth rate before 1973 but then slowed and stagnated during the 1990s.

(b) No catch-up?

Among a wider range of countries shown in part (b), growth rates have been lower than that of the United States. The gaps between the real GDP per person in the United States and in these countries have widened. The gaps between the real GDP per person in the United States and Africa has widened by a large amount.

Sources of data: (1960–2000) Alan Heston, Robert Summers, and Bettina Aten, Penn World Table Version 6.1, Center for International Comparisons at the University of Pennsylvania (CICUP), October 2002; and (2001–2005) International Monetary Fund, *World Economic Outlook*, April 2006.

A group of Asian economies provides a strong contrast to the persistent and growing gaps between the United States and other economies shown in Fig. 8.3(b). Hong Kong, Korea, Singapore, and Taiwan have experienced spectacular growth, which you can see in Fig. 8.4. During the 1960s, real GDP per person in these economies ranged from 13 to 30 percent of that in the United States. But by 2005, real GDP per person in Hong Kong and Singapore had reached 80 percent of that in the United States.

Figure 8.4 shows that China is catching up but from a long way behind. China's real GDP per person increased from 5 percent of the U.S. level in 1960 to 15 percent in 2005.

The Asian economies shown in Fig. 8.4 are like fast trains running on the same track at similar speeds and with a roughly constant gap between them. Hong Kong is the lead train and runs about 15 years in front of Korea and 40 years in front of the rest of China, which is the last train. Real GDP per person in Korea in 2005 was similar to that in Hong Kong in 1985, and real GDP in China in 2005 was similar to that of Hong Kong in 1965. Between 1965 and 2005, Hong Kong transformed itself from a poor developing economy into one of the richest economies in the world.

The rest of China is now doing what Hong Kong has done. If China continues its rapid growth, the world economy will change dramatically. China has a population 200 times that of Hong Kong and more than 4 times that of the United States.

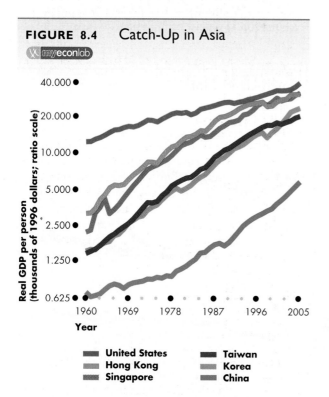

FIGURE 8.4   Catch-Up in Asia

myeconlab

Year

United States   Taiwan
Hong Kong   Korea
Singapore   China

Catch-up has occurred in five economies in Asia. After starting out in 1960 with real GDP per person as low as 13 percent of that in the United States, Hong Kong, Korea, Singapore, and Taiwan have substantially narrowed the gap between them and the United States. And from being a very poor developing country in 1960, China now has a real GDP per person that equals that of Hong Kong in 1965. China is growing at a rate that is enabling it to continue to catch up with the United States.

Sources of data: See Fig. 8.3.

REVIEW QUIZ

1   What has been the average economic growth rate in the United States over the past 100 years? In which periods was growth the most rapid and in which periods was it the slowest?

2   Describe the gaps between the levels of real GDP per person in the United States and other countries. For which countries are the gaps narrowing? For which countries are the gaps widening? And for which countries are the gaps remaining unchanged?

3   Compare the growth rates and levels of real GDP per person in Hong Kong, Korea, Singapore, Taiwan, China, and the United States. How far is China's real GDP per person behind that of the other Asian economies?

myeconlab   Study Plan 8.2

The facts about economic growth in the United States and around the world raise some big questions that we're now going to answer. We'll study the causes of economic growth in three stages. First, we'll look at the preconditions for growth and the activities that sustain it. Second, we'll learn how economists measure the relative contributions of the sources of growth—an activity called *growth accounting*. And third, we'll study three theories of economic growth that seek to explain how the influences on growth interact to determine the growth rate. Let's take our first look at the causes of economic growth.

The Sources of Economic Growth

For thousands of years, most human societies have lived like Li River fisherman Songman Yang, with no economic growth. Why?

Real GDP grows when the quantities of the factors of production grow or when persistent advances in technology make factors of production increasingly productive. So to understand what determines the growth rate of real GDP, we must understand what determines the growth rates of the factors of production and rate of increase in their productivity.

We are interested in real GDP growth because it contributes to improvements in our standard of living. But our standard of living improves only if we produce more goods and services per person. So our main concern is to understand the forces that make our labor more productive. We begin by dividing all the influences on real GDP growth into those that increase

- Aggregate hours
- Labor productivity

Aggregate Hours

Aggregate hours are the total number of hours worked by all the people employed during a year (see Chapter 6, p. 135). We calculate aggregate hours as the number of people employed multiplied by average hours per worker. But the number of people employed equals the working-age population multiplied by the *employment-to-population ratio* (see Chapter 6, p. 134). So aggregate hours change as a result of

1. Working-age population growth
2. Changes in the employment-to-population ratio
3. Changes in average hours per worker

Aggregate hours grow at the growth rate of the working-age population, adjusted for changes in the employment-to-population ratio and changes in average hours per worker.

With steady population growth, the working-age population grows at the same rate as the total population. But in the United States in recent years, the working-age population has grown faster than the total population because of the baby boom—the burst in the birth rate during the years that followed the end of World War II. Through the 1960s and

early 1970s, an increasing number of "baby-boomers" entered the working-age group and the working-age population increased from 65 percent of the total population in 1960 to 77 percent in 2005.

The employment-to-population ratio has increased during the past few decades as the labor force participation rate has increased. But average hours per worker have decreased as the workweek has become shorter and more people have become part-time workers. The combined effects of a rising employment-to-population ratio and falling average hours per worker have kept the average hours per working-age person surprisingly constant at about 1,100 hours a year.

So the growth of aggregate hours comes from population growth rather than from changes in average hours per person.

Population growth increases aggregate hours and real GDP. But to increase real GDP per person, labor must become more productive.

Labor Productivity

Labor productivity is the quantity of real GDP produced by an hour of labor. It is calculated by dividing real GDP by aggregate labor hours. For example, if real GDP is $10,000 billion and aggregate hours are 200 billion, labor productivity is $50 per hour.

When labor productivity grows, real GDP per person grows and brings a rising standard of living.

The growth of labor productivity depends on three things:

- Physical capital growth
- Human capital growth
- Technological advances

These three sources of growth, which interact with each other, are the primary sources of the extraordinary growth in labor productivity during the past 200 years. Let's look at each in turn.

Physical Capital Growth

Physical capital growth results from saving and investment decisions. As the amount of capital per worker increases, labor productivity also increases. Labor productivity took the most dramatic upturn when the amount of capital per worker increased during the Industrial Revolution. Production processes that use hand tools can create beautiful objects, but production methods that use large amounts of capital per worker, such as auto plant assembly lines, are much more productive. The accumulation of capital on farms, in textile factories, in iron foundries and steel mills, in coal mines, on building sites, in chemical plants, in auto plants, in banks and insurance companies, and in shopping malls has added incredibly to the productivity of our economy. The next time you see a movie that is set in the Old West or colonial times, look carefully at the small amount of capital around. Try to imagine how productive you would be in such circumstances compared with your productivity today.

Human Capital Growth

Human capital—the accumulated skill and knowledge of human beings—is the most fundamental source of economic growth. It is a source of both increased labor productivity and technological advance.

The development of one of the most basic human skills—writing—was the source of some of the earliest major gains in productivity. The ability to keep written records made it possible to reap ever-larger gains from specialization and trade. Imagine how hard it would be to do any kind of business if all the accounts, invoices, and agreements existed only in people's memories.

Later, the development of mathematics laid the foundation for the eventual extension of knowledge about physical forces and chemical and biological processes. This base of scientific knowledge was the foundation for the technological advances of the Industrial Revolution 200 years ago and of today's information revolution.

But a lot of human capital that is extremely productive is much more humble. It takes the form of millions of individuals learning and repetitively doing simple production tasks and becoming remarkably more productive in those tasks.

One carefully studied example illustrates the importance of this kind of human capital. Between 1941 and 1944 (during World War II), U.S. shipyards produced some 2,500 units of a cargo ship, called the Liberty Ship, to a standardized design. In 1941, it took 1.2 million person-hours to build one ship. By 1942, it took 600,000 person-hours, and by 1943, it took only 500,000. Not much change occurred in the capital employed during these years.

But an enormous amount of human capital was accumulated. Thousands of workers and managers learned from experience and accumulated human capital that more than doubled their productivity in two years.

Technological Advances

The accumulation of physical capital and human capital have made a large contribution to economic growth. But technological change—the discovery and the application of new technologies and new goods—has made an even greater contribution.

People are many times more productive today than they were a hundred years ago. We are not more productive because we have more steam engines and more horse-drawn carriages per person. Rather, it is because we have engines and transportation equipment that use technologies that were unknown a hundred years ago and that are more productive than the old technologies were. Technological change makes an enormous contribution to our increased productivity. Technological advance arises from formal research and development programs and from informal trial and error, and it involves discovering new ways of getting more out of our resources.

To reap the benefits of technological change, capital must increase. Some of the most powerful and far-reaching fundamental technologies are embodied in human capital—for example, language, writing, and mathematics. But most technologies are embodied in physical capital. For example, to reap the benefits of the internal combustion engine, millions of horse-drawn carriages and horses were replaced by automobiles; and to reap the benefits of digital music, millions of Walkmans were replaced by iPods.

Figure 8.5 summarizes the sources of economic growth that we've just described. It also emphasizes that for real GDP per person to grow, real GDP growth must exceed the population growth rate.

We began this account of the sources of economic growth by noting that for thousands of years, no growth occurred. You've seen that economic growth results from productivity growth. Why is productivity growth a relatively recent phenomenon?

The reason is that early humans (like many people today) lacked the fundamental social institutions and arrangements that are essential preconditions for economic growth. Let's end our discussion of the sources of growth by examining its preconditions.

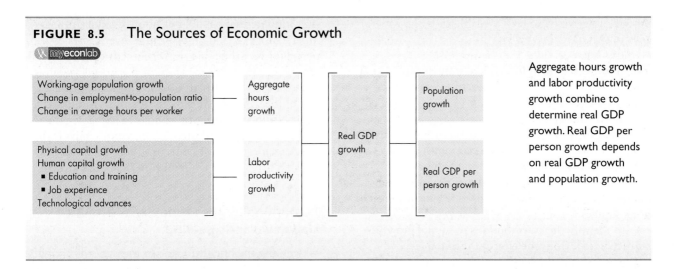

FIGURE 8.5   The Sources of Economic Growth

Aggregate hours growth and labor productivity growth combine to determine real GDP growth. Real GDP per person growth depends on real GDP growth and population growth.

Preconditions for Economic Growth

The most basic precondition for economic growth is an appropriate *incentive* system. Three institutions are crucial to the creation of incentives:

1. Markets
2. Property rights
3. Monetary exchange

Markets enable buyers and sellers to get information and to do business with each other, and market prices send signals to buyers and sellers that create incentives to increase or decrease the quantities demanded and supplied. Markets enable people to specialize and trade and to save and invest. But markets need property rights and monetary exchange.

Property rights are the social arrangements that govern the ownership, use, and disposal of factors of production and goods and services. They include the rights to physical property (land, buildings, and capital equipment), to financial property (claims by one person against another), and to intellectual property (such as inventions). Clearly established and enforced property rights give people an assurance that a capricious government will not confiscate their income or savings.

Monetary exchange facilitates transactions of all kinds, including the orderly transfer of private property from one person to another. Property rights and monetary exchange create incentives for people to specialize and trade, to save and invest, and to discover new technologies.

No unique political system is necessary to deliver the preconditions for economic growth. Liberal democracy, founded on the fundamental principle of the rule of law, is the system that does the best job. It provides a solid base on which property rights can be established and enforced. But authoritarian political systems have sometimes provided an environment in which economic growth has occurred.

Early human societies, based on hunting and gathering, did not experience economic growth because they lacked these preconditions. Economic growth began when societies evolved the three key institutions that create incentives. But the presence of an incentive system and the institutions that create it does not guarantee that economic growth will occur. It permits economic growth but does not make that growth inevitable.

Next you'll learn how we measure the quantitative contributions of the sources of economic growth.

Growth Accounting

The accumulation of physical and human capital and the discovery of new technologies bring economic growth. But how much does each of these sources of growth contribute? The answer to this question is a crucial input in the design of policies to achieve faster growth. Edward F. Denison, an economist at the Brookings Institution, provided the answer by developing **growth accounting**, a tool that calculates the quantitative contribution to real GDP growth of each of its sources.

To identify the contributions of capital growth and separate it from the effect of technological change and human capital growth, we need to know how labor productivity changes when capital changes.

The *law of diminishing returns*, which states that as the quantity of one input increases with the quantities of all other inputs remaining the same, output increases but by ever smaller increments, applies to capital just as it applies to labor. You saw this law in action in the labor market in Chapter 7 (p. 161).

Applied to capital, the law of diminishing returns states that if a given number of hours of labor use more capital (with the same technology), the *additional* output that results from the *additional* capital gets smaller as the amount of capital increases. One person working with two computers types fewer than twice as many pages a day as one person working with one computer. More generally, one hour of labor working with $40 of capital produces less than twice the output of one hour of labor working with $20 of capital. But how much less? The answer is given by the *one third rule*.

The One Third Rule

Using data on capital, labor hours, and real GDP in the U.S. economy, Robert Solow of MIT estimated the effect of capital on real GDP per hour of labor, or labor productivity. In doing so, he discovered the **one third rule**, that on the average, with no change in technology, a 1 percent increase in capital per hour of labor brings a *1/3 percent increase* in labor productivity. The one third rule is used to calculate the contributions of an increase in capital per hour of labor and technological change to the growth of labor productivity. Let's do such a calculation.

Suppose that capital per hour of labor grows by 3 percent a year and labor productivity grows by 2.5 percent a year. The one third rule tells us that capital growth contributed one third of 3 percent, which is 1 percent, to the growth of labor productivity. The rest of the 2.5 percent growth of labor productivity comes from technological change. That is, technological change contributed 1.5 percent, which is the 2.5 percent growth of labor productivity minus the estimated 1 percent contribution of capital growth.

Accounting for the Productivity Growth Slowdown and Speedup

We can use the one third rule to measure the contributions to U.S. productivity growth. Figure 8.6 shows the results for the years 1960 through 2005. Between 1960 and 1973, labor productivity grew by 3.7 percent a year and capital growth and technological change contributed equally to this growth.

Between 1973 and 1983, labor productivity growth slowed to 1.7 percent a year and a collapse of the contributions of human capital and technological change brought this slowdown. Technological change did not stop during the productivity growth slowdown. But its focus changed from increasing labor productivity to coping with energy price shocks and environmental protection.

Between 1983 and 1993, labor productivity growth speeded to 2 percent a year, and between 1993 and 2005, it speeded to a bit more than 2.4 percent a year. Although growth in the "new economy" of the 1990s and 2000s was stronger than that of the 1970s, growth lagged a long way behind that of the booming sixties.

Achieving Faster Growth

Growth accounting tells us that to achieve faster economic growth, we must increase the growth rate of physical capital, the pace of technological advance, or the growth rate of human capital.

The main suggestions for achieving these objectives are

- Stimulate saving
- Stimulate research and development
- Target high-technology industries
- Encourage international trade
- Improve the quality of education

FIGURE 8.6   Labor Productivity Growth

(a) Labor productivity growth

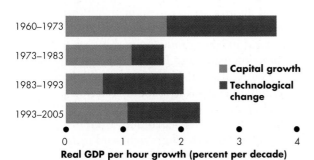

(b) The contributions to labor productivity growth

Labor productivity grew most quickly during the 1960s and most slowly between 1973 and 1983. Changes in the pace of technological change were the biggest source of fluctuations in labor productivity growth.

Sources of data: Bureau of Economic Analysis, Bureau of Labor Statistics, and author's calculations.

Stimulate Saving Saving finances investment, which brings capital accumulation. So stimulating saving can increase economic growth. The East Asian economies have the highest growth rates and the highest saving rates. Some African economies have the lowest growth rates and the lowest saving rates.

Tax incentives can increase saving. Individual Retirement Accounts (IRAs) are a tax incentive to save. Economists claim that a tax on consumption rather than income provides the best saving incentive.

Stimulate Research and Development Everyone can use the fruits of *basic* research and development efforts. For example, all biotechnology firms can use advances in gene-splicing technology. Because basic inventions can be copied, the inventor's profit is limited and the market allocates too few resources to this activity.

Governments can direct public funds toward financing basic research, but this solution is not foolproof. It requires a mechanism for allocating the public funds to their highest-valued use. The National Science Foundation is one possibly efficient channel for allocating public funds to universities to finance and stimulate basic research.

Target High-Technology Industries Some people say that by providing public funds to high-technology firms and industries, a country can become the first to exploit a new technology and can earn above-average profits for a period while others are busy catching up. This strategy is risky and just as likely to use resources inefficiently as to speed growth.

Encourage International Trade Free international trade stimulates growth by extracting all the available gains from specialization and trade. The fastest-growing nations today are those with the fastest-growing exports and imports.

Improve the Quality of Education The free market produces too little education because it brings benefits beyond those valued by the people who receive the education. By funding basic education and by ensuring high standards in basic skills such as language, mathematics, and science, governments can contribute to a nation's growth potential. Education can also be stimulated and improved by using tax incentives to encourage improved private provision.

REVIEW QUIZ

1 How does the one third rule isolate the contribution of capital growth and separate it from the other factors that make productivity grow?
2 Why did labor productivity grow slowly between 1973 and 1983?
3 What are the policy actions that might speed productivity growth?

Study Plan 8.4

Growth Theories

You've seen that real GDP grows when the quantities of labor, physical capital, and human capital grow and when technology advances. Does this mean that the growth of labor and capital and technological advances *cause* economic growth? It might. But there are other possibilities. *Some* of these factors might be the causes of real GDP growth, and the others might be the *effect*. We must try to discover how the influences on economic growth interact with each other to make some economies grow quickly and others grow slowly. And we must probe the reasons why a country's long-term growth rate sometimes speeds up and sometimes slows down.

To explain economic growth, we need a theory of economic growth that explains the interactions among the several factors that contribute to it and disentangles cause and effect.

Economists seek a universal theory of economic growth. They want to understand the growth of poor countries and rich countries—why and how poor countries become rich and rich countries continue to get richer.

Economic growth occurs when real GDP increases. But a one-shot increase in real GDP in a recovery from recession isn't economic growth. Economic growth is a sustained, year-after-year increase in *potential GDP*.

We're going to begin our explanation of growth theory by studying the effects and interactions that occur when labor productivity increases.

Increase in Labor Productivity

How does an increase in labor productivity change real GDP? How does it change aggregate hours? And how does it influence the real wage rate—the income from labor?

We can answer these questions by using the classical model that you studied in Chapter 7. This model of the full-employment economy is ideally suited to studying economic growth because sustained real GDP growth can occur only when potential GDP grows.

If labor productivity increases, production possibilities expand. The real GDP that any given quantity of labor can produce increases. The *marginal product of labor* also increases, which increases the demand for labor.

With an increase in the demand for labor and *no change in the supply of labor*, the real wage rate rises and the quantity of labor supplied increases. Employment (aggregate hours) increases.

Potential GDP increases for two reasons. First, because labor is more productive, a given amount of employment produces more real GDP. Second, equilibrium employment increases.

Illustrating the Effects of an Increase in Labor Productivity

Figure 8.7 illustrates the effects of an increase in labor productivity that results from an increase in physical capital or human capital or an advance in technology.

In part (a), the production function initially is PF_0. With 200 billion hours of labor employed, potential GDP is $12 trillion at point A.

In part (b), the demand for labor curve is LD_0 and the supply of labor curve is LS. The real wage rate is $35 an hour, and equilibrium employment is 200 billion hours a year.

Now an increase in capital or an advance in technology increases the labor productivity. In Fig. 8.7(a), the increase in labor productivity shifts the production function upward to PF_1. At each quantity of labor, more real GDP can be produced. For example, at 200 billion hours, the economy can now produce $17 trillion of real GDP at point B.

In Fig. 8.7(b), the demand for labor increases and the demand curve shifts rightward to LD_1. At the original real wage rate of $35 an hour, there is now a shortage of labor. So the real wage rate rises. In this example, the real wage rate keeps rising until it reaches $45 an hour. At $45 an hour, the quantity of labor demanded equals the quantity of labor supplied and aggregate hours at equilibrium employment increase to 225 billion a year.

Figure 8.7(a) shows the effects of the increase in labor productivity on potential GDP. There are two effects. At the initial quantity of labor, real GDP increases to point B on the new production function. But as aggregate hours increase from 200 billion to 225 billion, potential GDP increases further to $18 trillion at point C.

Potential GDP per hour of labor also increases. You can see this increase by dividing potential GDP by aggregate hours. Initially, with potential GDP at $12 trillion and aggregate hours at 200 billion, potential GDP per hour of labor was $60. With the

FIGURE 8.7 The Effects of an Increase in Labor Productivity

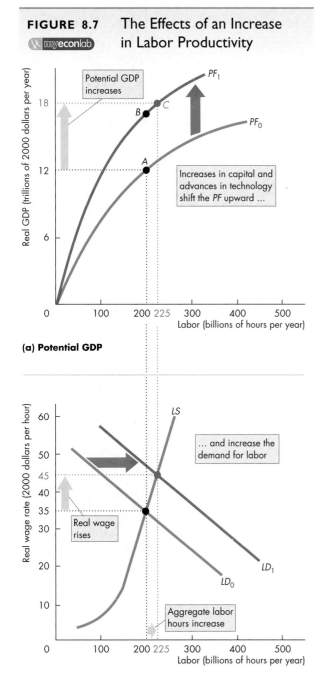

(a) Potential GDP

(b) The labor market

An increase in labor productivity shifts the production function upward from PF_0 to PF_1 in part (a) and shifts the demand for labor curve rightward from LD_0 to LD_1 in part (b). The real wage rate rises to $45 an hour, and aggregate hours increase from 200 billion to 225 billion. Potential GDP increases from $12 trillion to $18 trillion.

increase in labor productivity, potential GDP is $18 trillion and aggregate hours are 225 billion, so potential GDP per hour of labor is $80.

You've now seen the effects of an increase in labor productivity. If labor productivity grows, potential GDP grows, the real wage rate rises, and aggregate hours increase.

There is a limit to the increase in aggregate hours and if the process of labor productivity growth continues with no change in the supply of labor, eventually, at some higher real wage rate, the labor supply curve becomes vertical. At this point, as labor productivity continues to grow, the real wage rate rises, potential GDP increases, but aggregate hours remain constant.

You've just seen that aggregate hours can increase as a consequence of an increase in labor productivity. This interaction of aggregate hours and labor productivity is an example of the interaction effects that economists seek to identify in their search for the ultimate causes of economic growth. In the case that we've just studied, aggregate hours increase but that increase is a consequence, not a cause, of real GDP growth. The source of the real GDP increase is an increase in capital or technological advances that increase labor productivity.

But aggregate hours can increase if the population increases. Let's now examine the effects of this source of an increase in aggregate hours.

An Increase in Population

As the population increases and the additional people reach working age, the supply of labor increases. With more labor available, the economy's production possibilities expand. But does the expansion of production possibilities mean that potential GDP increases? And does it mean that potential GDP *per hour of labor* increases?

The answers to these questions have intrigued economists for many years. And they cause heated political debate today. In China, for example, families are under enormous pressure to limit the number of children they have. In other countries, such as France, the government encourages large families. In the United States and the United Kingdom, immigration and its effects on the population and the labor market are a big concern.

Again, we can analyze the effects of an increase in population by using the classical model of the full-employment economy that you studied in Chapter 7.

If the population increases, the supply of labor increases. There is no change in the demand for labor and no change in the production function. The economy can produce more output by using more labor (a movement along the production function), but there is no change in the quantity of real GDP that a given quantity of labor can produce.

With an increase in the supply of labor and no change in the demand for labor, the real wage rate falls and equilibrium employment (aggregate hours) increases. The increased labor hours produce more output and potential GDP increases.

Illustrating the Effects of an Increase in Population

Figure 8.8 illustrates the effects of an increase in the population. In Fig. 8.8(a), the demand for labor curve is LD and initially the supply of labor curve is LS_0. The equilibrium real wage rate is $35 an hour and aggregate hours are 200 billion a year. In Fig. 8.8(b), the production function (PF) shows that with 200 billion hours of labor employed, potential GDP is $12 trillion at point A.

An increase in the population increases the number of people of working age, and the supply of labor increases. The supply of labor curve shifts rightward to LS_1. At a real wage rate of $35 an hour, there is now a surplus of labor. So the real wage rate falls. In this example, the real wage rate falls until it reaches $25 an hour. At $25 an hour, the quantity of labor demanded equals the quantity of labor supplied. Aggregate hours increase to 300 billion a year.

Figure 8.8(b) shows the effect of the increase in aggregate hours on real GDP. As aggregate hours increase from 200 billion to 300 billion, potential GDP increases from $12 trillion to $15 trillion at point B.

So an increase in the population increases aggregate hours, increases potential GDP, and lowers the real wage rate.

An increase in the population also decreases potential GDP per hour of labor. You can see this decrease by dividing potential GDP by aggregate hours. Initially, with potential GDP at $12 trillion and aggregate hours at 200 billion, potential GDP per hour of labor was $60. With the increase in the population, potential GDP is $15 trillion and aggregate hours are 300 billion. Potential GDP per hour

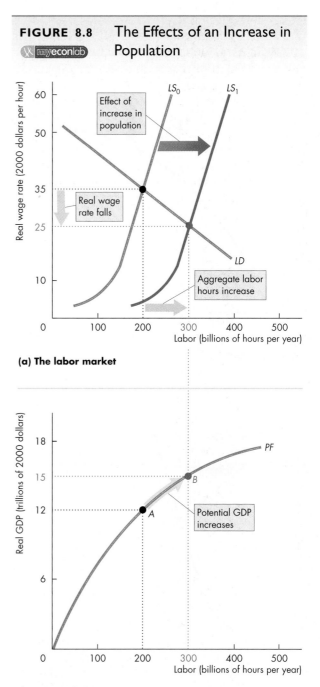

FIGURE 8.8   The Effects of an Increase in Population

(a) The labor market

(b) Potential GDP

An increase in the population increases the supply of labor. In part (a), the real wage rate falls and employment (aggregate hours) increases. In part (b), the increase in aggregate hours increases potential GDP. Because the marginal product of labor diminishes, the increased population increases real GDP but real GDP per hour of labor decreases.

of labor is $50. Diminishing returns are the source of the decrease in potential GDP per hour of labor.

Economic growth theory builds on the effects of labor productivity growth and population growth that you've just reviewed.

You're going to study three theories of economic growth, each of which gives some insights into the process of economic growth. But none provides a complete and definite answer to the basic questions: What causes economic growth and why do growth rates vary? Economics has some way to go before it can provide a definite answer to these questions. The three growth theories we study are

- Classical growth theory
- Neoclassical growth theory
- New growth theory

Classical Growth Theory

Classical growth theory is the view that the growth of real GDP per person is temporary and that when it rises above the subsistence level, a population explosion eventually brings it back to the subsistence level. Adam Smith, Thomas Robert Malthus, and David Ricardo—the leading economists of the late eighteenth century and early nineteenth century—proposed this theory, but the view is most closely associated with the name of Malthus and is sometimes called the *Malthusian theory*.

Modern-Day Malthusians Many people today are Malthusians! They say that if today's global population of 6.2 billion explodes to 11 billion by 2200, we will run out of resources, real GDP per person will decline, and we will return to a primitive standard of living. We must act, say the Malthusians, to contain the population growth.

Modern-day Malthusians also point to global warming and climate change as reasons to believe that eventually, real GDP per person will decrease. They believe that as the planet becomes hotter, the polar ice caps melt, and the oceans' water levels rise, food production will decrease, the land area will shrink, and production possibilities will decrease.

These doomsday conditions, they believe, arise as a direct consequence of today's economic growth and the vast and growing amounts of activity that are increasing the amount of carbon dioxide in the earth's atmosphere.

The Basic Classical Idea To understand classical growth theory, let's transport ourselves back to the world of 1776, when Adam Smith is first explaining the idea. Most of the 2.5 million people who live in the newly independent United States of America work on farms or on their own land and perform their tasks using simple tools and animal power. They earn an average of 2 shillings (a bit less than 12 dollars in today's money) for working a 10-hour day.

Then advances in farming technology bring new types of plows and seeds that increase farm productivity. As farm productivity increases, farm production increases and some farm workers move from the land to the cities, where they get work producing and selling the expanding range of farm equipment. Incomes rise, and the people seem to be prospering. But will the prosperity last? Classical growth theory says it will not.

Advances in technology—in both agriculture and industry—lead to an investment in new capital, which makes labor more productive. More and more businesses start up and hire the now more productive labor. The greater demand for labor raises the real wage rate and increases employment.

At this stage, economic growth has occurred and everyone has benefited from it. Real GDP has increased, and the real wage rate has increased. But the classical economists believe that this new situation can't last because it will induce a population explosion.

Classical Theory of Population Growth When the classical economists were developing their ideas about population growth, an unprecedented population explosion was under way. In Britain and other Western European countries, improvements in diet and hygiene had lowered the death rate while the birth rate remained high. For several decades, population growth was extremely rapid. For example, after being relatively stable for several centuries, the population of Britain increased by 40 percent between 1750 and 1800 and by a further 50 percent between 1800 and 1830. Meanwhile, an estimated 1 million people (about 20 percent of the 1750 population) left Britain for America and Australia before 1800, and outward migration continued on a similar scale through the nineteenth century. These facts are the empirical basis for the classical theory of population growth.

To explain the high rate of population growth, the classical economists used the idea of a **subsistence**

real wage rate, which is the minimum real wage rate needed to maintain life. If the actual real wage rate is less than the subsistence real wage rate, some people cannot survive and the population decreases. In classical theory, when the real wage rate exceeds the subsistence real wage rate, the population grows. But an increasing population brings diminishing returns to labor. So labor productivity eventually decreases. This dismal implication led to economics being called the *dismal science*. The dismal implication is that no matter how much technological change occurs, real wage rates are always pushed back toward the subsistence level.

The dismal conclusion of classical growth theory is a direct consequence of the assumption that the population explodes if real GDP per hour of labor exceeds the subsistence level. To avoid this conclusion, we need a different view of population growth.

The neoclassical growth theory that we'll now study provides a different view.

Neoclassical Growth Theory

Neoclassical growth theory is the proposition that real GDP per person grows because technological change induces a level of saving and investment that makes capital per hour of labor grow. Growth ends only if technological change stops.

Robert Solow of MIT suggested the most popular version of neoclassical growth theory in the 1950s. But Frank Ramsey of Cambridge University in England first developed this theory in the 1920s.

Neoclassical growth theory's big break with its classical predecessor is its view about population growth. We'll begin our account of neoclassical theory by examining its views about population growth.

The Neoclassical Economics of Population Growth
The population explosion of eighteenth century Europe that created the classical theory of population eventually ended. The birth rate fell, and while the population continued to increase, its rate of increase became moderate. This slowdown in population growth seemed to make the classical theory less relevant. It also eventually led to the development of a modern economic theory of population growth.

The modern view is that although the population growth rate is influenced by economic factors, the influence is not a simple and mechanical one like that proposed by the classical economists. Key among the economic influences on population growth is the opportunity cost of a woman's time. As women's wage rates increase and their job opportunities expand, the opportunity cost of having children increases. Faced with a higher opportunity cost, families choose to have fewer children and the birth rate falls.

A second economic influence works on the death rate. The technological advance that brings increased productivity and increased incomes brings advances in health care that extends lives.

These two opposing economic forces influence the population growth rate. As incomes increase, both the birth rate and the death rate decrease. It turns out that these opposing forces almost offset each other, so the rate of population growth is independent of the economic growth rate.

This modern view of population growth and the historical trends that support it contradict the views of the classical economists. They also call into question the modern doomsday conclusion that the planet will one day be swamped with more people than it can support. Neoclassical growth theory adopts this modern view of population growth. Forces other than real GDP and its growth rate determine population growth.

Technological Change In neoclassical growth theory, the rate of technological change influences the economic growth rate but economic growth does not influence the pace of technological change. It is assumed that technological change results from chance. When we're lucky, we have rapid technological change, and when bad luck strikes, the pace of technological advance slows.

Target Rate of Return and Saving The key assumption in neoclassical growth theory concerns saving. Other things remaining the same, the higher the real interest rate, the greater is the amount that people save (see Chapter 7, pp. 171–172). But in the long run, saving is highly responsive to the real interest rate. To decide how much to save, people compare the real interest rate with a *target rate of return*. If the real interest rate exceeds the target rate of return, saving is sufficient to make capital per hour of labor grow. If the target rate of return exceeds the real interest rate, saving is not sufficient to maintain the current level of capital per hour of labor, so capital per hour of labor shrinks. And if the real interest rate equals a target rate of return, saving is just sufficient to maintain the quantity of capital per hour of labor at its current level.

The Basic Neoclassical Idea To understand neoclassical growth theory, imagine the world of the mid-1950s, when Robert Solow is explaining his idea. Americans are enjoying post–World War II prosperity. Income per person is around $12,000 a year in today's money. The population is growing at about 1 percent a year. Saving and investment are about 18 percent of GDP, enough to keep the quantity of capital per hour of labor constant. Income per person is growing but not by much.

Then technology begins to advance at a more rapid pace across a range of activities. The transistor revolutionizes an emerging electronics industry. New plastics revolutionize the manufacture of household appliances. The interstate highway system revolutionizes road transportation. Jet airliners start to replace piston-engine airplanes and speed air transportation.

These technological advances bring new profit opportunities. Businesses expand, and new businesses are created to exploit the newly available profitable technologies. Investment and saving increase. The economy enjoys new levels of prosperity and growth. But will the prosperity last? And will the growth last? Neoclassical growth theory says that the *prosperity* will last but the *growth* will not last unless technology keeps advancing.

According to neoclassical growth theory, the prosperity will persist because there is no classical population growth to induce the wage rate to fall.

But growth will stop if technology stops advancing, for two related reasons. First, high profit rates that result from technological change bring increased saving and capital accumulation. But second, capital accumulation eventually results in diminishing returns that lower the real interest rate and that eventually decrease saving and slow the rate of capital accumulation.

A Problem with Neoclassical Growth Theory
All economies have access to the same technologies, and capital is free to roam the globe, seeking the highest available real interest rate. Given these facts, neoclassical growth theory implies that growth rates and income levels per person around the globe will converge. While there is some sign of convergence among the rich countries, as Fig. 8.3(a) shows, convergence is slow, and it does not appear to be imminent for all countries, as Fig. 8.3(b) shows.

New growth theory overcomes this shortcoming of neoclassical growth theory. It also explains what determines the rate of technological change.

New Growth Theory

New growth theory holds that real GDP per person grows because of the choices people make in the pursuit of profit and that growth can persist indefinitely. Paul Romer of Stanford University developed this theory during the 1980s, but the ideas go back to the work by Joseph Schumpeter during the 1930s and 1940s.

The theory begins with two facts about market economies:

- Discoveries result from choices.
- Discoveries bring profit, and competition destroys profit.

Discoveries and Choices When people discover a new product or technique, they think of themselves as being lucky. They are right. But the pace at which new discoveries are made—and at which technology advances—is not determined by chance. It depends on how many people are looking for a new technology and how intensively they are looking.

Discoveries and Profits Profit is the spur to technological change. The forces of competition squeeze profits, so to increase profit, people constantly seek either lower-cost methods of production or new and better products for which people are willing to pay a higher price. Inventors can maintain a profit for several years by taking out a patent or a copyright. But eventually, a new discovery is copied, and profits disappear.

Two further facts play a key role in the new growth theory:

- Discoveries are a public capital good.
- Knowledge is capital that is not subject to the law of diminishing returns.

Discoveries Are a Public Capital Good Economists call a good a *public good* when no one can be excluded from using it and when one person's use does not prevent others from using it. National defense is one example of a public good. Knowledge is another.

When in 1992, Marc Andreesen and his friend Eric Bina developed a browser they called Mosaic, they laid the foundation for Netscape Navigator and Internet Explorer, two pieces of capital that have increased productivity unimaginably.

While patents and copyrights protect the inventors or creators of new products and production processes and enable them to reap the returns from their innovative ideas, once a new discovery has been made, everyone can benefit from its use. And one person's use of a new discovery does not prevent others from using it. Your use of a Web browser doesn't prevent someone else from using that same code simultaneously.

Because knowledge is a public good, as the benefits of a new discovery spread, free resources become available. These resources are free because nothing is given up when they are used. They have a zero opportunity cost. Knowledge is even more special because it is not subject to diminishing returns.

Knowledge Capital Is Not Subject to Diminishing Returns Production is subject to diminishing returns when one resource is fixed and the quantity of another resource changes. Adding labor to a fixed amount of capital or adding capital to a fixed amount of labor both bring diminishing marginal product—diminishing returns.

But increasing the stock of knowledge makes labor and machines more productive. Knowledge capital does not bring diminishing returns.

The fact that knowledge capital does *not* experience diminishing returns is the central novel proposition of new growth theory. And the implication of this simple and appealing idea is astonishing. Unlike the other two theories, new growth theory has no growth-stopping mechanism. As physical capital accumulates, the return to capital—the real interest rate—falls. But the incentive to innovate and earn a higher profit becomes stronger. So innovation occurs, capital become more productive, the demand for capital increases, and the real interest rate rises again.

Labor productivity grows indefinitely as people discover new technologies that yield a higher real interest rate. This growth rate depends on people's ability to innovate.

Over the years, the ability to innovate has changed. The invention of language and writing (the two most basic human capital tools) and later the development of the scientific method and the establishment of universities and research institutions brought huge increases in the pace of innovation. Today, a deeper understanding of genes is bringing profit in a growing biotechnology industry. And advances in computer technology are creating an explosion of profit opportunities in a wide range of information-age industries.

A Perpetual Motion Economy New growth theory sees the economy as a perpetual motion machine, which Fig. 8.9 illustrates.

No matter how rich we become, our wants will always exceed our ability to satisfy them. We will always want a higher standard of living.

In the pursuit of a higher standard of living, human societies have developed incentive systems—property rights and voluntary monetary exchange in markets—that enable people to profit from innovation.

Innovation leads to the development of new and better techniques of production and new and better products.

To take advantage of new techniques and to produce new products, new firms start up and old firms go out of business—firms are born and die.

As old firms die and new firms are born, some jobs are destroyed and others are created. The new jobs created are better than the old ones and they pay higher real wage rates. Also, with higher wage rates and more productive techniques, leisure increases.

New and better jobs and new and better products lead to more consumption goods and services and, combined with increased leisure, bring a higher standard of living.

But our insatiable wants are still there, so the process continues, going round and round a circle of wants, incentives, innovation, and new and better products, and a yet higher standard of living.

New Growth Theory Versus Malthusian Theory

The contrast between the Malthusian theory and new growth theory couldn't be more sharp. Malthusians see the end of prosperity as we know it today and new growth theorists see unending plenty. The contrast becomes clearest by thinking about the differing views about population growth.

To a Malthusian, population growth is part of the problem. To a new growth theorist, population growth is part of the solution! People are the ultimate economic resource. A larger population brings forth more wants. But it also brings a greater amount of scientific discovery and technological advance. So rather than being the source of falling real GDP per person, population growth generates faster productivity growth and rising real GDP per person. Resources are limited, but the human imagination and ability to increase productivity are unlimited.

FIGURE 8.9   A Perpetual Motion Machine

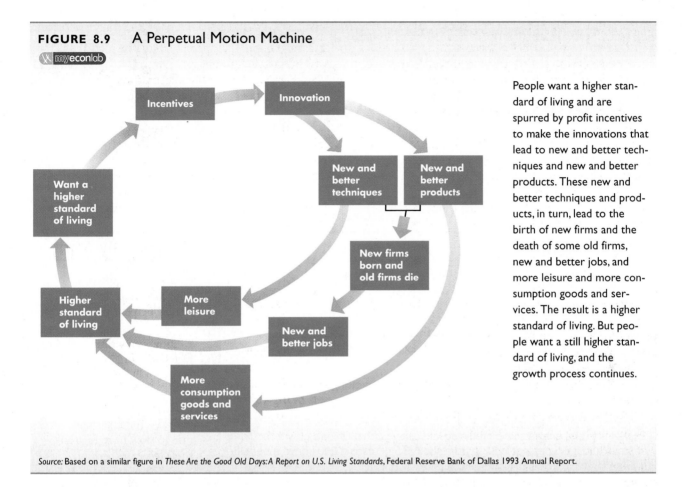

People want a higher standard of living and are spurred by profit incentives to make the innovations that lead to new and better techniques and new and better products. These new and better techniques and products, in turn, lead to the birth of new firms and the death of some old firms, new and better jobs, and more leisure and more consumption goods and services. The result is a higher standard of living. But people want a still higher standard of living, and the growth process continues.

Source: Based on a similar figure in *These Are the Good Old Days: A Report on U.S. Living Standards,* Federal Reserve Bank of Dallas 1993 Annual Report.

Sorting Out the Theories

Which theory is correct? Probably none tells us the whole story, but they all teach us something of value.

Classical growth theory reminds us that our physical resources are limited and that without advances in technology, we must eventually hit diminishing returns.

Neoclassical growth theory reaches the same conclusion but not because of a population explosion. Instead, it emphasizes diminishing returns to capital and reminds us that we cannot keep growth going just by accumulating physical capital. We must also advance technology and accumulate human capital. We must become more creative in our use of scarce resources.

New growth theory emphasizes the possible capacity of human resources to innovate at a pace that offsets diminishing returns.

New growth theory probably fits the facts of today's world more closely than either of the other two theories do. But that doesn't make it correct.

REVIEW QUIZ

1 What are the effects of an increase in labor productivity on economic growth?
2 What are the effects of an increase in the population on economic growth?
3 What is the key idea of classical growth theory that leads to the dismal outcome?
4 What, according to neoclassical growth theory, is the fundamental cause of economic growth?
5 What is the key proposition of new growth theory that makes growth persist?

myeconlab Study Plan 8.5

To complete your study of economic growth, take a look at *Reading Between the Lines* on pp. 200–201 and see how economic growth is transforming the economy of China.

Economic Growth in Asia

---

http://www.nytimes.com

China's Economy Surges 9.4% in 3rd Quarter

October 21, 2005

China's roaring economy grew 9.4 percent in the third quarter of this year, fueled by surging exports, strong investments in infrastructure and solid retail sales, according to government figures released Thursday.

The figures indicate that China's economy, the fastest-growing major economy in the world, shows no sign of moderating, despite repeated attempts by the government to ease growth as a way to head off inflation or overheating.

Economists and analysts who predicted late last year that China's growth would abate to about 8.5 percent in 2005 from about 9.5 percent in 2004 have repeatedly been forced to adjust their forecasts upward.

Thursday, more analysts raised their forecasts.

"This is much stronger growth than the market expected," said Hong Liang, an economist at Goldman Sachs, who expects the Chinese economy to grow 9.4 percent this year and 9 percent in 2006. . . .

Many experts say China seems to be locked into 9 percent economic growth—even after its economy has advanced at a faster pace over the last 20 years than any other major country in modern history, even outpacing the earlier decades long expansions of Japan and South Korea.

"It's not going to change," said Yiping Huang, an economist at Citigroup in Hong Kong. "At the moment, the government is trying to slow momentum a bit, but we're not seeing slowing." . . .

Essence of the Story

▶ Real GDP growth in China is running at more than 9 percent per year.

▶ China's economy is the fastest-growing major economy in the world.

▶ Economists who expected China's growth rate to slow have revised their forecasts upward.

▶ China is now expected to continue to achieve 9 percent economic growth.

▶ Government attempts to slow the growth rate are expected to have little effect.

In 1949, when Mao Zedong established the People's Republic of China, incomes in China were among the lowest in the world.

From 1949 until 1978, China operated a planned economy with little private enterprise. Economic growth was modest, and in some years, real GDP decreased.

In 1978, under the leadership of Deng Xiaoping, China embarked on a program of economic reform.

Gradually, state-owned monopolies were replaced by private competitive businesses, often financed with foreign capital and operated as joint ventures with foreign firms.

By the early 1980s, China's real GDP was growing at one of the fastest rates in the world and the fastest ever known.

In 2005, China's real GDP was more than $9 trillion (using U.S. dollars and PPP prices in 2000—see Chapter 5, p. 124).

U.S. real GDP in 2005 was almost $12 trillion (2000 dollars).

Although China's real GDP was not far behind U.S. real GDP in 2005, China used much more labor than the United States used.

Aggregate labor hours in the United States in 2005 were about 250 billion.

We don't know what China's aggregate labor hours were. But employment was 790 million and with an average workweek of 40 hours (an assumption), aggregate hours would be around 1,650 billion—more than 6 times the U.S. hours.

So real GDP per hour of labor in China in 2005 was around $5 compared to about $48 in the United States.

But China's real GDP is growing at about 9 percent a year. In contrast, U.S. real GDP is growing at about 2.5 percent a year.

If these growth rates persist, China's real GDP will surpass that of the United States within the next decade.

But China's real GDP per hour of labor will continue to lag well behind that of the United States.

The figure shows the situation in China and the United States in 2005.

The U.S. production function is PF_{US05}, and China's production function is PF_{C05}.

With employment of 250 billion hours, the

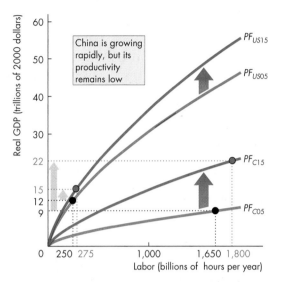

Figure 1 Growth in China and the United States

United States produces $12 trillion of real GDP, and with employment of 1,650 billion hours, China produces $9 trillion of real GDP.

That is, an hour of labor in the United States produces around 10 times as much as an hour of labor in China produces.

The figure also shows the situation in the United States and China in 2015 if current growth rates persist.

The U.S. production function will be PF_{US15}, and China's production function will be PF_{C15}.

With population growth at about 1 percent a year in both countries, labor hours will increase and so will real GDP.

In 2015, China will be producing a larger real GDP than the United States but real GDP per hour of labor in China will still lag that in the United States.

You're the Voter

Do you think the United States can learn any lessons from China about how to make the U.S. economy grow faster?

Can you think of any tax reforms that might increase the U.S. growth rate? Would you vote for these reforms? Why or why not?

SUMMARY

Key Points

The Basics of Economic Growth (pp. 182–183)

- Economic growth is the sustained expansion of production possibilities and is measured as the annual percentage rate of change of real GDP.
- Sustained growth transforms poor nations into rich ones.
- The Rule of 70 tells us the number of years in which real GDP doubles—70 divided by the annual percentage growth rate.

Economic Growth Trends (pp. 184–186)

- Between 1905 and 2005, real GDP per person in the United States grew at an average rate of 2 percent a year. Growth was rapid during the 1960s and late 1990s.
- The gap in real GDP per person between the United States and Central and South America has persisted. The gaps between the United States and Hong Kong, Korea, Taiwan, and China have narrowed. The gaps between the United States and Africa and Central Europe have widened.

The Sources of Economic Growth (pp. 187–189)

- The sources of economic growth are increases in aggregate hours and labor productivity. Labor productivity depends on physical capital and human capital growth and advances in technology.
- Economic growth requires an incentive system created by markets, property rights, and monetary exchange.

Growth Accounting (pp. 190–191)

- Growth accounting measures the contributions of capital accumulation and technological change to the growth of labor productivity.
- Growth accounting uses the one third rule: A 1 percent increase in capital per hour of labor brings a 1/3 percent increase in labor productivity.
- During the productivity growth slowdown of the 1970s, technological change did not stop growing but its focus changed to coping with energy price shocks and environmental protection.

- Stimulating saving and research, targeting high-technology industries, encouraging international trade, and improving education might boost economic growth.

Growth Theories (pp. 192–199)

- An increase in labor productivity increases employment, the real wage rate, and potential GDP.
- An increase in the population increases employment and potential GDP, but the real wage rate and real GDP per hour of labor decrease.
- In classical theory, real GDP per person returns to the subsistence level.
- In neoclassical growth theory, without further technological change, diminishing returns to capital bring economic growth to a halt.
- In new growth theory, economic growth persists indefinitely at a rate determined by decisions that lead to innovation and technological change.

Key Figures

Key Terms

PROBLEMS

1. Japan's real GDP was 515 trillion yen in 2003 and 529 trillion yen in 2004. Japan's population was 127.7 million in 2003 and 127.9 million in 2004. Calculate
   a. Japan's economic growth rate in 2004.
   b. The growth rate of real GDP per person in Japan in 2004.
   c. The approximate number of years it takes for real GDP per person in Japan to double if the 2004 economic growth rate and population growth rate are maintained.

2. If China's real GDP is growing at 9 percent a year, its population is growing at 1 percent a year, and these growth rates continue, in what year will China's real GDP per person be twice what it is in 2006?

3. The following information has been discovered about the economy of Longland:

Capital per hour of labor (2000 dollars)	Real GDP per hour of labor (2000 dollars)
10	3.80
20	5.70
30	7.13
40	8.31
50	9.35
60	10.29
70	11.14
80	11.94

   a. Does this economy conform to the one third rule? If so, explain why. If not, explain why not and explain what rule, if any, it does conform to.
   b. Explain how you would do the growth accounting for this economy.

4. In Longland, described in problem 3, capital per hour of labor in 2004 was $40 and real GDP per hour of labor was $8.31. In 2006, capital per hour of labor was $50 and real GDP per hour of labor was $10.29 an hour.
   a. Does Longland experience diminishing returns? Explain why or why not.

   b. Use growth accounting to find the contribution of capital growth between 2004 and 2006 to labor productivity growth.
   c. Use growth accounting to find the contribution of technological change between 2004 and 2006 to labor productivity growth.

5. If the United States cracks down on illegal immigrants and returns millions of workers to their countries of origin, explain what will happen to
   a. U.S. potential GDP?
   b. U.S. employment?
   c. The U.S. real wage rate?
   In the countries to which the immigrants return, explain what will happen to
   d. Potential GDP?
   e. Employment?
   f. The real wage rate?

6. If a large increase in investment increases labor productivity, explain what will happen to
   a. Potential GDP?
   b. Employment?
   c. The real wage rate?
   If a severe drought decreases labor productivity, explain what will happen to
   d. Potential GDP?
   e. Employment?
   f. The real wage rate?

7. In the economy of Cape Despair, the subsistence real wage rate is $15 an hour. Whenever real GDP per hour rises above $15, the population grows, and whenever real GDP per hour of labor falls below this level, the population falls. The production function in Cape Despair is as follows:

Labor (billions of hours per year)	Real GDP (billions of 2000 dollars)
0.5	8
1.0	15
1.5	21
2.0	26
2.5	30
3.0	33
3.5	35

Initially, the population of Cape Despair is constant and real GDP per hour of labor is at the subsistence level of $15. Then a technological advance shifts the production function upward by 50 percent at each level of labor.

a. What are the initial levels of real GDP and labor productivity?

b. What happens to labor productivity immediately following the technological advance?

c. What happens to the population growth rate following the technological advance?

d. What are the eventual levels of real GDP and real GDP per hour of labor?

8. Explain the processes that will bring the growth of real GDP per person to a stop according to

a. Classical growth theory

b. Neoclassical growth theory

c. New growth theory

CRITICAL THINKING

1. After studying *Reading Between the Lines* on pp. 200–201, answer the following questions:

a. What was the growth rate of real GDP in China in 2005?

b. Is real GDP per hour of labor in China growing because labor productivity is increasing or only because the population is increasing? How would you determine the contribution of each factor?

c. Is China narrowing the gap between real GDP per person in China and real GDP per person in the United States?

d. At the current rate of convergence, how long will it take for real GDP per person in China to equal that in the United States?

2. **The productivity watch**

According to former Federal Reserve chairman Alan Greenspan in the 1990s IT investments boosted productivity, which boosted corporate profits, which led to more IT investments, and so on, leading to a nirvana of high growth.

Fortune Magazine, 4 September 2006

Which of the growth theories that you have studied in this chapter best corresponds to the explanation given by Mr. Greenspan?

3. Is faster economic growth always a good thing? Argue the case for faster growth and the case for slower growth. Then reach a conclusion on whether growth should be increased or slowed.

4. **Make Way for India—The Next China**

. . .China . . . growing at around 9 percent a year. . . .the one-child policy will start to reduce the size of China's working population within the next 10 years. India, by contrast, will have an increasing working population for another generation at least.

The Independent, 1 March 2006

a. Given the expected population changes, do you think China or India will have the greater economic growth rate? Why?

b. Would China's growth rate remain at 9 percent a year without the restriction on its population growth rate?

c. India's population growth rate is 1.6 percent a year, and in 2005 its economic growth rate was 8 percent a year. China's population growth rate is 0.6 percent a year, and in 2005 its economic growth rate was 9 percent a year. In what year will real GDP per person double in each country?

WEB ACTIVITIES

myeconlab Links to Web sites

1. Obtain data on real GDP per person for the United States, China, South Africa, and Mexico since 1960.

a. Draw a graph of the data.

b. Which country has the lowest real GDP per person and which has the highest?

c. Which country has experienced the fastest growth rate since 1960 and which the slowest?

d. Explain why the growth rates in these four countries are ranked in the order you have discovered.

e. Return to the Web site and obtain data for any four other countries that interest you. Describe and explain the patterns that you find for these countries.

2. Write a memo to your member of Congress in which you set out the policies you believe the U.S. government must follow to speed up the growth rate of real GDP in the United States.

Money, the Price Level, and Inflation

Money Makes the World Go Around

Money, like fire and the wheel, has been around for a long time. And it has taken many forms. Money was wampum (beads made  from shells) for North American Indians, whale's teeth for Fijians, and tobacco for early American colonists. Cakes of salt served as money in Ethiopia and Tibet. Today, when we want to buy something, we use coins or dollar bills, write a check, or present a debit card or a credit card. Soon, we'll be using a "smart card" that keeps track of spending and that our pocket computer can read. Are all these things money?

When we deposit some coins or notes into a bank, is that still money? And what happens when the bank lends the money we've deposited to someone else? How can we get our money back if it has been lent out?

The quantity of money in our economy is regulated by the Federal Reserve—the Fed. How does the Fed influence the quantity of money? And what happens if the Fed creates too much money or too little money?

◆ In this chapter, we study the functions of money, the banks that create it, the Federal Reserve and its influence on the quantity of money, and the long-run consequences of changes in the quantity of money. In *Reading Between the Lines* at the end of the chapter, we look at a spectacular example of money and inflation in action in the African nation Zimbabwe.

After studying this chapter, you will be able to

▶ Define money and describe its functions

▶ Explain the economic functions of banks and other depository institutions

▶ Describe the structure and functions of the Federal Reserve System (the Fed)

▶ Explain how the banking system creates money

▶ Explain what determines the demand for money, the supply of money, and the nominal interest rate

▶ Explain how the quantity of money influences the price level and the inflation rate in the long run

What Is Money?

What do wampum, tobacco, and nickels and dimes have in common? They are all examples of **money**, which is defined as any commodity or token that is generally acceptable as a means of payment. A **means of payment** is a method of settling a debt. When a payment has been made, there is no remaining obligation between the parties to a transaction. So what wampum, tobacco, and nickels and dimes have in common is that they have served (or still do serve) as the means of payment. Money serves three other functions:

- Medium of exchange
- Unit of account
- Store of value

Medium of Exchange

A *medium of exchange* is any object that is generally accepted in exchange for goods and services. Without a medium of exchange, goods and services must be exchanged directly for other goods and services—an exchange called **barter**. Barter requires a *double coincidence of wants*, a situation that rarely occurs. For example, if you want a hamburger, you might offer a CD in exchange for it. But you must find someone who is selling hamburgers and who wants your CD.

A medium of exchange overcomes the need for a double coincidence of wants. And money acts as a medium of exchange because people with something to sell will always accept money in exchange for it. But money isn't the only medium of exchange. You can buy with a credit card. But a credit card isn't money. It doesn't make a final payment, and the debt it creates must eventually be settled by using money.

Unit of Account

A *unit of account* is an agreed measure for stating the prices of goods and services. To get the most out of your budget, you have to figure out whether seeing one more movie is worth its opportunity cost. But that cost is not dollars and cents. It is the number of ice-cream cones, sodas, or cups of coffee that you must give up. It's easy to do such calculations when all these goods have prices in terms of dollars and cents (see Table 9.1). If a movie costs $6 and a six-pack of soda costs $3, you know right away that

TABLE 9.1   The Unit of Account Function of Money Simplifies Price Comparisons

Good	Price in money units	Price in units of another good
Movie	$6.00 each	2 six-packs of soda
Soda	$3.00 per six-pack	2 ice-cream cones
Ice cream	$1.50 per cone	3 packs of jelly beans
Jelly beans	$0.50 per pack	2 sticks of gum
Gum	$0.25 per stick	1 local phone call

Money as a unit of account: The price of a movie is $6 and the price of a stick of gum is 25¢, so the opportunity cost of a movie is 24 sticks of gum ($6.00 ÷ 25¢ = 24).

No unit of account: You go to a movie theater and learn that the price of a movie is 2 six-packs of soda. You go to a candy store and learn that a pack of jelly beans costs 2 sticks of gum. But how many sticks of gum does seeing a movie cost you? To answer that question, you go to the convenience store and find that a six-pack of soda costs 2 ice-cream cones. Now you head for the ice-cream shop, where an ice-cream cone costs 3 packs of jelly beans. Now you get out your pocket calculator: 1 movie costs 2 six-packs of soda, or 4 ice-cream cones, or 12 packs of jelly beans, or 24 sticks of gum!

seeing one more movie costs you 2 six-packs of soda. If jelly beans are 50¢ a pack, one more movie costs 12 packs of jelly beans. You need only one calculation to figure out the opportunity cost of any pair of goods and services.

But imagine how troublesome it would be if your local movie theater posted its price as 2 six-packs of soda, the convenience store posted the price of a six-pack of soda as 2 ice-cream cones, the ice-cream shop posted the price of an ice-cream cone as 3 packs of jelly beans, and the candy store priced a pack of jelly beans as 2 sticks of gum! Now how much running around and calculating will you have to do to figure out how much that movie is going to cost you in terms of the soda, ice cream, jelly beans, or gum that you must give up to see it? You get the answer for soda right away from the sign posted on the movie theater. But for all the other goods, you're going to have to visit many different stores to establish the price of each commodity in terms of another and then calculate prices in units that are relevant for your own decision. Cover up the column labeled "Price in money units" in Table 9.1 and see how hard it is to figure out the number of local phone calls it costs to see one movie. It's enough to make a person swear off movies! You can see how much simpler it is if all the prices are expressed in dollars and cents.

Store of Value

Money is a *store of value* in the sense that it can be held and exchanged later for goods and services. If money were not a store of value, it could not serve as a means of payment.

Money is not alone in acting as a store of value. A house, a car, and a work of art are other examples.

The more stable the value of a commodity or token, the better it can act as a store of value and the more useful it is as money. No store of value has a completely stable value. The value of a house, a car, or a work of art fluctuates over time. The value of the commodities and tokens that are used as money also fluctuate over time. And when there is inflation, their values persistently fall.

Because inflation brings a falling value of money, a low inflation rate is needed to make money as useful as possible as a store of value.

Money in the United States Today

In the United States today, money consists of

- Currency
- Deposits at banks and other depository institutions

Currency The notes and coins held by individuals and businesses are known as **currency**. Notes are money because the government declares them so with the words "This note is legal tender for all debts, public and private." You can see these words on every dollar bill. Notes and coins *inside* banks are not counted as money.

Deposits Deposits at banks and other depository institutions such as savings and loan associations are also money. Deposits are money because they can be used to make payments.

Official Measures of Money The two main official measures of money in the United States today are known as M1 and M2. Figure 9.1 shows the items that make up these two measures. **M1** consists of currency and traveler's checks plus checking deposits owned by individuals and businesses. M1 does *not* include currency held by banks, and it does not include currency and checking deposits owned by the U.S. government. **M2** consists of M1 plus time deposits, savings deposits, and money market mutual funds and other deposits. You can see that M2 is almost five times as large as M1. You can also see that currency is a small part of our money.

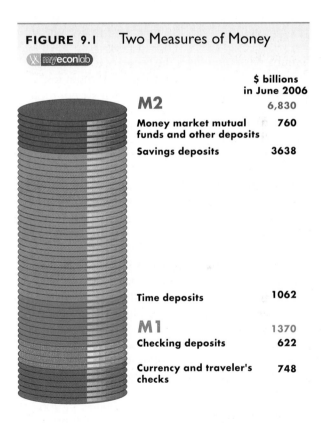

FIGURE 9.1   Two Measures of Money

myeconlab

	$ billions in June 2006
M2	6,830
Money market mutual funds and other deposits	760
Savings deposits	3638
Time deposits	1062
M1	1370
Checking deposits	622
Currency and traveler's checks	748

M1   ■ Currency and traveler's checks

   ■ Checking deposits at commercial banks, savings and loan associations, savings banks, and credit unions

M2   ■ M1

   ■ Time deposits

   ■ Savings deposits

   ■ Money market mutual funds and other deposits

Source of data: The Federal Reserve Board.

Are M1 and M2 Really Money? Money is the means of payment. So the test of whether an asset is money is whether it serves as a means of payment. Currency passes the test. But what about deposits? Checking deposits are money because they can be transferred from one person to another by writing a check or using a debit card. Such a transfer of ownership is equivalent to handing over currency. Because M1 consists of currency plus checking deposits and each of these is a means of payment, *M1 is money.*

But what about M2? Some of the savings deposits in M2 are just as much a means of payment as the checking deposits in M1. You can use the ATM at the grocery store checkout or gas station and transfer funds directly from your savings account to pay for your purchase. But some savings deposits are not means of payment. These deposits are known as liquid assets. *Liquidity* is the property of being easily convertible into a means of payment without loss in value. Because the deposits in M2 that are not means of payment are quickly and easily converted into a means of payment—into currency or checking deposits—they are counted as money.

Deposits Are Money but Checks Are Not In defining money, we include, along with currency, deposits at banks and other depository institutions. But we do not count the checks that people write as money. Why are deposits money and checks not?

To see why deposits are money but checks are not, think about what happens when Colleen buys some roller-blades for $200 from Rocky's Rollers. When Colleen goes to Rocky's shop, she has $500 in her deposit account at the Laser Bank. Rocky has $1,000 in his deposit account—at the same bank, as it happens. The total deposits of these two people are $1,500. Colleen writes a check for $200. Rocky takes the check to the bank right away and deposits it. Rocky's bank balance rises from $1,000 to $1,200, and Colleen's balance falls from $500 to $300. The total deposits of Colleen and Rocky are still the same as before: $1,500. Rocky now has $200 more than before, and Colleen has $200 less.

This transaction has transferred money from Colleen to Rocky. The check itself was never money. There wasn't an extra $200 worth of money while the check was in circulation. The check instructs the bank to transfer money from Colleen to Rocky.

If Colleen and Rocky use different banks, there is an extra step. Rocky's bank credits the check to

Rocky's account and then takes the check to a check-clearing center. The check is then sent to Colleen's bank, which pays Rocky's bank $200 and then debits Colleen's account $200. This process can take a few days, but the principles are the same as when two people use the same bank.

Credit Cards Are Not Money So checks are not money. But what about credit cards? Isn't having a credit card in your wallet and presenting the card to pay for your roller-blades the same thing as using money? Why aren't credit cards somehow valued and counted as part of the quantity of money?

When you pay by check, you are frequently asked to prove your identity by showing your driver's license. It would never occur to you to think of your driver's license as money. It's just an ID card. A credit card is also an ID card but one that lets you take out a loan at the instant you buy something. When you sign a credit card sales slip, you are saying, "I agree to pay for these goods when the credit card company bills me." Once you get your statement from the credit card company, you must make at least the minimum payment due. To make that payment, you need money—you need to have currency or a checking deposit to pay the credit card company. So although you use a credit card when you buy something, the credit card is not the *means of payment* and it is not money.

REVIEW QUIZ

1 What makes something money? What functions does money perform? Why do you think packs of chewing gum don't serve as money?
2 What are the problems that arise when a commodity is used as money?
3 What are the main components of money in the United States today?
4 What are the official measures of money? Are all the measures really money?
5 Why are checks and credit cards not money?

 **Study Plan 9.1**

We've seen that the main component of money in the United States is deposits at banks and other depository institutions. Let's take a closer look at these institutions.

Depository Institutions

A firm that takes deposits from households and firms and makes loans to other households and firms is called a **depository institution**. The deposits of three types of depository institutions make up the nation's money:

- Commercial banks
- Thrift institutions
- Money market mutual funds

Commercial Banks

A *commercial bank* is a firm that is licensed by the Comptroller of the Currency (at the U.S. Treasury) or by a state agency to receive deposits and make loans. About 8,000 commercial banks operate in the United States today.

Profit and Prudence: A Balancing Act The aim of a bank is to maximize the net worth of its stockholders. To achieve this objective, the interest rate at which a bank lends exceeds the interest rate at which it borrows. But a bank must perform a delicate balancing act. Lending is risky, and the more a bank ties up its deposits in high-risk, high-interest rate loans, the bigger is its chance of not being able to repay its depositors. And if depositors perceive a high risk of not being repaid, they withdraw their funds and create a crisis for the bank. So a bank must be prudent in the way it uses its deposits, balancing security for the depositors against profit for its stockholders.

Reserves and Loans To achieve security for its depositors, a bank divides the funds it receives in deposits into two parts: reserves and loans. *Reserves* are the cash in a bank's vault plus its deposits at Federal Reserve banks. (We'll study the Federal Reserve banks later in this chapter.) The cash in a bank's vaults is a reserve to meet its depositors' demands for currency. This cash keeps the ATM replenished after you and your friends raid it for money for a midnight pizza. The account of a bank at the Federal Reserve is similar to your own bank account. Banks use these accounts to receive and make payments. A commercial bank deposits cash into or draws cash out of its account at the Federal Reserve and writes checks on that account to settle debts with other banks.

If a bank kept all its deposits as reserves, it wouldn't make any profit. In fact, a bank keeps only a small fraction of its funds in reserves and lends the rest. A bank has three types of assets:

1. *Liquid assets* are U.S. government Treasury bills and commercial bills. These assets are the banks' first line of defense if they need cash. Liquid assets can be sold and instantly converted into cash with virtually no risk of loss. Because they are virtually risk free, they have a low interest rate.
2. *Investment securities* are longer-term U.S. government bonds and other bonds. These assets can be sold quickly and converted into cash but at prices that fluctuate. Because their prices fluctuate, these assets are riskier than liquid assets, but they also have a higher interest rate.
3. Loans are commitments of fixed amounts of money for agreed-upon periods of time. Most bank loans are made to corporations to finance the purchase of capital equipment and inventories and to households—personal loans—to finance consumer durable goods, such as cars or boats. The outstanding balances on credit card accounts are also bank loans. Loans are the riskiest assets of a bank because they cannot be converted into cash until they are due to be repaid. And some borrowers default and never repay. Because they are the riskiest of a bank's assets, loans carry the highest interest rate.

Thrift Institutions

The thrift institutions are

- Savings and loan associations
- Savings banks
- Credit unions

Savings and Loan Association A *savings and loan association* (S&L) is a depository institution that receives checking and savings deposits and that makes personal, commercial, and home-purchase loans.

Savings Bank A *savings bank* is a depository institution that accepts savings deposits and makes mostly home-purchase loans. Some savings banks (called *mutual* savings banks) are owned by their depositors.

Credit Union A *credit union* is a depository institution owned by a social or economic group such as a firm's employees that accepts savings deposits and makes mostly personal loans.

Money Market Mutual Funds

A *money market mutual fund* is a fund operated by a financial institution that sells shares in the fund and holds liquid assets such as U.S. Treasury bills or short-term commercial bills.

Money market mutual fund shares act like bank deposits. Shareholders can write checks on their money market mutual fund accounts. But there are restrictions on most of these accounts. For example, the minimum deposit accepted might be $2,500, and the smallest check a depositor is permitted to write might be $500.

The Economic Functions of Depository Institutions

All depository institutions make a profit from the spread between the interest rate they pay on deposits and the interest rate at which they lend. Why can depository institutions get deposits at a low interest rate and lend at a higher one? What services do they perform that make their depositors willing to put up with a low interest rate and their borrowers willing to pay a higher one?

Depository institutions provide four main services that people are willing to pay for:

- Creating liquidity
- Minimizing the cost of obtaining funds
- Minimizing the cost of monitoring borrowers
- Pooling risk

Creating Liquidity Depository institutions create liquidity. *Liquid assets* are those that are easily convertible into money with little loss of value. Some of the liabilities of depository institutions are themselves money; others are highly liquid assets that are easily converted into money.

Depository institutions create liquidity by borrowing short and lending long. *Borrowing short* means taking deposits but standing ready to repay them on short notice (and even on no notice in the case of checking deposits). *Lending long* means making loan commitments for a prearranged, and often quite long, period of time. For example, when a per-

son makes a deposit with a savings and loan association, that deposit can be withdrawn at any time. But the S&L makes a lending commitment for perhaps more than 20 years to a homebuyer.

Minimizing the Cost of Obtaining Funds Finding someone from whom to borrow can be a costly business. Imagine how troublesome it would be if there were no depository institutions. A firm that was looking for $1 million to buy a new factory would probably have to hunt around for several dozen people from whom to borrow to acquire enough funds for its capital project. Depository institutions lower the costs of this search. The firm that needs $1 million can go to a single depository institution to obtain those funds. The depository institution has to borrow from a large number of people, but it's not doing that just for this one firm and the million dollars it wants to borrow. The depository institution can establish an organization that is capable of raising funds from a large number of depositors and can spread the cost of this activity over a large number of borrowers.

Minimizing the Cost of Monitoring Borrowers Lending money is a risky business. There's always a danger that the borrower will not repay. Most of the money that is lent gets used by firms to invest in projects that they hope will return a profit. But sometimes those hopes are not fulfilled. Checking up on the activities of a borrower and ensuring that the best possible decisions are being made for making a profit and avoiding a loss are costly and specialized activities. Imagine how costly it would be if each household that lent money to a firm had to incur the costs of monitoring that firm directly. By depositing funds with a depository institution, households avoid those costs. The depository institution performs the monitoring activity by using specialized resources that have a much lower cost than what the households would incur if they had to undertake the activity individually.

Pooling Risk As we noted above, lending money is risky. There is always a chance of not being repaid—of default. Lending to a large number of different individuals can reduce the risk of default. In such a situation, if one person defaults on a loan, it is a nuisance but not a disaster. In contrast, if only one person borrows and that person defaults on the loan, the entire loan is a write-off. Depository institutions enable people to pool risk in an efficient way. Thousands of people lend money to any one institution, and, in turn, the institution relends the money to hundreds, perhaps thousands, of individual firms. If any one firm defaults on its loan, that default is spread across all the people who deposited money with the institution, and no individual depositor is left exposed to a high degree of risk.

Financial Innovation

The deposits that form the bulk of the nation's money are financial products' and depository institutions are constantly seeking ways to improve their products and earn larger profits. The process of developing new financial products is called *financial innovation*. The aim of financial innovation is to lower the cost of deposits or to increase the return from lending or, more simply, to increase the profit from financial intermediation. The three main influences on financial innovation are

- Economic environment
- Technology
- Regulation

The pace of financial innovation was remarkable during the 1980s and 1990s, and all three of these forces played a role.

Economic Environment During the late 1970s and early 1980s, a high inflation rate brought high interest rates. For example, the interest rate on home-purchase loans was as high as 15 percent a year.

High inflation and high interest rates created an incentive for financial innovation. Traditionally, house purchases were financed by loans at a guaranteed interest rate. The high interest rates of the early 1980s brought high borrowing costs for S&Ls. But because they were committed to low fixed interest rates on their outstanding home-purchase loans, the industry incurred severe losses.

To overcome this situation, the S&Ls developed variable interest rate mortgages—loans on which the interest rate would change in response to changing economic conditions. The creation of variable interest rate mortgages has taken some of the risk out of long-term lending for house purchases.

Technology The major technological change of the 1980s and 1990s was the development of low-cost computing and long-distance communication. These new technologies had profound effects on financial products and led to much financial innovation.

Some examples of financial innovation that resulted from these new technologies are the widespread use of credit cards and the spread of daily interest deposit accounts.

The cost of keying in transactions data and of calculating interest on deposits or on outstanding credit card balances was too great to make these financial products widely available before the 1980s. But with today's technologies, these products are highly profitable for banks and widely used.

Regulation A good deal of financial innovation takes place to avoid regulation. For example, a regulation known as Regulation Q prevented banks from paying interest on checking deposits. This restriction created an incentive for the banks to devise new types of deposits on which checks could be written and interest paid, thereby getting around the regulation.

Financial Innovation and Money

Financial innovation has brought changes in the composition of the nation's money. Checking deposits at S&Ls, savings banks, and credit unions have become an increasing percentage of M1 while checking deposits at commercial banks have become a decreasing percentage. The composition of M2 has also changed as savings deposits have decreased, while time deposits and money market mutual funds have expanded.

REVIEW QUIZ

1 What are the functions of depository institutions?
2 What is liquidity and how do depository institutions create it?
3 How do depository institutions lower the cost of borrowing and lending and of monitoring borrowers?
4 How do depository institutions pool risks?

myeconlab Study Plan 9.2

You now know what money is and that the bulk of the nation's money is deposits in banks and other institutions. Your next task is to learn about the Federal Reserve System and the ways in which it can influence the quantity of money.

The Federal Reserve System

The central bank of the United States is the **Federal Reserve System** (usually called the **Fed**). A **central bank** is a bank's bank and a public authority that regulates a nation's depository institutions and controls the quantity of money. As the banks' bank, the Fed provides banking services to commercial banks such as Citibank. A central bank is not a citizens' bank. That is, the Fed does not provide general banking services for businesses and individual citizens.

The Fed's Goals and Targets

The Fed conducts the nation's *monetary policy,* which means that it adjusts the quantity of money in circulation. The Fed's goals are to keep inflation in check, maintain full employment, moderate the business cycle, and contribute toward achieving long-term growth. Complete success in the pursuit of these goals is impossible, and the Fed's more modest goal is to improve the performance of the economy and to get closer to the goals than a hands-off approach would achieve. Whether the Fed succeeds in improving economic performance is a matter on which there is a range of opinion.

In pursuit of its ultimate goals, the Fed pays close attention to interest rates and pays special attention to one interest rate, the **federal funds rate**, which is the interest rate that the banks charge each other on overnight loans of reserves. The Fed sets a target for the federal funds rate that is consistent with its ultimate goals and then takes actions to achieve its target.

This section examines the Fed's policy tools. Later in this chapter, we look at the long-run effects of the Fed's actions, and in Chapter 15, we look at the short-run context in which the Fed conducts monetary policy. We begin by describing the structure of the Fed.

The Structure of the Fed

The key elements in the structure of the Federal Reserve System are

- The Board of Governors
- The regional Federal Reserve banks
- The Federal Open Market Committee

The Board of Governors The Board of Governors has seven members, who are appointed by the President of the United States and confirmed by the Senate, each for a 14-year term. The terms are staggered so that one seat on the board becomes vacant every two years. The President appoints one of the board members as chairman for a term of four years, which is renewable.

The Federal Reserve Banks There are 12 Federal Reserve banks, one for each of 12 Federal Reserve districts shown in Fig. 9.2. These Federal Reserve banks provide check-clearing services to commercial banks and other depository institutions, hold the reserve accounts of commercial banks, lend reserves to banks, and issue the bank notes that circulate as currency.

One of the district banks, the Federal Reserve Bank of New York (known as the New York Fed), occupies a special place in the Federal Reserve System because it implements the policy decisions of the Federal Open Market Committee.

The Federal Open Market Committee The **Federal Open Market Committee** (FOMC) is the main policy-making organ of the Federal Reserve System. The FOMC consists of the following voting members:

- The chairman and the other six members of the Board of Governors
- The president of the Federal Reserve Bank of New York
- The presidents of the other regional Federal Reserve banks (of whom, on a yearly rotating basis, only four vote)

The FOMC meets approximately every six weeks to review the state of the economy and to decide the actions to be carried out by the New York Fed.

The Fed's Power Center

A description of the formal structure of the Fed gives the impression that power in the Fed resides with the Board of Governors. In practice, it is the chairman of the Board of Governors who has the largest influence on the Fed's monetary policy actions, and some remarkable individuals have held this position. The current chairman is Ben Bernanke, a former economics professor at Princeton University, who was

FIGURE 9.2   The Federal Reserve System

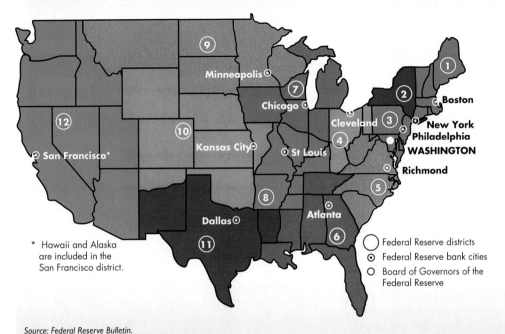

The nation is divided into 12 Federal Reserve districts, each having a Federal Reserve bank. (Some of the larger districts also have branch banks.) The Board of Governors of the Federal Reserve System is located in Washington, D.C.

* Hawaii and Alaska are included in the San Francisco district.

○ Federal Reserve districts
◉ Federal Reserve bank cities
○ Board of Governors of the Federal Reserve

Source: Federal Reserve Bulletin.

appointed by President George W. Bush in 2006. Bernanke's predecessors were Alan Greenspan (1987–2006) and Paul Volker (1979–1987).

The chairman's power and influence stem from three sources. First, it is the chairman who controls the agenda and who dominates the meetings of the FOMC. Second, day-to-day contact with a large staff of economists and other technical experts provides the chairman with detailed background briefings on monetary policy issues. Third, the chairman is the spokesperson for the Fed and the main point of contact of the Fed with the President and government and with foreign central banks and governments.

The Fed's Policy Tools

The Federal Reserve System has many responsibilities, but we'll examine its single most important one: regulating the amount of money floating around in the United States. How does the Fed control the quantity of money? It does so by adjusting the reserves of the banking system. Also, it is by adjusting the reserves of the banking system and by standing ready to make loans to banks that the Fed is able to prevent

bank failures. The Fed uses three main policy tools to achieve its objectives:

- Required reserve ratios
- Discount rate
- Open market operations

Required Reserve Ratios All depository institutions are required to hold a minimum percentage of deposits as reserves. This minimum percentage is known as a **required reserve ratio**. The Fed determines a required reserve ratio for each type of deposit. In 2006, banks were required to hold minimum reserves equal to 3 percent of checking deposits between $7.8 million and $48.3 million and 10 percent of these deposits in excess of $48.3 million. The required reserves on other types of deposits are zero.

Discount Rate The **discount rate** is the interest rate at which the Fed stands ready to lend reserves to depository institutions. A change in the discount rate is proposed to the FOMC by the Board of Directors of at least one of the 12 Federal Reserve banks and is approved by the Board of Governors.

Open Market Operations An **open market operation** is the purchase or sale of government securities— U.S. Treasury bills and bonds—by the Federal Reserve System in the open market. When the Fed conducts an open market operation, it makes a transaction with a bank or some other business but it does not transact with the federal government.

Figure 9.3 summarizes the structure and policy tools of the Fed. To understand how the tools work, we need to know about the Fed's balance sheet.

The Fed's Balance Sheet

Table 9.2 shows the balance sheet of the Federal Reserve System for June 2006. The assets on the left side are what the Fed owns, and the liabilities on the right side are what it owes. The Fed's assets are

1. Gold and foreign exchange
2. U.S. government securities
3. Loans to banks

Gold and foreign exchange are the Fed's holdings of international reserves, which consist of deposits at other central banks and an account called Special Drawing Rights, which the Fed holds at the International Monetary Fund.

The Fed's major assets are U.S. government securities. These securities are short-term Treasury bills and long-term Treasury bonds.

When the banks are short of reserves, they can borrow reserves from the Fed. These borrowed reserves are an asset, "loans to banks," in the Fed's balance sheet.

The Fed's assets are the backing for its liabilities:

1. Federal Reserve notes
2. Banks' deposits

The Federal Reserve notes are the dollar bills that we use in our daily transactions. Some of these notes are held by the public; others are in the tills and vaults of banks and other financial institutions. Banks' deposits are part of the banks' reserves.

You might be wondering why Federal Reserve notes are considered a liability of the Fed. When bank notes were invented, they gave their owner a claim on the gold reserves of the issuing bank. Such notes were *convertible paper money*. The holder of such a note could convert the note on demand into gold (or some other commodity such as silver) at a guaranteed price. So when a bank issued a note, it was holding itself

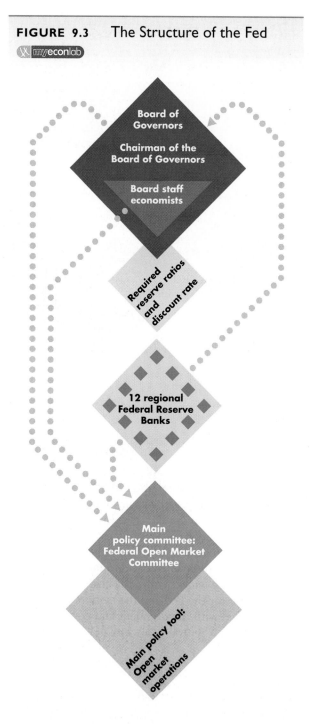

FIGURE 9.3   The Structure of the Fed

The Board of Governors sets required reserve ratios and, on the proposal of the 12 Federal Reserve banks, sets the discount rate. The Board of Governors and presidents of the regional Federal Reserve banks sit on the FOMC to determine open market operations.

TABLE 9.2	The Fed's Balance Sheet, June 2006		
Assets (billions of dollars)		**Liabilities** (billions of dollars)	
Gold and foreign exchange	13	Federal Reserve notes	754
U.S. government securities*	762	Banks' deposits	21
Loans to banks	—		—
Total assets	775	Total liabilities	775

*Includes other (net) assets
Source of data: Federal Reserve Board.

liable to convert that note into gold or silver. Modern bank notes are nonconvertible. A *nonconvertible note* is a bank note that is not convertible into any commodity and that obtains its value by government order and is called "fiat money." Such notes are the legal liability of the bank that issues them, and they are backed by holdings of securities and loans. Federal Reserve notes are backed by the Fed's holdings of U.S. government securities.

The Fed's liabilities together with coins in circulation (coins are issued by the Treasury and are not liabilities of the Fed) make up the monetary base. That is, the **monetary base** is the sum of Federal Reserve notes, coins, and banks' deposits at the Fed. The monetary base is so named because it acts like a base that supports the nation's money. When the monetary base changes, so does the quantity of money, as you're about to see.

REVIEW QUIZ

1 What is the central bank of the United States and what functions does it perform?
2 Who appoints the Fed board members and chairman and for how long do they serve?
3 What are the Fed's three policy tools?
4 What is the Federal Open Market Committee and what are its main functions?

myeconlab Study Plan 9.3

Next, we're going to see how the banking system—the banks and the Fed—creates money.

How Banks Create Money

Banks create money. But this doesn't mean that they have smoke-filled back rooms in which counterfeiters are busily working. Remember, most money is deposits, not currency. What banks create is deposits, and they do so by making loans.

Creating Deposits by Making Loans

The easiest way to see that banks create deposits is to think about what happens when Andy, who has a Visa card issued by Citibank, uses his card to buy a tank of gas from Chevron. When Andy signs the card sales slip, he takes a loan from Citibank and obligates himself to repay the loan at a later date. At the end of the business day, a Chevron clerk takes a pile of signed credit card sales slips, including Andy's, to Chevron's bank. For now, let's assume that Chevron also banks at Citibank. The bank immediately credits Chevron's account with the value of the slips (minus the bank's commission).

You can see that these transactions have created a bank deposit and a loan. Andy has increased the size of his loan (his credit card balance), and Chevron has increased the size of its bank deposit. And because deposits are money, Citibank has created money.

If, as we've just assumed, Andy and Chevron use the same bank, no further transactions take place. But the outcome is essentially the same when two banks are involved. If Chevron's bank is the Bank of America, then Citibank uses its reserves to pay the Bank of America. Citibank has an increase in loans and a decrease in reserves; the Bank of America has an increase in reserves and an increase in deposits. And the banking system as a whole has an increase in loans and deposits and no change in reserves.

If Andy had swiped his card at an automatic payment pump, all these transactions would have occurred at the time he filled his tank, and the quantity of money would have increased by the amount of his purchase (minus the bank's commission for conducting the transactions).

Three factors limit the quantity of deposits that the banking system can create:

■ The monetary base
■ Desired reserves
■ Desired currency holdings

The Monetary Base You've seen that the *monetary base* is the sum of Federal Reserve notes, coins, and banks' deposits at the Fed. The size of the monetary base limits the total quantity of money that the banking system can create because banks have a desired level of reserves, households and firms have a desired level of currency holding, and both of these desired holdings of the monetary base depend on the quantity of money.

Desired Reserves A bank's *actual* **reserves** consist of the notes and coins in its vaults and its deposit at the Federal Reserve. A bank uses its reserves to meet depositors' demand for currency and to make payments to other banks.

You've also seen that banks don't have $100 of reserves for every $100 that people have deposited with them. If the banks did behave that way, they wouldn't earn any profit.

Banks today have reserves of $3 for every $100 of M1 deposits and 60¢ for every $100 of M2 deposits. Most of these reserves are currency. You saw in the previous section that reserves in the form of deposits at the Federal Reserve are tiny. But there's no need for panic. These reserve levels are adequate for ordinary business needs.

The fraction of a bank's total deposits that are held in reserves is called the **reserve ratio**. So with reserves of $3 for every $100 of M1 deposits, the M1 reserve ratio is 0.03 or 3 percent, and with reserves of 60¢ for every $100 of M2 deposits, the M2 reserve ratio is 0.006 or 0.6 percent.

A bank's desired reserves are the reserves that it wishes to hold. The banks are required to hold a level of reserves that does not fall below a specified percentage of total deposits. This percentage is the *required reserve ratio*.

The **desired reserve ratio** is the ratio of reserves to deposits that a bank wants to hold. This ratio exceeds the required reserve ratio by an amount that the banks determine to be prudent on the basis of their daily business requirements.

A bank's reserve ratio changes when its customers make a deposit or a withdrawal. If a bank's customer makes a deposit, reserves and deposits increase by the same amount, so the bank's reserve ratio increases. Similarly, if a bank's customer makes a withdrawal, reserves and deposits decrease by the same amount, so the bank's reserve ratio decreases.

A bank's **excess reserves** are its actual reserves minus its desired reserves. Whenever the banking system as a whole has excess reserves, the banks are able to create money. Banks increase their loans and deposits when they have excess reserves and they decrease their loans and deposits when they are short of reserves—when desired reserves exceed actual reserves.

But the greater the desired reserve ratio, the smaller is the quantity of deposits and money that the banking system can create from a given amount of monetary base.

Desired Currency Holding We hold our money in the form of currency and bank deposits. The proportion of money held as currency isn't constant but at any given time, people have a definite view as to how much they want to hold in each form of money.

In 2006, for every dollar of M1 deposits held, we held $1.20 of currency and for every dollar of M2 deposits, we held 12¢ of currency.

Because households and firms want to hold some proportion of their money in the form of currency, when the total quantity of bank deposits increases, so does the quantity of currency that they want to hold. Because desired currency holding increases when deposits increase, currency leaves the banks when loans are made and deposits increase. We call the leakage of currency from the banking system the *currency drain*. And we call the ratio of currency to deposits the **currency drain ratio**.

The greater the currency drain ratio, the smaller is the quantity of deposits and money that the banking system can create from a given amount of monetary base.

The Money Creation Process

The money creation process begins when the monetary base increases and the banking system has excess reserves. These excess reserves come from a purchase of securities by the Fed from a bank. (Chapter 15, pp. 375–376, explains exactly how the Fed conducts such a purchase, called an open-market operation.)

When the Fed buys securities from a bank, the bank's reserves increase but its deposits do not change. So the bank has excess reserves and it lends those excess reserves. A sequence of events then plays out.

The sequence, which keeps repeating until all the reserves are desired and no excess reserves are being held, has nine steps. They are

1. Banks have excess reserves.

2. Banks lend excess reserves.

3. Bank deposits increase.

4. The quantity of money increases.

5. New money is used to make payments.

6. Some of the new money remains on deposit.

7. Some of the new money is a *currency drain*.

8. Desired reserves increase because deposits have increased.

9. Excess reserves decrease but remain positive.

The sequence repeats in a series of rounds, but each round begins with a smaller quantity of excess reserves than did the previous one. The process continues until excess reserves have finally been eliminated. Figure 9.4 illustrates this process.

To make the process of money creation more concrete, let's work through an example for a banking system in which each bank has a desired reserve ratio of 10 percent and the currency drain ratio is 50 per-cent or 0.5. (Although these ratios are larger than the ones in the U.S. economy, they make the process end more quickly and enable you to see more clearly the principles at work.)

Figure 9.5 will keep track of the numbers. The process begins when all the banks have zero excess reserves except one bank, and it has excess reserves of $100,000. When the bank lends $100,000 of excess reserves, $33,333 drains off and is held outside the banks as currency. The other $66,667 remains in the banks as deposits. The quantity of money has now increased by $100,000—the increase in deposits plus the increase in currency holdings.

The increased bank deposits of $66,667 generate an increase in desired reserves of 10 percent of that amount, which is $6,667. Actual reserves have increased by the same amount as the increase in deposits: $66,667. So the banks now have excess reserves of $60,000. At this stage, we have gone around the circle shown in Fig. 9.4 once. The process we've just described repeats but begins with excess reserves of $60,000. Figure 9.5 shows the next two rounds. At the

---

FIGURE 9.4   How the Banking System Creates Money by Making Loans

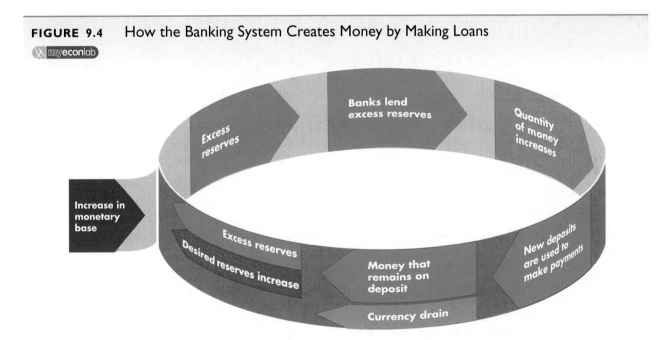

The Federal Reserve increases the monetary base which increases bank reserves and creates excess reserves. Banks lend the excess reserves, new deposits are created, and the quantity of money increases. New deposits are used to make payments. Some of the new money remains on deposit at banks and some leaves the banks in a currency drain. The increase in bank deposits increases banks' desired reserves. But the banks still have excess reserves, though less than before. The process repeats until excess reserves have been eliminated.

FIGURE 9.5   The Money Creation Process: An Example

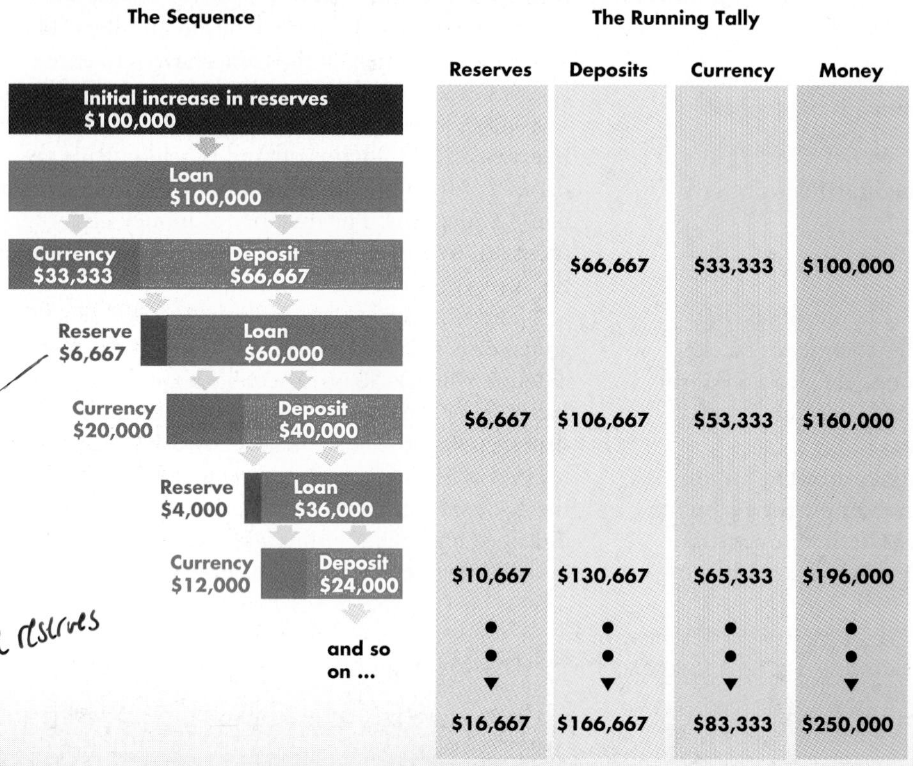

When the Fed provides the banks with $100,000 of additional reserves, the banks lend those reserves. Of the amount lent, $33,333 (50 percent of deposits) leaves the banks in a currency drain and $66,667 remains on deposit. With additional deposits, desired reserves increase by $6,667 (10 percent desired reserve ratio) and the banks lend $60,000. Of this amount, $20,000 leaves the banks in a currency drain and $40,000 remains on deposit. The process repeats until the banks have created enough deposits to eliminate their excess reserves. An additional $100,000 of reserves creates $250,000 of money.

end of the process, the quantity of money has increased by a multiple of the increase in the monetary base. In this case, the increase is $250,000, which is 2.5 times the increase in the monetary base.

The Money Multiplier

The sequence in Fig. 9.5 is the first four stages of the process that finally reaches the totals shown in the final row of the running tally. To figure out the entire process, look closely at the numbers in the figure. The initial increase in reserves is $100,000 (call it A). At each stage, the loan is 60 percent (0.6) of the previous loan and the quantity of money increases by 0.6 of the previous increase. Call that proportion L ($L = 0.6$). We can write down the complete sequence for the increase in the quantity of money as

$$A + AL + AL^2 + AL^3 + AL^4 + AL^5 + \dots .$$

Remember, L is a fraction, so at each stage in this sequence, the amount of new loans and new money

gets smaller. The total value of loans made and money created at the end of the process is the sum of the sequence, which is[1]

$$A/(1 - L).$$

If we use the numbers from the example, the total increase in the quantity of money is

---

[1] The sequence of values is called a convergent geometric series. To find the sum of a series such as this, begin by calling the sum S. Then write the sum as

$$S = A + AL + AL^2 + AL^3 + AL^4 + AL^5 + \dots .$$

Multiply by L to get,

$$LS = AL + AL^2 + AL^3 + AL^4 + AL^5 + \dots .$$

and then subtract the second equation from the first to get

$$S(1 - L) = A$$

or

$$S = A/(1 - L).$$

$100,000 + 60,000 + 36,000 + ...

$$= \$100,000 \ (1 + 0.6 + 0.36 + ...)$$

$$= \$100,000 \ (1 + 0.6 + 0.6^2 + ...)$$

$$= \$100,000 \times 1/(1 - 0.6)$$

$$= \$100,000 \times 1/(0.4)$$

$$= \$100,000 \times 2.5$$

$$= \$250,000.$$

The **money multiplier** is the ratio of the change in the quantity of money to the change in monetary base. Here, the monetary base increased by $100,000 and the quantity of money increased by $250,000 so the money multiplier is 2.5.

The magnitude of the money multiplier depends on the desired reserve ratio and the currency drain ratio. Call the monetary base MB and the quantity of money M. When there are no excess reserves,

MB = Desired currency holding + Desired reserves.

Also,

M = Deposits + Desired currency holding.

Call the currency drain ratio a and the desired reserve ratio b. Then

$$\text{Desired currency holding} = a \times \text{Deposits}$$

$$\text{Desired reserves} = b \times \text{Deposits}$$

$$MB = (a + b) \times \text{Deposits}$$

$$M = (1 + a) \times \text{Deposits}.$$

Call the change in monetary base ΔMB and the change in the quantity of money ΔM. Then

$$\Delta MB = (a + b) \times \text{Change in deposits}$$

$$\Delta M = (1 + a) \times \text{Change in deposits}.$$

Divide the above equation for ΔM by the one for ΔMB, and you see that the money multiplier, which is the ratio of ΔM to ΔMB, is

$$\text{Money multiplier} = (1 + a)/(a + b).$$

If we use the values of the example summarized in Fig. 9.5, $a = 0.5$ and $b = 0.1$, the

$$\text{Money multiplier} = (1 + 0.5)/(0.5 + 0.1).$$

$$= 1.5/0.6 = 2.5.$$

The U.S. Money Multiplier

The money multiplier in the United States can be found by using the formula above along with the values of a and b in the U.S. economy.

Because we have two definitions of money, M1 and M2, we have two money multipliers. The numbers for M1 in 2006 are $a = 1.20$ and $b = 0.03$. So

$$\text{M1 multiplier} = (1 + 1.20)/(1.20 + 0.03)$$

$$= 2.20/1.23 = 1.8.$$

For M2 in 2006, $a = 0.12$ and $b = 0.006$, so

$$\text{M2 multiplier} = (1 + 0.12)/(0.12 + 0.006)$$

$$= 1.12/0.126 = 8.9.$$

REVIEW QUIZ

1 How does the banking system create money?
2 What limits the quantity of money that the banking system can create?
3 A bank manager tells you that she doesn't create money. She just lends the money that people deposit. Explain why she's wrong.
4 If people decide to hold less currency and more deposits, how does the quantity of money change?

 myeconlab **Study Plan 9.4**

You now know how money gets created. Your next task is to study the demand and supply in the "market" for money and money market equilibrium.

The Market for Money

There is no limit to the amount of money we would like to *receive* in payment for our labor or as interest on our savings. But there *is* a limit to how big an inventory of money—the money in our wallet or in a deposit account at the bank—we would like to *hold* and neither spend nor use to buy assets that generate an income. The *quantity of money demanded* is the inventory of money that people plan to hold. The quantity of money held must equal the quantity supplied, and the forces that bring about this equality in the money market have powerful effects on the economy, as you will see in the rest of this chapter.

But first, we need to explain what determines the amount of money that people plan to hold.

The Influences on Money Holding

The quantity of money that people plan to hold depends on four main factors:

- The price level
- The *nominal* interest rate
- Real GDP
- Financial innovation

The Price Level The quantity of money measured in dollars is *nominal money*. The quantity of nominal money demanded is proportional to the price level, other things remaining the same. If the price level rises by 10 percent, people hold 10 percent more nominal money than before, other things remaining the same. If you hold $20 to buy your weekly movies and soda, you will increase your money holding to $22 if the prices of movies and soda—and your wage rate—increase by 10 percent.

The quantity of money measured in constant dollars (for example, in 2000 dollars) is *real money*. Real money is equal to nominal money divided by the price level and is the quantity of money measured in terms of what it will buy. In the above example, when the price level rises by 10 percent and you increase your money holding by 10 percent, your *real* money holding is constant. Your $22 at the new price level buys the same quantity of goods and is the same quantity of *real money* as your $20 at the original price level. The quantity of real money demanded is independent of the price level.

The *Nominal* Interest Rate A fundamental principle of economics is that as the opportunity cost of something increases, people try to find substitutes for it. Money is no exception. The higher the opportunity cost of holding money, other things remaining the same, the smaller is the quantity of real money demanded. The nominal interest rate on other assets minus the nominal interest rate on money is the opportunity cost of holding money.

The interest rate that you earn on currency and checking deposits is zero. So the opportunity cost of holding these items is the nominal interest rate on other assets such as a savings bond or Treasury bill. By holding money instead, you forgo the interest that you otherwise would have received.

Money loses value because of inflation. So why isn't the inflation rate part of the cost of holding money? It is. Other things remaining the same, the higher the expected inflation rate, the higher is the nominal interest rate.

Real GDP The quantity of money that households and firms plan to hold depends on the amount they are spending, and the quantity of money demanded in the economy as a whole depends on aggregate expenditure—real GDP.

Again, suppose that you hold an average of $20 to finance your weekly purchases of movies and soda. Now imagine that the prices of these goods and of all other goods remain constant but that your income increases. As a consequence, you now spend more and you also keep a larger amount of money on hand to finance your higher volume of expenditure.

Financial Innovation Technological change and the arrival of new financial products change the quantity of money held. Financial innovations include

1. Daily interest checking deposits
2. Automatic transfers between checking and saving deposits
3. Automatic teller machines
4. Credit cards and debit cards
5. Internet banking and bill paying

These innovations have occurred because of the development of computing power that has lowered the cost of calculations and record keeping.

We summarize the effects of the influences on money holding by using a demand for money curve.

The Demand for Money

The **demand for money** is the relationship between the quantity of real money demanded and the nominal interest rate when all other influences on the amount of money that people wish to hold remain the same.

Figure 9.6 shows a demand for money curve, *MD*. When the interest rate rises, everything else remaining the same, the opportunity cost of holding money rises and the quantity of real money demanded decreases—there is a movement up along the demand for money curve. Similarly, when the interest rate falls, the opportunity cost of holding money falls, and the quantity of real money demanded increases—there is a movement down along the demand for money curve.

When any influence on money holding other than the interest rate changes, there is a change in the demand for money and the demand for money curve shifts. Let's study these shifts.

Shifts in the Demand for Money Curve

A change in real GDP or financial innovation changes the demand for money and shifts the demand curve for real money.

Figure 9.7 illustrates the change in the demand for money. A decrease in real GDP decreases the demand for money and shifts the demand curve leftward from MD_0 to MD_1. An increase in real GDP has the opposite effect: It increases the demand for money and shifts the demand curve rightward from MD_0 to MD_2.

The influence of financial innovation on the demand for money curve is more complicated. It decreases the demand for currency and might increase the demand for some types of deposits and decrease the demand for others. But generally, financial innovation decreases the demand for money.

We'll look at the effects of changes in real GDP and financial innovation by studying the demand for money in the United States.

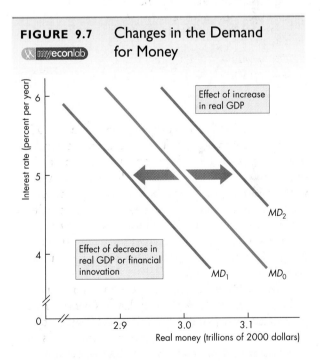

FIGURE 9.6 The Demand for Money

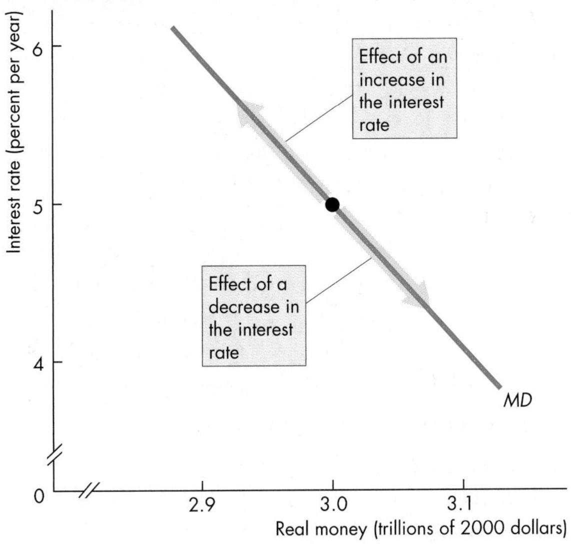

The demand for money curve, *MD*, shows the relationship between the quantity of real money that people plan to hold and the interest rate, other things remaining the same. The interest rate is the opportunity cost of holding money. A change in the interest rate brings a movement along the demand for money curve.

FIGURE 9.7 Changes in the Demand for Money

A decrease in real GDP decreases the demand for money. The demand curve shifts leftward from MD_0 to MD_1. An increase in real GDP increases the demand for money. The demand curve shifts rightward from MD_0 to MD_2. Financial innovation generally decreases the demand for money.

The Demand for Money in the United States

Figure 9.8 shows the relationship between the interest rate and the quantity of real money demanded in the United States from 1970 to 2005. Each dot shows the interest rate and the real money held in a given year. In 1970, the demand for M1 curve, in part (a), was MD_0. During the early 1970s, the spread of credit cards decreased the demand for M1 (currency and checking deposits) and shifted the demand for M1 curve leftward to MD_1. But over the years, real GDP growth increased the demand for M1, and by 1994, the demand for M1 curve had shifted rightward to MD_2. A continued increase in the use of credit cards and the spread of ATMs decreased the demand for M1 and shifted the demand curve leftward again during the 1990s and 2000s to MD_3.

In 1970, the demand for M2 curve, in part (b) was MD_0. New interest-bearing deposits increased the demand for M2 from 1970 through 1989 and shifted the demand curve rightward to MD_1. But between 1989 and 1994, innovations in financial products that compete with deposits of all kinds occurred and the demand for M2 decreased. The demand for M2 curve shifted leftward to MD_2. After 1994, the expanding economy brought rising real GDP and the demand for M2 increased. By 2005, the demand for M2 curve was MD_3.

You now know what determines the demand for money. And you've seen how the banking system creates money. Let's now see how the money market reaches an equilibrium in the short run and in the long run.

FIGURE 9.8   The Demand for Money in the United States

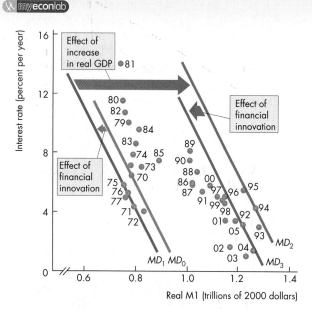

(a) M1 demand

The dots show the quantity of real money and the interest rate in each year between 1970 and 2005. In 1970, the demand for M1 curve was MD_0 in part (a). The demand for M1 decreased during the early 1970s because of financial innovation, and the demand curve shifted leftward to MD_1. But real GDP growth increases the demand for M1, and by 1994, the demand curve had shifted rightward to MD_2. Further financial innovation decreased the demand for M1 during the 1990s and 2000s and shifted the demand curve

Sources of data: Bureau of Economic Analysis and Federal Reserve Board.

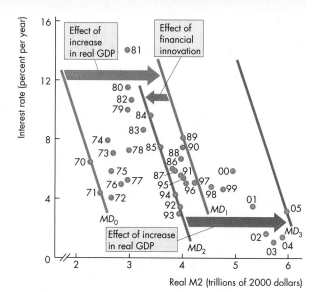

(b) M2 demand

leftward again to MD_3.

In 1970, the demand for M2 curve was MD_0 in part (b). The growth of real GDP increased the demand for M2, and by 1989, the demand curve had shifted rightward to MD_1. During the early 1990s, new substitutes for M2 decreased the demand for M2 and the demand curve shifted leftward to MD_2. But during the late 1990s, rapid growth of real GDP increased the demand for M2. By 2005, the demand curve had shifted rightward to MD_3.

Money Market Equilibrium

Money market equilibrium occurs when the quantity of money demanded equals the quantity of money supplied. The adjustments that occur to bring money market equilibrium are fundamentally different in the short run and the long run. Our primary focus here is the long run. (We explore short-run issues in Chapters 11–15.) But we need to say a little bit about the short run so that you can appreciate how the long-run equilibrium comes about.

Short-Run Equilibrium The quantity of money supplied is determined by the actions of the banks and the Fed. Each day, the Fed adjusts the quantity of money to hit its interest rate target. In Fig. 9.9, with demand for money curve *MD*, if the Fed wants the

interest rate to be 5 percent, it adjusts the quantity of money so that the quantity of real money supplied is $3.0 trillion and the supply of money curve is *MS*.

The equilibrium interest rate is 5 percent. If the interest rate were 6 percent, people would want to hold less money than exists. They would buy bonds, bid up their price, and lower the interest rate. If the interest rate were 4 percent, people would want to hold more money than exists. They would sell bonds, bid down their price, and raise the interest rate.

Long-Run Equilibrium In the long run, supply and demand in the loanable funds market determines the interest rate. The nominal interest rate equals the equilibrium real interest rate plus the expected inflation rate. Real GDP, which influences the demand for money, equals potential GDP. So the only variable that is left to adjust in the long run is the price level. The price level adjusts to make the quantity of real money supplied equal to the quantity demanded. If the Fed changes the nominal quantity of money, the price level changes (in the long run) by the same percentage as the percentage change in the quantity of nominal money. In the long run, the change in the price level is proportional to the change in the quantity of money.

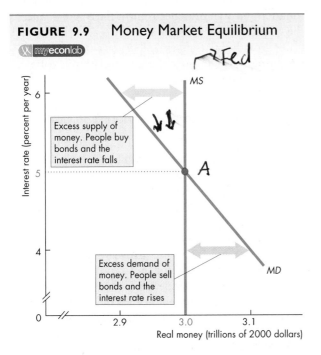

FIGURE 9.9   Money Market Equilibrium

Money market equilibrium occurs when the quantity of money demanded equals the quantity supplied.

Short run: In the short run, the quantity of real money and real GDP are given and the interest rate adjusts to achieve equilibrium, here 5 percent a year.

Long run: In the long run, supply and demand in the loanable funds market determines the interest rate, real GDP equals potential GDP, and the price level adjusts to make the quantity of real money supplied equal the quantity demanded, here $3 trillion.

Let's explore the long-run link between money and the price level a bit more thoroughly.

The Quantity Theory of Money

In the long run, the price level adjusts to make the quantity of real money demanded equal the quantity supplied. A special theory of the price level and inflation—the quantity theory of money—explains this long-run adjustment of the price level.

The **quantity theory of money** is the proposition that in the long run, an increase in the quantity of money brings an equal percentage increase in the price level. To explain the quantity theory of money, we first need to define *the velocity of circulation*.

The **velocity of circulation** is the average number of times a dollar of money is used annually to buy the goods and services that make up GDP. But GDP equals the price level (*P*) multiplied by *real* GDP (*Y*). That is,

$$GDP = PY.$$

Call the quantity of money *M*. The velocity of circulation, *V*, is determined by the equation

$$V = PY/M.$$

For example, if GDP is $1,000 billion (*PY* = $1,000 billion) and the quantity of money is $250 billion, the velocity of circulation is 4.

From the definition of the velocity of circulation, the *equation of exchange* tells us how *M*, *V*, *P*, and *Y* are connected. This equation is

$$MV = PY.$$

Given the definition of the velocity of circulation, the equation of exchange is always true—it is true by definition. It becomes the quantity theory of money if the quantity of money does not influence the velocity of circulation or real GDP. In this case, the equation of exchange tells us that in the long run, the price level is determined by the quantity of money. That is,

$$P = M(V/Y),$$

where (*V*/*Y*) is independent of *M*. So a change in *M* brings a proportional change in *P*.

We can also express the equation of exchange in growth rates,[1] in which form it states that

$$\frac{\text{Money}}{\text{growth rate}} + \frac{\text{Rate of}}{\text{velocity}}_{\text{change}} = \frac{\text{Inflation}}{\text{rate}} + \frac{\text{Real GDP}}{\text{growth rate}}$$

Solving this equation for the inflation rate gives

$$\frac{\text{Inflation}}{\text{rate}} = \frac{\text{Money}}{\text{growth rate}} + \frac{\text{Rate of}}{\text{velocity}}_{\text{change}} - \frac{\text{Real GDP}}{\text{growth rate}}$$

In the long run, the rate of velocity change is not influenced by the money growth rate. More strongly, in the long run, the rate of velocity change is approximately zero. With this assumption, the inflation rate in the long run is determined as

$$\frac{\text{Inflation}}{\text{rate}} = \frac{\text{Money}}{\text{growth rate}} - \frac{\text{Real GDP}}{\text{growth rate}}.$$

In the long run, fluctuations in the money growth rate minus the real GDP growth rate bring equal fluctuations in the inflation rate.

Also, in the long run, with the economy at full employment, real GDP equals potential GDP, so the real GDP growth rate equals the potential GDP growth rate. This growth rate might be influenced by inflation but the influence is most likely small, and the quantity theory assumes that it is zero. So the real GDP growth rate is given and doesn't change when the money growth rate changes—inflation is correlated with money growth.

Evidence on the Quantity Theory of Money

Figure 9.10 summarizes some U.S. evidence on the quantity theory of money. The figure reveals that on the average, as predicted by the quantity theory of money, the inflation rate fluctuates in line with fluctuations in the money growth rate minus the real GDP growth rate.

Figure 9.11 shows two scatter diagrams of the inflation rate and the money growth rate for 134 countries in part(a) and for those countries with inflation rates below 20 percent a year in part (b). You can see a general tendency for money growth and inflation to be correlated but the quantity theory (the red lines) does not predict inflation precisely.

The correlation between money growth and inflation isn't perfect. Nor does it tell us that money

---

[1] To obtain this equation, begin with

$$MV = PY$$

and then changes in these variables are related by the equation

$$\Delta MV + M\Delta V = \Delta PY + P\Delta Y$$

Divide this equation by the equation of exchange to obtain

$$\Delta M/M + \Delta V/V = \Delta P/P + \Delta Y/Y$$

The term $\Delta M/M$ is the money growth rate, $\Delta V/V$ is the rate of velocity change, $\Delta P/P$ is the inflation rate, and $\Delta Y/Y$ is the real GDP growth rate.

FIGURE 9.10
U. S. Money Growth and Inflation

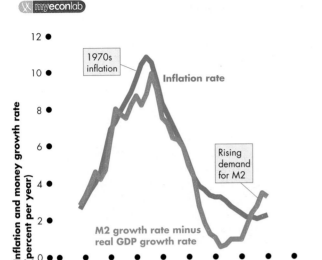

On the average, the inflation rate and the money growth rate minus real GDP growth are correlated—they rise and fall together.

Source of data: Federal Reserve and Bureau of Labor Statistics.

growth *causes* inflation. Money growth might cause inflation; inflation might cause money growth; or some third variable might cause both inflation and money growth.

REVIEW QUIZ

1 What is the quantity theory of money?
2 What is the velocity of circulation and how is it calculated?
3 What is the equation of exchange? Can the equation of exchange be wrong?
4 What do the long-run historical evidence and international evidence tell us about the quantity theory of money?

myeconlab Study Plan 9.6

◆ You now know what money is, how banks create it, and how the quantity of money influences the interest rate in the short-run and the price level in the long run. *Reading Between the Lines* rounds out the chapter by looking at the quantity theory of money in action in Zimbabwe today.

FIGURE 9.11
Money Growth and Inflation in the World

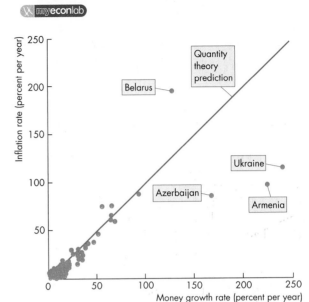

(a) 134 Countries: 1990–2005

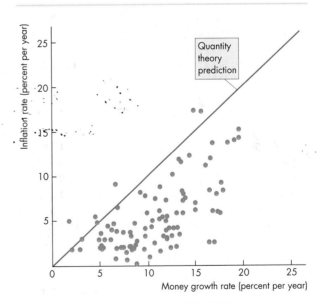

(b) 104 Lower-inflation countries: 1990–2005

Inflation and money growth in 134 countries in part (a) and low-inflation countries in part (b) show a clear positive relationship between money growth and inflation.

Sources of data: International Financial Statistics Yearbook, 2006 and International Monetary Fund, World Economic Outlook, April 2006.

The Quantity Theory of Money in Zimbabwe

Zimbabwe's Prices Rise 900%, Turning Staples Into Luxuries

April 25, 2006

How bad is inflation in Zimbabwe? Well, consider this: at a supermarket near the center of this tatterdemalion capital, toilet paper costs $417.

No, not per roll. Four hundred seventeen Zimbabwean dollars is the value of a single two-ply sheet. A roll costs $145,750—in American currency, about 69 cents.

The price of toilet paper, like everything else here, soars almost daily, spawning jokes about an impending better use for Zimbabwe's $500 bill, now the smallest in circulation.

But what is happening is no laughing matter. For untold numbers of Zimbabweans, toilet paper—and bread, margarine, meat, even the once ubiquitous morning cup of tea—have become unimaginable luxuries. All are casualties of the hyperinflation that is roaring toward 1,000 percent a year, a rate usually seen only in war zones.

Zimbabwe has been tormented this entire decade by both deep recession and high inflation, but in recent months the economy seems to have abandoned whatever moorings it had left. The national budget for 2006 has already been largely spent. Government services have started to crumble.

The purity of Harare's drinking water, siphoned from a lake downstream of its sewer outfall, has been unreliable for months, and dysentery and cholera swept the city in December and January. The city suffers rolling electrical blackouts. Mounds of uncollected garbage pile up on the streets of the slums.

Zimbabwe's inflation is hardly history's worst—in Weimar Germany in 1923, prices quadrupled each month, compared with doubling about once every three or four months in Zimbabwe. That said, experts agree that Zimbabwe's inflation is currently the world's highest, and has been for some time. . . .

Essence of the Story

▸ In April 2006, in Zimbabwe, a single two-ply sheet of toilet paper cost $417 and a roll cost $145,750 (in Zimbabwe dollars).

▸ Zimbabwe is suffering a 1,000 percent per year inflation.

▸ The government had spent its 2006 budget by April, and public services were crumbling.

▸ Zimbabwe's inflation isn't the highest in history, but it is the highest in the world today.

The quantity theory of money explains inflation trends. A low growth rate of the quantity of money keeps inflation low. A rapid growth rate of the quantity of money brings a high inflation rate.

The quantity theory of money is most visible when money growth is rapid and the inflation rate is high.

Zimbabwe has the highest inflation rate in the world today, so it provides a good example of the quantity theory of money in action.

During 2006, the inflation rate averaged close to 1,000 percent a year and exceeded that rate in some months.

To appreciate an inflation rate of 1,000 percent a year, translate it to a monthly inflation rate. Every month, on the average, prices rise by 20 percent. A cup of coffee that costs $3 in January costs $9 in June and $27 in December!

When people expect prices to rise rapidly, they expect the money they hold to fall in value rapidly. So they spend and hold goods rather than money.

The velocity of circulation begins to rise. The velocity of circulation is independent of the quantity of money but not independent of the money growth rate.

Figure 1 shows the inflation rate and money growth rate record in Zimbabwe since 2000.

Between 2000 and 2005, the money growth rate increased from a bit more than 100 percent a year to 475 percent a year. (The Reserve Bank of Zimbabwe—the country's central bank—stopped reporting the money data in 2006.)

The inflation rate increased slowly at first, from about 50 percent a year in 2000 to 100 percent a year in 2002.

In 2003, the inflation rate took off as people started to dump their dollars and scramble to buy goods and services before their prices increased too much.

The inflation rate continued to increase until it hit 1,000 percent a year in some months of 2006.

By 2006, prices had risen to the point that even a small item such as a sheet of toilet paper

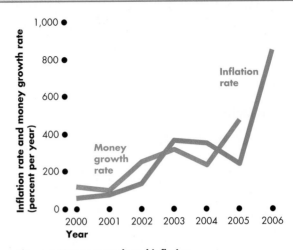

Figure 1 Money growth and inflation

cost hundreds of dollars and a big item such as a pair of jeans cost $10,000,000!

To cope with all the zeroes, the Reserve Bank of Zimbabwe launched "Project Sunrise," which redefined the Zimbabwe dollar by knocking off three zeroes.

In new dollars, a pair of jeans cost only $10,000!

The bank notes issued by the Reserve Bank of Zimbabwe are time limited and worthless after December 31, 2006, when they will be replaced by some other "new" dollars.

Knocking off three zeroes doesn't solve Zimbabwe's inflation problem. It only makes it a bit easier to live with.

An inflation such as Zimbabwe's doesn't happen because the central bank wants to create inflation. It occurs because the government can't raise enough tax revenue, so the central bank makes loans to the government, which means that the government spends newly created money.

SUMMARY

Key Points

What Is Money? (pp. 206–208)

- Money is the means of payment. It functions as a medium of exchange, a unit of account, and a store of value.
- Today, money consists of currency and deposits.

Depository Institutions (pp. 209–211)

- Commercial banks, S&Ls, savings banks, credit unions, and money market mutual funds are depository institutions whose deposits are money.
- Depository institutions provide four main economic services: They create liquidity, minimize the cost of obtaining funds, minimize the cost of monitoring borrowers, and pool risks.

The Federal Reserve System (pp. 212–215)

- The Federal Reserve System is the central bank of the United States.
- The Fed influences the quantity of money by setting the required reserve ratio, the discount rate, and by conducting open market operations.

How Banks Create Money (pp. 215–219)

- Banks create money by making loans.
- The total quantity of money that can be created depends on the monetary base, the desired reserve ratio, and the currency drain ratio.

The Market for Money (pp. 220–223)

- The quantity of money demanded is the amount of money that people plan to hold.
- The quantity of real money equals the quantity of nominal money divided by the price level.
- The quantity of real money demanded depends on the nominal interest rate, real GDP, and financial innovation. A rise in the nominal interest rate brings a decrease in the quantity of real money demanded.
- In the short run, the Fed sets the quantity of money to hit a target nominal interest rate.

- In the long run, the loanable funds market determines the interest rate and money market equilibrium determines the price level.

The Quantity Theory of Money (pp. 224–225)

- The quantity theory of money is the proposition that money growth and inflation move up and down together in the long run.
- The U.S. and international evidence is consistent with the quantity theory, on the average.

Key Figures

Key Terms

PROBLEMS

myeconlab **Tests, Study Plan, Solutions***

1. In the United States today, money includes which of the following items?
   a. Federal Reserve banknotes in Citibank's cash machines
   b. Your Visa card
   c. The quarters inside public phones
   d. U.S. dollar bills in your wallet
   e. The check you have just written to pay for your rent
   f. The loan you took out last August to pay for your school fees

2. Sara withdraws $1,000 from her savings account at the Lucky S&L, keeps $50 in cash, and deposits the balance in her checking account at the Bank of Illinois. What is the immediate change in M1 and M2?

3. The commercial banks in Zap have

Reserves	$250 million
Loans	$1,000 million
Deposits	$2,000 million
Total assets	$2,500 million

   Calculate the banks' desired reserve ratio.

4. Banks in New Transylvania have a desired reserve ratio of 10 percent and no excess reserves. The currency drain ratio is 50 percent. Then the central bank increases bank reserves by $1,200.
   a. What is the initial increase in the monetary base?
   b. How much do the banks lend in the first round of the money creation process?
   c. How much of the amount initially lent does not return to the banks but is held as currency?
   d. Set out the transactions that take place and calculate the amount of deposits created and the increase in the amount of currency held after the second round of the money creation process.

5. You are given the following information about the economy of Nocoin: The banks have deposits of $300 billion. Their reserves are $15 billion, two thirds of which is in deposits with the central bank. Households and firms hold $30 billion in banknotes. There are no coins! Calculate

*Solutions to odd-numbered problems are provided.

   a. The monetary base.
   b. The quantity of money.
   c. The banks' reserve ratio (as a percentage).
   d. The currency drain ratio (as a percentage).

6. In problem 5, the banks have no excess reserves. Suppose that the Bank of Nocoin, the central bank, increases bank reserves by $0.5 billion.
   a. What happens to the quantity of money?
   b. Explain why the change in the quantity of money is not equal to the change in the monetary base.
   c. Calculate the money multiplier.

7. In problem 5, the banks have no excess reserves. Suppose that the Bank of Nocoin, the central bank, decreases bank reserves by $0.5 billion.
   a. What happens to the quantity of deposits?
   b. What happens to the quantity of currency?
   c. What happens to the quantity of money?
   d. Calculate the money multiplier.

8. In the United Kingdom, the currency drain ratio is 0.38 and the desired reserve ratio is 0.002. Calculate the U.K. money multiplier.

9. In Australia, the quantity of M1 is $150 billion, the currency drain ratio is 33 percent and the desired reserve ratio is 8 percent. Calculate the monetary base in Australia.

10. The spreadsheet provides information about the demand for money in Minland.

	A	B	C
1	r	Y_0	Y_1
2	7	1.0	1.5
3	6	1.5	2.0
4	5	2.0	2.5
5	4	2.5	3.0
6	3	3.0	3.5
7	2	3.5	4.0
8	1	4.0	4.5

Column A is the nominal interest rate, r. Columns B and C show the quantity of money demanded at two different levels of real GDP: Y_0 is $10 billion and Y_1 is $20 billion. The quantity of money is $3 billion. Initially, real GDP is $20 billion. What happens in Minland if the interest rate
   a. Exceeds 4 percent a year?
   b. Is less than 4 percent a year?
   c. Equals 4 percent a year?

11. The Minland economy in problem 10 experiences a severe recession. Real GDP decreases to $10 billion. If the quantity of money supplied does not change,
    a. What happens in Minland if the interest rate is 4 percent a year?
    b. Do people buy bonds or sell bonds?
    c. Will the interest rate rise or fall? Why?
12. Quantecon is a country in which the quantity theory of money operates. The country has a constant population, capital stock, and technology. In year 1, real GDP was $400 million, the price level was 200, and the velocity of circulation was 20. In year 2, the quantity of money was 20 percent higher than in year 1. What was
    a. The quantity of money in year 1?
    b. The quantity of money in year 2?
    c. The price level in year 2?
    d. The level of real GDP in year 2?
    e. The velocity of circulation in year 2?
13. In Quantecon described in problem 12, in year 3, the quantity of money falls to one fifth of its level in year 2.
    a. What is the quantity of money in year 3?
    b. What is the price level in year 3?
    c. What is the level of real GDP in year 3?
    d. What is the velocity of circulation in year 3?
    e. If it takes more than one year for the full quantity theory effect to occur, what do you predict happens to real GDP in Quantecon in year 3? Why?

CRITICAL THINKING

1. Study *Reading Between the Lines* on pp. 226–227 and then
    a. Describe the money growth rate and the inflation rate in Zimbabwe since 2000.
    b. Why will knocking three zeroes off all prices not stop Zimbabwe's inflation?
    c. What must be done to stop Zimbabwe's inflation?
2. Rapid inflation in Brazil in the early 1990s caused the cruzeiro to lose its ability to function as money. Which of the following commodities do you think would most likely have taken the place of the cruzeiro in the Brazilian economy? Explain why.

a. Tractor parts
b. Packs of cigarettes
c. Loaves of bread
d. Impressionist paintings
e. Baseball trading cards

3. The table provides some data for the United States in the first decade following the Civil War.

	1869	1879
Quantity of money	$1.3 billion	$1.7 billion
Real GDP (1929 dollars)	$7.4 billion	Z
Price level (1929 = 100)	X	54
Velocity of circulation	4.50	4.61

Source: Milton Friedman and Anna J. Schwartz, *A Monetary History of the United States 1867-1960*

a. Calculate the value of X in 1869.
b. Calculate the value of Z in 1879.
c. Are the data consistent with the quantity theory of money? Explain your answer.

4. **From paper-clip to house, in 14 trades**
    A 26-year-old Montreal man appears to have succeeded in his quest to barter a single, red paper-clip all the way up to a house. It took almost a year and 14 trades, . . .
    CBC News, 7 July 2006
    a. Is barter a means of payment?
    b. Is barter just as efficient as money when trading on e-Bay? Explain.

WEB ACTIVITIES

myeconlab Links to Web sites

1. Visit Roy Davies's Web site, "Money—Past, Present, and Future," and study the section on e-money. Then answer the following questions:
    a. What is e-money and what are the alternative forms that it takes?
    b. Do you think that the widespread use of e-money will limit the ability of the Federal Reserve to control the quantity of money? Why or why not?
    c. When you buy an item on the Internet and pay for it using PayPal, are you using money? Explain why or why not.
    d. Why might e-money be superior to cash as a means of payment?

CHAPTER 10

The Exchange Rate and the Balance of Payments

Many Monies!

The dollar (\$), the yen (¥), and the euro (€) are three of the world's monies. But they are three among a world of more than 100 different monies. The dollar (the currency of the United States) and the yen (the currency of Japan) have been around for a long time. The euro (the currency of 12 members of the European Union) is new. It was created in the 1990s but didn't come into everyday use as notes and coins until January 1, 2002. Most of the world's international payments are made using these three currencies.

In August 2002, one U.S. dollar bought 1.02 euros. From 2002 through 2005, the dollar sank against the euro, and by August 2006, one U.S. dollar bought only 78 euro cents. But against the yen, the U.S. dollar held its value at about 117 yen per dollar.

Why did the dollar fall in value against the euro? Is there anything we can do or should do to stabilize the value of the dollar?

Before 1988, American ownership of foreign assets exceeded foreign ownership of U.S. assets. But in 1988, the value of foreign assets owned by Americans just equaled the value of the assets that foreigners owned in the United States. And every year since 1988, the balance has tipped increasingly the other way. Foreign entrepreneurs have roamed the United States with giant virtual shopping carts and loaded them up with Gerber, Firestone, Chrysler, Columbia Pictures, and Ben & Jerry's, all of which are now controlled by Japanese or European companies. Why have foreigners been buying U.S. businesses?

◆ In this chapter, you're going to discover why the U.S. economy has become attractive to foreign investors, what determines the amount of international borrowing and lending, and why the dollar fluctuates against other currencies. At the end of the chapter, in *Reading Between the Lines*, we'll look at China's foreign exchange rate policy and see why many Americans are troubled by it.

After studying this chapter, you will be able to

▶ Describe the foreign exchange market, define the exchange rate, and distinguish between the nominal exchange rate and the real exchange rate

▶ Explain how the exchange rate is determined day by day

▶ Explain the long-run trends in the exchange rate and explain interest rate parity and purchasing power parity

▶ Describe the balance of payments accounts and explain what causes an international deficit

▶ Describe the alternative exchange rate policies and explain their long-run effects

231

Currencies and Exchange Rates

When Wal-Mart imports DVD players from Japan, it pays for them using Japanese yen. And when Japan Airlines buys an airplane from Boeing, it pays using U.S. dollars. Whenever people buy things from another country, they use the currency of that country to make the transaction. It doesn't make any difference what the item is that is being traded internationally. It might be a DVD player, an airplane, insurance or banking services, real estate, the stocks and bonds of a government or corporation, or even an entire business.

Foreign money is just like U.S. money. It consists of notes and coins issued by a central bank and mint and deposits in banks and other depository institutions. When we described U.S. money in Chapter 9, we distinguished between currency (notes and coins) and deposits. But when we talk about foreign money, we refer to it as foreign currency. **Foreign currency** is the money of other countries regardless of whether that money is in the form of notes, coins, or bank deposits.

We get these foreign currencies and foreigners get U.S. dollars in the foreign exchange market.

The Foreign Exchange Market

The **foreign exchange market** is the market in which the currency of one country is exchanged for the currency of another. The foreign exchange market is not a place like a downtown flea market or a fruit and vegetable market. The foreign exchange market is made up of thousands of people—importers and exporters, banks, international travelers, and specialist traders called *foreign exchange brokers.*

The foreign exchange market opens on Monday morning in Sydney, Australia, and Hong Kong, which is still Sunday evening in New York. As the day advances, markets open in Singapore, Tokyo, Bahrain, Frankfurt, London, New York, Chicago, and San Francisco. As the West Coast markets close, Sydney is only an hour away from opening for the next day of business. The sun barely sets in the foreign exchange market. Dealers around the world are in continual contact by telephone and computer, and on a typical day in 2006, close to $2 trillion (of all currencies) were traded in the foreign exchange market—or more than $400 trillion in a year.

Exchange Rates

An **exchange rate** is the price at which one currency exchanges for another currency in the foreign exchange market. For example, on September 1, 2006, $1 would buy 117 Japanese yen or 78 euro cents. So the exchange rate was 117 yen per dollar or, equivalently, 78 euro cents per dollar.

The exchange rate fluctuates. Sometimes it rises and sometimes it falls. A rise in the exchange rate is called an *appreciation* of the dollar, and a fall in the exchange rate is called a *depreciation* of the dollar. For example, when the exchange rate rises from 117 yen to 130 yen per dollar, the dollar appreciates, and when the exchange rate falls from 117 yen to 100 yen per dollar, the dollar depreciates.

Figure 10.1 shows the U.S. dollar exchange rate against the five currencies that feature most prominently in U.S. imports—the Canadian dollar, the Chinese yuan, the European euro, the Mexican peso, and the Japanese yen—between 1995 and 2005.

The figure shows that the U.S. dollar has generally appreciated against the Mexican peso, been constant against the Chinese yuan, and fluctuated in both directions against the other three currencies. But since 2002, the dollar has depreciated against the currencies of Canada, Europe, and Japan.

The quantity of foreign money that we get for our dollar changes when the dollar appreciates or depreciates. But a change in the value of the dollar might not change what we *really* pay for our imports and earn from our exports. The reason is that prices might change to offset the change in the exchange rate and leave the terms on which we trade with other countries unchanged.

To determine whether a change in the exchange rate changes what we earn from exports and pay for imports, we need to distinguish between the *nominal* exchange rate and the *real* exchange rate.

Nominal and Real Exchange Rates

The **nominal exchange rate** is the value of the U.S. dollar expressed in units of foreign currency per U.S. dollar. It is a measure of how much of one money exchanges for a unit of another money.

The **real exchange rate** is the relative price of foreign-produced goods and services to U.S.-produced goods and services. It is a measure of the quantity of the real GDP of other countries that we get for a unit of U.S. real GDP.

FIGURE 10.1   The U.S. Dollar Against Five Currencies

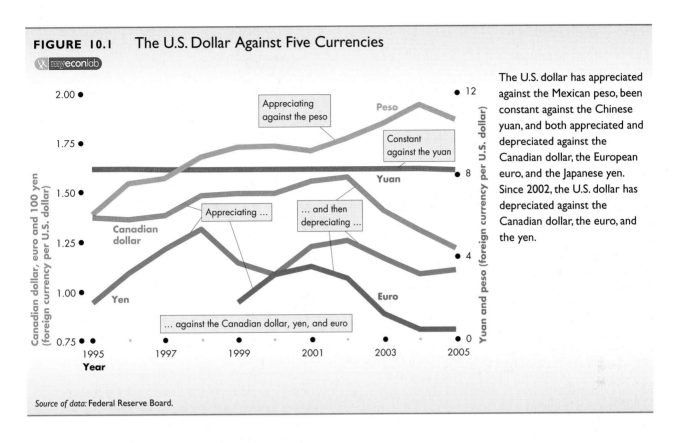

The U.S. dollar has appreciated against the Mexican peso, been constant against the Chinese yuan, and both appreciated and depreciated against the Canadian dollar, the European euro, and the Japanese yen. Since 2002, the U.S. dollar has depreciated against the Canadian dollar, the euro, and the yen.

Source of data: Federal Reserve Board.

The exchange rates that we've just discussed and that are graphed in Fig. 10.1 are *nominal* exchange rates. To understand the real exchange rate, suppose that Japan produces only DVD players and the United States produces only airplanes. The price of a DVD player is 10,000 yen, and the price of an airplane is $100 million. Also suppose that the exchange rate—the *nominal* exchange rate—is 100 yen per dollar. With this information, we can calculate the *real* exchange rate, which is the number DVD players that one airplane buys. Let's do this calculation.

At the price of 10,000 yen and an exchange rate of 100 yen per dollar, the price of a DVD player is $100. At a price of $100 million for an airplane and $100 for a DVD player, one airplane buys 1 million DVD players. The real exchange rate is 1 million DVD players per airplane.

In our example, airplanes represent U.S. real GDP, and DVD players represent Japanese real GDP. So the price of a DVD player in Japan and the price of an airplane in the United States represent the price levels (GDP deflators) in the two countries.

Call the U.S. price level *P*, the Japanese price level P^*, the nominal exchange rate *E* yen per dollar and

the real exchange rate *RER* (Japanese real GDP per unit of U.S. real GDP). Then the real exchange rate is

$$RER = E \times (P/P^*).$$

In words, the real exchange rate is the nominal exchange rate multiplied by the ratio of the U.S. price level to the foreign price level.

The real exchange rate changes if the nominal exchange rate changes and prices remain constant. But if the dollar appreciates (*E* rises) and foreign prices rise (P^* rises) by the same percentage, the real exchange rate doesn't change. In the above example, if the exchange rate rises to 120 yen per dollar and the price of a DVD player rises to 12,000 yen, one airplane still buys 1 million DVD players.

How has the real exchange rate changed? Has it changed in the same way as the nominal exchange rate? We could answer these questions by calculating a real exchange rate in terms of each of the currencies in Fig. 10.1. But there is a more efficient way of measuring the real exchange rate. Instead of looking at the exchange rates between many different currencies, we can look at an average of the exchange rates against all the currencies in which the United States trades.

Trade-Weighted Index

The average exchange rate of the U.S. dollar against other currencies, with individual currencies weighted by their importance in U.S. international trade, is called the **trade-weighted index**. The trade-weighted index of major currencies is an index based on the currencies of Europe, Australia, Canada, Japan, Sweden, Switzerland, and the United Kingdom.

This index started in 1973, and it is defined to be 100 in that year. So the index tells us the value of the U.S. dollar against these currencies as a percentage of its 1973 value.

The blue line in Fig. 10.2 shows the nominal trade-weighted index since 1995. The index shows that the dollar appreciated from 1995 through 2000 and then started to depreciate in 2001. The red line in Fig. 10.2 shows the real trade-weighted index. You can see that the nominal and real exchange rates moved in the same direction. But the nominal exchange rate appreciated less and depreciated more than the real exchange rate. The gap between the real exchange rate and the nominal exchange rate arises because the inflation rate in the rest of the world is below the U.S. inflation rate.

Questions About the Exchange Rate

The performance of the U.S. dollar in the foreign exchange market raises a number of questions that we address in the rest of this chapter.

First, how are the nominal exchange rate and real exchange rate determined? Why did the dollar appreciate during the 1990s and depreciate during the 2000s? And why did the dollar appreciate against the Mexican peso but depreciate against other currencies?

Second, how do exchange rate fluctuations influence our international trade and international payments? In particular, could we eliminate, or at least decrease, our international deficit by changing the exchange rate?

Third, how do the Fed and other central banks operate in the foreign exchange market? In particular, how was the exchange rate between the U.S. dollar and the Chinese yuan fixed and why did it remain constant for many years? Would an appreciation of the yuan change the balance of trade and payments between the United States and China?

We begin by learning how trading in the foreign exchange market determines the exchange rate.

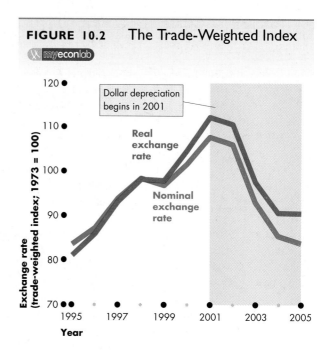

FIGURE 10.2 The Trade-Weighted Index

The nominal trade-weighted index of major currencies (blue line) and the real trade-weighted index of major currencies (red line) appreciated through 2000 and then depreciated. The nominal exchange rate appreciated less and depreciated more than the real exchange rate because the U.S. inflation rate exceeded the inflation rate in the other major economies.

Source of data: Economic Report of the President, 2006.

REVIEW QUIZ

1 What is the foreign exchange market and what prices are determined in this market?
2 Distinguish between appreciation and depreciation of the dollar.
3 What are the world's major currencies?
4 Against which currencies and during which years has the U.S. dollar appreciated since 1995?
5 Against which currencies and during which years has the U.S. dollar depreciated since 1995?
6 What is the distinction between the nominal exchange rate and the real exchange rate?
7 What does the trade-weighted index measure?

myeconlab Study Plan 10.1

The Foreign Exchange Market

An exchange rate is a price—the price of one currency in terms of another. And like all prices, an exchange rate is determined in a market—the foreign exchange market.

The U.S. dollar trades in the foreign exchange market and is supplied and demanded by tens of thousands of traders every hour of every business day. Because it has many traders and no restrictions on who may trade, the foreign exchange market is a *competitive market*.

In a competitive market, demand and supply determine the price. So to understand the forces that determine the exchange rate, we need to study the factors that influence demand and supply in the foreign exchange market. But there is a feature of the foreign exchange market that makes it special.

The Demand for One Money Is the Supply of Another Money

When people who are holding the money of some other country want to exchange it for U.S. dollars, they demand U.S. dollars and supply that other country's money. And when people who are holding U.S. dollars want to exchange them for the money of

Dealers in the foreign exchange market.

some other country, they supply U.S. dollars and demand that other country's money.

So the factors that influence the demand for U.S. dollars also influence the supply of European Union euros, Canadian dollars, or Japanese yen. And the factors that influence the demand for that other country's money also influence the supply of U.S. dollars.

We'll first look at the influences on the demand for U.S. dollars in the foreign exchange market.

Demand in the Foreign Exchange Market

People buy U.S. dollars in the foreign exchange market so that they can buy U.S.-produced goods and services—U.S. exports. They also buy U.S. dollars so that they can buy U.S. assets such as bonds, stocks, businesses, and real estate or so that they can keep part of their money holding in a U.S. dollar bank account.

The quantity of U.S. dollars demanded in the foreign exchange market is the amount that traders plan to buy during a given time period at a given exchange rate. This quantity depends on many factors, but the main ones are

1. The exchange rate
2. World demand for U.S. exports
3. Interest rates in the United States and other countries
4. The expected future exchange rate

So that we can first isolate the exchange rate and see how it is determined, we'll look first at the relationship between the quantity of U.S. dollars demanded in the foreign exchange market and the exchange rate when the other three influences remain the same—the law of demand in the foreign exchange market. In the next section, we'll consider what happens when these other influences change.

The Law of Demand for Foreign Exchange

The law of demand applies to U.S. dollars just as it does to anything else that people value. Other things remaining the same, the higher the exchange rate, the smaller is the quantity of U.S. dollars demanded in the foreign exchange market. For example, if the price of the U.S. dollar rises from 100 yen to 120 yen but nothing else changes, the quantity of U.S. dollars that people plan to buy in the foreign exchange market decreases. The exchange rate influences the quantity of U.S. dollars demanded for two reasons:

- Exports effect
- Expected profit effect

Exports Effect The larger the value of U.S. exports, the larger is the quantity of U.S. dollars demanded in the foreign exchange market. But the value of U.S. exports depends on the prices of U.S.-produced goods and services *expressed in the currency of the foreign buyer.* And these prices depend on the exchange rate. The lower the exchange rate, other things remaining the same, the lower are the prices of U.S.-produced goods and services to foreigners and the greater is the volume of U.S. exports. So if the exchange rate falls (and other influences remain the same), the quantity of U.S. dollars demanded in the foreign exchange market increases.

To see this effect at work, think about orders for Boeing's new 787 airplane. If the price of a 787 is $100 million and the exchange rate is 90 euro cents per U.S. dollar, the price of this airplane to KLM, a European airline, is €900,000. KLM decides that this price is too high, so it doesn't buy a new 787. If the exchange rate falls to 80 euro cents per U.S. dollar and other things remain the same, the price of a 787 now falls to €800,000. KLM now decides to buy a 787 and buys U.S. dollars in the foreign exchange market.

Expected Profit Effect The larger the expected profit from holding U.S. dollars, the greater is the quantity of U.S. dollars demanded in the foreign exchange market. But expected profit depends on the exchange rate. For a given expected future exchange rate, the lower the exchange rate today, the larger is the expected profit from buying U.S. dollars today and holding them, so the greater is the quantity of U.S. dollars demanded in the foreign exchange market today.

To see this effect at work, suppose that Mizuho Bank, a Japanese bank, expects the exchange rate to be 120 yen per U.S. dollar at the end of the year. If today's exchange rate is also 120 yen per U.S. dollar, Mizuho Bank expects no profit from buying U.S. dollars and holding them until the end of the year. But if the exchange rate is 100 yen per U.S. dollar

and Mizuho Bank buys U.S. dollars, it expects to sell those dollars at the end of the year for 120 yen per dollar and make a profit of 20 yen per U.S. dollar.

The lower the exchange rate today, other things remaining the same, the greater is the expected profit from holding U.S. dollars and the greater is the quantity of U.S. dollars demanded in the foreign exchange market today.

Demand Curve for U.S. Dollars

Figure 10.3 shows the demand curve for U.S. dollars in the foreign exchange market. A change in the exchange rate, other things remaining the same, brings a change in the quantity of U.S. dollars demanded and a movement along the demand curve as shown by the arrows.

We will look at the factors that change demand in the next section of this chapter. But first, let's see what determines the supply of U.S. dollars.

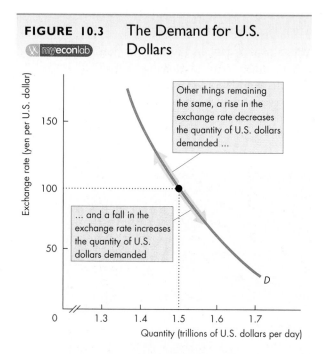

FIGURE 10.3   The Demand for U.S. Dollars

The quantity of U.S. dollars demanded depends on the exchange rate. Other things remaining the same, if the exchange rate rises, the quantity of U.S. dollars demanded decreases and there is a movement up along the demand curve for U.S. dollars. If the exchange rate falls, the quantity of U.S. dollars demanded increases and there is a movement down along the demand curve for U.S. dollars.

Supply in the Foreign Exchange Market

People sell U.S. dollars and buy other currencies so that they can buy foreign-produced goods and services—U.S. imports. People also sell U.S. dollars and buy foreign currencies so that they can buy foreign assets such as bonds, stocks, businesses, and real estate or so that they can hold part of their money in bank deposits denominated in a foreign currency.

The quantity of U.S. dollars supplied in the foreign exchange market is the amount that traders plan to sell during a given time period at a given exchange rate. This quantity depends on many factors, but the main ones are

1. The exchange rate
2. U.S. demand for imports
3. Interest rates in the United States and other countries
4. The expected future exchange rate

Let's look at the relationship between the quantity of U.S. dollars supplied in the foreign exchange market and the exchange rate when the other three influences remain the same—the law of supply in the foreign exchange market.

The Law of Supply of Foreign Exchange

Other things remaining the same, the higher the exchange rate, the greater is the quantity of U.S. dollars supplied in the foreign exchange market. For example, if the exchange rate rises from 100 yen to 120 yen per U.S. dollar and other things remain the same, the quantity of U.S. dollars that people plan to sell in the foreign exchange market increases.

The exchange rate influences the quantity of dollars supplied for two reasons:

■ Imports effect
■ Expected profit effect

Imports Effect The larger the value of U.S. imports, the larger is the quantity of U.S. dollars supplied in the foreign exchange market. But the value of U.S. imports depends on the prices of foreign-produced goods and services *expressed in U.S. dollars*. These prices depend on the exchange rate. The higher the exchange rate, other things remaining the same, the lower are the prices of foreign-produced goods and services to Americans and the greater is the volume of U.S. imports. So if the exchange rate rises (and

other influences remain the same), the quantity of U.S. dollars supplied in the foreign exchange market increases.

Expected Profit Effect This effect works just like that on the demand for the U.S. dollar but in the opposite direction. The higher the exchange rate today, other things remaining the same, the larger is the expected profit from selling U.S. dollars today and holding foreign currencies, so the greater is the quantity of U.S. dollars supplied.

Supply Curve for U.S. Dollars

Figure 10.4 shows the supply curve of U.S. dollars in the foreign exchange market. A change in the exchange rate, other things remaining the same, brings a change in the quantity of U.S. dollars supplied and a movement along the supply curve as shown by the arrows.

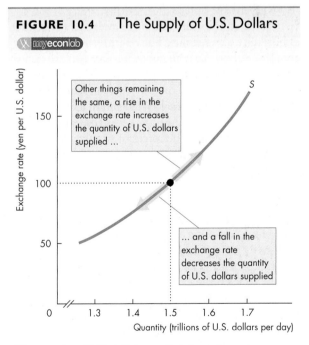

FIGURE 10.4   The Supply of U.S. Dollars

Other things remaining the same, a rise in the exchange rate increases the quantity of U.S. dollars supplied ...

... and a fall in the exchange rate decreases the quantity of U.S. dollars supplied

The quantity of U.S. dollars supplied depends on the exchange rate. Other things remaining the same, if the exchange rate rises, the quantity of U.S. dollars supplied increases and there is a movement up along the supply curve of U.S. dollars. If the exchange rate falls, the quantity of U.S. dollars supplied decreases and there is a movement down along the supply curve of U.S. dollars.

Market Equilibrium

Equilibrium in the foreign exchange market depends on how the Federal Reserve and other central banks operate. Here, we will study equilibrium when central banks keep out of this market. In a later section (on pp. 249–251), we examine the effects of alternative actions that the Fed or another central bank might take in the foreign exchange market.

Figure 10.5 shows the demand curve for U.S. dollars, *D*, from Fig. 10.3 and the supply curve of U.S. dollars, *S*, from Fig. 10.4, and the equilibrium exchange rate.

The exchange rate acts as a regulator of the quantities demanded and supplied. If the exchange rate is too high, there is a surplus—the quantity supplied exceeds the quantity demanded. For example, in Fig. 10.5, if the exchange rate is 150 yen per U.S. dollar, there is a surplus of U.S. dollars. If the exchange rate is too low, there is a shortage—the quantity supplied is less than the quantity demanded. For example, if the exchange rate is 50 yen per U.S. dollar, there is a shortage of U.S. dollars.

At the equilibrium exchange rate, there is neither a shortage nor a surplus. The quantity supplied equals the quantity demanded. In Fig. 10.5, the equilibrium exchange rate is 100 yen per U.S. dollar. At this exchange rate, the quantity demanded and the quantity supplied are each $1.5 trillion a day.

The foreign exchange market is constantly pulled to its equilibrium by the forces of supply and demand. Foreign exchange dealers are constantly looking for the best price they can get. If they are selling, they want the highest price available. If they are buying, they want the lowest price available. Information flows from dealer to dealer through the worldwide computer network, and the price adjusts minute by minute to keep buying plans and selling plans in balance. That is, the price adjusts minute by minute to keep the exchange rate at its equilibrium.

Figure 10.5 shows how the exchange rate between the U.S. dollar and the Japanese yen is determined. The exchange rates between the U.S. dollar and all other currencies are determined in a similar way. So are the exchange rates among the other currencies. But the exchange rates are tied together so that no profit can be made by buying one currency, selling it for a second one, and then buying back the first one. If such a profit were available, traders would spot it, demand and supply would change, and the exchange rates would snap into alignment.

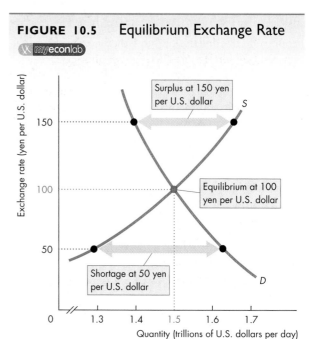

FIGURE 10.5   Equilibrium Exchange Rate

The demand curve for U.S. dollars is *D*, and the supply curve of U.S. dollars is *S*. If the exchange rate is 150 yen per U.S. dollar, there is a surplus of U.S. dollars and the exchange rate falls. If the exchange rate is 50 yen per U.S. dollar, there is a shortage of U.S. dollars and the exchange rate rises. If the exchange rate is 100 yen per dollar, there is neither a shortage nor a surplus of U.S. dollars and the exchange rate remains constant. The foreign exchange market is in equilibrium.

REVIEW QUIZ

1 What are the influences on the demand for U.S. dollars in the foreign exchange market?
2 Provide an example of the exports effect on the demand for U.S. dollars.
3 What are the influences on the supply of U.S. dollars in the foreign exchange market?
4 Provide an example of the imports effect on the supply of U.S. dollars.
5 How is the equilibrium exchange rate determined?
6 What happens if there is a shortage or a surplus of U.S. dollars in the foreign exchange market?

myeconlab **Study Plan 10.2**

Changes in Demand and Supply: Exchange Rate Fluctuations

When the demand for U.S. dollars or the supply of U.S. dollars changes, the exchange rate changes. We'll now look at the factors that make demand and supply change, starting with the demand side of the market.

Changes in the Demand for U.S. Dollars

The demand for U.S. dollars in the foreign exchange market changes when there is a change in

■ World demand for U.S. exports
■ U.S. interest rate relative to the foreign interest rate
■ The expected future exchange rate

World Demand for U.S. Exports An increase in world demand for U.S. exports increases the demand for U.S. dollars. To see this effect, think about Boeing's airplane sales. An increase in demand for air travel in Australia sends that country's airlines on a global shopping spree. They decide that the 787 is the ideal product, so they order 50 airplanes from Boeing. The demand for U.S. dollars now increases.

U.S. Interest Rate Relative to the Foreign Interest Rate People and businesses buy financial assets to make a return. The higher the interest rate that people can make on U.S. assets compared with foreign assets, the more U.S. assets they buy.

What matters is not the *level* of the U.S. interest rate, but the U.S. interest rate minus the foreign interest rate—a gap that is called the **U.S. interest rate differential**. If the U.S. interest rate rises and the foreign interest rate remains constant, the U.S. interest rate differential increases. The larger the U.S. interest rate differential, the greater is the demand for U.S. assets and the greater is the demand for U.S. dollars in the foreign exchange market.

The Expected Future Exchange Rate For a given current exchange rate, other things remaining the same, a rise in the expected future exchange rate increases the profit that people expect to earn by holding U.S. dollars and increases the demand for U.S. dollars today.

Figure 10.6 summarizes the influences on the demand for U.S. dollars. An increase in the demand

for U.S. exports, a rise in the U.S. interest rate differential, or a rise in the expected future exchange rate increases the demand for U.S. dollars today and shifts the demand curve rightward from D_0 to D_1. A decrease in the demand for U.S. exports, a fall in the U.S. interest rate differential, or a fall in the expected future exchange rate decreases the demand for U.S. dollars today and shifts the demand curve leftward from D_0 to D_2.

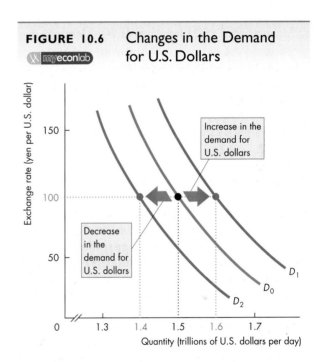

FIGURE 10.6   Changes in the Demand for U.S. Dollars

myeconlab

A change in any influence on the quantity of U.S. dollars that people plan to buy, other than the exchange rate, brings a change in the demand for U.S. dollars.

The demand for U.S. dollars

Increases if:	Decreases if:
■ World demand for U.S. exports increases	■ World demand for U.S. exports decreases
■ The U.S. interest rate differential rises	■ The U.S. interest rate differential falls
■ The expected future exchange rate rises	■ The expected future exchange rate falls

Changes in the Supply of U.S. Dollars

The supply of U.S. dollars in the foreign exchange market changes when there is a change in

- U. S. demand for imports
- U.S. interest rate relative to the foreign interest rate
- The expected future exchange rate

U.S. Demand for Imports An increase in U.S. demand for imports increases the supply of U.S. dollars in the foreign exchange market. To see why, think about Wal-Mart's purchase of DVD players. An increase in the demand for DVD players sends Wal-Mart out on a global shopping spree. Wal-Mart decides that Panasonic DVD players produced in Japan are the best buy, so Wal-Mart increases its purchases of these players. The supply of U.S. dollars now increases as Wal-Mart goes to the foreign exchange market for Japanese yen to pay Panasonic.

U.S. Interest Rate Relative to the Foreign Interest Rate
The effect of the U.S. interest rate differential on the supply of U.S. dollars is the opposite of its effect on the demand for U.S. dollars. The larger the U.S. interest rate differential, the *smaller* is the supply of U.S. dollars in the foreign exchange market. The supply of U.S. dollars is smaller because the demand for *foreign* assets is smaller. If people spend less on foreign assets, the quantity of U.S. dollars they supply in the foreign exchange market decreases. So, a rise in the U.S. interest rate, other things remaining the same, increases the U.S. interest rate differential and decreases the supply of U.S. dollars in the foreign market.

The Expected Future Exchange Rate For a given current exchange rate, other things remaining the same, a fall in the expected future exchange rate decreases the profit that can be earned by holding U.S. dollars and decreases the quantity of U.S. dollars that people want to hold. To lower their holdings of U.S. dollar assets, people must sell U.S. dollars. When they do so, the supply of U.S. dollars in the foreign exchange market increases.

Figure 10.7 summarizes the influences on the supply of U.S. dollars. If the supply of U.S. dollars decreases, the supply curve shifts leftward from S_0 to S_1. And if the supply of U.S. dollars increases, the supply curve shifts rightward from S_0 to S_2.

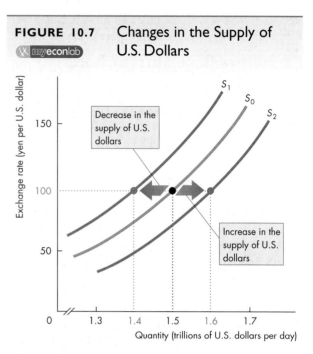

FIGURE 10.7   Changes in the Supply of U.S. Dollars

A change in any influence on the quantity of dollars that people plan to sell, other than the exchange rate, brings a change in the supply for dollars.

The supply of U.S. dollars

Increases if:

- U.S. import demand increases
- The U.S. interest rate differential falls
- The expected future exchange rate falls

Decreases if:

- U.S. import demand decreases
- The U.S. interest rate differential rises
- The expected future exchange rate rises

Changes in the Exchange Rate

If the demand for U.S. dollars increases and the supply does not change, the exchange rate rises. If the demand for U.S. dollars decreases and the supply does not change, the exchange rate falls. Similarly, if the supply of U.S. dollars decreases and the demand does not change, the exchange rate rises. If the supply of U.S. dollars increases and the demand does not change, the exchange rate falls.

These predictions are exactly the same as those for any other market. Let's now look at two episodes in the life of the U.S. dollar.

An Appreciating U.S. Dollar: 2000–2002 Between 2000 and 2002, the U.S. dollar appreciated against the yen. It rose from 108 yen to 127 yen per U.S. dollar. Figure 10.8(a) provides a possible explanation for this appreciation.

In 2000, the demand and supply curves were those labeled D_{00} and S_{00}. The exchange rate was 108 yen per U.S. dollar.

During 2001, real GDP growth slowed in both the United States and Japan. But growth slowed by more in Japan. International investors believed that they would make a bigger profit from U.S. assets than from Japanese assets. So funds flowed into the United States. Also, currency traders, aware of these profit assessments, expected the dollar to appreciate against the yen. The demand for U.S. dollars increased, and the supply of U.S. dollars decreased.

In Fig. 10.8(a), the demand curve shifted rightward from D_{00} to D_{02} and the supply curve shifted leftward from S_{00} to S_{02}. The exchange rate rose to 127 yen per U.S. dollar. In the figure, the equilibrium quantity remained unchanged—an assumption.

A Depreciating U.S. Dollar: 2002–2004 Between 2002 and 2004, the U.S. dollar depreciated against the yen. It fell from 127 yen to 108 yen per U.S. dollar. Figure 10.8(b) provides a possible explanation for this depreciation.

In 2002, the demand and supply curves were those labeled D_{02} and S_{02}. The exchange rate was 127 yen per U.S. dollar.

During 2003, real GDP growth remained low in the United States but increased in Japan. Investors gradually changed their views about the profit they could earn from U.S. assets and Japanese assets and saw increasing profits in Japan. Also, the U.S. interest rate differential narrowed as the U.S. interest rate fell. Funds flowed into Japan. And assessing this situation, currency traders expected the U.S. dollar to depreciate against the yen. The demand for U.S. dollars decreased and the supply of U.S. dollars increased.

In Fig. 10.8(b), the demand curve shifted leftward from D_{02} to D_{04}, the supply curve shifted rightward from S_{02} to S_{04}, and the exchange rate fell to 108 yen per dollar.

FIGURE 10.8   Exchange Rate Fluctuations

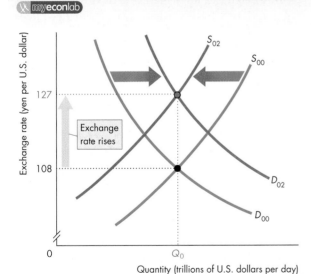

(a) 2000 to 2002

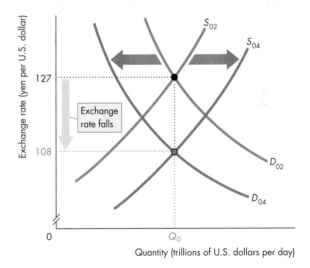

(b) 2002 to 2004

Between 2000 and 2002 (in part a), investors expected higher profits in the United States than in Japan and currency traders expected the U.S. dollar to appreciate. The demand for U.S. dollars increased, the supply of U.S. dollars decreased, and the U.S. dollar appreciated.

Between 2002 and 2004 (in part b), investors began to expect higher profits in Japan and currency traders expected the U.S. dollar to depreciate. The demand for U.S. dollars decreased, the supply of U.S. dollars increased, and the U.S. dollar depreciated.

Exchange Rate Expectations

The changes in the exchange rate that we've just examined occurred in part because the exchange rate was *expected to change*. This explanation sounds a bit like a self-fulfilling prophecy. So what makes expectations change? The answer is new information about the deeper forces that influence the value of one money relative to the value of another money. There are two such forces:

- Interest rate parity
- Purchasing power parity

Interest Rate Parity One definition of what money is worth is what it can earn. Two kinds of money—U.S. dollars and Japanese yen, for example—might earn different amounts. For example, suppose a yen bank deposit in Tokyo earns 1 percent a year and a U.S. dollar bank deposit in New York earns 3 percent a year. In this situation, why does anyone deposit money in Tokyo? Why doesn't all the money flow to New York? The answer is because of exchange rate expectations. Suppose people expect the yen to appreciate by 2 percent a year. American investors expect that if they buy and hold yen for a year, they will earn 1 percent interest and 2 percent from the higher yen (lower dollar) to give a total return of 3 percent. So the interest rate in terms of U.S. dollars is the same in Tokyo and New York. This situation is one of **interest rate parity**, which means equal rates of return.

Adjusted for risk, interest rate parity always prevails. Funds move to get the highest return available. If for a few seconds a higher return is available in New York than in Tokyo, the demand for U.S. dollars increases and the exchange rate rises until expected rates of return are equal.

Purchasing Power Parity Another definition of what money is worth is what it will buy. But two kinds of money—U.S. dollars and Japanese yen, for example—might buy different amounts of goods and services. Suppose a memory stick costs 5,000 yen in Tokyo and $50 in New York. If the exchange rate is 100 yen per dollar, the two monies have the same value. You can buy a memory stick in either Tokyo or New York for the same price. You can express that price as either 5,000 yen or $50, but the price is the same in the two currencies.

The situation we've just described is called **purchasing power parity**, which means *equal value of money*. If purchasing power parity does not prevail, some powerful forces go to work. To understand these forces, let's suppose that the price of a memory stick in New York rises to $60, but in Tokyo it remains at 5,000 yen. Further, suppose the exchange rate remains at 100 yen per dollar. In this case, a memory stick in Tokyo still costs 5,000 yen or $50. But in New York, it costs $60 or 6,000 yen. Money buys more in Japan than in the United States. Money is not of equal value in the two countries.

If all (or most) prices have increased in the United States and not increased in Japan, then people will generally expect that the value of the U.S. dollar in the foreign exchange market must fall. In this situation, the exchange rate is expected to fall. The demand for U.S. dollars decreases, and the supply of U.S. dollars increases. The exchange rate falls, as expected. If the exchange rate falls to 83.33 yen per dollar and there are no further price changes, purchasing power parity is restored. A memory stick that costs $60 in New York also costs the equivalent of $60 ($60 \times 83.33 = 5,000$) in Tokyo.

If prices increase in Japan and other countries but remain constant in the United States, then people will generally expect that the value of the U.S. dollar in the foreign exchange market is too low and that it is going to rise. In this situation, the exchange rate is expected to rise. The demand for U.S. dollars increases, and the supply of U.S. dollars decreases. The exchange rate rises, as expected.

Instant Exchange Rate Response

The exchange rate responds instantly to news about changes in the variables that influence demand and supply in the foreign exchange market. You can see why the response is immediate by thinking about the expected profit opportunities that such news creates.

Suppose that the Bank of Japan is reported to be considering raising the interest rate next week. If this move is regarded as likely, then traders expect the demand for yen to increase and the demand for dollars to decrease. They also expect the yen to appreciate and the dollar to depreciate.

But to benefit from a yen appreciation and to avoid the loss from a dollar depreciation, yen must be bought and dollars must be sold *before* the exchange rate changes. Each trader knows that all the other traders share the same information and have similar expectations. And each trader knows that when people begin to sell dollars and buy yen, the exchange rate will change. To transact before the exchange rate changes means transacting right away, as soon as the information that changes expectations is received.

The Nominal and Real Exchange Rates in the Short Run and in the Long Run

Earlier in this chapter, we distinguished between the nominal exchange rate and the real exchange rate. So far we've explained only how the nominal exchange rate is determined. And we've focused on the day-to-day fluctuations in the nominal exchange rate. We're going to turn now to the real exchange rate and explain how it is determined. We're also going to distinguish between the short run and the long run.

Recall the equation that links the nominal and real exchange rates. That equation is

$$RER = E \times (P/P^*),$$

where P is the U.S. price level, P^* is the Japanese price level, E is the nominal exchange rate (yen per U.S. dollar), and RER is the real exchange rate (the quantity of Japanese real GDP per unit of U.S. real GDP).

In the short run, this equation determines the real exchange rate. The price levels in the United States and Japan don't change every time the nominal exchange rate changes. So a change in E brings an equivalent change in RER.

But in the long run, the situation is radically different. The classical dichotomy that we described in Chapter 7 (see p. 158) holds in the foreign exchange market just as it does in other markets. In the long run, the real exchange rate is determined by demand and supply in the markets for goods and services. If Japan and the United States produced identical goods (if GDP in both countries consisted only of memory sticks for example), purchasing power parity would make the real exchange rate equal 1. One Japanese memory stick would exchange for one U.S. memory stick. In reality, although there is overlap in what each country produces, U.S. real GDP is a different bundle of goods and services from Japanese real GDP. So the relative price of Japanese and U.S. real GDP—the real exchange rate—is not 1 and it fluctuates. But the forces of demand and supply in the markets for the millions of goods and services that make up real GDP determine these relative prices.

In the long run, with the real exchange rate determined by the real forces of demand and supply in markets for goods and services, the above equation must be turned around to determine the nominal exchange rate. That is, the nominal exchange rate is

$$E = RER \times (P^*/P).$$

This equation tells us that in the long run, the nominal exchange rate is determined by the equilibrium real exchange rate and the price levels in the two countries. A rise in the Japanese price level, P^*, brings dollar appreciation—a rise in E; and a rise in the U.S. price level, P, brings dollar depreciation—a fall in E.

You learned in Chapter 9 (see pp. 224–225) that in the long run, the quantity of money determines the price level. But the quantity theory of money applies to all countries. So the quantity of money in Japan determines the price level in Japan, and the quantity of money in the United States determines the price level in the United States.

A nominal exchange rate, then, in the long run, is a monetary phenomenon. It is determined by the quantities of money in two countries.

The long-run forces that we've just described explain the broad trends in exchange rates. For example, the U.S dollar has generally appreciated against the Mexican peso because Mexico has created money at a faster pace than has the United States and the price level in Mexico has risen more rapidly than the U.S. price level. The U.S. dollar has been depreciating since 2002 because U.S. prices have been rising faster, on the average, than European, Canadian, and Japanese prices.

REVIEW QUIZ

1 Why does the demand for U.S. dollars change?
2 Why does the supply of U.S. dollars change?
3 What makes the U.S. dollar exchange rate fluctuate?
4 What is interest rate parity and what happens when this condition doesn't hold?
5 What is purchasing power parity and what happens when this condition doesn't hold?
6 What determines the real exchange rate and the nominal exchange rate in the short run?
7 What determines the real exchange rate and the nominal exchange rate in the long run?

 myeconlab Study Plan 10.3

Financing International Trade

You have seen how the exchange rate is determined. But what is the effect of the exchange rate? How does currency depreciation or currency appreciation influence our international trade and payments? We're going to lay the foundation for addressing these questions by looking at the scale of international trading, borrowing, and lending and at the way in which we keep our records of international transactions. These records are called the balance of payments accounts.

Balance of Payments Accounts

A country's **balance of payments accounts** records its international trading, borrowing, and lending in three accounts:

1. Current account
2. Capital account
3. Official settlements account

The **current account** records receipts from exports of goods and services sold abroad, payments for imports of goods and services from abroad, net interest income paid abroad, and net transfers (such as foreign aid payments). The *current account balance* equals the sum of exports minus imports, net interest income, and net transfers.

The **capital account** records foreign investment in the United States minus U.S. investment abroad. (This account also has a statistical discrepancy that arises from errors and omissions in measuring capital transactions.)

The **official settlements account** records the change in **U.S. official reserves**, which are the government's holdings of foreign currency. If U.S. official reserves *increase*, the official settlements account balance is *negative*. The reason is that holding foreign money is like investing abroad. U.S. investment abroad is a minus item in the capital account and in the official settlements account.

The sum of the balances on the three accounts always equals zero. That is, to pay for our current account deficit, either we must borrow more from abroad than we lend abroad or our official reserves must decrease to cover the shortfall.

Table 10.1 shows the U.S. balance of payments accounts in 2005. Items in the current account and

capital account that provide foreign currency to the United States have a plus sign; items that cost the United States foreign currency have a minus sign. The table shows that in 2005, U.S. imports exceeded U.S. exports and the current account had a deficit of $792 billion. How do we pay for imports that exceed the value of our exports? That is, how do we pay for our current account deficit?

We pay by borrowing from the rest of the world. The capital account tells us by how much. We borrowed $1,212 billion (foreign investment in the United States) but made loans of $444 billion (U.S. investment abroad). Our *net* foreign borrowing was $1,212 billion minus $444 billion, which equals $768 billion. There is almost always a statistical discrepancy between our capital account and current account transactions, and in 2005, the discrepancy was $10 billion. Combining the discrepancy with the measured net foreign borrowing gives a capital account balance of $778 billion.

TABLE 10.1   U.S. Balance of Payments Accounts in 2005

Current account	Billions of dollars
Exports of goods and services	+1,275
Imports of goods and services	−1,992
Net interest income	+11
Net transfers	−86
Current account balance	−792

Capital account	
Foreign investment in the United States	+1,212
U.S. investment abroad	−444
Statistical discrepancy	10
Capital account balance	+778

Official settlements account	
Official settlements account balance	14

Source of data: Bureau of Economic Analysis.

Our capital account balance plus our current account balance equals the change in U.S. official reserves. In 2005, our capital account balance of $778 billion plus our current balance of −$792 billion equaled −$14 billion. Our official reserves *decreased* in 2005 by $14 billion. This amount appears in Table 10.1 as +$14 billion. When our reserves *decrease*, we record this as a positive number in our international accounts because a decrease in our reserves is like borrowing from the rest of the world—the government decreases its deposits in foreign central banks.

The numbers in Table 10.1 give a snapshot of the balance of payments accounts in 2005. Figure 10.9 puts that snapshot into perspective by showing the balance of payments between 1980 and 2005. Because the economy grows and the price level rises, changes in the dollar value of the balance of payments do not convey much information. To remove the influences of growth and inflation, Fig. 10.9 shows the balance of payments as a percentage of nominal GDP.

As you can see, the capital account balance is almost a mirror image of the current account balance. The official settlements balance is very small in comparison with the balances on these other two

accounts. A large current account deficit (and capital account surplus) emerged during the 1980s but declined from 1987 to 1991. The current account deficit then increased every year through 2000, decreased slightly in 2001, and then increased again.

To see more clearly what the nation's balance of payments accounts mean, think about your own balance of payments accounts.

An Individual's Balance of Payments Accounts An individual's current account records the income from supplying the services of factors of production and the expenditure on goods and services. Consider Jackie, for example. She worked in 2005 and earned an income of $25,000. Jackie has $10,000 worth of investments that earned her an interest income of $1,000. Jackie's current account shows an income of $26,000. Jackie spent $18,000 buying goods and services for consumption. She also bought a new house, which cost her $60,000. So Jackie's total expenditure was $78,000. Jackie's expenditure minus her income is $52,000 ($78,000 minus $26,000). This amount is Jackie's current account deficit.

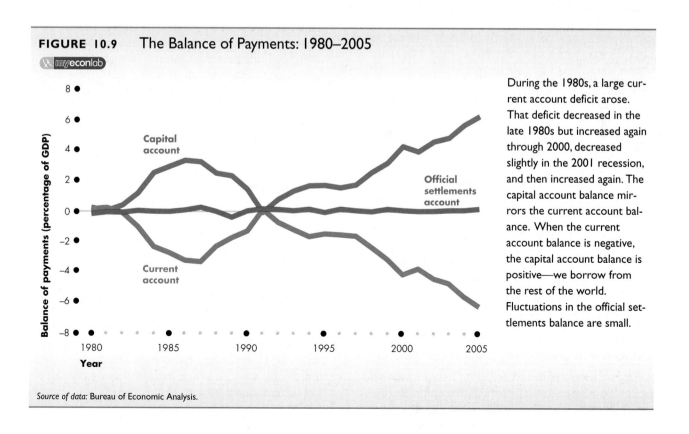

FIGURE 10.9   The Balance of Payments: 1980–2005

During the 1980s, a large current account deficit arose. That deficit decreased in the late 1980s but increased again through 2000, decreased slightly in the 2001 recession, and then increased again. The capital account balance mirrors the current account balance. When the current account balance is negative, the capital account balance is positive—we borrow from the rest of the world. Fluctuations in the official settlements balance are small.

Source of data: Bureau of Economic Analysis.

To pay for expenditure of $52,000 in excess of her income, Jackie must either use the money that she has in the bank or take out a loan. Suppose that Jackie took out a loan of $50,000 to help buy her house and that this loan was the only borrowing that she did. Borrowing is an *inflow* in the capital account, so Jackie's capital account *surplus* was $50,000. With a current account deficit of $52,000 and a capital account surplus of $50,000, Jackie was still $2,000 short. She got that $2,000 from her own bank account. Her cash holdings decreased by $2,000.

Jackie's income from her work is like a country's income from its exports. Her income from her investments is like a country's interest income from foreigners. Her purchases of goods and services, including her purchase of a house, are like a country's imports. Jackie's loan—borrowing from someone else—is like a country's borrowing from the rest of the world. The change in Jackie's bank account is like the change in the country's official reserves.

Borrowers and Lenders

A country that is borrowing more from the rest of the world than it is lending to the rest of the world is called a **net borrower**. Similarly, a **net lender** is a country that is lending more to the rest of the world than it is borrowing from the rest of the world.

The United States is a net borrower, but it has not always been in this situation. Throughout the 1960s and most of the 1970s, the United States was a net lender to the rest of the world—the United States had a current account surplus and a capital account deficit. But from the early 1980s, with the exception of only a single year, 1991, the United States has been a net borrower from the rest of the world. And during the years since 1992, the scale of U.S. borrowing has mushroomed.

Most countries are net borrowers like the United States. But a few countries, including China, Japan, and oil-rich Saudi Arabia, are net lenders. In 2005, when the United States borrowed almost $800 billion from the rest of the world, these three countries lent $400 billion. China alone lent $160 billion.

Debtors and Creditors

A net borrower might be decreasing its net assets held in the rest of the world, or it might be going deeper into debt. A nation's total stock of foreign investment determines whether it is a debtor or creditor. A **debtor nation** is a country that during its entire history has borrowed more from the rest of the world than it has lent to it. It has a stock of outstanding debt to the rest of the world that exceeds the stock of its own claims on the rest of the world. A **creditor nation** is a country that during its entire history has invested more in the rest of the world than other countries have invested in it.

The United States was a debtor nation through the nineteenth century as we borrowed from Europe to finance our westward expansion, railroads, and industrialization. We paid off our debt and became a creditor nation for most of the twentieth century. But following a string of current account deficits, we became a debtor nation again in 1986.

Since 1986, the total stock of U.S. borrowing from the rest of the world has exceeded U.S. lending to the rest of the world. The largest debtor nations are the capital-hungry developing countries (such as the United States was during the nineteenth century). The international debt of these countries grew from less than a third to more than a half of their gross domestic product during the 1980s and created what was called the "Third World debt crisis."

Should we be concerned that the United States is a net borrower and a debtor? The answer to this question depends mainly on what the net borrower is doing with the borrowed money. If borrowing is financing investment that in turn is generating economic growth and higher income, borrowing is not a problem. It earns a return that more than pays the interest. But if borrowed money is used to finance consumption, to pay the interest and repay the loan, consumption will eventually have to be reduced. In this case, the more the borrowing and the longer it goes on, the greater is the reduction in consumption that will eventually be necessary.

Is U.S. Borrowing for Consumption?

In 2005, we borrowed almost $800 billion from abroad. In that year, private investment in buildings, plant, and equipment was $2,270 billion and government investment in defense equipment and social projects was $430 billion. All this investment added to the nation's capital, and much of it increased productivity. Government also spends on education and health care services, which increase *human capital*. Our international borrowing is financing private and public investment, not consumption.

Current Account Balance

What determines a country's current account balance and net foreign borrowing? You've seen that net exports (*NX*) is the main item in the current account. We can define the current account balance (*CAB*) as

$$CAB = NX + \text{Net interest income} + \text{Net transfers.}$$

We can study the current account balance by looking at what determines net exports because the other two items are small and do not fluctuate much.

Net Exports

Net exports are determined by the government budget and private saving and investment. To see how net exports are determined, we need to recall some of the things that we learned about the *National Income and Product Accounts* in Chapter 5. Table 10.2 will refresh your memory and summarize some calculations.

Part (a) lists the national income variables that are needed, with their symbols. Part (b) defines three balances. **Net exports** is exports of goods and services minus imports of goods and services.

The **government sector surplus or deficit** is equal to net taxes minus government expenditures on goods and services. If that number is positive, a government sector surplus is lent to other sectors; if that number is negative, a government deficit must be financed by borrowing from other sectors. The government sector deficit is the sum of the deficits of the federal, state, and local governments.

The **private sector surplus or deficit** is saving minus investment. If saving exceeds investment, a private sector surplus is lent to other sectors. If investment exceeds saving, a private sector deficit is financed by borrowing from other sectors.

Part (b) also shows the values of these balances for the United States in 2006. As you can see, net exports were −$784 billion, a deficit of $784 billion. The government sector's revenue from net taxes was $2,161 billion, and government expenditure was $2,474 billion. The government sector deficit was $313 billion. The private sector saved $1,799 billion and invested $2,270 billion, so it had a deficit of $471 billion.

Part (c) shows the relationship among the three balances. From the *National Income and Product Accounts*, we know that real GDP, *Y*, is the sum of consumption expenditure (*C*), investment, government expenditures, and net exports. It also equals the

TABLE 10.2   Net Exports, the Government Budget, Saving, and Investment

	Symbols and equations	United States in 2006 (billions of dollars)
(a) Variables		
Exports*	X	1,395
Imports*	M	2,179
Government expenditures	G	2,474
Net taxes	T	2,161
Investment	I	2,270
Saving	S	1,799
(b) Balances		
Net exports	X − M	1,395 − 2,179 = −784
Government sector	T − G	2,161 − 2,474 = −313
Private sector	S − I	1,799 − 2,270 = −471
(c) Relationship among balances		
National accounts	$Y = C + I + G + X - M$	
	$= C + S + T$	
Rearranging:	$X - M = S - I + T - G$	
Net exports	X − M	−784
equals:		
Government sector	T − G	−313
plus		
Private sector	S − I	−471

Source of data: Bureau of Economic Analysis. The data are for 2006, second quarter, seasonally adjusted at annual rate.

* The *National Income and Product Accounts* measures of exports and imports are slightly different from the balance of payments accounts measures in Table 10.1 on p. 244.

sum of consumption expenditure, saving, and net taxes. Rearranging these equations tells us that net exports is the sum of the government sector deficit and the private sector deficit. In the United States in

2006, the government sector deficit was $313 billion and the private sector deficit was $471 billion. The government sector deficit plus the private sector deficit equaled net exports of −$784 billion.

The Three Sector Balances

You've seen that net exports equal the sum of the government sector balance and the private sector balance. How do these three sector balances fluctuate over time? Figure 10.10 answers this question. It shows the government sector balance (the red line), net exports (the blue line), and the private sector balance (the green line).

The private sector balance and the government sector balance move in opposite directions. When the government sector deficit increased during the late 1980s and early 1990s, the private sector surplus

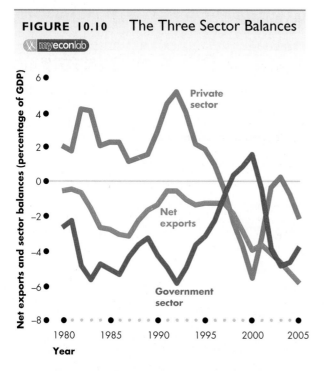

FIGURE 10.10   The Three Sector Balances

The private sector balance and the government sector balance tend to move in opposite directions. Net exports respond to the *sum* of the government sector and private sector balances. When the private sector and the government sector together are in deficit, that deficit is financed by net foreign borrowing.

Source of data: Bureau of Economic Analysis.

increased. And when the government sector deficit decreased and became a surplus during the 1990s and early 2000s, the private sector's surplus decreased and became a deficit.

Sometimes, when the government sector deficit increases, as it did during the first half of the 1980s, net exports become more negative. But after the early 1990s, net exports did not follow the government sector balance closely. Rather, net exports respond to the *sum* of the government sector and private sector balances. When both the private sector and the government sector have a deficit, net exports are negative and the combined private and government deficit is financed by borrowing from the rest of the world.

Where Is the Exchange Rate?

In explaining the current account balance, we have not mentioned the exchange rate. Doesn't the exchange rate play a role?

In the short run, a fall in the nominal exchange rate lowers the real exchange rate, which makes our imports more costly and our exports more competitive. A higher price of imported consumer goods might induce a decrease in consumption and an increase in saving. And a higher price of imported capital goods might induce a decrease in investment. Other things remaining the same, an increase in saving or a decrease in investment decreases the current account deficit.

But in the long run, a change in the nominal exchange rate leaves the real exchange rate and all other real variables unchanged. So in the long run, the nominal exchange rate plays no role in influencing the current account balance.

Exchange Rate Policy

Because the exchange rate is the price of a country's money in terms of another country's money, governments and central banks must have a policy toward the exchange rate. Three possible exchange rate policies are

- Flexible exchange rate
- Fixed exchange rate
- Crawling peg

Flexible Exchange Rate

A **flexible exchange rate** policy is one that permits the exchange rate to be determined by demand and supply with no direct intervention in the foreign exchange market by the central bank. Most countries —and the United States is among them—operate a flexible exchange rate, and the foreign exchange market that we have studied so far in this chapter is an example of a flexible exchange rate regime.

But even a flexible exchange rate is influenced by central bank actions. If the Fed raises the U.S. interest rate and other countries keep their interest rates unchanged, the demand for U.S. dollars increases, the supply of U.S. dollars decreases, and the exchange rate rises. (Similarly, if the Fed lowers the U.S. interest rate, the demand for U.S. dollars decreases, the supply increases, and the exchange rate falls.)

In a flexible exchange rate regime, when the central bank changes the interest rate, its purpose is not to influence the exchange rate. It is to achieve some other monetary policy objective. (We return to this topic at length in Chapter 15.)

Fixed Exchange Rate

A **fixed exchange rate** policy is one that pegs the exchange rate at a value decided by the government or central bank and that blocks the unregulated forces of demand and supply by direct intervention in the foreign exchange market. The world economy operated a fixed exchange rate regime from the end of World War II to the early 1970s. China had a fixed exchange rate until recently. And Hong Kong has had a fixed exchange rate for many years and continues with that policy today.

A fixed exchange rate requires active intervention in the foreign exchange market.

If the Fed wanted to fix the U.S. dollar exchange rate against the Japanese yen, the Fed would have to sell U.S. dollars to prevent the exchange rate from rising above the target value and buy U.S. dollars to prevent the exchange rate from falling below the target value.

There is no limit to the quantity of U.S. dollars that the Fed can *sell*. The Fed creates U.S. dollars and can create any quantity it chooses. But there is a limit to the quantity of U.S. dollars the Fed can *buy*. That limit is set by U.S. official holdings of foreign currency reserves. If reserves run dry, intervention to buy U.S. dollars would stop.

Let's look at the foreign exchange interventions that the Fed can make.

Suppose the Fed wants the exchange rate to be steady at 100 yen per U.S. dollar. If the exchange rate rises above 100 yen, the Fed sells dollars. If the exchange rate falls below 100 yen, the Fed buys dollars. By these actions, the Fed changes the supply of dollars and keeps the exchange rate close to its target rate of 100 yen per U.S dollar.

Figure 10.11 shows the Fed's intervention in the foreign exchange market. The supply of dollars is S and initially the demand for dollars is D_0. The equilibrium exchange rate is 100 yen per dollar. This exchange rate is also the Fed's target exchange rate, shown by the horizontal red line.

When the demand for U.S. dollars increases and the demand curve shifts rightward to D_1, the Fed sells $10 billion. This action increases the supply of U.S. dollars by $10 billion and prevents the exchange rate from rising. When the demand for U.S. dollars decreases and the demand curve shifts leftward to D_2, the Fed buys $10 billion. This action decreases the supply of U.S. dollars by $10 billion and prevents the exchange rate from falling.

If the demand for U.S. dollars fluctuates between D_1 and D_2 and on the average is D_0, the Fed can repeatedly intervene in the way we've just seen. Sometimes the Fed buys and sometimes it sells but, on the average, it neither buys nor sells.

But suppose the demand for U.S. dollars *increases permanently* from D_0 to D_1. To maintain the exchange rate at 100 yen per U.S. dollar, the Fed must sell dollars and buy foreign currency, so U.S. official foreign currency reserves would be increasing. At some point, the Fed would abandon the exchange rate of 100 yen per U.S. dollar and stop piling up foreign currency reserves.

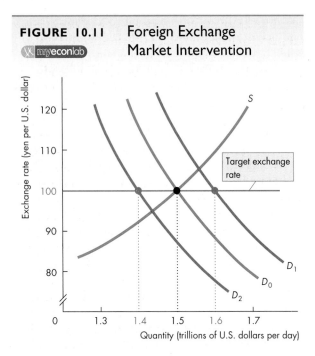

FIGURE 10.11   Foreign Exchange Market Intervention

Initially, the demand for U.S. dollars is D_0, the supply of U.S. dollars is S, and the exchange rate is 100 yen per U.S. dollar. The Fed can intervene in the foreign exchange market to keep the exchange rate close to its target rate (100 yen in this example). If demand increases from D_0 to D_1, the Fed sells dollars to increase supply. If demand decreases from D_0 to D_2, the Fed buys dollars to decrease supply. Persistent intervention on one side of the market cannot be sustained.

Now suppose the demand for U.S. dollars *decreases permanently* from D_0 to D_2. In this situation, the Fed *cannot* maintain the exchange rate at 100 yen per U.S. dollar indefinitely. To hold the exchange rate at 100 yen, the Fed must *buy* U.S. dollars. When the Fed buys U.S. dollars in the foreign exchange market, it uses U.S. official foreign currency reserves. So the Fed must decrease its foreign currency reserves. Eventually, the Fed would run out of foreign currency and would then have to abandon the 100 yen per U.S. dollar exchange rate.

Crawling Peg

A **crawling peg** exchange rate policy is one that selects a target path for the exchange rate with intervention in the foreign exchange market to achieve that path. The Fed has never operated a crawling peg. But some

prominent countries do use this system. When China abandoned its fixed exchange rate, it replaced it with a crawling peg. Several other developing countries use a crawling peg.

A crawling peg works like a fixed exchange rate except that the target value changes. Sometimes the target changes once a month, and sometimes it changes every day.

The idea behind a crawling peg is to prevent fluctuating expectations from making the exchange rate fluctuate and to avoid the problems that can occur with a fixed exchange rate of running out of reserves or piling up reserves. (A crawling peg is also sometimes used to control inflation, a role that we examine in Chapter 15, p. 386.)

The People's Bank of China in the Foreign Exchange Market

You saw in Fig. 10.1 that the exchange rate between the U.S. dollar and the Chinese yuan has been constant for several years. The reason for this near constant exchange rate is that China's central bank, the People's Bank of China, has intervened to operate a fixed exchange rate policy. From 1997 until 2005, the yuan was pegged at 8.28 yuan per U.S. dollar. Since 2005, the yuan has appreciated slightly but has not been permitted to fluctuate freely. Since 2005, the yuan has been on a crawling peg.

The immediate consequence of the fixed yuan exchange rate (and crawling exchange rate) is that since 2000, China has piled up U.S dollar reserves on a huge scale. By mid-2006, China's official foreign currency reserves approached $1 trillion!

Figure 10.12(a) shows the scale of China's increase in official foreign currency (mainly U.S. dollar) reserves. You can see that in 2004 and 2005, its reserves increased by $200 billion a year.

Figure 10.12(b) illustrates what is happening in the market for U.S. dollars priced in terms of the yuan and explains why China's reserves have increased. The demand curve D and supply curve S intersect at 5 yuan per U.S. dollar. If the People's Bank of China takes no actions in the foreign exchange market, this exchange rate is the equilibrium rate. (This particular value is only an example. No one knows what the yuan–U.S. dollar exchange rate would be with no intervention.)

By intervening in the foreign exchange market and buying U.S. dollars, the People's Bank pegs the

FIGURE 10.12 China's Foreign Exchange Market Intervention

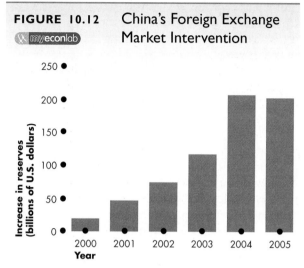

(a) Increase in U.S. dollar reserves

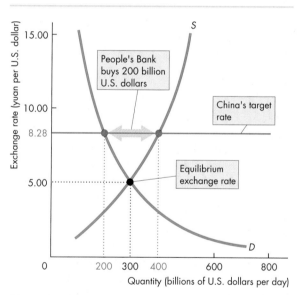

(b) Pegging the yuan

Part (a) shows the annual increase in China's reserves of U.S. dollars.

Part (b) shows the market for U.S. dollars in terms of the Chinese yuan. (Note that a higher exchange rate means a higher value of the U.S. dollar and a lower value of the yuan.) With demand curve *D* and supply curve *S*, the equilibrium exchange rate is below China's target exchange rate of 8.28 yuan per dollar. To keep the exchange rate pegged at its target level, the People's Bank of China must buy U.S. dollars and increase its foreign currency reserves.

yuan at 8.28 yuan per U.S. dollar. But to do so, it must keep piling up U.S. dollars. In Fig. 10.12(b), the People's Bank buys $200 billion a year.

If the People's Bank stops buying U.S. dollars and piling up U.S. dollar reserves, the U.S. dollar will depreciate and the yuan will appreciate.

Why Does China Fix Its Exchange Rate? The popular story is that China fixes its exchange rate to keep its export prices low and to make it easier to compete in world markets. You've seen that this story might have some truth in the short run. With prices in China and the rest of the world given, a low yuan–U.S. dollar exchange rate brings lower U.S. dollar prices for China's exports. But the yuan–U.S. dollar exchange rate has been fixed for almost 10 years. This long period of a fixed exchange rate has long-run, not short-run, effects. And in the long run, the exchange rate has no effect on competitiveness. The reason is that prices adjust to reflect the exchange rate and the real exchange rate is unaffected by the nominal exchange rate.

So why does China fix its exchange rate? The more convincing answer is that China sees a fixed exchange rate as a way of achieving a low inflation rate. By fixing the yuan against the U.S. dollar, China's inflation rate is anchored to the U.S. inflation rate and will not wander too far from that rate.

Similarly, countries that use a crawling peg keep their inflation rates close to that of the country against which they crawl. The bottom line is that exchange rate policy is monetary policy, not balance of payments policy. To change its balance of payments, a country must change its saving and investment.

Reading Between the Lines on pp. 252–253 looks further at China's exchange rate policy.

REVIEW QUIZ

1 What is a flexible exchange rate and how does it work?
2 What is a fixed exchange rate and how does it get fixed?
3 What is a crawling peg and how does it work?
4 How has China operated in the foreign exchange market, why, and with what effect?

myeconlab Study Plan 10.5

The Sinking Dollar

http://www.nytimes.com

Bush Aides Struggling with Yuan

May 10, 2006

After nearly three years of pushing China to let its currency float more freely, with only modest results, the Bush administration still appears reluctant to accuse China of manipulating its exchange rate. ...

American manufacturers and many members of Congress have complained for years that China has kept its currency, the yuan, at an artificially low exchange rate to the dollar as a way of selling its exports at cheap prices.

Treasury Secretary John W. Snow has resisted demands to threaten Beijing, arguing that Chinese leaders are making "progress" toward a more flexible exchange rate and a more open financial system.

This week, a Treasury official again emphasized China's steps toward openness.

"If you look at what China is doing in exercising their commitment on putting in place a foreign-exchange regime that has greater flexibility," Mr. Snow's principal spokesman, Tony Fratto, told reporters on Monday, "you see some evidence that they're doing that."

But changes in the yuan's value have been relatively minor. Chinese leaders let the yuan climb about 2 percent against the dollar last July, and another similarly small amount more recently.

When President Hu Jintao visited President Bush in Washington last month, top Chinese officials re-emphasized a need for "stability" and offered no hint of when they might let the yuan move more freely. ...

The United States' trade deficit with China ballooned to $202 billion in 2005, an imbalance that might ordinarily have pushed up the value of the yuan in relation to the dollar. China has prevented the yuan from rising by buying hundreds of billions in dollar-denominated reserves. ...

Essence of the Story

▶ U.S. producers and members of Congress complain that China has kept the yuan artificially low to sell exports at low prices.

▶ Treasury Secretary John W. Snow says that China is moving toward a more flexible exchange rate.

▶ Changes in the yuan–dollar exchange rate have been small.

▶ The yuan appreciated in July 2005 and by small amounts more recently.

▶ The U.S. trade deficit with China was $202 billion in 2005.

▶ This imbalance should have pushed up the value of the yuan, but China prevented that from happening and increased its U.S. dollar reserves.

▶ China's exchange rate was pegged at 8.28 yuan per U.S. dollar until July 2005.

▶ In July 2005, the yuan was appreciated (the dollar depreciated) by 2.1 percent.

▶ Since July 2005, the yuan has persistently but slowly risen against the dollar (the dollar has fallen against the yuan).

▶ Figure 1 shows the path of the falling dollar against the yuan.

▶ To peg the yuan before July 2005 and to keep the exchange rate from rising more than it wants, the People's Bank of China buys U.S. dollars in the foreign exchange market.

▶ The result of these foreign exchange market transactions has been a strong growth in reserves.

▶ Figure 2 shows the buildup of China's reserves, which, by 2006, were almost $1 trillion.

▶ Americans are concerned about the yuan because China has a large trade surplus with the United States.

▶ But China's overall current account surplus is not large and is a fraction of the large U.S. current account deficit.

▶ Figure 3 shows the U.S. current account deficit and China's current account surplus.

▶ The analysis in this chapter explains that a current account deficit results from too little private and government saving relative to investment.

▶ China saves more than it invests, and the United States invests more than it saves.

▶ A change in the nominal exchange rate between the U.S. dollar and the Chinese yuan cannot make a large contribution to changing these imbalances.

▶ The main effect of the appreciation of the yuan will be to slow China's inflation rate relative to the the U.S. inflation rate.

You're the Voter

▶ Do you think the United States should pressure China to raise the value of the yuan substantially?

▶ Do you think it would be in China's interest to raise the value of the yuan substantially?

▶ How would a substantially higher valued yuan affect world trade?

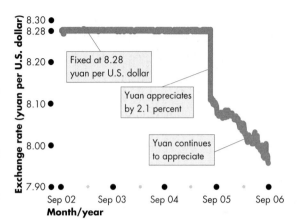

Figure 1 The yuan–U.S. dollar exchange rate

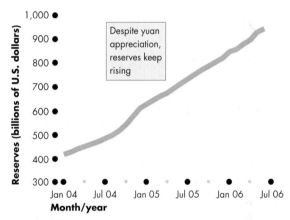

Figure 2 China's reserves pile up

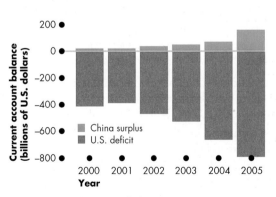

Figure 3 Current account balances

SUMMARY

Key Points

Currencies and Exchange Rates (pp. 232–234)

- Foreign currency is obtained in exchange for domestic currency in the foreign exchange market.
- The nominal exchange rate is the value of one currency in terms of another currency.
- The real exchange rate is the price of one country's real GDP in terms of another country's real GDP.

The Foreign Exchange Market (pp. 235–238)

- Demand and supply in the foreign exchange market determine the exchange rate.
- The higher the exchange rate, the smaller is the quantity of U.S. dollars demanded and the greater is the quantity of U.S. dollars supplied.
- The equilibrium exchange rate makes the quantity of U.S. dollars demanded equal the quantity of U.S. dollars supplied.

Changes in Demand and Supply: Exchange Rate Fluctuations (pp. 239–243)

- Changes in the the world demand for U.S. exports, the U.S. interest rate differential, or the expected future exchange rate change the demand for U.S. dollars.
- Changes in U.S. demand for imports, the U.S. interest rate differential, or the expected future exchange rate change the supply of U.S. dollars.
- Exchange rate expectations are influenced by purchasing power parity and interest rate parity.
- In the long run, the nominal exchange rate is a monetary phenomenon and the real exchange rate is independent of the nominal exchange rate.

Financing International Trade (pp. 244–248)

- International trade, borrowing, and lending are financed by using foreign currency.
- A country's international transactions are recorded in its current account, capital account, and official settlements account.
- The current account balance is similar to net exports and is determined by the government sector balance plus the private sector balance.

Exchange Rate Policy (pp. 249–251)

- An exchange rate can be flexible, fixed, or a crawling peg.
- To achieve a fixed or a crawling exchange rate, a central bank must intervene in the foreign exchange market and either buy or sell foreign currency.

Key Figures and Table

Key Terms

PROBLEMS

myeconlab Tests, Study Plan, Solutions*

1. The U.S. dollar exchange rate decreased from $1.30 Canadian in 2004 to $1.21 Canadian in 2005, and it increased from 108.15 Japanese yen in 2004 to 110.11 Japanese yen in 2005.
   a. Did the U.S. dollar appreciate or depreciate against of the Canadian dollar?
   b. Did the U.S. dollar appreciate or depreciate against of the Japanese yen?
   c. What was the value of the Canadian dollar in terms of U.S. dollars in 2004 and 2005?
   d. What was the value of 100 Japanese yen in terms of U.S. dollars in 2004 and 2005?
   e. Did the Canadian dollar appreciate or depreciate against the U.S. dollar in 2005?
   f. Did the Japanese yen appreciate or depreciate against the U.S. dollar in 2005?

2. In 2004, the price level in the Eurozone is 112.4, the price level in the United States was 109.1, and the nominal exchange rate was 80 euro cents per U.S. dollar. What was the real exchange rate expressed as Eurozone real GDP per unit of U.S. real GDP?

3. In 2003, the price level in the United States was 106.3, the price level in Japan was 95.4, and the real exchange rate expressed as Japan real GDP per unit of U.S. real GDP was 103.6. What is the nominal exchange rate?

4. There is a large increase in the global demand for roses and Colombia is the biggest producer of roses. At the same time, the central bank of Colombia increases the interest rate. What happens in the foreign exchange market for Colombian pesos to
   a. The demand for pesos?
   b. The supply of pesos?
   c. The quantity of pesos demanded?
   d. The quantity of pesos supplied?
   e. The exchange rate of the pesos against the U.S. dollar?

5. In 2002, a euro deposit in a bank in Paris, France, earns interest of 2.8 percent a year and a yen deposit in Tokyo, Japan, earns 0.036 percent a year. Everything else remaining the same and adjusted for risk, what is the exchange rate expectation of the Japanese yen?

*Solutions to odd-numbered problems are provided.

6. The U.K. pound is trading at 1.82 U.S. dollars per U.K. pound. There is purchasing power parity at this exchange rate. The interest rate in the United States is 2.5 percent a year and the interest rate in the United Kingdom is 3 percent a year.
   a. Calculate the U.S. interest rate differential.
   b. What is the U.K. pound expected to be worth in terms of U.S. dollars one year from now?
   c. Which country more likely has the lower inflation rate? How can you tell?

7. You can purchase a laptop in Mexico City for 12,960 Mexican pesos. If the exchange rate is 10.8 Mexican pesos per U.S. dollar and if purchasing power parity prevails, at what price can you buy an identical computer in Dallas, Texas?

8. The table gives some information about the U.S. international transactions in 2003.

Item	Billions of dollars
Imports of goods and services	1,487
Foreign investment in the United States	1,051
Exports of goods and services	990
U.S. investment abroad	456
Net interest income	7
Net transfers	–68
Statistical discrepancy	–36

   a. Calculate the current account balance.
   b. Calculate the capital account balance.
   c. Are U.S. official reserves increasing or decreasing?
   d. Was the United States a net borrower or a net lender in 2003? Explain your answer.

9. The table gives some information about the U.K. economy in 2003:

Item	Billions of U.K. pounds
Consumption expenditure	721
Exports of goods and services	277
Government expenditures	230
Net taxes	217
Investment	181
Saving	162

   a. Calculate the private sector balance.
   b. Calculate the government sector balance.
   c. Calculate net exports.
   d. What is the relationship between the government sector balance and net exports?

10. A country's currency appreciates, and its official holdings of foreign currency increase. What can you say about:
   a. The central bank's intervention in the foreign exchange market?
   b. The country's current account balance?
   c. The country's official settlements account?

11. A country has a lower inflation rate than all other countries. It has more rapid economic growth. The central bank does not intervene in the foreign exchange market. What can you say (and why) about:
   a. The exchange rate?
   b. The current account balance?
   c. The expected exchange rate?
   d. The interest rate differential?
   e. Interest rate parity?
   f. Purchasing power parity?

CRITICAL THINKING

1. Study *Reading Between the Lines* on pp. 252–253 and then answer the following questions.
   a. Do you think the yuan is a problem for Americans or the source of the U.S. current account deficit?
   b. Do you think that yuan appreciation can help the United States to get rid of its current account deficit?
   c. What do you predict would be the main effects of an increase in the yuan–U.S. dollar exchange rate?
   d. What, if anything, could U.S. policy do to reduce the U.S. current account deficit?

2. **The lesson: Buy Ruffles in Myanmar**
   . . . A small bag of cheese-flavored Ruffles potato chips is $1.69 in Japan and only 8 cents in Myanmar. A plain white T-shirt costs $16 in a mall in Cape Town, South Africa, and . . . The price of spending 1 hour at an Internet cafe in Vietnam is $0.62 U.S., in China is $1.48 U.S., and in South Africa is $3.40 U.S.

   The Los Angeles Times, April 23, 2006

   Do these prices indicate that purchasing power parity does not prevail? Why or why not?

3. The *Economist* magazine uses the price of a Big Mac to determine whether a currency is undervalued or overvalued. In May 2006, the price of a Big Mac was $3.10 in New York, 10.5 yuan in Beijing, and 6.30 Swiss francs in Geneva. The exchanges rates were 8.03 yuan per U.S. dollar and 1.21 Swiss francs per U.S. dollar.
   a. Was the yuan undervalued or overvalued relative to purchasing power parity?
   b. Was the Swiss franc undervalued or overvalued relative to purchasing power parity?
   c. Do you think the price of a Big Mac in different countries provides a valid test of purchasing power parity?

WEB ACTIVITIES
myeconlab Links to Web sites

1. Visit PACIFIC (an exchange rate service) and read the page on purchasing power parity.
   a. What is purchasing power parity?
   b. Which currencies are the most overvalued relative to the U.S. dollar today?
   c. Which currencies are the most undervalued relative to the U.S. dollar today?
   d. Can you offer some suggestions as to why some currencies are overvalued and some are undervalued?
   e. Do you think that the information on overvaluation and undervaluation is useful to currency speculators? Why or why not?

2. Visit the Bureau of Economic Analysis and find data on the U.S. balance of payments accounts.
   a. When did the United States last have a current account surplus?
   b. Does the United States have a surplus or a deficit in trade in goods?
   c. Does the United States have a surplus or a deficit in trade in services?
   d. What has happened to foreign investment in the United States during the past 10 years?
   e. Do you think the U.S. balance of payments record is a matter for concern? Why or why not?

Expanding the Frontier

Economics is about how we cope with scarcity. We cope as individuals by making choices that balance marginal benefits and marginal costs so that we use our scarce resources efficiently. We cope as societies by creating incentive systems and social institutions that encourage specialization and exchange.

These choices and the incentive systems that guide them determine what we specialize in; how much work we do; how hard we work at school to learn the mental skills that form our human capital and that determine the kinds of jobs we get and the incomes we earn; how much we save for future big-ticket expenditures; how much businesses and governments spend on new capital—on auto assembly lines, computers and fiber cables for improved Internet services, shopping malls, highways, bridges, and tunnels; how intensively existing capital and natural resources are used and how quickly they wear out or are used up; and the problems that scientists, engineers, and other inventors work on to develop new technologies.

All the choices we've just described combine to determine the standard of living and the rate at which it improves—the economic growth rate.

Economic growth, maintained at a steady rate over a number of decades, is the single most powerful influence on any society. It brings a transformation that continues to amaze thoughtful people. Maintained at a rapid rate, economic growth transforms a society in years, not decades. Such transformations are taking place right now in many Asian countries. These transformations are economic miracles.

The first two chapters in this part dealt with the standard of living and the miracle of rapid economic growth. Chapter 7 explained how potential GDP and the full-employment quantity of labor, employment, and unemployment are determined by equilibrium in the labor market. This chapter also explained how capital accumulation results from saving and investment decisions that are coordinated in the capital market. Chapter 8 studied the process of economic growth in the fast-growing economies of Asia and the United States. It explained how growth is influenced by technological change and the incentives that stimulate it.

Money that makes possible specialization and exchange in markets is a huge contributor to economic growth. But too much money brings a rising cost of living with no improvement in the standard of living.

The second two chapters in this part explained the role of money and its influence on the price level and the exchange rate. Chapter 9 explained exactly what money is, how banks create it, how the Federal Reserve influences its quantity, and how in the long run, the quantity of money influences the price level. Chapter 10 broadens the canvas and looks at the world of many moneys: their exchange rates and the deficits and surpluses that arise from international trade and investment.

Incentives to Innovate, Save, and Invest

"Economic progress, in capitalist society, means turmoil."

JOSEPH SCHUMPETER
Capitalism, Socialism, and Democracy

The Economist

Joseph Schumpeter, *the son of a textile factory owner, was born in Austria in 1883. He moved from Austria to Germany during the tumultuous 1920s when those two countries experienced hyperinflation. In 1932, in the depths of the Great Depression, he came to the United States and became a professor of economics at Harvard University.*

This creative economic thinker wrote about economic growth and development, business cycles, political systems, and economic biography. He was a person of strong opinions who expressed them strongly and delighted in verbal battles.

Schumpeter has become the unwitting founder of modern growth theory. He saw the development and diffusion of new technologies by profit-seeking entrepreneurs as the source of economic progress. But he saw economic progress as a process of creative destruction—the creation of new profit opportunities and the destruction of currently profitable businesses. For Schumpeter, economic growth and the business cycle were a single phenomenon.

When Schumpeter died, in 1950, he had achieved his self-expressed life ambition: He was regarded as the world's greatest economist.

The Issues

Technological change, capital accumulation, and population growth all interact to produce economic growth. But what is cause and what is effect? And can we expect productivity and income per person to keep growing?

The classical economists of the eighteenth and nineteenth centuries believed that technological advances and capital accumulation were the engines of growth. But they also believed that no matter how successful people were at inventing more productive technologies and investing in new capital, they were destined to live at the subsistence level. These economists based their conclusion on the belief that productivity growth causes population growth, which in turn causes productivity to decline. These classical economists believed that whenever economic growth raises incomes above the subsistence level, the population will increase. They went on to reason that the increase in population brings diminishing returns that lower productivity. As a result, incomes must always return to the subsistence level. Only when incomes are at the subsistence level is population growth held in check.

A new approach, called neoclassical growth theory, was developed by Robert Solow of MIT, during the 1950s. Solow, who was one of Schumpeter's students, received the Nobel Prize for Economic Science for this work.

Solow challenged the conclusions of the classical economists. But the new theories of economic growth that were developed during the 1980s and 1990s went further. They stand the classical belief on its head. Today's theory of population growth is that rising income slows the population growth rate because it increases the opportunity cost of having children and lowers the opportunity cost of investing in children and equipping them with more human capital, which makes them more productive. Productivity and income grow because technology advances, and the scope for further productivity growth, which is stimulated by the search for profit, is practically unlimited.

Then

In 1830, a strong and experienced farm worker could harvest three acres of wheat in a day. The only capital employed was a scythe to cut the wheat, which had been used since Roman times, and a cradle on which the stalks were laid, which had been invented by Flemish farmers in the fifteenth century. With newly developed horse-drawn plows, harrows, and planters, farmers could plant more wheat than they could harvest. But despite big efforts, no one had been able to make a machine that could replicate the swing of a scythe. Then in 1831, 22-year-old Cyrus McCormick built a machine that worked. It scared the horse that pulled it, but it did in a matter of hours what three men could accomplish in a day. Technological change has increased productivity on farms and brought economic growth. Do the facts about productivity growth mean that the classical economists, who believed that diminishing returns would push us relentlessly back to a subsistence living standard, were wrong?

Now

Today's technologies are expanding our horizons beyond the confines of our planet and are expanding our minds. Geosynchronous satellites bring us global television, voice and data communication, and more accurate weather forecasts, which, incidentally, increase agricultural productivity. In the foreseeable future, we might have superconductors that revolutionize the use of electric power, virtual reality theme parks and training facilities, pollution-free hydrogen cars, wristwatch telephones, and optical computers that we can talk to. Equipped with these new technologies, our ability to create yet more dazzling technologies increases. Technological change begets technological change in an (apparently) unending process and makes us ever more productive and brings ever higher incomes.

Several people have contributed to today's revolution in the way economists think about economic growth. Xavier Sala-i-Martin, a professor of economics at Columbia University, whom you can meet on the following pages, is one of them.

Xavier Sala-i-Martin

Xavier Sala-i-Martin is Professor of Economics at Columbia University. He is also a Research Associate at the National Bureau of Economic Research, Senior Economic Advisor to the World Economic Forum, Associate Editor of the Journal of Economic Growth, *founder and CEO of Umbele Foundation: A Future for Africa, and President of the Economic Commission of the Barcelona football club.*

Professor Sala-i-Martin was an undergraduate at Universitat Autonoma de Barcelona and a graduate student at Harvard University, where he obtained his Ph.D. in 1990.

In 2004, he was awarded the Premio Juan Carlos I de Economía, a biannual prize given by the Bank of Spain to the best economist in Spain and Latin America.

With Robert Barro, he is the author of Economic Growth Second Edition *(MIT Press, 2003), the definitive graduate level text on this topic.*

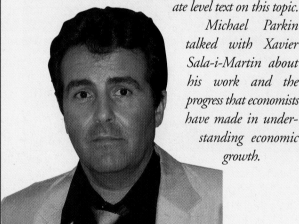

Michael Parkin talked with Xavier Sala-i-Martin about his work and the progress that economists have made in understanding economic growth.

What attracted you to economics?

It was a random event. I wanted to be rich, so I asked my mom, "In my family, who is the richest guy?" She said, "Your uncle John." And I asked, "What did he study?" And she said, "Economics." So I went into economics!

In Spain, there are no liberal arts colleges where you can study lots of things. At age 18, you must decide what career you will follow. If you choose economics, you go to economics school and take economics five years in a row. So you have to make a decision in a crazy way, like I did.

How did economic growth become your major field of research?

I studied economics. I liked it. I studied mathematical economics. I liked it too, and I went to graduate school. In my second year at Harvard, Jeffrey Sachs hired me to go to Bolivia. I saw poor people for the first time in my life. I was shocked. I decided I should try to answer the question "Why are these people so poor and why are we so rich, and what can we do to turn their state into our state?" We live in a bubble world in the United States and Europe, and we don't realize how poor people really are. When you see poverty at first hand, it is very hard to think about something else. So I decided to study economic growth. Coincidentally, when I returned from Bolivia, I was assigned to be Robert Barro's teaching assistant He was teaching economic growth, so I studied with him and eventually wrote books and articles with him.

In your first research on economic growth, you tested the neoclassical growth model using data for a number of countries and for the states of the United States. What did you discover?

Neoclassical theory was criticized on two grounds. First, its source of growth, technological change, is exogenous—not explained. Second, its assumption of diminishing marginal returns to capital seems to imply that income per person should converge to the same level in every country. If you are poor, your marginal product should be high. Every cookie that you save should generate huge growth. If you are rich, your marginal product should be low. Every cookie you save should generate very little growth. Therefore poor countries should grow faster than rich countries, and convergence of income levels should occur. Convergence doesn't occur, so, said its critics, neoclassical theory must be wrong.

It turned out that it was this criticism that was wrong. Growth depends on the productivity of your cookies and on how many cookies you save. If you don't save any cookies, you don't grow, even if your marginal product is large.

Conditional convergence is the idea that income per person will converge only if countries have similar savings rates, similar technologies, and similar everything. That's what I tested. To hold every relevant factor equal, I tested the hypothesis using regions: states within the United States or countries that are similar. And once you're careful to hold other things equal, you see a perfect negative relationship between growth rates and income levels.

As predicted by neoclassical theory, poor countries grow faster than rich countries if they are similar. So my research shows that it is not so easy to reject neoclassical theory. The law of diminishing returns that comes from Adam Smith and Malthus and Ricardo is very powerful. Growth through capital accumulation is very, very hard. Growth has to come from other things, such as technological change.

> Growth through capital accumulation is very, very hard. Growth has to come from other things, such as technological change.

What do we know today about the nature and causes of the wealth of nations that Adam Smith didn't know?

Actually, even though over the last two hundred years some of the best minds have looked at the question, we know surprisingly little. We have some general principles that are not very easy to apply in practice. We know, for example, that markets are good. We know that for the economy to work, we need property rights to be guaranteed. If there are thieves—government or private thieves—that can steal the proceeds of the investment, there's no invest-ment and there's no growth. We know that the incentives are very important.

These are general principles. Because we know these principles we should ask: How come Africa is still poor? The answer is, it is very hard to translate "Markets are good" and "Property rights work" into practical actions. We know that Zimbabwe has to guarantee property rights. With the government it has, that's not going to work. The U.S. constitution works in the United States. If you try to copy the constitution and impose the system in Zimbabwe, it's not going to work.

You've done a lot of work on distribution of income, and you say we've made a lot of progress. What is the evidence to support this conclusion?

There are two issues: poverty and inequality. When in 2001 I said poverty is going down, everyone said I was crazy. The United Nations Development Report, which uses World Bank data, was saying the exact opposite. I said the World Bank methodology was flawed. After a big public argument that you can see in *The Economist*, the World Bank revised their poverty numbers and they now agree with me that poverty rates are falling.

Now why is poverty falling? In 1970, 80 percent of the world's poor were in Asia—in China, India, Bangladesh, and Indonesia. China's "Great Leap Forward" was a great leap backward. People were starving to death. Now, the growth of these countries has been spectacular and the global poverty rate has fallen. Yes, if you look at Africa, Africa is going backwards. But Africa has 700 million people. China has 1.3 billion. India has 1.1 billion. Indonesia has 300 million. Asia has 4 billion of the world's 6 billion people. These big guys are growing. It's impossible that global poverty is not going down.

But what we care about is poverty in different regions of the world. Asia has been doing very well, but Africa has not. Unfortunately, Africa is still going in the wrong direction.

You've made a big personal commitment to Africa. What is the Africa problem? Why does this continent lag behind Asia? Why, as you've just put it, is Africa going in the wrong direction?

Number one, Africa is a very violent continent. There are twenty-two wars in Africa as we speak. Two, nobody will invest in Africa. Three, we in the rich world—the United States, Europe, and Japan—won't let them trade. Because we have agricultural subsidies, trade barriers, and tariffs for their products, they can't sell to us.

Africans should globalize themselves. They should open, and we should let them open. They should introduce markets. But to get markets, you need legal systems, police, transparency, less red tape. You need a lot of the things we have now. They have corrupt economies, very bureaucratic, with no property rights, the judiciary is corrupt. All of that has to change.

They need female education. One of the biggest rates of return that we have is educating girls. To educate girls, they'll need to build schools, they need to pay teachers, they need to buy uniforms, they need to provide the incentives for girls to go to school, which usually is like a string. You pull it, you don't push it. Pushing education doesn't work. What you need is: Let the girls know that the rate of return on education is very high by providing jobs after they leave school. So you need to change the incentives of the girls to go to school and educate themselves. That's going to increase the national product, but it will also increase health, and it will also reduce fertility.

Question! Question everything!

Returning to the problems of poverty and inequality, how can inequality be increasing within countries but decreasing globally— across countries?

Because most inequality comes from the fact that some people live in rich countries and some people live in poor countries. The big difference across people is not that there are rich Americans and poor Americans. Americans are very close to each other relative to the difference between Americans and people from Senegal. What is closing today is the gap *across* countries—and for the first time in history. Before the Industrial Revolution, everybody was equal. Equal and poor. Equally poor. People were living at subsistence levels, which means you eat, you're clothed, you have a house, you die. No movies, no travel, no music, no toothbrush. Just subsist. And if the weather is not good, one third of the population dies. That was the history of the world between 10,000 B.C. and today.

Yes, there was a king, there was Caesar, but the majority of the population were peasants.

All of a sudden, the Industrial Revolution means that one small country, England, takes off and there is 2 percent growth every year. The living standard of the workers of England goes up and up and up. Then the United States, then France, then the rest of Europe, then Canada all begin to grow.

In terms of today's population, one billion people become rich and five billion remain poor. Now for the first time in history, the majority of these five billion people are growing more rapidly than the rich guys. They're catching up quickly. The incomes of the majority of poor citizens of the world are growing faster than those of Americans.

What advice do you have for someone who is just beginning to study economics?

Question! Question everything! Take some courses in history and math. And read my latest favorite book, Bill Easterly's *White Man's Burden.** It shows why we have not been doing the right thing in the aid business. I'm a little bit less dramatic than he is. He says that nothing has worked. I think some things have worked, and we have to take advantage of what has worked to build on it. But I agree with the general principle that being nice, being good, doesn't necessarily mean doing good. Lots of people with good intentions do harm. Economic science teaches us that incentives are the key.

*William Easterly, *The White Man's Burden: Why the West's Efforts to Aid the Rest Have Done So Much Ill and So Little Good*. New York, Penguin Books, 2006.

Aggregate Supply and Aggregate Demand

Production and Prices

Production grows and prices rise. But the pace at which production grows and prices rise is uneven. In 1997, measured by real GDP, production grew by 4.5 percent. At this growth rate, real GDP doubles

in about 16 years. But in 2001, growth slowed to less than 1 percent, a rate that takes about 70 years for real GDP to double!

Similarly, during recent years, prices have increased at rates ranging from less than 2 percent to almost 4 percent. An inflation rate of 2 percent a year is barely noticed. But at 4 percent a year, inflation becomes a problem, not least because people begin to wonder where it is heading next.

The uneven pace of economic growth and inflation—the business cycle—is the subject of this chapter and the two that follow it. Here, you will discover the forces that bring fluctuations in the pace of real GDP growth and inflation and associated fluctuations in employment and unemployment.

◆ This chapter explains a *model* of real GDP and the price level—the *aggregate supply–aggregate demand model* or *AS-AD model*. This model represents the consensus view of macroeconomists on how real GDP and the price level are determined. The model provides a framework for understanding the forces that make our economy expand, that bring inflation, and that cause business cycle fluctuations. The *AS-AD* model also provides a framework within which we can see the range of views of macroeconomists in different schools of thought.

After studying this chapter, you will be able to

▶ Distinguish between the macroeconomic long run and short run

▶ Explain what determines aggregate supply

▶ Explain what determines aggregate demand

▶ Explain how real GDP and the price level are determined and how changes in aggregate supply and aggregate demand bring economic growth, inflation, and the business cycle

▶ Describe the main schools of thought in macroeconomics today

The Macroeconomic Long Run and Short Run

The economy is constantly bombarded by events that move real GDP away from potential GDP and employment away from full employment. Natural shocks, such as Hurricane Katrina, and shocks that are born from a clash of cultures and ideologies, such as terrorist attacks, lower real GDP and employment and send the unemployment rate above the natural rate. Technological shocks, such as the discovery and widespread application of computer and related information technologies, raise real GDP and employment and lower the unemployment rate.

Whatever the source of a shock or its direction, once it hits, real GDP and employment begin an adjustment process. In the previous part (in Chapters 7 through 10), we ignored the shocks that hit the economy and studied the long run. The long run is like an anchor point around which the economy tosses and turns like a boat on an ocean. We're now going to study those tosses and turns. But first, let's be clear about the distinction between the macroeconomic long run and short run.

The Macroeconomic Long Run

The **macroeconomic long run** is a time frame that is sufficiently long for the real wage rate to have adjusted to achieve full employment: real GDP equals potential GDP, unemployment is at the natural rate, the price level is proportional to the quantity of money, and the inflation rate equals the money growth rate minus the real GDP growth rate.

The Macroeconomic Short Run

The **macroeconomic short run** is a period during which some *money* prices are sticky so that real GDP might be below, above, or at potential GDP and the unemployment rate might be above, below, or at the natural unemployment rate.

The aggregate supply–aggregate demand model that you are about to study explains the behavior of real GDP and the price level in the short run. It also explains how the economy adjusts to eventually restore long-run equilibrium and full employment.

We'll begin by learning about aggregate supply.

myeconlab **Study Plan 11.1**

Aggregate Supply

The *quantity of real GDP supplied* (Y) is the total quantity that firms plan to produce during a given period. This quantity depends on the quantity of labor employed; the quantity of capital, both physical and human; and the state of technology.

At any given time, the quantity of capital and the state of technology are fixed. They depend on decisions that were made in the past. The population is also fixed. But the quantity of labor is not fixed. It depends on decisions made by people and firms about the supply of and demand for labor.

The labor market can be in any one of three states: at full employment, above full employment, or below full employment.

The quantity of real GDP at full employment is *potential GDP*, which depends on the full-employment quantity of labor, the quantity of capital, and the state of technology (see Chapter 7, pp. 165–166). Over the business cycle, employment fluctuates around full employment and real GDP fluctuates around potential GDP.

To study aggregate supply in different states of the labor market, we distinguish two time frames for aggregate supply:

- Long-run aggregate supply
- Short-run aggregate supply

Long-Run Aggregate Supply

Long-run aggregate supply is the relationship between the quantity of real GDP supplied and the price level in the long run when real GDP equals potential GDP. The long-run aggregate supply curve in Fig. 11.1 illustrates this relationship.

The long-run aggregate supply curve is the vertical line at potential GDP labeled *LAS*. Along the long-run aggregate supply curve, as the price level changes, real GDP remains at potential GDP, which in Fig. 11.1 is $12 trillion. The long-run aggregate supply curve is always vertical and is always located at potential GDP.

The long-run aggregate supply curve is vertical because potential GDP is independent of the price level. The reason for this independence is that a movement along the *LAS* curve is accompanied by a change in *two* sets of prices: the prices of goods and

FIGURE 11.1 Long-Run Aggregate Supply

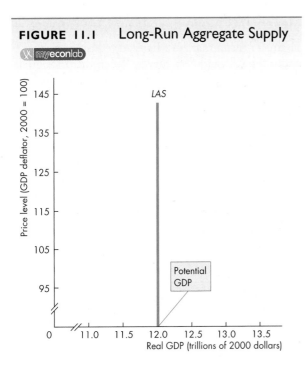

The long-run aggregate supply curve (LAS) shows the relationship between potential GDP and the price level. Potential GDP is independent of the price level, so the LAS curve is vertical at potential GDP.

services—the price level—and the prices of the factors of production, most notably, the money wage rate. A 10 percent increase in the prices of goods and services is matched by a 10 percent increase in the money wage rate. Because the price level and the money wage rate change by the same percentage, the *real wage rate* remains constant at its full-employment equilibrium level. So when the price level changes and the real wage rate remains constant, employment remains constant and real GDP remains constant at potential GDP.

Production at a Pepsi Plant You can see more clearly why real GDP remains constant when all prices change by the same percentage by thinking about production decisions at a Pepsi bottling plant. The plant is producing the quantity of Pepsi that maximizes profit. If the price of Pepsi and the wage rate of workers at the bottling plant rise by the same percentage, the firm has no incentive to change production.

Short-Run Aggregate Supply

Short-run aggregate supply is the relationship between the quantity of real GDP supplied and the price level when the money wage rate, the prices of other resources, and potential GDP remain constant. The short-run aggregate supply curve in Fig. 11.2 illustrates this relationship as the short-run aggregate supply curve *SAS* and the short-run aggregate supply schedule. Each point on the *SAS* curve corresponds to a row of the short-run aggregate supply schedule. For example, point *A* on the *SAS* curve and row *A* of the schedule tell us that if the price level is 105, the quantity of real GDP supplied is $11 trillion. In the short run, a rise in the price level brings an increase in the quantity of real GDP supplied. The short-run aggregate supply curve slopes upward.

With a given money wage rate, there is one price level at which the real wage rate is at its full-employment equilibrium level. At this price level, the quantity of real GDP supplied equals potential GDP and the *SAS* curve intersects the *LAS* curve. In this example, that price level is 115. At price levels higher than 115, the quantity of real GDP supplied exceeds potential GDP; at price levels below 115, the quantity of real GDP supplied is less than potential GDP.

Back at the Pepsi Plant You can see why the short-run aggregate supply curve slopes upward by returning to the Pepsi bottling plant. The greater the rate of production, the higher is the marginal cost (see Chapter 2, p. 37). The plant maximizes its profit by producing the quantity at which price equals marginal cost. If the price of Pepsi rises while the money wage rate and other costs remain constant, Pepsi has an incentive to increase production because the higher price covers the higher marginal cost. And because Pepsi is in business to maximize its profit, it increases production.

Similarly, if the price of Pepsi falls while the money wage rate and other costs remain constant, Pepsi can avoid a loss by decreasing production. The lower price weakens the incentive to produce, so Pepsi decreases production.

What's true for Pepsi bottlers is true for the producers of all goods and services. When all prices rise, the *price level rises*. If the price level rises and the money wage rate and other factor prices remain constant, all firms increase production and the quantity of real GDP supplied increases. A fall in the price level has the opposite effect and decreases real GDP.

FIGURE 11.2   Short-Run Aggregate Supply

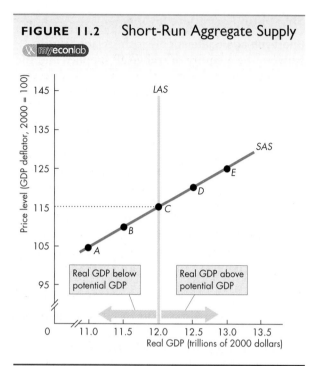

	Price level (GDP deflator)	Real GDP supplied (trillions of 2000 dollars)
A	105	11.0
B	110	11.5
C	115	12.0
D	120	12.5
E	125	13.0

The short-run aggregate supply curve, *SAS*, and the short-run aggregate supply schedule show the relationship between the quantity of real GDP supplied and the price level when the money wage rate, other factor prices, and potential GDP remain the same. A rise in the price level brings an increase in the quantity of real GDP supplied: the short-run aggregate supply curve slopes upward.

At the price level that makes the given money wage rate equal the full-employment equilibrium real wage rate, the quantity of real GDP supplied equals potential GDP and the *SAS* curve intersects the *LAS* curve. Here, that price level is 115. At price levels higher than 115, the quantity of real GDP supplied exceeds potential GDP; at price levels below 115, the quantity of real GDP supplied is less than potential GDP.

Movements Along the *LAS* and *SAS* Curves

Figure 11.3 summarizes what you've just learned about the *LAS* and *SAS* curves. When the price level, the money wage rate, and other factor prices rise by the same percentage, relative prices remain constant and the quantity of real GDP supplied equals potential GDP. There is a *movement along* the *LAS* curve.

When the price level rises but the money wage rate and other factor prices remain the same, the quantity of real GDP supplied increases and there is a *movement along* the *SAS* curve.

Let's next study the influences that bring changes in aggregate supply.

FIGURE 11.3   Movements Along the Aggregate Supply Curves

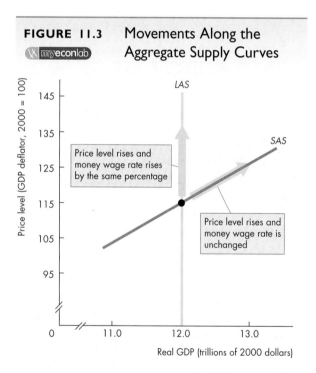

A rise in the price level with no change in the money wage rate and other factor prices brings an increase in the quantity of real GDP supplied and a movement along the short-run aggregate supply curve, *SAS*.

A rise in the price level with equal percentage increases in the money wage rate and other factor prices keeps the quantity of real GDP supplied constant at potential GDP and brings a movement along the long-run aggregate supply curve, *LAS*.

Changes in Aggregate Supply

You've just seen that a change in the price level brings a movement along the aggregate supply curves but does not change aggregate supply. Aggregate supply changes when influences on production plans other than the price level change. Let's begin by looking at factors that change potential GDP.

Changes in Potential GDP When potential GDP changes, aggregate supply changes. An increase in potential GDP increases both long-run aggregate supply and short-run aggregate supply.

Figure 11.4 shows these effects of an increase in potential GDP. Initially, the long-run aggregate supply curve is LAS_0 and the short-run aggregate supply curve is SAS_0. If an increase in the full-employment quantity of labor, an increase in the quantity of capital, or an advance in technology increases potential GDP to $13 trillion, long-run aggregate supply increases and the long-run aggregate supply curve shifts rightward to LAS_1. Short-run aggregate supply also increases, and the short-run aggregate supply curve shifts rightward to SAS_1. The two supply curves shift by the same amount only if the full-employment price level remains constant, which we will assume to be the case.

Potential GDP can increase for any of three reasons:

- The full-employment quantity of labor increases.
- The quantity of capital increases.
- Technology advances.

Let's look at these influences on potential GDP and the aggregate supply curves.

An Increase in the Full-Employment Quantity of Labor A Pepsi bottling plant that employs 100 workers bottles more Pepsi than does an otherwise identical plant that employs 10 workers. The same is true for the economy as a whole. The larger the quantity of labor employed, the greater is real GDP.

Over time, potential GDP increases because the labor force increases. But (with constant capital and technology) *potential* GDP increases only if the full-employment quantity of labor increases. Fluctuations in employment over the business cycle bring fluctuations in real GDP. But these changes in real GDP are fluctuations around potential GDP. They are not changes in potential GDP and long-run aggregate supply.

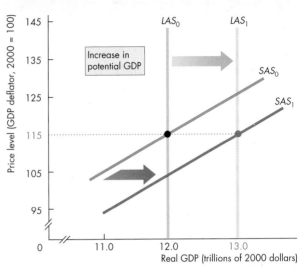

FIGURE 11.4   A Change in Potential GDP

An increase in potential GDP increases both long-run aggregate supply and short-run aggregate supply and shifts both aggregate supply curves rightward from LAS_0 to LAS_1 and from SAS_0 to SAS_1.

An Increase in the Quantity of Capital A Pepsi bottling plant with two production lines bottles more Pepsi than does an otherwise identical plant that has only one production line. For the economy, the larger the quantity of capital, the more productive is the labor force and the greater is its potential GDP. Potential GDP per person in the capital-rich United States is vastly greater than that in capital-poor China and Russia.

Capital includes *human capital*. One Pepsi plant is managed by an economics major with an MBA and has a labor force with an average of 10 years of experience. This plant produces a larger output than does an otherwise identical plant that is managed by someone with no business training or experience and that has a young labor force that is new to bottling. The first plant has a greater amount of human capital than the second. For the economy as a whole, the larger the quantity of *human capital*—the skills that people have acquired in school and through on-the-job training—the greater is potential GDP.

An Advance in Technology A Pepsi plant that has pre-computer age machines produces less than one that uses the latest robot technology. Technological change enables firms to produce more from any given amount of inputs. So even with fixed quantities of labor and capital, improvements in technology increase potential GDP.

Technological advances are by far the most important source of increased production over the past two centuries. As a result of technological advances, one farmer in the United States today can feed 100 people and one autoworker can produce almost 14 cars and trucks in a year.

Let's now look at the effects of changes in the money wage rate.

Changes in the Money Wage Rate and Other Factor Prices

When the money wage rate (or the money price of any other factor of production such as oil) changes, short-run aggregate supply changes but long-run aggregate supply does not change.

Figure 11.5 shows the effect of an increase in the money wage rate. Initially, the short-run aggregate supply curve is SAS_0. A rise in the money wage rate *decreases* short-run aggregate supply and shifts the short-run aggregate supply curve leftward to SAS_2.

A rise in the money wage rate decreases short-run aggregate supply because it increases firms' costs. With increased costs, the quantity that firms are willing to supply at each price level decreases, which is shown by a leftward shift of the *SAS* curve.

A change in the money wage rate does not change long-run aggregate supply because on the *LAS* curve, the change in the money wage rate is accompanied by an equal percentage change in the price level. With no change in *relative* prices, firms have no incentive to change production and real GDP remains constant at potential GDP. With no change in potential GDP, the long-run aggregate supply curve remains at *LAS*.

What Makes the Money Wage Rate Change?

The money wage rate can change for two reasons: departures from full employment and expectations about inflation. Unemployment above the natural rate puts downward pressure on the money wage rate, and unemployment below the natural rate puts upward pressure on the money wage rate. An expected increase in the inflation rate makes the money wage rate rise faster, and an expected decrease in the inflation rate slows the rate at which the money wage rate rises.

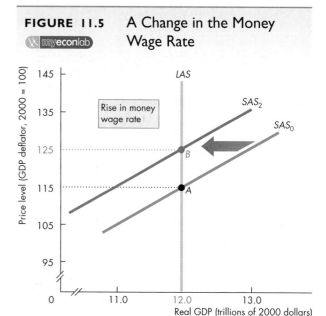

FIGURE 11.5   A Change in the Money Wage Rate

A rise in the money wage rate decreases short-run aggregate supply and shifts the short-run aggregate supply curve leftward from SAS_0 to SAS_2. A rise in the money wage rate does not change potential GDP, so the long-run aggregate supply curve does not shift.

REVIEW QUIZ

1 If the price level rises and the money wage rate rises by the same percentage, what happens to the quantity of real GDP supplied? Along which aggregate supply curve does the economy move?

2 If the price level rises and the money wage rate remains constant, what happens to the quantity of real GDP supplied? Along which aggregate supply curve does the economy move?

3 If potential GDP increases, what happens to aggregate supply? Does the *LAS* curve shift or is there a movement along the *LAS* curve? Does the *SAS* curve shift or is there a movement along the *SAS* curve?

4 If the money wage rate rises and potential GDP remains the same, does the *LAS* curve or the *SAS* curve shift or is there a movement along the *LAS* curve or the *SAS* curve?

⊗ myeconlab **Study Plan 11.2**

Aggregate Demand

The quantity of real GDP demanded is the sum of the real consumption expenditure (C), investment (I), government expenditure (G), and exports (X) minus imports (M). That is,

$$Y = C + I + G + X - M.$$

The *quantity of real GDP demanded* is the total amount of final goods and services produced in the United States that people, businesses, governments, and foreigners plan to buy.

These buying plans depend on many factors. Some of the main ones are

- The price level
- Expectations
- Fiscal policy and monetary policy
- The world economy

We first focus on the relationship between the quantity of real GDP demanded and the price level. To study this relationship, we keep all other influences on buying plans the same and ask: How does the quantity of real GDP demanded vary as the price level varies?

The Aggregate Demand Curve

Other things remaining the same, the higher the price level, the smaller is the quantity of real GDP demanded. This relationship between the quantity of real GDP demanded and the price level is called **aggregate demand**. Aggregate demand is described by an *aggregate demand schedule* and an *aggregate demand curve*.

Figure 11.6 shows an aggregate demand curve (*AD*) and an aggregate demand schedule. Each point on the *AD* curve corresponds to a row of the schedule. For example, point C' on the *AD* curve and row C' of the schedule tell us that if the price level is 115, the quantity of real GDP demanded is $12 trillion.

The aggregate demand curve slopes downward for two reasons:

- Wealth effect
- Substitution effects

Wealth Effect When the price level rises but other things remain the same, *real* wealth decreases. Real

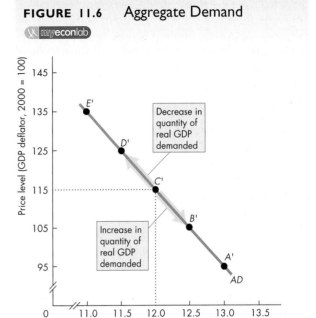

FIGURE 11.6   Aggregate Demand

	Price level (GDP deflator)	Real GDP demanded (trillions of 2000 dollars)
A'	95	13.0
B'	105	12.5
C'	115	12.0
D'	125	11.5
E'	135	11.0

The aggregate demand curve (*AD*) shows the relationship between the quantity of real GDP demanded and the price level. The aggregate demand curve is based on the aggregate demand schedule in the table. Each point A' through E' on the curve corresponds to the row in the table identified by the same letter. When the price level is 115, the quantity of real GDP demanded is $12 trillion, as shown by point C' in the figure. A change in the price level, when all other influences on aggregate buying plans remain the same, brings a change in the quantity of real GDP demanded and a movement along the *AD* curve.

wealth is the amount of money in the bank, bonds, stocks, and other assets that people own, measured not in dollars but in terms of the goods and services that the money, bonds, and stock will buy.

People save and hold money, bonds, and stocks for many reasons. One reason is to build up funds for education expenses. Another reason is to build up enough funds to meet possible medical expenses or other big bills. But the biggest reason is to build up enough funds to provide a retirement income.

If the price level rises, real wealth decreases. People then try to restore their wealth. To do so, they must increase saving and, equivalently, decrease current consumption. Such a decrease in consumption is a decrease in aggregate demand.

Maria's Wealth Effect You can see how the wealth effect works by thinking about Maria's buying plans. Maria lives in Moscow, Russia. She has worked hard all summer and saved 20,000 rubles (the ruble is the currency of Russia), which she plans to spend attending graduate school when she has finished her economics degree. So Maria's wealth is 20,000 rubles. Maria has a part-time job, and her income from this job pays her current expenses. The price level in Russia rises by 100 percent, and now Maria needs 40,000 rubles to buy what 20,000 once bought. To try to make up some of the fall in value of her savings, Maria saves even more and cuts her current spending to the bare minimum.

Substitution Effects When the price level rises and other things remain the same, interest rates rise. The reason is related to the wealth effect that you've just studied. A rise in the price level decreases the real value of the money in people's pockets and bank accounts. With a smaller amount of real money around, banks and other lenders can get a higher interest rate on loans. But faced with higher interest rates, people and businesses delay plans to buy new capital and consumer durable goods and cut back on spending.

This substitution effect involves substituting goods in the future for goods in the present and is called an *intertemporal* substitution effect—a substitution across time. Saving increases to increase future consumption.

To see this intertemporal substitution effect more clearly, think about your own plan to buy a new computer. At an interest rate of 5 percent a year, you might borrow $2,000 and buy the new computer. But at an interest rate of 10 percent a year, you might decide that the payments would be too high. You don't abandon your plan to buy the computer, but you decide to delay your purchase.

A second substitution effect works through international prices. When the U.S. price level rises and other things remain the same, U.S.-made goods and services become more expensive relative to foreign-made goods and services. This change in *relative prices* encourages people to spend less on U.S.-made items and more on foreign-made items. For example, if the U.S. price level rises relative to the Canadian price level, Canadians buy fewer U.S.-made cars (U.S. exports decrease) and Americans buy more Canadian-made cars (U.S. imports increase). U.S. GDP decreases.

Maria's Substitution Effects In Moscow, Russia, Maria makes some substitutions. She was planning to trade in her old motor scooter and get a new one. But with a higher price level and higher interest rates, she decides to make her old scooter last one more year. Also, with the prices of Russian goods sharply increasing, Maria substitutes a low-cost dress made in Malaysia for the Russian-made dress she had originally planned to buy.

Changes in the Quantity of Real GDP Demanded
When the price level rises and other things remain the same, the quantity of real GDP demanded decreases—a movement up along the aggregate demand curve as shown by the arrow in Fig. 11.6. When the price level falls and other things remain the same, the quantity of real GDP demanded increases—a movement down the aggregate demand curve.

We've now seen how the quantity of real GDP demanded changes when the price level changes. How do other influences on buying plans affect aggregate demand?

Changes in Aggregate Demand

A change in any factor that influences buying plans other than the price level brings a change in aggregate demand. The main factors are

- Expectations
- Fiscal policy and monetary policy
- The world economy

Expectations An increase in expected future income increases the amount of consumption goods (especially big-ticket items such as cars) that people plan to buy today and increases aggregate demand.

An increase in the expected future inflation rate increases aggregate demand because people decide to buy more goods and services at today's relatively lower prices.

An increase in expected future profits increases the investment that firms plan to undertake today and increases aggregate demand.

Fiscal Policy and Monetary Policy The government's attempt to influence the economy by setting and changing taxes, making transfer payments, and purchasing goods and services is called **fiscal policy**. A tax cut or an increase in transfer payments—for example, unemployment benefits or welfare payments—increases aggregate demand. Both of these influences operate by increasing households' *disposable* income. **Disposable income** is aggregate income minus taxes plus transfer payments. The greater the disposable income, the greater is the quantity of consumption goods and services that households plan to buy and the greater is aggregate demand.

Government expenditure on goods and services is one component of aggregate demand. So if the government spends more on spy satellites, schools, and highways, aggregate demand increases.

Monetary policy consists of changes in interest rates and in the quantity of money in the economy. The quantity of money is determined by the Federal Reserve (the Fed) and the banks (in a process described in Chapters 9 and 15). An increase in the quantity of money in the economy increases aggregate demand. To see why money affects aggregate demand, imagine that the Fed borrows the army's helicopters, loads them with millions of new $10 bills, and sprinkles them like confetti across the nation. People gather the newly available money and plan to spend some of it. So the quantity of goods and services demanded increases. But people don't plan to spend all the new money. They plan to save some of it and lend it to others through the banks. Interest rates fall, and with lower interest rates, people plan to buy more consumer durables and firms plan to increase their investment.

The World Economy Two main influences that the world economy has on aggregate demand are the exchange rate and foreign income. The *exchange rate* is the amount of a foreign currency that you can buy with a U.S. dollar. Other things remaining the same, a rise in the exchange rate decreases aggregate

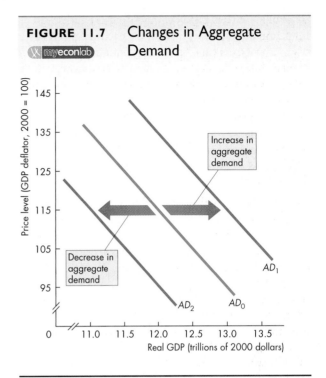

FIGURE 11.7 **Changes in Aggregate Demand**

myeconlab

Aggregate demand

Decreases if:

- Expected future income, inflation, or profits decrease

- Fiscal policy decreases government expenditure, increases taxes, or decreases transfer payments

- Monetary policy decreases the quantity of money and increases interest rates

- The exchange rate increases or foreign income decreases

Increases if:

- Expected future income, inflation, or profits increase

- Fiscal policy increases government expenditure, decreases taxes, or increases transfer payments

- Monetary policy increases the quantity of money and decreases interest rates

- The exchange rate decreases or foreign income increases

demand. To see how the exchange rate influences aggregate demand, suppose that the exchange rate is 1.20 euros per U.S. dollar. A Nokia cell phone made in Finland costs 120 euros, and an equivalent Motorola phone made in the United States costs $110. In U.S. dollars, the Nokia phone costs $100, so people around the world buy the cheaper phone from Finland. Now suppose the exchange rate falls to 1 euro per U.S. dollar. The Nokia phone now costs $120 and is more expensive than the Motorola phone. People will switch from the Nokia phone to the Motorola phone. U.S. exports will increase and U.S. imports will decrease, so U.S. aggregate demand will increase.

An increase in foreign income increases U.S. exports and increases U.S. aggregate demand. For example, an increase in income in Japan and Germany increases Japanese and German consumers' and producers' planned expenditures on U.S.-produced goods and services.

Shifts of the Aggregate Demand Curve When aggregate demand changes, the aggregate demand curve shifts. Figure 11.7 shows two changes in aggregate demand and summarizes the factors that bring about such changes.

Aggregate demand increases and the aggregate demand curve shifts rightward from AD_0 to AD_1 when expected future income, inflation, or profit increases; government expenditure on goods and services increases; taxes are cut; transfer payments increase; the quantity of money increases and interest rates fall; the exchange rate falls; or foreign income increases.

Aggregate demand decreases and the aggregate demand curve shifts leftward from AD_0 to AD_2 when expected future income, inflation, or profit decreases; government expenditure on goods and services decreases; taxes increase; transfer payments decrease; the quantity of money decreases and interest rates rise; the exchange rate rises; or foreign income decreases.

REVIEW QUIZ

1 What does the aggregate demand curve show? What factors change and what factors remain the same when there is a movement along the aggregate demand curve?

2 Why does the aggregate demand curve slope downward?

3 How do changes in expectations, fiscal policy and monetary policy, and the world economy change aggregate demand and the aggregate demand curve?

myeconlab Study Plan 11.3

Macroeconomic Equilibrium

The purpose of the aggregate supply–aggregate demand model is to explain changes in real GDP and the price level. To achieve this purpose, we combine aggregate supply and aggregate demand and determine macroeconomic equilibrium. There is a macroeconomic equilibrium for each of the time frames for aggregate supply: a long-run equilibrium and a short-run equilibrium. Long-run equilibrium is the state toward which the economy is heading. Short-run equilibrium is the normal state of the economy as it fluctuates around potential GDP.

We'll begin our study of macroeconomic equilibrium by looking first at the short run.

Short-Run Macroeconomic Equilibrium

The aggregate demand curve tells us the quantity of real GDP demanded at each price level, and the short-run aggregate supply curve tells us the quantity of real GDP supplied at each price level. **Short-run macroeconomic equilibrium** occurs when the quantity of real GDP demanded equals the quantity of real GDP supplied. That is, short-run macroeconomic equilibrium occurs at the point of intersection of the AD curve and the SAS curve. Figure 11.8 shows such an equilibrium at a price level of 115 and real GDP of $12 trillion (points C and C').

To see why this position is the equilibrium, think about what happens if the price level is something other than 115. Suppose, for example, that the price level is 125 and that real GDP is $13 trillion (at point E on the SAS curve). The quantity of real GDP demanded is less than $13 trillion, so firms are unable to sell all their output. Unwanted inventories pile up, and firms cut both production and prices. Production and prices are cut until firms can sell all their output. This situation occurs only when real GDP is $12 trillion and the price level is 115.

Now suppose the price level is 105 and real GDP is $11 trillion (at point A on the SAS curve). The quantity of real GDP demanded exceeds $11 trillion, so firms are unable to meet the demand for their output. Inventories decrease, and customers clamor for goods and services. So firms increase production and raise prices. Production and prices increase until firms can meet the demand for their

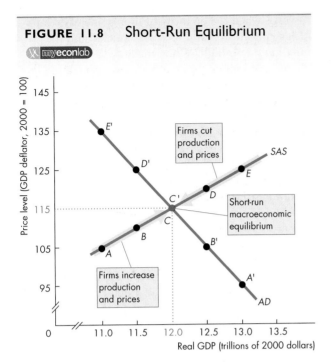

FIGURE 11.8   Short-Run Equilibrium

Short-run macroeconomic equilibrium occurs when real GDP demanded equals real GDP supplied—at the intersection of the aggregate demand curve (*AD*) and the short-run aggregate supply curve (*SAS*). Here, such an equilibrium occurs at points *C* and *C'*, where the price level is 115 and real GDP is $12 trillion. If the price level is 125 and real GDP is $13 trillion (point *E*), firms will not be able to sell all their output. They will decrease production and cut prices. If the price level is 105 and real GDP is $11 trillion (point *A*), people will not be able to buy all the goods and services they demand. Firms will increase production and raise their prices. Only when the price level is 115 and real GDP is $12 trillion can firms sell all that they produce and can people buy all the goods and services they demand. This is the short-run macroeconomic equilibrium.

output. This situation occurs only when real GDP is $12 trillion and the price level is 115.

In the short run, the money wage rate is fixed. It does not adjust to move the economy to full employment. So in the short run, real GDP can be greater than or less than potential GDP. But in the long run, the money wage rate does adjust and real GDP moves toward potential GDP. We are going to study this adjustment process. But first, let's look at the economy in long-run equilibrium.

Long-Run Macroeconomic Equilibrium

Long-run macroeconomic equilibrium occurs when real GDP equals potential GDP—equivalently, when the economy is on its *long-run* aggregate supply curve. Figure 11.9 shows the long-run macroeconomic equilibrium, which occurs at the intersection of the *AD* curve and the *LAS* curve (the blue curves). Long-run macroeconomic equilibrium comes about because the money wage rate adjusts. Potential GDP and aggregate demand determine the price level, and the price level influences the money wage rate. In long-run equilibrium, the money wage rate has adjusted to put the (green) *SAS* curve through the long-run equilibrium point.

We'll look at this money wage adjustment process later in this chapter. But first, let's see how the *AS-AD* model helps us to understand economic growth and inflation.

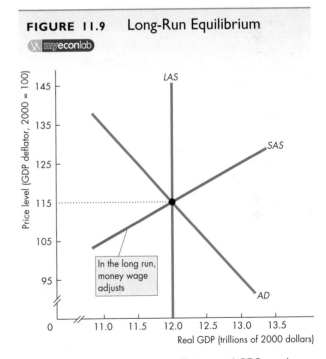

FIGURE 11.9   Long-Run Equilibrium

In long-run macroeconomic equilibrium, real GDP equals potential GDP. So long-run equilibrium occurs where the aggregate demand curve *AD* intersects the long-run aggregate supply curve *LAS*. In the long run, aggregate demand determines the price level and has no effect on real GDP. The money wage rate adjusts in the long run, so the *SAS* curve intersects the *LAS* curve at the long-run equilibrium price level.

Economic Growth and Inflation

Economic growth occurs because over time, the quantity of labor grows, capital is accumulated, and technology advances. These changes increase potential GDP and shift the *LAS* curve rightward. Figure 11.10 shows such a shift. The growth rate of potential GDP is determined by the pace at which labor grows, capital is accumulated, and technology advances.

Inflation occurs when over time, the increase in aggregate demand is greater than the increase in long-run aggregate supply. That is, inflation occurs if the *AD* curve shifts rightward by more than the rightward shift in the *LAS* curve. Figure 11.10 shows such shifts.

If aggregate demand increased at the same pace as long-run aggregate supply, we would experience real GDP growth with no inflation.

In the long run, the main influence on aggregate demand is the growth rate of the quantity of money.

At times when the quantity of money increases rapidly, aggregate demand increases quickly and the inflation rate is high. When the growth rate of the quantity of money slows, other things remaining the same, the inflation rate eventually decreases.

Our economy experiences periods of growth and inflation, like those shown in Fig. 11.10. But it does not experience *steady* growth and *steady* inflation. Real GDP fluctuates around potential GDP in a business cycle, and inflation fluctuates. When we study the business cycle, we ignore economic growth. By doing so, we can see the business cycle more clearly.

The Business Cycle

The business cycle occurs because aggregate demand and short-run aggregate supply fluctuate but the money wage rate does not adjust quickly enough to keep real GDP at potential GDP. Figure 11.11 shows three types of short-run macroeconomic equilibrium.

In part (a), there is a below full-employment equilibrium. A **below full-employment equilibrium** is a macroeconomic equilibrium in which potential GDP exceeds real GDP. The gap between real GDP and potential GDP is the **output gap.** When potential GDP exceeds real GDP, the output gap is also called a **recessionary gap.** This name reminds us that a gap has opened up between potential GDP and real GDP either because the economy has experienced a recession or because real GDP, while growing, has grown more slowly than potential GDP.

The below full-employment equilibrium shown in Fig. 11.11(a) occurs where the aggregate demand curve AD_0 intersects the short-run aggregate supply curve SAS_0 at a real GDP of $11.8 trillion. Potential GDP is $12 trillion, so the recessionary gap is $0.2 trillion. The U.S. economy was in a situation similar to that shown in Fig. 11.11(a) in the early 2000s.

Figure 11.11(b) is an example of **full-employment equilibrium,** in which real GDP equals potential GDP. In this example, the equilibrium occurs where the aggregate demand curve AD_1 intersects the short-run aggregate supply curve SAS_1 at an actual and potential GDP of $12 trillion. The U.S. economy was in a situation such as that shown in Fig. 11.11(b) in 1998.

Figure 11.11(c) shows an above full-employment equilibrium. An **above full-employment equilibrium** is a macroeconomic equilibrium in which real GDP

FIGURE 11.10 Economic Growth and Inflation

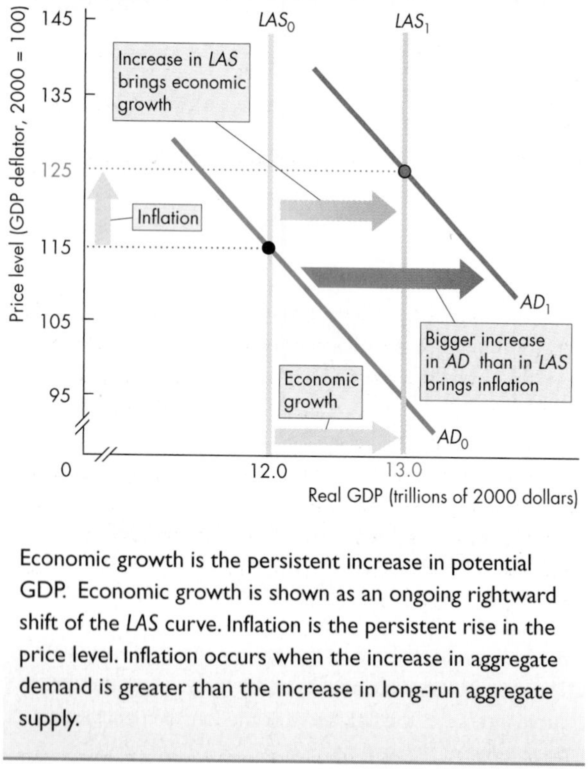

Economic growth is the persistent increase in potential GDP. Economic growth is shown as an ongoing rightward shift of the *LAS* curve. Inflation is the persistent rise in the price level. Inflation occurs when the increase in aggregate demand is greater than the increase in long-run aggregate supply.

exceeds potential GDP. When real GDP exceeds potential GDP, the output gap is called an **inflationary gap**. This name reminds us that a gap has opened up between real GDP and potential GDP and that this gap creates inflationary pressure.

The above full-employment equilibrium shown in Fig. 11.11(c) occurs where the aggregate demand curve AD_2 intersects the short-run aggregate supply curve SAS_2 at a real GDP of $12.2 trillion. There is an inflationary gap of $0.2 trillion. The U.S. econ-

omy was in a situation similar to that depicted in Fig. 11.11(c) in 1999 and 2000.

The economy moves from one type of macroeconomic equilibrium to another as a result of fluctuations in aggregate demand and in short-run aggregate supply. These fluctuations produce fluctuations in real GDP. Figure 11.11(d) shows how real GDP fluctuates around potential GDP.

Let's now look at some of the sources of these fluctuations around potential GDP.

FIGURE 11.11   The Business Cycle

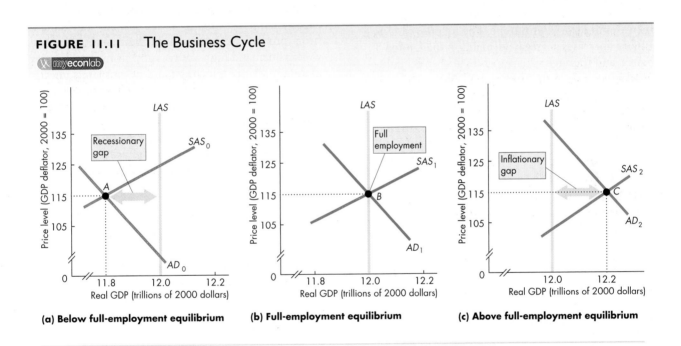

(a) Below full-employment equilibrium

(b) Full-employment equilibrium

(c) Above full-employment equilibrium

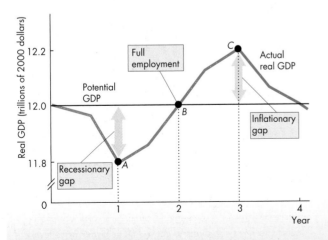

(d) Fluctuations in real GDP

Part (a) shows a below full-employment equilibrium in year 1; part (b) shows a full-employment equilibrium in year 2; and part (c) shows an above full-employment equilibrium in year 3. Part (d) shows how real GDP fluctuates around potential GDP in a business cycle.

In year 1, a recessionary gap exists and the economy is at point A (in parts a and d). In year 2, the economy is at full employment and the economy is at point B (in parts b and d). In year 3, an inflationary gap exists and the economy is at point C (in parts c and d).

Fluctuations in Aggregate Demand

One reason real GDP fluctuates around potential GDP is that aggregate demand fluctuates. Let's see what happens when aggregate demand increases.

Figure 11.12(a) shows an economy at full employment. The aggregate demand curve is AD_0, the short-run aggregate supply curve is SAS_0, and the long-run aggregate supply curve is LAS. Real GDP equals potential GDP at $12 trillion, and the price level is 115.

Now suppose that the world economy expands and that the demand for U.S.-produced goods increases in Japan and Europe. The increase in U.S. exports increases aggregate demand in the United States, and the aggregate demand curve shifts rightward from AD_0 to AD_1 in Fig. 11.12(a).

Faced with an increase in demand, firms increase production and raise prices. Real GDP increases to $12.5 trillion, and the price level rises to 120. The economy is now in an above full-employment equilibrium. Real GDP exceeds potential GDP, and there is an inflationary gap.

The increase in aggregate demand has increased the prices of all goods and services. Faced with higher prices, firms have increased their output rates. At this stage, prices of goods and services have increased but the money wage rate has not changed. (Recall that as we move along a short-run aggregate supply curve, the money wage rate is constant.)

The economy cannot produce in excess of potential GDP forever. Why not? What are the forces at work that bring real GDP back to potential GDP?

Because the price level has increased and the money wage rate is unchanged, workers have experienced a fall in the buying power of their wages and firms' profits have increased. In these circumstances, workers demand higher wages and firms, anxious to maintain their employment and output levels, meet those demands. If firms do not raise the money wage rate, they will either lose workers or have to hire less productive ones.

As the money wage rate rises, the short-run aggregate supply curve begins to shift leftward. In Fig. 11.12(b), the short-run aggregate supply curve shifts

---

FIGURE 11.12   An Increase in Aggregate Demand

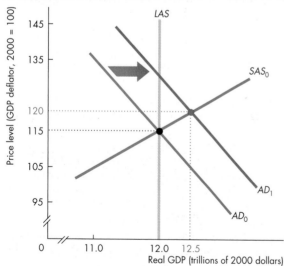

(a) Short-run effect

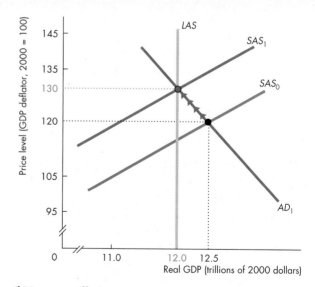

(b) Long-run effect

An increase in aggregate demand shifts the aggregate demand curve from AD_0 to AD_1. In short-run equilibrium, real GDP increases to $12.5 trillion and the price level rises to 120. In this situation, an inflationary gap exists. In the long run, the money wage rate rises and the short-run aggregate supply

curve shifts leftward in part (b). As short-run aggregate supply decreases, the SAS curve shifts from SAS_0 to SAS_1 and intersects the aggregate demand curve AD_1 at higher price levels and real GDP decreases. Eventually, the price level rises to 130 and real GDP decreases to $12 trillion—potential GDP.

from SAS_0 toward SAS_1. The rise in the money wage rate and the shift in the SAS curve produce a sequence of new equilibrium positions. Along the adjustment path, real GDP decreases and the price level rises. The economy moves up along its aggregate demand curve as shown by the arrowheads in the figure.

Eventually, the money wage rate rises by the same percentage as the price level. At this time, the aggregate demand curve AD_1 intersects SAS_1 at a new full-employment equilibrium. The price level has risen to 130, and real GDP is back where it started, at potential GDP.

A decrease in aggregate demand has effects similar but opposite to those of an increase in aggregate demand. That is, a decrease in aggregate demand shifts the aggregate demand curve leftward. Real GDP decreases to less than potential GDP, and a recessionary gap emerges. Firms cut prices. The lower price level increases the purchasing power of wages and increases firms' costs relative to their output prices because the money wage rate is unchanged. Eventually, the money wage rate falls and the short-run aggregate supply curve shifts rightward.

Let's now work out how real GDP and the price level change when aggregate supply changes.

Fluctuations in Aggregate Supply

Fluctuations in short-run aggregate supply can bring fluctuations in real GDP around potential GDP. Suppose that initially real GDP equals potential GDP. Then there is a large but temporary rise in the price of oil. What happens to real GDP and the price level?

Figure 11.13 answers this question. The aggregate demand curve is AD_0, the short-run aggregate supply curve is SAS_0, and the long-run aggregate supply curve is LAS. Real GDP is $12 trillion, which equals potential GDP, and the price level is 115. Then the price of oil rises. Faced with higher energy and transportation costs, firms decrease production. Short-run aggregate supply decreases, and the short-run aggregate supply curve shifts leftward to SAS_1. The price level rises to 125, and real GDP decreases to $11.5 trillion. Because real GDP decreases, the economy experiences recession. Because the price level increases, the economy experiences inflation. A combination of recession and inflation, called **stagflation**, actually occurred in the United States in the mid-1970s and early 1980s. But events like this are not common.

When the price of oil returns to its original level, the economy returns to full employment.

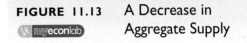

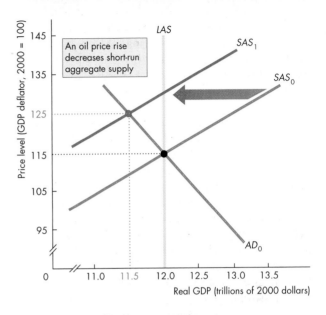

FIGURE 11.13   A Decrease in Aggregate Supply

An increase in the price of oil decreases short-run aggregate supply and shifts the short-run aggregate supply curve from SAS_0 to SAS_1. Real GDP falls from $12 trillion to $11.5 trillion, and the price level increases from 115 to 125. The economy experiences stagflation.

REVIEW QUIZ

1 Does economic growth result from increases in aggregate demand, short-run aggregate supply, or long-run aggregate supply?

2 Does inflation result from increases in aggregate demand, short-run aggregate supply, or long-run aggregate supply?

3 Describe three types of short-run macroeconomic equilibrium.

4 How do fluctuations in aggregate demand and short-run aggregate supply bring fluctuations in real GDP around potential GDP?

myeconlab Study Plan 11.4

We can use the *AS–AD* model to explain and illustrate the views of the alternative schools of thought in macroeconomics. That is your next task.

Macroeconomic Schools of Thought

Macroeconomics is an active field of research, and much remains to be learned about the forces that make our economy grow and fluctuate. There is a greater degree of consensus and certainty about economic growth and inflation—the longer-term trends in real GDP and the price level—than there is about the business cycle—the short-term fluctuations in these variables. Here, we'll look only at differences of view about short-term fluctuations.

The aggregate supply–aggregate demand model that you've studied in this chapter provides a good foundation for understanding the range of views that macroeconomists hold about this topic. But what you will learn here is just a first glimpse at the scientific controversy and debate. We'll return to these issues at various points later in the text and deepen your appreciation of the alternative views.

Classification usually requires simplification. And classifying macroeconomists is no exception to this general rule. The classification that we'll use here is simple, but it is not misleading. We're going to divide macroeconomists into three broad schools of thought and examine the views of each group in turn. The groups are

- Classical
- Keynesian
- Monetarist

The Classical View

A **classical** macroeconomist believes that the economy is self-regulating and always at full employment. The term "classical" derives from the name of the founding school of economics that includes Adam Smith, David Ricardo, and John Stuart Mill.

A **new classical** view is that business cycle fluctuations are the efficient responses of a well-functioning market economy that is bombarded by shocks that arise from the uneven pace of technological change.

The classical view can be understood in terms of beliefs about aggregate demand and aggregate supply.

Aggregate Demand Fluctuations In the classical view, technological change is the most significant influence on both aggregate demand and aggregate

supply. For this reason, classical macroeconomists don't use the *AS-AD* framework. But their views can be interpreted in this framework. A technological change that increases the productivity of capital brings an increase in aggregate demand because firms increase their expenditure on new plant and equipment. A technological change that lengthens the useful life of existing capital decreases the demand for new capital, which decreases aggregate demand.

Aggregate Supply Response In the classical view, the money wage rate that lies behind the short-run aggregate supply curve is instantly and completely flexible. The money wage rate adjusts so quickly to maintain equilibrium in the labor market that real GDP always adjusts to equal potential GDP.

Potential GDP itself fluctuates for the same reasons that aggregate demand fluctuates: technological change. When the pace of technological change is rapid, potential GDP increases quickly and so does real GDP. And when the pace of technological change slows, so does the growth rate of potential GDP.

Classical Policy The classical view of policy emphasizes the potential for taxes to stunt incentives and create inefficiency. By minimizing the disincentive effects of taxes, employment, investment, and technological advance are at their efficient levels and the economy expands at an appropriate and rapid pace.

The Keynesian View

A **Keynesian** macroeconomist believes that left alone, the economy would rarely operate at full employment and that to achieve and maintain full employment, active help from fiscal policy and monetary policy is required.

The term "Keynesian" derives from the name of one of the twentieth century's most famous economists, John Maynard Keynes (see p. 338).

The Keynesian view is based on beliefs about the forces that determine aggregate demand and short-run aggregate supply.

Aggregate Demand Fluctuations In the Keynesian view, *expectations* are the most significant influence on aggregate demand. And expectations are based on herd instinct, or what Keynes himself called "animal spirits." A wave of pessimism about future profit prospects can lead to a fall in aggregate demand and plunge the economy into recession.

Aggregate Supply Response In the Keynesian view, the money wage rate that lies behind the short-run aggregate supply curve is extremely sticky in the downward direction. Basically, the money wage rate doesn't fall. So if there is a recessionary gap, there is no automatic mechanism for getting rid of it. If it were to happen, a fall in the money wage rate would increase short-run aggregate supply and restore full employment. But the money wage rate doesn't fall, so the economy remains stuck in recession.

A modern version of the Keynesian view known as the **new Keynesian** view holds not only that the money wage rate is sticky but also that prices of goods and services are sticky. With a sticky price level, the short-run aggregate supply curve is horizontal at a fixed price level.

Policy Response Needed The Keynesian view calls for fiscal policy and monetary policy to actively offset changes in aggregate demand that bring recession.

By stimulating aggregate demand in a recession, full employment can be restored.

The Monetarist View

A **monetarist** is a macroeconomist who believes that the economy is self-regulating and that it will normally operate at full employment, provided that monetary policy is not erratic and that the pace of money growth is kept steady.

The term "monetarist" was coined by an outstanding twentieth-century economist, Karl Brunner, to describe his own views and those of Milton Friedman (see p. 394).

The monetarist view can be interpreted in terms of beliefs about the forces that determine aggregate demand and short-run aggregate supply.

Aggregate Demand Fluctuations In the monetarist view, *the quantity of money* is the most significant influence on aggregate demand. And the quantity of money is determined by the Federal Reserve (the Fed). If the Fed keeps money growing at a steady pace, aggregate demand fluctuations will be minimized and the economy will operate close to full employment. But if the Fed decreases the quantity of money or even just slows its growth rate too abruptly, the economy will go into recession. In the monetarist view, all recessions result from inappropriate monetary policy.

Aggregate Supply Response The monetarist view of short-run aggregate supply is the same as the Keynesian view: the money wage rate is sticky. If the economy is in recession, it will take an unnecessarily long time for it to return unaided to full employment.

Monetarist Policy The monetarist view of policy is the same as the classical view on fiscal policy. Taxes should be kept low to avoid disincentive effects that decrease potential GDP. Provided that the quantity of money is kept on a steady growth path, no active stabilization is needed to offset changes in aggregate demand.

The Way Ahead

In the chapters that follow, you're going to encounter Keynesian, classical, and monetarist views again. In the next chapter, we study the original Keynesian model of aggregate demand. This model remains useful today because it explains how expenditure fluctuations get magnified and bring larger changes in aggregate demand. We then go on to apply the *AS-AD* model to a deeper look at U.S. inflation and business cycles.

Our attention then turns to short-run macroeconomic policy—the fiscal policy of the Administration and Congress and the monetary policy of the Fed.

REVIEW QUIZ

1 What are the defining features of classical macroeconomics and what policies do classical macroeconomists recommend?
2 What are the defining features of Keynesian macroeconomics and what policies do Keynesian macroeconomists recommend?
3 What are the defining features of monetarist macroeconomics and what policies do monetarist macroeconomists recommend?

myeconlab **Study Plan 11.5**

To complete your study of the aggregate supply–aggregate demand model, take a look at the U.S. economy in 2006 through the eyes of this model in *Reading Between the Lines* on pp. 280–281.

Aggregate Supply and Aggregate Demand in Action

Revised Growth Data Eases Inflation Fear

May 26, 2006

Concerns the economy might have overheated in the first quarter eased yesterday after revised economic growth figures showed that expansion was indeed strong, but not too strong. . . .

The Commerce Department said yesterday that the nation's gross domestic product expanded 5.3 percent in the first quarter, up from the 4.8 percent first reported last month. That is the fastest rate of growth since 2003. Still, many expected a growth rate of 5.8 percent, according to a survey of economists by Bloomberg News.

But instead of showing signs that inflation was even more of a problem in the first quarter than initially thought, the revised numbers suggested fairly tame price pressures. Consumer spending, which accounts for the bulk of the gross domestic product, contributed 3.63 percentage points to the overall 5.3 percent growth. Initially, the government said consumer spending contributed slightly more.

And core consumer spending, which excludes energy and food, rose 2 percent in the first quarter—unchanged from the first report. Investors looking for signs that inflationary pressures had ebbed were also reassured by a letter to the chairman of the Congressional Joint Economic Committee, from Ben S. Bernanke, the Federal Reserve chairman, that said core inflation appeared stable. . . .

Although his tone was upbeat, Mr. Bernanke did not indicate what the Fed might do when it meets late next month to discuss raising the benchmark short-term interest rate. "Of course, inflation expectations will remain low only so long as the Federal Reserve demonstrates its commitment to price stability," he wrote. . . .

Essence of the Story

▶ Real GDP grew at a 5.3 percent annual rate during the first quarter of 2006, the fastest since 2003.

▶ Consumer spending (the largest component of GDP) contributed 3.63 percentage points to the overall growth.

▶ Federal Reserve chairman Ben S. Bernanke eased concerns about inflation.

▶ He said that core inflation appeared to be stable and low but would remain so only as long as the Federal Reserve demonstrates commitment to price stability.

▶ The data showed a strong expansion but eased fears that the economy might have overheated.

▶ U.S. real GDP grew at a 5.3 percent annual rate during the first quarter of 2006, the fastest since the spectacular 8.2 percent annual growth rate in 2003.

▶ Real GDP had increased steadily throughout 2005 and the inflation rate was steady.

▶ In 2006, most forecasters were confident that real GDP growth was not greater than the growth of potential GDP and that there was little fear of inflation breaking out.

▶ The Congressional Budget Office (CBO) estimate of potential GDP and its implied output gap are consistent with this view.

▶ Despite the strong growth, the CBO estimated that real GDP was below potential GDP—that there was a recessionary gap—in 2006.

▶ Figure 1 illustrates the CBO estimate of the recessionary gap through 2005 and in the first quarter of 2006.

▶ Real GDP (the red line) grew faster than potential GDP (the gray line), so the recessionary gap narrowed. But it didn't disappear.

▶ Another number estimated by the CBO places a question mark on the output gap estimate.

▶ The CBO's estimate of the natural unemployment rate suggests that by mid-2005, the economy was at full employment and that by 2006, there was an inflationary gap.

▶ Figure 2 shows the actual unemployment rate and the CBO's estimate of the natural rate.

▶ Whether inflation is likely to remain constant, increase, or decrease depends on the output gap.

▶ Figure 3 illustrates the three possibilities.

▶ In the second quarter of 2006, real GDP was $11.4 trillion and the price level was 116 at the intersection of the short-run aggregate supply curve SAS and the aggregate demand curve AD.

▶ The CBO estimate of potential GDP was $11.5 trillion with the long-run aggregate supply curve at LAS_A.

▶ If the CBO's estimate of the natural unemployment rate provides a better estimate of the output gap, the LAS curve might be LAS_B.

▶ But with stable inflation, it seems more likely that the economy is actually at full employment with the LAS curve at LAS_C.

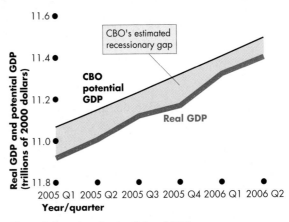

Figure 1 Actual and potential real GDP

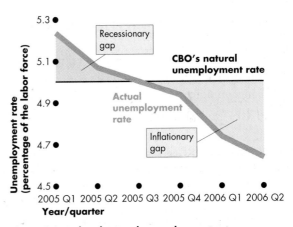

Figure 2 Actual and natural unemployment rate

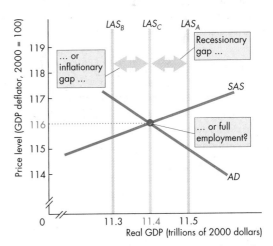

Figure 3 Aggregate supply and aggregate demand in 2006

SUMMARY

Key Points

The Macroeconomic Long Run and Short Run (p. 264)

- The macroeconomic long run is a time frame in which prices adjust to achieve full employment.
- The macroeconomic short run is a time frame in which some money prices are sticky so that the economy might be below, at, or above full employment.

Aggregate Supply (pp. 264–268)

- In the long run, the quantity of real GDP supplied is potential GDP.
- In the short run, a rise in the price level increases the quantity of real GDP supplied.
- A change in potential GDP changes long-run and short-run aggregate supply. A change in the money wage rate changes only short-run aggregate supply.

Aggregate Demand (pp. 269–272)

- A rise in the price level decreases the quantity of real GDP demanded.
- Changes in expected future income, inflation, and profits; in fiscal policy and monetary policy; and in world real GDP and the exchange rate change aggregate demand.

Macroeconomic Equilibrium (pp. 272–277)

- Aggregate demand and short-run aggregate supply determine real GDP and the price level.
- In the long run, real GDP equals potential GDP and aggregate demand determines the price level.
- The business cycle occurs because aggregate demand and aggregate supply fluctuate.

Macroeconomic Schools of Thought (pp. 278–279)

- Classical economists believe that the economy is self-regulating and always at full employment.
- Keynesian economists believe that full employment can be achieved only with active policy.
- Monetarist economists believe that recessions result from inappropriate monetary policy.

Key Figures

Key Terms

PROBLEMS

1. The following events have occurred at times in the history of the United States:
   - A deep recession hits the world economy.
   - The world oil price rises sharply.
   - U.S. businesses expect future profits to fall.
   a. Explain for each event whether it changes short-run aggregate supply, long-run aggregate supply, aggregate demand, or some combination of them.
   b. Explain the separate effects of each event on U.S. real GDP and the price level, starting from a position of long-run equilibrium.
   c. Explain the combined effects of these events on U.S. real GDP and the price level, starting from a position of long-run equilibrium.
   d. Describe what a classical macroeconomist, a Keynesian, and a monetarist would want to do in response to each of the above events.

2. The following events have occurred at times in the history of the United States:
   - The world economy goes into an expansion.
   - U.S. businesses expect future profits to rise.
   - The government increases its expenditure on goods and services in a time of war or increased international tension.
   a. Explain for each event whether it changes short-run aggregate supply, long-run aggregate supply, aggregate demand, or some combination of them.
   b. Explain the separate effects of each event on U.S. real GDP and the price level, starting from a position of long-run equilibrium.
   c. Explain the combined effects of these events on U.S. real GDP and the price level, starting from a position of long-run equilibrium.

3. In the United Kingdom, potential GDP is 1,050 billion pounds and the table in the next column shows aggregate demand and short-run aggregate supply.
   a. What is the short-run equilibrium real GDP and price level?
   b. Does the United Kingdom have an inflationary gap or a recessionary gap and what is its magnitude?

*Solutions to odd-numbered problems are provided.

Price level	Real GDP demanded	Real GDP supplied in the short run
	(billions of 2001 pounds)	
100	1,150	1,050
110	1,100	1,100
120	1,050	1,150
130	1,000	1,200
140	950	1,250
150	900	1,300
160	850	1,350

4. In Japan, potential GDP is 600 trillion yen and the table shows aggregate demand and short-run aggregate supply.

Price level	Real GDP demanded	Real GDP supplied in the short run
	(trillions of 2000 yen)	
75	600	400
85	550	450
95	500	500
105	450	550
115	400	600
125	350	650
135	300	700

   a. Draw a graph of the aggregate demand curve and the short-run aggregate supply curve.
   b. What is the short-run equilibrium real GDP and price level?
   c. Does Japan have an inflationary gap or a recessionary gap and what is its magnitude?

5. In September 2006, the Bureau of Economic Analysis reported that real GDP during the second quarter of 2006 was $11,388 billion compared to $11,002 billion in the same quarter of 2005. The GDP deflator was 115.9, up from 112.2 in the second quarter of 2005. The Congressional Budget Office estimated potential GDP to be $11,491 billion in the second quarter of 2006 and $11,146 billion a year earlier.

   a. Draw a graph of the aggregate demand curve, the short-run aggregate supply curve, and the long-run aggregate supply curve in 2005 that is consistent with these numbers.
   b. On the graph, show how the aggregate demand curve, the short-run aggregate supply curve, and the long-run aggregate supply curve shifted during the year to the second quarter of 2006.

6. Initially, short-run aggregate supply is SAS_0 and aggregate demand is AD_0. Some events change aggregate demand, and later, some other events change aggregate supply.

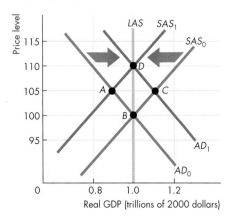

a. What is the equilibrium after the change in aggregate demand?
b. What is the equilibrium after the change in aggregate supply?
c. Describe two events that could have changed aggregate demand from AD_0 to AD_1.
d. Describe two events could have changed aggregate supply from SAS_0 to SAS_1.

CRITICAL THINKING

1. After you have studied the account of the U.S. economy in 2006 in *Reading Between the Lines* on pp. 280–281,
   a. Describe the main features of the U.S. economy in the first quarter of 2006.
   b. Did the United States have a recessionary gap or an inflationary gap in 2006? How do you know?
   c. Use the *AS-AD* model to show the changes in aggregate demand and aggregate supply that brought the increase in real GDP and modest rise in the price level between the fourth quarter of 2005 and the first quarter of 2006.
   d. Use the *AS-AD* model to show the changes in aggregate demand and aggregate supply that would occur if the Federal Reserve raised the interest rate.
   e. Use the *AS-AD* model to show the changes in aggregate demand and aggregate supply that would occur if the federal government increased its expenditure on goods and services or cut taxes further.

2. The International Monetary Fund's World Economic Outlook database provides the following data for India in 2004, 2005, and 2006.

	2004	2005	2006
Real GDP growth rate	8.1	8.3	7.3
Inflation rate	4.2	4.7	4.6

   a. What changes in long-run and short-run aggregate supply and aggregate demand are consistent with these numbers?
   b. Draw a graph to illustrate your answer to part (a).
   c. List the main factors that might have produced the changes in aggregate supply and aggregate demand that you have described in your answer to part (a).
   d. From the above data, do you think India has an inflationary gap, a recessionary gap, or is at full employment?

WEB ACTIVITIES

myeconlab **Links to Web sites**

1. Find data on recent changes in and forecasts of real GDP and the price level in the United States.
   a. What is your forecast of next year's real GDP?
   b. What is your forecast of next year's price level?
   c. What is your forecast of the inflation rate?
   d. What is your forecast of the growth rate of real GDP?
   e. Do you think there will be a recessionary gap or an inflationary gap next year?
2. Find data on recent changes in and forecasts of real GDP and the price level in another economy that you find interesting.
   a. What is your forecast of next year's real GDP?
   b. What is your forecast of next year's price level?
   c. What is your forecast of the inflation rate?
   d. What is your forecast of the growth rate of real GDP?
   e. Compare and contrast the forecasts for the U.S. economy and the other economy you've selected.

Expenditure Multipliers: The Keynesian Model

Economic Amplifier or Shock Absorber?

Erykah Badu sings into a microphone in a barely audible whisper. Increasing in volume, through the magic of electronic amplification, her voice fills Central Park.

Michael Bloomberg, the mayor of New York, and a secretary are being driven to a business meeting along one of the city's less well-repaired streets. The car's wheels bounce and vibrate over some of the worst potholes in the nation, but its passengers are completely undisturbed and the secretary's notes are written without a ripple, thanks to the car's efficient shock absorbers.

Investment and exports fluctuate like the volume of Erykah Badu's voice and the uneven surface of a New York City street. How does the economy react to those fluctuations? Does it behave like an amplifier, blowing up the fluctuations and spreading them out to affect the many millions of participants in an economic rock concert? Or does it react like a limousine, absorbing the shocks and providing a smooth ride for the economy's passengers?

◆ You will explore these questions in this chapter. You will learn how a recession or an expansion begins when a change in investment or exports induces an amplified change in aggregate expenditure and real GDP. *Reading Between the Lines* at the end of the chapter looks at the role played by business inventories during 2005 as the economy boomed.

After studying this chapter, you will be able to

▶ Explain how expenditure plans are determined when the price level is fixed

▶ Explain how real GDP is determined when the price level is fixed

▶ Explain the expenditure multiplier when the price level is fixed

▶ Explain the relationship between aggregate expenditure and aggregate demand and explain the multiplier when the price level changes

Fixed Prices and Expenditure Plans

The Keynesian model that we study in this chapter describes the economy in the very short run. It isolates and places in focus the forces that operate at a business cycle peak, when an expansion ends and a recession begins, and at a trough, when a recession turns into an expansion.

In this model, all the firms are like your local supermarket. They set their prices, advertise their products and services, and sell the quantities their customers are willing to buy. If firms persistently sell a greater quantity than they plan to and are constantly running out of inventory, they eventually raise their prices. And if firms persistently sell a smaller quantity than they plan to and have inventories piling up, they eventually cut their prices. But in the very short term, their prices are fixed. Firms hold the prices they have set, and the quantities they sell depend on demand, not supply.

Fixed prices have two immediate implications for the economy as a whole:

1. Because each firm's price is fixed, the *price level* is fixed.

2. Because demand determines the quantities that each firm sells, *aggregate demand* determines the aggregate quantity of goods and services sold, which equals real GDP.

So to understand the fluctuations in real GDP when the price level is fixed, we must understand aggregate demand fluctuations. The Keynesian aggregate expenditure model explains fluctuations in aggregate demand by identifying the forces that determine expenditure plans.

Expenditure Plans

Aggregate expenditure has four components:

1. Consumption expenditure
2. Investment
3. Government expenditure on goods and services
4. Net exports (exports *minus* imports)

These four components of aggregate expenditure sum to real GDP (see Chapter 5, pp. 113–114).

Aggregate planned expenditure is equal to *planned* consumption expenditure plus *planned* investment plus *planned* government expenditure on goods and services plus *planned* exports minus *planned* imports. Planned investment, government expenditure, and exports don't depend on the current level of real GDP. But planned consumption expenditure does depend on real GDP because it depends on income. Also, because some consumer goods are imported, planned imports depend on real GDP.

A Two-Way Link Between Aggregate Expenditure and GDP   Because real GDP influences consumption expenditure and imports, and because consumption expenditure and imports are components of aggregate expenditure, there is a two-way link between aggregate expenditure and GDP. Other things remaining the same,

■ An increase in real GDP increases aggregate expenditure, and

■ An increase in aggregate expenditure increases real GDP.

You are going to learn how this two-way link between aggregate expenditure and real GDP determines real GDP when the price level is fixed. The starting point is to consider the first piece of the two-way link: the influence of real GDP on planned consumption expenditure and saving.

Consumption Function and Saving Function

Several factors influence consumption expenditure and saving. The more important ones are

■ Disposable income
■ Real interest rate
■ Wealth
■ Expected future income

Disposable income is aggregate income minus taxes plus transfer payments. Aggregate income equals real GDP, so disposable income depends on real GDP. To explore the two-way link between real GDP and planned consumption expenditure, we focus on the relationship between consumption expenditure and disposable income when the other three factors listed above are constant.

Consumption and Saving Plans   The table in Fig. 12.1 shows an example of the relationship among planned consumption expenditure, planned saving, and disposable income. It lists the consumption expenditure and the saving that people plan to undertake at each level of disposable income. Notice that at each level of disposable income, consumption expenditure plus saving always equals disposable income. Households can only consume or save their disposable income, so planned consumption expenditure plus planned saving always equals disposable income.

The relationship between consumption expenditure and disposable income, other things remaining the same, is called the **consumption function.** The relationship between saving and disposable income, other things remaining the same, is called the **saving function.** Let's begin by studying the consumption function.

Consumption Function Figure 12.1(a) shows a consumption function. The y-axis measures consumption

---

FIGURE 12.1   Consumption Function and Saving Function

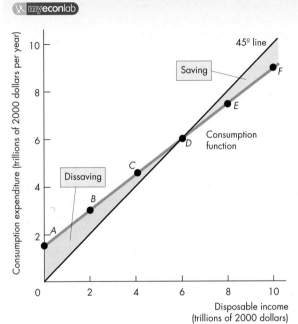

(a) Consumption function

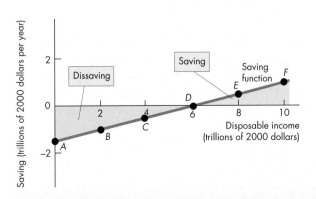

(b) Saving function

	Disposable income	Planned consumption expenditure	Planned saving
		(trillions of 2000 dollars)	
A	0	1.5	−1.5
B	2	3.0	−1.0
C	4	4.5	−0.5
D	6	6.0	0
E	8	7.5	0.5
F	10	9.0	1.0

The table shows consumption expenditure and saving plans at various levels of disposable income. Part (a) of the figure shows the relationship between consumption expenditure and disposable income (the consumption function). The height of the consumption function measures consumption expenditure at each level of disposable income. Part (b) shows the relationship between saving and disposable income (the saving function). The height of the saving function measures saving at each level of disposable income. Points A through F on the consumption and saving functions correspond to the rows in the table.

The height of the 45° line in part (a) measures disposable income. So along the 45° line, consumption expenditure equals disposable income. Consumption expenditure plus saving equals disposable income. When the consumption function is above the 45° line, saving is negative (dissaving occurs). When the consumption function is below the 45° line, saving is positive. At the point where the consumption function intersects the 45° line, all disposable income is consumed and saving is zero.

expenditure, and the x-axis measures disposable income. Along the consumption function, the points labeled A through F correspond to the rows of the table. For example, point E shows that when disposable income is $8 trillion, consumption expenditure is $7.5 trillion. Along the consumption function, as disposable income increases, consumption expenditure also increases.

At point A on the consumption function, consumption expenditure is $1.5 trillion even though disposable income is zero. This consumption expenditure is called *autonomous consumption*, and it is the amount of consumption expenditure that would take place in the short run even if people had no current income. Consumption expenditure in excess of this amount is called *induced consumption*, which is expenditure that is induced by an increase in disposable income.

45° Line Figure 12.1(a) also contains a 45° line, the height of which measures disposable income. At each point on this line, consumption expenditure equals disposable income. In the range over which the consumption function lies above the 45° line—between A and D—consumption expenditure exceeds disposable income. In the range over which the consumption function lies below the 45° line—between D and F—consumption expenditure is less than disposable income. And at a point at which the consumption function intersects the 45° line—at point D—consumption expenditure equals disposable income.

Saving Function Figure 12.1(b) shows a saving function. The x-axis is exactly the same as that in part (a). The y-axis measures saving. Again, the points marked A through F correspond to the rows of the table. For example, point E shows that when disposable income is $8 trillion, saving is $0.5 trillion. Along the saving function, as disposable income increases, saving also increases. At disposable income less than $6 trillion (point D), saving is negative. Negative saving is called *dissaving*. At disposable income greater than $6 trillion, saving is positive, and at $6 trillion, saving is zero.

Notice the connection between the two parts of Fig. 12.1. When consumption expenditure exceeds disposable income in part (a), saving is negative in part (b). When disposable income exceeds consump-

tion expenditure in part (a), saving is positive in part (b). And when consumption expenditure equals disposable income in part (a), saving is zero in part (b).

When saving is negative (when consumption expenditure exceeds disposable income), past savings are used to pay for current consumption. Such a situation cannot last forever, but it can occur if disposable income falls temporarily.

Marginal Propensities to Consume and Save

The extent to which consumption expenditure changes when disposable income changes depends on the marginal propensity to consume. The **marginal propensity to consume** (MPC) is the fraction of a *change* in disposable income that is consumed. It is calculated as the *change* in consumption expenditure (ΔC) divided by the *change* in disposable income (ΔYD) that brought it about. That is,

$$MPC = \frac{\Delta C}{\Delta YD}.$$

In the table in Fig. 12.1, when disposable income increases from $6 trillion to $8 trillion, consumption expenditure increases from $6 trillion to $7.5 trillion. The $2 trillion increase in disposable income increases consumption expenditure by $1.5 trillion. The MPC is $1.5 trillion divided by $2 trillion, which equals 0.75.

The **marginal propensity to save** (MPS) is the fraction of a *change* in disposable income that is saved. It is calculated as the *change* in saving (ΔS) divided by the *change* in disposable income (ΔYD) that brought it about. That is,

$$MPS = \frac{\Delta S}{\Delta YD}.$$

In the table in Fig. 12.1, an increase in disposable income from $6 trillion to $8 trillion increases saving from zero to $0.5 trillion. The $2 trillion increase in disposable income increases saving by $0.5 trillion. The MPS is $0.5 trillion divided by $2 trillion, which equals 0.25.

The marginal propensity to consume plus the marginal propensity to save always equals 1. They sum to 1 because consumption expenditure and saving exhaust disposable income. Part of each dollar increase in disposable income is consumed, and the remaining part is saved. You can see that these two marginal propensities sum to 1 by using the equation:

$$\Delta C + \Delta S = \Delta YD.$$

Divide both sides of the equation by the change in disposable income to obtain

$$\frac{\Delta C}{\Delta YD} + \frac{\Delta S}{\Delta YD} = 1.$$

$\Delta C/\Delta YD$ is the marginal propensity to consume (*MPC*), and $\Delta S/\Delta YD$ is the marginal propensity to save (*MPS*), so

$$MPC + MPS = 1.$$

Slopes and Marginal Propensities

The slope of the consumption function is the marginal propensity to consume, and the slope of the saving function is the marginal propensity to save. Figure 12.2(a) shows the *MPC* as the slope of the consumption function. A $2 trillion increase in disposable income from $6 trillion to $8 trillion is the base of the red triangle. The increase in consumption expenditure that results from this increase in disposable income is $1.5 trillion and is the height of the triangle. The slope of the consumption function is given by the formula "slope equals rise over run" and is $1.5 trillion divided by $2 trillion, which equals 0.75—the *MPC*.

Figure 12.2(b) shows the *MPS* as the slope of the saving function. A $2 trillion increase in disposable income from $6 trillion to $8 trillion (the base of the red triangle) increases saving by $0.5 trillion (the height of the triangle). The slope of the saving function is $0.5 trillion divided by $2 trillion, which equals 0.25—the *MPS*.

Other Influences on Consumption Expenditure and Saving

A change in disposable income changes consumption expenditure and saving and brings movements along the consumption function and saving function.

Along the consumption function and the saving function, all other influences on consumption expenditure and saving (such as the real interest rate, wealth, and expected future income) are fixed. A change in any of these other influences shifts both the consumption function and the saving function.

FIGURE 12.2   Marginal Propensities to Consume and Save
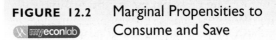

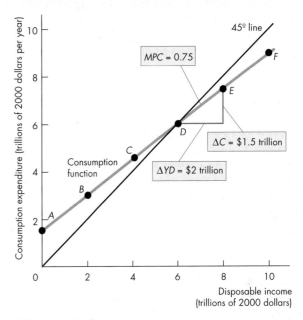

(a) Consumption function

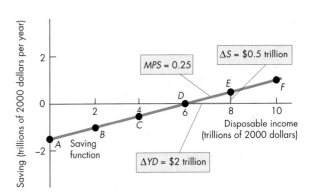

(b) Saving function

The marginal propensity to consume, *MPC*, is equal to the change in consumption expenditure divided by the change in disposable income, other things remaining the same. It is measured by the slope of the consumption function. In part (a), the *MPC* is 0.75. The marginal propensity to save, *MPS*, is equal to the change in saving divided by the change in disposable income, other things remaining the same. It is measured by the slope of the saving function. In part (b), the *MPS* is 0.25.

When the real interest rate falls or when wealth or expected future income increases, consumption expenditure increases and saving decreases. Figure 12.3 shows the effects of these changes on the consumption function and the saving function. The consumption function shifts upward from CF_0 to CF_1, and the saving function shifts downward from SF_0 to SF_1. Such shifts commonly occur during the expansion phase of the business cycle because, at such a time, expected future income increases.

When the real interest rate rises or when wealth or expected future income decreases, consumption expenditure decreases and saving increases. The consumption function shifts downward, and the saving function shifts upward. Such shifts often occur when a recession begins because, at such a time, expected future income decreases.

We've studied the theory of the consumption function. Let's now see how that theory applies to the U.S. economy.

The U.S. Consumption Function

Figure 12.4 shows the U.S. consumption function. Each point identified by a blue dot represents consumption expenditure and disposable income for a particular year. (The dots are for the years 1965 to 2005, and the dots of five of the years are identified in the figure.) The line labeled CF_0 is an estimate of the U.S. consumption function in 1965 and the line labeled CF_1 is an estimate of the U.S. consumption function in 2005.

The slope of the consumption function in Fig. 12.4 is 0.9, which means that a $1 trillion increase in disposable income brings a $0.9 trillion increase in consumption expenditure. This slope, which is an estimate of the marginal propensity to consume, is an assumption that is at the upper end of the range of values that economists have estimated for the marginal propensity to consume.

The consumption function shifts upward over time as other influences on consumption expenditure change. Of these other influences, the real interest rate and wealth fluctuate and so bring upward and downward shifts in the consumption function. But rising expected future income brings a steady upward shift in the consumption function. As the consumption function shifts upward, autonomous consumption increases.

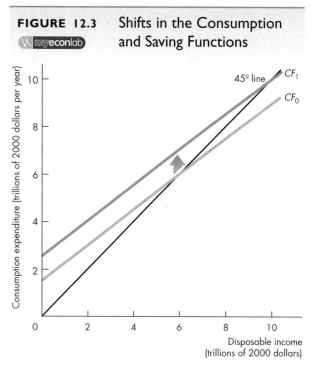

FIGURE 12.3 Shifts in the Consumption and Saving Functions

(a) Consumption function

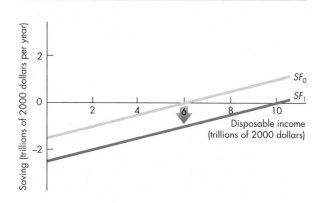

(b) Saving function

A fall in the real interest rate, an increase in wealth, or an increase in expected future income increases consumption expenditure and decreases saving. The consumption function shifts upward from CF_0 to CF_1 and the saving function shifts downward from SF_0 to SF_1.

A rise in the real interest rate, a decrease in wealth, or a decrease in expected future income decreases consumption expenditure and increases saving. The consumption function shifts downward and the saving function shifts upward.

FIGURE 12.4 The U.S. Consumption Function

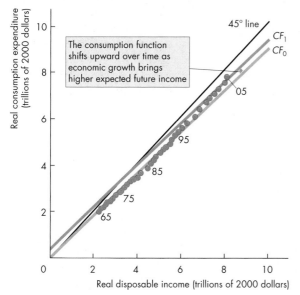

The consumption function shifts upward over time as economic growth brings higher expected future income

Each blue dot shows consumption expenditure and disposable income for a particular year. The lines CF_0 and CF_1 are estimates of the U.S. consumption function in 1965 and 2005, respectively. Here, the (assumed) marginal propensity to consume is 0.9.

Consumption as a Function of Real GDP

You've seen that consumption expenditure changes when disposable income changes. Disposable income changes when either real GDP changes or net taxes change. If tax rates don't change, real GDP is the only influence on disposable income. So consumption expenditure depends not only on disposable income but also on real GDP. We use this link between consumption expenditure and real GDP to determine equilibrium expenditure. But before we do so, we need to look at one further component of aggregate expenditure: imports. Like consumption expenditure, imports are influenced by real GDP.

Import Function

U.S. imports are determined by many factors, but in the short run, one factor dominates: U.S. real GDP.

Other things remaining the same, the greater the U.S. real GDP, the larger is the quantity of U.S. imports.

The relationship between imports and real GDP is determined by the marginal propensity to import. The **marginal propensity to import** is the fraction of an increase in real GDP that is spent on imports. It is calculated as the change in imports divided by the change in real GDP that brought it about, other things remaining the same. For example, if a $1 trillion increase in real GDP increases imports by $0.25 trillion, the marginal propensity to import is 0.25.

In recent years, since the North American Free Trade Agreement (NAFTA) was implemented, U.S. imports have surged. For example, between 1991 and 2001, real GDP increased by $2,657 billion and imports increased by $861 billion. If no factors other than real GDP influenced imports during the 1990s, these numbers would imply a marginal propensity to import of 0.32. But other factors, such as NAFTA, increased imports, so the marginal propensity to import is smaller than 0.32. The marginal propensity to import is probably as large as 0.2, and it has been increasing as the global economy has become more integrated.

REVIEW QUIZ

1 Which components of aggregate expenditure are influenced by real GDP?
2 Define the marginal propensity to consume. What is your estimate of your own marginal propensity to consume? After you graduate, will it change? Why or why not?
3 How do we calculate the effects of real GDP on consumption expenditure and imports by using the marginal propensity to consume and the marginal propensity to import?

myeconlab Study Plan 12.1

Real GDP influences consumption expenditure and imports. But consumption expenditure and imports along with investment, government expenditure, and exports influence real GDP. Your next task is to study this second piece of the two-way link between aggregate expenditure and real GDP and see how all the components of aggregate planned expenditure interact to determine real GDP.

Real GDP with a Fixed Price Level

You are now going to discover how aggregate expenditure plans interact to determine real GDP when the price level is fixed. First, we will study the relationship between aggregate planned expenditure and real GDP.

Second, we'll learn about the key distinction between *planned* expenditure and *actual* expenditure.

And third, we'll study equilibrium expenditure, a situation in which aggregate planned expenditure and actual expenditure are equal.

The relationship between aggregate planned expenditure and real GDP can be described by either an aggregate expenditure schedule or an aggregate expenditure curve. The *aggregate expenditure schedule* lists aggregate planned expenditure generated at each level of real GDP. The *aggregate expenditure curve* is a graph of the aggregate expenditure schedule.

FIGURE 12.5   Aggregate Expenditure

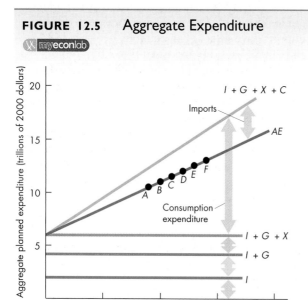

Aggregate planned expenditure is the sum of planned consumption expenditure, investment, government expenditure on goods and services, and exports minus imports. For example, in row *B* of the table, when real GDP is $10 trillion, planned consumption expenditure is $7.0 trillion, planned investment is $2.0 trillion, planned government expenditure is $2.2 trillion, planned exports are $1.8 trillion, and planned imports are $2.0 trillion. So when real GDP is $10 trillion, aggregate planned expenditure is $11 trillion ($7.0 + $2.0 + $2.2 + $1.8 − $2.0). The schedule shows that aggregate planned expenditure increases as real GDP increases. This relationship is graphed as the aggregate expenditure curve *AE*. The components of aggregate expenditure that increase with real GDP are consumption expenditure and imports. The other components—investment, government expenditure, and exports—do not vary with real GDP.

	Real GDP **(Y)**	**Consumption expenditure** **(C)**	**Investment** **(I)**	**Government expenditure** **(G)**	**Exports** **(X)**	**Imports** **(M)**	**Aggregate planned expenditure** **(AE = C + I + G + X − M)**
				(trillions of 2000 dollars)			
	0	0	2.0	2.2	1.8	0.0	6.0
A	9	6.3	2.0	2.2	1.8	1.8	10.5
B	10	7.0	2.0	2.2	1.8	2.0	11.0
C	11	7.7	2.0	2.2	1.8	2.2	11.5
D	12	8.4	2.0	2.2	1.8	2.4	12.0
E	13	9.1	2.0	2.2	1.8	2.6	12.5
F	14	9.8	2.0	2.2	1.8	2.8	13.0

Aggregate Planned Expenditure and Real GDP

The table in Fig. 12.5 sets out an aggregate expenditure schedule together with the components of aggregate planned expenditure. To calculate aggregate planned expenditure at a given real GDP, we add the various components together. The first column of the table shows real GDP, and the second column shows the consumption expenditure generated by each level of real GDP. A $1 trillion increase in real GDP generates a $0.7 trillion increase in consumption expenditure—the *MPC* is 0.7.

The next two columns show investment and government expenditure on goods and services. Investment depends on the real interest rate and the expected rate of profit (see Chapter 7, p. 171). At a given point in time, these factors generate a particular level of investment. Suppose this level of investment is $2.0 trillion. Also, suppose that government expenditure is $2.2 trillion.

The next two columns show exports and imports. Exports are influenced by events in the rest of the world, prices of foreign-produced goods and services relative to the prices of similar U.S.-produced goods and services, and exchange rates. But they are not directly affected by U.S. real GDP. Exports are a constant $1.8 trillion. Imports increase as U.S. real GDP increases. A $1 trillion increase in U.S. real GDP generates a $0.2 trillion increase in imports— the marginal propensity to import is 0.2.

The final column shows aggregate planned expenditure—the sum of planned consumption expenditure, investment, government expenditure on goods and services, and exports minus imports.

Figure 12.5 plots an aggregate expenditure curve. Real GDP is shown on the *x*-axis, and aggregate planned expenditure is shown on the *y*-axis. The aggregate expenditure curve is the red line *AE*. Points *A* through *F* on that curve correspond to the rows of the table. The *AE* curve is a graph of aggregate planned expenditure (the last column) plotted against real GDP (the first column).

Figure 12.5 also shows the components of aggregate expenditure. The constant components—investment (*I*), government expenditure on goods and services (*G*), and exports (*X*)—are shown by the horizontal lines in the figure. Consumption expenditure (*C*) is the vertical gap between the lines labeled *I* + *G* + *X* and *I* + *G* + *X* + *C*.

To construct the *AE* curve, subtract imports (*M*) from the *I* + *G* + *X* + *C* line. Aggregate expenditure is expenditure on U.S.-produced goods and services. But the components of aggregate expenditure—*C*, *I*, and *G*—include expenditure on imported goods and services. For example, if you buy a new cell phone, your expenditure is part of consumption expenditure. But if the cell phone is a Nokia made in Finland, your expenditure on it must be subtracted from consumption expenditure to find out how much is spent on goods and services produced in the United States—on U.S. real GDP. Money paid to Nokia for cell phone imports from Finland does not add to aggregate expenditure in the United States.

Because imports are only a part of aggregate expenditure, when we subtract imports from the other components of aggregate expenditure, aggregate planned expenditure still increases as real GDP increases, as you can see in Fig. 12.5.

Consumption expenditure minus imports, which varies with real GDP, is called **induced expenditure.** The sum of investment, government expenditure, and exports, which does not vary with real GDP, is called **autonomous expenditure.** Consumption expenditure and imports can also have an autonomous component—a component that does not vary with real GDP. Another way of thinking about autonomous expenditure is that it would be the level of aggregate planned expenditure if real GDP were zero.

In Fig. 12.5, autonomous expenditure is $6 trillion—aggregate planned expenditure when real GDP is zero. For each $1 trillion increase in real GDP, induced expenditure increases by $0.5 trillion.

The aggregate expenditure curve summarizes the relationship between aggregate *planned* expenditure and real GDP. But what determines the point on the aggregate expenditure curve at which the economy operates? What determines *actual* aggregate expenditure?

Actual Expenditure, Planned Expenditure, and Real GDP

Actual aggregate expenditure is always equal to real GDP, as we saw in Chapter 5 (p. 114). But aggregate *planned* expenditure is not necessarily equal to actual aggregate expenditure and therefore is not necessarily equal to real GDP. How can actual expenditure and planned expenditure differ from each other? Why don't expenditure plans get implemented? The main reason is that firms might end up with inventories that are greater or smaller than planned. People carry out their consumption expenditure plans, the government implements its planned expenditure on goods and services, and net exports are as planned. Firms carry out their plans to purchase new buildings, plant, and equipment. But one component of investment is the change in firms' inventories of goods. If aggregate planned expenditure is less than real GDP, firms don't sell all the goods they planned to sell and

they end up with unplanned inventories. If aggregate planned expenditure exceeds real GDP, firms sell more than they planned to sell and inventories decrease below the level that firms had planned.

Equilibrium Expenditure

Equilibrium expenditure is the level of aggregate expenditure that occurs when aggregate *planned* expenditure equals real GDP. Equilibrium expenditure is a

---

FIGURE 12.6   Equilibrium Expenditure

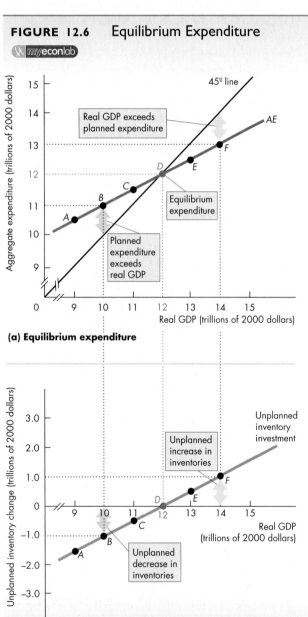

(a) Equilibrium expenditure

(b) Unplanned inventory changes

	Real GDP (Y)	Aggregate planned expenditure (AE)	Unplanned inventory change (Y – AE)
		(trillions of 2000 dollars)	
A	9	10.5	−1.5
B	10	11.0	−1.0
C	11	11.5	−0.5
D	12	12.0	0
E	13	12.5	0.5
F	14	13.0	1.0

The table shows expenditure plans at different levels of real GDP. When real GDP is $12 trillion, aggregate planned expenditure equals real GDP.

Part (a) of the figure illustrates equilibrium expenditure, which occurs when aggregate planned expenditure equals real GDP at the intersection of the 45° line and the AE curve. Part (b) of the figure shows the forces that bring about equilibrium expenditure. When aggregate planned expenditure exceeds real GDP, inventories decrease—for example, at point B in both parts of the figure. Firms increase production, and real GDP increases.

When aggregate planned expenditure is less than real GDP, inventories increase—for example, at point F in both parts of the figure. Firms decrease production, and real GDP decreases. When aggregate planned expenditure equals real GDP, there are no unplanned inventory changes and real GDP remains constant at equilibrium expenditure.

level of aggregate expenditure and real GDP at which everyone's spending plans are fulfilled. When the price level is fixed, equilibrium expenditure determines real GDP. When aggregate planned expenditure and actual aggregate expenditure are unequal, a process of convergence toward equilibrium expenditure occurs. And throughout this convergence process, real GDP adjusts. Let's examine equilibrium expenditure and the process that brings it about.

Figure 12.6(a) illustrates equilibrium expenditure. The table sets out aggregate planned expenditure at various levels of real GDP. These values are plotted as points A through F along the AE curve. The 45° line shows all the points at which aggregate planned expenditure equals real GDP. So where the AE curve lies above the 45° line, aggregate planned expenditure exceeds real GDP; where the AE curve lies below the 45° line, aggregate planned expenditure is less than real GDP; and where the AE curve intersects the 45° line, aggregate planned expenditure equals real GDP. Point D illustrates equilibrium expenditure. At this point, real GDP is $12 trillion.

Convergence to Equilibrium

What are the forces that move aggregate expenditure toward its equilibrium level? To answer this question, we must look at a situation in which aggregate expenditure is away from its equilibrium level. Suppose that in Fig. 12.6, real GDP is $10 trillion. With real GDP at $10 trillion, actual aggregate expenditure is also $10 trillion. But aggregate *planned* expenditure is $11 trillion, point B in Fig. 12.6(a). Aggregate planned expenditure exceeds *actual* expenditure. When people spend $11 trillion and firms produce goods and services worth $10 trillion, firms' inventories fall by $1 trillion, point B in Fig. 12.6(b). Because the change in inventories is part of investment, *actual* investment is $1 trillion less than *planned* investment.

Real GDP doesn't remain at $10 trillion for very long. Firms have inventory targets based on their sales. When inventories fall below target, firms increase production to restore inventories to the target level. To increase inventories, firms hire additional labor and increase production. Suppose that they increase production in the next period by $1 trillion. Real GDP increases by $1.0 trillion to $11.0 trillion. But again, aggregate planned expenditure exceeds real GDP. When real GDP is $11.0 trillion, aggregate planned expenditure is $11.5 trillion, point C in Fig.

12.6(a). Again, inventories decrease, but this time by less than before. With real GDP of $11.0 trillion and aggregate planned expenditure of $11.5 trillion, inventories decrease by $0.5 trillion, point C in Fig. 12.6(b). Again, firms hire additional labor and production increases; real GDP increases yet further.

The process that we've just described—planned expenditure exceeds real GDP, inventories decrease, and production increases to restore inventories—ends when real GDP has reached $12 trillion. At this real GDP, there is equilibrium. Unplanned inventory changes are zero. Firms do not change their production.

You can do an experiment similar to the one we've just done but starting with a level of real GDP greater than equilibrium expenditure. In this case, planned expenditure is less than actual expenditure, inventories pile up, and firms cut production. As before, real GDP keeps on changing (decreasing this time) until it reaches its equilibrium level of $12 trillion.

REVIEW QUIZ

1 What is the relationship between aggregate planned expenditure and real GDP at equilibrium expenditure?
2 How does equilibrium expenditure come about? What adjusts to achieve equilibrium?
3 If real GDP and aggregate expenditure are less than equilibrium expenditure, what happens to firms' inventories? How do firms change their production? And what happens to real GDP?
4 If real GDP and aggregate expenditure are greater than equilibrium expenditure, what happens to firms' inventories? How do firms change their production? And what happens to real GDP?

myeconlab Study Plan 12.2

We've learned that when the price level is fixed, real GDP is determined by equilibrium expenditure. And we have seen how unplanned changes in inventories and the production response they generate bring a convergence toward equilibrium expenditure. We're now going to study *changes* in equilibrium expenditure and discover an economic amplifier called the *multiplier*.

The Multiplier

Investment and exports can change for many reasons. A fall in the real interest rate might induce firms to increase their planned investment. A wave of innovation, such as occurred with the spread of multimedia computers in the 1990s, might increase expected future profits and lead firms to increase their planned investment. An economic boom in Western Europe and Japan might lead to a large increase in their expenditure on U.S.-produced goods and services—on U.S. exports. These are all examples of increases in autonomous expenditure.

When autonomous expenditure increases, aggregate expenditure increases and so does equilibrium expenditure and real GDP. But the increase in real GDP is *larger* than the change in autonomous expenditure. The **multiplier** is the amount by which a change in autonomous expenditure is magnified or multiplied to determine the change in equilibrium expenditure and real GDP.

To get the basic idea of the multiplier, we'll work with an example economy in which there are no income taxes and no imports. So we'll first assume that these factors are absent. Then, when you understand the basic idea, we'll bring these factors back into play and see what difference they make to the multiplier.

The Basic Idea of the Multiplier

Suppose that investment increases. The additional expenditure by businesses means that aggregate expenditure and real GDP increase. The increase in real GDP increases disposable income, and with no income taxes, real GDP and disposable income increase by the same amount. The increase in disposable income brings an increase in consumption expenditure. And the increased consumption expenditure adds even more to aggregate expenditure. Real GDP and disposable income increase further, and so does consumption expenditure. The initial increase in investment brings an even bigger increase in aggregate expenditure because it induces an increase in consumption expenditure. The magnitude of the increase in aggregate expenditure that results from an increase in autonomous expenditure is determined by the *multiplier*.

The table in Fig. 12.7 sets out an aggregate planned expenditure schedule. Initially, when real GDP is $11 trillion, aggregate planned expenditure is $11.25 trillion. For each $1 trillion increase in real GDP, aggregate planned expenditure increases by $0.75 trillion. This aggregate expenditure schedule is shown in the figure as the aggregate expenditure curve AE_0. Initially, equilibrium expenditure is $12 trillion. You can see this equilibrium in row B of the table and in the figure where the curve AE_0 intersects the 45° line at the point marked B.

Now suppose that autonomous expenditure increases by $0.5 trillion. What happens to equilibrium expenditure? You can see the answer in Fig. 12.7. When this increase in autonomous expenditure is added to the original aggregate planned expenditure, aggregate planned expenditure increases by $0.5 trillion at each level of real GDP. The new aggregate expenditure curve is AE_1. The new equilibrium expenditure, highlighted in the table (row D'), occurs where AE_1 intersects the 45° line and is $14 trillion (point D'). At this real GDP, aggregate planned expenditure equals real GDP.

The Multiplier Effect

In Fig. 12.7, the increase in autonomous expenditure of $0.5 trillion increases equilibrium expenditure by $2 trillion. That is, the change in autonomous expenditure leads, like Erykah Badu's electronic equipment, to an amplified change in equilibrium expenditure. This amplified change is the *multiplier effect*—equilibrium expenditure increases by *more than* the increase in autonomous expenditure. The multiplier is greater than 1.

Initially, when autonomous expenditure increases, aggregate planned expenditure exceeds real GDP. As a result, inventories decrease. Firms respond by increasing production so as to restore their inventories to the target level. As production increases, so does real GDP. With a higher level of real GDP, *induced expenditure* increases. Thus equilibrium expenditure increases by the sum of the initial increase in autonomous expenditure and the increase in induced expenditure. In this example, induced expenditure increases by $1.5 trillion, so equilibrium expenditure increases by $2 trillion.

Although we have just analyzed the effects of an *increase* in autonomous expenditure, the same analysis applies to a decrease in autonomous expenditure. If initially the aggregate expenditure curve is AE_1, equilibrium expenditure and real GDP are $14 trillion. A decrease in autonomous expenditure of $0.5 trillion shifts the aggregate expenditure curve downward by

Why Is the Multiplier Greater Than 1?

We've seen that equilibrium expenditure increases by more than the increase in autonomous expenditure. This makes the multiplier greater than 1. How come? Why does equilibrium expenditure increase by more than the increase in autonomous expenditure?

The multiplier is greater than 1 because induced expenditure increases—an increase in autonomous expenditure *induces* further increases in expenditure. The NASA space shuttle program costs about $5 billion a year. This expenditure adds $5 billion a year directly to real GDP. But that is not the end of the story. Astronauts and engineers now have more income, and they spend part of the extra income on goods and services. Real GDP now rises by the initial $5 billion plus the extra consumption expenditure induced by the $5 billion increase in income. The producers of cars, flat-screen TVs, vacations, and other goods and services now have increased incomes, and they, in turn, spend part of the increase in their incomes on consumption goods and services. Additional income induces additional expenditure, which creates additional income.

We have seen that a change in autonomous expenditure has a multiplier effect on real GDP. But how big is the multiplier effect?

The Size of the Multiplier

Suppose that the economy is in a recession. Profit prospects start to look better, and firms are making plans for large increases in investment. The world economy is also heading toward expansion, and exports are increasing. The question on everyone's lips is: How strong will the expansion be? This is a hard question to answer. But an important ingredient in the answer is working out the size of the multiplier.

The *multiplier* is the amount by which a change in autonomous expenditure is multiplied to determine the change in equilibrium expenditure that it generates. To calculate the multiplier, we divide the change in equilibrium expenditure by the change in autonomous expenditure. Let's calculate the multiplier for the example in Fig. 12.7. Initially, equilibrium expenditure is $12 trillion. Then autonomous expenditure increases by $0.5 trillion, and equilibrium expenditure increases by $2 trillion, to $14 trillion. Then

$$\text{Multiplier} = \frac{\text{Change in equilibrium expenditure}}{\text{Change in autonomous expenditure}}$$

FIGURE 12.7   The Multiplier

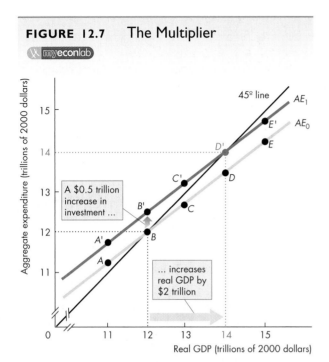

Real GDP (Y)	Aggregate planned expenditure			
	Original (AE₀)		New (AE₁)	
	(trillions of 2000 dollars)			
11	A	11.25	A'	11.75
12	B	12.00	B'	12.50
13	C	12.75	C'	13.25
14	D	13.50	D'	14.00
15	E	14.25	E'	14.75

A $0.5 trillion increase in autonomous expenditure shifts the AE curve upward by $0.5 trillion from AE₀ to AE₁. Equilibrium expenditure increases by $2 trillion from $12 trillion to $14 trillion. The increase in equilibrium expenditure is 4 times the increase in autonomous expenditure, so the multiplier is 4.

$0.5 trillion to AE_0. Equilibrium expenditure decreases from $14 trillion to $12 trillion. The decrease in equilibrium expenditure ($2 trillion) is larger than the decrease in autonomous expenditure that brought it about ($0.5 trillion).

$$\text{Multiplier} = \frac{\$2 \text{ trillion}}{\$0.5 \text{ trillion}} = 4.$$

The Multiplier and the Slope of the *AE* Curve

The magnitude of the multiplier depends on the slope of the *AE* curve. The steeper the slope of the *AE* curve, the larger is the multiplier. To see why, let's do a calculation.

Aggregate expenditure and real GDP change because induced expenditure and autonomous expenditure change. The change in real GDP (ΔY) equals the change in induced expenditure (ΔN) plus the change in autonomous expenditure (ΔA). That is,

$$\Delta Y = \Delta N + \Delta A.$$

But the change in induced expenditure is determined by the change in real GDP and the slope of the *AE* curve. To see why, begin with the fact that the slope of the *AE* curve equals the "rise," ΔN, divided by the "run," ΔY. That is

$$\text{Slope of } AE \text{ curve} = \Delta N \div \Delta Y.$$

So

$$\Delta N = \text{Slope of } AE \text{ curve} \times \Delta Y.$$

Now, use this equation to replace ΔN in the first equation above to give

$$\Delta Y = \text{Slope of } AE \text{ curve} \times \Delta Y + \Delta A.$$

Now, solve for ΔY as

$$(1 - \text{Slope of } AE \text{ curve}) \times \Delta Y = \Delta A$$

and rearrange to give

$$\Delta Y = \frac{\Delta A}{1 - \text{Slope of } AE \text{ curve}}.$$

Finally, divide both sides of this equation by ΔA to give

$$\text{Multiplier} = \frac{\Delta Y}{\Delta A} = \frac{1}{1 - \text{Slope of } AE \text{ curve}}.$$

If we use the example in Fig. 12.7, the slope of the *AE* curve is 0.75, so

$$\text{Multiplier} = \frac{1}{1 - 0.75} = \frac{1}{0.25} = 4.$$

Where there are no income taxes and no imports, the slope of the *AE* curve equals the marginal propensity to consume (*MPC*). So

$$\text{Multiplier} = \frac{1}{1 - MPC}.$$

But ($1 - MPC$) equals *MPS*. So another formula is

$$\text{Multiplier} = \frac{1}{MPS}.$$

Again using the numbers in Fig. 12.7, we have

$$\text{Multiplier} = \frac{1}{0.25} = 4.$$

Because the marginal propensity to save (*MPS*) is a fraction—a number between 0 and 1—the multiplier is greater than 1.

Imports and Income Taxes

The multiplier is determined, in general, not only by the marginal propensity to consume but also by the marginal propensity to import and by the income tax rate. Imports make the multiplier smaller than it otherwise would be. To see why, think about what happens following an increase in investment. An increase in investment increases real GDP, which in turn increases consumption expenditure. But part of the increase in investment and consumption expenditure is expenditure on imported goods and services, not U.S.-produced goods and services. Only expenditure on U.S.-produced goods and services increases U.S. real GDP. The larger the marginal propensity to import, the smaller is the change in U.S. real GDP.

Income taxes also make the multiplier smaller than it otherwise would be. Again, think about what happens following an increase in investment. An increase in investment increases real GDP. But because income taxes increase, disposable income increases by less than the increase in real GDP. Consequently, consumption expenditure increases by less than it would if taxes had not changed. The larger the income tax rate, the smaller is the change in disposable income and real GDP.

The marginal propensity to import and the income tax rate together with the marginal propensity to consume determine the multiplier. And their combined influence determines the slope of the *AE* curve.

Figure 12.8 compares two situations. In Fig. 12.8(a), there are no imports and no taxes. The slope of the *AE* curve equals the marginal propensity to consume, which is 0.75, and the multiplier is 4. In Fig. 12.8(b), imports and income taxes decrease the slope of the *AE* curve to 0.5. The multiplier is 2.

FIGURE 12.8   The Multiplier and the Slope of the AE Curve

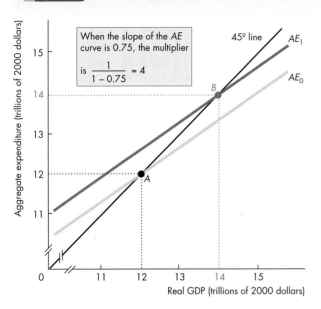

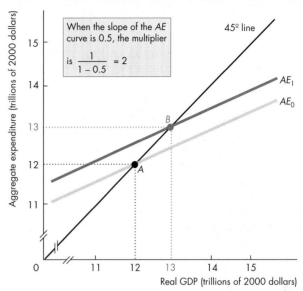

(a) Multiplier is 4

(b) Multiplier is 2

Imports and income taxes make the AE curve less steep and reduce the value of the multiplier. In part (a), with no imports and income taxes, the slope of the AE curve is 0.75 (the marginal propensity to consume) and the multiplier is 4.

But with imports and income taxes, the slope of the AE curve is less than the marginal propensity to consume. In part (b), the slope of the AE curve is 0.5. In this case, the multiplier is 2.

Over time, the value of the multiplier changes as tax rates change and as the marginal propensity to consume and the marginal propensity to import change. These ongoing changes make the multiplier hard to predict. But they do not change the fundamental fact that an initial change in autonomous expenditure leads to a magnified change in aggregate expenditure and real GDP.

Pages 308–309 of the math note show the effects of taxes, imports, and the *MPC* on the multiplier.

The Multiplier Process

The multiplier effect isn't a one-shot, overnight event. It is a process that plays out over a few months. Figure 12.9 illustrates the multiplier process. Autonomous expenditure increases by $0.5 trillion. At this time, real GDP increases by $0.5 trillion (the green bar in round 1). This increase in real GDP increases induced expenditure in round 2. With the slope of the AE curve equal to 0.75, induced expenditure

increases by 0.75 times the increase in real GDP, so the increase in real GDP of $0.5 trillion induces a further increase in expenditure of $0.375 trillion. This change in induced expenditure (the green bar in round 2) when added to the previous increase in expenditure (the blue bar in round 2) increases real GDP by $0.875 trillion. The round 2 increase in real GDP induces a round 3 increase in induced expenditure. The process repeats through successive rounds. Each increase in real GDP is 0.75 times the previous increase and eventually real GDP increases by $2 trillion.

Now that you've studied the multiplier we can use it to gain some insights into what happens at business cycle turning points.

Business Cycle Turning Points

At business cycle turning points, the economy moves from expansion to recession or from recession to expansion. Economists understand these turning

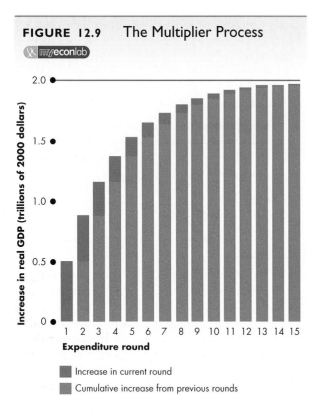

FIGURE 12.9   The Multiplier Process

Increase in real GDP (trillions of 2000 dollars)

Expenditure round

■ Increase in current round

■ Cumulative increase from previous rounds

Autonomous expenditure increases by $0.5 trillion. In round 1, real GDP increases by the same amount. With the slope of the *AE* curve equal to 0.75, each additional dollar of real GDP induces an additional 0.75 of a dollar of induced expenditure. The round 1 increase in real GDP brings an increase in induced expenditure of $0.375 trillion in round 2. At the end of round 2, real GDP has increased by $0.875 trillion. The extra $0.375 trillion of real GDP in round 2 brings a further increase in induced expenditure of $0.281 trillion in round 3. Real GDP increases yet further to $1.156 trillion. This process continues with real GDP increasing by ever-smaller amounts. When the process comes to an end, real GDP has increased by a total of $2 trillion.

points as seismologists understand earthquakes. They know quite a lot about the forces and mechanisms that produce them, but they can't predict them. The forces that bring business cycle turning points are the swings in autonomous expenditure such as investment and exports. The mechanism that gives momentum to the economy's new direction is the multiplier. Let's use what we've now learned to examine these turning points.

A Recession Begins A recession is triggered by a decrease in autonomous expenditure that decreases aggregate planned expenditure. At the moment the economy turns the corner into recession, real GDP exceeds aggregate planned expenditure. In this situation, firms see unplanned inventories piling up. The recession now begins. To reduce their inventories, firms cut production, and real GDP begins to decrease. This initial decrease in real GDP brings lower incomes that cut consumption expenditure. The multiplier process kicks in, and the recession takes hold.

An Expansion Begins The process we've just described works in reverse at a business cycle trough. An expansion is triggered by an increase in autonomous expenditure that increases aggregate planned expenditure. At the moment the economy turns the corner into an expansion, aggregate planned expenditure exceeds real GDP. In this situation, firms see their inventories taking an unplanned dive. The expansion now begins. To meet their inventory targets, firms increase production, and real GDP begins to increase. This initial increase in real GDP brings higher incomes that stimulate consumption expenditure. The multiplier process kicks in, and the expansion picks up speed.

The 2002–2006 Expansion The National Bureau of Economic Research declared November 2001 as the start of the most recent expansion. During 2001, the year before the expansion, business inventories fell relative to their desired levels. From 2002 through 2006, inventories increased, but not by as much as planned. So during these years, firms stepped up production to increase inventories toward their planned levels.

REVIEW QUIZ

1 What is the multiplier? What does it determine? Why does it matter?
2 How do the marginal propensity to consume, the marginal propensity to import, and the income tax rate influence the multiplier?
3 How do fluctuations in autonomous expenditure influence real GDP? If autonomous expenditure decreases, which phase of the business cycle does the economy enter?

Ⓧ myeconlab **Study Plan 12.3**

The Multiplier and the Price Level

We have just considered adjustments in spending that occur in the very short run when the price level is fixed. In this time frame, the economy's potholes, which are changes in investment and exports, are not smoothed by shock absorbers like those on Michael Bloomberg's car. Instead, they are amplified like Erykah Badu's voice. But these outcomes occur only when the price level is fixed. We now investigate what happens after a long enough time lapse for the price level to change.

Adjusting Quantities *and* Prices

When firms can't keep up with sales and their inventories fall below target, they increase production, but at some point, they raise their prices. Similarly, when firms find unwanted inventories piling up, they decrease production, but eventually they cut their prices. So far, we've studied the macroeconomic consequences of firms changing their production levels when their sales change, but we haven't looked at the effects of price changes. When individual firms change their prices, the economy's price level changes.

To study the simultaneous determination of real GDP and the price level, we use the *aggregate supply– aggregate demand model*, which is explained in Chapter 11. But to understand how aggregate demand adjusts, we need to work out the connection between the aggregate supply–aggregate demand model and the equilibrium expenditure model that we've used in this chapter. The key to understanding the relationship between these two models is the distinction between the aggregate *expenditure* and aggregate *demand* and the related distinction between the aggregate *expenditure curve* and the aggregate *demand curve*.

Aggregate Expenditure and Aggregate Demand

The aggregate expenditure curve is the relationship between the aggregate planned expenditure and real GDP, all other influences on aggregate planned expenditure remaining the same. The aggregate demand curve is the relationship between the aggregate quantity of goods and services demanded and the price level, all other influences on aggregate demand remaining the same. Let's explore the links between these two relationships.

Deriving the Aggregate Demand Curve

When the price level changes, aggregate planned expenditure changes and the quantity of real GDP demanded changes. The aggregate demand curve slopes downward. Why? There are two main reasons:

- Wealth effect
- Substitution effects

Wealth Effect Other things remaining the same, the higher the price level, the smaller is the purchasing power of wealth. For example, suppose you have $100 in the bank and the price level is 105. If the price level rises to 125, your $100 buys fewer goods and services. You are less wealthy. With less wealth, you will probably want to try to spend a bit less and save a bit more. The higher the price level, other things remaining the same, the lower is aggregate planned expenditure.

Substitution Effects For a given expected future price level, a rise in the price level today makes current goods and services more expensive relative to future goods and services and results in a delay in purchases—an *intertemporal substitution*. A rise in the U.S. price level, other things remaining the same, makes U.S.-produced goods and services more expensive relative to foreign-produced goods and services. As a result, U.S. imports increase and U.S. exports decrease—an *international substitution*.

When the price level rises, each of these effects reduces aggregate planned expenditure at each level of real GDP. As a result, when the price level *rises*, the aggregate expenditure curve shifts *downward*. A fall in the price level has the opposite effect. When the price level *falls*, the aggregate expenditure curve shifts *upward*.

Figure 12.10(a) shows the shifts of the *AE* curve. When the price level is 115, the aggregate expenditure curve is AE_0, which intersects the 45° line at point *B*. Equilibrium expenditure is $12 trillion. If the price level increases to 135, the aggregate expenditure curve shifts downward to AE_1, which intersects the 45° line at point *A*. Equilibrium expenditure decreases to $11 trillion. If the price level decreases to 95, the aggregate expenditure curve shifts upward to AE_2, which intersects the 45° line at point C. Equilibrium expenditure increases to $13 trillion.

We've just seen that when the price level changes, other things remaining the same, the aggregate expenditure curve shifts and the equilibrium expenditure changes. But when the price level changes, other things remaining the same, there is a movement along the aggregate demand curve.

Figure 12.10(b) shows the movements along the aggregate demand curve. At a price level of 115, the aggregate quantity of goods and services demanded is $12 trillion—point B on the AD curve. If the price level rises to 135, the aggregate quantity of goods and services demanded decreases to $11 trillion. There is a movement up along the aggregate demand curve to point A. If the price level falls to 95, the aggregate quantity of goods and services demanded increases to $13 trillion. There is a movement down along the aggregate demand curve to point C.

Each point on the aggregate demand curve corresponds to a point of equilibrium expenditure. The equilibrium expenditure points A, B, and C in Fig. 12.10(a) correspond to the points A, B, and C on the aggregate demand curve in Fig. 12.10(b).

Changes in Aggregate Expenditure and Aggregate Demand

When any influence on aggregate planned expenditure other than the price level changes, both the aggregate expenditure curve and the aggregate demand curve shift. For example, an increase in investment or exports increases both aggregate planned expenditure and aggregate demand and shifts both the AE curve and the AD curve. Figure 12.11 illustrates the effect of such an increase.

Initially, the aggregate expenditure curve is AE_0 in part (a) and the aggregate demand curve is AD_0 in part (b). The price level is 115, real GDP is $12 trillion, and the economy is at point A in both parts of Fig. 12.11. Now suppose that investment increases by $1 trillion. At a constant price level of 115, the aggregate expenditure curve shifts upward to AE_1. This curve intersects the 45° line at an equilibrium expenditure of $14 trillion (point B). This equilibrium expenditure of $14 trillion is the aggregate quantity of goods and services demanded at a price level of 115, as shown by point B in part (b). Point B lies on

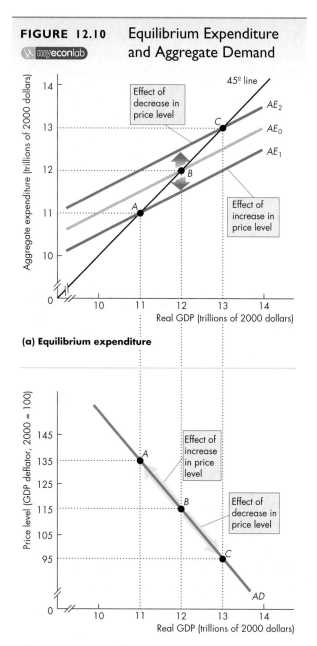

FIGURE 12.10 myeconlab   Equilibrium Expenditure and Aggregate Demand

(a) Equilibrium expenditure

(b) Aggregate demand

A change in the price level *shifts* the AE curve and results in a *movement along* the AD curve. When the price level is 115, the AE curve is AE_0 and equilibrium expenditure is $12 trillion at point B. When the price level rises to 135, the AE curve is AE_1 and equilibrium expenditure is $11 trillion at point A. When the price level falls to 95, the AE curve is AE_2 and equilibrium expenditure is $13 trillion at point C. Points A, B, and C on the AD curve in part (b) correspond to the equilibrium expenditure points A, B, and C in part (a).

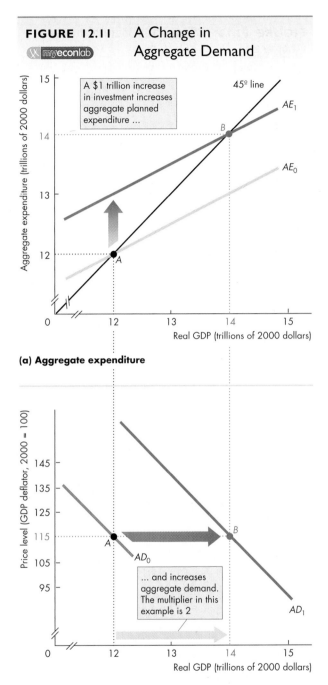

FIGURE 12.11 myeconlab A Change in Aggregate Demand

A $1 trillion increase in investment increases aggregate planned expenditure ...

45° line

AE₁

B

AE₀

A

(a) Aggregate expenditure

A

B

AD₀

... and increases aggregate demand. The multiplier in this example is 2.

AD₁

(b) Aggregate demand

The price level is 115. When the aggregate expenditure curve is AE_0 (part a), the aggregate demand curve is AD_0 (part b). An increase in autonomous expenditure shifts the AE curve upward to AE_1. In the new equilibrium, real GDP is $14 trillion (at point B). Because the quantity of real GDP demanded at a price level of 115 increases to $14 trillion, the AD curve shifts rightward to AD_1.

a new aggregate demand curve. The aggregate demand curve has shifted rightward to AD_1.

But how do we know by how much the AD curve shifts? The multiplier determines the answer. The larger the multiplier, the larger is the shift in the aggregate demand curve that results from a given change in autonomous expenditure. In this example, the multiplier is 2. A $1 trillion increase in investment produces a $2 trillion increase in the aggregate quantity of goods and services demanded at each price level. That is, a $1 trillion increase in autonomous expenditure shifts the aggregate demand curve rightward by $2 trillion.

A decrease in autonomous expenditure shifts the aggregate expenditure curve downward and shifts the aggregate demand curve leftward. You can see these effects by reversing the change that we've just described. If the economy is initially at point B on the aggregate expenditure curve AE_1 and on the aggregate demand curve is AD_1, a decrease in autonomous expenditure shifts the aggregate expenditure curve downward to AE_0. The aggregate quantity of goods and services demanded decreases from $14 trillion to $12 trillion, and the aggregate demand curve shifts leftward to AD_0.

Let's summarize what we have just discovered:

If some factor other than a change in the price level increases autonomous expenditure, the AE curve shifts upward and the AD curve shifts rightward. The size of the AD curve shift equals the change in autonomous expenditure multiplied by the multiplier.

Equilibrium Real GDP and the Price Level

In Chapter 11, we learned that aggregate demand and short-run aggregate supply determine equilibrium real GDP and the price level. We've now put aggregate demand under a more powerful microscope and have discovered that a change in investment (or in any component of autonomous expenditure) changes aggregate demand and shifts the aggregate demand curve. The magnitude of the shift depends on the multiplier. But whether a change in autonomous expenditure results ultimately in a change in real GDP, a change in the price level, or a combination of the two depends on aggregate supply. There are two time frames to consider: the short run and the long run. First we'll see what happens in the short run.

An Increase in Aggregate Demand in the Short Run
Figure 12.12 describes the economy. Initially, in part
(a), the aggregate expenditure curve is AE_0 and equilibrium expenditure is $12 trillion—point A. In part
(b), aggregate demand is AD_0 and the short-run
aggregate supply curve is SAS. (Chapter 11,
pp. 265–266 explains the SAS curve.) Equilibrium
is at point A, where the aggregate demand and short-
run aggregate supply curves intersect. The price level
is 115, and real GDP is $12 trillion.

Now suppose that investment increases by $1 tril-
lion. With the price level fixed at 115, the aggregate
expenditure curve shifts upward to AE_1. Equilibrium
expenditure increases to $14 trillion—point B in part
(a). In part (b), the aggregate demand curve shifts
rightward by $2 trillion, from AD_0 to AD_1. How far
the aggregate demand curve shifts is determined by the
multiplier when the price level is fixed.

But with this new aggregate demand curve, the
price level does not remain fixed. The price level rises,
and as it does, the aggregate expenditure curve shifts
downward. The short-run equilibrium occurs when
the aggregate expenditure curve has shifted downward to AE_2 and the new aggregate demand curve,
AD_1, intersects the short-run aggregate supply curve
at point C in both part (a) and part (b). Real GDP is
$13.3 trillion, and the price level is 128.

When price level effects are taken into account,
the increase in investment still has a multiplier effect
on real GDP, but the multiplier is smaller than it
would be if the price level were fixed. The steeper the
slope of the short-run aggregate supply curve, the
larger is the increase in the price level and the smaller
is the multiplier effect on real GDP.

An Increase in Aggregate Demand in the Long Run
Figure 12.13 illustrates the long-run effect of an
increase in aggregate demand. In the long run, real
GDP equals potential GDP and there is full employment. Potential GDP is $12 trillion, and the long-
run aggregate supply curve is LAS. Initially, the
economy is at point A in parts (a) and (b).

Investment increases by $1 trillion. In Fig. 12.13,
the aggregate expenditure curve shifts to AE_1 and the
aggregate demand curve shifts to AD_1. With no
change in the price level, the economy would move to
point B and real GDP would increase to $14 trillion.
But in the short run, the price level rises to 128 and
real GDP increases to only $13.3 trillion. With the
higher price level, the AE curve shifts from AE_1 to

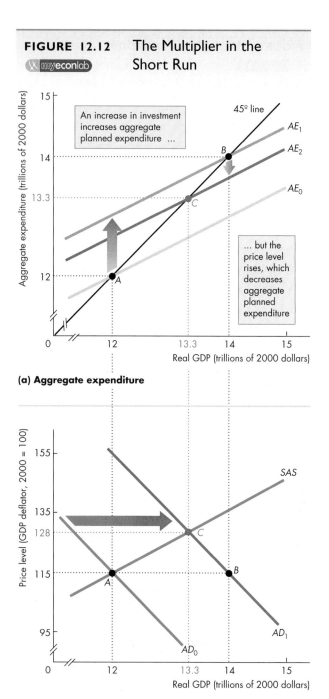

**FIGURE 12.12   The Multiplier in the
Short Run**

(a) Aggregate expenditure

(b) Aggregate demand

An increase in investment shifts the AE curve from AE_0 to
AE_1 and the AD curve from AD_0 to AD_1. The price level
rises, and the higher price level shifts the AE curve downward from AE_1 to AE_2. The economy moves to point C in
both parts. In the short run, when prices are flexible, the
multiplier effect is smaller than when the price level is fixed.

FIGURE 12.13   The Multiplier in the Long Run

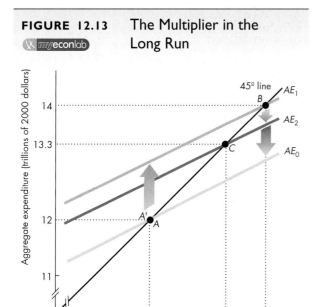

(a) Aggregate expenditure

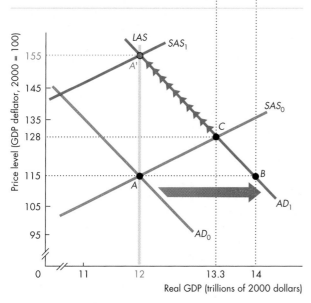

(b) Aggregate demand

Starting from point A, an increase in investment shifts the AE curve to AE_1 and the AD curve to AD_1. In the short run, the economy moves to point C. In the long run, the money wage rate rises and the SAS curve shifts to SAS_1. As the price level rises, the AE curve shifts back to AE_0 and the economy moves to point A'. In the long run, the multiplier is zero.

AE_2. The economy is now in a short-run equilibrium at point C in both part (a) and part (b).

Real GDP now exceeds potential GDP. The labor force is more than fully employed, and in the long run, shortages of labor increase the money wage rate. The higher money wage rate increases firms' costs, which decreases short-run aggregate supply and shifts the SAS curve leftward to SAS_1. The price level rises further, and real GDP decreases. There is a movement along AD_1, and the AE curve shifts downward from AE_2 toward AE_0. When the money wage rate and the price level have increased by the same percentage, real GDP is again equal to potential GDP and the economy is at point A'. In the long run, the multiplier is zero.

REVIEW QUIZ

1 How does a change in the price level influence the AE curve and the AD curve?

2 If autonomous expenditure increases with no change in the price level, what happens to the AE curve and the AD curve? Which curve shifts by an amount that is determined by the multiplier and why?

3 How does an increase in autonomous expenditure change real GDP in the short run? Does real GDP change by the same amount as the change in aggregate demand? Why or why not?

4 How does real GDP change in the long run when autonomous expenditure increases? Does real GDP change by the same amount as the change in aggregate demand? Why or why not?

 myeconlab Study Plan 12.4

◆ You are now ready to build on what you've learned about aggregate expenditure fluctuations and study the business cycle and the roles of fiscal policy and monetary policy in smoothing the cycle, while achieving price stability and sustained economic growth. In Chapter 13, we study the U.S. business cycle and inflation, and in Chapters 14 and 15, we study fiscal policy and monetary policy respectively. But before you leave the current topic, look at *Reading Between the Lines* on pp. 306–307 and see the Keynesian model in action in the U.S. economy during 2005.

Inventories in Expansion

Economy Shows Some Resilience in Quarter

December 1, 2005

The economy grew at a 4.3 percent annual rate from July through September, the Commerce Department reported yesterday, the fastest since the first quarter of last year and evidence of resilience in the face of hurricanes and record energy costs. . . .

"The economy is booming," said Mike Englund, chief economist at Action Economics in Boulder, Colo. "'As much as people may have been concerned about gas prices, consumers took the hit and now gas prices are falling." . . .

In addition, the Federal Reserve said yesterday in its regional survey of businesses that retailers were optimistic about the holiday shopping season. At the same time, the report showed that consumer prices "remained stable or experienced generally modest increases." . . .

According to the Commerce Department, the gross domestic product rose to $11.2 trillion when annualized and adjusted for inflation. Without adjustment, the economy grew at a 7.4 percent annual pace, to $12.6 trillion, for the quarter.

The government's personal consumption expenditures price index, a measure of prices tied to consumer spending, rose 3.6 percent, compared with a 3.7 percent rise reported last month and a 3.3 percent second-quarter gain.

Business inventories fell at a $13.4 billion annual rate, compared with the $16.6 billion downward pace previously reported.

Consumer spending, which accounts for about 70 percent of the economy, expanded at a 4.2 percent annual pace, compared with the 3.9 percent estimated in October and the 3.4 percent pace for the second quarter. Economists had expected consumer spending to set a 3.9 percent annual pace.

Essence of the Story

▸ Real GDP increased to $11.2 trillion (per year) in the third quarter of 2005, an annual rate of increase of 4.3 percent.

▸ Real consumer expenditure grew at a 4.2 percent annual rate.

▸ The prices of consumer goods and services increased at a 3.6 percent annual rate.

▸ The Federal Reserve reported increased expenditure with generally stable prices.

▸ Business inventories fell at a $13.4 billion annual rate.

▸ One economist said "The economy is booming."

▶ We can use the aggregate expenditure model to interpret this news article.

▶ The article reports that the economy is booming and business inventories have decreased.

▶ The effect of a decrease in inventories on real GDP depends on whether the decrease is planned or unplanned.

▶ A planned decrease in inventories decreases aggregate planned expenditure, shifts the *AE* curve downward, and decreases equilibrium expenditure.

▶ An unplanned decrease in inventories has no direct effect on the *AE* curve but means that actual expenditure is less than planned expenditure.

▶ When actual expenditure is less than planned expenditure, real GDP grows more quickly.

▶ The news article does not (and cannot) say whether the decrease in inventories was planned or unplanned.

▶ But the other features of real GDP in the third quarter of 2005 are consistent with the change in inventories being unplanned.

▶ The figures illustrate why.

▶ In the third quarter of 2005 (the quarter that ended on September 30, 2005), real GDP was $11,115 billion, up $113 billion from the second quarter. (All the values are 2000 dollars.)

▶ Business inventories decreased during the third quarter by $13 billion.

▶ But with real GDP increasing, firms planned larger inventories.

▶ On the basis of trends in the ratio of inventories to sales, we can estimate that planned inventory investment during the third quarter of 2005 was $11 billion.

▶ If this estimate is correct, there was an unplanned decrease in inventories of $24 billion—see Fig. 2.

▶ Aggregate *planned* expenditure was $24 billion greater than actual expenditure and was $11,139 billion—in Fig. 1.

▶ With an assumption about the slope of the *AE* curve, we can calculate equilibrium expenditure.

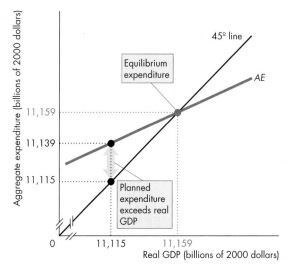

Figure 1 Equilibrium expenditure

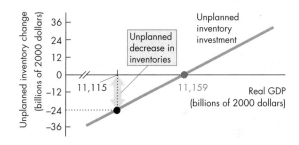

Figure 2 Unplanned inventory changes

▶ In Fig. 1, the slope of the *AE* curve is 0.457 (a value that is based on the assumption that the *MPC* is 0.9, the income tax rate is 0.27, and the marginal propensity to import is 0.2).

▶ Equilibrium expenditure, based on these assumptions, is $11,159 billion.

▶ Regardless of the exact values, equilibrium expenditure exceeds actual expenditure and the pace of real GDP growth is increasing.

▶ The economy is booming, as stated in the news article.

Mathematical Note:
The Algebra of the Keynesian Model

This mathematical note derives formulas for equilibrium expenditure and the multipliers. We begin by defining the symbols we need:

- Aggregate planned expenditure, AE
- Real GDP, Y
- Consumption expenditure, C
- Investment, I
- Government expenditure, G
- Exports, X
- Imports, M
- Net taxes, T
- Autonomous consumption expenditure, a
- Autonomous taxes, T_a
- Marginal propensity to consume, b
- Marginal propensity to import, m
- Marginal tax rate, t
- Autonomous expenditure, A

Aggregate Expenditure

Aggregate planned expenditure (AE) is the sum of the planned amounts of consumption expenditure (C), investment (I), government expenditure (G), and exports (X) minus the planned amount of imports (M).

$$AE = C + I + G + X - M.$$

Consumption Function Consumption expenditure (C) depends on disposable income (YD), and we write the consumption function as

$$C = a + bYD.$$

Disposable income (YD) equals real GDP minus net taxes ($Y - T$). So if we replace YD with ($Y - T$), the consumption function becomes

$$C = a + b(Y - T).$$

Net taxes, T, equal autonomous taxes (that are independent of income), T_a, plus induced taxes (that vary with income), tY. So

$$T = T_a + tY.$$

Use this last equation to replace T in the consumption function. The consumption function becomes

$$C = a - bT_a + b(1 - t)Y.$$

This equation describes consumption expenditure as a function of real GDP.

Import Function Imports depend on real GDP, and the import function is

$$M = mY.$$

Aggregate Expenditure Curve Use the consumption function and the import function to replace C and M in the AE equation. That is,

$$AE = a - bT_a + b(1 - t)Y + I + G + X - mY.$$

Collect the terms on the right side of the equation that involve Y to obtain

$$AE = (a - bT_a + I + G + X) + [b(1 - t) - m]Y.$$

Autonomous expenditure (A) is ($a - bT_a + I + G + X$), and the slope of the AE curve is $[b(1 - t) - m]$. So the equation for the AE curve, which is shown in Fig. 1, is

$$AE = A + [b(1 - t) - m]Y.$$

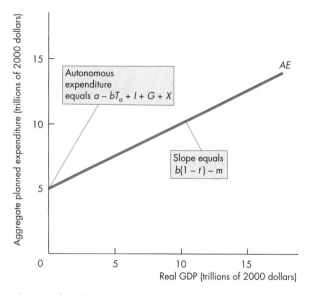

Figure 1 The AE curve

Equilibrium Expenditure

Equilibrium expenditure occurs when aggregate planned expenditure (AE) equals real GDP (Y). That is,

$$AE = Y.$$

In Fig. 2, the scales of the x-axis (real GDP) and the y-axis (aggregate planned expenditure) are identical, so the 45° line shows the points at which aggregate planned expenditure equals real GDP.

Figure 2 shows the point of equilibrium expenditure at the intersection of the AE curve and the 45° line.

To calculate equilibrium expenditure, solve the equations for the AE curve and the 45° line for the two unknown quantities AE and Y. So starting with

$$AE = A + [b(1 - t) - m]Y$$
$$AE = Y,$$

replace AE with Y in the AE equation to obtain

$$Y = A + [b(1 - t) - m]Y.$$

The solution for Y is

$$Y = \frac{1}{1 - [b(1 - t) - m]}A.$$

The Multiplier

The multiplier equals the change in equilibrium expenditure and real GDP (Y) that results from a change in autonomous expenditure (A) divided by the change in autonomous expenditure.

A change in autonomous expenditure (ΔA) changes equilibrium expenditure and real GDP by

$$\Delta Y = \frac{1}{1 - [b(1 - t) - m]}\Delta A,$$

$$\text{Multiplier} = \frac{1}{1 - [b(1 - t) - m]}.$$

The size of the multiplier depends on the slope of the AE curve, $b(1 - t) - m$. The larger the slope, the larger is the multiplier. So the multiplier is larger,

- The greater the marginal propensity to consume (b)
- The smaller the marginal tax rate (t)
- The smaller the marginal propensity to import (m)

An economy with no imports and no income taxes has $m = 0$ and $t = 0$. In this special case, the multiplier equals $1/(1 - b)$. If b is 0.75, then the multiplier is 4, as shown in Fig. 3.

In an economy with imports and income taxes, if $b = 0.75$, $t = 0.2$, and $m = 0.1$, the multiplier equals 1 divided by $[1 - 0.75(1 - 0.2) - 0.1]$, which equals 2. Make up some more examples to show the effects of b, t, and m on the multiplier.

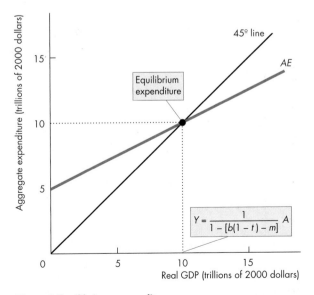

Figure 2 Equilibrium expenditure

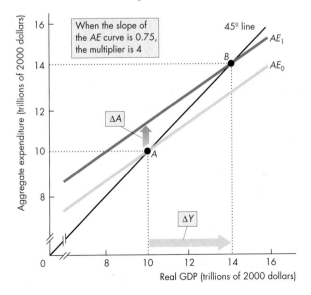

Figure 3 The multiplier

Government Expenditure Multiplier

The government expenditure multiplier equals the change in equilibrium expenditure (Y) that results from a change in government expenditure (G) divided by the change in government expenditure. Because autonomous expenditure is equal to

$$A = a - bT_a + I + G + X,$$

the change in autonomous expenditure equals the change in government expenditure. That is,

$$\Delta A = \Delta G.$$

You can see from the solution for equilibrium expenditure Y that

$$\Delta Y = \frac{1}{1 - [b(1 - t) - m]}\Delta G.$$

The government expenditure multiplier equals

$$Y = \frac{1}{1 - [b(1 - t) - m]}.$$

In an economy in which $t = 0$ and $m = 0$, the government expenditure multiplier is $1/(1 - b)$. With $b = 0.75$, the government expenditure multiplier is 4, as Fig. 4 shows. Make up some examples and use the above formula to show how b, m, and t influence the government expenditure multiplier.

Autonomous Tax Multiplier

The autonomous tax multiplier equals the change in equilibrium expenditure (Y) that results from a change in autonomous taxes (T_a) divided by the change in autonomous taxes. Because autonomous expenditure is equal to

$$A = a - bT_a + I + G + X,$$

the change in autonomous expenditure equals *minus* b multiplied by the change in autonomous taxes. That is,

$$\Delta A = -b\Delta T_a.$$

You can see from the solution for equilibrium expenditure Y that

$$\Delta Y = \frac{-b}{1 - [b(1 - t) - m]}\Delta T_a.$$

The autonomous tax multiplier equals

$$\frac{-b}{1 - [b(1 - t) - m]}.$$

In an economy in which $t = 0$ and $m = 0$, the autonomous tax multiplier is $-b/(1 - b)$. In this special case, with $b = 0.75$, the autonomous tax multiplier equals -3, as Fig. 5 shows. Make up some examples and use the above formula to show how b, m, and t influence the autonomous tax multiplier.

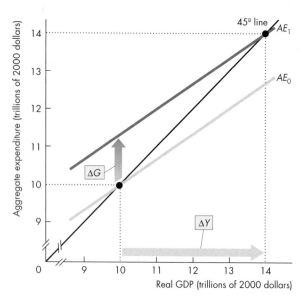

Figure 4 Government expenditure multiplier

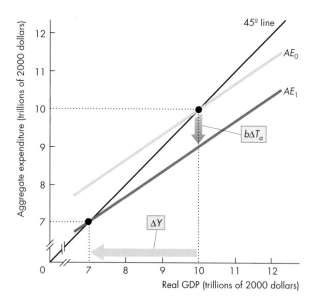

Figure 5 Autonomous tax multiplier

Balanced Budget Multiplier

The balanced budget multiplier equals the change in equilibrium expenditure (Y) that results from equal changes in government expenditure and lump-sum taxes divided by the change in government expenditure. Because government expenditure and autonomous taxes change by the same amount, the budget balance does not change.

The change in equilibrium expenditure that results from the change in government expenditure is

$$\Delta Y = \frac{1}{1 - [b(1 - t) - m]}\Delta G.$$

And the change in equilibrium expenditure that results from the change in autonomous taxes is

$$\Delta Y = \frac{-b}{1 - [b(1 - t) - m]}\Delta T_a.$$

So the change in equilibrium expenditure resulting from the changes in government expenditure and autonomous taxes is

$$\Delta Y = \frac{1}{1 - [b(1 - t) - m]}\Delta G +$$

$$\frac{-b}{1 - [b(1 - t) - m]}\Delta T_a.$$

Notice that

$$\frac{1}{1 - [b(1 - t) - m]}$$

is common to both terms on the right side. So we can rewrite the equation as

$$\Delta Y = \frac{1}{1 - [b(1 - t) - m]}[\Delta G - b\Delta T_a]$$

The AE curve shifts upward by $\Delta G - b\Delta T_a$ as shown in Fig. 6.

But the change in government expenditure equals the change in autonomous taxes. That is,

$$\Delta G = \Delta T_a.$$

And

$$\Delta Y = \frac{1 - b}{1 - [b(1 - t) - m]}\Delta G.$$

The balanced budget multiplier equals

$$\frac{1 - b}{1 - [b(1 - t) - m]}.$$

In an economy in which $t = 0$ and $m = 0$, the balanced budget multiplier is $(1 - b)/(1 - b)$, which equals 1, as Fig. 6 shows. Make up some examples and use the above formula to show how b, m, and t influence the balanced budget multiplier.

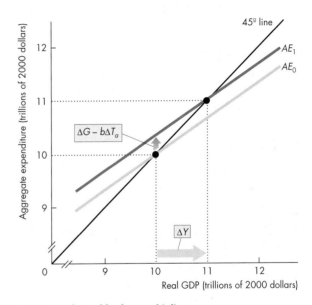

Figure 6 Balanced budget multiplier

SUMMARY

Key Points

Fixed Prices and Expenditure Plans (pp. 286–291)

- When the price level is fixed, expenditure plans determine real GDP.
- Consumption expenditure is determined by disposable income, and the marginal propensity to consume (*MPC*) determines the change in consumption expenditure brought about by a change in disposable income. Real GDP determines disposable income.
- Imports are determined by real GDP, and the marginal propensity to import determines the change in imports brought about by a change in real GDP.

Real GDP with a Fixed Price Level (pp. 292–295)

- Aggregate *planned* expenditure depends on real GDP.
- Equilibrium expenditure occurs when aggregate planned expenditure equals actual expenditure and real GDP.

The Multiplier (pp. 296–300)

- The multiplier is the magnified effect of a change in autonomous expenditure on equilibrium expenditure and real GDP.
- The multiplier is determined by the slope of the *AE* curve.
- The slope of the *AE* curve is influenced by the marginal propensity to consume, the marginal propensity to import, and the income tax rate.

The Multiplier and the Price Level (pp. 301–305)

- The aggregate demand curve is the relationship between the quantity of real GDP demanded and the price level, other things remaining the same.
- The aggregate expenditure curve is the relationship between aggregate planned expenditure and real GDP, other things remaining the same.

- At a given price level, there is a given aggregate expenditure curve. A change in the price level changes aggregate planned expenditure and shifts the aggregate expenditure curve. A change in the price level also creates a movement along the aggregate demand curve.
- A change in autonomous expenditure that is not caused by a change in the price level shifts the aggregate expenditure curve and shifts the aggregate demand curve. The magnitude of the shift of the aggregate demand curve depends on the multiplier and on the change in autonomous expenditure.
- The multiplier decreases as the price level changes, and the long-run multiplier is zero.

Key Figures

Key Terms

PROBLEMS

Tests, Study Plan, Solutions*

1. You are given the following information about the economy of the United Kingdom.

Disposable income	Consumption expenditure
(billions of pounds per year)	
300	340
400	420
500	500
600	580
700	660

   a. Calculate the marginal propensity to consume.
   b. Calculate saving at each level of disposable income.
   c. Calculate the marginal propensity to save.

2. You are given the following information about the economy of Australia.

Disposable income	Saving
(billions of dollars per year)	
0	−5
100	20
200	45
300	70
400	95

   a. Calculate the marginal propensity to save.
   b. Calculate consumption at each level of disposable income.
   c. Calculate the marginal propensity to consume.

3. The figure illustrates the components of aggregate planned expenditure on Turtle Island.

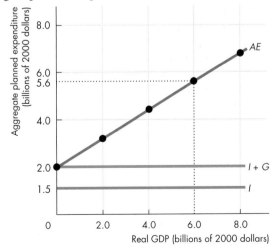

Turtle Island has no imports or exports, the people of Turtle Island pay no incomes taxes, and the price level is fixed.

   a. Calculate autonomous expenditure.
   b. Calculate the marginal propensity to consume.
   c. What is aggregate planned expenditure when real GDP is $6 billion?
   d. If real GDP is $4 billion, what is happening to inventories?
   e. If real GDP is $6 billion, what is happening to inventories?
   f. Calculate the multiplier.

4. The spreadsheet lists the components of aggregate planned expenditure in the United Kingdom. The numbers are in billions of pounds.

	A	B	C	D	E	F	G
		Y	C	I	G	X	M
1							
2	A	100	110	50	60	60	15
3	B	200	170	50	60	60	30
4	C	300	230	50	60	60	45
5	D	400	290	50	60	60	60
6	E	500	350	50	60	60	75
7	F	600	410	50	60	60	90

   a. Calculate autonomous expenditure.
   b. Calculate the marginal propensity to consume.
   c. What is aggregate planned expenditure when real GDP is 200 billion pounds?
   d. If real GDP is 200 billion pounds, what is happening to inventories?
   e. If real GDP is 500 billion pounds, what is happening to inventories?
   f. Calculate the multiplier.

5. You are given the following information about the Canadian economy: Autonomous consumption expenditure is $50 billion, investment is $200 billion, and government expenditure is $250 billion. The marginal propensity to consume is 0.7 and net taxes are $250 billion—net taxes are assumed to be constant and not vary with income. Exports are $500 billion and imports are $450 billion.

   a. What is the consumption function?
   b. What is the equation of the *AE* curve?
   c. Calculate equilibrium expenditure.
   d. If investment decreases to $150 billion, what is the change in equilibrium expenditure?
   e. Describe the process in part (d) that moves the economy to its new equilibrium expenditure.
   f. Calculate the multiplier.

*Solutions to odd-numbered problems are provided.

6. Suppose that the economy is at full employment, the price level is 100, and the investment multiplier is 2. Investment increases by $100 billion.
   a. What is the change in equilibrium expenditure?
   b. What is the immediate change in the quantity of real GDP demanded?
   c. In the short run, does real GDP increase by more than, less than, or the same amount as the increase in the quantity of real GDP demanded in part (b)?
   d. In the short run, does the price level remain at 100? Explain why or why not.
   e. In the long run, does real GDP increase by more than, less than, or the same amount as the increase in the quantity of real GDP demanded in part (b)?
   f. Explain how the price level changes in the long run.
   g. Compare the multipliers in the short run and the long run with the investment multiplier.

   a. Does the increase in U.S. exports create a movement along the *AE* curve or does it shift the *AE* curve?
   b. Suppose that U.S. exports increase by $120 billion in 2006 and the multiplier is 1.5. If other things remain the same, what is the increase in real GDP?
   c. Suppose that U.S. exports increase by $120 billion in 2006 and U.S. imports increase by the same amount. Will there still be a multiplier effect in the U.S. economy?
   d. Suppose that the U.S. economy is at full employment in 2006 when exports increase by $120 billion. Will there still be a multiplier effect?
   e. Suppose that the U.S. economy is above full employment in 2006 when exports increase by $120 billion in 2006. What in this case will happen to aggregate expenditure, aggregate demand, real GDP, and the price level?

CRITICAL THINKING

1. Study *Reading Between the Lines* on pp. 306–307 and then answer the following questions:
   a. If the 2005 changes in inventories were part of *planned* investment, what role did they play in shifting the *AE* curve and changing equilibrium expenditure? Use a figure similar to that on p. 307 to answer this question.
   b. If the 2005 changes in inventories were part of *unplanned* investment, what role did they play in shifting the *AE* curve and changing equilibrium expenditure? Use a figure similar to that on p. 307 to answer this question.
   c. What do you think will happen to real GDP, aggregate expenditure, and inventory investment in 2006? What clues do you get from the news article?
   d. Is a decrease in business inventories a cause or a consequence of expansion?

2. **U.S. Economy Is Still Growing at Rapid Pace**
   . . . strong global growth is lifting American exports, economists say. Last week the International Monetary Fund predicted that the world economy would grow at 4.9 percent this year, up from 4.8 percent in 2005.
   The New York Times, April 28, 2006

WEB ACTIVITIES

⟨X⟩ myeconlab Links to Web sites

1. Obtain data on real GDP per person and consumption as a percentage of real GDP for the United States, China, South Africa, and Mexico since 1960.
   a. In a spreadsheet, multiply your real GDP data by the consumption percentage and divide by 100 to obtain data on real consumption expenditure per person for each country.
   b. Make graphs like Fig. 12.4 to show the relationship between real consumption expenditure and real GDP for these four countries.
   c. On the basis of the numbers you've obtained, in which country do you expect the multiplier to be largest (other things remaining the same)?
   d. What other data would you need to be able to calculate the multipliers for these countries?

2. You are a research assistant in the office of the President's Council of Economic Advisors. Draft a note for the President that explains the power and limitations of the multiplier. The President wants only 250 words of crisp, clear, jargon-free explanation together with a lively example. He also wants to know if the multiplier has any policy relevance for the United States today and why or why not.

U.S. Inflation, Unemployment, and Business Cycles

Inflation Plus Unemployment Equals Misery!

Back in the 1970s, when inflation was raging at a double-digit rate, economist Arthur M. Okun proposed what he called the Misery Index. Misery, he suggested, could be measured as the sum of the infla-

tion rate and the unemployment rate. At its peak, in 1980, the Misery Index hit 21. In 2006, it was 9. At its lowest, in 1964 and again in 1999, the Misery Index was 6.

Inflation and unemployment make us miserable for good reasons. We care about inflation because it raises our cost of living. And we care about unemployment because either it hits us directly and takes our jobs or it scares us into thinking that we might lose our jobs.

We want rapid income growth, low unemployment, and low inflation. But can we have all these things at the same time? Or do we face a tradeoff among them?

◆ This chapter applies the *aggregate supply–aggregate demand model* that you studied in Chapter 11 to explain the patterns in inflation and output that occur in our economy. The chapter also looks at a related model, the Phillips curve, which illustrates a short-run tradeoff between inflation and unemployment. The chapter then applies the classical model of Chapter 7 to explain how business cycle fluctuations can arise from the normal working of the economy and independently of fluctuations in cost-push forces or aggregate demand.

We begin by looking at the evolving U.S. economy. At the end of the chapter, in *Reading Between the Lines*, we examine the state of the economy in 2006 as some people began to fear both inflation and recession.

The Evolving U.S. Economy

Real GDP and the price level are continually changing. Let's see how we can use the aggregate supply–aggregate demand model of Chapter 11 to explain these changes.

Imagine the economy as a video and think of the aggregate supply–aggregate demand figure as a freeze-frame. We can run this video—run an instant replay—but keep our finger on the freeze-frame button and look at some important parts of the previous action. Let's run the video from 1960.

Figure 13.1 shows the economy in 1960 at the point of intersection of its aggregate demand curve, AD_{60}, and short-run aggregate supply curve, SAS_{60}. Real GDP was $2.5 trillion, and the GDP deflator was 21. In 1960, real GDP equaled potential GDP—the economy was on its long-run aggregate supply curve, LAS_{60}.

By 2005, the economy had reached the point marked by the intersection of the aggregate demand curve AD_{05} and the short-run aggregate supply curve SAS_{05}. Real GDP was $11.1 trillion, and the GDP deflator was 112. The Congressional Budget Office estimated potential GDP in 2005 to be $11.3 trillion, so equilibrium real GDP was less than potential GDP on LAS_{05}.

The path traced by the blue and red dots in Fig. 13.1 shows three key features:

■ Economic growth
■ Inflation
■ Business cycles

Economic Growth

Over the years, real GDP grows—shown in Fig. 13.1 by the rightward movement of the dots. The faster real GDP grows, the larger is the horizontal distance between successive dots. The forces that generate economic growth are those that increase potential GDP that we explored in Chapter 8. Potential GDP grows because the quantity of labor grows and because capital accumulation (physical capital and human capital) and technological change increase labor productivity.

These forces that bring economic growth were strongest during the 1960s. They strengthened again during the 1990s. But during the 1970s, early 1980s, and early 2000s, economic growth was slow.

Inflation

The price level rises over the years—shown in Fig. 13.1 by the upward movement of the points. The larger the rise in the price level, the larger is the vertical distance between successive dots in the figure. The main force generating the persistent increase in the price level is a tendency for aggregate demand to increase at a faster pace than the increase in potential GDP. All of the factors that increase aggregate demand and shift the aggregate demand curve influence the pace of inflation. But one factor—the growth of the quantity of money—is the main source of *persistent* increases in aggregate demand and persistent inflation.

Business Cycles

Over the years, the economy grows and shrinks in cycles—shown in Fig. 13.1 by the wavelike pattern made by the dots, with the recessions highlighted. The cycles arise because both the expansion of short-run aggregate supply and the growth of aggregate demand do not proceed at a fixed, steady pace.

The Evolving Economy: 1960–2005

From 1960 to 1967, real GDP growth was rapid and inflation was low. This was a period of rapid increases in potential GDP and of moderate increases in aggregate demand. The pace of inflation increased in the late 1960s.

In the mid-1970s, a series of massive oil price increases decreased short-run aggregate supply and rapid increases in the quantity of money increased aggregate demand. The decrease in short-run aggregate supply was greater than the increase in aggregate demand and the result was a combination of rapid inflation *and* recession—stagflation.

The rest of the 1970s saw high inflation—the price level increased quickly—but slow real GDP growth. By 1980, inflation was a major problem and the Fed decided to take strong action. The Fed drove interest rates to previously unknown levels and decreased aggregate demand. By 1982, the decrease in aggregate demand put the economy in a deep recession.

During the years 1983–1990, capital accumulation and steady technological change resulted in a sustained increase in potential GDP. Wage growth was moderate, the price of oil fell, and short-run aggregate supply increased. Aggregate demand

FIGURE 13.1   Economic Growth, Inflation, and Cycles: 1960–2005

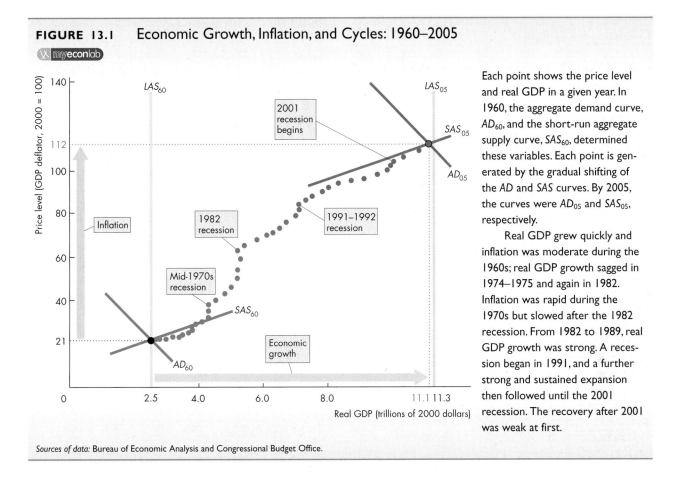

Each point shows the price level and real GDP in a given year. In 1960, the aggregate demand curve, AD_{60}, and the short-run aggregate supply curve, SAS_{60}, determined these variables. Each point is generated by the gradual shifting of the AD and SAS curves. By 2005, the curves were AD_{05} and SAS_{05}, respectively.

Real GDP grew quickly and inflation was moderate during the 1960s; real GDP growth sagged in 1974–1975 and again in 1982. Inflation was rapid during the 1970s but slowed after the 1982 recession. From 1982 to 1989, real GDP growth was strong. A recession began in 1991, and a further strong and sustained expansion then followed until the 2001 recession. The recovery after 2001 was weak at first.

Sources of data: Bureau of Economic Analysis and Congressional Budget Office.

growth kept pace with the growth of potential GDP. Sustained but steady growth in aggregate supply and aggregate demand kept real GDP growing and inflation steady. The economy moved from a recession in 1982 to above full employment in 1990.

The economy was in this condition when a decrease in aggregate demand led to the 1991 recession. The economy again embarked on a path of expansion through 2001. During the late 1990s and 2000, the expansion increased real GDP to a level that exceeded potential GDP and took employment to above full employment. Then in late 2000 and early 2001, aggregate demand decreased and another recession occurred. This recession was mild and was followed by a slow recovery. By 2005, although real GDP had grown, it remained below potential GDP.

You've seen how the *AS-AD* model can provide an account of the forces that move real GDP and the price level to bring economic growth, inflation, and business cycles. We're now going to use this model to explore the cycles in inflation and real GDP more

closely. We're then going to use a related model (the Phillips curve) that focuses on the tradeoff between unemployment and inflation. But the *AS-AD* and Phillips curve models are not the only ones that economists use to study cycles. We'll end this chapter by looking at an alternative real business cycle theory that extends the classical model and applies it to explain cycles as well as growth in a unified framework.

REVIEW QUIZ

1 In which period since 1960 was U.S. economic growth (i) fastest and (ii) slowest?
2 In which period since 1960 was U.S. inflation (i) fastest and (ii) slowest?
3 In which years did recessions occur in the United States?

 myeconlab **Study Plan 13.1**

Inflation Cycles

In the long run, inflation is a monetary phenomenon. It occurs if the quantity of money grows faster than potential GDP. But in the short run, many factors can start an inflation, and real GDP and the price level interact. To study these interactions, we distinguish two sources of inflation:

- Demand-pull inflation
- Cost-push inflation

Demand-Pull Inflation

An inflation that starts because aggregate demand increases is called **demand-pull inflation**. Demand-pull inflation can be kicked off by *any* of the factors that change aggregate demand. Examples are a cut in the interest rate, an increase in the quantity of money, an increase in government expenditure, a tax cut, an increase in exports, or an increase in investment stimulated by an increase in expected future profits.

Initial Effect of an Increase in Aggregate Demand
Suppose that last year the price level was 115 and real GDP was $12 trillion. Potential GDP was also $12 trillion. Figure 13.2(a) illustrates this situation. The aggregate demand curve is AD_0, the short-run aggregate supply curve is SAS_0, and the long-run aggregate supply curve is LAS.

Now suppose that the Fed cuts the interest rate and increases the quantity of money and aggregate demand increases to AD_1. With no change in potential GDP and no change in the money wage rate, the long-run aggregate supply curve and the short-run aggregate supply curve remain at LAS and SAS_0, respectively.

The price level and real GDP are determined at the point where the aggregate demand curve AD_1 intersects the short-run aggregate supply curve. The price level rises to 118, and real GDP increases above potential GDP to $12.5 trillion. Unemployment falls below its natural rate. The economy is at an above full-employment equilibrium and there is an inflationary gap. The next step in the unfolding story is a rise in the money wage rate.

FIGURE 13.2   A Demand-Pull Rise in the Price Level

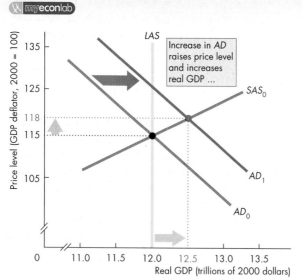

(a) Initial effect

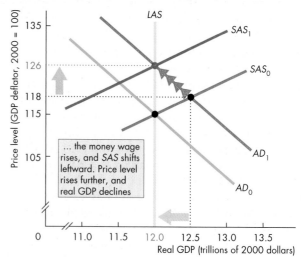

(b) The money wage adjusts

In part (a), the aggregate demand curve is AD_0, the short-run aggregate supply curve is SAS_0, and the long-run aggregate supply curve is LAS. The price level is 115, and real GDP is $12 trillion, which equals potential GDP. Aggregate demand increases to AD_1. The price level rises to 118, and real GDP increases to $12.5 trillion.

In part (b), starting from above full employment, the money wage rate begins to rise and the short-run aggregate supply curve shifts leftward toward SAS_1. The price level rises further, and real GDP returns to potential GDP.

Money Wage Rate Response Real GDP cannot remain above potential GDP forever. With unemployment below its natural rate, there is a shortage of labor. In this situation, the money wage rate begins to rise. As it does so, short-run aggregate supply decreases and the *SAS* curve starts to shift leftward. The price level rises further, and real GDP begins to decrease.

With no further change in aggregate demand—that is, the aggregate demand curve remains at AD_1—this process ends when the short-run aggregate supply curve has shifted to SAS_1 in Fig. 13.2(b). At this time, the price level has increased to 126 and real GDP has returned to potential GDP of $12 trillion, the level from which it started.

A Demand-Pull Inflation Process The events that we've just described bring a *one-time rise in the price level*, not an inflation. For inflation to proceed, aggregate demand must *persistently* increase.

The only way in which aggregate demand can persistently increase is if the quantity of money persistently increases. Suppose the government has a budget deficit that it finances by selling bonds. Also suppose that the Fed buys some of these bonds. When the Fed buys bonds, it creates more money. In this situation, aggregate demand increases year after year. The aggregate demand curve keeps shifting rightward. This persistent increase in aggregate demand puts continual upward pressure on the price level. The economy now experiences demand-pull inflation.

Figure 13.3 illustrates the process of demand-pull inflation. The starting point is the same as that shown in Fig. 13.2. The aggregate demand curve is AD_0, the short-run aggregate supply curve is SAS_0, and the long-run aggregate supply curve is *LAS*. Real GDP is $12 trillion, and the price level is 115. Aggregate demand increases, shifting the aggregate demand curve to AD_1. Real GDP increases to $12.5 trillion, and the price level rises to 118. The economy is at an above full-employment equilibrium. There is a shortage of labor, and the money wage rate rises. The short-run aggregate supply curve shifts to SAS_1. The price level rises to 126, and real GDP returns to potential GDP.

But the Fed increases the quantity of money again, and aggregate demand continues to increase. The aggregate demand curve shifts rightward to AD_2. The price level rises further to 130, and real GDP again exceeds potential GDP at $12.5 trillion. Yet

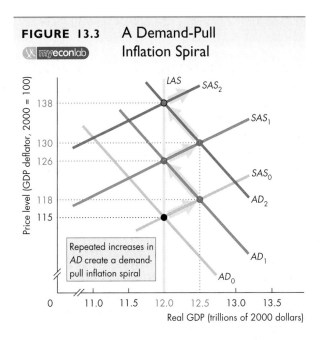

FIGURE 13.3   A Demand-Pull Inflation Spiral

myeconlab

Each time the quantity of money increases, aggregate demand increases and the aggregate demand curve shifts rightward from AD_0 to AD_1 to AD_2, and so on. Each time real GDP increases above potential GDP, the money wage rate rises and the short-run aggregate supply curve shifts leftward from SAS_0 to SAS_1 to SAS_2, and so on. The price level rises from 115 to 118, 126, 130, 138, and so on. There is a demand-pull inflation spiral. Real GDP fluctuates between $12 trillion and $12.5 trillion.

again, the money wage rate rises and decreases short-run aggregate supply. The *SAS* curve shifts to SAS_2, and the price level rises further, to 138. As the quantity of money continues to grow, aggregate demand increases and the price level rises in an ongoing demand-pull inflation process.

The process you have just studied generates inflation—an ongoing process of a rising price level.

Demand-Pull Inflation in Kalamazoo You may better understand the inflation process that we've just described by considering what is going on in an individual part of the economy, such as a Kalamazoo soda-bottling plant. Initially, when aggregate demand increases, the demand for soda increases and the price of soda rises. Faced with a higher price, the soda plant works overtime and increases production. Conditions are good for workers in Kalamazoo, and the soda factory finds it hard to hang on to its best people. To do so, it offers a higher money wage rate. As the wage rate rises, so do the soda factory's costs.

What happens next depends on aggregate demand. If aggregate demand remains constant, the firm's costs increase but the price of soda does not increase as quickly as its costs. So the firm cuts production. Eventually, the money wage rate and costs increase by the same percentage as the rise in the price of soda. In real terms, the soda factory is in the same situation as it was initially. It produces the same amount of soda and employs the same amount of labor as before the increase in demand.

But if aggregate demand continues to increase, so does the demand for soda and the price of soda rises at the same rate as wages. The soda factory continues to operate above full employment, and there is a persistent shortage of labor. Prices and wages chase each other upward in a demand-pull inflation spiral.

Demand-Pull Inflation in the United States

A demand-pull inflation like the one you've just studied in the United States during the late 1960s. In 1960, inflation was a moderate 2 percent a year, but its rate increased slowly to 3 percent by 1966. Then, in 1967, a large increase in government expenditure on the Vietnam War and an increase in spending on social programs, together with an increase in the growth rate of the quantity of money, increased aggregate demand more quickly. Consequently, the rightward shift of the aggregate demand curve speeded up and the price level increased more quickly. Real GDP moved above potential GDP, and the unemployment rate fell below its natural rate.

With unemployment below its natural rate, the money wage rate started to rise more quickly and the short-run aggregate supply curve shifted leftward. The Fed responded with a further increase in the money growth rate, and a demand-pull inflation spiral unfolded. By 1970, the inflation rate had reached 5 percent a year.

For the next few years, aggregate demand grew even more quickly and the inflation rate kept rising. By 1974, the inflation rate had reached 11 percent a year.

Next, let's see how shocks to aggregate supply can create cost-push inflation.

Cost-Push Inflation

An inflation that is kicked off by an increase in costs is called **cost-push inflation**. The two main sources of cost increases are

1. An increase in the money wage rate
2. An increase in the money prices of raw materials

At a given price level, the higher the cost of production, the smaller is the amount that firms are willing to produce. So if the money wage rate rises or if the prices of raw materials (for example, oil) rise, firms decrease their supply of goods and services. Aggregate supply decreases, and the short-run aggregate supply curve shifts leftward.[1] Let's trace the effects of such a decrease in short-run aggregate supply on the price level and real GDP.

Initial Effect of a Decrease in Aggregate Supply

Suppose that last year the price level was 115 and real GDP was $12 trillion. Potential real GDP was also $12 trillion. Figure 13.4(a) illustrates this situation. The aggregate demand curve was AD_0, the short-run aggregate supply curve was SAS_0, and the long-run aggregate supply curve was LAS. In the current year, the world's oil producers form a price-fixing organization that strengthens their market power and increases the relative price of oil. They raise the price of oil, and this action decreases short-run aggregate supply. The short-run aggregate supply curve shifts leftward to SAS_1. The price level rises to 122, and real GDP decreases to $11.5 trillion. The economy is at a below full-employment equilibrium and there is a recessionary gap.

This event is a *one-time rise in the price level*. It is not inflation. In fact, a supply shock on its own cannot cause inflation. Something more must happen to enable a one-time supply shock, which causes a one-time rise in the price level, to be converted into a process of ongoing inflation. The quantity of money must persistently increase. And it sometimes does increase, as you will now see.

---

[1] Some cost-push forces, such as an increase in the price of oil accompanied by a decrease in the availability of oil, can also decrease long-run aggregate supply. We'll ignore such effects here and examine cost-push factors that change only short-run aggregate supply. Later in the chapter, we study the effects of shocks to long-run aggregate supply.

FIGURE 13.4   A Cost-Push Rise in the Price Level

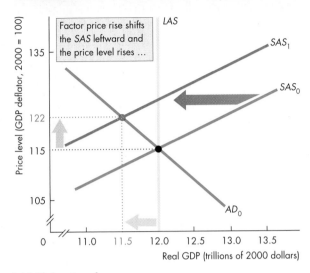

(a) Initial cost push

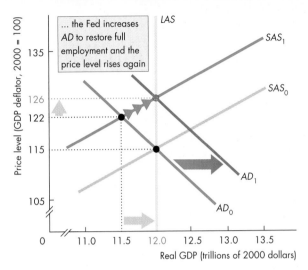

(b) The Fed responds

Initially, the aggregate demand curve is AD_0, the short-run aggregate supply curve is SAS_0, and the long-run aggregate supply curve is LAS. A decrease in aggregate supply (for example, resulting from a rise in the world price of oil) shifts the short-run aggregate supply curve to SAS_1. The economy moves to the point where the short-run aggregate supply curve SAS_1 intersects the aggregate demand curve AD_0. The

price level rises to 122, and real GDP decreases to $11.5 trillion.

In part (b), if the Fed responds by increasing aggregate demand to restore full employment, the aggregate demand curve shifts rightward to AD_1. The economy returns to full employment, but the price level rises further to 126.

Aggregate Demand Response When real GDP decreases, unemployment rises above its natural rate. In such a situation, there is often an outcry of concern and a call for action to restore full employment. Suppose that the Fed cuts the interest rate and increases the quantity of money. Aggregate demand increases. In Fig. 13.4(b), the aggregate demand curve shifts rightward to AD_1 and full employment is restored. But the price level rises further to 126.

A Cost-Push Inflation Process The oil producers now see the prices of everything they buy increasing. So OPEC increases the price of oil again to restore its new high relative price. Figure 13.5 continues the story. The short-run aggregate supply curve now shifts to SAS_2. The price level rises and real GDP decreases.

The price level rises further, to 134, and real GDP decreases to $11.5 trillion. Unemployment

increases above its natural rate. If the Fed responds yet again with an increase in the quantity of money, aggregate demand increases and the aggregate demand curve shifts to AD_2. The price level rises even higher—to 138—and full employment is again restored. A cost-push inflation spiral results. The combination of a rising price level and decreasing real GDP is called **stagflation.**

You can see that the Fed has a dilemma. If it does not respond when OPEC raises the price of oil, the economy remains below full employment. If the Fed increases the quantity of money to restore full employment, it invites another oil price hike that will call forth yet a further increase in the quantity of money.

If the Fed responds to each oil price hike by increasing the quantity of money, inflation will rage along at a rate decided by OPEC. But if the Fed keeps the lid on money growth, the economy remains below full employment.

FIGURE 13.5   A Cost-Push Inflation Spiral

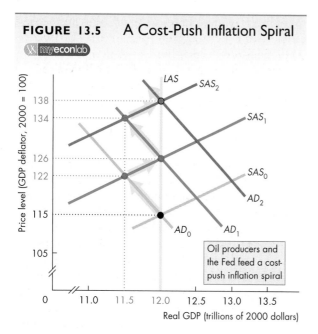

Each time a cost increase occurs, the short-run aggregate supply curve shifts leftward from SAS_0 to SAS_1 to SAS_2, and so on. Each time real GDP decreases below potential GDP, the Fed increases the quantity of money and the aggregate demand curve shifts rightward from AD_0 to AD_1 to AD_2, and so on. The price level rises from 115 to 122, 126, 134, 138, and so on. There is a cost-push inflation spiral. Real GDP fluctuates between $12 trillion and $11.5 trillion.

Cost-Push Inflation in Kalamazoo What is going on in the Kalamazoo soda-bottling plant when the economy is experiencing cost-push inflation?

When the oil price increases, so do the costs of bottling soda. These higher costs decrease the supply of soda, increasing its price and decreasing the quantity produced. The soda plant lays off some workers.

This situation persists until either the Fed increases aggregate demand or the price of oil falls. If the Fed increases aggregate demand, the demand for soda increases and so does its price. The higher price of soda brings higher profits, and the bottling plant increases its production. The soda factory rehires the laid-off workers.

Cost-Push Inflation in the United States A cost-push inflation like the one you've just studied occurred in the United States during the 1970s. It began in 1974

when the Organization of the Petroleum Exporting Countries (OPEC) raised the price of oil fourfold. The higher oil price decreased aggregate supply, which caused the price level to rise more quickly and real GDP to shrink. The Fed then faced a dilemma: Would it increase the quantity of money and accommodate the cost-push forces, or would it keep aggregate demand growth in check by limiting money growth? In 1975, 1976, and 1977, the Fed repeatedly allowed the quantity of money to grow quickly and inflation proceeded at a rapid rate. In 1979 and 1980, OPEC was again able to push oil prices higher. On that occasion, the Fed decided not to respond to the oil price hike with an increase in the quantity of money. The result was a recession but also, eventually, a fall in inflation.

Expected Inflation

If inflation is expected, the fluctuations in real GDP that accompany demand-pull and cost-push inflation that you've just studied don't occur. Instead, inflation proceeds as it does in the long run, with real GDP equal to potential GDP and unemployment at its natural rate. Figure 13.6 explains why.

Suppose that last year the aggregate demand curve was AD_0, the aggregate supply curve was SAS_0, and the long-run aggregate supply curve was LAS. The price level was 115, and real GDP was $12 trillion, which is also potential GDP.

To keep things as simple as possible, suppose that potential GDP does not change, so the LAS curve doesn't shift. Also suppose that aggregate demand is *expected to increase* to AD_1.

In anticipation of this increase in aggregate demand, the money wage rate rises and the short-run aggregate supply curve shifts leftward. If the money wage rate rises by the same percentage as the price level is expected to rise, the short-run aggregate supply curve for next year is SAS_1.

If aggregate demand turns out to be the same as expected, the aggregate demand curve is AD_1. The short-run aggregate supply curve, SAS_1, and AD_1 determine the actual price level at 126. Between last year and this year, the price level increased from 115 to 126 and the economy experienced an inflation rate equal to that expected. If this inflation is ongoing, aggregate demand increases (as expected) in the following year and the aggregate demand curve shifts to AD_2. The money wage rate rises to reflect the expected inflation, and the short-run aggregate sup-

FIGURE 13.6   Expected Inflation

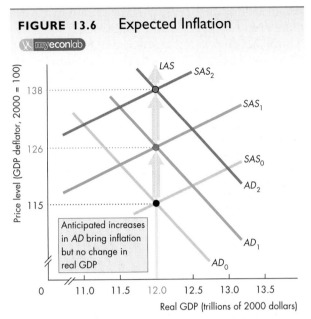

Potential real GDP is $12 trillion. Last year, aggregate demand was AD_0 and the short-run aggregate supply curve was SAS_0. The actual price level was the same as the expected price level: 115. This year, aggregate demand is expected to increase to AD_1 and the price level is expected to rise from 115 to 126. As a result, the money wage rate rises and the short-run aggregate supply curve shifts to SAS_1. If aggregate demand actually increases as expected, the actual aggregate demand curve AD_1 is the same as the expected aggregate demand curve. Real GDP is $12 trillion, and the actual price level rises to 126. The inflation is expected. Next year, the process continues with aggregate demand increasing as expected to AD_2 and the money wage rate rising to shift the short-run aggregate supply curve to SAS_2. Again, real GDP remains at $12 trillion, and the price level rises, as expected, to 138.

ply curve shifts to SAS_2. The price level rises, as expected, to 138.

What caused this inflation? The immediate answer is that because people expected inflation, the money wage rate increased and the price level increased. But the expectation was correct. Aggregate demand was expected to increase, and it did increase. It is the actual and expected increase in aggregate demand that caused the inflation.

An expected inflation at full employment is exactly the process that the quantity theory of money predicts. To review the quantity theory of money, see Chapter 9, pp. 224–225.

This broader account of the inflation process and its short-run effects explains why the quantity theory predictions don't explain the cycles in inflation. Only if aggregate demand growth is correctly forecasted does the economy follow the course described in Fig. 13.6 and accord with the quantity theory of money.

Forecasting Inflation

To anticipate inflation, people must forecast it. Some economists who work for macroeconomic forecasting agencies, banks, insurance companies, labor unions, and large corporations specialize in inflation forecasting. The best forecast available is one that is based on all the relevant information and is called a **rational expectation**. A rational expectation is not necessarily a correct forecast. It is simply the best forecast with the information available. It will often turn out to be wrong, but no other forecast that could have been made with the information available could do better.

Inflation and the Business Cycle

When the inflation forecast is correct, the economy operates at full employment. If aggregate demand grows faster than expected, real GDP moves above potential GDP, the inflation rate exceeds its expected rate, and the economy behaves like it does in a demand-pull inflation. If aggregate demand grows more slowly than expected, real GDP falls below potential GDP, the inflation rate slows, and the economy behaves like it does in a cost-push inflation.

REVIEW QUIZ

1 How does demand-pull inflation begin?
2 What must happen to create a demand-pull inflation spiral?
3 How does cost-push inflation begin?
4 What must happen to create a cost-push inflation spiral?
5 What is stagflation and why does cost-push inflation cause stagflation?
6 How does expected inflation occur?
7 How do real GDP and the price level change if the forecast of inflation turns out to be incorrect?

myeconlab Study Plan 13.2

Inflation and Unemployment: The Phillips Curve

Another way of studying inflation cycles focuses on the relationship and the short-run tradeoff between inflation and unemployment, a relationship called the **Phillips curve**—so named because it was first suggested by New Zealand economist A.W. Phillips.

Why do we need another way of studying inflation? What is wrong with the *AS-AD* explanation of the fluctuations in inflation and real GDP? The first answer to both questions is that we often want to study changes in both the expected and actual inflation rates and for this purpose the Phillips curve provides a simpler tool and clearer insights than what the *AS-AD* model provides. The second answer to both questions is that we often want to study changes in the short-run tradeoff between inflation and real economic activity (real GDP and unemployment) and again, the Phillips curve serves this purpose well.

To begin our explanation of the Phillips curve, we distinguish between two time frames (similar to the two aggregate supply time frames). We study

- The short-run Phillips curve
- The long-run Phillips curve

The Short-Run Phillips Curve

The **short-run Phillips curve** shows the relationship between inflation and unemployment, holding constant:

1. The expected inflation rate
2. The natural unemployment rate

You've just seen what determines the expected inflation rate. The natural unemployment rate and the factors that influence it are explained in Chapter 7, pp. 166–168.

Figure 13.7 shows a short-run Phillips curve, *SRPC*. Suppose that the expected inflation rate is 10 percent a year and the natural unemployment rate is 6 percent, point *A* in the figure. A short-run Phillips curve passes through this point. If inflation rises above its expected rate, unemployment falls below its natural rate. This joint movement in the inflation rate and the unemployment rate is illustrated as a movement up along the short-run Phillips curve from point *A* to point *B*. Similarly, if

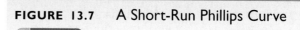

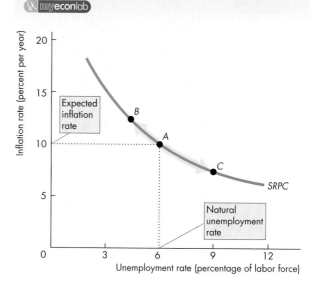

FIGURE 13.7   A Short-Run Phillips Curve

The short-run Phillips curve (*SRPC*) shows the relationship between inflation and unemployment at a given expected inflation rate and a given natural unemployment rate. With an expected inflation rate of 10 percent a year and a natural unemployment rate of 6 percent, the short-run Phillips curve passes through point *A*.

An unexpected increase in aggregate demand lowers unemployment and increases the inflation rate—a movement up along the short-run Phillips curve to point *B*. An unexpected decrease in aggregate demand increases unemployment and lowers the inflation rate—a movement down along the short-run Phillips curve to point *C*.

inflation falls below its expected rate, unemployment rises above its natural rate. In this case, there is movement down along the short-run Phillips curve from point *A* to point *C*.

The short-run Phillips curve is like the short-run aggregate supply curve. A movement along the *SAS* curve that brings a higher price level and an increase in real GDP is equivalent to a movement along the short-run Phillips curve from *A* to *B* that brings an increase in the inflation rate and a decrease in the unemployment rate.

Similarly, a movement along the *SAS* curve that brings a lower price level and a decrease in real GDP is equivalent to a movement along the short-run Phillips curve from *A* to *C* that brings a decrease in the inflation rate and an increase in the unemployment rate.

The Long-Run Phillips Curve

The **long-run Phillips curve** shows the relationship between inflation and unemployment when the actual inflation rate equals the expected inflation rate. The long-run Phillips curve is vertical at the natural unemployment rate. In Fig. 13.8, it is the vertical line *LRPC*. The long-run Phillips curve tells us that any expected inflation rate is possible at the natural unemployment rate. This proposition is consistent with the *AS-AD* model, which predicts that when inflation is expected, real GDP equals potential GDP and unemployment is at its natural rate.

The short-run Phillips curve intersects the long-run Phillips curve at the expected inflation rate. A change in the expected inflation rate shifts the short-run Phillips curve but it does not shift the long-run Phillips curve.

In Fig. 13.8, if the expected inflation rate is 10 percent a year, the short-run Phillips curve is $SRPC_0$. If the expected inflation rate falls to 6 percent a year, the short-run Phillips curve shifts downward to $SRPC_1$. The vertical distance by which the short-run

Phillips curve shifts from point *A* to point *D* is equal to the change in the expected inflation rate. If the actual inflation rate also falls from 10 percent to 6 percent, there is a movement down the long-run Phillips curve from *A* to *D*. An increase in the expected inflation rate has the opposite effect to that shown in Fig. 13.8.

The other source of a shift in the Phillips curve is a change in the natural unemployment rate.

Changes in the Natural Unemployment Rate

The natural unemployment rate changes for many reasons (see Chapter 7, pp. 166–168). A change in the natural unemployment rate shifts both the short-run and long-run Phillips curves. Figure 13.9 illustrates such shifts. If the natural unemployment rate increases from 6 percent to 9 percent, the long-run Phillips curve shifts from $LRPC_0$ to $LRPC_1$, and if expected inflation is constant at 10 percent a year, the short-run Phillips curve shifts from $SRPC_0$ to

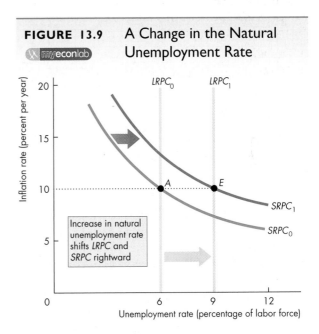

FIGURE 13.8   Short-Run and Long-Run Phillips Curves

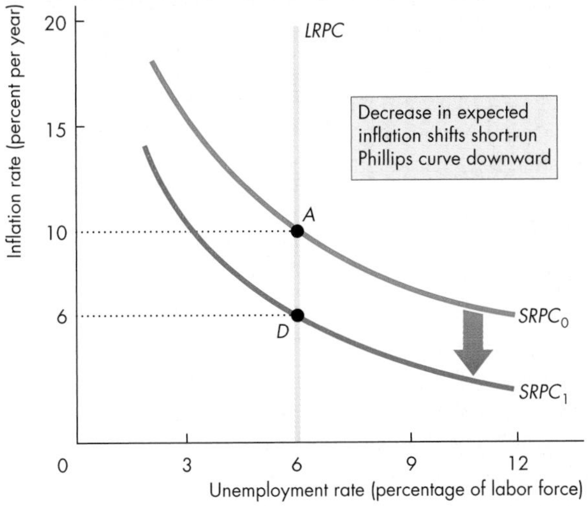

The long-run Phillips curve is *LRPC*. A fall in expected inflation from 10 percent a year to 6 percent a year shifts the short-run Phillips curve downward from $SRPC_0$ to $SRPC_1$. The long-run Phillips curve does not shift. The new short-run Phillips curve intersects the long-run Phillips curve at the new expected inflation rate—point *D*.

FIGURE 13.9   A Change in the Natural Unemployment Rate

A change in the natural unemployment rate shifts both the short-run and long-run Phillips curves. An increase in the natural unemployment rate from 6 percent to 9 percent shifts the Phillips curves rightward to $SRPC_1$ and $LRPC_1$. The new long-run Phillips curve intersects the new short-run Phillips curve at the expected inflation rate—point *E*.

FIGURE 13.10   Phillips Curves in the United States

myeconlab

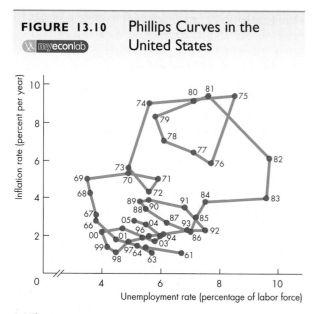

(a) Time sequence

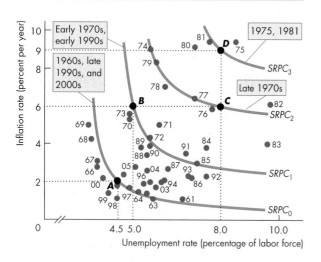

(b)

In part (a), each dot represents the combination of inflation and unemployment for a particular year. Part (b) interprets the data with a shifting short-run Phillips curve. The black dots A, B, C, and D show the combination of the natural unemployment rate and the expected inflation rate in different periods. The short-run Phillips curve was $SRPC_0$ during the 1960s and the late 1990s and early 2000s. It was $SRPC_1$ during the early 1970s and early 1990s, $SRPC_2$ during the late 1970s, and $SRPC_3$ (briefly) in 1975 and 1981.

Source of data: Bureau of Labor Statistics and the author's calculations and assumptions.

$SRPC_1$. Because the expected inflation rate is constant, the short-run Phillips curve $SRPC_1$ intersects the long-run curve $LRPC_1$ (point E) at the same inflation rate at which the short-run Phillips curve $SRPC_0$ intersects the long-run curve $LRPC_0$ (point A).

The U.S. Phillips Curve

Figure 13.10(a) is a scatter diagram of the inflation rate and the unemployment rate since 1961. We can interpret the data in terms of the shifting short-run Phillips curve in Fig. 13.10(b). During the 1960s, the short-run Phillips curve was $SRPC_0$, with a natural unemployment rate of 4.5 percent and an expected inflation rate of 2 percent a year (point A). During the early 1970s, the short-run Phillips curve was $SRPC_1$ with a natural unemployment rate of 5 percent and an expected inflation rate of 6 percent a year (point B). During the late 1970s, the natural unemployment rate increased to 8 percent (point C) and the short-run Phillips curve was $SRPC_2$. And briefly in 1975 and again in 1981, the expected inflation rate surged to 9 percent a year (point D) and the short-run Phillips curve was $SRPC_3$. During the 1980s and 1990s, the expected inflation rate and the natural unemployment rate decreased and the short-run Phillips curve shifted leftward. By the early 1990s, it was back at $SRPC_1$. And by the mid-1990s, it was again $SRPC_0$, where it has remained into the 2000s.

REVIEW QUIZ

1. How would you use the Phillips curve to illustrate an unexpected change in inflation?
2. If the expected inflation rate increases by 10 percentage points, how do the short-run Phillips curve and the long-run Phillips curve change?
3. If the natural unemployment rate increases, what happens to the short-run Phillips curve, the long-run Phillips curve, and the expected inflation rate?
4. Does the United States have a stable short-run Phillips curve? Explain why or why not.
5. Does the United States have a stable long-run Phillips curve?

myeconlab **Study Plan 13.3**

Business Cycles

Business cycles are easy to describe but hard to explain and business cycle theory remains unsettled and a source of controversy. We'll look at two approaches to understanding business cycles:

- Mainstream business cycle theory
- Real business cycle theory

Mainstream Business Cycle Theory

The mainstream business cycle theory is that potential GDP grows at a steady rate while aggregate demand grows at a fluctuating rate. Because the money wage rate is sticky, if aggregate demand grows faster than potential GDP, real GDP moves above potential GDP and an inflationary gap emerges. And if aggregate demand grows slower than potential GDP, real GDP moves below potential GDP and a recessionary gap emerges. If aggregate demand decreases, real GDP also decreases in a recession.

Figure 13.11 illustrates this cycle theory. Initially, actual and potential GDP are $9 trillion, and the long-run aggregate supply curve is LAS_0. Aggregate demand curve is AD_0, and the price level is 105. The economy is at full employment at point A.

An expansion occurs when potential GDP increases and the LAS curve shifts rightward to LAS_1. During an expansion, aggregate demand also increases, and usually by more than potential GDP, so the price level rises. Assume that in the current expansion, the price level is expected to rise to 115 and that the money wage rate has been set on that expectation. The short-run aggregate supply curve is SAS_1.

If aggregate demand increases to AD_1, real GDP increases to $12 trillion, the new level of potential GDP, and the price level rises, as expected, to 115. The economy remains at full employment but now at point B.

If aggregate demand increases more slowly to AD_2, real GDP grows by less than potential GDP and the economy moves to point C, with real GDP at $11.5 trillion and the price level at 112. Real GDP growth is slower and inflation is lower than expected.

If aggregate demand increases more quickly to AD_3, real GDP grows by more than potential GDP and the economy moves to point D, with real GDP at $12.5 trillion and the price level at 118. Real GDP growth is faster and inflation is higher than expected.

Growth, inflation, and business cycles arise from the relentless increases in potential GDP, faster (on the average) increases in aggregate demand, and fluctuations in the pace of aggregate demand growth.

FIGURE 13.11   The Mainstream Business Cycle Theory

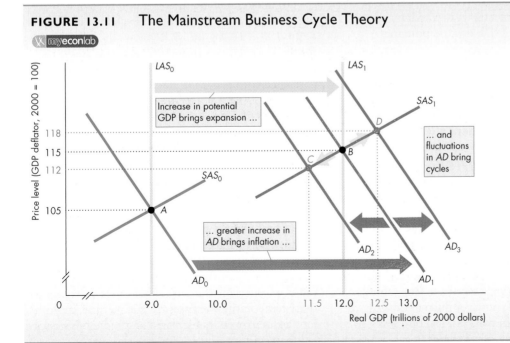

In a business cycle expansion, potential GDP increases and the LAS curve shifts rightward from LAS_0 to LAS_1. A greater than expected increase in aggregate demand brings inflation.

If the aggregate demand curve shifts to AD_1, the economy remains at full employment. If the aggregate demand curve shifts to AD_2, a recessionary gap arises. If the aggregate demand curve shifts to AD_3, an inflationary gap arises.

This mainstream theory comes in a number of special forms that differ in what is regarded as the source of fluctuations in aggregate demand growth and the source of money wage stickiness.

Keynesian Cycle Theory

In **Keynesian cycle theory**, fluctuations in investment driven by fluctuations in business confidence—summarized in the phrase "animal spirits"—are the main source of fluctuations in aggregate demand.

Monetarist Cycle Theory

In **monetarist cycle theory**, fluctuations in both investment and consumption expenditure, driven by fluctuations in the growth rate of the quantity of money, are the main source of fluctuations in aggregate demand.

Both the Keynesian and monetarist cycle theories simply assume that the money wage rate is rigid and don't explain that rigidity.

Two newer theories seek to explain money wage rate rigidity and to be more careful about working out its consequences.

New Classical Cycle Theory

In **new classical cycle theory**, the rational expectation of the price level, which is determined by potential GDP and *expected* aggregate demand, determines the money wage rate and the position of the *SAS* curve. In this theory, only *unexpected* fluctuations in aggregate demand bring fluctuations in real GDP around potential GDP.

New Keynesian Cycle Theory

The **new Keynesian cycle theory** emphasizes the fact that today's money wage rates were negotiated at many past dates, which means that *past* rational expectations of the current price level influence the money wage rate and the position of the *SAS* curve. In this theory, both unexpected and currently expected fluctuations in aggregate demand bring fluctuations in real GDP around potential GDP.

The mainstream cycle theories don't rule out the possibility that occasionally an aggregate supply shock might occur. An oil price rise, a widespread drought, a major hurricane, or another natural disaster, could, for example, bring a recession. But supply shocks are not the normal source of fluctuations in the mainstream theories. In contrast, real business cycle theory puts supply shocks at center stage.

Real Business Cycle Theory

The newest theory of the business cycle, known as **real business cycle theory** (or RBC theory), regards random fluctuations in productivity as the main source of economic fluctuations. These productivity fluctuations are assumed to result mainly from fluctuations in the pace of technological change, but they might also have other sources, such as international disturbances, climate fluctuations, or natural disasters. The origins of RBC theory can be traced to the rational expectations revolution set off by Robert E. Lucas, Jr., but the first demonstrations of the power of this theory were given by Edward Prescott and Finn Kydland and by John Long and Charles Plosser. Today, RBC theory is part of a broad research agenda called dynamic general equilibrium analysis, and hundreds of young macroeconomists do research on this topic.

We'll explore RBC theory by looking first at its impulse and then at the mechanism that converts that impulse into a cycle in real GDP.

The RBC Impulse

The impulse in RBC theory is the growth rate of productivity that results from technological change. RBC theorists believe this impulse to be generated mainly by the process of research and development that leads to the creation and use of new technologies.

To isolate the RBC theory impulse, economists use growth accounting, which is explained in Chapter 8, pp. 190–191. Figure 13.12 shows the RBC impulse for the United States from 1960 through 2005. You can see that fluctuations in productivity growth are correlated with real GDP fluctuations.

Most of the time, technological change is steady and productivity grows at a moderate pace. But sometimes productivity growth speeds up, and occasionally productivity *decreases*—labor becomes less productive, on the average. A period of rapid productivity growth brings a business cycle expansion, and a *decrease* in productivity triggers a recession.

It is easy to understand why technological change brings productivity growth. But how does it *decrease* productivity? All technological change eventually increases productivity. But if initially, technological change makes a sufficient amount of existing capital—especially human capital—obsolete, productivity temporarily decreases. At such a time, more jobs are destroyed than created and more businesses fail than start up.

FIGURE 13.12   The Real Business Cycle Impulse

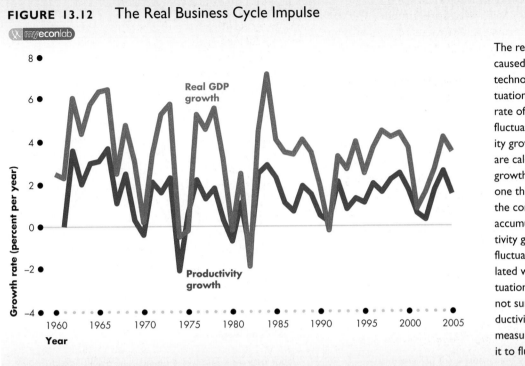

Source of data: Bureau of Economic Analysis and author's assumptions and calculations.

The real business cycle is caused by changes in technology that bring fluctuations in the growth rate of productivity. The fluctuations in productivity growth shown here are calculated by using growth accounting (the one third rule) to remove the contribution of capital accumulation to productivity growth. Productivity fluctuations are correlated with real GDP fluctuations. Economists are not sure what the productivity variable actually measures or what causes it to fluctuate.

The RBC Mechanism Two effects follow from a change in productivity that gets an expansion or a contraction going:

1. Investment demand changes.
2. The demand for labor changes.

We'll study these effects and their consequences during a recession. In an expansion, they work in the direction opposite to what is described here.

Technological change makes some existing capital obsolete and temporarily decreases productivity. Firms expect the future profits to fall and see their labor productivity falling. With lower profit expectations, they cut back their purchases of new capital, and with lower labor productivity, they plan to lay off some workers. So the initial effect of a temporary fall in productivity is a decrease in investment demand and a decrease in the demand for labor.

Figure 13.13 illustrates these two initial effects of a decrease in productivity. Part (a) shows the effects of a decrease in investment demand in the loanable funds market. The demand for loanable funds is DLF and the supply of loanable funds is SLF (both of which are explained in Chapter 7, pp. 169–174).

Initially, the demand for loanable funds is DLF_0 and the equilibrium quantity of funds is $2 trillion at a real interest rate of 6 percent a year. A decrease in productivity decreases investment demand, and the demand for loanable funds curve DLF shifts leftward to DLF_1. The real interest rate falls to 4 percent a year, and the equilibrium quantity of loanable funds decreases to $1.7 trillion.

Figure 13.13(b) shows the demand for labor curve LD and the supply of labor curve LS (which are explained in Chapter 7, pp. 160–164). Initially, the demand for labor curve is LD_0, and equilibrium employment is 200 billion hours a year at a real wage rate of $35 an hour. The decrease in productivity decreases the demand for labor, and the LD curve shifts leftward to LD_1.

Before we can determine the new level of employment and real wage rate, we need to take a ripple effect into account—the key effect in RBC theory.

The Key Decision: When to Work? According to RBC theory, people decide *when* to work by doing a cost-benefit calculation. They compare the return from

FIGURE 13.13   Loanable Funds and Labor Markets in a Real Business Cycle

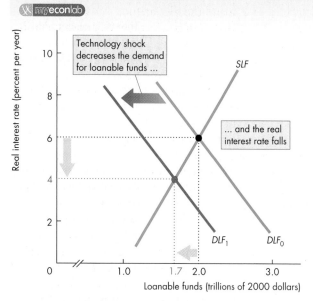

(a) Loanable funds and interest rate

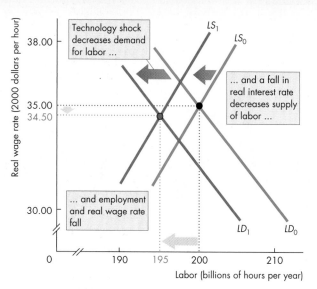

(b) Labor and wage rate

In part (a), the supply of loanable funds SLF and initial demand for loanable funds DLF_0 determine the real interest rate at 6 percent a year. In part (b), the initial demand for labor LD_0 and supply of labor, LS_0, determine the real wage rate at $35 an hour and employment at 200 billion hours. A technological change temporarily decreases productivity, and both the demand for loanable funds and the demand for

labor decrease. The two demand curves shift leftward to DLF_1 and LD_1. In part (a), the real interest rate falls to 4 percent a year. In part (b), the fall in the real interest rate decreases the supply of labor (the when-to-work decision) and the supply of labor curve shifts leftward to LS_1. Employment decreases to 195 billion hours, and the real wage rate falls to $34.50 an hour. A recession is underway.

working in the current period with the *expected* return from working in a later period. You make such a comparison every day in school. Suppose your goal in this course is to get an A. To achieve this goal, you work hard most of the time. But during the few days before the midterm and final exams, you work especially hard. Why? Because you believe that the return from studying close to the exam is greater than the return from studying when the exam is a long time away. So during the term, you take time off for the movies and other leisure pursuits, but at exam time, you study every evening and weekend.

RBC theory says that workers behave like you. They work fewer hours, sometimes zero hours, when the real wage rate is temporarily low, and they work more hours when the real wage rate is temporarily high. But to properly compare the current wage rate with the expected future wage rate, workers must use

the real interest rate. If the real interest rate is 6 percent a year, a real wage of $1 an hour earned this week will become $1.06 a year from now. If the real wage rate is expected to be $1.05 an hour next year, today's real wage of $1 looks good. By working longer hours now and shorter hours a year from now, a person can get a 1 percent higher real wage. But suppose the real interest rate is 4 percent a year. In this case, $1 earned now is worth $1.04 next year. Working fewer hours now and more next year is the way to get a 1 percent higher real wage.

So the when-to-work decision depends on the real interest rate. The lower the real interest rate, other things remaining the same, the smaller is the supply of labor today. Many economists believe this *intertemporal substitution* effect to be of negligible size. RBC theorists believe that the effect is large, and it is the key feature of the RBC mechanism.

You saw in Fig. 13.13(a) that the decrease in the demand for loanable funds lowers the real interest rate. This fall in the real interest rate lowers the return to current work and decreases the supply of labor.

In Fig. 13.13(b), the labor supply curve shifts leftward to LS_1. The effect of the decrease in productivity on the demand for labor is larger than the effect of the fall in the real interest rate on the supply of labor. That is, the LD curve shifts farther leftward than does the LS curve. As a result, the real wage rate falls to $34.50 an hour and employment decreases to 195 billion hours. A recession has begun and is intensifying.

What Happened to Money? The name *real* business cycle theory is no accident. It reflects the central prediction of the theory. Real things, not nominal or monetary things, cause business cycles. If the quantity of money changes, aggregate demand changes. But if there is no real change—with no change in the use of resources and no change in potential GDP—the change in the quantity of money changes only the price level. In RBC theory, this outcome occurs because the aggregate supply curve is the LAS curve, which pins real GDP down at potential GDP, so when aggregate demand changes, only the price level changes.

Cycles and Growth The shock that drives the business cycle of RBC theory is the same as the force that generates economic growth: technological change. On the average, as technology advances, productivity grows. But it grows at an uneven pace. You saw this fact when you studied growth accounting in Chapter 8, pp. 190–191. There, we focused on slow-changing trends in productivity growth. RBC theory uses the same idea but says that there are frequent shocks to productivity that are mostly positive but that are occasionally negative.

Criticisms and Defenses of RBC Theory The three main criticisms of RBC theory are that (1) the money wage rate *is* sticky, and to assume otherwise is at odds with a clear fact; (2) intertemporal substitution is too weak a force to account for large fluctuations in labor supply and employment with small real wage rate changes; and (3) productivity shocks are as likely to be caused by *changes in aggregate demand* as by technological change.

If the fluctuations in productivity are caused by aggregate demand fluctuations, then the traditional aggregate demand theories are needed to explain them. Fluctuations in productivity do not cause business cycles but are caused by them!

Building on this theme, the critics point out that the so-called productivity fluctuations that growth accounting measures are correlated with changes in the growth rate of money and other indicators of changes in aggregate demand.

The defenders of RBC theory claim that the theory explains the macroeconomic facts about business cycles and is consistent with the facts about economic growth. In effect, a single theory explains *both growth and cycles*. The growth accounting exercise that explains slowly changing trends also explains the more frequent business cycle swings. Its defenders also claim that RBC theory is consistent with a wide range of *micro*economic evidence about labor supply decisions, labor demand and investment demand decisions, and information on the distribution of income between labor and capital.

REVIEW QUIZ

1 Explain the mainstream theory of the business cycle.
2 What are the four varieties of the mainstream theory of the business cycle and how do they differ?
3 According to RBC theory, what causes the business cycle? What is the role of fluctuations in the rate of technological change?
4 According to RBC theory, how does a fall in productivity growth influence investment demand, the market for loanable funds, the real interest rate, the demand for labor, the supply of labor, employment, and the real wage rate?
5 What are the main criticisms of RBC theory and how do its supporters defend it?

myeconlab Study Plan 13.4

You can complete your study of inflation and the business cycle in *Reading Between the Lines* on pp. 332–333, which reviews the tradeoff between inflation and unemployment in the United States in 2006.

The Short-Run Inflation–Unemployment Tradeoff in 2006

http://www.nytimes.com

A Modest Rise Still Amplifies Inflation Fears

June 15, 2006

. . . After taking over as Fed chairman this year, Ben S. Bernanke indicated that he believed the underlying rate of inflation should not exceed 2 percent a year. That tough goal, which most other Fed policy makers share, reflects a major shift in attitude about the risks of inflation.

Much as the 1930s Depression seared an entire generation of Americans who lived through it, the stagflation of the 1970s and the acute recession of the early 1980s indelibly marked an entire generation of economists.

"It's a complete regime change," said Barry P. Bosworth, a top economic adviser to President Jimmy Carter during the worst years of soaring inflation.

"Back then, we were arguing about the trade-off between unemployment and inflation, and we weren't clear about which one was more important," he explained. "Today, there is no question: you cannot run the economy without the primacy of the goal of price stability."

These days, the Fed's goal is to reduce "inflation expectations," even though the effect could be to slow down an economy that already seems to be slowing, to send another icy chill through the housing market and possibly to increase unemployment. All that, even though hourly wages have barely kept up with consumer prices, which, including energy and food costs, rose 0.4 percent in May, leaving them 4.2 percent higher than a year earlier.

The effort to keep inflation so low is not without controversy, however. Some argue that the Fed should tolerate a slightly higher range, worrying that if the Fed establishes a narrow comfort zone of zero to 2 percent, it runs the risk of something worse—actual deflation—if the economy hits a bump in the road. . . .

Essence of the Story

▶ The Fed wants to keep the inflation rate close to 2 percent a year.

▶ The stagflation of the 1970s and the recession of the early 1980s have left an indelible mark on Bernanke's generation of economists.

▶ During the 1970s, economists were arguing about the tradeoff between unemployment and inflation and weren't clear about which one was more important.

▶ Today, economists agree that the primary goal is price stability.

▶ The Fed wants to lower inflation expectations, even if the effect is to slow further an already slowing economy.

▶ Some economists think the Fed should tolerate a slightly higher inflation rate because a negative shock might bring deflation.

▶ The inflation rate (CPI) in July 2006 was 0.4 percent, which translates to an annual inflation rate of almost 5 percent.

▶ The unemployment rate in July 2006 was 4.7 percent.

▶ The Congressional Budget Office's estimate of the natural unemployment rate is 5.5 percent.

▶ Using this estimate of the natural rate, the economy was in an above-full employment equilibrium in the summer of 2006.

▶ Figure 1 illustrates the state of the U.S. economy in July 2006 using the Phillips curve model.

▶ The long-run Phillips curve is $LRPC$ at the natural unemployment rate of 5.5 percent.

▶ The short-run Phillips curve is $SRPC_0$, which is based on an assumed expected inflation rate of 3 percent a year.

▶ The actual inflation rate exceeds the expected inflation rate.

▶ If the Fed takes no action and if the economy doesn't slow on its own, the expected inflation rate will rise and the short-run Phillips curve will shift upward and make the trade-off between inflation and unemployment more unfavorable.

▶ Figure 2 shows what happens if the Fed slows the growth rate of aggregate demand and pushes the unemployment rate up.

▶ The inflation rate slows and the economy moves down the short-run Phillips curve $SRPC_0$.

▶ Figure 3 shows the longer run effects of slowing inflation.

▶ When the unemployment rate rises above the natural rate, the inflation rate slows to less than the expected inflation rate.

▶ Eventually, the expected inflation rate begins to fall, and the short-run Phillips curve shifts downward.

▶ If the Fed can lower the expected inflation rate to 2 percent a year, the short-run Phillips curve shifts downward to $SRPC_1$.

▶ It is unlikely that a negative shock would bring deflation, as the article says some fear.

▶ But if the Fed failed to act to lower the inflation rate, it is most likely that inflation expectations would become unanchored and increase.

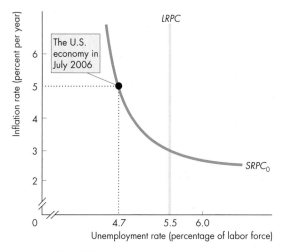

Figure 1 The Phillips curves

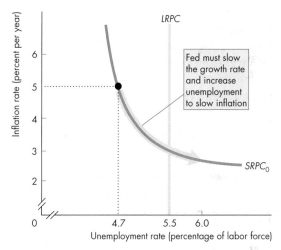

Figure 2 The Fed decreases the money growth rate

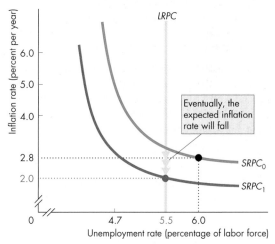

Figure 3 In the long run, inflation slows

SUMMARY

Key Points

The Evolving U.S. Economy (pp. 316–317)

- Potential GDP grows.
- Inflation persists because aggregate demand grows faster than potential GDP.
- Business cycles occur because potential GDP and aggregate demand change at an uneven pace.

Inflation Cycles (pp. 318–323)

- Demand-pull inflation is triggered by an increase in aggregate demand and fueled by ongoing money growth. Real GDP cycles above full employment.
- Cost-push inflation is triggered by an increase in the money wage rate or raw material prices and is fueled by ongoing money growth. Real GDP cycles below full employment in a stagflation.
- When inflation is expected correctly, real GDP remains at potential GDP.

Inflation and Unemployment: The Phillips Curve (pp. 324–326)

- The short-run Phillips curve shows the tradeoff between inflation and unemployment when the expected inflation rate and the natural unemployment rate are constant.
- The long-run Phillips curve, which is vertical, shows that when the actual inflation rate equals the expected inflation rate, the unemployment rate equals the natural unemployment rate.

Business Cycles (pp. 327–331)

- The mainstream business cycle theory explains business cycles as fluctuations of real GDP around potential GDP and as arising from a steady expansion of potential GDP combined with an expansion of aggregate demand at a fluctuating rate.
- Real business cycle theory explains business cycles as fluctuations of potential GDP, which arise from fluctuations in the influence of technological change on productivity growth.

Key Figures

Key Terms

PROBLEMS

1. The spreadsheet provides information about the economy in Argentina. Column A is the year, Column B is real GDP in billions of 2000 pesos, and Column C is the price level.

	A	B	C
1	1993	244	97.2
2	1994	257	99.9
3	1995	250	103.1
4	1996	264	103.1
5	1997	286	102.6
6	1998	297	100.8
7	1999	297	99.0
8	2000	284	100.0
9	2001	272	98.9
10	2002	242	129.1
11	2003	263	142.7
12	2004	287	155.8

a. In which years did Argentina experience inflation? In which years did it experience deflation?
b. In which years did recessions occur? In which years did expansions occur?
c. In which years do you expect the unemployment rate was highest? Why?
d. Do these data show a relationship between unemployment and inflation in Argentina?

Use the following figure to answers problems 2, 3, 4, and 5.

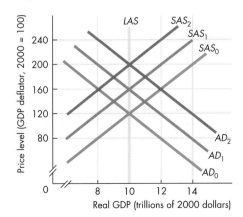

2. The economy starts out on the curves AD_0 and SAS_0. Some events then occur that generate a demand-pull inflation.
   a. List the events that might cause a demand-pull inflation.
   b. Using the figure, describe the initial effects of a demand-pull inflation.
   c. Using the figure, describe what happens as a demand-pull inflation spiral unwinds.
3. The economy starts out on the curves AD_0 and SAS_0. Some events then occur that generate a cost-push inflation.
   a. List the events that might cause a cost-push inflation.
   b. Using the figure, describe the initial effects of a cost-push inflation.
   c. Using the figure, describe what happens as a cost-push inflation spiral unwinds.
4. The economy starts out on the curves AD_0 and SAS_0. Some events then occur that generate an expected inflation.
   a. List the events that might cause an expected inflation.
   b. Using the figure, describe the initial effects of an expected inflation.
   c. Using the figure, describe what happens as an expected inflation proceeds.
5. Suppose that people expect deflation (a falling price level), but aggregate demand remains at AD_0.
   a. What happens to the short-run and long-run aggregate supply curves? (Draw some new curves if you need to.)
   b. Use the figure to describe the initial effects of an expected deflation.
   c. Use the figure to describe what happens as it becomes obvious to everyone that the expected deflation is not going to occur.
6. The Reserve Bank of New Zealand signed an agreement with the New Zealand government in which the Bank agreed to maintain inflation inside a low target range. Failure to achieve the target would result in the governor of the Bank (the equivalent of the chairman of the Fed) losing his job.
   a. Explain how this arrangement might have influenced New Zealand's short-run Phillips curve.
   b. Explain how this arrangement might have influenced New Zealand's long-run Phillips curve.

*Solutions to odd-numbered problems are provided.

7. An economy has an unemployment rate of 4 percent and an inflation rate of 5 percent a year at point *A* in the figure.

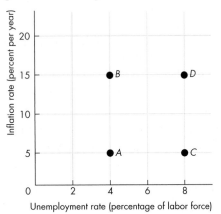

Some events occur that move the economy in a clockwise loop from *A* to *B* to *D* to *C* and back to *A*.

a. Describe the events that could create this sequence.

b. Draw in the figure the sequence of the economy's short-run and long-run Phillips curves.

c. Has the economy experienced demand-pull inflation, cost-push inflation, expected inflation, or none of these?

8. Suppose that the business cycle in the United States is best described by RBC theory. An advance in technology increases productivity.

a. Draw a diagram to show the effect of the advance in technology in the market for loanable funds.

b. Draw a diagram to show the effect of the advance in technology in the labor market.

c. What is the when-to-work decision when technology advances?

CRITICAL THINKING

1. After you have studied the account of the U.S. economy in 2006 in *Reading Between the Lines* on pp. 332–333,

a. Describe the main features of the U.S. economy in July 2006.

b. Did the United States have a recessionary gap or an inflationary gap in July 2006? How do you know?

c. Use the *AS-AD* model to show the changes in aggregate demand and aggregate supply that

brought the low unemployment and higher inflation rate in 2006.

d. Use the *AS-AD* model to show the changes in aggregate demand and aggregate supply that would occur if the Federal Reserve raised the interest rate and slowed the money growth rate during 2006 and 2007.

e. Use the Phillips curve model to show the changes in the inflation rate and the unemployment rate that would occur if the Federal Reserve raised the interest rate and slowed the money growth rate during 2006 and 2007.

2. **Real Wages Fail to Match a Rise in Productivity**

For most of the last century, wages and productivity—the key measure of the economy's efficiency—have risen together, increasing rapidly through the 1950s and 60s and far more slowly in the 1970s and 80s. But in recent years, the productivity gains have continued while the pay increases have not kept up.

The New York Times, August 28, 2006

Explain the relationship between wages and productivity in this news article in terms of real business cycle theory.

WEB ACTIVITIES

myeconlab Links to Web sites

1. Find data on recent changes in and forecasts of real GDP and the price level in the United States.

a. What is your forecast of next year's real GDP?

b. What is your forecast of next year's price level?

c. What is your forecast of the inflation rate?

d. What is your forecast of the growth rate of real GDP?

e. Do you think there will be a recessionary gap or an inflationary gap next year?

2. Find data on recent changes in and forecasts of real GDP and the price level in Japan.

a. What is your forecast of next year's real GDP?

b. What is your forecast of next year's price level?

c. What is your forecast of the inflation rate?

d. What is your forecast of the growth rate of real GDP?

e. Compare and contrast the forecasts for the U.S. and Japanese economies.

Boom and Bust

To cure a disease, doctors must first understand how the disease responds to different treatments. It helps to understand the mechanisms that operate to cause the disease, but sometimes, a workable cure can be found even before the full story of the causes has been told.

Curing economic ills is similar to curing our medical ills. We need to understand how the economy responds to the treatments we might prescribe for it. And sometimes, we want to try a cure even though we don't fully understand the reasons for the problem we're trying to control.

You've seen how the pace of capital accumulation and technological change determine the long-term growth trend. You've learned how fluctuations around the long-term trend can be generated by changes in aggregate demand and aggregate supply. And you've learned about the key sources of fluctuations in aggregate demand and aggregate supply.

The three chapters in this part have explained the alternative theories of economic fluctuations. We began in Chapter 11 by studying the *AS-AD* model. This model explains the forces that determine real GDP and the price level in the short run. The model also enables us to see the big picture or grand vision of the different schools of macroeconomic thought concerning the sources of aggregate fluctuations.

Chapter 12 explained the Keynesian aggregate expenditure model. This model provides an account of the factors that determine aggregate demand and make it fluctuate. The Keynesian model also explains how inventory changes trigger changes in production and bring a multiplier effect when investment, exports, or government expenditure on goods and services changes.

In Chapter 13, you learned about alternative theories of inflation and business cycles. All of these theories can be translated into the *AS-AD* model. And doing so helps us to compare and contrast the competing visions. But the new real business cycle theory is more at home with the demand and supply model of microeconomics than with the *AS-AD* model. Most economists have not embraced the real business cycle approach. It is an extreme view. But the *method* that real business cycle theory uses is here to stay. This method is to build a mathematical model of the entire economy and then to see, in a computer simulation, what kind of cycle the model creates. The economy on the computer is calibrated to the real economy, and the cycles are compared. The computer model can be treated with a variety of "medications," and their effects are then observed. This new style of business cycle research cannot be explained in detail without using advanced mathematical ideas. But Chapter 13 explained the economics that underlies it and showed you the type of model that real business cycle theorists use.

The economist you're going to meet on the next page, John Maynard Keynes, was the first to lay the foundations of the *AS-AD* model, although his version of the model was difficult to understand. Nonetheless, he revolutionized macroeconomics.

Business Cycles

> "The ideas of economists and political philosophers, both when they are right and when they are wrong, are more powerful than is commonly understood. Indeed the world is ruled by little else."

JOHN MAYNARD KEYNES
The General Theory of Employment, Interest, and Money

The Economist

John Maynard Keynes, *born in England in 1883, was one of the outstanding minds of the twentieth century. He wrote on probability as well as economics, represented Britain at the Versailles peace conference at the end of World War I, was a master speculator on international financial markets (an activity he conducted from bed every morning and which made and lost him several fortunes), and played a prominent role in creating the International Monetary Fund.*

He was a member of the Bloomsbury Group, a circle of outstanding artists and writers that included E. M. Forster, Bertrand Russell, and Virginia Woolf.

Keynes was a controversial and quick-witted figure. A critic once complained that Keynes had changed his opinion on some matter, to which Keynes retorted: "When I discover I am wrong, I change my mind. What do you do?"

Keynes' book, The General Theory of Employment, Interest and Money, *written during the Great Depression and published in 1936, was the origin of macroeconomics as a distinct branch of economics.*

The Issues

During the Industrial Revolution, as technological change created new jobs and destroyed old ones, people began to wonder whether the economy could create enough jobs and sufficient demand to buy all the things that the new industrial economy could produce.

Jean-Baptiste Say argued that production creates incomes that are sufficient to buy everything that is produced—supply creates its own demand—an idea that came to be called Say's Law.

Say and Keynes would have had a lot to disagree about. Jean-Baptiste Say, born in Lyon, France, in 1767 (he was 9 years old when Adam Smith's *Wealth of Nations* was published), suffered the wrath of Napoleon for his views on government and the economy. In today's world, Say would be leading a radical conservative charge for a smaller and leaner government. Say was the most famous economist of his era on both sides of the Atlantic. His book *Traité d'économie politique* (*A Treatise in Political Economy*), published in 1803, became a best-selling university economics textbook in both Europe and North America.

As the Great Depression of the 1930s became more severe and more prolonged, Say's Law looked less and less relevant. John Maynard Keynes revolutionized macroeconomic thinking by turning Say's Law on its head, arguing that supply does not create its own demand. Instead, aggregate production depends on what people are willing to buy—on aggregate demand. Or as Keynes put it, production depends on *effective* demand. It is possible, argued Keynes, for people to refuse to spend all of their incomes. If businesses fail to spend on new capital the amount that people plan to save, demand might be less than supply. In this situation, resources might go unemployed and remain unemployed indefinitely.

The influence of Keynes persists even today, more than 60 years after the publication of his main work. But during the past 20 years, Nobel Laureate Robert E. Lucas, Jr., with significant contributions from a list of outstanding macroeconomists too long to name, has further revolutionized macroeconomics. Today, we know a lot about economic fluctuations. But we don't yet have all the answers. Macroeconomics remains a field of lively controversy and exciting research.

Then

The Great Depression that Keynes tried to understand and help to avoid was a period of prolonged and extreme economic hardship that lasted from 1929 until the end of the 1930s.

By 1933, the worst of the Depression years, real GDP had fallen by a huge 30 percent. The people in the photograph were among the one in four workers who wanted jobs but couldn't find them.

The horrors of the Great Depression led to the New Deal and shaped political attitudes that persist today.

Now

How can a building designed as a shop have no better use than to be boarded up and left empty? Not enough aggregate demand, say the Keynesians. Not so, say the real business cycle theorists. Technological change has reduced the building's current productivity as a shop to zero. But its expected future productivity is sufficiently high that it is not efficient to refit the building for some other purpose. So it stays boarded up.

All unemployment, whether of buildings or of people, can be explained in a similar way. For example, how can it be that during a recession, a person trained as a shop clerk is without work? Not enough aggregate demand is one answer. Another is that the current productivity of shop clerks is low but their expected future productivity is sufficiently high that it does not pay an unemployed clerk to retrain for a job that is currently available.

It is now over 75 years since the Great Depression began. Although we've had many recessions since then, none of them compare with the severity of that event. But we still experience economic fluctuations. On the following pages, you can meet Ricardo Caballero, a professor at MIT and one of today's most distinguished economists and experts on economic fluctuations.

Ricardo J. Caballero

Ricardo J. Caballero is Ford Professor of International Economics at MIT. He has received many honors, the most notable of which are the Frisch Medal of the Econometric Society (2002) and being named Chile's Economist of the Year (2001). A highly regarded teacher, he is much sought as a special lecturer and in 2005 gave the prestigious Yrjo Jahnsson Lecture at the University of Helsinki.

Professor Caballero earned his B.S. degree in 1982 and M.A. in 1983 at Pontificia Universidad Católica de Chile. He then moved to the United States and obtained his Ph.D. at MIT in 1988.

Michael Parkin talked with Ricardo Caballero about his work and the progress that economists have made in understanding economic fluctuations.

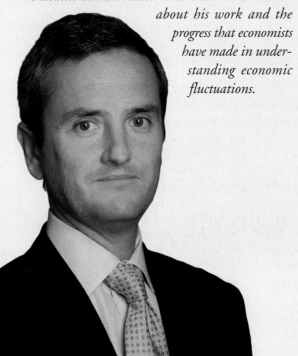

Professor Caballero, why did you decide to become an economist?
Did I decide? I'm convinced that one is either born an economist or not. I began studying business, but as soon as I took the first course in economics, I was captivated by the simple but elegant logic of (good) economic reasoning. Given the complexity of the real world, economic analysis is necessarily abstract. But at the same time, economics is mostly about concrete and important issues that affect the lives of millions of people. Abstraction and relevance—this is a wonderful but strange combination. Not everybody feels comfortable with it, but if you do, economics is for you.

Most of your work has been on business cycles and other high-frequency phenomena. Can we begin by reviewing the costs of recessions? Robert Lucas says that postwar U.S. recessions have cost very little. Do you agree?
No . . . but I'm not sure Robert Lucas was really trying to say that. My sense is that he was trying to push the profession to focus a bit more on long-run growth issues. Putting down the costs of recessions was a useful debating device to make his important point.

I believe that the statement that recessions are not costly is incorrect. First, I think his calculation of this magnitude reflects some fundamental flaw in the way the workhorse models we use in economics fail to account for the costs of risk and volatility. This flaw shows up in many different puzzles in economics, including the well-known equity premium puzzle. Economic models underestimate, by an order of magnitude, how unhappy agents are about facing uncertainty. Second, it is highly unlikely that recessions and medium-term growth are completely separable. In particular, the ongoing process of restructuring, which is central to productivity growth, is severely hampered by deep recessions.

Recessions are costly because they waste enormous resources, affect physical and human investment decisions, have large negative distributional consequences, influence political outcomes, and so on.

What about the costs of recessions in other parts of the world, especially Latin America?
The cost of recessions grows exponentially with their size and the country's inability to soften the impact on the most affected. Less developed economies suffer much larger shocks because their economies are not well diversified, and they experience capital outflows that exacerbate the impact of recessionary shocks. Their domestic financial sectors are small and often become strained during recessions, making it difficult to reallocate scarce resources toward those who need them the most. To make matters worse, the government's ability to use fiscal policy becomes impaired by the capital outflows, and monetary policy is also out of the question when the currency is in free fall and liabilities are dollarized. There are many things that we take for granted in the United States that simply are not feasible for emerging markets in distress. One has to be careful with extrapolating too directly the countercyclical recipes used for developed economies to these countries.

Your first work, in your M.A. dissertation, was to build a macroeconomic model of the economy of Chile? What do we learn by comparing economies? Does the Chilean economy behave essentially like the U.S. economy or are there fundamental differences?
Chile is a special economy among emerging markets. It began pro-market reforms many years before the rest and has had very prudent macroeconomic management for several decades by now. For that reason, it is a bit more "like the U.S. economy" than most other emerging market economies. However there are still important differences, of the sort

> Recessions are costly because they waste enormous resources [and] affect physical and human investment decisions.

described in my answer to the previous question.

Beyond the specifics of Chile, at some deep level, macroeconomic principles, and economic principles more generally, are the same everywhere. It is all about incentives, tradeoffs, effort, commitment, discipline, transparency, insurance, and so on. But different economies hurt in different places, and hence the practice of economics has plenty of diversity.

During the most recent U.S. expansion, some asset prices—especially house prices—have looked as if they might be experiencing a speculative bubble, and you've done some recent work on bubbles. How can we tell whether we're seeing a bubble or just a rapid increase that is being driven by fundamental market forces?
First things first. I think we need to get used to the presence of speculative bubbles. The reason is that the world today has a massive shortage of financial assets that savers can use to store value. Because of this shortage, "artificial" assets are ready to emerge at all times. Specific bubbles come and go—from the NASDAQ, to real estate, to commodities—but the total is much more stable.

I do not think the distinction between bubbles and fundamentals is as clear-cut as people describe. Probably outside periods of liquidity crises, all assets have some bubble component in them. The question is how much.

You've studied situations in which capital suddenly stops flowing into an economy from abroad. What are the lessons you've learned from this research?
The most basic lesson for emerging markets is that capital flows are volatile. Sometimes they simply magnify domestic problems, but in many other cases, they are the direct source of volatility.

> The most basic lesson for emerging markets is that capital flows are volatile.

However the conclusion from this observation is not that capital flows should be limited, just as we do not close the banks in the United States to eliminate the possibility of bank runs. On the contrary, much of the volatility comes from insufficient integration with international capital markets, which makes emerging markets illiquid and the target of specialists and speculators. For the short and medium run, the main policy lesson is that sudden stops to the inflow of capital must be put at the center of macroeconomic policy design in emerging markets. This has deep implications for the design of monetary and fiscal policy, as well as for international reserves management practices and domestic financial markets regulation.

The U.S. current account deficit has been large and increasing for many years, and dollar debt levels around the world have increased. Do you see any danger in this process for either the United States or the rest of the world?
I believe the persistent current account deficits in the United States are not the result of an anomaly that, as such, must go away in a sudden crash, as the conventional view has it. Instead, my view is that these deficits are just the counterpart of large capital inflows resulting from the global shortage of financial assets that I mentioned earlier. Good growth potential in the United States over that of Europe and Japan and the much better quality of its financial assets over those of emerging Asian and oil-producing countries make

... Good growth of potential in the United States over that of Europe and Japan and the much better quality of its financial assets over those of emerging Asian and oil-producing countries make the United States very attractive to international private and public investors.

Almost everything in life has an economic angle to it—look for it ...

the United States very attractive to international private and public investors.

Absent major shocks, this process may still last for quite some time. But of course shocks do happen, and in that sense, leverage is dangerous. However there isn't much we can or should do, short of implementing structural reforms around the world aimed at improving growth potential in some cases and domestic financial development in others.

What advice do you have for someone who is just beginning to study economics but who wants to become an economist? If they are not in the United States, should they come here for graduate work as you did?
There is no other place in the world like the United States to pursue a Ph.D. and do research in economics. However, this is only the last stage in the process of becoming an economist. There are many superb economists, especially applied ones, all around the world.

I believe the most important step is to learn to think like an economist. I heard Milton Friedman say that he knows many economists who have never gone through a Ph.D. program, and equally many who have completed their Ph.D. but are not really economists. I agree with him on this one. A good undergraduate program and talking about economics is a great first step. Almost everything in life has an economic angle to it—look for it and discuss it with your friends. It will not improve your social life, but it will make you a better economist.

Fiscal Policy

Balancing Acts on Capitol Hill

In 2007, the federal government planned to collect in

taxes 18.2 cents of every dollar Americans earned and to spend 21.1 cents of

every dollar that Americans earned. So the government planned a deficit of almost 3 cents of every dollar earned—a total deficit of $370 billion. Federal government deficits are not new. Aside from the four years 1998–2001, the government's budget has been in deficit every year since 1970. Deficits bring debts, and your share of the federal government's debt is around $29,000.

What are the effects of taxes on the economy? Do they harm employment and production?

Does it matter if the government doesn't balance its books? What are the effects of an ongoing government deficit and accumulating debt? Do they slow economic growth? Do they impose a burden on future generations—on you and your children?

What are the effects of government spending on the economy? Does a dollar spent by the government on goods and services have the same effect as a dollar spent by someone else? Does it create jobs, or does it destroy them?

◆ These are the fiscal policy issues that you will study in this chapter. In *Reading Between the Lines* at the end of the chapter, we look at the federal budget in 2007 and compare it with that of 2000, the last year of the Clinton administration.

After studying this chapter, you will be able to

▶ Describe the federal budget process and the recent history of outlays, tax revenues, deficits, and debt

▶ Explain the supply-side effects of fiscal policy on employment and potential GDP

▶ Explain the effects of deficits on investment, saving, and economic growth

▶ Explain how fiscal policy choices redistribute benefits and costs across generations

▶ Explain how fiscal policy can be used to stabilize the business cycle

The Federal Budget

The annual statement of the outlays and tax revenues of the government of the United States together with the laws and regulations that approve and support those outlays and tax revenues make up the **federal budget**. The federal budget has two purposes:

1. To finance the activities of the federal government
2. To achieve macroeconomic objectives

The first purpose of the federal budget was its only purpose before the Great Depression years of the 1930s. The second purpose arose as a reaction to the Great Depression. The use of the federal budget to achieve macroeconomic objectives such as full employment, sustained economic growth, and price level stability is called **fiscal policy**. It is on this second purpose that we focus in this chapter.

The Institutions and Laws

Fiscal policy is made by the President and Congress on an annual timeline that is shown in Fig. 14.1 for the 2007 budget.

The Roles of the President and Congress

The President *proposes* a budget to Congress each February and, after Congress has passed the budget acts in September, either signs those acts into law or vetoes the *entire* budget bill. The President does not have the veto power to eliminate specific items in a budget bill and approve others—known as a *line-item veto*. Many state governors have long had line-item veto authority, and Congress attempted to grant these powers to the President of the United States in 1996. But in a 1998 Supreme Court ruling, the line-item veto for the President was declared unconstitutional. Although the President proposes and ultimately approves the budget, the task of making the tough decisions on spending and taxes rests with Congress.

Congress begins its work on the budget with the President's proposal. The House of Representatives and the Senate develop their own budget ideas in their respective House and Senate Budget Committees. Formal conferences between the two houses eventually resolve differences of view, and a series of spending acts and an overall budget act are usually passed by both houses before the start of the fiscal year. A

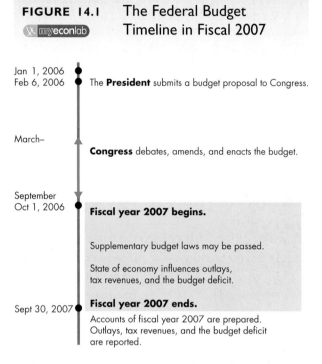

FIGURE 14.1   The Federal Budget Timeline in Fiscal 2007

Jan 1, 2006
Feb 6, 2006 — The **President** submits a budget proposal to Congress.

March– — **Congress** debates, amends, and enacts the budget.

September
Oct 1, 2006 — **Fiscal year 2007 begins.**

Supplementary budget laws may be passed.

State of economy influences outlays, tax revenues, and the budget deficit.

Sept 30, 2007 — **Fiscal year 2007 ends.**
Accounts of fiscal year 2007 are prepared. Outlays, tax revenues, and the budget deficit are reported.

The federal budget process begins with the President's proposals in February. Congress debates and amends these proposals and enacts a budget before the start of the fiscal year on October 1. The President signs the budget acts into law or vetoes the entire budget bill. Throughout the fiscal year, Congress might pass supplementary budget laws. The budget outcome is calculated after the end of the fiscal year.

fiscal year is a year that runs from October 1 to September 30 in the next calendar year. *Fiscal* 2007 is the fiscal year that *begins* on October 1, 2006.

During a fiscal year, Congress often passes supplementary budget laws, and the budget outcome is influenced by the evolving state of the economy. For example, if a recession begins, tax revenues fall and welfare payments increase.

The Employment Act of 1946 Fiscal policy operates within the framework of the landmark **Employment Act of 1946** in which Congress declared that

> . . . it is the continuing policy and responsibility of the Federal Government to use all practicable means . . . to coordinate and utilize all its plans, functions, and resources . . . to promote maximum employment, production, and purchasing power.

This act recognized a role for government actions to keep unemployment low, the economy expanding, and inflation in check. The *Full Employment and Balanced Growth Act of 1978*, more commonly known as the *Humphrey-Hawkins Act*, went farther than the Employment Act of 1946 and set a specific target of 4 percent for the unemployment rate. But this target has never been treated as an unwavering policy goal. Under the 1946 act, the President must describe the current economic situation and the policies he believes are needed in the annual *Economic Report of the President*, which the Council of Economic Advisers writes.

The Council of Economic Advisers The President's Council of Economic Advisers was established in the Employment Act of 1946. The Council consists of a chairperson and two other members, all of whom are economists on a one- or two-year leave from their regular university or public service jobs. In 2006, the chair of President Bush's Council of Economic Advisers was Edward P. Lazear of Stanford University. The **Council of Economic Advisers** monitors the economy and keeps the President and the public well informed about the current state of the economy and the best available forecasts of where it is heading. This economic intelligence activity is one source of data that informs the budget-making process.

Let's look at the most recent federal budget.

Highlights of the 2007 Budget

Table 14.1 shows the main items in the federal budget proposed by President Bush for 2007. The numbers are projected amounts for the fiscal year beginning on October 1, 2006—fiscal 2007. Notice the three main parts of the table: *Tax revenues* are the government's receipts, *outlays* are the government's payments, and the *deficit* is the amount by which the government's outlays exceed its tax revenues.

Tax Revenues Tax revenues were projected to be $2,521 billion in fiscal 2007. These revenues come from four sources:

1. Personal income taxes
2. Social security taxes
3. Corporate income taxes
4. Indirect taxes

The largest source of revenue is *personal income taxes*, which in 2007 are expected to be $1,098 billion. These taxes are paid by individuals on their incomes. The second largest source is *social security taxes*. These taxes are paid by workers and their employers to finance the government's social security programs. Third in size are *corporate income taxes*. These taxes are paid by companies on their profits. Finally, the smallest source of federal revenue is what are called *indirect taxes*. These taxes are on the sale of gasoline, alcoholic beverages, and a few other items.

Outlays Outlays are classified in three categories:

1. Transfer payments
2. Expenditure on goods and services
3. Debt interest

The largest item of outlays, *transfer payments*, are payments to individuals, businesses, other levels of government, and the rest of the world. In 2007, this item is expected to be $1,738 billion. It includes Social Security benefits, Medicare and Medicaid, unemployment checks, welfare payments, farm subsidies, grants to state and local governments, aid to developing countries, and dues to international organizations such as the United Nations. Transfer

TABLE 14.1	Federal Budget in Fiscal 2007
Item	**Projections** (billions of dollars)
Tax Revenues	**2,521**
Personal income taxes	1,098
Social security taxes	949
Corporate income taxes	297
Indirect taxes	177
Outlays	**2,891**
Transfer payments	1,738
Expenditure on goods and services	837
Debt interest	316
Deficit	**370**

Source of data: Budget of the United States Government, Fiscal Year 2007, Table 14.1.

payments, especially those for Medicare and Medicaid, are sources of persistent growth in government expenditures and are a major source of concern and political debate.

Expenditure on goods and services is the expenditure on final goods and services, and in 2007, it is expected to total $837 billion. This expenditure, which includes that on national defense, homeland security, research on cures for AIDS, computers for the Internal Revenue Service, government cars and trucks, federal highways, and dams, has decreased in recent years. This component of the federal budget is the *government expenditure on goods and services* that appears in the circular flow of expenditure and income and in the National Income and Product Accounts (see Chapter 5, pp. 113–114 and 117).

Debt interest is the interest on the government debt. In 2007, this item is expected to be $316 billion—about 10 percent of total expenditure. This interest payment is large because the government has a debt of more than $4 trillion, which has arisen from many years of budget deficits during the 1970s, 1980s, 1990s, and 2000s.

Surplus or Deficit   The government's budget balance is equal to tax revenues minus outlays.

   Budget balance = Tax revenues − Outlays.

If tax revenues exceed outlays, the government has a **budget surplus**. If outlays exceed tax revenues, the government has a **budget deficit**. If tax revenues equal outlays, the government has a **balanced budget**. In fiscal 2007, with projected outlays of $2,891 billion and tax revenues of $2,521 billion, the government projected a budget deficit of $370 billion.

Big numbers like these are hard to visualize and hard to compare over time. To get a better sense of the magnitude of tax revenues, outlays, and the deficit, we often express them as percentages of GDP. Expressing them in this way lets us see how large government is relative to the size of the economy and also helps us to study *changes* in the scale of government over time.

How typical is the federal budget of 2007? Let's look at the recent history of the budget.

The Budget in Historical Perspective

Figure 14.2 shows the government's tax revenues, outlays, and budget surplus or deficit since 1980. Through 1997, there was a budget deficit. The federal government began running a deficit in 1970, and the 1983 deficit shown in the figure was the highest on record at 5.2 percent of GDP. The deficit declined through 1989 but climbed again during the 1990–1991 recession. During the 1990s expansion,

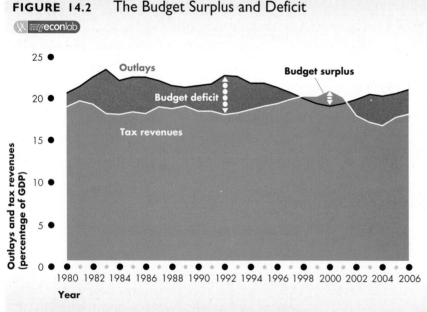

FIGURE 14.2   The Budget Surplus and Deficit

The figure records the federal government's outlays, tax revenues, and budget balance from 1980 to 2006. During the 1980s, a large and persistent budget deficit arose from the combination of falling tax revenues and rising outlays. In 1998, rising tax revenues and falling outlays (as percentages of GDP) created a budget surplus, but a deficit emerged again in 2002 as expenditure on security increased and taxes were cut.

Source of data: *Budget of the United States Government, Fiscal Year 2007*, Table 14.2.

the deficit gradually shrank, and in 1998, the first budget surplus since 1969 emerged. But by 2002, the budget was again in deficit.

Why did the budget deficit grow during the 1980s and vanish in the late 1990s? The answer lies in the changes in outlays and tax revenues. But which components of outlays and tax revenues changed to swell and then shrink the deficit? Let's look at tax revenues and outlays in a bit more detail.

Tax Revenues Figure 14.3(a) shows the components of tax revenues as percentages of GDP from 1980 to 2006. Cuts in corporate and personal income taxes lowered total tax revenues between 1983 and 1986. The decline resulted from tax cuts that had been passed during 1981. From 1986 through 1991, tax revenues did not change much as a percentage of GDP. Personal income tax payments increased through the 1990s but fell sharply after 2000.

FIGURE 14.3   Federal Government Tax Revenues and Outlays

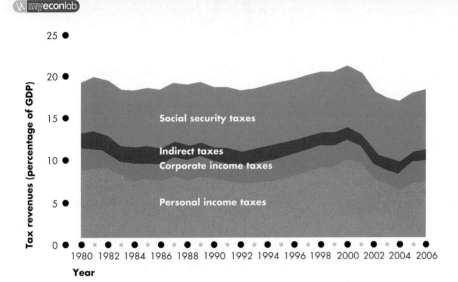

(a) Tax revenues

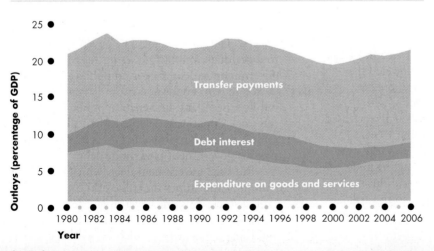

(b) Outlays

In part (a), revenues from personal and corporate income taxes as a percentage of GDP were approximately constant during the 1980s, increased during the 1990s, and decreased sharply from 2000 to 2004 but then increased again. The other components of tax revenues remained steady.

In part (b), expenditure on goods and services as a percentage of GDP decreased through 2001 but then increased because expenditure on security-related goods and services increased sharply after 2001. Transfer payments increased over the entire period. Debt interest held steady during the 1980s and decreased during the 1990s and 2000s, helped by a shrinking budget deficit during the 1990s and low interest rates during 2002 and 2003.

Source of data: Budget of the United States Government, Fiscal Year 2007 Table 14.2.

Outlays Figure 14.3(b) shows the components of government outlays as percentages of GDP from 1980 to 2006. Total outlays decreased slightly through 1989, increased during the early 1990s, decreased steadily until 2000, and then increased again. Expenditure on goods and services decreased through 2001. It increased when expenditure on security-related goods and services increased sharply in 2002 in the wake of the attacks that occurred on September 11, 2001. Transfer payments increased over the entire period. Debt interest was a constant percentage of GDP during the 1980s and fell slightly during the late 1990s and 2000s. To understand the role of debt interest, we need to see the connection between the government's budget balance and debt.

Budget Balance and Debt The government borrows when it has a budget deficit and makes repayments when it has a budget surplus. **Government debt** is the total amount that the government has borrowed. It is the sum of past budget deficits minus the sum of past budget surpluses. A government budget deficit increases government debt. A persistent budget deficit feeds itself: The budget deficit leads to increased borrowing; increased borrowing leads to larger interest payments; and larger interest payments lead to a larger deficit. That is the story of the increasing budget deficit during the 1970s and 1980s.

Figure 14.4 shows two measures of government debt since 1940. Gross debt includes the amounts that the government owes to future generations in social security payments. Net debt is the debt held by the public, and it excludes social security obligations.

Government debt (as a percentage of GDP) was at an all-time high at the end of World War II. Budget surpluses and rapid economic growth lowered the debt-to-GDP ratio through 1974. Small budget deficits increased the debt-to-GDP ratio slightly through the 1970s, and large budget deficits increased it dramatically during the 1980s and the 1990–1991 recession. The growth rate of the debt-to-GDP ratio slowed as the economy expanded during the mid-1990s, fell when the budget went into surplus in the late 1990s and early 2000s, and began to rise again as the budget turned in deficit.

Debt and Capital Businesses and individuals incur debts to buy capital—assets that yield a return. In fact, the main point of debt is to enable people to

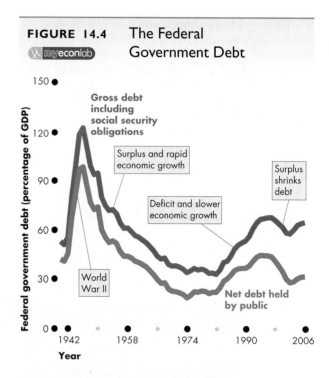

FIGURE 14.4   The Federal Government Debt

Gross and net government debt (the accumulation of past budget deficits less past budget surpluses) was at its highest at the end of World War II. Debt as a percentage of GDP fell through 1974 but then started to increase. After a further brief decline during the late 1970s, it exploded during the 1980s and continued to increase through 1995, after which it fell. After 2002, it began to rise again.

Source of data: Budget of the United States Government, Fiscal Year 2007, Table 7.1.

buy assets that will earn a return that exceeds the interest paid on the debt. The government is similar to individuals and businesses in this regard. Much government expenditure is on public assets that yield a return. Highways, major irrigation schemes, public schools and universities, public libraries, and the stock of national defense capital all yield a social rate of return that probably far exceeds the interest rate the government pays on its debt.

But total government debt, which exceeds $4 trillion, is four times the value of the government's capital stock. So some government debt has been incurred to finance public consumption expenditure and transfer payments, which do not have a social return. Future generations bear the cost of this debt.

How does the U.S. government budget balance compare with those in other countries?

The U.S. Government Budget in Global Perspective

Figure 14.5 places the U.S. government budget of 2006 in a global perspective. In that year, almost all countries had budget deficits. Summing the deficits of all the governments, the world as a whole had a deficit of 3 percent of world GDP—a total government deficit of close to $2 trillion.

The government of Japan had the largest deficit, as a percentage of GDP. The United States, Italy, and Germany came next, followed by the developing countries. Of the other advanced economies, the United Kingdom, France, and the entire European Union had large deficits.

Even the newly industrialized economies of Asia (Hong Kong, South Korea, Singapore, and Taiwan) had deficits. The other advanced countries as a group and Canada had surpluses in 2006.

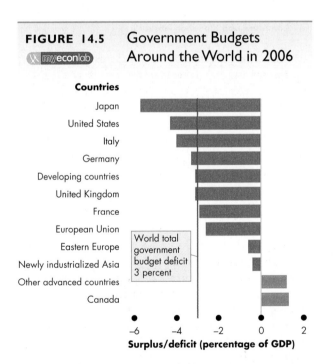

FIGURE 14.5
Government Budgets Around the World in 2006

Governments in most countries had budget deficits in 2006. The largest ones were in Japan, followed by the United States, Italy, and Germany. The developing countries, the United Kingdom, and France also had large deficits. Other advanced economies and Canada had budget surpluses.

Source of data: International Monetary Fund, *World Economic Outlook*, April 2006.

State and Local Budgets

The *total government* sector of the United States includes state and local governments as well as the federal government. In 2005, when federal government outlays were about $2,500 billion, state and local outlays were almost $1,700 billion. Most of these expenditures were on public schools, colleges, and universities ($550 billion); local police and fire services; and roads.

It is the combination of federal, state, and local government tax revenues, outlays, and budget deficits that influences the economy. But state and local budgets are not designed to stabilize the aggregate economy or to make it more efficient. So sometimes, when the federal government cuts taxes or outlays, state and local governments do the reverse and, to a degree, cancel out the effects of the federal actions. For example, during 2001, when federal taxes began to decrease as a percentage of GDP, state and local taxes increased.

REVIEW QUIZ

1. What is fiscal policy, who makes it, and what is it designed to influence?
2. What special role does the President play in creating fiscal policy?
3. What special roles do the Budget Committees of the House of Representatives and the Senate play in creating fiscal policy?
4. What is the timeline for the U.S. federal budget each year? When does a fiscal year begin and end?
5. Is the federal government budget today in surplus or deficit?

myeconlab Study Plan 14.1

Now that you know what the federal budget is and what the main components of tax revenues and outlay are, it is time to study the *effects* of fiscal policy. We'll begin by learning about the effects of taxes on employment, aggregate supply, and potential GDP. Then we'll study the effects of budget deficits and see how fiscal policy brings redistribution across generations. Finally, we'll look at the demand-side effects of fiscal policy and see how it provides a tool for stabilizing the business cycle.

The Supply Side: Employment and Potential GDP

Fiscal policy has important effects on employment, potential GDP, and aggregate supply that we'll now examine. These effects are known as **supply-side effects**, and economists who believe these effects to be large ones are generally referred to as *supply-siders*. To study these effects, we'll begin with a refresher on how full employment and potential GDP are determined in the absence of taxes. Then we'll introduce an income tax and see how it changes the economic outcome.

Full Employment and Potential GDP

You learned in Chapter 7 (pp. 164–165) how the full-employment quantity of labor and potential GDP are determined. At full employment, the real wage rate adjusts to make the quantity of labor demanded equal the quantity of labor supplied. Potential GDP is the real GDP that the full-employment quantity of labor produces.

Figure 14.6 illustrates a full-employment situation. In part (a), the demand for labor curve is *LD*, the supply of labor curve is *LS*. At a real wage rate of $30 an hour and 250 billion hours of labor a year employed, the economy is at full employment.

In Fig. 14.6(b), the production function is *PF*. When 250 billion hours of labor are employed, real GDP—which is also potential GDP—is $13 trillion.

Let's now see how an income tax changes potential GDP.

The Effects of the Income Tax

The tax on labor income influences potential GDP and aggregate supply by changing the full-employment quantity of labor. The income tax weakens the incentive to work and drives a wedge between the take-home wage of workers and the cost of labor to firms. The result is a smaller quantity of labor and a lower potential GDP.

Figure 14.6 shows this outcome. In the labor market, the income tax has no effect on the demand for labor, which remains at *LD*. The reason is that the quantity of labor that firms plan to hire depends only on how productive labor is and what it costs—its real wage rate.

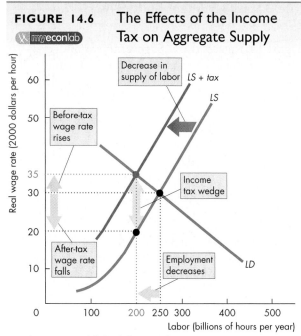

FIGURE 14.6   The Effects of the Income Tax on Aggregate Supply

(a) Income tax and the labor market

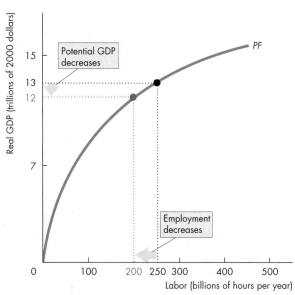

(b) Income tax and potential GDP

In part (a), with no income tax, the real wage rate is $30 an hour and employment is 250 billion hours. In part (b), potential GDP is $13 trillion. An income tax shifts the supply of labor curve leftward to *LS + tax*. The before-tax wage rate rises to $35 an hour, the after-tax wage rate falls to $20 an hour, and the quantity of labor employed decreases to 200 billion hours. With less labor, potential GDP decreases.

But the supply of labor *does* change. With no income tax, the real wage rate is $30 an hour and 250 billion hours of labor a year are employed. An income tax weakens the incentive to work and decreases the supply of labor. The reason is that for each dollar of before-tax earnings, workers must pay the government an amount determined by the income tax code. So workers look at the after-tax wage rate when they decide how much labor to supply. An income tax shifts the supply curve leftward to *LS + tax*. The vertical distance between the *LS* curve and the *LS + tax* curve measures the amount of income tax. With the smaller supply of labor, the *before-tax* wage rate rises to $35 an hour but the *after-tax* wage rate falls to $20 an hour. The gap created between the before-tax and after-tax wage rates is called the **tax wedge**.

The new equilibrium quantity of labor employed is 200 billion hours a year—less than in the no-tax case. Because the full-employment quantity of labor decreases, so does potential GDP. And a decrease in potential GDP decreases aggregate supply.

In this example, the tax rate is high—$15 tax on a $35 wage rate, about 43 percent. A lower tax rate would have a smaller effect on employment and potential GDP.

An increase in the tax rate to above 43 percent would decrease the supply of labor by more than the decrease shown in Fig. 14.6. Equilibrium employment and potential GDP would also decrease still further. A tax cut would increase the supply of labor, increase equilibrium employment, and increase potential GDP.

Taxes on Expenditure and the Tax Wedge

The tax wedge that we've just considered is only a part of the wedge that affects labor-supply decisions. Taxes on consumption expenditure add to the wedge. The reason is that a tax on consumption raises the prices paid for consumption goods and services and is equivalent to a cut in the real wage rate.

The incentive to supply labor depends on the goods and services that an hour of labor can buy. The higher the taxes on goods and services and the lower the after-tax wage rate, the less is the incentive to supply labor. If the income tax rate is 25 percent and the tax rate on consumption expenditure is 10 percent, a dollar earned buys only 65 cents worth of goods and services. The tax wedge is 35 percent.

Some Real World Tax Wedges

Edward C. Prescott of Arizona State University, who shared the 2004 Nobel Prize for Economic Science, has estimated the tax wedges for a number of countries. The U.S. tax wedge is a combination of 13 percent tax on consumption and 32 percent tax on incomes. The income tax rate includes Social Security taxes and is a *marginal* tax rate.

Among the industrial countries, the U.S. tax wedge is relatively small. Prescott estimates that in France, taxes on consumption are 33 percent and taxes on incomes are 49 percent. The estimates for the United Kingdom fall between those for the United States and France. Figure 14.7 shows these components of the tax wedges in the three countries.

Does the Tax Wedge Matter?

According to Prescott's estimates, the tax wedge has a powerful effect on employment and potential GDP. Potential GDP in France is 14 percent below that of the United States (per person), and the entire difference can be attributed to the difference in the tax wedge in the two countries.

Potential GDP in the United Kingdom is 41 percent below that of the United States (per person), and about a third of the difference arises from the different tax wedges. (The rest is due to different productivities.)

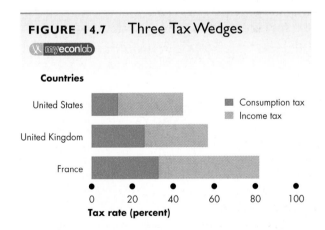

FIGURE 14.7 Three Tax Wedges

Tax rates are much higher in France and the United Kingdom than in the United States and can account for much of the difference in potential GDP per person.

Source of data: Edward C. Prescott, *American Economic Review*, 2003.

Tax Revenues and the Laffer Curve

An interesting consequence of the effect of a tax on employment is that a higher tax *rate* does not always bring greater tax *revenue*. A higher tax rate brings in more revenue per dollar earned. But because a higher tax rate decreases the number of dollars earned, two forces operate in opposite directions on the tax revenue collected.

The relationship between the tax rate and the amount of tax revenue collected is called the **Laffer curve**. The curve is so named because Arthur B. Laffer, a member of President Reagan's Economic Policy Advisory Board, drew such a curve on a table napkin and launched the idea that tax *cuts* could *increase* tax revenue.

Figure 14.8 shows a Laffer curve. The tax *rate* is on the *x*-axis, and total tax *revenue* is on the *y*-axis. For tax rates below T^*, an increase in the tax rate increases tax revenue; at T^*, tax revenue is maximized; and a tax rate increase above T^* decreases tax revenue.

Most people think that the United States is on the upward-sloping part of the Laffer curve. So is the United Kingdom. But France might be close to the maximum point or perhaps even beyond it.

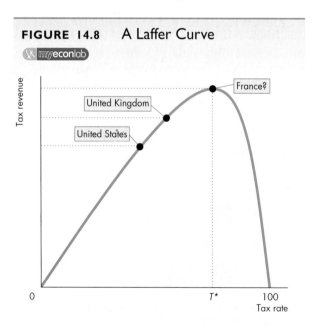

FIGURE 14.8   A Laffer Curve

A Laffer curve shows the relationship between the tax rate and tax revenues. For tax rates below T^*, an increase in the tax rate increases tax revenue. At the tax rate T^*, tax revenue is maximized. For tax rates above T^*, an increase in the tax rate decreases tax revenue.

The Supply-Side Debate

Before 1980, few economists paid attention to the supply-side effects of taxes on employment and potential GDP. Then, when Ronald Reagan took office as President, a group of supply-siders began to argue the virtues of cutting taxes. Arthur Laffer was one of them. Laffer and his supporters were not held in high esteem among mainstream economists, but they were influential for a period. They correctly argued that tax cuts would increase employment and increase output. But they incorrectly argued that tax cuts would increase tax revenues and decrease the budget deficit. For this prediction to be correct, the United States would have had to be on the "wrong" side of the Laffer curve. Given that U.S. tax rates are among the lowest in the industrial world, it is unlikely that this condition was met. And when the Reagan administration did cut taxes, the budget deficit increased, a fact that reinforces this view.

Supply-side economics became tarnished because of its association with Laffer and came to be called "voodoo economics." But mainstream economists, including Martin Feldstein, a Harvard professor who was Reagan's chief economic advisor, recognized the power of tax cuts as incentives but took the standard view that tax cuts without spending cuts would swell the budget deficit and bring serious further problems. This view is now widely accepted by economists of all political persuasions.

You now know the effects of taxes on potential GDP. The effects that we've studied influence the *level* of real GDP but not its *growth rate*. We're now going to look at the effects of taxes and the budget deficit on saving and investment, which in turn influence the pace of economic growth.

The Supply Side: Investment, Saving, and Economic Growth

You learned in Chapter 5 how investment is financed by national saving and borrowing from the rest of the world. In Chapter 7, you studied the factors that influence investment and saving decisions and how the real interest rate adjusts in the loanable funds market to coordinate saving and lending and investment and borrowing plans. Then in Chapter 8, you saw how investment increases the capital stock and contributes to real GDP growth.

When we studied the loanable funds market in Chapter 7, we noted that a government budget deficit (or surplus) influences the loanable funds market but we studied equilibrium in a market in which the government budget is balanced. We're now going to see how a government budget deficit changes the equilibrium in the loanable funds market. We'll begin by reviewing the sources of investment finance.

The Sources of Investment Finance

GDP equals the sum of consumption expenditure, C, investment, I, government expenditure on goods and services, G, and net exports, $(X - M)$. That is,

$$\text{GDP} = C + I + G + (X - M).$$

GDP also equals the sum of consumption expenditure, saving, S, and net taxes, T. That is,

$$\text{GDP} = C + S + T.$$

By combining these two ways of looking at GDP, you can see that

$$I + G + (X - M) = S + T$$

or

$$I = S + (T - G) + (M - X).$$

This equation tells us that investment, I, is financed by saving, S, government saving, $T - G$, and borrowing from the rest of the world, $(M - X)$. Saving and borrowing from the rest of the world are the private sources of saving, PS, and

$$PS = S + (M - X).$$

Investment is equal to the sum of private saving and government saving. That is,

$$I = PS + (T - G).$$

■ If T exceeds G, the government sector has a budget surplus and government saving is positive.
■ If G exceeds T, the government sector has a budget deficit and government saving is negative.

When the government sector has a budget surplus, it contributes toward financing investment. But when the government sector has a budget deficit, it competes with businesses for private saving.

Figure 14.9 shows the sources of investment finance in the United States from 1973 to 2005. It shows that during the 1990s, a sharp increase in investment was financed by an increase in borrowing from the rest of the world and a decrease in the government deficit. During the 2000s, private saving and borrowing from the rest of the world financed both investment and a growing government deficit.

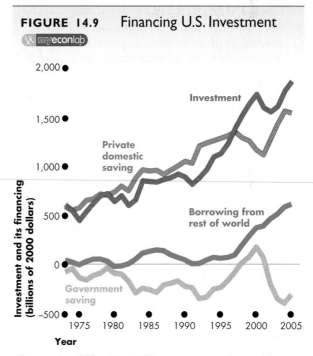

FIGURE 14.9   Financing U.S. Investment

During the 1990s, rising U.S. investment was financed by a rise in borrowing from the rest of the world and a fall in the budget deficit. During the 2000s, U.S. investment and a rising budget deficit were financed by a surge in borrowing from the rest of the world and a rise in private saving.

Sources of data: Bureau of Economic Analysis and Office of Management and Budget.

Fiscal policy influences investment and saving in two ways:

■ Taxes affect the incentive to save and change the supply of loanable funds.
■ Government saving—the budget surplus or deficit—is a component of total saving and the supply of loanable funds.

Taxes and the Incentive to Save

A tax on interest income weakens the incentive to save and drives a wedge between the after-tax interest rate earned by savers and the interest rate paid by firms. These effects are analogous to those of a tax on labor income. But they are more serious for two reasons.

First, a tax on labor income lowers the quantity of labor employed and lowers potential GDP, while a tax on capital income lowers the quantity of saving and investment and *slows the growth rate of real GDP*. A tax on capital income creates a Lucas wedge (Chapter 4, p. 95)—an ever widening gap between potential GDP and the potential GDP that might have been.

Second, the true tax rate on interest income is much higher than that on labor income because of the way in which inflation and taxes on interest income interact. We'll examine this interaction before we study the effects of taxes on saving and investment.

Tax Rate on Real Interest Rate   The interest rate that influences investment and saving plans is the *real after-tax interest rate*. The real *after-tax* interest rate subtracts the income tax paid on interest income from the real interest rate. But the taxes depend on the nominal interest rate, not the real interest rate. So the higher the inflation rate, the higher is the true tax rate on interest income. Here is an example. Suppose the real interest rate is 4 percent a year and the tax rate is 40 percent.

If there is no inflation, the nominal interest rate equals the real interest rate. The tax on 4 percent interest is 1.6 percent (40 percent of 4 percent), so the real after-tax interest rate is 4 percent minus 1.6 percent, which equals 2.4 percent.

If the inflation rate is 6 percent a year, the nominal interest rate is 10 percent. The tax on 10 percent interest is 4 percent (40 percent of 10 percent), so the real after-tax interest rate is 4 percent minus 4 percent, which equals zero. The true tax rate in this case is not 40 percent but 100 percent!

Effect of Income Tax on Saving and Investment   In Fig. 14.10, initially there are no taxes. Also, the government has a balanced budget. The demand for loanable funds curve, which is also the investment demand curve, is *DLF*. The supply of loanable funds curve, which is also the saving supply curve, is *SLF*. The equilibrium interest rate is 3 percent a year, and the quantity of funds borrowed and lent is $2 trillion a year.

A tax on interest income has no effect on the demand for loanable funds. The quantity of investment and borrowing that firms plan to undertake depends only on how productive capital is and what it costs—its real interest rate. But a tax on interest income weakens the incentive to save and lend and decreases the supply of loanable funds. For each dollar of before-tax earnings, savers must pay the government an amount deter-

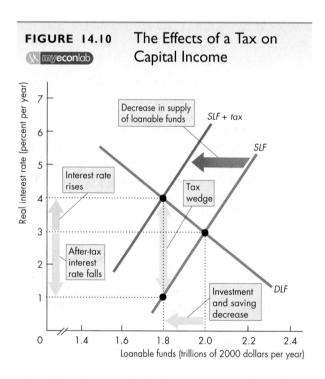

FIGURE 14.10   The Effects of a Tax on Capital Income

The demand for loanable funds and investment demand curve is *DLF*, and the supply of loanable funds and saving supply curve is *SLF*. With no income tax, the real interest rate is 3 percent a year and investment is $2 trillion. An income tax shifts the supply curve leftward to *SLF + tax*. The interest rate rises to 4 percent a year, the after-tax interest rate falls to 1 percent a year, and investment decreases to $1.8 trillion. With less investment, the real GDP growth rate decreases.

mined by the tax code. So savers look at the after-tax real interest rate when they decide how much to save.

When a tax is imposed, saving decreases and the supply of loanable funds curve shifts leftward to *SLF + tax*. The amount of tax payable is measured by the vertical distance between the *SLF* curve and the *SLF + tax* curve. With this smaller supply of loanable funds, the interest rate rises to 4 percent a year but the *after-tax* interest rate falls to 1 percent a year. A tax wedge is driven between the interest rate and the after-tax interest rate, and the equilibrium quantity of loanable funds decreases. Saving and investment also decrease.

The effects of the income tax on saving and investment are likely to be large. And at a high inflation rate, these effects are likely to be especially large.

You've seen how taxes affect private saving. Let's now see how government saving affects the loanable funds market.

Government Saving

Government saving is positive when the government has a budget surplus, negative when it has a budget deficit, and zero when it has a balanced budget.

In Fig. 14.11, *DLF* is the demand of loanable funds curve. The curve labeled *PSLF* is the *private* supply of loanable funds generated by private saving. With a balanced government budget, the *PSLF* curve is the market supply curve, the real interest rate is 4 percent a year, and the quantity of loanable funds, saving, and investment are $1.8 trillion a year.

When the government has a budget deficit, we must subtract the budget deficit from private saving to find the supply of loanable funds—the curve labeled *SLF*. The horizontal distance between the *PSLF* curve and the *SLF* curve is government saving, which in this example is a negative $0.3 trillion. (This number, like all the other numbers in Fig. 14.11, is similar to the actual value in the United States in 2006.)

The effect of negative government saving, which is also called *dissaving*, is to decrease the supply of loanable funds and increase the real interest rate. The quantity of loanable funds demanded and the investment that it finances decrease. In Fig. 14.11, with a government deficit of $0.3 trillion, the supply of loanable funds curve shifts leftward and the real interest rate rises from 4 percent to 5 percent a year. The equilibrium quantity of borrowing and investment decrease from $1.8 trillion to $1.6 trillion. Investment does not decrease by the full amount of the govern-

ment deficit because the higher real interest rate induces an increase in private saving. In Fig. 14.11, private saving increases by $0.1 trillion to $1.9 trillion.

The tendency for a government budget deficit to decrease investment is called a **crowding-out effect**. By raising the real interest rate, the government budget deficit crowds out private investment. A government budget surplus has the opposite effect to what we've just seen. It increases the supply of loanable funds, lowers the real interest rate, and increases investment.

In the crowding-out case, the *quantity of private saving* changes because the real interest rate changes. There is a movement along the *PSLF* curve. But the private supply of loanable funds does not change. That is, the *PSLF* curve does not shift. But suppose that a change in government saving changes private saving and shifts the *PSLF* curve. This possibility is called the Ricardo-Barro effect, so named because it

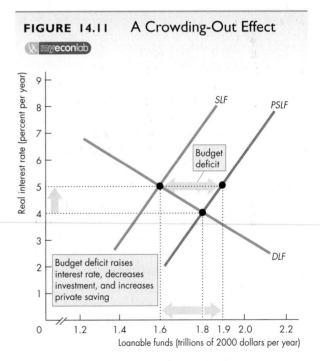

FIGURE 14.11   A Crowding-Out Effect

The demand for loanable funds curve is *DLF*, and the private supply of loanable funds is *PSLF*. With a balanced government budget, the real interest rate is 4 percent a year and investment is $1.8 trillion a year. A government budget deficit is negative government saving (dissaving). We subtract the budget deficit from private saving to determine the supply of loanable funds curve *SLF*. The real interest rate rises, investment decreases (is crowded out), and private saving increases.

was first suggested by the English economist David Ricardo in the eighteenth century and refined by Robert J. Barro of Harvard University during the 1970s and 1980s. **Ricardo-Barro equivalence** is the proposition that taxes and government borrowing are equivalent—budget deficit has no effect on the real interest rate or investment.

The reasoning behind Ricardo-Barro equivalence is the following. A government that has a budget deficit must sell bonds to pay for the goods and services that are not paid for by taxes. And the government must pay interest on those bonds. It must also collect more taxes *in the future* to pay the interest on the larger quantity of bonds that are outstanding. Taxpayers are rational and have good foresight. They can see that their taxes will be higher in the future and so their disposable income will be lower. Lower expected future disposable income increases saving. And if taxpayers want to neutralize the effects of the budget deficit on their own consumption plans, they increase their own saving by the same amount that the government is dissaving through its deficit.

This outcome is extreme and probably does not actually occur. Taxpayers probably respond in the *direction* suggested by Ricardo and Barro but not in the *amount* they suggest. So the effect of a budget deficit probably lies between the case shown in Fig. 14.11 and the Ricardo-Barro case. A budget deficit increases the real interest rate and partly crowds out private investment, but it also induces an increase in private saving in anticipation of higher future taxes.

REVIEW QUIZ

1 Why does the tax on interest income have more serious effects than the tax on labor income?
2 How does a tax on interest income affect the real interest rate, saving, and investment?
3 Does a government budget deficit crowd out investment? How?
4 What is the Ricardo-Barro equivalence and why is it unlikely to operate fully?

myeconlab Study Plan 14.3

You now know how a government budget deficit influences saving and investment. Because a budget deficit crowds out investment, it slows the growth rate of real GDP. Next we'll look at the effects of fiscal policy on intergenerational redistribution.

Generational Effects of Fiscal Policy

Is a budget deficit a burden on future generations? If it is, how will the burden be borne? And is the budget deficit the only burden on future generations? What about the deficit in the Social Security fund? Does it matter who owns the bonds that the government sells to finance its deficit? What about the bonds owned by foreigners? Won't repaying those bonds impose a bigger burden than repaying bonds owned by Americans?

To answer questions like these, we use a tool called **generational accounting**—an accounting system that measures the lifetime tax burden and benefits of each generation. This accounting system was developed by Alan Auerbach of the University of Pennsylvania and Laurence Kotlikoff of Boston University. Generational accounts for the United States have been prepared by Jagadeesh Gokhale of the Federal Reserve Bank of Cleveland and Kent Smetters of the University of Pennsylvania.

Generational Accounting and Present Value

Income taxes and social security taxes are paid by people who have jobs. Social security benefits are paid to people after they retire. So to compare taxes and benefits, we must compare the value of taxes paid by people during their working years with the benefits received in their retirement years. To compare the value of an amount of money at one date with that at a later date, we use the concept of present value. A **present value** is an amount of money that, if invested today, will grow to equal a given future amount when the interest that it earns is taken into account. We can compare dollars today with dollars in 2030 or any other future year by using present values.

For example, if the interest rate is 5 percent a year, $1,000 invested today will grow, with interest, to $11,467 after 50 years. So the present value (in 2006) of $11,467 in 2056 is $1,000.

By using present values, we can assess the magnitude of the government's debts to older Americans in the form of pensions and medical benefits.

But the assumed interest rate and growth rate of taxes and benefits critically influence the answers we get. For example, at an interest rate of 3 percent a year, the present value (in 2006) of $11,467 in 2056 is $2,616. The lower the interest rate, the greater is the present value of a given future amount.

Because there is uncertainty about the proper interest rate to use to calculate present values, plausible alternative numbers are used to estimate a range of present values.

Using generational accounting and present values, economists have studied the situation facing the federal government arising from its social security obligations. And they have found a time bomb!

The Social Security Time Bomb

When social security was introduced in the New Deal of the 1930s, today's demographic situation was not envisaged. The age distribution of the U.S. population today is dominated by the surge in the birth rate after World War II that created what is called the "baby boom generation." There are 77 million "baby boomers."

In 2008, the first of the baby boomers will start collecting Social Security pensions and in 2011, they will become eligible for Medicare benefits. By 2030, all the baby boomers will have retired and, compared to 2006, the population supported by social security will have doubled.

Under the existing Social Security laws, the federal government has an obligation to these citizens to pay pensions and Medicare benefits on an already declared scale. These obligations are a debt owed by the government and are just as real as the bonds that the government issues to finance its current budget deficit.

To assess the full extent of the government's obligations, economists use the concept of fiscal imbalance. **Fiscal imbalance** is the present value of the government's commitments to pay benefits minus the present value of its tax revenues. Fiscal imbalance is an attempt to measure the scale of the government's true liabilities.

Gokhale and Smetters estimated that the fiscal imbalance was $45 trillion in 2003. (Using alternative assumptions about interest rates and growth rates, the number might be as low as $29 trillion or as high as $65 trillion.) To put the $45 trillion in perspective, note that U.S. GDP in 2003 was $11 trillion. So the fiscal imbalance was 4 times the value of one year's production.

How can the federal government meet its social security obligations? Gokhale and Smetters consider

four alternative fiscal policy changes that might be made:

- Raise income taxes
- Raise social security taxes
- Cut social security benefits
- Cut federal government discretionary spending

They estimated that starting in 2003 and making only one of these changes, income taxes would need to be raised by 69 percent, or social security taxes raised by 95 percent, or social security benefits cut by 56 percent. Even if the government stopped all its discretionary spending, including that on national defense, it would not be able to pay its bills.

Of course, by combining the four measures, the pain from each could be lessened. But the pain would still be severe. And worse, delay makes all these numbers rise. With no action, the fiscal imbalance climbs from the $45 trillion of 2003 to $54 trillion in 2008.

Generational Imbalance

A fiscal imbalance must eventually be corrected and when it is, people either pay higher taxes or receive lower benefits. The concept of generational imbalance tells us who will pay. **Generational imbalance** is the division of the fiscal imbalance between the current and future generations, assuming that the current generation will enjoy the existing levels of taxes and benefits.

Figure 14.12 shows an estimate of how the fiscal imbalance is distributed across the current (born before 1988) and future (born in or after 1988) generations. It also shows that the major source of the imbalances is Medicare. Social Security pension benefits create a fiscal imbalance, but these benefits will be more than fully paid for by the current generation. But the current generation will pay less than 50 percent of its Medicare costs, and the balance will fall on future generations. If we sum all the items, the current generation will pay 43 percent and future generations will pay 57 percent of the fiscal imbalance.

Because the estimated fiscal imbalance is so large, it is not possible to predict how it will be resolved. But we can predict that the outcome will involve both lower benefits and higher taxes. One of these taxes could be the inflation tax—paying bills with new money and creating inflation. But the Fed will resist inflation being used to deal with the imbalance, as you will see in the next chapter.

FIGURE 14.12   Fiscal and Generational
Imbalances

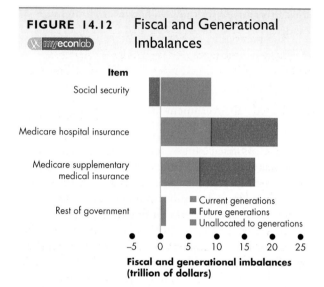

The bars show the scale of the fiscal imbalance. The largest component is the more than $20 trillion of Medicare benefits. These benefits are also the main component of the generational imbalance. Social security pensions are paid for entirely by the current generation.

Source of data: Jagadeesh Gokhale and Kent Smetters, *Fiscal and Generational Imbalances: New Budget Measures for New Budget Priorities,* Washington, D.C: The AEI Press, April 2003.

International Debt

So far in our discussion of government deficits and debts, we've ignored the role played by the rest of the world. We'll conclude this discussion by considering the role and magnitude of international debt.

You've seen that borrowing from the rest of the world is one source of investment finance. And you've also seen that this source of investment finance became larger during the late 1990s and 2000s.

How large is the contribution of the rest of the world? How much investment have we paid for by borrowing from the rest of the world? And how much U.S. government debt is held abroad?

Table 14.2 answers these questions. In June 2006, the United States had a net debt to the rest of the world of $5.2 trillion. Of that debt, $2.2 trillion was U.S. government debt. U.S. corporations had used $4.4 trillion of foreign funds ($2.1 trillion in bonds and $2.3 trillion in equities). More than half of the outstanding government debt is held by foreigners.

The international debt of the United States is important because, when that debt is repaid, the United States will transfer real resources to the rest of the world. Instead of running a large net exports

TABLE 14.2   What the United States Owed the Rest of the World in June 2006

	$ trillions
(a) U.S. Liabilities	
Deposits in U.S. banks	0.8
U.S. government securities	2.2
U.S. corporate bonds	2.1
U.S. corporate equities	2.3
Other (net)	− 2.2
Total	**5.2**
(b) U.S. government securities	
Held by rest of world	2.2
Held in the United States	1.9
Total	**4.1**

Source of data: Federal Reserve Board.

deficit, the United States will need a surplus of exports over imports. To make a surplus possible, U.S. saving must increase and consumption must decrease. Some tough choices lie ahead.

REVIEW QUIZ

1 What is a present value?
2 Distinguish between fiscal imbalance and generational imbalance.
3 How large was the estimated U.S. fiscal imbalance in 2003 and how did it divide between current and future generations?
4 What is the source of the U.S. fiscal imbalance and what are the painful choices that face current and future generations?
5 How much of U.S. government debt is held by the rest of the world?

myeconlab Study Plan 14.4

You now know how economists assess fiscal imbalance and how they divide the cost of covering an imbalance across generations. And you've seen the extent and implication of U.S. debt held in the rest of the world. We conclude this chapter by looking at fiscal policy as a tool for stabilizing the business cycle.

Stabilizing the Business Cycle

Fiscal policy actions influence both aggregate supply and aggregate demand. Policies that seek to stabilize the business cycle work by changing aggregate demand.

- Discretionary or
- Automatic

A fiscal action initiated by an act of Congress is called **discretionary fiscal policy**. It requires a change in a spending program or in a tax law. For example, an increase in defense spending or a cut in the income tax rate is a discretionary fiscal policy.

A fiscal action that is triggered by the state of the economy is called **automatic fiscal policy**. For example, an increase in unemployment induces an increase in payments to the unemployed. A fall in incomes induces a decrease in tax revenues.

Changes in government expenditure and changes in taxes have multiplier effects on aggregate demand. Chapter 12 explains the basic idea of the multiplier and the math note on pp. 310–311 shows the algebra of the fiscal policy multipliers that we'll now study.

Government Expenditure Multiplier

The **government expenditure multiplier** is the magnification effect of a change in government expenditure on goods and services on aggregate demand. Government expenditure is a component of aggregate expenditure, so when government expenditure changes, aggregate demand changes. Real GDP changes and induces a change in consumption expenditure, which brings a further change in aggregate expenditure. A multiplier process ensues.

A Homeland Security Multiplier The terrorist attacks of September 11, 2001, brought a reappraisal of the nation's homeland security requirements and an increase in government expenditure. This increase initially increased the incomes of producers of airport and border security equipment and security workers. Better-off security workers increased their consumption expenditure. With rising revenues, other businesses in all parts of the nation boomed and expanded their payrolls. A second round of increased consumption expenditure increased incomes yet further. This multiplier effect helped to end the 2001 recession.

The Autonomous Tax Multiplier

The **autonomous tax multiplier** is the magnification effect of a change in autonomous taxes on aggregate demand. A *decrease* in taxes *increases* disposable income, which increases consumption expenditure. A decrease in taxes works like an increase in government expenditure. But the magnitude of the autonomous tax multiplier is smaller than the government expenditure multiplier. The reason is that a $1 tax cut generates *less than* $1 of additional expenditure. The marginal propensity to consume determines the increase in consumption expenditure induced by a tax cut. For example, if the marginal propensity to consume is 0.75, then a $1 tax cut increases consumption expenditure by only 75 cents. In this case, the tax multiplier is 0.75 times the magnitude of the government expenditure multiplier.

A Bush Tax Cut Multiplier Congress enacted the Bush tax cut package that lowered taxes starting in 2002. These tax cuts had a multiplier effect. With more disposable income, people increased consumption expenditure. This spending increased other people's incomes, which spurred yet more consumption expenditure. Like the increase in security expenditures, the tax cut and its multiplier effect helped to end the 2001 recession.

The Balanced Budget Multiplier

The **balanced budget multiplier** is the magnification effect on aggregate demand of a *simultaneous* change in government expenditure and taxes that leaves the budget balance unchanged. The balanced budget multiplier is positive because a $1 increase in government expenditure increases aggregate demand by more than a $1 increase in taxes decreases aggregate demand. So when both government expenditure and taxes increase by $1, aggregate demand increases.

Discretionary Fiscal Stabilization

If real GDP is below potential GDP, discretionary fiscal policy might be used in an attempt to restore full employment. The government might increase its expenditure on goods and services, cut taxes, or do some of both. These actions would increase aggregate demand. If they were timed correctly and were of the correct magnitude, they could restore full employment. Figure 14.13 shows how. Potential GDP is $12 trillion, but real GDP is below potential at $11 trillion and there is a $1 trillion *recessionary gap* (see

Chapter 11, p. 274). To restore full employment, the government takes a discretionary fiscal policy action. An increase in government expenditure or a tax cut increases aggregate expenditure by ΔE. If this were the only change in spending plans, the AD curve would become $AD_0 + \Delta E$ in Fig. 14.13. But the fiscal policy action sets off a multiplier process, which increases consumption expenditure. As the multiplier process plays out, aggregate demand increases further and the AD curve shifts rightward to AD_1.

With no change in the price level, the economy would move from point A to point B on AD_1. But the increase in aggregate demand combined with the upward-sloping SAS curve brings a rise in the price level. The economy moves to point C, and the economy returns to full employment.

Figure 14.14 illustrates the opposite case in which discretionary fiscal policy is used to eliminate inflationary pressure. The government decreases its expenditure on goods and services or raises taxes to decrease aggregate demand. In the figure, the fiscal policy action decreases aggregate expenditure by ΔE and the AD curve shifts to $AD_0 - \Delta E$. The initial decrease in aggregate expenditure sets off a multiplier process, which decreases consumption expenditure. The multiplier process decreases aggregate demand further and the AD curve shifts leftward to AD_1.

With no change in the price level, the economy would move from point A to point B on AD_1 in Fig. 14.14. But the decrease in aggregate demand combined with the upward-sloping SAS curve brings a fall in the price level. So the economy moves to point C, where the inflationary gap has been eliminated, inflation has been avoided, and the economy is back at full employment.

Figures 14.13 and 14.14 make fiscal policy look easy: Calculate the recessionary gap or the inflationary gap and the multiplier, change government expenditure or taxes, and eliminate the gap. In reality, things are not that easy.

FIGURE 14.13   Expansionary Fiscal Policy

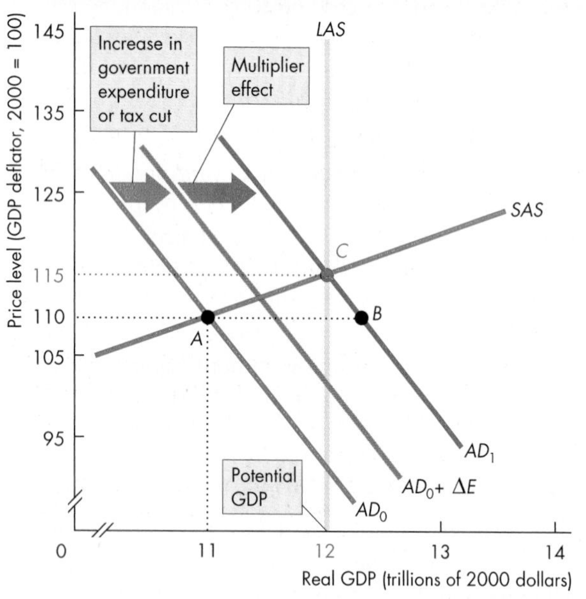

Potential GDP is $12 trillion, real GDP is $11 trillion, and there is a $1 trillion recessionary gap. An increase in government expenditure or a tax cut increases expenditure by ΔE. The multiplier increases induced expenditure. The AD curve shifts rightward to AD_1, the price level rises to 115, real GDP increases to $12 trillion, and the recessionary gap is eliminated.

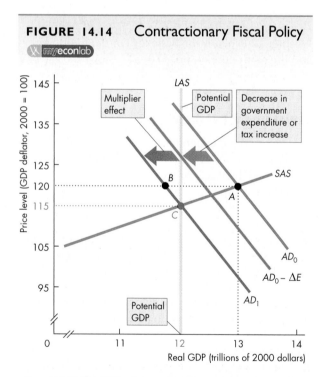

FIGURE 14.14   Contractionary Fiscal Policy

Potential GDP is $12 trillion, real GDP is $13 trillion, and there is a $1 trillion inflationary gap. A decrease in government expenditure or a rise in taxes decreases expenditure by ΔE. The multiplier decreases induced expenditure. The AD curve shifts leftward to AD_1, the price level falls to 115, real GDP decreases to $12 trillion, and the inflationary gap is eliminated.

Limitations of Discretionary Fiscal Policy

The use of discretionary fiscal policy is seriously hampered by three time lags:

- Recognition lag
- Law-making lag
- Impact lag

Recognition Lag The recognition lag is the time it takes to figure out that fiscal policy actions are needed. This process has two aspects: assessing the current state of the economy and forecasting its future state.

Law-Making Lag The law-making lag is the time it takes Congress to pass the laws needed to change taxes or spending. This process takes time because each member of Congress has a different idea about what is the best tax or spending program to change, so long debates and committee meetings are needed to reconcile conflicting views. The economy might benefit from fiscal stimulation today, but by the time Congress acts, a different fiscal medicine is needed.

Impact Lag The impact lag is the time it takes from passing a tax or spending change to its effects on real GDP being felt. This lag depends partly on the speed with which government agencies can act and partly on the timing of changes in spending plans by households and businesses.

Economic forecasting has improved in recent years, but it remains inexact and subject to error. So because of these three time lags, discretionary fiscal action might end up moving real GDP *away* from potential GDP and creating the very problems it seeks to correct.

Let's now look at automatic fiscal policy.

Automatic Stabilizers

Automatic fiscal policy is a consequence of tax revenues and outlays that fluctuate with real GDP. These features of fiscal policy are called **automatic stabilizers** because they work to stabilize real GDP without explicit action by the government. Their name is borrowed from engineering and conjures up images of shock absorbers, thermostats, and sophisticated devices that keep airplanes and ships steady in turbulent air and seas.

Induced Taxes On the revenues side of the budget, tax laws define tax *rates*, not tax *dollars*. Tax dollars paid depend on tax rates and incomes. But incomes vary with real GDP, so tax revenues depend on real GDP. Taxes that vary with real GDP are called **induced taxes**. When real GDP increases in an expansion, wages and profits rise, so the taxes on these incomes—induced taxes—rise. When real GDP decreases in a recession, wages and profits fall, so the induced taxes on these incomes fall.

Needs-Tested Spending On the outlays side of the budget, the government creates programs that pay benefits to suitably qualified people and businesses. The spending on such programs is called **needs-tested spending**, and it results in transfer payments that depend on the economic state of individual citizens and businesses. When the economy is in a recession, unemployment is high and the number of people experiencing economic hardship increases, and needs-tested spending on unemployment benefits and food stamps also increases. When the economy expands, unemployment falls, the number of people experiencing economic hardship decreases, and needs-tested spending decreases.

Induced taxes and needs-tested spending decrease the multiplier effects of changes in autonomous expenditure (such as investment and exports). So they moderate both expansions and recessions and make real GDP more stable. They achieve this outcome by weakening the link between real GDP and disposable income and so reduce the effect of a change in real GDP on consumption expenditure. When real GDP increases, induced taxes increase and needs-tested spending decreases, so disposable income does not increase by as much as the increase in real GDP. As a result, consumption expenditure does not increase by as much as it otherwise would and the multiplier effect is reduced.

We can see the effects of automatic stabilizers by looking at the way in which the government budget deficit fluctuates over the business cycle.

Budget Deficit Over the Business Cycle Figure 14.15 shows the business cycle in part (a) and fluctuations in the budget deficit in part (b) between 1983 and 2005. Both parts highlight recessions by shading those periods. By comparing the two parts of the figure, you can see the relationship between the business cycle and the budget deficit. When the economy is in

FIGURE 14.15   The Business Cycle and the Budget Deficit

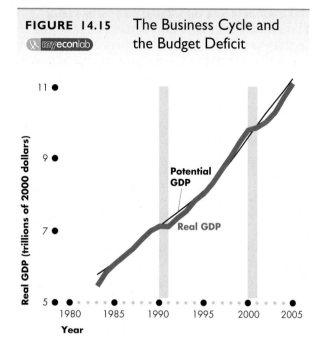

(a) Growth and recessions

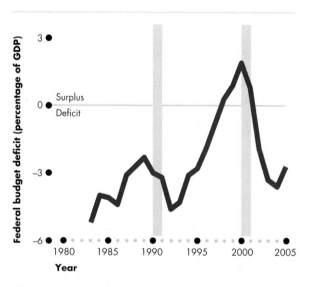

(b) Federal budget deficit

As real GDP fluctuates around potential GDP (part a), the budget deficit fluctuates (part b). During a recession (shaded years), tax revenues decrease, transfer payments increase, and the budget deficit increases. The deficit also increases *before* a recession as real GDP growth slows and *after* a recession before real GDP growth speeds up.

Sources of data: Bureau of Economic Analysis, Congressional Budget Office, and Office of Management and the Budget.

an expansion, the budget deficit declines. (In the figure, a declining deficit means a deficit that is getting closer to zero.) As the expansion slows before the recession begins, the budget deficit increases. It continues to increase during the recession and for a period after the recession is over. Then, when the expansion is well under way, the budget deficit declines again.

The budget deficit fluctuates with the business cycle because both tax revenues and outlays fluctuate with real GDP. As real GDP increases during an expansion, tax revenues increase and transfer payments decrease, so the budget deficit automatically decreases. As real GDP decreases during a recession, tax revenues decrease and transfer payments increase, so the budget deficit automatically increases. Fluctuations in investment and exports have a multiplier effect on real GDP. But fluctuations in the budget deficit decrease the swings in disposable income and make the multiplier effect smaller. They dampen both expansions and recessions.

Cyclical and Structural Balances Because the government budget balance fluctuates with the business cycle, we need a method of measuring the balance that tells us whether it is a temporary cyclical phenomenon or a persistent phenomenon. A temporary cyclical surplus or deficit vanishes when full employment returns. A persistent surplus or deficit requires government action to remove it.

To determine whether the budget balance is persistent or temporary and cyclical, economists have developed the concepts of the structural budget balance and the cyclical budget balance. The **structural surplus or deficit** is the budget balance that would occur if the economy were at full employment and real GDP were equal to potential GDP. The **cyclical surplus or deficit** is the actual surplus or deficit minus the structural surplus or deficit. That is, the cyclical surplus or deficit is the part of the budget balance that arises purely because real GDP does not equal potential GDP. For example, suppose that the budget deficit is $100 billion. And suppose that economists have determined that there is a structural deficit of $25 billion. Then there is a cyclical deficit of $75 billion.

Figure 14.16 illustrates the concepts of the cyclical surplus or deficit and the structural surplus or deficit. The blue curve shows government outlays. The outlays curve slopes downward because transfer payments, a component of government outlays, decreases as real GDP increases. The green curve

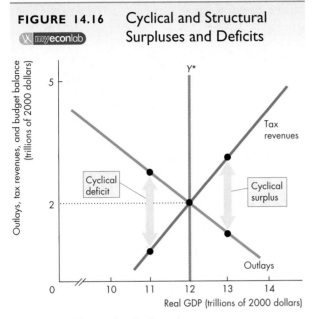

FIGURE 14.16 **Cyclical and Structural Surpluses and Deficits**

(a) Cyclical deficit and cyclical surplus

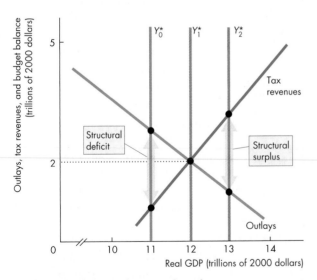

(b) Structural deficit and structural surplus

In part (a), potential GDP is $12 trillion. When real GDP is less than potential GDP, the budget is in a *cyclical deficit*. When real GDP exceeds potential GDP, the budget is in a *cyclical surplus*. The government has a *balanced budget* when real GDP equals potential GDP. In part (b), if real GDP and potential GDP are $11 trillion, there is a *structural deficit*. But if real GDP and potential GDP are $13 trillion, there is a *structural surplus*.

shows tax revenues. The tax revenues curve slopes upward because most components of tax revenues increase as incomes and real GDP increase.

In Fig. 14.16(a), potential GDP is $12 trillion. If real GDP equals potential GDP, the government has a *balanced budget*. Outlays and tax revenues each equal $2 trillion. If real GDP is less than potential GDP, outlays exceed tax revenues and there is a *cyclical deficit*. If real GDP is greater than potential GDP, outlays are less than tax revenues and there is a *cyclical surplus*.

In Fig. 14.16(b), if both real GDP and potential GDP are $11 trillion ($Y^*_0$), the government has a budget deficit and it is a *structural deficit*. If both real GDP and potential GDP are $12 trillion ($Y^*_1$), the budget is balanced—a *structural balance* of zero. If both real GDP and potential GDP are $13 trillion ($Y^*_2$), the government has a budget surplus and it is a *structural surplus*.

The U.S. federal budget is a structural deficit and has been in that state since the early 1970s. The structural deficit decreased from 1992 to 2000 and was almost eliminated in 2000. But since 2000, the structural deficit has increased. The cyclical deficit is estimated to be small relative to the structural deficit.

The federal government faces some tough fiscal policy challenges.

REVIEW QUIZ

1 How can the federal government use fiscal policy to stabilize the business cycle?

2 Why is the government expenditure multiplier larger than the autonomous tax multiplier?

3 Why does a balanced budget increase in spending and taxes increase aggregate demand?

4 How do induced taxes and needs-tested programs work as automatic stabilizers to dampen the business cycle?

5 How do we tell whether a budget deficit needs government action to remove it?

Wmyeconlab Study Plan 14.5

◆ You've seen how fiscal policy influences potential GDP, the growth rate of real GDP, and real GDP fluctuations. *Reading Between the Lines* on pp. 364–365 looks further at the 2007 budget and contrasts it with fiscal policy in the Clinton years.

▶ ## Fiscal Policy Today

80% of Budget Effectively Off Limits to Cuts

April 6, 2006

. . . Since President Bush took office, overall federal spending has risen 33 per-cent, twice as fast as under President Bill Clinton and faster than any other presi-dent since Lyndon B. Johnson.

But the biggest growth has come in areas that Republicans, by and large, have supported: the military, domestic security and the biggest expansion of Medicare in 40 years.

The military and so-called entitlement programs like Medicare now account for about four-fifths of the government's $2.7 trillion budget, and they are set to keep increasing much faster than inflation or the economy. Given the political realities, they are effectively off limits for now to budget cutters.

With tax cuts putting a squeeze on government revenues, almost all the battle to shrink the budget deficit is therefore focused on the less than one-fifth of govern-ment spending that goes to domestic "discretionary" programs like education, sci-entific research, national parks and space programs.

Spending on domestic discretionary programs—the ones that Congress must ap-propriate money for each year—climbed 31 percent from 2001 through 2005.

A result is a pitched battle over tiny corners of budget—whether to shift $7 billion out of more than $500 billion in military spending into health and education pro-grams—rather than to attack the broader issues.

If House Republican leaders get their way, for example, Congress would trim about $6.8 billion over the next five years from the expected growth in entitlement programs like Medicare and Medicaid.

But those savings would be obliterated by the $385 billion in additional spending over five years for the Medicare prescription drug benefits that the Republican-led Congress passed in 2003. . . .

Essence of the Story

▶ Federal spending has increased by 33 percent since 2000.

▶ This percentage increase is twice that of the 1990s under President Bill Clinton and the fastest since the 1960s under President Lyndon B. Johnson.

▶ The biggest growth has been in expenditure on the military, domestic security, and Medicare.

▶ The military and enti-tlement programs ac-count for 80 percent of the $2.7 trillion budget and are off limits for cuts.

▶ Tax cuts have decreased government revenues, so spending must be cut.

▶ The spending cuts that are under consideration are swamped by the growth in spending over the next five years for the Medicare prescription drug benefits that Con-gress passed in 2003.

▶ The news article compares expenditure growth during the Bush years with that during the Clinton years.

▶ Figure 1 shows the broad facts about the federal budget in 2000 and 2007. The 2000 numbers are those for the last Clinton year, and the 2007 numbers are for the current year.

▶ Outlays have increased substantially. Transfer payments increased by $484 billion; defense spending increased by $234 billion; and other expenditures increased by $121 billion. Total outlays were up by $1,039 billion.

▶ Tax revenues increased by much less than outlays. Personal income taxes *decreased* by $2 billion. Corporate income taxes increased by $91 billion, and social security taxes and indirect taxes increased by $224 billion. Total taxes increased by $480 billion.

▶ The balance of the federal budget turned from a surplus of $189 billion in 2000 to a deficit of $370 billion in 2007.

▶ Figure 2 expresses the budget data as percentages of GDP. This way of looking at the budget highlights the allocation of resources between the

federal government and the rest of the economy.

▶ Relative to GDP, the increase in outlays is small. You can see that transfer payments and nondefense expenditures increased by more than the increase in defense expenditures.

▶ Figure 2 also highlights the decrease in personal income taxes. These tax cuts and the consequent swing from surplus to deficit are the major fiscal policy events of the Bush administration.

▶ These fiscal policy actions have supply-side effects on the labor market and capital market, generational effects, and stabilization effects.

▶ The swing from surplus to deficit, a swing of $559 billion, has been financed by a $300 billion *increase* in borrowing from the rest of the world and a $259 billion crowding out of private expenditures.

▶ The tax cuts have positive supply-side effects, but the government spending increase has a negative crowding-out effect.

▶ The increased deficit increases the burden that is transferred to future generations.

▶ The combined spending increase and tax cut in-

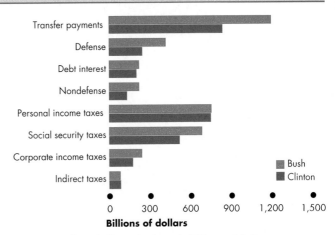

Figure 1 Bush and Clinton budgets in billions of dollars

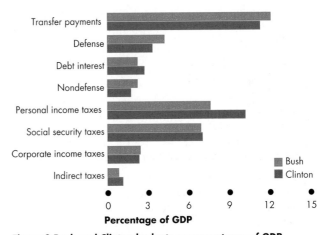

Figure 2 Bush and Clinton budgets as percentages of GDP

creased aggregate demand and helped to bring the economy back from recession.

▶ But according to the Congressional Budget Office, real GDP remained below potential GDP in 2006.

You're the Voter

▶ Do you think the current federal fiscal policy is appropriate?

▶ Would you vote for further tax cuts and spending cuts or for tax and spending increases or for tax increases and spending cuts? Explain.

SUMMARY

Key Points

The Federal Budget (pp. 344–349)

- The federal budget is used to achieve macroeconomic objectives.
- Tax revenues can exceed, equal, or fall short of outlays—the budget can be in surplus, balanced, or deficit.
- Budget deficits create government debt.

The Supply Side: Employment and Potential GDP (pp. 350–352)

- Fiscal policy has supply-side effects because taxes weaken the incentive to work and decrease employment and potential GDP.
- The U.S. tax wedge is large but it is small compared to those of other industrial countries.
- The Laffer curve shows the relationship between the tax rate and the amount of tax revenue collected.

The Supply Side: Investment, Saving, and Economic Growth (pp. 353–356)

- Fiscal policy has supply-side effects because taxes weaken the incentive to save and invest, which lowers the growth rate of real GDP.
- A government budget deficit raises the real interest rate and crowds out some investment.
- If the Ricardo-Barro equivalence proposition is correct, a government budget deficit has no crowding-out effect.

Generational Effects of Fiscal Policy (pp. 356–358)

- Generational accounting measures the lifetime tax burden and benefits of each generation.
- In 2003, the U.S. fiscal imbalance was estimated to be $45 trillion—4 times the value of one year's production.
- Future generations will pay for 57 percent of the benefits of the current generation.
- About half of U.S. government debt is held by the rest of the world.

Stabilizing the Business Cycle (pp. 359–363)

- Fiscal stabilization can be discretionary or automatic.
- Discretionary changes in government expenditure or taxes can change aggregate demand but are hampered by law-making lags and the difficulty of correctly diagnosing and forecasting the state of the economy.
- Automatic changes in fiscal policy moderate the business cycle.

Key Figures

Figure 14.6   The Effects of the Income Tax on Aggregate Supply, 350
Figure 14.10 The Effects of a Tax on Capital Income, 354
Figure 14.13 Expansionary Fiscal Policy, 360
Figure 14.14 Contractionary Fiscal Policy, 360

Key Terms

Automatic fiscal policy, 359
Automatic stabilizers, 361
Autonomous tax multiplier, 359
Balanced budget, 346
Balanced budget multiplier, 359
Budget deficit, 346
Budget surplus, 346
Council of Economic Advisers, 345
Crowding-out effect, 355
Cyclical surplus or deficit, 362
Discretionary fiscal policy, 359
Employment Act of 1946, 344
Federal budget, 344
Fiscal imbalance, 357
Fiscal policy, 344
Generational accounting, 356
Generational imbalance, 357
Government debt, 348
Government expenditure multiplier, 359
Induced taxes, 361
Laffer curve, 352
Needs-tested spending, 361
Present value, 356
Ricardo-Barro equivalence, 356
Structural surplus or deficit, 362
Supply-side effects, 350
Tax wedge, 351

PROBLEMS

myeconlab Tests, Study Plan, Solutions*

1. The government is proposing to increase the tax rate on labor income and asks you to report on the supply-side effects of such an action. Answer the following questions using appropriate diagrams. You are being asked about directions of change, not exact magnitudes.
   a. What will happen to the supply of labor and why?
   b. What will happen to the demand for labor and why?
   c. How will the equilibrium level of employment change and why?
   d. How will the equilibrium before-tax wage rate change and why?
   e. How will the equilibrium after-tax wage rate change and why?
   f. What will happen to potential GDP?
   g. How would your answers to the above questions change if at the same time as raising the tax rate on labor income, the government cut the rate of sales tax to keep the amount of tax collected constant?
   h. What evidence would you present to the government to support the view that a lower tax on labor income will increase employment, potential GDP, and aggregate supply?

2. Suppose that in the United States in 2007, investment is $1,600 billion, saving is $1,400 billion, government expenditure on goods and services is $1,500 billion, exports are $2,000 billion, and imports are $2,500 billion.
   a. What is the amount of tax revenue?
   b. What is the government budget balance?
   c. Is the government exerting a positive or negative impact on investment?
   d. What fiscal policy action might increase investment and speed economic growth? Explain how the policy action would work.

3. Suppose that in China in 2007, investment is $400 billion, saving is $400 billion, tax revenues are $500 billion, exports are $300 billion, and imports are $200 billion.
   a. Calculate government expenditure.
   b. What is the government budget balance?
   c. Is the government exerting a positive or negative impact on investment?

*Solutions to odd-numbered problems are provided.

   d. What fiscal policy action might increase investment and speed economic growth? Explain how the policy action would work.

4. The government increased its outlays by $100 billion with no change in tax revenues.
   a. Explain how the supply of loanable funds responds to this fiscal policy action.
   b. Explain how the real interest rate and the amounts of saving and investment respond to this fiscal policy action.
   c. How does your answer to part (a) depend on whether Ricardo-Barro equivalence holds?

5. Suppose that instead of taxing nominal capital income, the government changed the tax code so that the inflation rate is subtracted from the interest rate before the taxable income from capital is calculated. Use appropriate diagrams to explain and illustrate the effect that this change would have on
   a. The tax rate on capital income.
   b. The supply of loanable funds.
   c. The demand for loanable funds.
   d. Investment and the real interest rate.

6. Suppose that capital income taxes are based (as they are in the United States and most countries) on nominal interest rates. And suppose that the inflation rate increases by 5 percent. Use appropriate diagrams to explain and illustrate the effect that this change would have on
   a. The tax rate on capital income.
   b. The supply of loanable funds.
   c. The demand for loanable funds.
   d. Equilibrium investment.
   e. The equilibrium real interest rate.

7. The economy is in a recession, and the recessionary gap is large.
   a. Describe the discretionary and automatic fiscal policy actions that might occur.
   b. Describe a discretionary fiscal stimulation package that could be used that would *not* bring a budget deficit.
   c. Explain the risks of discretionary fiscal policy in this situation.

8. The economy is in a boom and the inflationary gap is large.
   a. Describe the discretionary and automatic fiscal policy actions that might occur.
   b. Describe a discretionary fiscal restraint package that could be used that would *not* produce serious negative supply-side effects.

c. Explain the risks of discretionary fiscal policy in this situation.

9. The economy is in a recession, the recessionary gap is large, and there is a budget deficit.
   a. Do we know whether the budget deficit is structural or cyclical? Explain your answer.
   b. Do we know whether automatic stabilizers are increasing or decreasing aggregate demand? Explain your answer.
   c. If a discretionary increase in government expenditure occurs, what happens to the structural deficit or surplus? Explain.

10. The economy is in a boom, the inflationary gap is large, and there is a budget deficit.
   a. Do we know whether the budget deficit is structural or cyclical? Explain your answer.
   b. Do we know whether automatic stabilizers are increasing or decreasing aggregate demand? Explain your answer.
   c. If a discretionary decrease in government expenditure occurs, what happens to the structural deficit or surplus? Explain your answer.

CRITICAL THINKING

1. Study *Reading Between the Lines* on pp. 364–365.
   a. Describe the main differences between the budgets of President Clinton in 2000 and President Bush in 2007.
   b. Does "a pitched battle over tiny corners of the budget" indicate that government spending is out of control? Explain why or why not.
   c. Do you think the 2007 budget should be balanced? If so, do you think the government should cut spending or raise taxes? If you think the budget should not be balanced, explain why.
2. Think about the supply-side effects of the 2007 U.S. budget.
   a. What would be the main effects of lower income tax rates on the level of potential GDP?
   b. How would lower income taxes influence the real wage rate and the real interest rate?
   c. What are the main costs of lower income taxes?

3. **Comprehensive Tax Code Overhaul Is Overdue**

   Some right-wingers in Congress claim that . . . tax cuts pay for themselves. Despite their insistence, there is ample evidence and general expert agreement that they do not. . . .

   Washington Post, April 24, 2006
   a. Explain what is meant by tax cuts paying for themselves. What does this statement imply about the tax multiplier?
   b. Why would tax cuts not pay for themselves?

4. **Brighter '06 Deficit Outlook, but Long Term Looks Grim**

   The federal budget deficit will shrink this year to its lowest level since 2001, . . . The budget office estimated the deficit for the 2006 fiscal year, which ends on Sept. 30, at $260 billion.

   The New York Times, August 18, 2006
   a. What events occurred in the U.S. economy in 2006 to make the federal budget deficit shrink to its lowest level since 2001?
   b. Do you think the 2006 federal budget deficit is a cyclical deficit or a structural deficit? Why?

WEB ACTIVITIES

myeconlab Links to Web sites

1. Visit the National Center for Policy Analysis Idea House. Click on "Dick Armey Flat Tax" and "The Liberal Case for a Flat Tax." When you have studied these two pages, answer the following questions:
   a. What are the main features of Dick Armey's plan?
   b. What is the liberal case for a flat tax?
   c. Why do you think a flat tax is usually supported by conservatives rather than liberals?
2. Visit the U.S. government budget Web site. Use the information that you can find on this site to
   a. Describe the main features of the budget for the current fiscal year.
   b. Analyze the demand-side effects of the current year's budget.
   c. Analyze the supply-side effects of the current year's budget.

CHAPTER 15

Monetary Policy

What Can Monetary Policy Do?

At eight regularly scheduled meetings a year, the Federal Reserve announces whether the interest rate will rise, fall, or remain constant until the next decision date. And every business day, the Federal

Reserve Bank of New York operates in financial markets to implement the Fed's decision and ensure that its target interest rate is achieved. Financial market traders and economic journalists watch the economy for clues about what the Fed will decide at its next meeting.

How does the Fed make its interest rate decision? What exactly does the New York Fed do every day to keep the interest rate where it wants it? And how do the Fed's interest rate changes influence the economy? Can the Fed speed up economic growth and lower unemployment by lowering the interest rate and keep inflation in check by raising the interest rate?

The Fed's monetary policy strategy gradually evolves. And the current strategy isn't the only one that might be used. Is the current monetary policy strategy the best one? What are the benefits and what are the risks associated with the alternative monetary policy strategies?

◆ You learned about the functions of the Federal Reserve and its long-run effects on the price level and inflation rate in Chapter 9. In this chapter, you will learn about the Fed's monetary policy in both the long run and the short run. You will learn how the Fed influences the interest rate and how the interest rate influences the economy. You will also review the alternative ways in which monetary policy might be conducted. In *Reading Between the Lines* at the end of the chapter, you will see the dilemma that the Fed sometimes faces as it tries to steer a steady course between inflation and recession.

After studying this chapter, you will be able to

▶ Describe the objectives of U.S. monetary policy and the framework for setting and achieving them

▶ Explain how the Federal Reserve makes its interest rate decision and achieves its interest rate target

▶ Explain the transmission channels through which the Federal Reserve influences the inflation rate

▶ Explain and compare alternative monetary policy strategies

Monetary Policy Objectives and Framework

A nation's monetary policy objectives and the framework for setting and achieving those objectives stem from the relationship between the central bank and the government.

We'll describe the objectives of U.S. monetary policy and the framework and assignment of responsibility for achieving those objectives.

Monetary Policy Objectives

The objectives of monetary policy are ultimately political. The objectives of U.S. monetary policy are set out in the mandate of the Board of Governors of the Federal Reserve System, which is defined by the Federal Reserve Act of 1913 and its subsequent amendments.

Federal Reserve Act The Fed's mandate was most recently clarified in amendments to the Federal Reserve Act passed by Congress in 2000. The 2000 law states that mandate in the following words:

> The Board of Governors of the Federal Reserve System and the Federal Open Market Committee shall maintain long-run growth of the monetary and credit aggregates commensurate with the economy's long-run potential to increase production, so as to promote effectively the goals of maximum employment, stable prices, and moderate long-term interest rates.

Goals and Means This description of the Fed's monetary policy objectives has two distinct parts: a statement of the goals, or ultimate objectives, and a prescription of the means by which the Fed should pursue its goals.

Goals of Monetary Policy The goals are "maximum employment, stable prices, and moderate long-term interest rates." In the long run, these goals are in harmony and reinforce each other. But in the short run, these goals might come into conflict. Let's examine these goals a bit more closely.

Achieving the goal of "maximum employment" means attaining the maximum sustainable growth rate of potential GDP and keeping real GDP close to potential GDP. It also means keeping the unemployment rate close to the natural unemployment rate.

Achieving the goal of "stable prices" means keeping the inflation rate low (and perhaps close to zero).

Achieving the goal of "moderate long-term interest rates" means keeping long-term *nominal* interest rates close to (or even equal to) long-term *real* interest rates.

Price stability is the key goal. It is the source of maximum employment and moderate long-term interest rates. Price stability provides the best available environment for households and firms to make the saving and investment decisions that bring economic growth. So price stability encourages the maximum sustainable growth rate of potential GDP.

Price stability delivers moderate long-term interest rates because the nominal interest rate reflects the inflation rate. The nominal interest rate equals the real interest rate plus the inflation rate. With stable prices, the nominal interest rate is close to the real interest rate, and most of the time, this rate is likely to be moderate.

In the short run, the Fed faces a tradeoff between inflation and interest rates and between inflation and real GDP, employment, and unemployment. Taking an action that is designed to lower the inflation rate and achieve stable prices might mean raising interest rates, which lowers employment and real GDP and increases the unemployment rate in the short run.

Means for Achieving the Goals The 2000 law instructs the Fed to pursue its goals by "maintain[ing] long-run growth of the monetary and credit aggregates commensurate with the economy's long-run potential to increase production." You can perhaps recognize this statement as being consistent with the quantity theory of money that you studied in Chapter 9 (see pp. 224–225). The "economy's long-run potential to increase production" is the growth rate of potential GDP. The "monetary and credit aggregates" are the quantities of money and loans. By keeping the growth rate of the quantity of money in line with the growth rate of potential GDP, the Fed is expected to be able to maintain full employment and keep the price level stable.

To pursue the goals of monetary policy, the Fed must make the general concepts of price stability and maximum employment precise and operational.

Operational "Stable Prices" Goal

The Fed uses the Consumer Price Index (CPI) to determine whether the goal of stable prices is being achieved. But the Fed pays closest attention to the *core CPI*—the CPI excluding food and fuel. The rate of increase in the core CPI is the **core inflation rate**.

The Fed focuses on the core inflation rate because it is less volatile than the total CPI inflation rate and the Fed believes that it provides a better indication of whether price stability is being achieved.

Figure 15.1 shows the core inflation rate alongside the total CPI inflation rate since 1990. You can see why the Fed says that the core rate is a better indicator. Its fluctuations are smoother and represent a sort of trend through the wider fluctuations in total CPI inflation.

The Fed has not defined price stability. But it almost certainly doesn't regard price stability as meaning a core inflation rate equal to zero. Former Fed Chairman Alan Greenspan suggests that "price stability is best thought of as an environment in which inflation is so low and stable over time that it does not materially enter into the decisions of households and firms." He also believes that a "specific numerical inflation target would represent an unhelpful and false precision."[1]

Ben Bernanke, Alan Greenspan's successor, has been more precise and suggested that a core inflation rate of between 1 and 2 percent a year is the equivalent of price stability. This rate takes account of the upward bias in the CPI measure of inflation that you met in Chapter 6 (see p. 145).

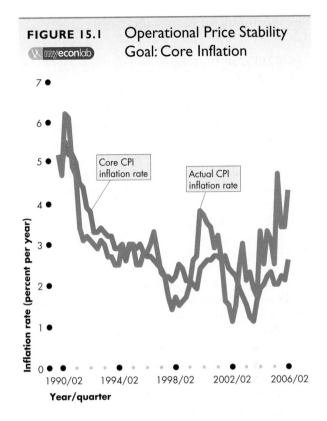

FIGURE 15.1   Operational Price Stability Goal: Core Inflation

The CPI inflation rate fluctuates more than the core inflation rate. If a 1 to 2 percent core inflation rate is price stability, the Fed has achieved stable prices in 1999 and between 2002 and 2005. In all the other years, the inflation rate was above the level consistent with price stability.

Source of data: Bureau of Labor Statistics.

Operational "Maximum Employment" Goal

The Fed regards stable prices (a core inflation rate of 1 to 2 percent a year) as the primary goal of monetary policy and as a means to achieving the other two goals. But the Fed also pays attention to the business cycle and tries to steer a steady course between inflation and recession. To gauge the state of output and employment relative to full employment, the Fed looks at a large number of indicators that include the labor force participation rate, the unemployment rate, measures of capacity utilization, activity in the housing market, the stock market, and regional information gathered by the regional Federal Reserve Banks. All these data are summarized in the Fed's *Beige Book*.

While the Fed considers a vast range of data, one number stands out as a summary of the overall state of aggregate demand relative to potential GDP. That number is the *output gap*—the percentage deviation of real GDP from potential GDP.

When the output gap is positive, it is an inflationary gap that brings an increase in the inflation rate. And when the output gap is negative, it is a recessionary gap that results in lost output and in employment being below its full-employment equilibrium level. So the Fed tries to minimize the output gap.

[1] Alan Greenspan, "Transparency in Monetary Policy," *Federal Reserve of St. Louis Review*, 84(4), 5–6, July/August 2002.

Responsibility for Monetary Policy

Who is responsible for monetary policy in the United States? What are the roles of the Fed, the Congress, and the President?

The Role of the Fed The Federal Reserve Act makes the Board of Governors of the Federal Reserve System and the Federal Open Market Committee (FOMC) responsible for the conduct of monetary policy. We described the composition of the FOMC in Chapter 9 (see p. 212). The FOMC makes a monetary policy decision at eight scheduled meetings each year and communicates its decision with a brief explanation. Three weeks after an FOMC meeting, the full minutes are published.

The Role of Congress Congress plays no role in making monetary policy decisions but the Federal Reserve Act requires the Board of Governors to report on monetary policy to Congress. The Fed makes two reports each year, one in February and another in July. These reports and the Fed chairman's testimony before Congress along with the minutes of the FOMC communicate the Fed's thinking on monetary policy to lawmakers and the public.

The Role of the President The formal role of the President of the United States is limited to appointing the members and the Chairman of the Board of Governors. But some Presidents—Richard Nixon was one—have tried to influence Fed decisions.

You now know the objectives of monetary policy and can describe the framework and assignment of responsibility for achieving those objectives. Your next task is to see how the Federal Reserve conducts its monetary policy.

REVIEW QUIZ

1 What are the objectives of monetary policy?
2 Are the goals of monetary policy in harmony or in conflict (a) in the long run and (b) in the short run?
3 What is the core inflation rate and how does it differ from the overall CPI inflation rate?
4 Who is responsible for U.S. monetary policy?

⊗ myeconlab Study Plan 15.1

The Conduct of Monetary Policy

In this section, we describe the way in which the Federal Reserve conducts its monetary policy and we explain the Fed's monetary policy strategy. We evaluate the Fed's strategy in the final section of this chapter, where we describe and compare alternative monetary policy strategies.

Choosing a Policy Instrument

A **monetary policy instrument** is a variable that the Fed can directly control or closely target. As the sole issuer of the monetary base, the Fed is a monopoly. Like all monopolies, it can fix the quantity of its product and leave the market to determine the price; or it can fix the price of its product and leave the market to choose the quantity.

The first decision is whether to fix the price of U.S. money on the foreign exchange market—the exchange rate. A country that operates a fixed exchange rate cannot pursue an independent monetary policy. The United States has a flexible exchange rate and pursues an independent monetary policy. (Chapter 10 explains the foreign exchange market and the factors that influence the exchange rate.)

Even with a flexible exchange rate, the Fed still has a choice of policy instrument. It can decide to target the monetary base or a short-term interest rate. While the Fed can set either of these two variables, it cannot set both. The value of one is the consequence of the other. If the Fed decided to decrease the monetary base, the interest rate would rise. If the Fed decided to raise the interest rate, the monetary base would decrease. So the Fed must decide which of these two variables to target.

The Federal Funds Rate

The Fed's choice of monetary policy instrument, which is the same choice as that made by most other major central banks, is a short-term interest rate. Given this choice, the Fed permits the exchange rate and the quantity of money to find their own equilibrium values and has no preset views about what those values should be.

The interest rate that the Fed targets is the **federal funds rate**, which is the interest rate on overnight loans that banks make to each other.

Figure 15.2 shows the federal funds rate since 1990. You can see that the federal funds rate was 8.25 percent in 1990 and that it was increased to 6.5 percent in 2000. In both of these periods of a high federal funds rate, the Fed wanted to take actions that lowered the inflation rate.

Between 2002 and 2004, the federal funds rate was set at historically low levels. The reason is that with inflation well anchored close to 2 percent a year, the Fed was less concerned about inflation than it was about recession so it wanted to lean in the direction of avoiding recession.

Although the Fed can change the federal funds rate by any (reasonable) amount that it chooses, it normally changes the federal funds rate by only a quarter of a percentage point.[2]

FIGURE 15.2   The Federal Funds Rate

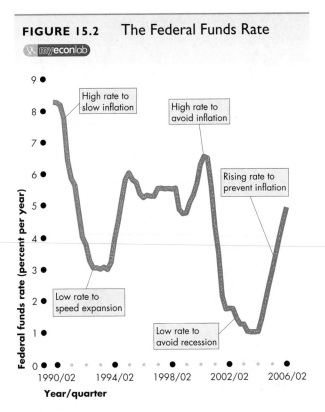

The Fed sets a target for the federal funds rate and then takes actions to keep the rate close to its target. When the Fed wants to slow inflation, it takes actions that raise the federal funds rate. When inflation is low and the Fed wants to avoid recession, it takes actions that lower the federal funds rate.

Source of data: Board of Governors of the Federal Reserve System.

How does the Fed decide the appropriate level for the federal funds rate? And how, having made that decision, does the Fed move the federal funds rate to its target level? We'll now answer these two questions.

The Fed's Decision-Making Strategy

Two alternative decision-making strategies might be used. They are summarized by the terms:

- Instrument rule
- Targeting rule

Instrument Rule An **instrument rule** is a decision rule for monetary policy that sets the policy instrument at a level that is based on the current state of the economy. The best-known instrument rule is the *Taylor rule*, in which the instrument is the federal funds rate and the rule is to make the federal funds rate respond by formula to the inflation rate and the output gap. (We describe the Taylor rule on the next page.)

To implement the Taylor instrument rule, the FOMC would simply get the best estimates available of the current inflation rate and output gap and then mechanically calculate the level at which to set the federal funds rate.

Targeting Rule A **targeting rule** is a decision rule for monetary policy that sets the policy instrument at a level that makes the forecast of the ultimate policy goal equal to its target. If the ultimate policy goal is a 2 percent inflation rate and the instrument is the federal funds rate, the targeting rule sets the federal funds rate at a level that makes the forecast of the inflation rate equal to 2 percent.

To implement such a targeting rule, the FOMC must gather and process a large amount of information about the economy, the way it responds to shocks, and the way it responds to policy. The FOMC must then process all these data and come to a judgment about the best level for the policy instrument.

The FOMC minutes suggest that the Fed follows a targeting rule strategy. But some economists think the interest rate settings decided by the FOMC are well described by the Taylor rule. The next section looks at the influences on the federal funds rate.

---

[2] A quarter of a percentage point is also called 25 *basis points*. A basis point is one hundredth of one percentage point.

Influences on the Federal Funds Rate

Stanford economist John B. Taylor has suggested a rule for the federal funds that that he says describes the *outcome* of the FOMC's complex decision-making deliberations. The **Taylor rule** sets the federal funds rate (*FFR*) at the equilibrium real interest rate (which Taylor says is 2 percent a year) plus amounts based on the inflation rate (*INF*), and the output gap (*GAP*) according to the following formula (all the values are percentages):

$$FFR = 2 + INF + 0.5(INF - 2) + 0.5GAP$$

In other words, the Taylor rule sets the federal funds rate at 2 percent plus the inflation rate plus one half of the deviation of inflation from its implicit target of 2 percent, plus one half of the output gap.

Taylor says that if the Fed followed this rule, the economy would perform better than it has performed historically. But he also says that the Fed comes close to following this rule.

Figure 15.3 shows how close the Fed has come to using the Taylor rule. Part (a) shows the extent to which the inflation rate has exceeded 2 percent a year—the extent to which the Fed has missed the goal of price stability. This variable has a downward trend. Part (b) shows the output gap—the extent to which the Fed missed its maximum employment goal. This variable cycles. Part (c) shows the federal funds rate that would have been set based on parts (a) and (b) if the Taylor rule had been followed (the green line) and the federal funds rate decisions of the FOMC (the blue line).

You can see that between 1991 and 1994, the Fed set the federal funds rate at a lower level than what the Taylor rule would have achieved. Between 1992 and 1994, the gap between the Fed's decision and the Taylor rule was especially wide. The reason for the discrepancy is that during the 1990–1991 recession, the Fed placed a greater weight on achieving the goal of "maximum employment" and a lower weight on lowering the inflation rate. In contrast, the Taylor rule places equal weight on the deviation of inflation from its target and the output gap.

After 9/11, the Fed also lowered the federal funds rate by more than what the Taylor rule required to ensure that financial markets did not collapse during a period of increased uncertainty and pessimism.

We've now described the Fed's monetary policy instrument and the FOMC's strategy for setting it. We next see how the Fed hits its instrument target.

FIGURE 15.3   Influences on the Federal Funds Rate

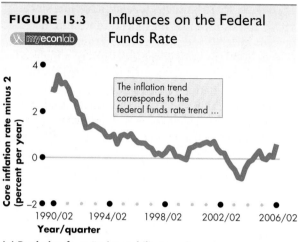

(a) **Deviation from "price stability" goal**

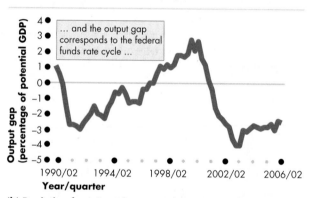

(b) **Deviation from "maximum employment" goal**

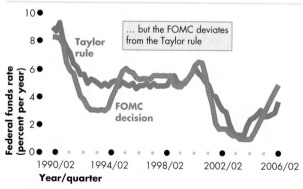

(c) **FOMC decisions and the Taylor rule**

The downward trend in the federal funds rate follows the downward trend in the inflation rate toward 2 percent in part (a), and the cycles in the federal funds rate follow the cycles in the output gap in part (b), but the FOMC decision in part (c) does not exactly match the Taylor rule formula.

Sources of data: Board of Governors of the Federal Reserve System, Congressional Budget Office, and Bureau of Labor Statistics.

Hitting the Federal Funds Rate Target: Open Market Operations

Once an interest rate decision has been made, the Fed achieves its target by instructing the New York Fed to make *open market operations*—to purchase or sell government securities from or to a commercial bank or the public. When the Fed buys securities, it pays for them with newly created reserves held by banks. When the Fed sells securities, it is paid for them with reserves held by banks. So open market operations directly influence the reserves of banks.

An Open Market Purchase To see how an open market operation changes bank reserves, suppose the Fed buys $100 million of government securities from the Bank of America. When the Fed makes this transaction, two things happen:

1. The Bank of America has $100 million less securities, and the Fed has $100 million more securities.

2. The Fed pays for the securities by placing $100 million in the Bank of America's deposit account at the Fed.

Figure 15.4 shows the effects of these actions on the balance sheets of the Fed and the Bank of America. Ownership of the securities passes from the Bank of America to the Fed, so the Bank of America's assets decrease by $100 million and the Fed's assets increase by $100 million, as shown by the blue arrow running from the Bank of America to the Fed.

The Fed pays for the securities by placing $100 million in the Bank of America's reserve account at the Fed, as shown by the green arrow running from the Fed to the Bank of America.

The Fed's assets and liabilities increase by $100 million. The Bank of America's total assets are unchanged: It sold securities to increase its reserves.

An Open Market Sale If the Fed *sells* $100 million of government securities in the open market:

1. The Bank of America has $100 million more securities, and the Fed has $100 million less securities.

2. The Bank of America pays for the securities by using $100 million of its reserves deposit account at the Fed.

Figure 15.5 shows the effects of these actions on the balance sheets of the Fed and the Bank of

---

FIGURE 15.4   The Fed Buys Securities in the Open Market

myeconlab

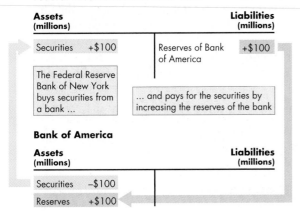

FIGURE 15.5   The Fed Sells Securities in the Open Market

myeconlab

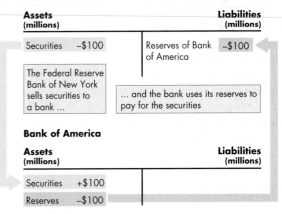

When the Fed buys securities in the open market, it creates bank reserves. Fed assets and liabilities increase, and the selling bank exchanges securities for reserves.

When the Fed sells securities in the open market, it reduces bank reserves. Fed assets and liabilities decrease, and the buying bank exchanges reserves for securities.

America. Ownership of the securities passes from the Fed to the Bank of America, so the Fed's assets decrease by $100 million and the Bank of America's assets increase by $100 million, as shown by the blue arrow running from the Fed to the Bank of America.

The Bank of America uses $100 million of its reserves to pay for the securities, as the green arrow running from the Bank of America to the Fed shows.

Both the Fed's assets and liabilities decrease by $100 million. The Bank of America's total assets are unchanged: It has used reserves to buy securities.

Equilibrium in the Market for Reserves

To see how an open market operation changes the federal funds rate, we must see what happens in the federal funds market—the market in which banks lend to and borrow from each other overnight—and in the market for bank reserves.

The higher the federal funds rate, the greater is the quantity of overnight loans supplied and the smaller is the quantity of overnight loans demanded in the federal funds market. The equilibrium federal funds rate balances the quantities demanded and supplied.

An equivalent way of looking at the forces that determine the federal funds rate is to consider the demand for and supply of bank reserves. Banks hold reserves to meet the required reserve ratio and so that they can make payments. But reserves are costly to hold. The alternative to holding reserves is to lend them in the federal funds market and earn the federal funds rate. The higher the federal funds rate, the higher is the opportunity cost of holding reserves and the greater is the incentive to economize on the quantity of reserves held.

So the quantity of reserves demanded by banks depends on the federal funds rate. The higher the federal funds rate, other things remaining the same, the smaller is the quantity of reserves demanded.

Figure 15.6 illustrates the market for bank reserves. The *x*-axis measures the quantity of reserves on deposit at the Fed, and the *y*-axis measures the federal funds rate. The demand for reserves is the curve labeled *RD*.

The Fed's open market operations determine the supply of reserves, which is shown by the supply curve *RS*. To decrease reserves, the Fed conducts an open market sale. To increase reserves, the Fed conducts an open market purchase.

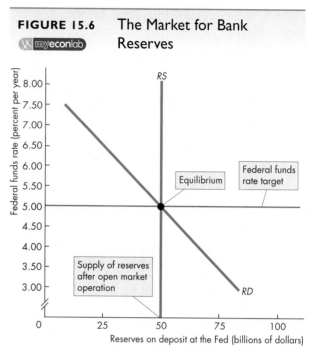

FIGURE 15.6   The Market for Bank Reserves

The demand curve for reserves is *RD*. The quantity of reserves demanded decreases as the federal funds rate rises because the federal funds rate is the opportunity cost of holding reserves. The supply curve of reserves is *RS*. The Fed uses open market operations to make the quantity of reserves supplied equal the quantity of reserves demanded ($50 billion in this case) at the federal funds rate target (5 percent a year in this case).

Equilibrium in the market for bank reserves determines the federal funds rate where the quantity of reserves demanded by the banks equals the quantity of reserves supplied by the Fed. By using open market operations, the Fed adjusts the supply of reserves to keep the federal funds rate on target.

REVIEW QUIZ

1 What is the Fed's monetary policy instrument?
2 What are the main influences on the FOMC federal funds rate decision?
3 What happens when the Fed buys or sells securities in the open market?
4 How is the federal funds rate determined in the federal funds market or the market for reserves?

Ⓧ myeconlab **Study Plan 15.2**

In Fig. 15.9(c), the supply of loanable funds curve shifts rightward from SLF_0 to SLF_1. With the demand for loanable funds at DLF, the real interest rate falls from 6 percent to 5.5 percent a year. (We're assuming a zero inflation rate so that the real interest rate equals the nominal interest rate.) The long-term interest rate changes by a smaller amount than the change in the short-term interest rate for the reason explained on p. 378.

The Market for Real GDP Figure 15.9(d) shows aggregate demand and aggregate supply—the demand for and supply of real GDP. Potential GDP is $12 trillion, where LAS is located. The short-run aggregate supply curve is SAS, and initially, the aggregate demand curve is AD_0. Real GDP is $11.8 trillion, which is less than potential GDP, so there is a recessionary gap. The Fed is reacting to this recessionary gap.

The increase in the supply of loans and the decrease in the real interest rate increase aggregate planned expenditure. (Not shown in the figure, a fall in the interest rate lowers the exchange rate, which increases net exports and aggregate planned expenditure.) The increase in aggregate expenditure, ΔE, increases aggregate demand and shifts the aggregate demand curve rightward to $AD_0 + \Delta E$. A multiplier process begins. The increase in expenditure increases income, which induces an increase in consumption expenditure. Aggregate demand increases further, and the aggregate demand curve eventually shifts rightward to AD_1.

The new equilibrium is at full employment. Real GDP is equal to potential GDP. The price level rises to 120 and then becomes stable at that level. So after a one-time adjustment, there is price stability.

In this example, we have given the Fed a perfect hit at achieving full employment and keeping the price level stable. It is unlikely that the Fed would be able to achieve the precision of this example. If the Fed stimulated demand by too little and too late, the economy would experience a recession. And if the Fed hit the gas pedal too hard, it would push the economy from recession to inflation.

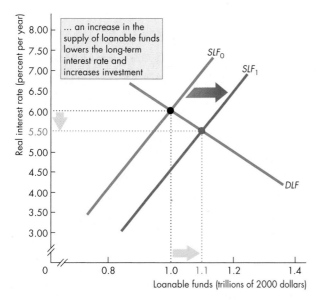

(c) The market for loanable funds

In part (c), an increase in the supply of bank loans increases the supply of loanable funds from SLF_0 to SLF_1 and the real interest rate falls. Investment increases.

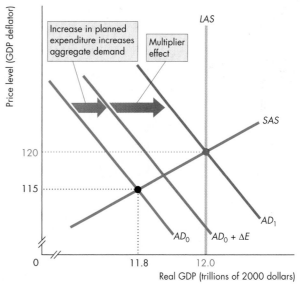

(d) Real GDP and the price level

In part (d), aggregate planned expenditure increases. The aggregate demand curve shifts to $AD_0 + \Delta E$ and eventually it shifts rightward to AD_1. Real GDP increases to potential GDP, and the price level rises.

The Fed Fights Inflation

If the inflation rate is too high and real GDP is above potential GDP, the Fed takes actions that are designed to lower the inflation rate and restore price stability. Figure 15.10 shows the effects of the Fed's actions starting in the market for reserves and ending in the market for real GDP.

Market for Bank Reserves In Fig. 15.10(a), which shows the market for bank reserves, the FOMC raises the target federal funds rate from 5 percent to 6 percent a year. To achieve the new target, the New York Fed sells securities and decreases the supply of reserves of the banking system from RS_0 to RS_1.

Money Market With decreased reserves, the banks shrink deposits by decreasing loans and the supply of money decreases. The short-term interest rate rises and the quantity of money demanded decreases. In Fig. 15.10(b), the supply of money decreases from MS_0 to MS_1, the interest rate rises from 5 percent to

6 percent a year and the quantity of money decreases from $3 trillion to $2.9 trillion.

Loanable Funds Market With a decrease in reserves, banks must decrease the supply of loans. The supply of (real) loanable funds decreases, and the supply of loanable funds curve shifts leftward in Fig. 15.10(c) from SLF_0 to SLF_1. With the demand for loanable funds at DLF, the real interest rate rises from 6 percent to 6.5 percent a year. (Again, we're assuming a zero inflation rate so that the real interest rate equals the nominal interest rate.)

The Market for Real GDP Figure 15.10(d) shows aggregate demand and aggregate supply in the market for real GDP. Potential GDP is $12 trillion where LAS is located. The short-run aggregate supply curve is SAS and initially the aggregate demand is AD_0. Now, real GDP is $12.2 trillion, which is greater than potential GDP, so there is an inflationary gap. The Fed is reacting to this inflationary gap.

FIGURE 15.10   The Fed Fights Inflation

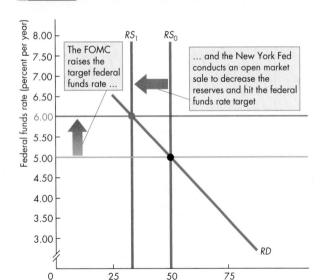

(a) The market for bank reserves

In part (a), the FOMC raises the federal funds rate from 5 percent to 6 percent. The New York Fed sells securities in an open market operation to decrease the supply of reserves from RS_0 to RS_1 and hit the new federal funds rate target.

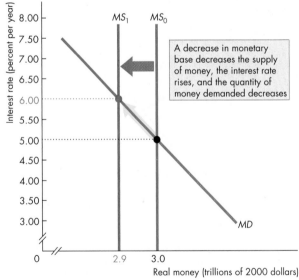

(b) Money market

In part (b), the supply of money decreases from MS_0 to MS_1, the short-term interest rate rises, and the quantity of money demanded decreases. The short-term interest rate and the federal funds rate change by similar amounts.

The increase in the short-term interest rate, the decrease in the supply of bank loans, and the increase in the real interest rate decrease aggregate planned expenditure. (Not shown in the figures, a rise in the interest rate raises the exchange rate, which decreases net exports and aggregate planned expenditure.)

The decrease in aggregate expenditure, ΔE, decreases aggregate demand and shifts the aggregate demand curve to $AD_0 - \Delta E$. A multiplier process begins. The decrease in expenditure decreases income, which induces a decrease in consumption expenditure. Aggregate demand decreases further, and the aggregate demand curve eventually shifts leftward to AD_1.

The economy returns to full employment. Real GDP is equal to potential GDP. The price level falls to 120 and then becomes stable at that level. So after a one-time adjustment, there is price stability.

Again, in this example, we have given the Fed a perfect hit at achieving full employment and keeping the price level stable. If the Fed decreased aggregate demand by too little and too late, the economy would

have remained with an inflationary gap and the inflation rate would have moved above the rate that is consistent with price stability. And if the Fed hit the brakes too hard, it would push the economy from inflation to recession.

Loose Links and Long and Variable Lags

The ripple effects of monetary policy that we've just analyzed with the precision of an economic model are, in reality, very hard to predict and anticipate.

To achieve its goals of price stability and full employment, the Fed needs a combination of good judgment and good luck. Too large an interest rate cut in an underemployed economy can bring inflation, as it did during the 1970s. And too large an interest rate rise in an inflationary economy can create unemployment, as it did in 1981 and 1991.

Loose links in the chain that runs from the federal funds rate to the ultimate policy goals make unwanted policy outcomes inevitable. And time lags

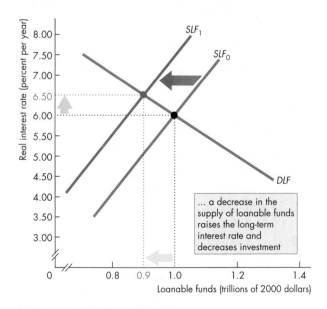

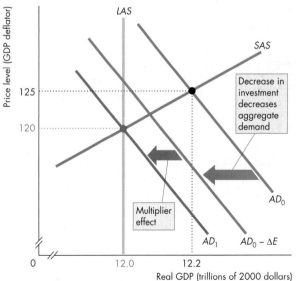

(c) The market for loanable funds

In part (c), a decrease in the supply of bank loans decreases the supply of loanable funds from SLF_0 to SLF_1 and the real interest rate rises. Investment decreases.

(d) Real GDP and the price level

In part (d), aggregate planned expenditure decreases. Aggregate demand decreases and the AD curve shifts leftward from AD_0 to AD_1. Real GDP decreases to potential GDP, and the price level falls.

that are both long and variable add to the Fed's challenges.

Loose Link from Federal Funds Rate to Spending
The real long-term interest rate that influences spending plans is linked only loosely to the federal funds rate. Also, the response of the *real* long-term interest rate to a change in the nominal interest rate depends on how inflation expectations change. And the response of expenditure plans to changes in the real interest rate depend on many factors that make the response hard to predict.

Time Lags in the Adjustment Process The Fed is especially handicapped by the fact that the monetary policy transmission process is long and drawn out. Also, the economy does not always respond in exactly the same way to a policy change. Further, many factors other than policy are constantly changing and bringing new situations to which policy must respond.

A Final Reality Check

You've studied the theory of monetary policy. Does it really work in the way we've described? It does. And Fig. 15.11 provides some evidence to support this claim.

In Fig.15.11, the blue line shows the federal funds rate that the Fed targets minus the long-term bond rate. We can view the gap between the long-term bond rate and the federal funds rate as a measure of how hard the Fed is trying to steer a change in course. When the federal funds rate falls relative to the long-term bond rate, the Fed is trying to stimulate real GDP growth. When the federal funds rate rises relative to the long-term bond rate, the Fed is trying to restrain inflation and slow real GDP growth.

The red line in Fig. 15.11 is the real GDP growth rate *one year later.* You can see that when the FOMC raises the federal funds rate, the real GDP growth rate slows one year later. And when the Fed lowers the federal funds rate, the real GDP growth rate speeds up one year later.

Not shown in Fig. 15.11, the inflation rate increases and decreases corresponding to the fluctuations in the real GDP growth rate. But the effects on the inflation rate take even longer.

You've seen how the Fed operates and the effects of its actions. We close this chapter by looking at alternative ways in which the Fed could operate.

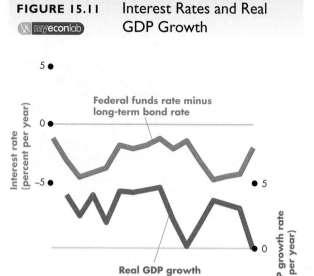

FIGURE 15.11   Interest Rates and Real GDP Growth

When the federal funds rate rises relative to the long-term bond rate, the real GDP growth rate usually slows about one year later. Similarly, when the federal funds rate falls relative to the long-term bond rate, the real GDP growth rate speeds up about one year later.

Sources of data: Interest rates, see Fig. 15.8; real GDP growth, Bureau of Economic Analysis.

REVIEW QUIZ

1 Describe the channels by which monetary policy ripples through the economy and explain why each channel operates.
2 Do interest rates fluctuate in response to the Fed's actions?
3 How do the Fed's actions change the exchange rate?
4 How do the Fed's actions influence real GDP and how long does it take for real GDP to respond to the Fed's policy changes?
5 How do the Fed's actions influence the inflation rate and how long does it take for inflation to respond to the Fed's policy changes?

myeconlab Study Plan 15.3

Alternative Monetary Policy Strategies

So far in this chapter, we've described and analyzed the Fed's method of conducting monetary policy. But the Fed does have choices among alternative monetary policy strategies. We're going to end our discussion of monetary policy by examining the alternatives and explaining why the Fed has rejected them in favor of the interest rate strategy that we've described.

You've seen that we can summarize monetary policy strategies in two broad categories: *instrument rules* and *targeting rules*. And you've seen that the Fed uses a *targeting rule* strategy but one that comes close to being the same as the Taylor rule, an instrument rule for the federal funds rate. So the Fed has rejected a pure or simple instrument rule. It has also rejected some other possible instrument and targeting rules.

The Fed might have chosen any of four alternative monetary policy strategies: One of them is an instrument rule, and three are alternative targeting rules. The four alternatives are

■ Monetary base instrument rule
■ Money targeting rule
■ Exchange rate targeting rule
■ Inflation rate targeting rule

Monetary Base Instrument Rule

Although the Fed uses open market operations to hit its federal funds rate target, it could instead shoot for a target level of the monetary base.

The idea of using a rule to set the monetary base has been suggested by Carnegie-Mellon University economist Bennet T. McCallum, and a monetary base rule bears his name.

The **McCallum rule** makes the growth rate of the monetary base respond to the long-term average growth rate of real GDP and medium-term changes in the velocity of circulation of the monetary base.

The rule is based on the *quantity theory of money* (see Chapter 9, pp 224–225). McCallum's idea is that by making the monetary base grow at a rate equal to a target inflation rate plus the long-term real GDP growth rate minus the medium-term growth rate of the velocity of circulation of the monetary base, infla-

tion will be kept close to target and the economy will be kept close to full employment.

The McCallum rule has some advantages over the Taylor rule. To target the interest rate using the Taylor rule, the Fed must estimate the long-run equilibrium real interest rate and the output gap.

In the Taylor rule, which we described on p. 374, the long-run equilibrium real interest rate is 2 percent a year. The federal funds rate is set at this level if the inflation rate and output gap are zero. But if the long-run equilibrium real interest rate is not 2 percent a year, the Taylor rule would set the interest rate either too high on the average and bring persistent recession or too low on the average and bring persistent and accelerating inflation.

Similarly, if the Fed overestimated the output gap, it would set the federal funds rate too high on the average and bring persistent recession. And if the Fed underestimated the output gap, it would set the federal funds rate too low on the average and bring persistent inflation.

Because the McCallum rule doesn't react to either the real interest rate or the output gap, the McCallum rule doesn't suffer from the problems of the Taylor rule.

A disadvantage of the McCallum rule compared to the Taylor rule is that it relies on the demand for money and demand for monetary base being reasonably stable.

The Fed believes that shifts in the demand for money and the demand for monetary base would bring large fluctuations in the interest rate, which in turn would bring large fluctuations in aggregate demand.

Money Targeting Rule

As long ago as 1948, Nobel Laureate Milton Friedman proposed a targeting rule for the quantity of money. Friedman's **k-percent rule** makes the quantity of money grow at a rate of k percent a year, where k equals the growth rate of potential GDP.

Like the McCallum rule, Friedman's k-percent rule relies on a stable demand for money, which translates to a stable velocity of circulation. Friedman had examined data on money and nominal GDP and argued that the velocity of circulation of money was one of the most stable macroeconomic variables and that it could be exploited to deliver a stable price level and small business cycle fluctuations.

Friedman's idea remained just that until the 1970s, when inflation increased to more than 10 percent a year in the United States and to much higher rates in some other major countries.

During the mid-1970s, in a bid to end the inflation, the central banks of most major countries adopted the *k*-percent rule for the growth rate of the quantity of money. The Fed, too, began to pay close attention to the growth rates of money aggregates, including M1 and M2.

Inflation rates fell during the early 1980s in the countries that had adopted a *k*-percent rule. But one by one, these countries abandoned the *k*-percent rule.

Money targeting works when the demand for money is stable and predictable—when the velocity of circulation is stable. But in the world of the 1980s, and possibly in the world of today, technological change in the banking system leads to large and unpredictable fluctuations in the demand for money, which make the use of monetary targeting unreliable. With monetary targeting, aggregate demand fluctuates because the demand for money fluctuates. With interest rate targeting, aggregate demand is insulated from fluctuations in the demand for money (and the velocity of circulation).

Exchange Rate Targeting Rule

The Fed could, if it wished to do so, intervene in the foreign exchange market to target the exchange rate. A fixed exchange rate is one possible exchange rate target. The Fed could fix the value of the U.S. dollar against a basket of other currencies such as the *trade-weighted index* (see Chapter 10, p. 234).

But with a fixed exchange rate, a country has no control over its inflation rate. The reason is that for internationally traded goods, *purchasing power parity* (see p. 242) moves domestic prices in line with foreign prices. If a computer chip costs $100 in Los Angeles and if the exchange rate is 120 yen per $1.00, then the computer chip will sell for 12,000 yen (ignoring local tax differences) in Tokyo. If this purchasing power parity didn't prevail, it would be possible to earn a profit by buying at the lower price and selling at the higher price. This trading would compete away the profit and price difference.

So prices of traded goods (and in the long run the prices of all goods and services) must rise at the same rate in the United States as they do on the aver-age in the other countries against which the value of the U.S. dollar is fixed.

The Fed could avoid a direct inflation link by using a *crawling peg exchange rate* (see Chapter 10, p. 250) as a means of achieving an inflation target. To do so, the Fed would make the exchange rate change at a rate equal to the U.S. inflation rate minus the target inflation rate. If other countries have an average inflation rate of 3 percent a year and the United States wants an inflation rate of 2 percent a year, the Fed would make the U.S. dollar appreciate at a rate of 1 percent a year against the trade-weighted index of other currencies.

Some developing countries that have an inflation problem use this monetary policy strategy to lower the inflation rate. The main reason for choosing this method is that these countries don't have well-functioning markets for bonds and overnight loans, so they cannot use the policy approach that relies on these features of a banking system.

A major disadvantage of a crawling peg to target the inflation rate is that the real exchange rate often changes in unpredictable ways. The **real exchange rate** between the United States and its trading partners is the relative price of the GDP basket of goods and services in the United States with respect to that in other countries. U.S. GDP contains a larger proportion of high-technology products and services than GDP in other countries contain. So when the relative prices of these items change, our real exchange rate changes. With a crawling peg targeting the inflation rate, we would need to be able to identify changes in the real exchange rate and offset them. This task is difficult to accomplish.

Inflation Rate Targeting Rule

Inflation rate targeting is a monetary policy strategy in which the central bank makes a public commitment

1. To achieve an explicit inflation target
2. To explain how its policy actions will achieve that target

Of the alternatives to the Fed's current strategy, inflation targeting is the most likely to be considered. In fact, some economists see it as a small step from what the Fed currently does. For these reasons, we'll explain this policy strategy in a bit of detail. Which countries practice inflation targeting, how do they do it, and what does it achieve?

Inflation Targeters Several major central banks practice inflation targeting and have done so since the mid-1990s. The best examples of central banks that use inflation targeting are the Bank of England, Bank of Canada, the Reserve Bank of New Zealand, and the Swedish Riksbank. The European Central Bank also practices inflation targeting. Japan and the United States are the most prominent major industrial economies that do not use this monetary policy strategy. But it is interesting to note that when the chairman of the Board of Governors of the Federal Reserve System, Ben Bernanke, and a member of the Board of Governors, Frederic S. Mishkin, were economics professors (at Princeton University and Columbia University, respectively), they did research together and wrote important articles and books on this topic. And their general conclusion was that inflation targeting is a sensible way in which to conduct monetary policy.

How Inflation Targeting is Conducted Inflation targets are specified in terms of a range for the CPI inflation rate. This range is typically between 1 percent and 3 percent a year, with an aim to achieve an average inflation rate of 2 percent per year. Because the lags in the operation of monetary policy are long, if the inflation rate falls outside the target range, the expectation is that the central bank will move the inflation rate back on target over the next two years.

All the inflation-targeting central banks use the overnight interest rate (the equivalent of the federal funds rate) as the policy instrument. And they use open market operations as the tool for achieving the desired overnight rate.

To explain their policy actions, inflation targeters publish an inflation report that describes the current state of the economy and its expected evolution over the next two years. The report also explains the central bank's current policy and how and why the central bank expects that its policy will achieve the inflation target.

What Does Inflation Targeting Achieve? The goals of inflation targeting are to state clearly and publicly the goals of monetary policy, to establish a framework of accountability, and to keep the inflation rate low and stable while maintaining a high and stable level of employment.

There is wide agreement that inflation targeting achieves its first two goals. And the inflation reports of inflation targeters have raised the level of discussion and understanding of the monetary policy process.

It is less clear whether inflation targeting does better than the implicit targeting that the Fed currently pursues in achieving low and stable inflation. The Fed's own record, without a formal inflation target, has been impressive over the past several years.

But monetary policy is about managing inflation expectations. And it seems clear that an explicit inflation target that is taken seriously and toward which policy actions are aimed and explained is a sensible way to manage expectations.

It is when the going gets tough that inflation targeting has the greatest attraction. It is difficult to imagine a serious inflation-targeting central bank permitting inflation to take off in the way that it did during the 1970s. And it is difficult to imagine deflation and ongoing recession such as Japan has endured for the past 10 years if monetary policy is guided by an explicit inflation target.

The debate on inflation targeting will continue!

Why Rules?

You might be wondering why all monetary policy strategies involve rules. Why doesn't the Fed just do what seems best every day, month, and year, at its discretion? The answer lies in what you've just read. Monetary policy is about managing inflation expectations. In both financial markets and labor markets, people must make long-term commitments. So these markets work best when plans are based on correctly anticipated inflation outcomes. A well-understood monetary policy rule helps to create an environment in which inflation is easier to forecast and manage.

REVIEW QUIZ

1 What are the four main alternative strategies for conducting monetary policy (other than the one used by the Fed)?
2 Briefly, why does the Fed reject each of these alternatives?

myeconlab Study Plan 15.4

As you complete your study of monetary policy, take a look at *Reading Between the Lines* on pages 388–389 and see the Fed's policy challenge in 2006.

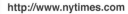

Monetary Policy in Action

In a Policy Shift, the Fed Halts a 2-Year String of Rate Increases

August 9, 2006

. . . After 17 consecutive increases [one] at each meeting since June 2004, the central bank voted to hold its benchmark interest rate steady at 5.25 percent. Policy makers suggested that they wanted more time to see where the economy was headed before deciding whether further increases might be necessary.

In a statement accompanying its decision, the Fed acknowledged that inflation had accelerated. But it predicted that slowing economic growth—led by the retreat of the housing market—would lead to smaller consumer price increases before long.

. . . The shift amounts to a bet by the Federal Reserve's chairman, Ben S. Bernanke, on an elusive goal in monetary policy: a "soft landing" in which the economy slows enough to cool spending and ease inflationary pressures but not enough to cause a big jump in unemployment.

. . . Many economists said they disagreed with the Fed's sanguine outlook, saying that prices and wages were both climbing significantly faster than just a year ago and showed no signs of slowing yet.

. . . Mr. Bernanke, both before and after he became Fed chairman, has said that his definition of price stability is a "core" inflation rate—excluding prices for energy and food—of 1 to 2 percent. But by the Fed's preferred measure of core inflation prices are about 2.9 percent higher than one year ago. That is the biggest year-over-year jump in 11 years.

. . . Laurence H. Meyer, a former Fed governor and now an economic forecaster at Macroeconomic Advisers, predicted that it would take more than a soft landing to reduce inflation significantly. For that to happen, he said, unemployment would have to rise for a sustained period. . . .

Essence of the Story

▶ In the summer of 2006, the core inflation rate was 2.9 percent.

▶ At its meeting on August 8, 2006, the Fed noted that the inflation rate was too high but said that it would fall without a further rise in the interest rate.

▶ So the Fed decided to hold the federal funds rate target at 5.25 percent.

▶ The hope was that the inflation rate would fall with no big jump in unemployment in a "soft landing."

▶ Many economists disagreed with the Fed and said that inflation showed no signs of slowing.

▶ Economist Laurence H. Meyer predicted that it would take more than a soft landing to reduce inflation, and that unemployment would have to rise for a sustained period.

▶ In mid-2006, the core inflation rate was above the rate consistent with price stability.

▶ Figure I illustrates the situation in the second quarter of 2006 compared with the second quarter of 2005.

▶ In 2005, the aggregate demand curve was AD_{05}, the short-run aggregate supply curve was SAS_{05}, real GDP was $11 trillion, and the price level was 112.

▶ In 2006, the aggregate demand curve was AD_{06}, the short-run aggregate supply curve was SAS_{06}, real GDP was $11.4 trillion, and the price level was 116.

▶ During the year, real GDP had grown by about 3.6 percent and the price level measured by the GDP deflator had increased by 3.6 percent.

▶ The core inflation rate was just below 3 percent a year. In this situation, the Fed wanted to lower the inflation rate.

▶ But the Fed faces an uncertain future and must set the interest rate based on its best forecast of how the economy will evolve over the coming year.

▶ In the summer of 2006, the Fed expected the economy to slow and the inflation rate to decrease

with no further monetary policy action. So the Fed kept the federal funds rate constant.

▶ Some economists thought that the Fed was incorrect and that further interest rate increases would be necessary to slow an economy that is growing too rapidly.

▶ Figure 2 illustrates the situation in the second quarter of 2007 if the Fed was wrong and inflation persisted at too high a rate.

▶ By mid-2007, the aggregate demand curve would be AD_{07}, the short-run aggregate supply curve would be SAS_{07}, real GDP would be $11.9 trillion, and the price level would be 122.

▶ Figure 2 also illustrates what the Fed expected by the second quarter of 2007.

▶ By mid-2007, aggregate demand growth would slow to AD_{07Fed}, the short-run aggregate supply curve would be SAS_{07Fed}, real GDP would be $11.7 trillion, and the price level would be 118.

▶ The inflation rate and real GDP growth rate would have slowed, and inflation would be back in the range consistent with price stability.

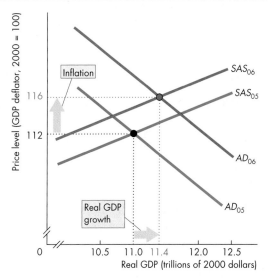

Figure 1 Real GDP and inflation 2005 to 2006

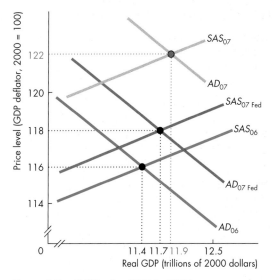

Figure 2 Possibilities for 2006 to 2007

You're the Voter

▶ Do you think the Fed was right to hold the interest rate constant in August 2006?

▶ If you were a member of the FOMC, what interest rate setting would you vote for today? Explain your decision.

389

SUMMARY

Key Points

Monetary Policy Objectives and Framework (pp. 370–372)

- The Federal Reserve Act requires the Fed to use monetary policy to achieve maximum employment, stable prices, and moderate long-term interest rates.
- The goal of stable prices delivers maximum employment and low interest rates in the long run but can conflict with the other goals in the short run.
- The Fed translates the goal of stable prices as an inflation rate of between 1 and 2 percent per year.
- The FOMC has the responsibility for the conduct of monetary policy, but the Fed reports to the public and to Congress.

The Conduct of Monetary Policy (pp. 372–376)

- The Fed's monetary policy instrument is the federal funds rate.
- The Fed sets the federal funds rate target and announces changes on eight dates each year.
- An *instrument rule* for monetary policy makes the instrument respond predictably to the state of the economy. The Fed does *not* use a mechanical instrument rule.
- A *targeting rule* for monetary policy sets the instrument to make the forecast of the inflation rate equal to the target inflation rate. The Fed *does* use such a rule, but its actions are similar to an instrument rule.
- The Fed hits its federal funds rate target by using open market operations.
- By buying or selling government securities in the open market, the Fed is able to change bank reserves and change the federal funds rate.

Monetary Policy Transmission (pp. 377–384)

- A change in the federal funds rate changes other interest rates, the exchange rate, the quantity of money and loans, aggregate demand, and eventually real GDP and the price level.
- Changes in the federal funds rate change real GDP about one year later and change the inflation rate with an even longer time lag.

Alternative Monetary Policy Strategies (pp. 385–387)

- The main alternatives to setting the federal funds rate are a monetary base instrument rule, a money targeting rule, an exchange rate targeting rule, or an inflation rate targeting rule.
- Rules dominate discretion in monetary policy because they better enable the central bank to manage inflation expectations.

Key Figures

Key Terms

PROBLEMS

myeconlab Tests, Study Plan, Solutions*

1. Suppose that the Fed is required to keep the inflation rate between 1 percent and 2 percent a year but with no requirement to keep trend inflation at the midpoint of this range. The Fed achieves its target.
   a. If initially the price level is 100,
      i. Calculate the highest price level that might occur after 10 years.
      ii. Calculate the lowest price level that might occur after 10 years.
      iii. What is the range of uncertainty about the price level after 10 years?
   b. Would this type of inflation goal serve the financial markets well and provide an anchor for inflation expectations?

2. Suppose the Fed is required to keep the inflation rate between 0 percent and 3 percent a year and is also required to keep trend inflation at the midpoint of the range. The Fed achieves its target.
   a. If initially the price level is 100, what is the likely price level after 10 years?
   b. Compare this economy with the economy in problem 1. Which economy has the greater certainty about inflation over the longer term? Which has the greater short-term certainty?

3. Suppose that the Bank of England decides to follow the Taylor rule. In 2005, the United Kingdom has an inflation rate of 2.1 percent a year and its output gap is –0.3 percent. At what level does the Bank of England set the repo rate (the U.K. equivalent of the federal funds rate)?

4. Suppose that the Reserve Bank of New Zealand is following the Taylor rule. In 2005, it sets the official cash rate (the N.Z. equivalent of the federal funds rate) at 5.8 percent a year. If the inflation rate in New Zealand is 3.0 percent a year, what is its output gap?

5. Suppose that the Bank of Canada is following the McCallum rule. The Bank of Canada has an inflation target range of between 1 percent a year and 3 percent a year. The long-term real GDP growth rate in Canada is 2.4 percent a year.

If the velocity of circulation of the monetary base is 2, what is the
   a. Highest growth rate of monetary base that will occur?
   b. Lowest growth rate of monetary base that will occur?

6. The figure shows the economy of Freezone. The aggregate demand curve is *AD*, and the short-run aggregate supply curve is *SAS_A*. Potential GDP is $300 billion.

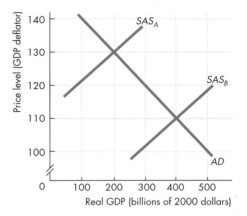

   a. What are the price level and real GDP?
   b. Does Freezone have an unemployment problem or an inflation problem? Why?
   c. What do you predict will happen in Freezone if the central bank takes no monetary policy actions?
   d. What monetary policy action would you advise the central bank to take and what do you predict will be the effect of that action?

7. Suppose that in Freezone, shown in problem 6, the aggregate demand curve is *AD* and potential GDP is $300 billion, but the short-run aggregate supply curve is *SAS_B*.
   a. What are the price level and real GDP?
   b. Does Freezone have an unemployment problem or an inflation problem? Why?
   c. What do you predict will happen in Freezone if the central bank takes no monetary policy actions?
   d. What monetary policy action would you advise the central bank to take and what do you predict will be the effect of that action?

8. Suppose that in Freezone, shown in problem 6, the short-run aggregate supply curve is *SAS_B* and potential GDP increases to $350 billion.
   a. What happens in Freezone if the central bank

* Solutions to odd-numbered problems are provided.

lowers the federal funds rate and buys securities on the open market?

b. What happens in Freezone if the central bank raises the federal funds rate and sells securities on the open market?

c. Do you recommend that the central bank lower or raise the federal funds rate? Why?

9. Suppose that in Freezone, shown in problem 6, the short-run aggregate supply curve is SAS_A and a drought decreases potential GDP to $250 billion.

a. What happens in Freezone if the central bank lowers the federal funds rate and buys securities on the open market?

b. What happens in Freezone if the central bank raises the federal funds rate and sells securities on the open market?

c. Do you recommend that the central bank lower or raise the federal funds rate? Why?

some variation of it appears five times in the minutes.

The New York Times, October 12, 2006

a. If the inflation rate rises, what effect will the Fed's decision not to change the federal funds rate have on the U.S. economy?

b. If the inflation rate falls, what effect will the Fed's decision not to change the federal funds rate have on the U.S. economy?

4. The Labor Department said overall U.S. consumer prices fell 0.5 percent in September though core prices, which exclude food and energy, kept edging up. . . .

CNN.com, October 18, 2006

If the Fed was following the Taylor rule, what adjustments would it make to the federal funds rate given the news in this article?

CRITICAL THINKING

1. Study *Reading Between the Lines* on pp. 388–389 and then answer the following questions.

a. How does the Fed's expectation about future inflation differ from that of some economists?

b. Why did the Fed keep the federal funds rate steady in August 2006?

c. Do you think the Fed made the correct decision, given the information then available? If so, why?

d. Do you think the Fed made the correct decision, given the information now available? If so, why?

2. When the Fed brought inflation under control during the early 1990s, it created a recession. Do you think a recession could have been avoided while still lowering the inflation rate? Explain why or why not.

3. **No Hurry to Cut Rates at the Fed**

Despite indications that inflation pressures may be starting to ease, the Federal Reserve is not inclined to lower short-term interest rates anytime soon, minutes from its most recent meeting show. The reason is uncertainty: uncertainty about the housing market, uncertainty about economic growth and most of all, uncertainty about inflation. . . . The word "uncertainty" or

WEB ACTIVITIES

myeconlab Links to Web sites

1. Visit the Fed and obtain the latest data on the core inflation rate and the overall CPI inflation rate as well as the federal funds rate. Then answer the following questions.

a. Is the Fed trying to slow the economy or speed it up? How can you tell?

b. What open market operations do you think the Fed has undertaken during the past few months?

c. In light of the Fed's recent actions, what ripple effects do you expect over the coming months?

d. What do you think the effects of the Fed's recent actions will be on bond prices, stock prices, and the exchange rate?

2. Visit the Bureau of Economic Analysis and the Bureau of Labor Statistics and look at the current economic conditions.

a. On the basis of the current state of the U.S. economy, do you predict that the Fed will raise interest rates, lower interest rates, or hold interest rates steady?

b. Write a brief summary of your predictions and reasons.

Tradeoffs or Free Lunches

A policy tradeoff arises if, in taking an action to achieve one goal, some other goal must be forgone. For example, the government might want to increase defense expenditure *and* stimulate business investment. But if defense expenditure is increased, either tax revenues must rise or government borrowing must increase. Either of these methods of financing the increase in defense expenditure raises the real interest rate, which decreases, or "crowds out," business investment. The government faces a tradeoff between defense expenditure and business investment.

Similarly, the Fed might want to avoid a rise in the inflation rate and a rise in the unemployment rate. But if the Fed raises the interest rate to curb inflation, it might lower expenditure and increase unemployment. In this example, the Fed faces a tradeoff between inflation and unemployment.

A policy free lunch arises if in taking actions to pursue one goal, some other (intended or unintended) goal is also achieved. For example, there might be mass unemployment that the government wants to cure. At the same time, the government wants to increase defense expenditure. If by increasing defense expenditure, the government stimulates aggregate demand and boosts employment, it enjoys a free lunch. It gets its higher defense expenditure and its lower unemployment.

Similarly, the Fed might want to keep inflation in check and, at the same time, to boost the economic growth rate. If lower inflation brings lower uncertainty about the future and stimulates saving and investment, the Fed gets both lower

inflation and faster real GDP growth. It enjoys a free lunch.

The two chapters in this part have described the institutional framework in which fiscal policy (Chapter 14) and monetary policy (Chapter 15) are made, described the instruments of policy, and analyzed the effects of policy. This exploration of economic policy draws on almost everything that you learned in previous chapters.

Fiscal policy influences both the level and the growth rate of potential GDP. Fiscal policy also influences the fluctuations of actual real GDP around potential GDP. So to study fiscal policy, we need the use the classical model of the full-employment economy, growth models, and the *AS-AD* model of economic fluctuations.

Monetary policy operates by changing the interest rate and influences the price level and inflation rate in the long run and the fluctuations of real GDP around potential GDP and cycles in the inflation rate in the short run. So to study monetary policy, we need to use the model of the loanable funds market in which the interest rate is determined, the quantity theory of money that governs the trends in inflation, and the *AS-AD* model of economic fluctuations.

These policy chapters serve as a capstone on your knowledge of macroeconomics and draw together all the strands in your study of the previous chapters.

Milton Friedman, whom you meet on the next page, has profoundly influenced our understanding of macroeconomic policy.

Incentives and Surprises

The Economist

Milton Friedman *was born into a poor immigrant family in New York City in 1912. He was an undergraduate at Rutgers and graduate student at Columbia University during the Great Depression. From 1977 until his death in 2006, Professor Friedman was a Senior Fellow at the Hoover Institution at Stanford University. But his reputation was built between 1946 and 1983, when he was a leading member of the "Chicago School," an approach to economics developed at the University of Chicago and based on the views that free markets allocate resources efficiently and that stable and low money supply growth delivers macroeconomic stability.*

Friedman has advanced our understanding of the forces that determine macroeconomic performance and clarified the effects of the quantity of money. And for this work, he was awarded the 1977 Nobel Prize for Economic Science.

By reasoning from basic economic principles, Friedman (along with Edmund S. Phelps, the 2006 Economics Nobel Laureate) predicted that persistent demand stimulation would not increase output but would cause inflation.

When output growth slowed and inflation broke out in the 1970s, Friedman seemed like a prophet, and for a time, his policy prescription, known as monetarism, was embraced around the world.

The Issues

The central challenges of fiscal policy and monetary policy are to contribute to achieving the fastest possible sustainable growth rate of real GDP, to maintain stable prices, and to minimize the volatility of real GDP fluctuations around potential GDP.

All fiscal policy and monetary policy actions work by influencing the incentives that people and businesses face. And these incentives can be influenced either in a well-understood and predictable manner or in a surprising manner.

Does it matter whether policy is predictable or a surprise?

Economists are agreed that it does matter and that predictable policy actions do a better job than do policy surprises.

A government that commits to a tax and spending regime that is predictable and not subject to capricious change creates an environment in which self-interest decisions can best serve the social interest.

A central bank that adopts a well-understood target, sets its policy instrument to achieve that target, and explains its policy choices in the framework of its target delivers a better outcome for all the goals of macroeconomic policy than does a central bank that acts capriciously and surprises financial markets by its actions.

But there remains much debate about just what the targets of policy should be. Should fiscal policy be aimed at long-run growth and generational balance objectives or short-run stabilization objectives? Should monetary policy be governed by an explicit inflation target, a money stock growth target, or some implicit targets that might include output and employment as well as the inflation rate? There is no settled answer to these questions.

Then

What happens to the economy when people lose confidence in banks? They withdraw their funds. These withdrawals feed on themselves, creating a snowball of withdrawals and, eventually, panic. Short of funds with which to repay depositors, banks call in loans and previously sound businesses are faced with financial distress. They close down and lay off workers. And recession deepens and turns into depression. Bank failures and the resulting decline in the nation's supply of money and credit were a significant factor in deepening and prolonging the Great Depression. But they taught us the importance of stable financial institutions and gave rise to the establishment of federal deposit insurance to prevent future financial collapse. The Great Depression also made the Fed much more aware of its power and its responsibility to influence and improve the performance of financial markets.

Now

By its careful analysis of the current and forecasted economic situation in the United States and around the world, the Board of Governors of the Federal Reserve seeks to maintain macroeconomic stability and avoid a disaster like the Great Depression.

During the years since the Great Depression, the Fed has managed the nation's banking and financial system with the aim of keeping the price level stable and avoiding a collapse of aggregate demand.

When a financial crisis in Asia in 1997 threatened the stability of the global financial system, the Fed injected reserves into the U.S. banks to ensure that they did not need to sell securities. Similarly, following the terrorist attacks of September 11, 2001, the Fed kept the banking system flush with reserves.

In recent years, we have enjoyed low inflation and sustained economic growth. Some credit for this macroeconomic performance must go to the Federal Reserve Board and the monetary policy that it has pursued. Next, you can meet Peter Ireland, a professor at Boston College and a former research economist at the Federal Reserve Bank of Richmond.

Peter N. Ireland

Peter N. Ireland is Professor of Economics at Boston College. Born in Cambridge, Massachusetts, he was an undergraduate and graduate student at the University of Chicago. Professor Ireland began his career as a research economist at the Federal Reserve Bank of Richmond and also taught at Rutgers University before returning home to the Boston area. His research has spanned a large range of theoretical, empirical, and policy issues in macro-economics and monetary economics.

Michael Parkin talked with Peter Ireland about his work and the challenges of conducting economic policy.

What attracted you to economics?

When I first started college, I wasn't quite sure which field I wanted to choose for my major. But after taking a number of courses in different fields, I decided that economics was what I liked best.

Most of all, I enjoyed how economics takes advantage of the quantitative precision of math and statistics—two other fields that I've always found interesting—while at the same time addressing many of the political and social issues that always seemed important to me.

Also, as an undergraduate at Chicago, I was lucky enough to work as a research assistant for Professor Robert Fogel who, as you know, went on to win the Nobel Prize in economics. That was a great experience; more than anything else, it taught me the value of patience and perseverance in conducting economic research. Often, the answer to a tough economics question is just waiting there for anyone to find—it's just a matter of who is willing to put the time and effort into finding and sifting though the relevant data.

What does a research economist at a regional Federal Reserve Bank do?

Reserve Bank economists perform many tasks. Through their writings and public speeches, they serve as liaisons between the Fed and the local communities. Also, through their basic research, they help find ways to improve monetary policymaking in the United States.

But perhaps the most important job that research economists at the Fed perform involves briefing their Reserve Bank president prior to each meeting of the Federal Open Market Committee. Eight times per year, members of each Bank's research staff sit down with their president to review the most recent economic data and to interpret those data using their theoretical and statistical models. All of the work that's done feeds into answering one important question: at the FOMC meeting, should the president recommend that interest rates be raised, lowered, or held steady?

I really enjoyed that part of my job at the Richmond Fed. It was exciting to be able to apply the economics that I learned in graduate school to address a specific policy issue. And it was nice to think that my work might be making a difference, however small, in helping senior Fed officials make the right policy decisions.

Can you summarize what you think we currently know about aggregate fluctuations? Do sticky wages have a role to play? What is the role of the technology shocks that real business cycle theory emphasizes?
Identifying the source of business cycle fluctuations remains an important and lively topic of research in macroeconomics. Different economists have different opinions on this issue, but I myself like to take a fairly eclectic view.

I agree with monetarist and Keynesian economists who argue that monetary policy can have important real effects in the short run, due to rigidity in nominal prices and wages. At the same time, however, I think that there is a strong element of truth in real business cycle theory, with its emphasis on technology shocks. In my view, perhaps the most important insight provided by real business cycle theory is the idea that there are some types of shocks that hit the economy to which monetary and fiscal policy makers cannot or should not respond.

Suppose, for example, that the price of imported oil rises sharply and suddenly, as it has done on a number of occasions in postwar U.S. history. When that type of shock—which resembles a negative technology shock—hits the economy, inflation and unemployment are both going to rise—one won't see the usual Phillips-curve tradeoff between those two variables. And anything that the Fed tries to do to offset the joint rise in inflation and unemployment is probably just going to make matters worse.

But there's a happy side to this same story. Suppose that the economy experiences a period of unusually rapid growth in productivity—like the one we enjoyed in the United States during the 1990s and may still be enjoying today. That's like a positive technology shock in the real business cycle model,

> … perhaps the most important insight provided by real business cycle theory is the idea that there are some types of shocks that hit the economy to which monetary and fiscal policy makers cannot or should not respond.

and it will be accompanied by low inflation and falling unemployment. Once again, there is no Phillips-curve tradeoff. In this case, the Fed can just sit back and enjoy the best of both worlds.

Some economists advocate a monetary policy rule that adjusts the federal funds rate in response to the latest inflation and output data—a Taylor rule. What is your view of such a rule?
I consider the Taylor rule to be very useful, because it gives monetary policy makers a simple but systematic way of comparing the present to the past. Suppose, for example, that today's federal funds rate turns out to be lower than the level that is recommended by the Taylor rule. Then FOMC members know that monetary policy today is more expansionary, relative to the state of the economy, than it has been in the past. So if FOMC members want policy to be more expansionary, then they can have confidence that they're on the right track. But if, on the other hand, FOMC members would prefer that policy be closer to neutral or even somewhat restrictive, then the Taylor rule warns them that the federal funds rate soon might need to move higher.

Other economists advocate a monetary policy rule that gradually adjusts the growth rate of the monetary base to long-term trends in real GDP and velocity—a McCallum rule. What is your view of this rule?
Again on this topic, my views are a bit eclectic. I also think that McCallum's rule is a valuable guide for monetary policy making—and for the very same reasons that I find the Taylor rule useful!

Too often, I think, economists fall into the trap of concluding that if there are two models—call them models A and B—and if model A has been helpful in understanding the data, then it necessarily follows that model B must be false. Of course, if model B has been shown to make predictions that are systematically inaccurate, then it should be abandoned in favor of its more successful competitor. But in many cases, different models can serve as complements rather than competitors.

Consider the situation that prevails in the U.S. economy today, in the Fall of 2003. The federal funds rate is unusually low, so the Taylor rule tells us that monetary policy is accommodative—as, presumably, it should be to help pull the economy out of recession. At the same time, the monetary base and the broader monetary aggregates are growing at a robust pace as well, so the McCallum rule leads us to the same conclusion that monetary policy is appropriately expansionary. So in this case, by seeing that two very different models lead to exactly the same conclusion, we can be all the more confident that the Fed is on track.

Thinking about what we know and don't know about aggregate fluctuations, how would you describe the task of macroeconomic stabilization policy?

Somewhat paradoxically, perhaps, the two most important lessons about stabilization policy that macroeconomists have learned in recent decades both apply to the long run. The first lesson is that in the long run, the inflation rate is constrained by the central bank's choice of money growth rate; put another way, the central bank is responsible for controlling inflation. And the second lesson is that in the long run, there is little or no tradeoff between inflation and unemployment.

Taken together, these two lessons imply that the Federal Reserve's job first and foremost is to provide for a low and stable rate of inflation. That is something that the Fed can achieve without sacrificing anything in terms of its goals for employment.

Constrained by that long-run objective, the Fed can then do what it can to help stabilize the real economy. But a difficult issue goes back to something that we talked about earlier: the fact that different shocks can call for different policy responses from the Fed. So Federal Reserve officials and their research advisors must work hard to continue building models that help us identify exactly what types of shocks might be hitting the economy at any given point in time. And above all, in pursuing its stabilization objectives, the Fed should act cautiously, so as to avoid repeating the large policy mistakes of the past—even if that means it can't always respond to developments in the economy as vigorously or as quickly as some observers might like.

What advice do you have for a student who is just starting to study economics? Is economics a good subject in which to major? What other subjects would you urge students to study alongside economics?

I definitely think that economics is a great choice for an undergraduate major. In addition to what I said before—about how economics combines some of the most interesting aspects of many other fields—an economics major can also serve as a stepping-stone toward a wide variety of careers. Of course, many economics majors go on to work in business or finance, but others find that they are equally well prepared for a career in law or in public policy. Or, if you major in economics today, who knows—you might even go on to graduate school and become the professor who writes the next best-selling Principles textbook! More seriously, the point is, you can do a lot of different things with an economics degree.

To someone who is just starting to study economics, I'd recommend taking at least a few additional courses in statistics, econometrics (which is just statistics applied specifically to economics), and mathematics—because the field continues to become more and more quantitative. But I'd also say that taking courses in political science, sociology, and psychology can also be really useful, especially if they suggest new problems that haven't yet been addressed from an economic point of view.

> … the Federal Reserve's job first and foremost is to provide for a low and stable rate of inflation.

Trading with the World

Silk Routes and Sucking Sounds

Since ancient times, people have expanded their trading as far as technology allowed. Marco Polo opened up the silk route between

Europe and China in the thirteenth century. Today, container ships laden with cars and electronics and Boeing 747s stuffed with farm-fresh foods ply sea and air routes, carrying billions of dollars worth of goods. Why do people go to such great lengths to trade with those in other nations?

In 1994, the United States entered into a free trade agreement with Canada and Mexico—the North American Free Trade Agreement, or NAFTA. Some people predicted a "giant sucking sound" as jobs were transferred from high-wage Michigan to low-wage Mexico. Can we compete with a country that pays its workers a fraction of U.S. wages?

Workers in China earn even less than those in Mexico, and today, just about every manufactured object that we buy seems to be made in China. How can we compete with low-wage China and the other low-wage Asian nations? Are there any industries, besides perhaps making Hollywood movies and building large passenger jets, in which we have an advantage?

Would it be a good idea to limit imports from China and other countries by putting a tariff or a quota on those imports?

◆ In this chapter, we're going to learn about international trade and discover how all nations can gain from trading with other nations. You will discover that all nations can compete, no matter how high their wages. But you will also learn why, despite the fact that international trade brings benefits to all, governments restrict trade. In *Reading Between the Lines* at the end of the chapter, we'll look at the growing trade with China and see why we all benefit from it.

After studying this chapter, you will be able to

▶ Describe the trends and patterns in international trade

▶ Explain comparative advantage and explain why all countries can gain from international trade

▶ Explain why international trade restrictions reduce the volume of imports and exports and reduce our consumption possibilities

▶ Explain the arguments that are used to justify international trade restrictions and show how they are flawed

▶ Explain why we have international trade restrictions

Patterns and Trends in International Trade

The goods and services that we buy from people in other countries are called **imports**. The goods and services that we sell to people in other countries are called **exports**. What are the most important things that we import and export? Most people would probably guess that a rich nation such as the United States imports raw materials and exports manufactured goods. Although that is one feature of U.S. international trade, it is not its most important feature. The bulk of our exports *and* imports is manufactured goods. We sell foreigners earth-moving equipment, airplanes, supercomputers, and scientific equipment, and we buy televisions, DVD players, blue jeans, and T-shirts from them. Also, we are a major exporter of agricultural products and raw materials. And we import and export a huge volume of services.

Trade in Goods

Manufactured goods account for 55 percent of our exports and 68 percent of our imports. Industrial materials (raw materials and semimanufactured items) account for 14 percent of our exports and 15 percent of our imports, and agricultural products account for only 8 percent of our exports and 4 percent of our imports. Our largest individual export and import items are capital goods and automobiles. But goods account for only 70 percent of our exports and 84 percent of our imports. The rest of our international trade is in services.

Trade in Services

You may be wondering how a country can "export" and "import" services. Here are some examples.

If you take a vacation in France and travel there on an Air France flight from New York, you import transportation services from France. The money you spend in France on hotel bills and restaurant meals is also classified as the import of services. Similarly, the money spent by a French student on vacation in the United States is a U.S. export of services to France.

When we import TV sets from South Korea, the owner of the ship that transports them might be Greek and the company that insures them might be British.

The payments that we make for transportation and insurance are imports of services. Similarly, when an American shipping company transports California wine to Tokyo, the transportation cost is a U.S. export of a service to Japan. Our international trade in these types of services is large and growing.

Geographical Patterns of International Trade

The United States has trading links with every part of the world, but Canada is our biggest trading partner. In 2006, 20 percent of our exports went to Canada and 17 percent of our imports came from Canada. Japan is our second biggest trading partner, accounting for 8 percent of exports and 9 percent of imports in 2006. The regions in which our trade is largest are the European Union—with 24 percent of our exports and 23 percent of our imports in 2006—and Latin America—with 20 percent of our exports and 18 percent of our imports in 2006.

Trends in the Volume of Trade

In 1960, we exported 3.5 percent of total output and imported 4 percent of the goods and services that we bought. In 2006, we exported 10 percent of total output and imported 15 percent of the goods and services that we bought.

On the export side, capital goods, automobiles, food, and raw materials have remained large items and held a roughly constant share of total exports. But the composition of imports has changed. Food and raw material imports have fallen steadily. Imports of fuel increased dramatically during the 1970s but fell during the 1980s. Imports of machinery have grown and today approach 50 percent of total imports.

Net Exports and International Borrowing

The value of exports minus the value of imports is called **net exports**. In 2006, U.S. net exports were a negative $780 billion. Our imports were $780 billion more than our exports. When we import more than we export, as we did in 2006, we borrow from foreigners or sell some of our assets to them. When we export more than we import, we make loans to foreigners or buy some of their assets.

myeconlab Study Plan 16.1

The Gains from International Trade

The fundamental force that generates international trade is *comparative advantage*. And the basis of comparative advantage is divergent *opportunity costs*. You met these ideas in Chapter 2 (pp. 42–45), when we learned about the gains from specialization and exchange between Joe and Liz.

Joe and Liz each specialize in producing just one good and then trade with each other. Most nations do not go to the extreme of specializing in a single good and importing everything else. But nations can increase the consumption of all goods if they redirect their scarce resources toward the production of those goods and services in which they have a comparative advantage.

To see how this outcome occurs, we'll apply the same basic ideas that we learned in the case of Joe and Liz to trade among nations. We'll begin by recalling how we can use the production possibilities frontier to measure opportunity cost. Then we'll see how divergent opportunity costs bring comparative advantage and gains from trade for countries as well as for individuals even though no country completely specializes in the production of just one good.

Opportunity Cost in Farmland

Farmland (a fictitious country) can produce grain and cars at any point inside or along its production possibilities frontier, *PPF*, shown in Fig. 16.1. (We're holding constant the output of all the other goods that Farmland produces.) The Farmers (the people of Farmland) are consuming all the grain and cars that they produce, and they are operating at point *A* in the figure. That is, Farmland is producing and consuming 15 billion bushels of grain and 8 million cars each year. What is the opportunity cost of a car in Farmland?

We can answer that question by calculating the slope of the production possibilities frontier at point *A*. The magnitude of the slope of the frontier measures the opportunity cost of one good in terms of the other. To measure the slope of the frontier at point *A*, place a straight line tangential to the frontier at point *A* and calculate the slope of that straight line. Recall that the formula for the slope of a line is the change in the value of the variable measured on the *y*-axis divided by the change in the value of the variable

measured on the *x*-axis as we move along the line. Here, the variable measured on the *y*-axis is billions of bushels of grain, and the variable measured on the *x*-axis is millions of cars. So the slope is the change in the number of bushels of grain divided by the change in the number of cars.

As you can see from the red triangle at point *A* in Fig. 16.1, if the number of cars produced increases by 2 million, grain production decreases by 18 billion bushels. Therefore the magnitude of the slope is 18 billion divided by 2 million, which equals 9,000. To get one more car, the people of Farmland must give up 9,000 bushels of grain. So the opportunity cost of 1 car is 9,000 bushels of grain. Equivalently, 9,000 bushels of grain cost 1 car. For the people of Farmland, these opportunity costs are the prices they face. The price of a car is 9,000 bushels of grain, and the price of 9,000 bushels of grain is 1 car.

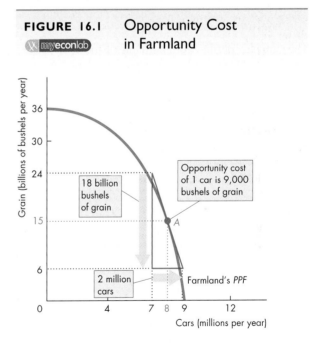

FIGURE 16.1 **Opportunity Cost in Farmland**

Farmland produces and consumes 15 billion bushels of grain and 8 million cars a year. That is, it produces and consumes at point A on its production possibilities frontier. Opportunity cost is equal to the magnitude of the slope of the *PPF*. The red triangle tells us that at point A, 18 billion bushels of grain must be forgone to get 2 million cars. That is, at point A, 2 million cars cost 18 billion bushels of grain. Equivalently, 1 car costs 9,000 bushels of grain or 9,000 bushels of grain cost 1 car.

Opportunity Cost in Mobilia

Figure 16.2 shows the production possibilities frontier of Mobilia (another fictitious country). Like the Farmers, the Mobilians consume all the grain and cars that they produce. Mobilia consumes 18 billion bushels of grain a year and 4 million cars, at point A'.

Let's calculate the opportunity costs in Mobilia. At point A', the opportunity cost of a car is equal to the magnitude of the slope of the red line tangential to Mobilia's *PPF*. You can see from the red triangle that the magnitude of the slope of Mobilia's *PPF* is 6 billion bushels of grain divided by 6 million cars, which equals 1,000 bushels of grain per car. To get one more car, the Mobilians must give up 1,000 bushels of grain. So the opportunity cost of 1 car is 1,000 bushels of grain, or equivalently, the opportunity cost of 1,000 bushels of grain is 1 car. These are the prices faced in Mobilia.

Comparative Advantage

Cars are cheaper in Mobilia than in Farmland. One car costs 9,000 bushels of grain in Farmland but only

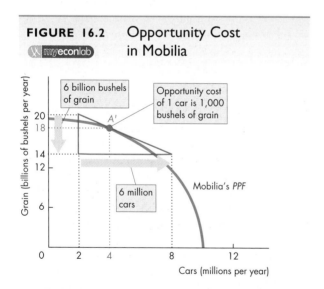

FIGURE 16.2   Opportunity Cost in Mobilia

Mobilia produces and consumes 18 billion bushels of grain and 4 million cars a year at point A' on its production possibilities frontier. Opportunity cost is equal to the magnitude of the slope of the *PPF* The red triangle tells us that at point A', 6 billion bushels of grain must be forgone to get 6 million cars. That is, at point A', 6 million cars cost 6 billion bushels of grain. Equivalently, 1 car costs 1,000 bushels of grain or 1,000 bushels of grain cost 1 car.

1,000 bushels of grain in Mobilia. But grain is cheaper in Farmland than in Mobilia—9,000 bushels of grain cost only 1 car in Farmland, while that same amount of grain costs 9 cars in Mobilia.

Mobilia has a comparative advantage in car production. Farmland has a comparative advantage in grain production. A country has a **comparative advantage** in producing a good if it can produce that good at a lower opportunity cost than any other country. Let's see how opportunity cost differences and comparative advantage generate gains from international trade.

The Gains from Trade: Cheaper to Buy Than to Produce

If Mobilia bought grain for what it costs Farmland to produce it, then Mobilia could buy 9,000 bushels of grain for 1 car. That is much lower than the cost of growing grain in Mobilia, where it costs 9 cars to produce 9,000 bushels of grain. If the Mobilians can buy grain at the low Farmland price, they will reap some gains.

If the Farmers can buy cars for what it costs Mobilia to produce them, they will be able to obtain a car for 1,000 bushels of grain. Because it costs 9,000 bushels of grain to produce a car in Farmland, the Farmers would gain from such an opportunity.

In this situation, it makes sense for Mobilians to buy their grain from Farmers and for Farmers to buy their cars from Mobilians. But at what price will Farmland and Mobilia engage in mutually beneficial international trade?

The Terms of Trade

The quantity of grain that Farmland must pay Mobilia for a car is Farmland's **terms of trade** with Mobilia. Because the United States exports and imports many different goods and services, we measure the terms of trade in the real world as an index number that averages the terms of trade over all the items we trade.

The forces of international supply and demand determine the terms of trade. Figure 16.3 illustrates these forces in the Farmland–Mobilia international car market. The quantity of cars *traded internationally* is measured on the *x*-axis. On the *y*-axis, we measure the price of a car. This price is expressed as the *terms of trade*: bushels of grain per car. If no international trade takes place, the price of a car in Farmland is 9,000

FIGURE 16.3   International Trade in Cars

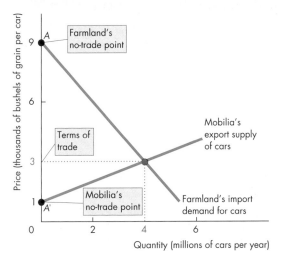

Farmland's import demand curve for cars is downward sloping, and Mobilia's export supply curve of cars is upward sloping. With no international trade, the price of a car is 9,000 bushels of grain in Farmland (point A) and 1,000 bushels of grain in Mobilia (point A').

With free international trade, the price (terms of trade) is determined where the export supply curve intersects the import demand curve: 3,000 bushels of grain per car. At that price, 4 million cars a year are imported by Farmland and exported by Mobilia. The value of grain exported by Farmland and imported by Mobilia is 12 billion bushels a year, the quantity required to pay for the cars imported.

bushels of grain, its opportunity cost, indicated by point *A*. The no-trade point *A* in Fig. 16.3 corresponds to point *A* in Fig. 16.1. The lower the price of a car in the international market (terms of trade), the greater is the quantity of cars that the Farmers are willing to import from the Mobilians. This fact is illustrated by the downward-sloping curve, which shows Farmland's import demand for cars.

Again, if no trade takes place, the price of a car in Mobilia is 1,000 bushels of grain, its opportunity cost, indicated by point *A'*. The no-trade point *A'* in Fig. 16.3 corresponds to point *A'* in Fig. 16.2. The higher the price of a car in the international market, the greater is the quantity of cars that Mobilians are willing to export to Farmers. This fact is illustrated by Mobilia's export supply of cars—the upward-sloping line in Fig. 16.3.

The international market in cars determines the equilibrium terms of trade (price) and quantity traded. This equilibrium occurs where the import demand curve intersects the export supply curve. In this case, the equilibrium terms of trade are 3,000 bushels of grain per car. Mobilia exports and Farmland imports 4 million cars a year. Notice that the terms of trade are lower than the no-trade price in Farmland but higher than the no-trade price in Mobilia.

Balanced Trade

The number of cars exported by Mobilia—4 million a year—is exactly equal to the number of cars imported by Farmland. How does Farmland pay for the cars it imports? The answer is by exporting grain. How much grain does Farmland export? You can find the answer by noticing that for 1 car, Farmland must pay 3,000 bushels of grain. So for 4 million cars, Farmland pays 12 billion bushels of grain. Farmland's exports of grain are 12 billion bushels a year, and Mobilia imports this same quantity of grain.

Mobilia exchanges 4 million cars for 12 billion bushels of grain each year, and Farmland exchanges 12 billion bushels of grain for 4 million cars. Trade is balanced. For each country, the value received from exports equals the value paid out for imports.

Changes in Production and Consumption

We've seen that international trade makes it possible for Farmers to buy cars at a lower price than what it costs them to produce a car and to sell their grain for a higher price. International trade also enables Mobilians to sell their cars for a higher price and buy grain for a lower price than it costs them to produce grain. Both countries gain. How is it possible for *both* countries to gain? What are the changes in production and consumption that accompany these gains?

An economy that does not trade with other economies has identical production and consumption possibilities. Without trade, the economy can consume only what it produces. But with international trade, an economy can consume different quantities of goods from those that it produces. The production possibilities frontier describes the limits of what a country can produce, but it does not describe the limits to what it can consume. Figure 16.4 will help you to see the distinction between production possibilities and consumption possibilities when a country trades with other countries.

FIGURE 16.4   Expanding Consumption Possibilities

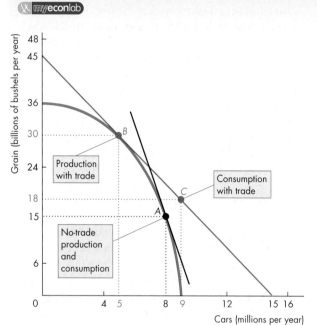

(a) Farmland

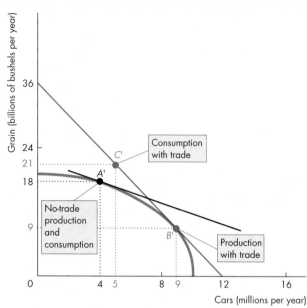

(b) Mobilia

With no international trade, the Farmers produce and consume at point *A* and the opportunity cost of a car is 9,000 bushels of grain (the slope of the black line in part a). Also, with no international trade, the Mobilians produce and consume at point *A'* and the opportunity cost of 1,000 bushels of grain is 1 car (the slope of the black line in part b).

Goods can be exchanged internationally at a price of 3,000 bushels of grain for 1 car along the red line in each part of the figure. In part (a), Farmland decreases its production of cars and increases its production of grain, moving

from *A* to *B*. Farmland exports grain and imports cars, and it consumes at point *C*. The Farmers have more of both cars and grain than they would if they produced all their own consumption goods—at point *A*.

In part (b), Mobilia increases car production and decreases grain production, moving from *A'* to *B'*. Mobilia exports cars and imports grain, and it consumes at point *C'*. The Mobilians have more of both cars and grain than they would if they produced all their own consumption goods— at point *A'*.

First, notice that Fig. 16.4 has two parts: part (a) for Farmland and part (b) for Mobilia. The production possibilities frontiers that you saw in Figs. 16.1 and 16.2 are reproduced here. The slopes of the two black lines represent the opportunity costs in the two countries when there is no international trade. Farmland produces and consumes at point *A*, and Mobilia produces and consumes at point *A'*. The opportunity cost of a car is 9,000 bushels of grain in Farmland and 1,000 bushels of grain in Mobilia.

Consumption Possibilities   The red line in each part of Fig. 16.4 shows the country's consumption possibilities with international trade. These two red lines

have the same slope, and the magnitude of that slope is the opportunity cost of a car in terms of grain on the world market: 3,000 bushels per car. The *slope* of the consumption possibilities line is common to both countries because its magnitude equals the *world* price. But the position of a country's consumption possibilities line depends on the country's production possibilities. A country cannot produce outside its production possibilities curve, so its consumption possibilities curve touches its production possibilities curve. So Farmland could choose to consume at point *B* with no international trade or, with international trade, at any point on its red consumption possibilities line.

Free Trade Equilibrium With international trade, the producers of cars in Mobilia can sell their cars for a higher price. As a result, they increase the quantity of cars they produce. At the same time, grain producers in Mobilia receive a lower price for their grain, and so they reduce the quantity of grain produced. Producers in Mobilia adjust their output by moving along their *PPF* until the opportunity cost in Mobilia equals the world price (the opportunity cost in the world market). This situation arises when Mobilia is producing at point *B'* in Fig. 16.4(b).

But the Mobilians do not consume at point *B'*. That is, they do not increase their consumption of cars and decrease their consumption of grain. Instead, they sell some of the cars they produce to Farmland in exchange for some of Farmland's grain. They trade internationally. But to see how that works out, we first need to check in with Farmland to see what's happening there.

In Farmland, producers of cars now receive a lower price and producers of grain can sell their grain for a higher price. As a consequence, producers in Farmland decrease car production and increase grain production. They adjust their outputs by moving along the *PPF* until the opportunity cost of a car in terms of grain equals the world price (the opportunity cost on the world market). They move to point *B* in part (a). But the Farmers do not consume at point *B*. Instead, they trade some of their additional grain production for the now cheaper cars from Mobilia.

The figure shows us the quantities consumed in the two countries. We saw in Fig. 16.3 that Mobilia exports 4 million cars a year and Farmland imports those cars. We also saw that Farmland exports 12 billion bushels of grain a year and Mobilia imports that grain. So Farmland's consumption of grain is 12 billion bushels a year less than it produces, and its consumption of cars is 4 million a year more than it produces. Farmland consumes at point *C* in Fig. 16.4(a).

Similarly, we know that Mobilia consumes 12 billion bushels of grain more than it produces and 4 million cars fewer than it produces. Mobilia consumes at point *C'* in Fig. 16.4(b).

Calculating the Gains from Trade

You can now literally see the gains from trade in Fig. 16.4. Without trade, Farmers produce and consume at *A* (part a)—a point on Farmland's production possibilities frontier. With international trade, Farmers consume at point *C* in part (a)—a point *outside* the production possibilities frontier. At point *C*, Farmers are consuming 3 billion bushels of grain a year and 1 million cars a year more than before. These increases in consumption of both cars and grain, beyond the limits of the production possibilities frontier, are the Farmers' gains from international trade.

Mobilians also gain. Without trade, they consume at point *A'* in part (b)—a point on Mobilia's production possibilities frontier. With international trade, they consume at point *C'*—a point *outside* their production possibilities frontier. With international trade, Mobilia consumes 3 billion bushels of grain a year and 1 million cars a year more than they would without trade. These are the gains from international trade for Mobilia.

Gains for Both Countries

Trade between the Farmers and the Mobilians does not create winners and losers. Both countries are winners. Farmers selling grain and Mobilians selling cars face an increased demand for their products because the demand by foreigners is added to domestic demand. With an increase in demand, the price rises.

Farmers buying cars and Mobilians buying grain face an increased supply of these products because the foreign supply is added to domestic supply. With an increase in supply, the price falls.

Gains from Trade in Reality

The gains from trade between Farmland and Mobilia that we have just studied occur in a model economy—in a world economy that we have imagined. But these same phenomena occur every day in the real global economy.

Comparative Advantage in the Global Economy We buy TVs and DVD players from Korea, machinery from Europe, and fashion goods from Hong Kong. In exchange, we sell machinery, grain and lumber, airplanes, computers, and financial services. All this international trade is generated by comparative advantage, just like the international trade between Farmland and Mobilia in our model economy. All international trade arises from comparative advantage, even when trade is in similar goods such as tools and machines. At first thought, it seems puzzling that countries exchange manufactured goods. Why doesn't each developed country produce all the manufactured goods its citizens want to buy?

Trade in Similar Goods Why does the United States produce automobiles for export and at the same time import large quantities of automobiles from Canada, Japan, Korea, and Western Europe? Wouldn't it make more sense to produce all the cars that we buy here in the United States? After all, we have access to the best technology available for producing cars. Autoworkers in the United States are surely as productive as their fellow workers in Canada, Western Europe, and Asia. So why does the United States have a comparative advantage in some types of cars and Asia and Europe in others?

Diversity of Taste and Economies of Scale The first part of the answer is that people have a tremendous diversity of taste. Let's stick with the example of cars. Some people prefer a sports car, some prefer a limousine, some prefer a regular, full-size car, some prefer a sport utility vehicle, and some prefer a minivan. In addition to size and type of car, there are many other dimensions in which cars vary. Some have low fuel consumption, some have high performance, some are spacious and comfortable, some have a large trunk, some have four-wheel drive, some have front-wheel drive, some have a radiator grill that looks like a Greek temple, others resemble a wedge. People's preferences across these many dimensions vary. The tremendous diversity in tastes for cars means that people value variety and are willing to pay for it in the marketplace.

The second part of the answer to the puzzle is *economies of scale*—the tendency for the average cost to be lower, the larger the scale of production. In such situations, larger and larger production runs lead to ever lower average costs. Production of many goods, including cars, involves economies of scale. For example, if a car producer makes only a few hundred (or perhaps a few thousand) cars of a particular type and design, the producer must use production techniques that are much more labor-intensive and much less automated than those employed to make hundreds of thousands of cars in a particular model. With short production runs and labor-intensive production techniques, costs are high. With very large production runs and automated assembly lines, production costs are much lower. But to obtain lower costs, the automated assembly lines have to produce a large number of cars.

It is the combination of diversity of taste and economies of scale that determines opportunity cost, produces comparative advantages, and generates such a large amount of international trade in similar commodities. With international trade, each car manufacturer has the whole world market to serve. Each producer can specialize in a limited range of products and then sell its output to the entire world market. This arrangement enables large production runs on the most popular cars and feasible production runs even on the most customized cars demanded by only a handful of people in each country.

The situation in the market for cars is also present in many other industries, especially those producing specialized equipment and parts. For example, the United States exports computer central processor chips but imports memory chips, exports mainframe computers but imports PCs, and exports specialized video equipment but imports DVD players. International trade in similar but slightly different manufactured products is profitable.

REVIEW QUIZ

1 What is the fundamental source of the gains from international trade?

2 In what circumstances can countries gain from international trade?

3 What determines the goods and services that a country will export?

4 What determines the goods and services that a country will import?

5 What is comparative advantage and what role does it play in determining the amount and type of international trade that occurs?

6 How can it be that all countries gain from international trade and that there are no losers?

7 Provide some examples of comparative advantage in today's world.

8 Why does the United States both export and import automobiles?

myeconlab Study Plan 16.2

You've now seen how free international trade brings gains for all countries. But international trade is not free in our world. We'll now take a brief look at the history and the effects of international trade restrictions. We'll see that free trade brings the greatest possible benefits and that international trade restrictions are costly.

International Trade Restrictions

Governments restrict international trade to protect domestic industries from foreign competition by using two main tools:

1. Tariffs
2. Nontariff barriers

A **tariff** is a tax that is imposed by the importing country when an imported good crosses its international boundary. A **nontariff barrier** is any action other than a tariff that restricts international trade. Examples of nontariff barriers are quantitative restrictions and licensing regulations limiting imports. First, let's look at tariffs.

The History of Tariffs

U.S. tariffs today are modest in comparison with their historical levels. Figure 16.5 shows the average tariff rate—total tariffs as a percentage of total imports. You can see in this figure that this average reached a peak of 20 percent in 1933. In that year,

three years after the passage of the Smoot-Hawley Act, one third of our imports was subject to a tariff and on those imports the tariff rate was 60 percent. The average tariff in Fig. 16.5 for 1933 is 60 percent multiplied by 1/3, which equals 20 percent. Today, the average tariff rate is less than 2 percent.

In 1947, the United States and 22 other countries signed the **General Agreement on Tariffs and Trade** (GATT). From its formation, GATT organized a series of "rounds" of negotiations that resulted in a steady process of tariff reduction. The final round, the Uruguay Round, started in 1986 and completed in 1994, led to the creation of the **World Trade Organization** (WTO).

In 2001, the WTO embarked on an ambitious program known as the *Doha Development Agenda*, which seeks to create free world trade in all goods and services, including agriculture. The major challenge of this program is to open markets for developing countries in the developed world. Limited progress has been made in this program in conferences held in Cancún in 2003, Geneva in 2004, and Hong Kong in 2005, and this program is ongoing.

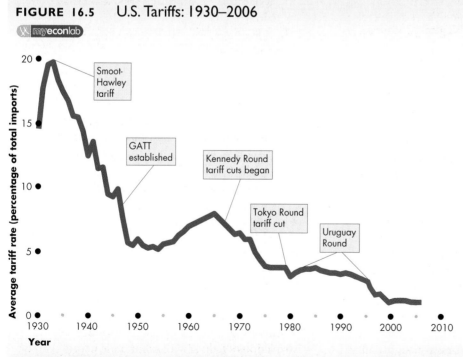

FIGURE 16.5   U.S. Tariffs: 1930–2006

The Smoot-Hawley Act, which was passed in 1930, took U.S. tariffs to a peak average rate of 20 percent in 1933. (One third of imports was subject to a tariff rate of 60 percent.) Since the establishment of GATT in 1947, tariffs have steadily declined in a series of negotiating rounds, the most significant of which are identified in the figure. Tariffs are now as low as they have ever been.

Sources of data: U.S. Bureau of the Census, *Historical Statistics of the United States, Colonial Times to 1970,* Bicentennial Edition, Part I (Washington, D.C., 1975); Series U-212: updated from *Statistical Abstract of the United States:* various editions.

In addition to the agreements under the GATT and the WTO, the United States is a party to the **North American Free Trade Agreement** (NAFTA), which became effective on January 1, 1994, and under which barriers to international trade between the United States, Canada, and Mexico will be virtually eliminated after a 15-year phasing-in period.

In other parts of the world, trade barriers have virtually been eliminated among the member countries of the European Union, which has created the largest unified tariff-free market in the world. In 1994, discussions among the Asia-Pacific Economic Cooperation (APEC) led to an agreement in principle to work toward a free-trade area that embraces China, all the economies of East Asia and the South Pacific, Chile, Peru, Mexico, and the United States and Canada. These countries include the fastest-growing economies and hold the promise of heralding a global free-trade area.

The effort to achieve freer trade underlines the fact that trade in some goods is still subject to a high tariff. Textiles and footwear are among the goods that face the highest tariffs, and rates on these items average more than 10 percent. Some individual items face a tariff much higher than the average. For example, when you buy a pair of blue jeans for $30, you pay about $7 more than you would if there were no tariffs on textiles. Other goods that are protected by tariffs are agricultural products, energy and chemicals, minerals, and metals. The meat, cheese, and sugar that you consume cost significantly more because of protection than they would with free international trade.

The temptation for governments to impose tariffs is a strong one. First, tariffs provide revenue to the government. Second, they enable the government to satisfy special interest groups in import-competing industries. But, as we'll see, free international trade brings enormous benefits that are reduced when tariffs are imposed. Let's see how.

How Tariffs Work

To see how tariffs work, let's return to the example of trade between Farmland and Mobilia. Figure 16.6 shows the international market for cars in which these two countries are the only traders. The volume of trade and the price of a car are determined at the point of intersection of Mobilia's export supply curve of cars and Farmland's import demand curve for cars.

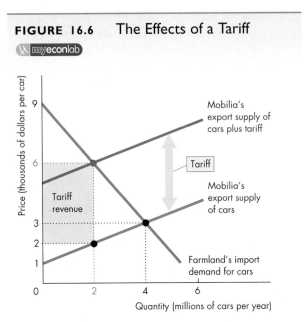

FIGURE 16.6   The Effects of a Tariff

Farmland imposes a tariff on car imports from Mobilia. The tariff increases the price that Farmers have to pay for a car and shifts the supply curve of cars in Farmland leftward. The vertical distance between the original supply curve and the new one is the amount of the tariff, $4,000 per car. The price of a car in Farmland increases, and the quantity of cars imported decreases. The government of Farmland collects a tariff revenue of $4,000 per car—a total of $8 billion on the 2 million cars imported. Farmland's exports of grain decrease because Mobilia now has a lower income from its exports of cars.

In Fig. 16.6, these two countries trade cars and grain in exactly the same way that we saw in Fig. 16.3: Mobilia exports cars, and Farmland exports grain. The volume of car imports into Farmland is 4 million a year, and the world market price of a car is 3,000 bushels of grain. Figure 16.6 expresses prices in dollars rather than in units of grain and is based on a money price of grain of $1 a bushel. With grain costing $1 a bushel, the money price of a car is $3,000.

Now suppose that the government of Farmland, perhaps under pressure from car producers, decides to impose a tariff on imported cars. In particular, suppose that a tariff of $4,000 per car is imposed. (This is a huge tariff, but the car producers of Farmland are fed up with competition from Mobilia.) What happens?

- The supply of cars in Farmland decreases.
- The price of a car in Farmland rises.
- The quantity of cars imported by Farmland decreases.
- The government of Farmland collects the tariff revenue.
- Resource use is inefficient.
- The *value* of exports changes by the same amount as the *value* of imports, and trade remains balanced.

Change in the Supply of Cars Farmland cannot import cars at Mobilia's export supply price. It must pay that price plus the $4,000 tariff. So the supply curve in Farmland shifts leftward. The new supply curve is labeled "Mobilia's export supply of cars plus tariff." The vertical distance between Mobilia's original export supply curve and the new supply curve is the tariff of $4,000 a car.

Rise in Price of a Car A new equilibrium occurs where the new supply curve intersects Farmland's import demand curve for cars. That equilibrium is at a price of $6,000 a car, up from $3,000 with free trade.

Fall in Imports Car imports fall from 4 million to 2 million cars a year. At the higher price of $6,000 a car, domestic car producers increase their production. Domestic grain production decreases as resources are moved into the expanding car industry.

Tariff Revenue Total expenditure on imported cars by the Farmers is $6,000 a car multiplied by the 2 million cars imported ($12 billion). But not all of that money goes to the Mobilians. They receive $2,000 a car, or $4 billion for the 2 million cars. The difference—$4,000 a car, or a total of $8 billion for the 2 million cars—is collected by the government of Farmland as tariff revenue.

Inefficiency The people of Farmland are willing to pay $6,000 for the marginal car imported. But the opportunity cost of that car is $2,000. So there is a gain from trading an extra car. In fact, there are gains—willingness to pay exceeds opportunity cost—all the way up to 4 million cars a year. Only when 4 million cars are being traded is the maximum price that a Farmer is willing to pay equal to the minimum price that is acceptable to a Mobilian. Restricting trade reduces the gains from trade.

Trade Remains Balanced With free trade, Farmland was paying $3,000 a car and buying 4 million cars a year from Mobilia. Farmland was paying Mobilia $12 billion a year for imported cars. With a tariff of $4,000 a car, Farmland's imports have decreased to 2 million cars a year and the price paid to Mobilia has fallen to $2,000 a car. The total amount Farmland has paid to Mobilia for imports has fallen to $4 billion a year. Doesn't this fact mean that Farmland now has a balance of trade surplus? It does not.

The price of a car in Mobilia has fallen but the price of grain remains at $1 a bushel. So the relative price of a car has fallen, and the relative price of grain has increased. With free trade, the Mobilians could buy 3,000 bushels of grain for one car. Now they can buy only 2,000 bushels for a car.

With a higher relative price of grain, the quantity demanded by the Mobilians decreases and Mobilia imports less grain. But because Mobilia imports less grain, Farmland exports less grain. In fact, Farmland's grain industry suffers from two sources. First, there is a decrease in the quantity of grain sold to Mobilia. Second, there is increased competition for resources from the now-expanded car industry. The tariff leads to a contraction in the scale of the grain industry in Farmland.

It seems paradoxical at first that a country imposing a tariff on cars hurts its own export industry, lowering its exports of grain. It might help to think of it this way: Mobilians buy grain with the money they make from exporting cars to Farmland. If they export fewer cars, they cannot afford to buy as much grain. In fact, in the absence of any international borrowing and lending, Mobilia must cut its imports of grain by exactly the same amount as the loss in revenue from its export of cars. Grain imports into Mobilia are cut back to a value of $4 billion, the amount that can be paid for by the new lower revenue from Mobilia's car exports. Trade is still balanced. The tariff cuts the value of imports and exports by the same amount. The tariff has no effect on the *balance* of trade, but it reduces the *volume* of trade.

The result that we have just derived is perhaps one of the most misunderstood aspects of international economics. On countless occasions, politicians and others call for tariffs to remove a balance of trade deficit or argue that lowering tariffs would produce a balance of trade deficit. They reach this conclusion by failing to work out all the implications of a tariff.

Let's now look at nontariff barriers.

Nontariff Barriers

The two main forms of nontariff barriers are

1. Quotas
2. Voluntary export restraints

A **quota** is a quantitative restriction on the import of a particular good, which specifies the maximum amount of the good that may be imported in a given period of time. A **voluntary export restraint** (VER) is an agreement between two governments in which the government of the exporting country agrees to restrain the volume of its own exports.

Quotas are especially prominent in textiles and agriculture. VERs have been used in U.S. trade with Japan in a wide range of products, and more recently in textile trade with China (see *Reading Between the Lines* on pp. 416–417).

How Quotas Work

Suppose that Farmland puts a quota on car imports of 2 million a year. Figure 16.7 shows the effects of this action. The quota is shown by the vertical red line at 2 million cars a year. Farmland car importers buy that quantity from Mobilia and pay $2,000 a car. But because the quantity of cars imported is restricted to 2 million cars a year, people in Farmland are willing to pay $6,000 per car. This is the price of a car in Farmland.

The value of imports falls to $4 billion (the same as in the case of the tariff). With lower incomes from car exports and with a higher relative price of grain, Mobilians cut back on their imports of grain in exactly the same way that they did under a tariff.

The key difference between a quota and a tariff lies in who collects the gap between the exporter's supply price and the domestic price. In the case of a tariff, the government of the importing country receives the gap. In the case of a quota, it goes to the importer.

How VERs Work

A VER is like a quota allocated to each exporter. The effects of a VER are similar to those of a quota but differ from them in that the gap between the domestic price and the export price is captured not by domestic importers but by the foreign exporter. The government of the exporting country has to establish procedures for allocating the restricted volume of exports among its producers.

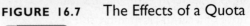

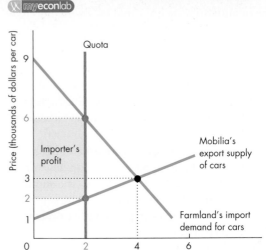

FIGURE 16.7   The Effects of a Quota

Farmland imposes a quota of 2 million cars a year on car imports from Mobilia. That quantity appears as the vertical line labeled "Quota." Because the quantity of cars imported by Farmland is restricted to 2 million, the price of a car in Farmland increases to $6,000. Importing cars is profitable because Mobilia is willing to supply cars at $2,000 each. There is competition for import quotas.

REVIEW QUIZ

1 What are the tools that a country can use to restrict international trade?
2 What do international trade restrictions do to the gains from international trade?
3 Which is best for a country: restricted trade, no trade, or free trade? Why?
4 What does a tariff on imports do to the volume of imports and the volume of exports?
5 In the absence of international borrowing and lending, how do tariffs and other international trade restrictions influence the total value of imports and exports and the balance of trade?

myeconlab Study Plan 16.3

We're now going to look at some commonly heard arguments for restricting international trade and see why they are almost never correct.

The Case Against Protection

For as long as nations and international trade have existed, people have debated whether a country is better off with free international trade or with protection from foreign competition. The debate continues, but for most economists, a verdict has been delivered and is the one you have just seen. Free trade promotes prosperity for all countries; protection is inefficient. We've seen the most powerful case for free trade in the example of how Farmland and Mobilia both benefit from their comparative advantage. But there is a broader range of issues in the free trade versus protection debate. Let's review these issues.

Three arguments for restricting international trade are

- The national security argument
- The infant-industry argument
- The dumping argument

The National Security Argument

The national security argument for protection is that a country must protect the industries that produce defense equipment and armaments and those on which the defense industries rely for their raw materials and other intermediate inputs. This argument for protection does not withstand close scrutiny.

First, it is an argument for international isolation, for in a time of war, there is no industry that does not contribute to national defense.

Second, if the case is made for boosting the output of a strategic industry, it is more efficient to achieve this outcome with a subsidy to the firms in the industry, with the subsidy financed out of taxes. Such a subsidy would keep the industry operating at the scale judged appropriate, and free international trade would keep the prices faced by consumers at their world market levels.

The Infant-Industry Argument

The so-called **infant-industry argument** for protection is that it is necessary to protect a new industry to enable it to grow into a mature industry that can compete in world markets. The argument is based on the idea of *dynamic comparative advantage*, which can arise from *learning-by-doing* (see Chapter 2).

Learning-by-doing is a powerful engine of productivity growth, and comparative advantage does evolve and change because of on-the-job experience. But these facts do not justify protection.

First, the infant-industry argument is valid only if the benefits of learning-by-doing *not only* accrue to the owners and workers of the firms in the infant industry but also *spill over* to other industries and parts of the economy. For example, there are huge productivity gains from learning-by-doing in the manufacture of aircraft. But almost all of these gains benefit the stockholders and workers of Boeing and other aircraft producers. Because the people making the decisions, bearing the risk, and doing the work are the ones who benefit, they take the dynamic gains into account when they decide on the scale of their activities. In this case, almost no benefits spill over to other parts of the economy, so there is no need for government assistance to achieve an efficient outcome.

Second, even if the case is made for protecting an infant industry, it is more efficient to do so by a subsidy to the firms in the industry, with the subsidy financed out of taxes. Such a subsidy would encourage the industry to mature and to compete with efficient world producers and keep the prices faced by consumers at their world market levels.

The Dumping Argument

Dumping occurs when a foreign firm sells its exports at a lower price than its cost of production. Dumping might be used by a firm that wants to gain a global monopoly. In this case, the foreign firm sells its output at a price below its cost to drive domestic firms out of business. When the domestic firms have gone, the foreign firm takes advantage of its monopoly position and charges a higher price for its product. Dumping is usually regarded as a justification for temporary tariffs, which are called *countervailing duties*.

But there are powerful reasons to resist the dumping argument for protection. First, it is virtually impossible to detect dumping because it is hard to determine a firm's costs. As a result, the test for dumping is whether a firm's export price is below its domestic price. But this test is a weak one because it can be rational for a firm to charge a low price in markets in which the quantity demanded is highly sensitive to price and a higher price in a market in which demand is less price-sensitive.

Second, it is hard to think of a good that is produced by a natural *global* monopoly. So even if all the domestic firms in some industry were driven out of business, it would always be possible to find many alternative foreign sources of supply and to buy the good at prices determined in competitive markets.

Third, if a good or service were a truly global natural monopoly, the best way of dealing with it would be by regulation—just as in the case of domestic monopolies. Such regulation would require international cooperation.

The three arguments for protection that we've just examined have an element of credibility. The counterarguments are in general stronger, however, so these arguments do not make the case for protection. But they are not the only arguments that you might encounter. There are many other new arguments against globalization and for protection. The most common of them are that protection

- Saves jobs
- Allows us to compete with cheap foreign labor
- Brings diversity and stability
- Penalizes lax environmental standards
- Protects national culture
- Prevents rich countries from exploiting developing countries

Saves Jobs

The argument is that when we buy shoes from Brazil or shirts from Taiwan, U.S. workers in these industries lose their jobs. With no earnings and poor prospects, these workers become a drain on welfare and spend less, causing a ripple effect of further job losses. The proposed solution is to ban imports of cheap foreign goods and protect U.S. jobs. This argument does not withstand scrutiny for three reasons.

First, free trade does cost some jobs, but it also creates other jobs. It brings about a global rationalization of labor and allocates labor resources to their highest-valued activities. International trade in textiles has cost tens of thousands of jobs in the United States as textile mills and other factories closed. But tens of thousands of jobs have been created in other countries as textile mills opened. And tens of thousands of U.S. workers got better-paying jobs than textile workers because U.S. export industries expanded and created new jobs. More jobs were created than destroyed.

Second, imports create jobs. They create jobs for retailers that sell imported goods and firms that service those goods. They also create jobs by creating incomes in the rest of the world, some of which are spent on imports of U.S.-made goods and services.

Although protection does save particular jobs, it does so at a high cost. For example, until 2005, textile jobs in the United States were protected by an international agreement called the Multifiber Arrangement. The U.S. International Trade Commission (ITC) has estimated that because of quotas, 72,000 jobs existed in textiles that would otherwise have disappeared and that the annual clothing expenditure in the United States was $15.9 billion, or $160 per family, higher than it will be with free trade. Equivalently, the ITC estimated that each textile job saved cost $221,000 a year.

Allows Us to Compete with Cheap Foreign Labor

With the removal of tariffs in U.S. trade with Mexico, people said we would hear a "giant sucking sound" as jobs rushed to Mexico (shown in the cartoon). Let's see what's wrong with this view.

The labor cost of a unit of output equals the wage rate divided by labor productivity. For example, if a U.S. autoworker earns $30 an hour and produces

"I don't know what the hell happened—one minute I'm at work in Flint, Michigan, then there's a giant sucking sound and suddenly here I am in Mexico."

© The New Yorker Collection 1993
Mick Stevens from Cartoonbank.com. All Rights Reserved.

15 units of output an hour, the average labor cost of a unit of output is $2. If a Mexican auto assembly worker earns $3 an hour and produces 1 unit of output an hour, the average labor cost of a unit of output is $3. Other things remaining the same, the higher a worker's productivity, the higher is the worker's wage rate. High-wage workers have high productivity. Low-wage workers have low productivity.

Although high-wage U.S. workers are more productive, on the average, than low-wage Mexican workers, there are differences across industries. U.S. labor is relatively more productive in some activities than in others. For example, the productivity of U.S. workers in producing movies, financial services, and customized computer chips is relatively higher than their productivity in the production of metals and some standardized machine parts. The activities in which U.S. workers are relatively more productive than their Mexican counterparts are those in which the United States has a *comparative advantage*. By engaging in free trade, increasing our production and exports of the goods and services in which we have a comparative advantage and decreasing our production and increasing our imports of the goods and services in which our trading partners have a comparative advantage, we can make ourselves and the citizens of other countries better off.

Brings Diversity and Stability

A diversified investment portfolio is less risky than one that has all the eggs in one basket. The same is true for an economy's production. A diversified economy fluctuates less than does an economy that produces only one or two goods.

But big, rich, diversified economies such as those of the United States, Japan, and Europe do not have this type of stability problem. Even a country such as Saudi Arabia that produces only one good (in this case, oil) can benefit from specializing in the activity at which it has a comparative advantage and then investing in a wide range of other countries to bring greater stability to its income and consumption.

Penalizes Lax Environmental Standards

Another argument for protection is that many poorer countries, such as Mexico, do not have the same environmental policies that we have and, because they are willing to pollute and we are not, we cannot compete with them without tariffs. So if they want free trade with the richer and "greener" countries, they must clean up their environments to our standards.

This argument for international trade restrictions is weak. First, not all poorer countries have significantly lower environmental standards than the United States has. Many poor countries and the former communist countries of Eastern Europe do have bad environmental records. But some countries enforce strict laws. Second, a poor country cannot afford to be as concerned about its environment as a rich country can. The best hope for a better environment in Mexico and in other developing countries is rapid income growth through free trade. As their incomes grow, developing countries will have the *means* to match their desires to improve their environment. Third, poor countries have a comparative advantage at doing "dirty" work, which helps rich countries to achieve higher environmental standards than they otherwise could.

Protects National Culture

The national culture argument for protection is not heard much in the United States, but it is a commonly heard argument in Canada and Europe.

The expressed fear is that free trade in books, magazines, movies, and television programs means U.S. domination and the end of local culture. So, the reasoning continues, it is necessary to protect domestic "culture" industries from free international trade to ensure the survival of a national cultural identity.

Protection of these industries is common and takes the form of nontariff barriers. For example, local content regulations on radio and television broadcasting and in magazines is often required.

The cultural identity argument for protection has no merit. Writers, publishers, and broadcasters want to limit foreign competition so that they can earn larger economic profits. There is no actual danger to national culture. In fact, many of the creators of so-called American cultural products are not Americans but the talented citizens of other countries, ensuring the survival of their national cultural identities in Hollywood! Also, if national culture is in danger, there is no surer way of helping it on its way out than by impoverishing the nation whose culture it is. And protection is an effective way of doing just that.

Prevents Rich Countries from Exploiting Developing Countries

Another argument for protection is that international trade must be restricted to prevent the people of the rich industrial world from exploiting the poorer people of the developing countries, forcing them to work for slave wages.

Child labor and near-slave labor is a serious problem that is rightly condemned. But by trading with poor countries, we increase the demand for the goods that these countries produce and, more significantly, we increase the demand for their labor. When the demand for labor in developing countries increases, the wage rate also increases. So, rather than exploiting people in developing countries, trade can improve their opportunities and increase their incomes.

We have reviewed the arguments that are commonly heard in favor of protection and the counterarguments against them. There is one counterargument to protection that is general and quite overwhelming. Protection invites retaliation and can trigger a trade war. The best example of a trade war occurred during the Great Depression of the 1930s when the Smoot-Hawley tariff was introduced in the United States. Country after country retaliated with its own tariff, and in a short period, world trade had almost disappeared. The costs to all countries were large and led to a renewed international resolve to avoid such self-defeating moves in the future. They also led to the creation of GATT and are the impetus behind NAFTA, APEC, and the European Union.

REVIEW QUIZ

1 Can we achieve national security goals, stimulate the growth of new industries, or restrain foreign monopoly by restricting international trade? If so, explain how.
2 Can we save jobs, compensate for low foreign wages, make the economy more diversified, compensate for costly environmental policies, protect national culture, or protect developing countries from being exploited by restricting international trade? If so, explain how.
3 What is the main argument against international trade restrictions?

 myeconlab Study Plan 16.4

Why Is International Trade Restricted?

Why, despite all the arguments against protection, is trade restricted? There are two key reasons:

- Tariff revenue
- Rent seeking

Tariff Revenue

Government revenue is costly to collect. In the developed countries such as the United States, a well-organized tax collection system is in place that can generate billions of dollars of income tax and sales tax revenues. This tax collection system is made possible by the fact that most economic transactions are done by firms that must keep properly audited financial records. Without such records, the revenue collection agencies (the Internal Revenue Service in the United States) would be severely hampered in the work. Even with audited financial accounts, some proportion of potential tax revenue is lost. Nonetheless, for the industrialized countries, the income tax and sales taxes are the major sources of revenue and the tariff plays a very small role.

But governments in developing countries have a difficult time collecting taxes from their citizens. Much economic activity takes place in an informal economy with few financial records, so only a small amount of revenue is collected from income taxes and sales taxes. The one area in which economic transactions are well recorded and audited is in international trade. So this activity is an attractive base for tax collection in these countries and is used much more extensively than it is in the developed countries.

Rent Seeking

Rent seeking is the major reason why international trade is restricted. **Rent seeking** is lobbying and other political activity that seek to capture the gains from trade. Free trade increases consumption possibilities *on the average*, but not everyone shares in the gain and some people even lose. Free trade brings benefits to some and imposes costs on others, with total benefits exceeding total costs. It is the uneven distribution of costs and benefits that is the principal source of impediment to achieving more liberal international trade.

Returning to our example of trade in cars and grain between Farmland and Mobilia, the benefits to Farmland from free trade accrue to all the producers of grain and to those producers of cars who do not bear the costs of adjusting to a smaller car industry. These costs are transition costs, not permanent costs. The costs of Farmland's move to free trade are borne by the car producers and their employees who have to become grain producers. In Mobilia, the benefits from free trade accrue to car producers and those grain producers who do not bear the transition costs to a small grain industry. The losers are the grain producers and their employees who have to produce cars.

The number of people who gain, in general, is large compared with the number who lose. So the gain per person is small but the loss per person to those who bear the loss is large. Because the loss that falls on those who bear it is large, it will pay those people to incur considerable expense to lobby against free trade. On the other hand, it will not pay those who gain to organize to achieve free trade. The gain from trade for any one person is too small for that person to spend much time or money on a political organization to achieve free trade. The loss from free trade will be seen as being so great by those bearing that loss that they *will* find it profitable to join a political organization to prevent free trade. Each group is optimizing—weighing benefits against costs and choosing the best action for themselves. The anti-free-trade group will, however, undertake a larger quantity of political lobbying than the pro-free-trade group.

Compensating Losers

If, in total, the gains from free international trade exceed the losses, why don't those who gain compensate those who lose so that everyone is in favor of free trade? To some degree, such compensation does take place. When Congress approved the NAFTA deal with Canada and Mexico, it set up a $56 million fund to support and retrain workers who lost their jobs as a result of the new trade agreement. During the first six months of the operation of NAFTA, only 5,000 workers applied for benefits under this scheme.

The losers from freer international trade are also compensated indirectly through the normal unemployment compensation arrangements. But only limited attempts are made to compensate those who lose. The main reason why full compensation is not attempted is that the costs of identifying all the losers and estimating the value of their losses would be

enormous. Also, it would never be clear whether a person who has fallen on hard times is suffering because of free trade or for other reasons that might be largely under his or her control. Furthermore, some people who look like losers at one point in time might, in fact, end up gaining. The young auto-worker who loses his job in Michigan and becomes a computer assembly worker in Minneapolis resents the loss of work and the need to move. But a year or two later, looking back on events, he counts himself fortunate. He has made a move that has increased his income and given him greater job security.

It is because we do not, in general, compensate the losers from free international trade that protectionism is such a popular and permanent feature of our national economic and political life.

REVIEW QUIZ

1 What are the two main reasons for imposing tariffs on imports?
2 What type of country benefits most from the revenue from tariffs? Provide some examples of such countries.
3 Does the United States need to use tariffs to raise revenue for the government? Explain why or why not.
4 If international trade restrictions are costly, why do we use them? Why don't the people who gain from trade organize a political force that is strong enough to ensure that their interests are protected?

myeconlab Study Plan 16.5

You've seen why all nations gain from specialization and trade. By producing goods in which we have a comparative advantage and trading some of our production for that of others, we expand our consumption possibilities. Placing restriction on that trade reduces our gains from international trade. By opening our country up to free trade, the market for the things that we sell expands and their relative price rises. The market for the things that we buy also expands, and their relative price falls.

Reading Between the Lines on pp. 416–417 looks at the globalization of production and the gains to Americans and Asians as production in China and trade between China and the United States expand.

The Gains from Globalization

http://www.nytimes.com

China and U.S. Expected to Reach Deal on Textiles

November 7, 2005

An agreement to limit for three years the surging growth of Chinese textile imports to the United States is expected to be completed as early as this week, Bush administration officials said yesterday.

. . . Worries that trade frictions could disrupt textile shipments from China have made some American retailers reluctant to place large orders. The deal is reportedly similar to an agreement reached last summer to limit Chinese clothing exports to the European Union, which followed disruption of supplies to retailers.

. . . China bought $278 million of American textile products in 2004, while selling 52 times that much, or $14.6 billion, to the United States, according to the United States trade representative's office. In 2002, the United States had 651,000 jobs in textile mills and apparel-making, less than half the number in 1990, data from the Census Bureau show.

. . . Overall Chinese textile exports to the United States surged 54 percent in the first eight months of this year, to $17.7 billion, the Chinese government reported last month. American officials put the figure at 46 percent.

. . . North Carolina had 350,000 textile jobs in 1972, but more than 90 percent of them will be gone by the end of this decade, Mark Vitner, a senior economist at Wachovia Bank in Charlotte, said yesterday. He said production had not declined as sharply because Chinese imports encouraged the state's companies to make investments in automated machinery, which cut payrolls.

China sold 700 million pairs of socks to the United States in the first eight months of this year, up from fewer than 12 million four years ago, and sales of jeans, underwear and other labor-intensive items are up as much as tenfold this year compared with 2004.

Essence of the Story

▶ China is expected to agree to limit textile exports to the United States.

▶ In 2004, for every $1 that China spent on U.S.-produced textiles, the United States spent $52 on textiles produced in China.

▶ Employment in textiles production in the United States has fallen, and it has done so especially strongly in North Carolina.

▶ Chinese textile exports to the United States grew by 54 percent in the first eight months of 2005.

▶ China sold 700 million pairs of socks to the United States in the first eight months of 2005, up from fewer than 12 million four years earlier.

▶ Sales of jeans and underwear were up tenfold in 2005 over 2004.

▶ With free trade, goods are produced where their opportunity cost of production is lowest.

▶ Clothing can be produced at a lower opportunity cost in China than in the United States.

▶ By specializing in items at which we have a comparative advantage and buying our clothes from China, we gain and China gains.

▶ We gain because our clothes cost less; China gains because it can sell clothing to us for a higher price than its cost of production.

▶ We also gain because we sell China items such as large passenger jets for more than our cost of production, and China gains because it can buy items like passenger jets for a lower price that its cost of producing them.

▶ Table 1 contains some illustrative numbers, and Fig. 1 shows these numbers graphically.

▶ The United States can produce Nike outfits or other goods and services. The opportunity cost in the United States of 1 unit of Nike outfits is 1 unit of other goods and services.

▶ China can also produce Nike outfits or other goods and services. The opportunity cost in China of 1 unit of Nike outfits is

0.5 unit of other goods and services.

▶ But if China produces Nike outfits and the United States produces other goods and services, the two countries can expand their consumption possibilities.

▶ In Fig. 2, China produces 40 units of Nike outfits and the United States produces 100 units of other goods and services.

▶ If the two countries trade 1 unit of Nike outfits for 0.75 unit of other goods and services, the United States gets Nike outfits for less than its opportunity cost of producing them and China sells the outfits for more than its opportunity cost of producing them.

▶ Table 1 shows the trading possibilities, and each country can trade along its trade line in Fig. 2.

▶ The United States buys goods from China, but China also buys goods from the United States.

You're the Voter

▶ Do you think that U.S. trade with China and other low-income Asian countries should be free?

▶ Would you vote for measures to keep the jobs that produce clothing in the United States? Explain why or why not.

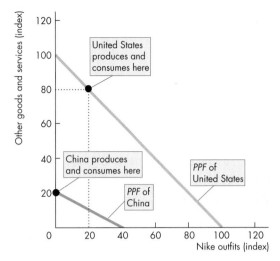

Figure 1 No trade

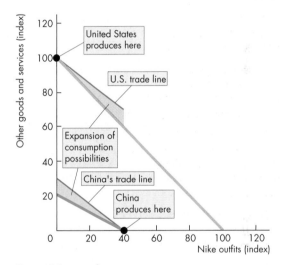

Figure 2 Free trade

	Other goods and services			
	Production possibilities		Trading possibilities	
Nike outfits	United States	China	United States	China
0	100	20	100	30
20	80	10	85	15
40	60	0	70	0
100	0			

Table 1 Production possibilities and trading possibilities for China and the United States

417

SUMMARY

Key Points

Patterns and Trends in International Trade (p. 400)

- Large flows of trade take place between countries, most of which is in manufactured goods exchanged among rich industrialized countries.
- Since 1960, the U.S. international trade has almost tripled.

The Gains from International Trade (pp. 401–406)

- Comparative advantage is the fundamental source of the gains from trade.
- Comparative advantage exists when opportunity costs between countries diverge.
- By increasing its production of goods and services in which it has a comparative advantage and then trading some of the increased output, a country can consume at points outside its production possibilities frontier.
- In the absence of international borrowing and lending, trade is balanced as prices adjust to reflect the international supply of and demand for goods and services.
- The world price balances the production and consumption plans of the trading parties. At the equilibrium price, trade is balanced.
- Comparative advantage explains the international trade that takes place in the world.
- But trade in similar goods arises from economies of scale in the face of diversified tastes.

International Trade Restrictions (pp. 407–410)

- Countries restrict international trade by imposing tariffs, quotas, and voluntary export restraints.
- International trade restrictions raise the domestic price of imported goods, lower the volume of imports, and reduce the total value of imports.
- International trade restrictions also reduce the total value of exports by the same amount as the reduction in the value of imports.

The Case Against Protection (pp. 411–414)

- Arguments that protection is necessary for national security, to protect infant industries, and to prevent dumping are weak.
- Arguments that protection saves jobs, allows us to compete with cheap foreign labor, makes the economy diversified and stable, penalizes lax environmental standards, protects national culture, and prevents rich countries from exploiting developing countries are fatally flawed.

Why Is International Trade Restricted? (pp. 414–415)

- Trade is restricted because tariffs raise government revenue and because protection brings a small loss to a large number of people and a large gain per person to a small number of people.

Key Figures

Key Terms

PROBLEMS

1. The table provides information about Virtual Reality's production possibilities.

TV sets (per day)		Computers (per day)
0	and	36
10	and	35
20	and	33
30	and	30
40	and	26
50	and	21
60	and	15
70	and	8
80	and	0

a. Calculate Virtual Reality's opportunity cost of a TV set when it produces 10 sets a day.

b. Calculate Virtual Reality's opportunity cost of a TV set when it produces 40 sets a day.

c. Calculate Virtual Reality's opportunity cost of a TV set when it produces 70 sets a day.

d. Using the answers to parts (a), (b), and (c), sketch the relationship between the opportunity cost of a TV set and the quantity of TV sets produced in Virtual Reality.

2. The table provides information about Vital Sign's production possibilities.

TV sets (per day)		Computers (per day)
0	and	18.0
10	and	17.5
20	and	16.5
30	and	15.0
40	and	13.0
50	and	10.5
60	and	7.5
70	and	4.0
80	and	0

a. Calculate Vital Sign's opportunity cost of a TV set when it produces 10 sets a day.

b. Calculate Vital Sign's opportunity cost of a TV set when it produces 40 sets a day.

c. Calculate Vital Sign's opportunity cost of a TV set when it produces 70 sets a day.

d. Using the answers to parts (a), (b), and (c), sketch the relationship between the opportunity cost of a TV set and the quantity of TV sets produced in Vital Sign.

3. Suppose that with no international trade, Virtual Reality in problem 1 produces and consumes 10 TV sets a day and Vital Signs in problem 2 produces and consumes 60 TV sets a day. Now suppose that the two countries begin to trade.

a. Which country exports TV sets?

b. What adjustments are made to the amount of each good produced by each country?

c. What adjustments are made to the amount of each good consumed by each country?

d. What can you say about the terms of trade (the price of a TV set expressed as computers per TV set) under free trade?

4. Suppose that with no international trade, Virtual Reality in problem 1 produces and consumes 50 TV sets a day and Vital Sign in problem 2 produces and consumes 20 TV sets a day. Now suppose that the two countries begin to trade.

a. Which country exports TV sets?

b. What adjustments are made to the amount of each good produced by each country?

c. What adjustments are made to the amount of each good consumed by each country?

d. What can you say about the terms of trade (the price of a TV set expressed as computers per TV set) under free trade?

5. Compare the total quantities of each good produced in problems 1 and 2 with the total quantities of each good produced in problems 3 and 4.

a. Does free trade increase or decrease the total quantities of TV sets and computers produced in both cases? Why?

b. What happens to the price of a TV set in Virtual Reality in the two cases? Why does it rise in one case and fall in the other?

c. What happens to the price of a computer in Vital Sign in the two cases? Why does it rise in one case and fall in the other?

6. Compare the international trade in problem 3 with that in problem 4.

a. Why does Virtual Reality export TV sets in one of the cases and import them in the other case?

b. Do the TV producers or the computer producers gain in each case?

c. Do consumers gain in each case?

*Solutions to odd-numbered problems are provided.

7. The figure depicts the world market for soybeans.

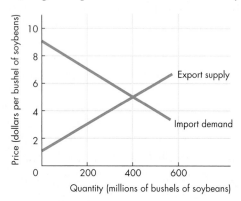

a. With no trade, what are the prices of soybeans in the two countries?
b. With free trade, what is the price of soybeans?
c. What quantity of soybeans is traded?

8. If the importer of soybeans in problem 7 imposes
   a. A tariff of $2 per bushel, what is the price of soybeans in the importing country and the tariff revenue?
   b. A quota of 300 million bushels, who gains from the quota?

CRITICAL THINKING

1. Study *Reading Between the Lines* on pp. 416–417 and then answer the following questions.
   a. What changes are occurring in the global market for clothing?
   b. Why is China going to become the biggest producer of clothing?
   c. Do you think that Americans should be concerned about who makes their clothes?
   d. Will the United States run out of activities at which it has a comparative advantage? Explain your answer.

2. **Trading Up**
   . . . the cost of protecting jobs in uncompetitive sectors through tariffs is foolishly high, . . .
   The Federal Reserve Bank of Dallas reported in 2002 that saving a job in the sugar industry cost American consumers $826,000 in higher prices a year, saving a dairy industry job cost $685,000 per year and saving a job in the manufacturing of women's handbags cost $263,000.
   The New York Times, June 26, 2006

   a. What are the arguments for saving the jobs mentioned in this news article?
   b. Explain why these arguments are faulty.
   c. Is there any merit to saving these jobs?

3. **Vows of New Aid to the Poor Leave the Poor Unimpressed**
   . . . the United States, the European Union and Japan [plan] to eliminate duties and quotas on almost all goods from up to 50 of the world's poor nations, . . . The proposal for duty-free, quota-free treatment is so divisive among developing countries that even some negotiators . . . are saying that the plan must be broadened. . . .
   The New York Times, December 15, 2005

   a. Why do the United States, the European Union, and Japan want to eliminate trade barriers on imports from only the poorest countries?
   b. Who will win from the elimination of these trade barriers? Who will lose?
   c. Why is the plan divisive among developing countries?

WEB APPLICATIONS

myeconlab   Links to Web sites

1. Study the *Reading Between the Lines* on steel dumping, then answer the following questions:
   a. What is the argument for limiting steel imports?
   b. Evaluate the argument. Is it correct or incorrect in your opinion? Why?
   c. Would you vote to eliminate steel imports? Why or why not?
   d. Would you vote differently if you lived in another steel-producing country? Why or why not?

2. Visit the Public Citizen Global Trade Watch, the Department of Commerce, and the government of Canada. Review the three assessments of NAFTA and then answer the following questions:
   a. What is the assessment of the Public Citizen Global Trade Watch?
   b. What are the assessments of the Department of Commerce and the government of Canada?
   c. Which view do you think is correct? Why?
   d. Would you vote to maintain NAFTA? Why or why not?

It's a Small World

The scale of international trade, borrowing, and lending, both in absolute dollar terms and as a percentage of total world production, expands every year. One country, Singapore, imports and exports goods and services in a volume that exceeds its gross domestic product. The world's largest nation, China, returned to the international economic stage during the 1980s and is now a major producer of manufactured goods.

International economic activity is large because today's economic world is small and because communication is so incredibly fast. But today's world is not a new world. From the beginning of recorded history, people have traded over large and steadily increasing distances. The great Western civilizations of Greece and Rome traded not only around the Mediterranean but also into the Gulf of Arabia. The great Eastern civilizations traded around the Indian Ocean. By the Middle Ages, the East and the West were routinely trading overland on routes pioneered by Venetian traders and explorers such as Marco Polo. When, in 1497, Vasco da Gama opened a sea route between the Atlantic and Indian Oceans around Africa, a new trade between East and West began, which brought tumbling prices of Eastern goods in Western markets.

The European discovery of the Americas and the subsequent opening up of Atlantic trade continued the process of steady globalization. So the developments of the 1990s, amazing though many of them are, represent a continuation of an ongoing expansion of human horizons.

Chapter 16 described and explained international trade in goods and services. In this chapter, you came face to face with one of the biggest policy issues of all ages: free trade versus protection and the globalization debate. The chapter explained how all nations can benefit from free international trade.

As you reflect on Chapter 16, remember Chapter 10, which explained the fundamentals of international borrowing and lending and the exchange rate. Recall how it explained the poorly understood fact that the size of a nation's international deficit depends not on how efficient it is, but on how much its citizens save relative to how much they invest. Nations with low saving rates, everything else being the same, have international deficits.

The global economy is big news these days. And it has always attracted attention. On the next pages, you can meet the economist who first understood comparative advantage: David Ricardo. And you can meet one of today's leading international economists: Jagdish Bhagwati of Columbia University.

Gains from International Trade

The Economist

David Ricardo *(1772–1832) was a highly successful 27-year-old stockbroker when he stumbled on a copy of Adam Smith's* Wealth of Nations *(see p. 54) on a weekend visit to the country. He was immediately hooked and went on to become the most celebrated economist of his age and one of the all-time great economists. One of his many contributions was to develop the principle of comparative advantage, the foundation on which the modern theory of international trade is built. The example he used to illustrate this principle was the trade between England and Portugal in cloth and wine.*

The General Agreement on Tariffs and Trade was established as a reaction against the devastation wrought by beggar-my-neighbor tariffs imposed during the 1930s. But it is also a triumph for the logic first worked out by Smith and Ricardo.

The Issues

Until the mid-eighteenth century, it was generally believed that the purpose of international trade was to keep exports greater than imports and pile up gold. If gold was accumulated, it was believed, the nation would prosper; if gold was lost through an international deficit, the nation would be drained of money and impoverished. These beliefs are called *mercantilism,* and the *mercantilists* were pamphleteers who advocated with missionary fervor the pursuit of an international surplus. If exports did not exceed imports, the mercantilists wanted imports restricted.

In the 1740s, David Hume explained that as the quantity of money (gold) changes, so also does the price level, and the nation's *real* wealth is unaffected. In the 1770s, Adam Smith argued that import restrictions would lower the gains from specialization and make a nation poorer. Thirty years later, David Ricardo proved the law of comparative advantage and demonstrated the superiority of free trade. Mercantilism was intellectually bankrupt but remained politically powerful.

Gradually, through the nineteenth century, the mercantilist influence waned and North America and Western Europe prospered in an environment of increasingly free international trade. But despite remarkable advances in economic understanding, mercantilism never quite died. It had a brief and devastating revival in the 1920s and 1930s when tariff hikes brought about the collapse of international trade and accentuated the Great Depression. It subsided again after World War II with the establishment of the General Agreement on Tariffs and Trade (GATT).

But mercantilism lingers on. The often expressed view that the United States should restrict Chinese imports and reduce its deficit with China and fears that NAFTA will bring economic ruin to the United States are modern manifestations of mercantilism. It would be interesting to have David Hume, Adam Smith, and David Ricardo commenting on these views. But we know what they would say: the same things that they said to the eighteenth century mercantilists. And they would still be right today.

Then

In the eighteenth century, when mercantilists and economists were debating the pros and cons of free international exchange, the transportation technology that was available limited the gains from international trade. Sailing ships with tiny cargo holds took close to a month to cross the Atlantic Ocean. But the potential gains were large, and so was the incentive to cut shipping costs. By the 1850s, the clipper ship had been developed, cutting the journey from Boston to Liverpool to only 12 days. Half a century later, 10,000-ton steamships were sailing between America and England in just 4 days. As sailing times and costs declined, the gains from international trade increased and the volume of trade expanded.

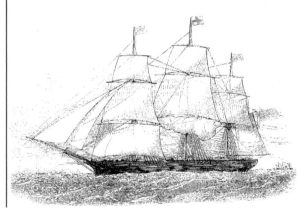

Now

The container ship has revolutionized international trade and contributed to its continued expansion. Today, most goods cross the oceans in containers—metal boxes—packed into and piled on top of ships like this one. Container technology has cut the cost of ocean shipping by economizing on handling and by making cargoes harder to steal, lowering insurance costs. It is unlikely that there would be much international trade in goods such as television sets and VCRs without this technology. High-value and perishable cargoes such as flowers and fresh foods, as well as urgent courier packages, travel by air. Every day, dozens of cargo-laden 747s fly between every major U.S. city and to destinations across the Atlantic and Pacific Oceans.

Jagdish Bhagwati, whom you can meet on the following pages, is one of the most distinguished international economists. He has contributed to our understanding of the effects of international trade and trade policy on economic growth and development and has played a significant role in helping to shape today's global trading arrangements.

Jagdish Bhagwati

Jagdish Bhagwati is University Professor at Columbia University. Born in India in 1934, he studied at Cambridge University in England, MIT, and Oxford University before returning to India. He returned to teach at MIT in 1968 and moved to Columbia in 1980. A prolific scholar, Professor Bhagwati also writes in leading newspapers and magazines throughout the world. He has been much honored for both his scientific work and his impact on public policy. His greatest contributions are in international trade but extend also to developmental problems and the study of political economy.

Michael Parkin talked with Jagdish Bhagwati about his work and the progress that economists have made in understanding the benefits of international economic integration since the pioneering work of Ricardo.

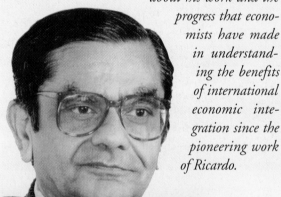

Professor Bhagwati, what attracted you to economics?
When you come from India, where poverty hits the eye, it is easy to be attracted to economics, which can be used to bring prosperity and create jobs to pull up the poor into gainful employment.

I learned later that there are two broad types of economist: those who treat the subject as an arid mathematical toy and those who see it as a serious social science.

If Cambridge, where I went as an undergraduate, had been interested in esoteric mathematical economics, I would have opted for something else. But the Cambridge economists from whom I learned— many among the greatest figures in the discipline— saw economics as a social science. I therefore saw the power of economics as a tool to address India's poverty and was immediately hooked.

Who had the greatest impact on you at Cambridge?
Most of all, it was Harry Johnson, a young Canadian of immense energy and profound analytical gifts. Quite unlike the shy and reserved British dons, Johnson was friendly, effusive, and supportive of students who flocked around him. He would later move to Chicago, where he became one of the most influential members of the market-oriented Chicago school. Another was Joan Robinson, arguably the world's most impressive female economist.

When I left Cambridge for MIT, going from one Cambridge to the other, I was lucky to transition from one phenomenal set of economists to another. At MIT, I learned much from future Nobel laureates Paul Samuelson and Robert Solow. Both would later become great friends and colleagues when I joined the MIT faculty in 1968.

After Cambridge and MIT, you went to Oxford and then back to India. What did you do in India?
I joined the Planning Commission in New Delhi, where my first big job was to find ways of raising the bottom 30 percent of India's population out of poverty to a "minimum income" level.

And what did you prescribe?
My main prescription was to "grow the pie." My research suggested that the share of the bottom 30 percent of the pie did not seem to vary dramatically

Above full-employment equilibrium A macroeconomic equilibrium in which real GDP exceeds potential GDP. (p. 274)

Absolute advantage A person has an absolute advantage if that person is more productive than another person. (p. 42)

Aggregate demand The relationship between the quantity of real GDP demanded and the price level. (p. 269)

Aggregate hours The total number of hours worked by all the people employed, both full time and part time, during a year. (p. 135)

Aggregate planned expenditure The sum of planned consumption expenditure, planned investment, planned government expenditure on goods and services, and planned exports minus planned imports. (p. 286)

Allocative efficiency A situation in which we cannot produce more of any good without giving up some of another good that we value more highly. (p. 39)

Automatic fiscal policy A fiscal policy action that is triggered by the state of the economy. (p. 359)

Automatic stabilizers Mechanisms that stabilize real GDP without explicit action by the government. (p. 361)

Autonomous expenditure The sum of those components of aggregate planned expenditure that are not influenced by real GDP. Autonomous expenditure equals the sum of investment, government expenditure, exports, and the autonomous parts of consumption expenditure and imports. (p. 293)

Autonomous tax multiplier The magnification effect of a change in taxes on aggregate demand. (p. 359)

Balanced budget A government budget in which tax revenues and outlays are equal. (p. 346)

Balanced budget multiplier The magnification effect on aggregate demand of a simultaneous change in government expenditure and taxes that leaves the budget balanced. (p. 359)

Balance of payments accounts A country's record of international trading, borrowing, and lending. (p. 244)

Barter The direct exchange of one good or service for other goods and services. (p. 206)

Below full-employment equilibrium A macroeconomic equilibrium in which potential GDP exceeds real GDP. (p. 274)

Big tradeoff The conflict between equality and efficiency. (p. 10)

Budget deficit A government's budget balance that is negative—outlays exceed tax revenues. (p. 346)

Budget surplus A government's budget balance that is positive—tax revenues exceed outlays. (p. 346)

Business cycle The periodic but irregular up-and-down movement in production. (p. 92)

Capital The tools, equipment, buildings, and other constructions that businesses use to produce goods and services. (p. 4)

Capital account A record of foreign investment in a country minus its investment abroad. (p. 244)

Capital accumulation The growth of capital resources, including human capital. (p. 40)

Capital stock The total quantity of plant, equipment, buildings, and business inventories. (p. 169)

Central bank A bank's bank and a public authority that regulates the nation's depository institutions and controls the quantity of money. (p. 212)

Ceteris paribus Other things being equal—all other relevant things remaining the same. (p. 13)

Chain-weighted output index An index that uses the prices of two adjacent years to calculate the real GDP growth rate. (p. 120)

Change in demand A change in buyers' plans that occurs when some influence on those plans other than the price of the good changes. It is illustrated by a shift of the demand curve. (p. 62)

Change in supply A change in sellers' plans that occurs when some influence on those plans other than the price of the good changes. It is illustrated by a shift of the supply curve. (p. 67)

Change in the quantity demanded A change in buyers' plans that occurs when the price of a good changes but all other influences on buyers' plans remain unchanged. It is illustrated by a movement along the demand curve. (p. 65)

Change in the quantity supplied A change in sellers' plans that occurs when the price of a good changes but all other influences on sellers' plans remain unchanged. It is illustrated by a movement along the supply curve. (p. 68)

Classical A macroeconomist who believes that the economy is self-regulating and that it is always at full employment. (p. 278)

Classical dichotomy At full employment, the forces that determine the real variables are independent of those that determine the nominal variables. (p. 158)

Classical growth theory A theory of economic growth based on the view that the growth of real GDP per person is temporary and that when it rises above subsistence level, a population explosion eventually brings it back to subsistence level. (p. 195)

Classical model A model of the economy that determines the real variables—real GDP, employment and unemployment, the real wage rate, consumption, saving, investment, and the real interest rate—at full employment. (p. 158)

Comparative advantage A person or country has a comparative advantage in an activity if that person or country can perform the activity at a lower opportunity cost than anyone else or any other country. (pp. 42, 402)

Competitive market A market that has many buyers and many sellers, so no single buyer or seller can influence the price. (p. 60)

Complement A good that is used in conjunction with another good. (p. 63)

Consumer Price Index (CPI) An index that measures the average of the prices paid by urban consumers for a fixed "basket" of the consumer goods and services. (p. 142)

Consumption expenditure The total payment for consumer goods and services. (p. 113)

Consumption function The relationship between consumption expenditure and disposable income, other things remaining the same. (p. 287)

Core inflation rate A measure of inflation based on the core CPI—the CPI excluding food and fuel. (p. 371)

Cost-push inflation An inflation that results from an initial increase in costs. (p. 320)

Council of Economic Advisers The President's council whose main work is to monitor the economy and keep the President and the public well informed about the current state of the economy and the best available forecasts of where it is heading. (p. 345)

Crawling peg A policy regime is one that selects a target path for the exchange rate with intervention in the foreign exchange market to achieve that path. (p. 250)

Creditor nation A country that during its entire history has invested more in the rest of the world than other countries have invested in it. (p. 246)

Cross-section graph A graph that shows the values of an economic variable for different groups or categories at a point in time. (p. 18)

Crowding-out effect The tendency for a government budget deficit to decrease investment. (p. 355)

Currency The notes and coins held by individuals and businesses. (p. 207)

Currency drain ratio The ratio of currency to deposits. (p. 216)

Current account A record of receipts from exports of goods and services, payments for imports of goods and services, net income and net transfers received from the rest of the world. (pp. 103, 244)

Cyclical surplus or deficit The actual surplus or deficit minus the structural surplus or deficit. (p. 362)

Cyclical unemployment The fluctuating unemployment over the business cycle. (p. 140)

Debtor nation A country that during its entire history has borrowed more in the rest of the world than other countries have lent in it. (p. 246)

Deflation A negative inflation rate—a process in which the price level is falling. (p. 99)

Demand The entire relationship between the price of the good the quantity demanded of it when all other influences on buyers' plans remain the same. It is illustrated by a demand curve and described by a demand schedule. (p. 61)

Demand curve A curve that shows the relationship between the quantity demanded of a good and its price when all other influences on consumers' planned purchases remain the same. (p. 62)

Demand for labor The relationship between the quantity of labor demanded and the real wage rate when all other influences on firms' hiring plans remain the same. (p. 160)

Demand for loanable funds The relationship between the quantity of loanable funds demanded and the real interest rate when all other influences on borrowing plans remain the same. (p. 169)

Demand for money The relationship between the quantity of money demanded and the nominal interest rate when all other influences on the amount of money that people wish to hold remain the same. (p. 221)

Demand-pull inflation An inflation that results from an initial increase in aggregate demand. (p. 318)

Depository institution A firm that takes deposits from households and firms and makes loans to other households and firms. (p. 209)

Depreciation The decrease in the capital stock that results from wear and tear and obsolescence. (p. 115)

Desired reserve ratio The ratio of reserves to deposits that banks want to hold. (p. 216)

Direct relationship A relationship between two variables that move in the same direction. (p. 20)

Discount rate The interest rate at which the Fed stands ready to lend reserves to depository institutions. (p. 213)

Discouraged workers People who are available and willing to work but have not made specific efforts to find a job within the previous four weeks. (p. 133)

Discretionary fiscal policy A fiscal action that is initiated by an act of Congress. (p. 359)

Disposable income Aggregate income minus taxes plus transfer payments. (pp. 271, 286)

Dumping The sale by a foreign firm of exports at a lower price than the cost of production. (p. 411)

Dynamic comparative advantage A comparative advantage that a person or country possesses as a result of having specialized in a particular activity and then, as a result of learning-by-doing, having become the producer with the lowest opportunity cost. (p. 45)

Economic growth The expansion of production possibilities that results from capital accumulation and technological change. (pp. 40, 91)

Economic growth rate The annual percentage change in real GDP. (p. 182)

Economic model A description of some aspect of the economic world that includes only those features of the world that are needed for the purpose at hand. (p. 12)

Economics The social science that studies the choices that we make as we cope with scarcity and the incentives that influence and reconcile those choices. (p. 2)

Economic theory A generalization that summarizes what we think we understand about the economic choices that people make and the performance of industries and entire economies. (p. 12)

Economic welfare A comprehensive measure of the general state of economic well-being. (p. 122)

Efficiency wage A real wage rate that is set above the equilibrium wage rate and that balances the costs and benefits of this higher wage rate to maximize the firm's profit. (p. 168)

Employment Act of 1946 A landmark Congressional act that recognizes a role for government actions to keep unemployment low, the economy expanding, and inflation in check. (p. 344)

Employment-to-population ratio The percentage of people of working age who have jobs. (p. 134)

Entrepreneurship The human resource that organizes the other three factors of production: labor, land, and capital. (p. 4)

Equilibrium expenditure The level of aggregate expenditure that occurs when aggregate planned expenditure equals real GDP. (p. 294)

Equilibrium price The price at which the quantity demanded equals the quantity supplied. (p. 70)

Equilibrium quantity The quantity bought and sold at the equilibrium price. (p. 70)

Excess reserves A bank's actual reserves minus its desired reserves. (p. 216)

Exchange rate The value of the U.S. dollar in terms of other currencies in the foreign exchange market. (pp. 101, 232)

Expansion A business cycle phase between a trough and a peak—a period in which real GDP increases. (p. 92)

Exports The goods and services that we sell to people in other countries. (pp. 114, 400)

Factors of production The resources used to produce goods and services. (p. 3)

Federal budget The annual statement of the outlays and tax revenues of the government of the United States, together with the laws and regulations that approve and support those outlays and taxes. (p. 344)

Federal funds rate The interest rate that the banks charge each other on overnight loans. (pp. 212, 372)

Federal Open Market Committee The main policy-making organ of the Federal Reserve System. (p. 212)

Federal Reserve System (the Fed) The central bank of the United States. (p. 212)

Final good An item that is bought by its final user during the specified time period. (p. 112)

Firm An economic unit that hires factors of production and organizes those factors to produce and sell goods and services. (p. 45)

Fiscal imbalance The present value of the government's commitments to pay benefits minus the present value of its tax revenues. (p. 357)

Fiscal policy The government's attempt to achieve macroeconomic objectives such as full employment, sustained long-term economic growth, and price level stability by setting and changing tax rates, making transfer payments, and purchasing goods and services. (pp. 105, 271, 344)

Fixed exchange rate An exchange rate pegged at a value decided by the government or central bank and that blocks the unregulated forces of demand and supply by direct intervention in the foreign exchange market. (p. 249)

Flexible exchange rate An exchange rate is determined by demand and supply with no direct intervention in the foreign exchange market by the central bank. (p. 249)

Foreign currency The money of other countries regardless of whether that money is in the form of notes, coins, or bank deposits. (p. 232)

Foreign exchange market The market in which the currency of one country is exchanged for the currency of another. (p. 232)

Frictional unemployment The unemployment that arises from normal labor turnover—from people entering and leaving the labor force and from the ongoing creation and destruction of jobs. (p. 139)

Full employment A situation in which the quantity of labor demanded equals the quantity supplied. At full employment, there is no cyclical unemployment—all unemployment is frictional and structural. (p. 140)

Full-employment equilibrium A macroeconomic equilibrium in which real GDP equals potential GDP. (p. 274)

GDP deflator One measure of the price level, which is the average of current-year prices as a percentage of base-year prices. (p. 120)

General Agreement on Tariffs and Trade An international agreement signed in 1947 to reduce tariffs on international trade. (p. 407)

Generational accounting An accounting system that measures the lifetime tax burden and benefits of each generation. (p. 356)

Generational imbalance The division of the fiscal imbalance between the current and future generations, assuming that the current generation will enjoy the existing levels of taxes and benefits. (p. 357)

Goods and services All the objects that people value and produce to satisfy human wants. (p. 3)

Government budget deficit The deficit that arises when the government spends more than it collects in taxes. (p. 102)

Government budget surplus The surplus that arises when the government collects more in taxes than it spends. (p. 102)

Government debt The total amount that the government has borrowed. It equals the sum of past budget deficits minus the sum of past budget surpluses. (p. 348)

Government expenditure Goods and services bought by the government. (p. 114)

Government expenditure multiplier The magnification effect of a change in government expenditure on goods and services on equilibrium expenditure and real GDP (p. 359)

Government sector surplus or deficit An amount equal to net taxes minus government expenditure on goods and services on aggregate demand. (p. 247)

Great Depression A decade (1929–1939) of high unemployment and stagnant production throughout the world economy. (p. 90)

Gross domestic product (GDP) The market value of all final goods and services produced within a country during a given time period. (p. 112)

Gross investment The total amount spent on purchases of new capital and on replacing depreciated capital. (p. 115)

Growth accounting A tool that calculates the contribution to real GDP growth of each of its sources. (p. 190)

Human capital The knowledge and skill that people obtain from education, on-the-job training, and work experience. (p. 3)

Hyperinflation An inflation that exceeds 50 percent a month. (p. 100)

Imports The goods and services that we buy from people in other countries. (pp. 114, 400)

Incentive A reward that encourages or a penalty that discourages an action. (p. 2)

Induced expenditure The sum of the components of aggregate planned expenditure that vary with real GDP. Induced expenditure equals consumption expenditure minus imports. (p. 293)

Induced taxes Taxes that vary with real GDP. (p. 361)

Infant-industry argument The argument that it is necessary to protect a new industry to enable it to grow into a mature industry that can compete in world markets. (p. 411)

Inferior good A good for which demand decreases as income increases. (p. 64)

Inflationary gap The amount by which real GDP exceeds potential GDP. (p. 275)

Inflation rate The annual percentage change in the price level. (pp. 99, 144)

Inflation rate targeting A monetary policy strategy in which the central bank makes a public commitment to achieve an explicit inflation rate and to explain how its policy actions will achieve that target. (p. 386)

Instrument rule A decision rule for monetary policy that sets the policy instrument at a level that is based on the current state of the economy. (p. 373)

Interest The income that capital earns. (p. 4)

Interest rate parity A situation in which the rates of return on assets in different currencies are equal. (p. 242)

Intermediate good An item that is produced by one firm, bought by another firm, and used as a component of a final good or service. (p. 112)

Inverse relationship A relationship between variables that move in opposite directions. (p. 21)

Investment The purchase of new plant, equipment, and buildings and additions to inventories. (p. 114)

Job rationing The practice of paying a real wage rate above the equilibrium level and then rationing jobs by some method. (p. 168)

Job search The activity of looking for an acceptable vacant job. (p. 166)

Keynesian A macroeconomist who believes that left alone, the economy would rarely operate at full employment and that to achieve full employ-

ment, active help from fiscal policy and monetary policy is required. (p. 278)

Keynesian cycle theory A theory that fluctuations in investment driven by fluctuations in business confidence—summarized in the phase "animal spirits"—are the main source of fluctuations in aggregate demand. (p. 328)

k-percent rule A rule that makes the quantity of money grow at a rate of k percent a year, where k equals the growth rate of potential GDP. (p. 385)

Labor The work time and work effort that people devote to producing goods and services. (p. 3)

Labor force The sum of the people who are employed and who are unemployed. (p. 132)

Labor force participation rate The percentage of the working-age population who are members of the labor force. (p. 133)

Labor market The market in which households supply and firms demand labor services. (p. 160)

Labor productivity The quantity of real GDP produced by an hour of labor. (p. 187)

Laffer curve The relationship between the tax rate and the amount of tax revenue collected. (p. 352)

Land All the gifts of nature that we use to produce goods and services. (p. 3)

Law of demand Other things remaining the same, the higher the price of a good, the smaller is the quantity demanded of it; the lower the price of a good, the larger is the quantity demanded of it. (p. 61)

Law of diminishing returns As a firm uses more of a variable input, with a given quantity of other inputs (fixed inputs), the marginal product of the variable input eventually diminishes. (p. 161)

Law of supply Other things remaining the same, the higher the price of a good, the greater is the quantity supplied of it. (p. 66)

Learning-by-doing People become more productive in an activity (learn) just by repeatedly producing a particular good or service (doing). (p. 45)

Linear relationship A relationship between two variables that is illustrated by a straight line. (p. 20)

Long-run aggregate supply The relationship between the quantity of real GDP supplied and the price level in the long run when real GDP equals potential GDP. (p. 264)

Long-run macroeconomic equilibrium A situation that occurs when real GDP equals potential GDP—the economy is on its long-run aggregate supply curve. (p. 273)

Long-run Phillips curve A curve that shows the relationship between inflation and unemployment when the actual inflation rate equals the expected inflation rate. (p. 325)

M1 A measure of money that consists of currency and traveler's checks plus checking deposits owned by individuals and businesses. (p. 207)

M2 A measure of money that consists of M1 plus time deposits, savings deposits, and money market mutual funds, and other deposits. (p. 207)

Macroeconomic long run A time frame that is sufficiently long for the real wage rate to have adjusted to achieve full employment: real GDP equal to potential GDP, unemployment equal to the natural unemployment rate, the price level is proportional to the quantity of money, and the inflation rate equal to the money growth rate minus the real GDP growth rate. (p. 264)

Macroeconomics The study of the performance of the national economy and the global economy. (p. 2)

Macroeconomic short run A period during which some money prices are sticky and real GDP might be below, above, or at potential GDP and unemployment might be above, below, or at the natural rate of unemployment. (p. 264)

Margin When a choice is changed by a small amount or by a little at a time, the choice is made at the margin. (p. 11)

Marginal benefit The benefit that a person receives from consuming one more unit of a good or service. It is measured as the maximum amount that a person is willing to pay for one more unit of the good or service. (pp. 11, 38)

Marginal benefit curve A curve that shows the relationship between the marginal benefit of a good and the quantity of that good consumed. (p. 38)

Marginal cost The opportunity cost of producing one more unit of a good or service. It is the best alternative forgone. It is calculated as the increase in total cost divided by the increase in output. (pp. 11, 37)

Marginal product of labor The change in real GDP that results from an additional hour of labor when all other influences on production remain the same. (p. 161)

Marginal propensity to consume The fraction of a change in disposable income that is consumed. It is calculated as the change in consumption expenditure divided by the change in disposable income. (p. 288)

Marginal propensity to import The fraction of an increase in real GDP that is spent on imports. (p. 291)

Marginal propensity to save The fraction of an increase in disposable income that is saved. It is calculated as the change in saving divided by the change in disposable income. (p. 288)

Market Any arrangement that enables buyers and sellers to get information and to do business with each other. (p. 46)

Market for loanable funds The markets in which households, firms, governments, banks, and other financial institutions borrow and lend. (p. 169)

McCallum rule A rule that makes the growth rate of the monetary base respond to the long-term average growth rate of real GDP and medium-term changes in the velocity of circulation of the monetary base. (p. 385)

Means of payment A method of settling a debt. (p. 206)

Microeconomics The study of the choices that individuals and businesses make, the way these choices interact in markets, and the influence governments. (p. 2)

Minimum wage A regulation that makes the hiring of labor below a specified wage rate illegal. The lowest wage at which a firm may legally hire labor. (p. 168)

Monetarist A macroeconomist who believes believes that the economy is self-regulating and that it will normally operate at full employment, provided that monetary policy is not erratic and that the pace of money growth is kept steady. (p. 279)

Monetarist cycle theory A theory that fluctuations in both investment and consumption expenditure, driven by fluctuations in the growth rate of the quantity of money, are the main source of fluctuations in aggregate demand. (p. 328)

Monetary base The sum of Federal Reserve notes, coins and banks' deposits at the Fed. (p. 215)

Monetary policy The Fed conducts the nation's monetary policy by changing interest rates and adjusting the quantity of money. (pp. 105, 271)

Monetary policy instrument A variable that the Fed can control directly or closely target. (p. 372)

Money Any commodity or token that is generally acceptable as the means of payment. (pp. 46, 206)

Money multiplier The ratio of the change in the quantity of money to the change in the monetary base. (p. 219)

Money price The number of dollars that must be given up in exchange for a good or service. (p. 60)

Money wage rate The number of dollars that an hour of labor earns. (p. 161)

Multiplier The amount by which a change in autonomous expenditure is magnified or multiplied to determine the change in equilibrium expenditure and real GDP. (p. 296)

National debt The amount that the government owes to all the people who have made loans to cover the government deficits. (p. 103)

National saving The sum of private saving (saving by households and businesses) and government saving. (p. 115)

Natural unemployment rate The unemployment rate when the economy is at full employment. There is no cyclical unemployment; all unemployment is frictional, structural, and seasonal. (p. 140)

Needs-tested spending Government spending on programs that pay benefits to suitably qualified people and businesses. (p. 361)

Negative relationship A relationship between variables that move in opposite directions. (p. 21)

Neoclassical growth theory A theory of economic growth that proposes that real GDP per person grows because technological change induces a level of saving and investment that makes capital per hour of labor grow. (p. 196)

Net borrower A country that is borrowing more from the rest of the world than it is lending to it. (p. 246)

Net exports The value of exports of goods and services minus the value of imports of goods and services. (pp. 114, 247, 400)

Net investment Net increase in the capital stock—gross investment minus depreciation. (p. 115)

Net lender A country that is lending more to the rest of the world than it is borrowing from it. (p. 246)

Net taxes Taxes paid to governments minus transfer payments received from governments. (p. 114)

New classical A macroeconomist who holds the view that business cycle fluctuations are the efficient responses of a well-functioning market economy bombarded by shocks that arise from the uneven pace of technological change. (p. 278)

New classical cycle theory A rational expectations theory of the business cycle that regards unexpected fluctuations in aggregate demand as the main source of fluctuations of real GDP around potential GDP. (p. 328)

New growth theory A theory of economic growth based on the idea that real GDP per person grows because of

the choices that people make in the pursuit of profit and that growth can persist indefinitely. (p. 197)

New Keynesian A macroeconomist who holds the view that not only is the money wage rate sticky but also that the prices of goods and services are sticky. (p. 279)

New Keynesian cycle theory A rational expectations theory of the business cycle that regards unexpected and currently expected fluctuations in aggregate demand as the main source of fluctuations of real GDP around potential GDP. (p. 328)

Nominal exchange rate The value of the U.S. dollar expressed in units of foreign currency per U.S. dollar. (p. 232)

Nominal GDP The value of the final goods and services produced in a given year valued at the prices that prevailed in that same year. It is a more precise name for GDP. (p. 119)

Nominal interest rate The number of dollars that a unit of capital earns. (p. 170)

Nontariff barrier Any action other than a tariff that restricts international trade. (p. 407)

Normal good A good for which demand increases as income increases. (p. 64)

North American Free Trade Agreement An agreement, which became effective on January 1, 1994, to eliminate all barriers to international trade between the United States, Canada, and Mexico after a 15-year phasing-in period. (p. 408)

Official settlements account A record of the change in official reserves, which are the government's holdings of foreign currency. (p. 244)

One third rule The rule that, on the average, with no change in technology, a 1 percent increase in capital per hour of labor brings a 1/3 percent increase in labor productivity. (p. 190)

Open market operation The purchase or sale of government securities—U.S. Treasury bills and bonds—by the Federal Reserve in the open market. (p. 214)

Opportunity cost The highest-valued alternative that we give up to get something. (p. 10)

Output gap Real GDP minus potential GDP. (pp. 95, 274)

Phillips curve A curve that shows a relationship between inflation and unemployment. (p. 324)

Positive relationship A relationship between two variables that move in the same direction. (p. 20)

Potential GDP The value of production when all the economy's labor, capital, land, and entrepreneurial ability are fully employed; the quantity of real GDP at full employment. (pp. 91, 141)

Preferences A description of a person's likes and dislikes. (p. 38)

Present value The amount of money that, if invested today, will grow to be as large as a given future amount when the interest that it will earn is taken into account. (p. 356)

Price level The average of the prices that people pay for all the goods an services that they buy as measured by a price index. (pp. 99, 120)

Private sector surplus or deficit An amount equal to saving minus investment. (p. 247)

Production efficiency A situation in which the economy cannot produce more of one good without producing less of some other good. (p. 35)

Production function The relationship between real GDP and the quantity of labor employed when all other influences on production remain the same. (p. 159)

Production possibilities frontier The boundary between the combinations of goods and services that can be produced and the combinations that cannot. (p. 34)

Productivity growth slowdown A situation in which the growth rate of output per person sags. (p. 91)

Profit The income earned by entrepreneurship. (p. 4)

Property rights Social arrangements that govern the ownership, use, and disposal of anything that people value that are enforceable in the courts. (p. 46)

Purchasing power parity The equal value of different monies. (p. 242)

Quantity demanded The amount of a good or service that consumers plan to buy during a given time period at a particular price. (p. 61)

Quantity supplied The amount of a good or service that producers plan to sell during a given time period at a particular price. (p. 66)

Quantity theory of money The proposition that in the long run, an increase in the quantity of money brings an equal percentage increase in the price level. (p. 224)

Quota A quantitative restriction on the import of a particular good, which specifies the maximum amount that can be imported in a given time period. (p. 410)

Rational expectation The most accurate forecast possible, a forecast that uses all the available information, including knowledge of the relevant economic forces that influence the variable being forecasted. (p. 323)

Real business cycle theory A theory of the business cycle that regards random fluctuations in productivity as the main source of economic fluctuations. (p. 328)

Real exchange rate The relative price of foreign-produced goods and services to U.S.-produced goods and services. (pp. 232, 386)

Real gross domestic product (real GDP) The value of final goods and services produced in a given year when valued at constant prices. (pp. 119)

Real GDP per person Real GDP divided by the population. (p. 182)

Real interest rate The quantity of goods and services that a unit of capital earns. It is the nominal interest rate adjusted for inflation and is approximately equal to the nominal interest rate minus the inflation rate. (p. 170)

Real wage rate The quantity of goods and services that an hour's work can buy. It is equal to the money wage rate divided by the price level and multiplied by 100. (pp. 135, 161)

Recession A business cycle phase in which real GDP decreases for at least two successive quarters. (p. 92)

Recessionary gap The amount by which potential GDP exceeds real GDP. (p. 274)

Reference base period The period in which the CPI is defined to be 100. (p. 142)

Relative price The ratio of the price of one good or service to the price of another good or service. A relative price is an opportunity cost. (p. 60)

Rent The income that land earns. (p. 4)

Rent seeking Any attempt to capture a consumer surplus, a producer surplus, or an economic profit. (p. 414)

Required reserve ratio The minimum percentage of deposits that banks are required to hold as reserves. (p. 213)

Reserve ratio The fraction of a bank's total deposits that are held in reserves. (p. 216)

Reserves A bank's reserves consist of notes and coins in its vaults plus its deposit at the Federal Reserve. (p. 216)

Ricardo-Barro equivalence The proposition that taxes and government borrowing are equivalent—a budget deficit has no effect on the real interest rate or investment. (p. 356)

Rule of 70 A rule that states that the number of years it takes for the level of a variable to double is approximately 70 divided by the annual percentage growth rate of the variable. (p. 182)

Saving The amount of income that households have left after they have paid their taxes and bought their consumer goods and services. (p. 114)

Saving function The relationship between saving and disposable income, other things remaining the same. (p. 287)

Scarcity Our inability to satisfy all our wants. (p. 2)

Scatter diagram A diagram that plots the value of one variable against the value of another. (p. 19)

Self-interest The choices that you think are best for you. (p. 5)

Short-run aggregate supply The relationship between the quantity of real GDP supplied and the price level when the money wage rate, the prices of other resources, and potential GDP remain constant. (p. 265)

Short-run macroeconomic equilibrium A situation that occurs when the quantity of real GDP demanded equals the quantity of real GDP supplied—at the point of intersection of the AD curve and the SAS curve. (p. 272)

Short-run Phillips curve A curve that shows the tradeoff between inflation and unemployment, when the expected inflation rate and the natural unemployment rate remain the same. (p. 324)

Slope The change in the value of the variable measured on the y-axis divided by the change in the value of the variable measured on the x-axis. (p. 24)

Social interest Choices that are the best for society as a whole. (p. 5)

Stagflation The combination of inflation and recession. (pp. 277, 321)

Structural surplus or deficit The budget balance that would occur if the economy were at full employment and real GDP were equal to potential GDP. (p. 362)

Structural unemployment The unemployment that arises when changes in technology or international competition change the skills needed to perform jobs or change the locations of jobs. (p. 140)

Subsistence real wage rate The minimum real wage rate needed to maintain life. (p. 195)

Substitute A good that can be used in place of another good. (p. 63)

Supply The entire relationship between the price of a good and the quantity supplied of it when all other influences on producers' planned sales remain the same. It is described by a supply schedule and illustrated by a supply curve. (p. 66)

Supply curve A curve that shows the relationship between the quantity supplied of a good and its price when all other influences on producers' planned sales remain the same. (p. 66)

Supply of labor The relationship between the quantity of labor supplied and the real wage rate when all other influences on work plans remain the same. (p. 163)

Supply of loanable funds The relationship between the quantity of loanable funds supplied and the real interest rate when all other influences on lending plans remain the same. (p. 171)

Supply-side effects The effects of fiscal policy on employment, potential GDP, and aggregate supply. (p. 350)

Targeting rule A decision rule for monetary policy that sets the policy instrument at a level that makes the forecast of the ultimate policy target equal to the target. (p. 373)

Tariff A tax that is imposed by the importing country when an imported good crosses its international boundary. (p. 407)

Tax wedge The gap between the before-tax and after-tax wage rates. (p. 351)

Taylor rule A rule that sets the federal funds rate at the equilibrium real interest rate (which Taylor says is 2 percent a year) plus amounts based on the inflation rate and the output gap. (p. 374)

Technological change The development of new goods and of better ways of producing goods and services. (p. 40)

Terms of trade The quantity of goods and services that a country exports to pay for its imports of goods and services. (p. 402)

Time-series graph A graph that measures time (for example, months or years) on the x-axis and the variable or variables in which we are interested on the y-axis. (p. 18)

Tradeoff A constraint that involves giving up one thing to get something else. (p. 9)

Trade-weighted index The average exchange rate, with individual currencies weighted by their importance in U.S. international trade. (p. 234)

Trend The general tendency for a variable to move in one direction. (p. 18)

Unemployment rate The number of unemployed people expressed as a percentage of all the people who have jobs or are looking for one. It is the percentage of the labor force who are unemployed. (pp. 97, 133)

U.S. interest rate differential The U.S. interest rate minus the foreign interest rate. (p. 239)

U.S. official reserves The government's holding of foreign currency. (p. 244)

Velocity of circulation The average number of times a dollar of money is used annually to buy the goods and services that make up GDP. (p. 224)

Voluntary export restraint An agreement between two governments in which the government of the exporting country agrees to restrain the volume of its own exports. (p. 410)

Wages The income that labor earns. (p. 4)

Wealth The value of all the things that people own—the market value of their assets. (p. 115)

Working-age population The total number of people aged 15 years and over. (p. 132)

World Trade Organization An international organization that places greater obligations on its member countries to observe the GATT rules. (p. 407)

INDEX

Adam Smith (p. 54) Corbis-Bettmann.

Pin factory (p. 55) Culver Pictures.

Silicon wafer (p. 55) Bruce Ando/Tony Stone Images.

Alfred Marshall (p. 84) Stock Montage.

Railroad bridge (p. 85) National Archives.

Airport (p. 85) PhotoDisc, Inc.

Charlie Holt (p. 86) University of Virginia/
Rebecca Arrington.

David Hume (p. 152) Library of Congress.

Playfair graph (p. 153) Annenberg Rare Book &
Manuscript Library, University of Pennsylvania.

Zimbabwe currency (p. 227) AP Wide World Photos.

Foreign exchange (p. 235) Currency
Market/APA555943/AP Wide World Photos.

Joseph Schumpeter (p. 258) Corbis-Bettmann.

McCormick's first reaping machine, ca. 1834
(p. 259) North Wind Picture Archives.

Fiber optics (p. 259) PhotoDisc, Inc.

John Maynard Keynes (p. 338) Stock Montage.

Boarded-up shop (p. 339) © Susan van Etten.

Soup kitchen (p. 339) Corbis-Bettmann.

Milton Friedman (p. 394) Marshall Henrichs/
Addison-Wesley.

Depositors outside door of closed bank (p. 395)
Corbis-Bettmann.

Federal Reserve Building (p. 395) Getty Images/
Photographer's Choice.

Peter N. Ireland (p. 396) L. Pellegrini.

David Ricardo (p. 422) Corbis-Bettmann.

Clipper ship (p. 423) North Wind Picture Archives.

Container ship (p. 423) © M. Timothy O'Keefe/
Weststock.

Macroeconomic Data

These macroeconomic data series show some of the trends in GDP and its components, the price level, and other variables that provide information about changes in the standard of living and the cost of living—the central questions of macroeconomics. You will find these data in a spreadsheet that you can download from your MyEconLab Web site.

	NATIONAL INCOME AND PRODUCT ACCOUNTS	1983	1984	1985	1986	1987	1988	1989	1990	1991	1992
	EXPENDITURES APPROACH										
the sum of	1 **Personal consumption expenditures**	2,290.6	2,503.3	2,720.3	2,899.7	3,100.2	3,353.6	3,598.5	3,839.9	3,986.1	4,235.3
	2 **Gross private domestic investment**	564.3	735.6	736.2	746.5	785.0	821.6	874.9	861.0	802.9	864.8
	3 **Government expenditures**	733.5	797.0	879.0	949.3	999.5	1,039.0	1,099.1	1,180.2	1,234.4	1,271.0
	4 **Exports**	277.0	302.4	302.0	320.5	363.9	444.1	503.3	552.4	596.8	635.3
less	5 **Imports**	328.6	405.1	417.2	453.3	509.1	554.5	591.5	630.3	624.3	668.6
equals	6 **Gross domestic product**	3,536.7	3,933.2	4,220.3	4,462.8	4,739.5	5,103.8	5,484.4	5,803.1	5,995.9	6,337.7
	INCOMES APPROACH										
	7 **Compensation of employees**	2,042.6	2,255.6	2,424.7	2,570.1	2,750.2	2,967.2	3,145.2	3,338.2	3,445.2	3,635.4
plus	8 **Net operating surplus**	779.8	929.2	975.8	995.5	1,070.9	1,200.1	1,265.1	1,311.2	1,306.9	1,373.4
equals	9 **Net domestic product at factor cost**	2,822.4	3,184.8	3,400.5	3,565.6	3,821.1	4,167.3	4,410.3	4,649.4	4,752.1	5,008.8
	10 **Indirect taxes less subsidies**	224.8	261.2	296.4	318.9	334.8	358.4	390.1	405.0	445.4	474.3
plus	11 **Depreciation (capital consumption)**	443.8	472.6	506.7	531.3	561.9	597.6	644.3	682.5	725.9	751.9
	12 **GDP (income approach)**	3,491.0	3,918.6	4,203.6	4,415.8	4,717.8	5,123.3	5,444.7	5,736.9	5,923.4	6,235.0
	13 **Statistical discrepancy**	45.7	14.6	16.7	47.0	21.7	–19.5	39.7	66.2	72.5	102.7
equals	14 **GDP (expenditure approach)**	3,536.7	3,933.2	4,220.3	4,462.8	4,739.5	5,103.8	5,484.4	5,803.1	5,995.9	6,337.7
	15 **Real GDP (billions of 2000 dollars)**	5,423.8	5,813.6	6,053.7	6,263.6	6,475.1	6,742.7	6,981.4	7,112.5	7,100.5	7,336.6
	16 **Real GDP growth rate (percent per year)**	4.5	7.2	4.1	3.5	3.4	4.1	3.5	1.9	-0.2	3.3
	OTHER DATA										
	17 **Population (millions)**	234.3	236.3	238.5	240.7	242.8	245.0	247.3	250.1	253.5	256.9
	18 **Labor force (millions)**	111.6	113.5	115.5	117.8	119.9	121.7	123.9	125.8	126.3	128.1
	19 **Employment (millions)**	100.8	105.0	107.2	109.6	112.4	115.0	117.3	118.8	117.7	118.5
	20 **Unemployment (millions)**	10.7	8.5	8.3	8.2	7.4	6.7	6.5	7.0	8.6	9.6
	21 **Labor force participation rate (percent of working-age population)**	64.0	64.4	64.8	65.3	65.6	65.9	66.5	66.5	66.2	66.4
	22 **Unemployment rate (percent of labor force)**	9.6	7.5	7.2	7.0	6.2	5.5	5.3	5.6	6.8	7.5
	23 **Real GDP per person (2000 dollars per year)**	23,148	24,598	25,386	26,028	26,668	27,519	28,226	28,435	28,011	28,559
	24 **Growth rate of real GDP per person (percent per year)**	3.6	6.3	3.2	2.5	2.5	3.2	2.6	0.7	–1.5	2.0
	25 **Quantity of money (M2, billions of dollars)**	2,126.5	2,310.0	2,495.7	2,732.3	2,831.5	2,994.5	3,158.5	3,278.8	3,379.7	3,433.1
	26 **GDP deflator (2000 = 100)**	65.2	67.7	69.7	71.3	73.2	75.7	78.6	81.6	84.4	86.4
	27 **GDP deflator inflation rate (percent per year)**	4.0	3.8	3.0	2.2	2.7	3.4	3.8	3.9	3.5	2.3
	28 **Consumer price index (1982–1984 = 100)**	99.6	103.9	107.6	109.6	113.6	118.3	124.0	130.7	136.2	140.3
	29 **CPI inflation rate (percent per year)**	3.2	4.3	3.6	1.9	3.6	4.1	4.8	5.4	4.2	3.0
	30 **Current account balance (billions of dollars)**	–38.7	–94.3	–118.2	–147.2	–160.7	–121.2	–99.5	–79.0	2.9	–50.1

The Addison-Wesley Series in Economics